ASCENT®
CENTER FOR TECHNICAL KNOWLEDGE

Creo Parametric 6.0
Design Documentation and Detailing

Learning Guide
1st Edition

ASCENT - Center for Technical Knowledge®
Creo Parametric 6.0
Design Documentation and Detailing
1st Edition

Prepared and produced by:

ASCENT Center for Technical Knowledge
630 Peter Jefferson Parkway, Suite 175
Charlottesville, VA 22911

866-527-2368
www.ASCENTed.com

Lead Contributor: Scott Hendren

ASCENT - Center for Technical Knowledge (a division of Rand Worldwide Inc.) is a leading developer of professional learning materials and knowledge products for engineering software applications. ASCENT specializes in designing targeted content that facilitates application-based learning with hands-on software experience. For over 25 years, ASCENT has helped users become more productive through tailored custom learning solutions.

We welcome any comments you may have regarding this guide, or any of our products. To contact us please email: feedback@ASCENTed.com.

General Disclaimer:

Notwithstanding any language to the contrary, nothing contained herein constitutes nor is intended to constitute an offer, inducement, promise, or contract of any kind. The data contained herein is for informational purposes only and is not represented to be error free. ASCENT, its agents and employees, expressly disclaim any liability for any damages, losses or other expenses arising in connection with the use of its materials or in connection with any failure of performance, error, omission even if ASCENT, or its representatives, are advised of the possibility of such damages, losses or other expenses. No consequential damages can be sought against ASCENT or Rand Worldwide, Inc. for the use of these materials by any third parties or for any direct or indirect result of that use.

The information contained herein is intended to be of general interest to you and is provided "as is", and it does not address the circumstances of any particular individual or entity. Nothing herein constitutes professional advice, nor does it constitute a comprehensive or complete statement of the issues discussed thereto. ASCENT does not warrant that the document or information will be error free or will meet any particular criteria of performance or quality. In particular (but without limitation) information may be rendered inaccurate by changes made to the subject of the materials (i.e. applicable software). Rand Worldwide, Inc. specifically disclaims any warranty, either expressed or implied, including the warranty of fitness for a particular purpose.

AS-CRP6-DDD1-SG // RS-CRP6-DDD1-SG

Contents

Preface ix

In This Guide xi

Practice Files xiii

Chapter 1: Views.. 1-1

   1.1 General Steps for Drawings 1-2

   1.2 Create a New Drawing 1-3

   1.3 Drawing Mode Interface... 1-6
       Pan, Zoom... 1-8
       Selection Tool 1-8
       Mini Toolbar 1-8
       Shortcut Menus 1-9
       Undo/Redo 1-10
       Drawing Tree.. 1-10

   1.4 Place the First Drawing View 1-12

   1.5 Place Additional Views 1-16

   1.6 Modify View Properties I... 1-21
       View Property Categories 1-22

   1.7 Drawing Options 1-33
       Config.pro File... 1-34

   Practice 1a Create a New Drawing.................................... 1-36

   Practice 1b Add a Drawing Format.................................... 1-45

   Practice 1c Create Views.. 1-57

   Practice 1d Create a Drawing.. 1-66

   Chapter Review Questions... 1-83

Chapter 2: View Manipulation... 2-1

   2.1 Modify View Properties II.. 2-2
       Additional Options 2-2

2.2 **Manipulate Drawing Views** **2-12**
    View Alignment 2-12
    Moving Views 2-12
    Delete Views 2-13
    Erasing Views 2-13
    Drawing Display 2-13

2.3 **Configuration Options** **2-16**

Practice 2a Move Drawing Views **2-18**

Practice 2b Move Broken Views **2-29**

Practice 2c Modify Drawing Views **2-32**

Practice 2d Modify View Boundaries **2-37**

Chapter Review Questions **2-39**

Chapter 3: Detailing a Drawing **3-1**

3.1 **Show Detail Items** **3-2**

3.2 **Create Dimensions** **3-7**
    Creating Dimensions 3-8
    Coordinate Dimensions 3-13

3.3 **Manipulate Detail Items** **3-14**
    Modify Dimensions 3-14
    Delete 3-17
    Move 3-17
    Edit Attachment 3-18
    Cross-Hatching Attributes 3-19
    Breaking Cross-Hatch Lines 3-24
    Break 3-24
    Clip 3-26
    Move Item to View 3-26
    Flip Arrows 3-26
    Make Jog 3-26
    Align Dimensions 3-27
    Snap Lines 3-28
    Cleaning Dimensions 3-28
    Erase Witness Lines 3-29
    Diameter/Linear Format 3-30
    Radial and Diameter Dimensions 3-31
    Automatic Clipped Dimensions 3-32

3.4 **Customizing Options** **3-33**

Practice 3a Detailing a Drawing I **3-35**

Practice 3b Detailing a Drawing II **3-47**

Practice 3c Creating Dimensions **3-62**

Practice 3d Ordinate Dimensions **3-68**

Chapter Review Questions **3-71**

Chapter 4: Project Labs 1 & 2 4-1

Practice 4a Creating a Detailed Drawing 4-2

Practice 4b Creating 3D Drawings 4-9

Chapter 5: Drawing Notes 5-1

5.1 Create and Modify Notes 5-2
Dimensions 5-5
System-defined Parameters 5-7
User-defined Parameters 5-8
Special Characters 5-9
User-defined Symbols 5-9
Note Handles 5-10
Editing Attachments 5-11
Modifying Text 5-12
Hyperlinks 5-13
Superscript and Subscript Text 5-13
Outlining a Note 5-13
Modifying Text Styles 5-14
Text Editor 5-15
Creating a Style Library 5-16
Saving Notes 5-18

5.2 Customizing Options 5-19

Practice 5a Creating Notes 5-21

Practice 5b Read a Note From File 5-28

Chapter Review Questions 5-32

Chapter 6: Tolerances 6-1

6.1 Showing Dimensional Tolerances 6-2

6.2 Set Tolerance Standards 6-3

6.3 Datum Feature Symbols 6-8
Automatic Naming 6-9
Additional Text 6-9
Adding Elbows 6-9

6.4 Create Geometric Tolerances 6-10
Showing Geometric Tolerances 6-15
Composite Geometric Tolerances 6-15
ISO GPS Indicators 6-16

6.5 Syntax Checking 6-17
Datum and Datum Target 6-17
Geometric Tolerance 6-18

6.6 Handling Legacy Datums 6-19

6.7 Datum Targets 6-27
   Specifying Datum References.. 6-27
   Intelligent Target Areas 6-28
   Datum Target Annotations 6-29

6.8 Drawing Configuration Options................................. 6-31

6.9 Drawing Setup File Options 6-33

Practice 6a Dimensional Tolerances 6-34

Practice 6b Geometric Tolerances 6-38

Practice 6c Handling Legacy Datums 6-53

Chapter Review Questions... 6-65

Chapter 7: Project Lab 3 7-1

Practice 7a Tolerancing a Drawing................................. 7-2

Chapter 8: Assembly Drawings... 8-1

8.1 Add Models.. 8-2

8.2 Explode Assembly Views 8-4

8.3 Change Component Display 8-6

8.4 Display Cross-Sections 8-9
   Cross-Section Material Files 8-10
   3D Cross-
   Sections 8-11

8.5 Modify Assembly Views 8-14
   View State 8-14
   Combined States... 8-15
   Z-Clipping.. 8-16

Practice 8a Assembly Drawing 8-17

Practice 8b Model Configurations on Drawings.............. 8-32

Chapter Review Questions... 8-43

Chapter 9: Drawing Tables 9-1

9.1 Create a Table.. 9-2
   Selection Methods... 9-10
   Copy Table 9-10
   Rotate.. 9-10
   Justification 9-11
   Size 9-12
   Insert 9-12
   Remove 9-12
   Merge 9-12
   Table Origin... 9-13
   Blank Line Display... 9-13

9.2 **Create Repeat Regions** **9-15**
    Filters 9-19
    Attributes 9-20
    Pagination 9-23
    Creating BOM Balloons.. 9-23
    Modifying BOM Balloons 9-24

9.3 **Create Hole, Point, and Axes Tables** **9-26**

Practice 9a Bill of Materials (BOM) **9-29**

Practice 9b Family Tables in Drawings **9-47**

Practice 9c Hole, Axis, and Datum Point Tables **9-51**

Chapter Review Questions **9-60**

Chapter 10: 2D Sketching **10-1**

10.1 **Create 2D Entities** **10-2**
    Line 10-5
    Circle 10-5
    Ellipse... 10-6
    Arc 10-7
    Construction Line 10-7
    Construction Circle 10-8
    Fillet.. 10-9
    Chamfer 10-9
    Spline 10-10
    Point 10-11
    Break 10-11
    Offset and Use Edge 10-12

10.2 **Modify 2D Entities** **10-13**
    Copy & Paste 10-13
    Edit Group 10-13
    Trim Group 10-15
    Format Group 10-16
    Line Style 10-16

10.3 **Group 2D Entities** **10-17**
    Create a Draft Group.. 10-18
    Relate Draft Items to a View 10-18
    Group Objects with Dimension Text.................................... 10-18
    Ungroup a Draft Group... 10-18
    Ungroup Items from a View.. 10-19
    Set Drawing View as Current Draft View 10-19
    Modify a Draft Group.. 10-19
    Suppress a Draft Group 10-19
    Resume a Suppressed Group... 10-19

10.4 Convert to Draft Entities **10-20**

10.5 Sketch Parametric Entities **10-21**

Practice 10a Drawing Sketches **10-22**

Chapter Review Questions **10-34**

Chapter 11: Symbols **11-1**

11.1 Create Symbol Geometry **11-2**

11.2 Place a Custom Symbol **11-10**

11.3 Symbol Palette **11-12**

11.4 Surface Finish Symbols **11-13**

Practice 11a Surface Symbols **11-14**

Practice 11b Custom Symbol Definition Palette **11-30**

Chapter Review Questions **11-37**

Chapter 12: Feature Management **12-1**

12.1 Hide Items **12-2**

12.2 Suppress Items **12-3**

12.3 Add Layers **12-6**
Active Layer 12-11
Default Layers 12-12
Display Status of Model Layers vs. Drawing Layers 12-12
Layers with the Same Name 12-13
Controlling Individual View Display 12-13
Active Layer 12-14

12.4 Create Assembly Simplified Representations **12-15**
Restrictions 12-18

12.5 Part Simplified Representations **12-19**
Creating Part Simplified Representations 12-19
Creating a Drawing including Part Simplified Representations 12-20

12.6 Review and Tools Tab **12-22**
Update.. 12-22
Compare 12-24
Information Tools 12-26

Practice 12a Drawing Layers **12-28**

**Practice 12b Drawing of an Assembly Simplified
Representation** **12-37**

Chapter Review Questions **12-43**

Appendix A: Drawing Formats and Templates **A-1**

  A.1 Create a Drawing Format...**A-2**

    Empty with Section...A-3

    Empty A-4

  A.2 Import Formats...**A-6**

  A.3 Add Tables to a Format **A-7**

  A.4 Parametric Text **A-8**

  A.5 Add a Drawing Format..**A-9**

  A.6 Create Drawing Templates **A-10**

  Practice A1 Drawing Formats **A-12**

  Practice A2 Formats with Imported Data **A-15**

  Practice A3 Drawing Templates.. **A-17**

  Chapter Review Questions...**A-23**

Appendix B: Object Linking and Embedding..........................**B-25**

  B.1 Object Linking and Embedding **B-26**

  Practice B1 Object Linking & Embedding.......................... **B-28**

Appendix C: Print and Export Options **C-31**

  C.1 Print and Export Options..**C-32**

    Print..C-32

    Export to DXF...C-34

Preface

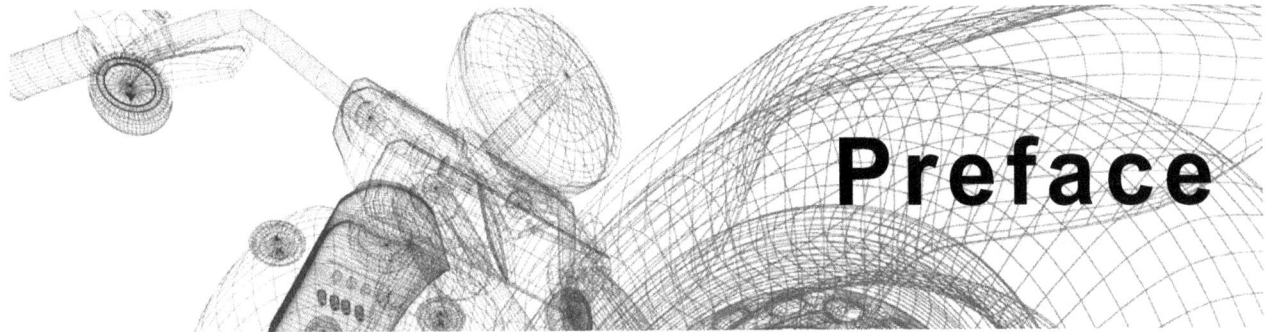

The *Creo Parametric 6.0: Design Documentation and Detailing* learning guide is designed for all draftspersons that document designs using Creo Parametric. It focuses on how to use Creo Parametric to communicate design information from your part and assembly models.

Topics Covered

- View creation
- View manipulation
- Detailing a drawing
- Drawing notes
- Tolerances
- Assembly drawings
- Drawing tables
- 2D sketching
- Symbols

Prerequisites

- Access to the Creo Parametric 6.0 software. The practices and files included with this guide might not be compatible with prior versions. Practice files included with this guide are compatible with the commercial version of the software, but not the student edition.

- Completing *Creo Parametric 6.0: Introduction to Solid Modeling* or equivalent Creo Parametric 6.0 experience.

Note on Software Setup

This guide assumes a standard installation of the software using the default preferences during installation. Lectures and practices use the standard software templates and default options for the Content Libraries.

This course was developed using Creo Parametric 6.0.4.0.

Lead Contributor: Scott Hendren

Scott Hendren has been a trainer and curriculum developer in the PLM industry for over 20 years, with experience on multiple CAD systems, including Pro/ENGINEER, Creo Parametric, and CATIA. Trained in Instructional Design, Scott uses his skills to develop instructor-led and web-based training products.

Scott has held training and development positions with several high profile PLM companies, and has been with the Ascent team since 2013.

Scott holds a Bachelor of Mechanical Engineering Degree as well as a Bachelor of Science in Mathematics from Dalhousie University, Nova Scotia, Canada.

Scott Hendren has been the Lead Contributor for *Creo Parametric: Design Documentation and Detailing* since 2013.

In This Guide

The following highlights the key features of this guide.

Feature	Description
Practice Files	The Practice Files page includes a link to the practice files and instructions on how to download and install them. The practice files are required to complete the practices in this guide.
Chapters	A chapter consists of the following - Learning Objectives, Instructional Content, Practices, Chapter Review Questions, and Command Summary. • **Learning Objectives** define the skills you can acquire by learning the content provided in the chapter. • **Instructional Content**, which begins right after Learning Objectives, refers to the descriptive and procedural information related to various topics. Each main topic introduces a product feature, discusses various aspects of that feature, and provides step-by-step procedures on how to use that feature. Where relevant, examples, figures, helpful hints, and notes are provided. • **Practice** for a topic follows the instructional content. Practices enable you to use the software to perform a hands-on review of a topic. It is required that you download the practice files (using the link found on the Practice Files page) prior to starting the first practice. • **Chapter Review Questions**, located close to the end of a chapter, enable you to test your knowledge of the key concepts discussed in the chapter.
Appendices	Appendices provide additional information to the main course content. It could be in the form of instructional content, practices, tables, projects, or skills assessment.

Practice Files

To download the practice files for this guide, use the following steps:

1. Type the URL *exactly as shown below* into the address bar of your Internet browser, to access the Course File Download page.

   Note: If you are using the ebook, you do not have to type the URL. Instead, you can access the page simply by clicking the URL below.

   ## https://www.ascented.com/getfile/id/muscari

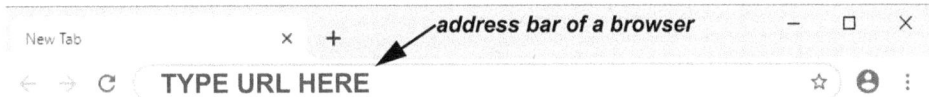

New Tab	×	+	*address bar of a browser*	—	☐	×
← → C	TYPE URL HERE			☆	😑	:

2. On the Course File Download page, click the **DOWNLOAD NOW** button, as shown below, to download the .ZIP file that contains the practice files.

   DOWNLOAD NOW ▶

3. Once the download is complete, unzip the file and extract its contents.

   The recommended practice files folder location is:
   C:\Creo Parametric Design Documentation and Detailing Practice Files

   Note: It is recommended that you do not change the location of the practice files folder. Doing so may cause errors when completing the practices.

Stay Informed!

To receive information about upcoming events, promotional offers, and complimentary webcasts, visit:

www.ASCENTed.com/updates

Views

Drawings are created to communicate information about how the model is to be built. Accurate representation of the model is key for manufacturing. In this chapter, you learn how to add basic model views to a new drawing.

Learning Objectives in This Chapter

- Learn the general steps to create a production drawing of a part or assembly.
- Create a new drawing using the template, format or empty option in the New Drawing dialog box.
- Learn to use the ribbon style interface to manipulate the drawing.
- Learn how to use the Drawing Tree and Model Tree in the drawing environment.
- Learn to create a General view and specify the orientation options to place the view in the drawing.
- Learn to create additional views using the *Layout* tab.
- Learn to refine any views using the different categories in the Drawing View dialog box.
- Use the drawing setup file to change drawing options that control the current drawing.
- Use the configuration file to change the environmental settings for the drawing.

1.1 General Steps for Drawings

Figure 1–1 illustrates the steps to follow when creating a drawing.

How To: Create a Production Drawing of a Part or Assembly Model

1. Create a drawing.
2. Place the first drawing view.
3. Place additional views.
4. Modify view properties.
5. Manipulate drawing views, as required.
6. Detail the drawing (e.g., dimensions, notes, tolerances, etc.).
7. Manipulate detail items, as required.
8. Print (or plot) the drawing.

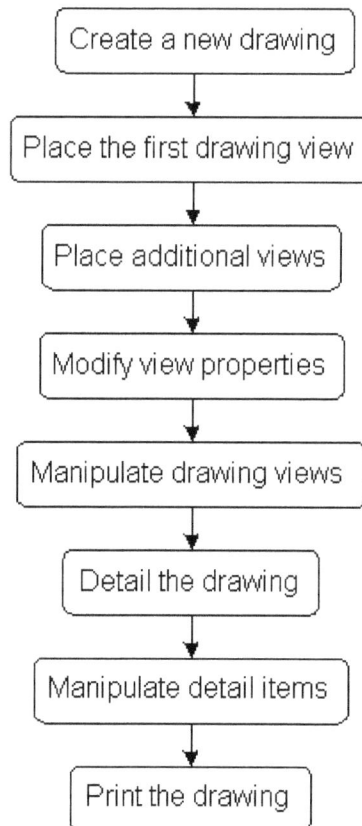

```
┌──────────────────────────┐
│   Create a new drawing    │
└──────────────────────────┘
             │
             ▼
┌──────────────────────────┐
│  Place the first drawing view │
└──────────────────────────┘
             │
             ▼
┌──────────────────────────┐
│  Place additional views   │
└──────────────────────────┘
             │
             ▼
┌──────────────────────────┐
│  Modify view properties   │
└──────────────────────────┘
             │
             ▼
┌──────────────────────────┐
│ Manipulate drawing views  │
└──────────────────────────┘
             │
             ▼
┌──────────────────────────┐
│    Detail the drawing     │
└──────────────────────────┘
             │
             ▼
┌──────────────────────────┐
│  Manipulate detail items  │
└──────────────────────────┘
             │
             ▼
┌──────────────────────────┐
│    Print the drawing      │
└──────────────────────────┘
```

Figure 1–1

1.2 Create a New Drawing

As with creating a new part or assembly file, you must go through a series of steps.

How To: Create a new drawing file:

The Common Name field is optional and enables you to assign a common (user- friendly) name to a new model for use with Windchill.

1. To create a new drawing, select **File>New** or click ☐ (New) in the Quick Access Toolbar or *Home* tab. The New dialog box opens.
2. Select **Drawing**. The **Use default template** option will create the drawing with a predefined set of views. Generally, this option is disabled in this content. You can enable the **Use drawing model file name** option to make the name of the drawing match the model, as shown in Figure 1–2, or disable this option and enter a name for the drawing.

Figure 1–2

3. Click **OK**.
4. The New Drawing dialog box opens as shown in Figure 1–3. The *Default Model* field defines the model to be represented in the drawing. To assign the model, enter the model name or click **Browse**. Additional models can be added once the drawing has been created.

   The template options include the following:

   • **Use Template**
   • **Empty with Format**
   • **Empty**

Use Template

To use a predefined drawing template, select **Use template** and select the template name in the *Template* area, as shown in Figure 1–3. Alternatively, you can click **Browse** and browse to other templates that are stored in other directories.

*If **Use default template** is selected in the New dialog box, the New Drawing dialog box defaults to the **Use Template** option, as shown in Figure 1–3. A predefined template is selected for use.*

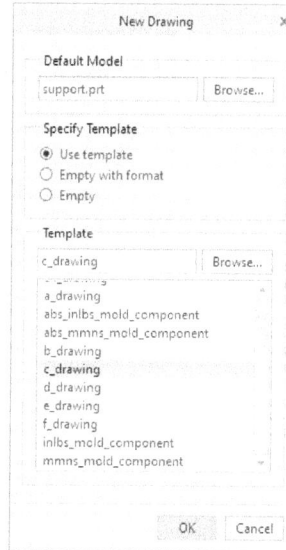

Figure 1–3

Empty with Format

To use a predefined drawing format, select **Empty with Format**. Enter the name of the format or click **Browse** to browse to a predefined format. The dialog box opens as shown in Figure 1–4.

A template can consist of placed views, predefined view displays, placed notes, defined tables, and displayed dimensions. A format generally contains standard information, such as borders, title blocks, tables, and company information.

Figure 1–4

Empty

To create a drawing without a template or format, select **Empty** and define the drawing size and orientation, as shown in Figure 1–5.

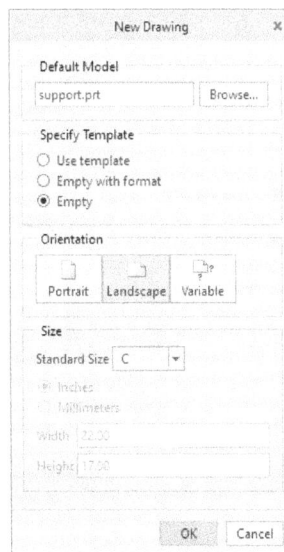

Figure 1–5

5. To create the new drawing, click **OK** in the New Drawing dialog box.

1.3 Drawing Mode Interface

Once the definition of the drawing and its templates have been completed, the Drawing mode user-interface displays. A variety of areas can be manipulated while working in the Drawing mode. Figure 1–6 shows the layout of the drawing environment.

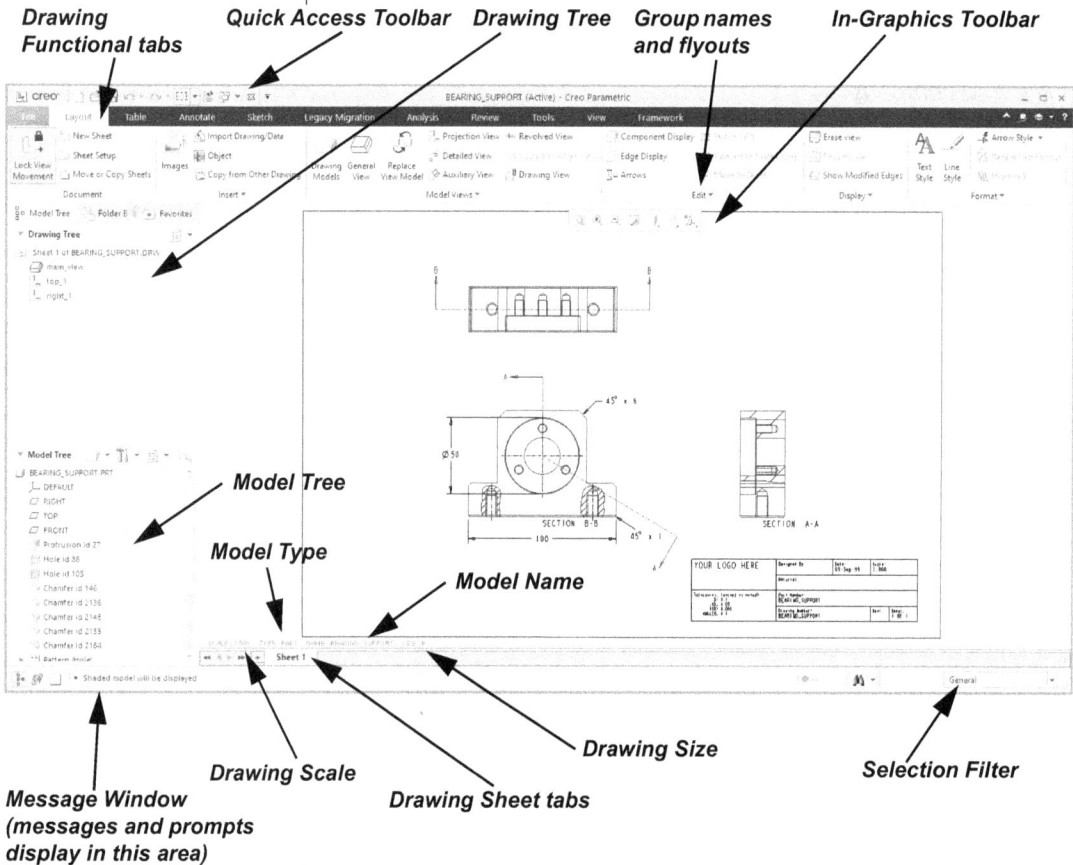

Figure 1–6

Drawing mode uses a ribbon style interface with tabs, as shown in Figure 1–7.

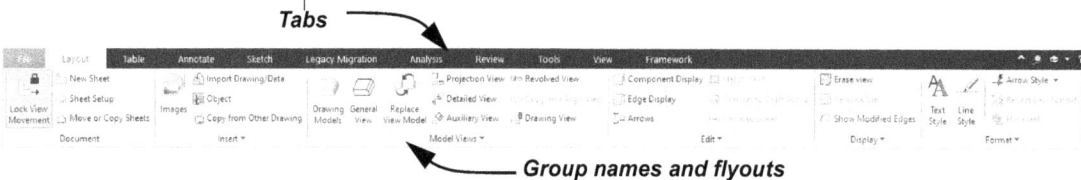

Figure 1–7

Tasks are grouped under tabs and common icons related to the task are grouped under the tab. For example, all of the View icons are located in the Model View group under the *Layout* tab. Only commands that are appropriate for the current task display at a specific time. The items available in the selection filter automatically change to suit the current task. The functionality found under some of the most frequently used tabs is shown in Figure 1–8.

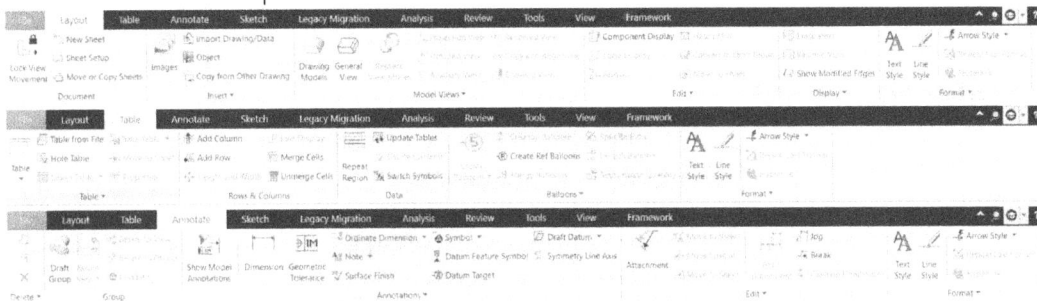

Figure 1–8

Commonly used icons are described as follows:

Icon	Description	Icon	Description
✕	Delete selected items.	A≡	Create notes.
	Drawing models.	↦	Create dimensions.
	Activate windows.		Insert a table.
	Lock or unlock view movement.	▷1M	Create geometric tolerance.
	Regenerate model.		Show.
?	Creo Help Center.		Insert custom drawing symbol.
	Opens the Show Model Annotations dialog box.		Insert general view.
	Aligns dimensions.	A	Text style.

Pan, Zoom

If you have a scroll wheel, use the following methods to pan and zoom a drawing:

- Hold the scroll wheel and drag the mouse to pan.
- Roll the scroll wheel to zoom.

If you do not have a scroll wheel, use the following methods to pan and zoom:

- Press the middle mouse button and drag the mouse to pan.
- Hold <Ctrl> and press the middle mouse button to zoom.

Selection Tool

The ⬚ ▾ (Selection) option in the Quick Access Toolbar provides you with various options for selecting items in a drawing. The default option is ⬚ (Inside/across Box), which enables you to draw a rectangular box. All of the items specified by the filter that lie entirely in the rectangular box are selected if you drag the box toward the right. To select items that lie across the sketched boundary, drag the box toward the left.

The ⬚ (Inside Polygon) option enables you to sketch a polygon that defines the selection area. The remaining selection options in this menu are available for facet surfaces.

Mini Toolbar

The mini toolbar is available for drawing objects and entities, as shown in Figure 1–9.

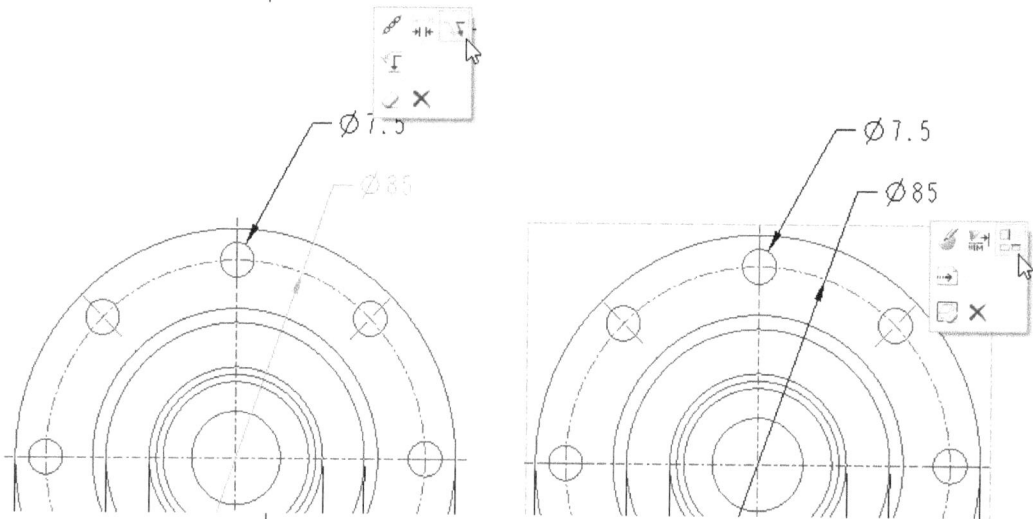

Figure 1–9

Objects and entities (such as annotations, views, and tables) are all supported with a corresponding mini toolbar. Note that the mini toolbar is also available for the 3D annotation environment.

The mini toolbar for entities and objects in the Drawing Tree is also supported, as shown in Figure 1–10.

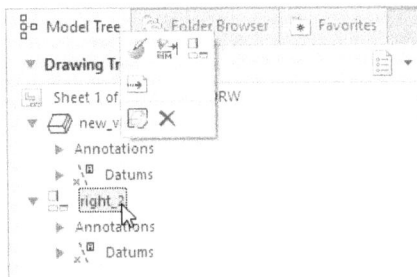

Figure 1–10

Shortcut Menus

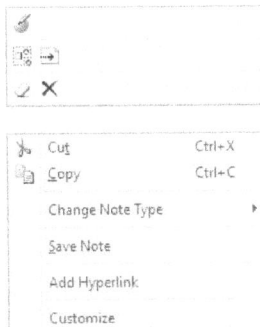

Many options are available in shortcut menus. To access these shortcuts, select an item and right-click. The options provided in the shortcut menu depend on which item is preselected. The options can also vary depending on what displays in the drawing. Several possible shortcut menus that display when different drawing objects are selected are described as follows:

Shortcut Menus

This menu displays when a drawing note is preselected.

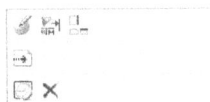

This menu displays when a drawing view is preselected.

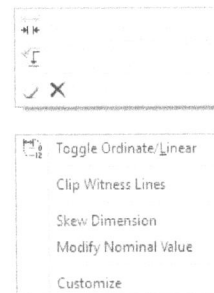

This menu displays when a drawing dimension is preselected.

Undo/Redo

The **Undo/Redo** functionality exists for drawings and works for editing and movement operations. For example, if you delete a dimension and click ↰ (Undo), the dimension will return to the drawing, or if you move a drawing view and click ↰ (Undo) the view will return to the previous location.

By default, the stack limit is 50 operations. This means that once 50 operations have been stored, the first is removed so that only 50 operations are stored in memory. The stack limit is controlled using the **general_undo_stack_limit** config.pro option.

Drawing Tree

The Model Tree is divided into two parts, the *Drawing Tree* area and the *Model Tree* area, as shown in Figure 1–11.

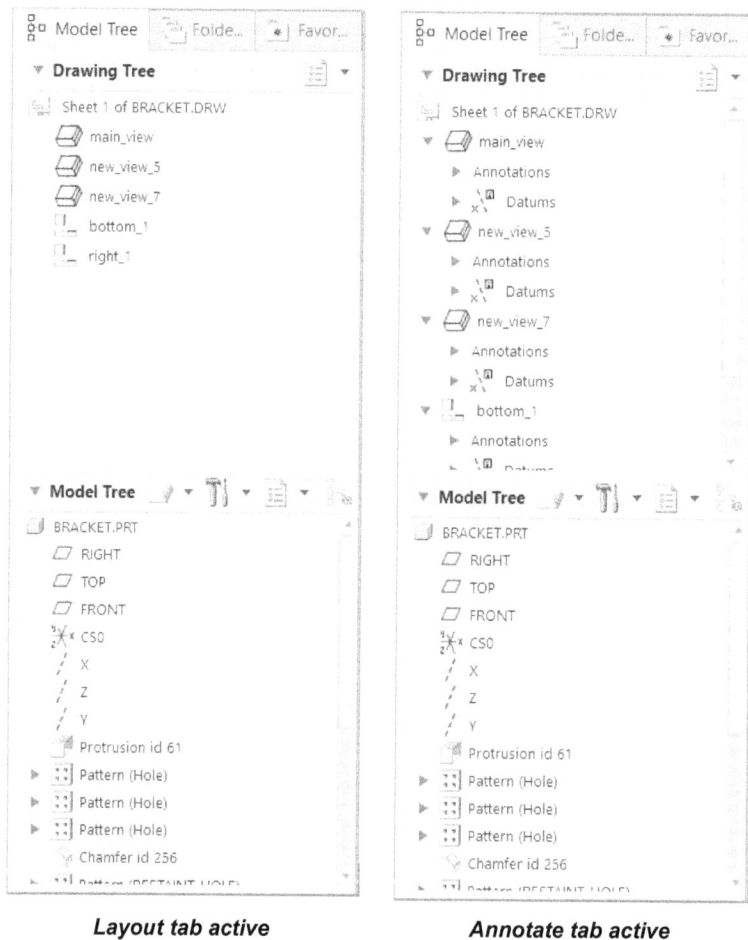

Layout tab active   Annotate tab active

Figure 1–11

The content in the Drawing Tree changes depending on the tab that is currently active. Selected objects highlight in both the Drawing Tree and Graphics window. Shortcut menus are available by right-clicking. The Drawing Tree displays the following drawing items:

- Sheets

- Views

- Tables

- Created/shown annotations

- Datums

- Draft entities

- Snap lines

- Sections

- Groups

- Overlays

1.4 Place the First Drawing View

A General view is always the first view that must be placed on a drawing. This view becomes the parent to other views in the drawing.

How To: Place the First (General) View

Drawings created using a template might already contain certain views. In these situations, you might not need to create the first drawing view, but can create additional General views if they are required in the drawing.

1. The *Layout* tab only displays commands relevant to that function and can be used to create and modify drawing views. The commands for the *Layout* tab are shown in Figure 1–12.

Figure 1–12

2. Use one of the following methods to create a General view:

   - Right-click and select **General View**.

   - Click ⊟ (General View) in the Model Views group in the *Layout* tab.

Select a location on the drawing to place the view. The **General** view is initially placed on the drawing sheet in the Standard Orientation of the model. Once the view has been placed, the Drawing View dialog box opens as shown in Figure 1–13.

Figure 1–13

By default, the *View Type* category settings display in the Drawing View dialog box. This area enables you to enter a name for the view and to define its view orientation. To modify the view orientation, select one the following orientation options in the *View orientation* area:

- View names from the model

- Geometry references

- Angles

View Names From the Model

The **View names from the model** option enables you to orient the General view on the drawing using a predefined view that has been saved in the model. The list of predefined views display in the Drawing View dialog box, as shown in Figure 1–14.

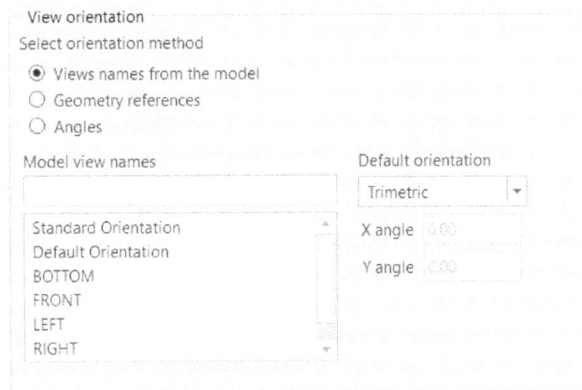

Figure 1–14

Geometry References

The **Geometry references** option enables you to orient the General view using the orientation tools that are used in other 3D models. You must select an orientation (e.g., Front, Top, Right, etc.), and then select a planar surface, coordinate system axis, or datum plane as its reference, as shown in Figure 1–15. The two references must be perpendicular to one another to orient the view into 2D.

Default datum planes are recommended to orient the model rather than planar surfaces. If the planar surfaces are later deleted, the orientation references are lost.

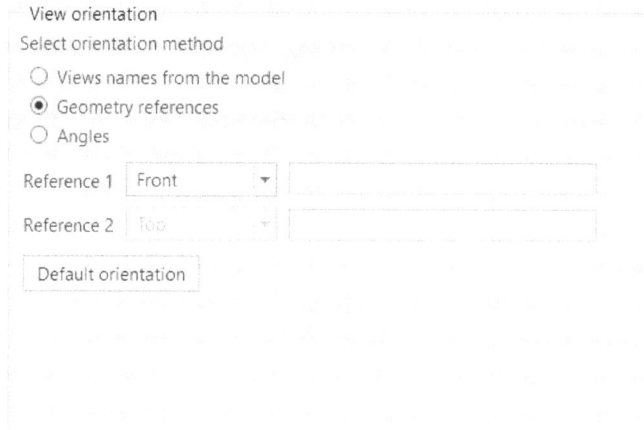

Figure 1–15

You can click **Default orientation** to return the view to the default orientation.

For example, the model shown in Figure 1–16 is oriented to 2D using the **Geometry references** option and by selecting references for the **Front** and **Top** reference options. Alternatively, you can select the **View names from the model** option if a predefined orientation exists that will orient the model the same way.

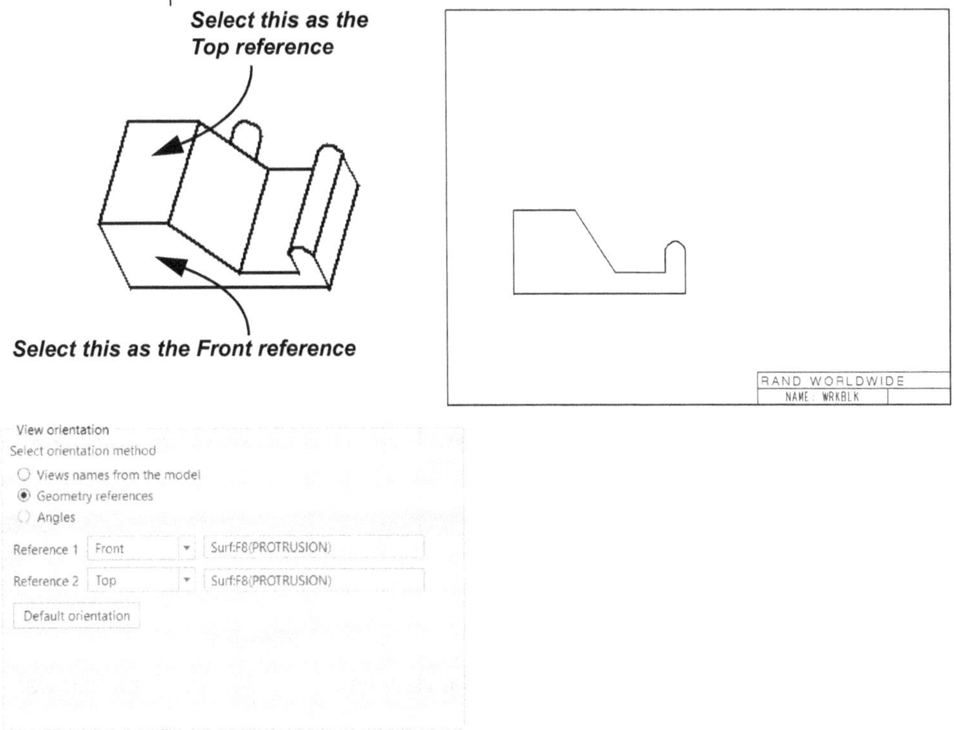

Select this as the Top reference

Select this as the Front reference

RAND WORLDWIDE
NAME: WRKBLK

View orientation

Select orientation method

○ Views names from the model
◉ Geometry references
○ Angles

| Reference 1 | Front | ▼ | Surf:F8(PROTRUSION) |
| Reference 2 | Top | ▼ | Surf:F8(PROTRUSION) |

Default orientation

Figure 1–16

Angles

The **Angles** option enables you to orient the General view by selecting a direction and entering angular values to place the view. The available directions are: **Normal**, **Vertical**, **Horizontal**, and **Edge/Axis**. The **Normal**, **Vertical**, and **Horizontal** directions are relative to the drawing sheet (monitor) and the **Edge/Axis** direction enables you to select a reference on the model from which to orient.

You can add and remove orientation angles as required using ✚ (Add Angle Entry) and ▬ (Remove Angle Entry).

To apply the new view orientation, select an option and click **Apply**.

- Once the orientation has been defined, click **OK** in the Drawing View dialog box to complete the view placement.

- Additional options and categories are available in the Drawing View dialog box.

1.5 Place Additional Views

Drawings usually contain multiple views to accurately represent the drawing model.

How To: Place Additional Views in a Drawing

1. The *Layout* tab only displays commands relevant to that function. This tab must be active if you want to create and modify views.
2. Once a General view has been added to the drawing, you can create additional General views or other types of views that reference the General view. The View icons are located in the *Layout* tab in the Model Views group, as shown in Figure 1–17.

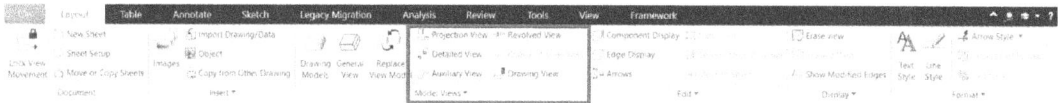

Figure 1–17

The additional view types are described as follows:

Option	Description
(General)	Creates an independent view of a model. The orientation of the General view is determined using the *View Type* category in the Drawing View dialog box. You can place several general views on a drawing, as shown. *General view* *General (Oriented) view*
(Projection)	Projects a view from an existing view, which creates orthogonal views, such as top, bottom, right, or left. A Projection view maintains the scale of its parent view as shown. *General view (Parent)* *Projection view (Child)*

◇ (Auxiliary)	Projects a view normal to a datum plane, edge, or axis of an existing view. This type of view can be used to display the actual size and form from an angled surface. Auxiliary views can be created by referencing a datum plane, edge, or axis of any other type of view as shown.

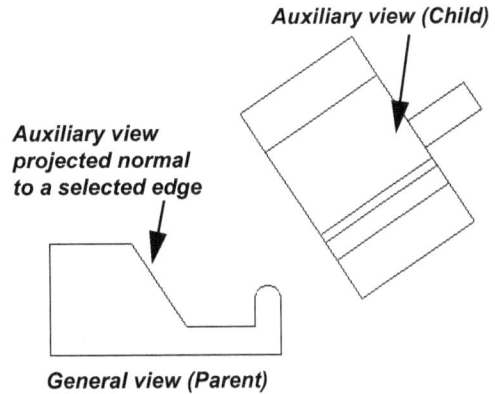

Auxiliary view (Child)

Auxiliary view projected normal to a selected edge

General view (Parent)

▱ (Detailed)	Creates a scaled view focusing on a specific area of an existing view. The Detailed view is created by sketching a spline on the parent view that encloses the area to be represented. To complete the view, assign a name, boundary type, and note location. The Detailed view is automatically labeled with its scale value and view name. Orientation of this view corresponds to the parent view as shown.

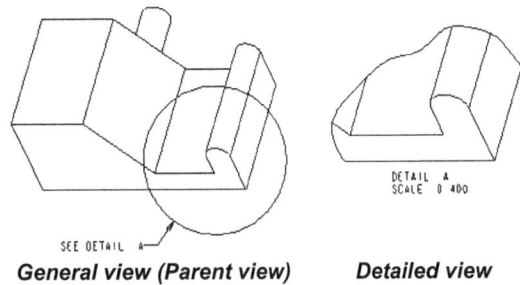

DETAIL A
SCALE 0.400

SEE DETAIL A

General view (Parent view)   **Detailed view**

⊶⊶ (Revolved)	Creates a planar area cross-section that is revolved 90° around the projection of the cutting plane as shown. Revolved views can be translated in the projection direction.

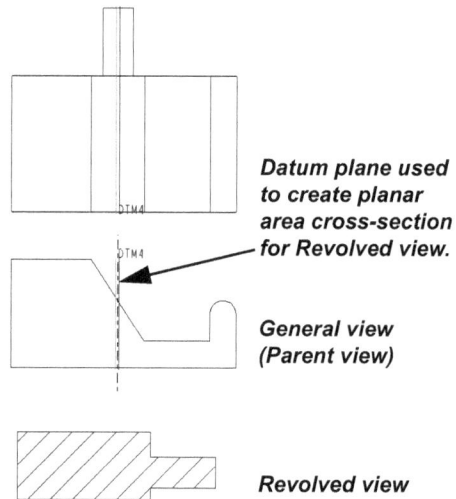

Datum plane used to create planar area cross-section for Revolved view.

General view (Parent view)

Revolved view

▽▽ (Copy and Align)	Creates a duplicate of an existing Partial or Detailed view. A new boundary spline can be sketched and the view is aligned to the parent view as shown. The Copy and Align view maintains the same scale as its parent view.

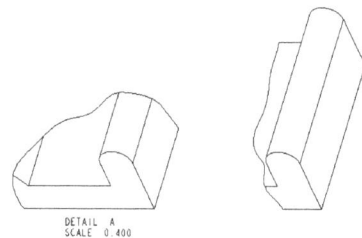

DETAIL A
SCALE 0.400

Detailed View (Parent view)   **Copy & Align view**

The methods of creating a new view vary depending on the type of view that is required. The methods include the following:

- To create an additional General view, right-click and select **General View**, and place the view. Alternatively, you can click ▱ (General View) in the *Layout* tab.

Drawings created using a template might already contain specific views. Additional views can be added at any time.

- To create a Projected view, select the parent view and click ⬚ (Projection View) in the mini toolbar or *Layout* tab.

- To create a Detailed, Auxiliary, or Revolved view, click the appropriate icon in the Model Views group in the *Layout* tab, and then access the options.

Visibility area is a category that can be customized for a drawing view.

- To create a Copy and Align view, preselect a Detailed view or a partial visibility area view, and click ▽▽ (Copy And Align) in the Model Views group in the *Layout* tab. This view type is not available unless a Detailed view or a partial visibility area view has been created in the drawing.

3. To obtain information about a view, right-click the view and click ⬚ (Drawing View) in the mini toolbar or the Model Views group>*Layout* tab. An information window opens as shown in Figure 1–18.

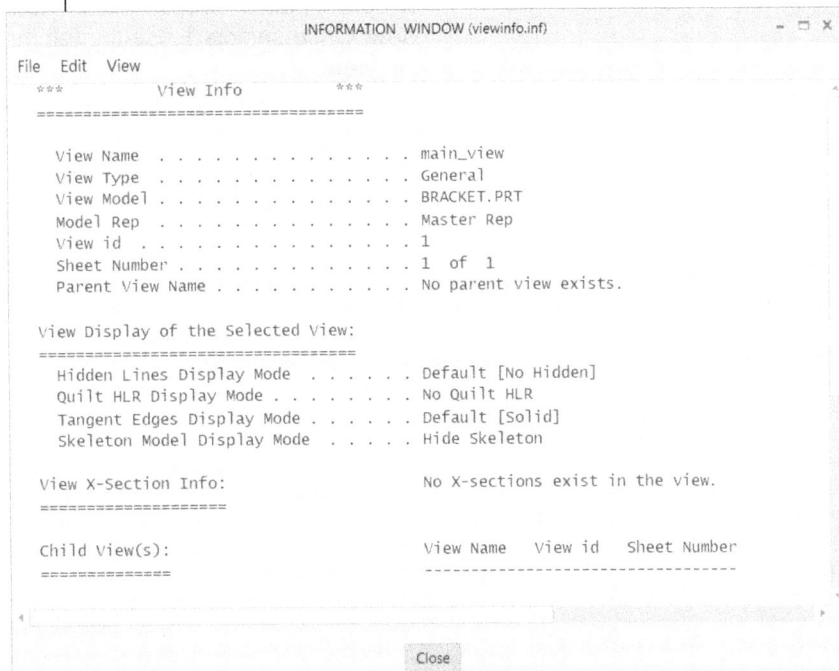

```
INFORMATION WINDOW (viewinfo.inf)                        - □ X

File  Edit  View
 ***          View Info          ***
 =====================================

    View Name  . . . . . . . . . . . . . main_view
    View Type  . . . . . . . . . . . . . General
    View Model . . . . . . . . . . . . . BRACKET.PRT
    Model Rep  . . . . . . . . . . . . . Master Rep
    View id  . . . . . . . . . . . . . . 1
    Sheet Number . . . . . . . . . . . . 1  of  1
    Parent View Name . . . . . . . . . . No parent view exists.


 View Display of the Selected View:
 ===================================
    Hidden Lines Display Mode  . . . . . . Default [No Hidden]
    Quilt HLR Display Mode . . . . . . . . No Quilt HLR
    Tangent Edges Display Mode . . . . . . Default [Solid]
    Skeleton Model Display Mode  . . . . . Hide Skeleton


 View X-Section Info:                      No X-sections exist in the view.
 ====================

 Child View(s):                           View Name   View id   Sheet Number
 ==============                           ---------------------------------------

                              Close
```

Figure 1–18

4. In general, views are placed using the left mouse button. Note the following additional information for placing specific view types:

- General views are placed using the left mouse button. Initially, the view is placed in its default orientation, but it can also be oriented into 2D.

- Projection views are placed using the left mouse button. They can only be placed horizontally or vertically relative to the parent view.

- Detailed views focus on a specific area. Therefore, you must first select a point on an existing view. The point represents the centerpoint for the new view. Once selected, sketch a spline around the point to define the extent (boundary) of the view. To complete the spline, press the middle mouse button. Once the spline has been completed, place the view using the left mouse button.

- Auxiliary views first require the selection of an edge, axis, or datum plane to represent the front surface of the new view. Once selected, use the left mouse button to place the view.

- Revolved views require the selection of a parent view followed by placement using the left mouse button. Once selected, the Drawing View dialog box opens. You can select the cross-section to be referenced or create a new one.

Additional options and categories are available in the Drawing View dialog box.

5. For many of the view types, the drawing view placement is complete on placement. However, for General and Revolved views that use the Drawing View dialog box, you must click **OK** to complete the view placement.

1.6 Modify View Properties I

All views except General and Revolved views are placed without using the Drawing Views dialog box. To further refine any views that do not use this dialog box, you can modify the view properties. You can use the *View Type* category or other categories in the Drawing View dialog box.

How To: Modify the View Properties

1. Use one of the following techniques to open the Drawing View dialog box, if it is not already open:

    • Double-click on the view that you are modifying.

    • Select the view that you are modifying and click

       (Properties) in the mini toolbar.

2. To modify a view property, you must select a category in the left column of the Drawing View dialog box. Once selected, the dialog box updates and displays the available options for the selected category.

    The following view property categories are available:

    • Visible Area

    • Scale

    • Sections

3. To complete the modification to the drawing view, click **OK** in the Drawing View dialog box.

View Property Categories

Visible Area

By default, views are created so that the entire model displays. You can customize how much of the model to display in a view using the *Visible Area* category. Once the *Visible Area* category is selected, the dialog box opens as shown in Figure 1–19.

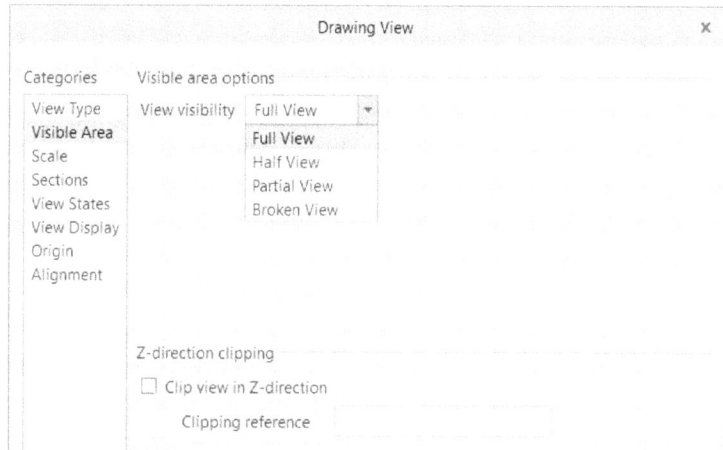

Figure 1–19

The **Visible area** options can be selected in the **View Visibility** menu. They are described as follows:

Option	Description
Full View	(Default option.) Displays a view of the entire model as shown.
Half View	Displays a view of the model about a line of symmetry as shown. The cutting plane used to define the half view can be a planar surface or datum plane. This option is available for Projection, Auxiliary, and General views.

Partial View	Displays a view focused on a specific location on the model. Bounding entities define the geometry that is represented as shown. This option is available for Projection, Auxiliary, General, and Revolved views.
Broken View	Displays a view in which break lines define the sections to be removed. Break lines can be horizontal and/or vertical as shown. This option is available for Projection and General views. You cannot break a horizontally projected view horizontally and you cannot break a vertically projected view vertically.

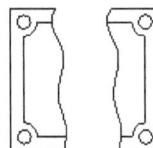

Scale

The *Scale* category in the Drawing View dialog box enables you to assign scales to General and Detailed views that are independent of the drawing scale. The scale for all other views in the drawing is determined by the parent view. Figure 1–20 shows the **Scale category** options in the Drawing View dialog box.

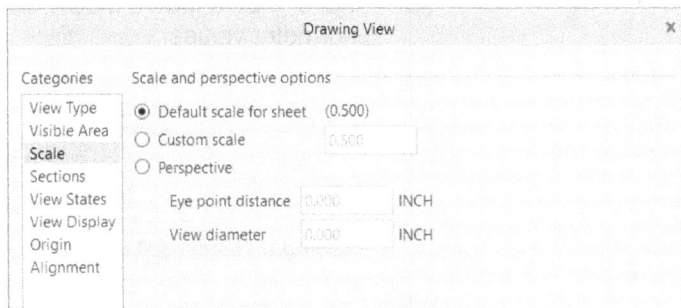

Figure 1–20

By default, all views except for Detailed views, are created using the scale that was assigned to the sheet (**Default scale for sheet**). Any changes made to the sheet scale updates these views. The **Custom scale** option enables you to assign an independent scale. Once assigned, the view scale is located directly under the view, as shown in Figure 1–21.

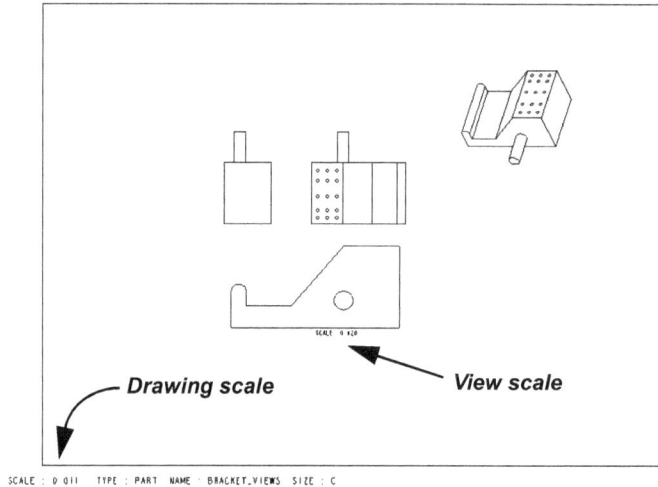

SCALE : 0 011   TYPE : PART   NAME : BRACKET_VIEWS   SIZE : C

Figure 1–21

The **Perspective** option enables you to change the viewing distance and diameter parameters of a General perspective view. The viewing distance is the distance (in model units) between the object and the viewer. The viewing diameter determines the actual size of the view based on drawing units. Figure 1–22 shows a model with different viewing distance parameter values.

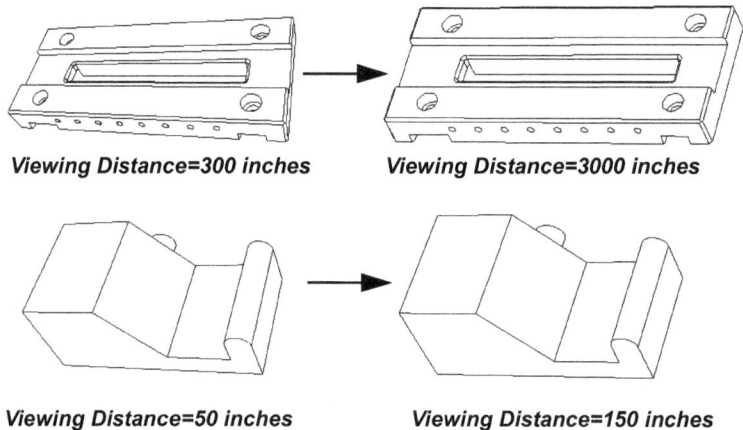

Viewing Distance=300 inches   *Viewing Distance=3000 inches*

Viewing Distance=50 inches   *Viewing Distance=150 inches*

Figure 1–22

Sections

By default, a view is created without any sectioning. To create a cross-section view, select the *Sections* category in the Drawing View dialog box and select **2D cross-section**. The dialog box opens as shown in Figure 1–23.

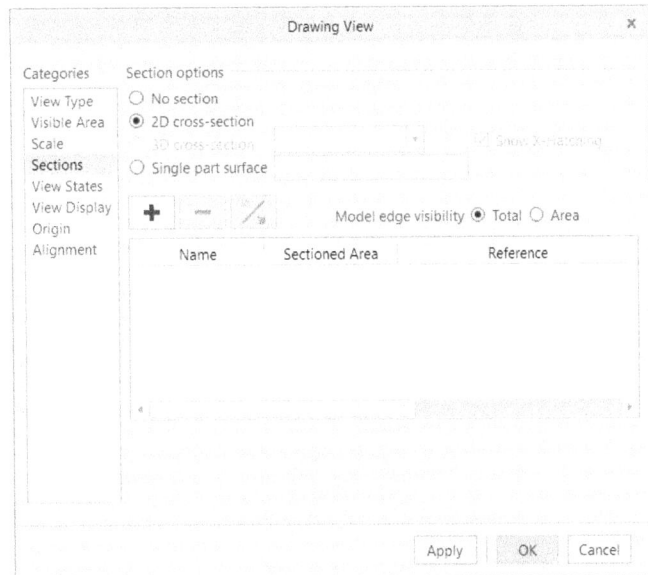

Figure 1–23

2D Cross-Sections

Click ✚ (Add Section) to assign a cross-section to the view. The dialog box updates as shown in Figure 1–24. You can select the section name in the **Name** menu or use **Create New** in this menu to create a new section. The options for creating a new section are the same as in Part or Assembly mode.

For simplicity, create and save your sections in the model and then place them in your drawing.

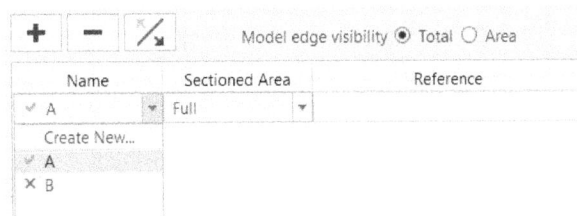

Figure 1–24

The edges that display in the cross-section view can be customized by selecting an edge visibility method. The **Total** option creates a cross-section that displays all of the edges that are behind the cutting plane, as shown on the left in Figure 1–25. The **Area** option creates a cross-section that only displays the material in the cutting plane, as shown on the right in Figure 1–25. Edges behind the cutting plane are not visible.

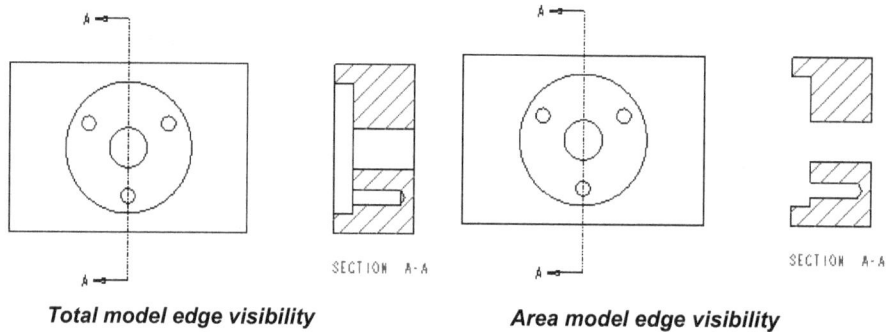

Total model edge visibility   *Area model edge visibility*

Figure 1–25

Once the cross-section has been selected, you can select an option in the **Sectioned Area** menu. The options are described as follows:

Option	Description
Full	Displays the cross-section on the entire view (default option) as shown.

Half	Displays the cross-section on one side of a boundary plane as shown. A datum plane is selected as the boundary for the cross-section. The material on the opposite side of the datum plane remains solid.

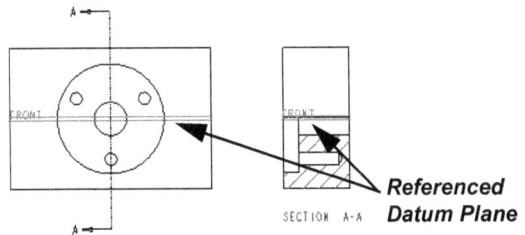

SECTION A-A   *Referenced Datum Plane*

Local	Displays the cross-section focusing on a specific area(s). A sketched spline defines the boundary of the local view. The material outside the boundary remains solid as shown.

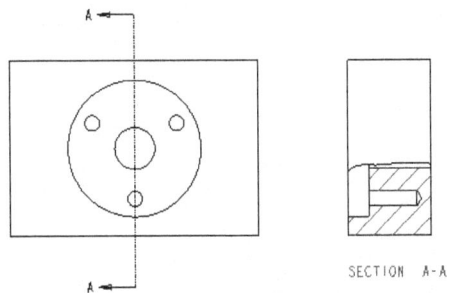

SECTION A-A

Full (Align)	Creates an area cross-section through the cutting planes of an offset cross-section until parallel to the screen. The planes are unfolded about an existing axis in the view as shown.

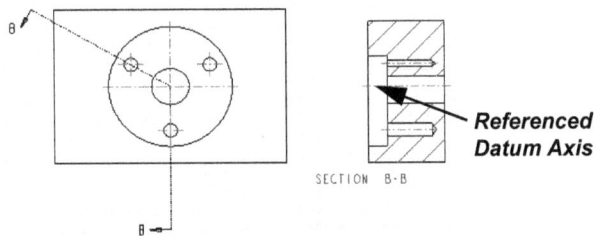

SECTION B-B   *Referenced Datum Axis*

Full (Unfold)	Creates an area cross-section where the cutting planes of an offset cross-section unfold until parallel to the screen. The planes are unfolded about the seams of the offset cutting line as shown.

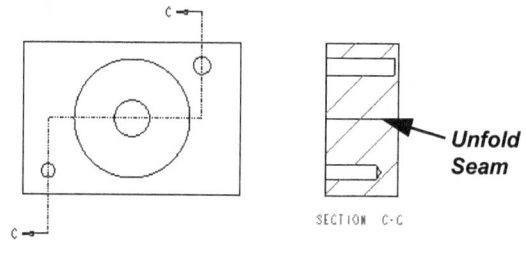

Once **Sectioned Area** has been selected, scroll to the right to display the remaining options for defining the section as shown in Figure 1–26.

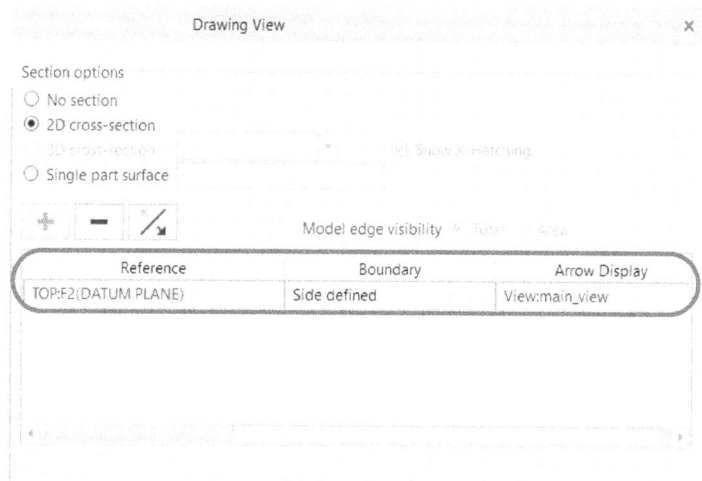

Figure 1–26

*Once a section view has been created, cross-section arrows can be added by right-clicking on the sectioned view and selecting **Add Arrows** or clicking ⬚ (Arrows) in the Layout tab.*

The *Arrow Display* column enables you to add cross-section arrows to a view, as shown in Figure 1–27. To place the arrows, select this cell and select the view to place the arrows.

To clear the arrows from the display, right-click on the reference view that was assigned and select **Remove**.

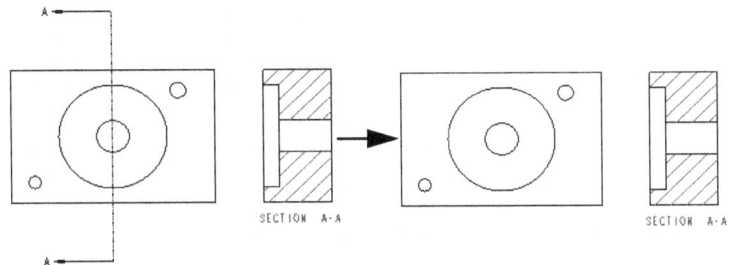

Figure 1–27

The *Reference* and *Boundary* columns are only available if you have selected a local cross-section. They enable you to define the center point for the breakout and its defining spline.

Multiple 2D Cross-Sections

Multiple cross-sections can be assigned to a view by clicking ✚ (Add Section) to define another cross-section. Creating multiple cross-sections in one view can help reduce the number of views on a drawing sheet. For example, Figure 1–28 shows a view that has two cross-sections: one is set as **Full** and the other as **Local**. To remove a cross-section from the view, select it and use ▬ (Remove Section).

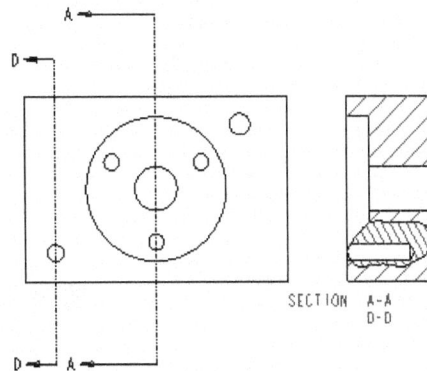

Figure 1–28

Single Part Surface

*A view to which the **Single part surface** option is applied cannot be converted back to a normal view.*

The **Single part surface** option in the *Section options* area in the dialog box provides an alternative to selecting or creating a cross-section. This option enables you to create a view of a single surface by projecting from the solid model surface or a datum quilt. Creo Parametric deletes all of the other geometry, as shown in Figure 1–29. This option is not available for Detailed views.

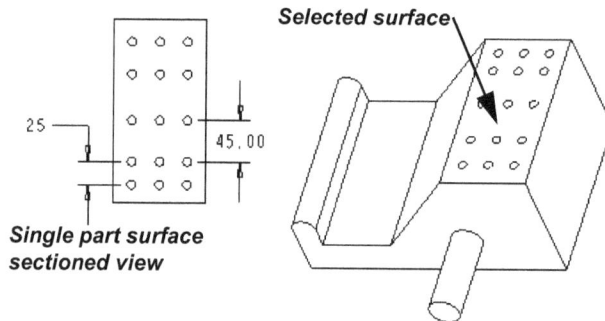

Figure 1–29

When you create a cross-section in Part mode or Assembly mode, the system automatically checks whether the parts intersected by the cross-section have assigned materials. If the material name matches the name of the saved cross-hatching pattern file (e.g., **copper.xch**), the cross-hatching pattern is automatically applied. The **pro_crosshatch_dir** config.pro option is used to point to a directory containing user-defined cross-hatching pattern files.

In Figure 1–30, the assembly drawing contains a section view. The materials assigned to the two components (i.e., aluminum and steel) match the names of saved cross-hatching files (i.e., **aluminum.xch** and **steel.xch**). When the section view was created and placed, these cross-hatching patterns were automatically applied.

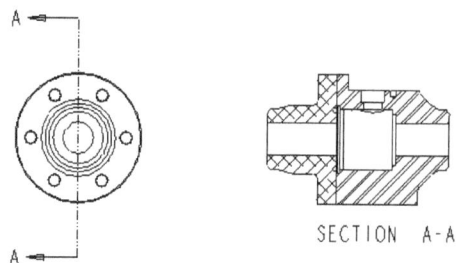

Figure 1–30

Cross-hatching

- You can hatch or fill flat surfaces by right-clicking on them and selecting **Hatch** or **Fill**.

- You can use the **X-Area** option in the **MOD XHATCH** menu to show or hide areas of component sections, as shown in Figure 1–31.

*To access the **MOD XHATCH** menu, right-click on the crosshatch/fill and select **Properties**.*

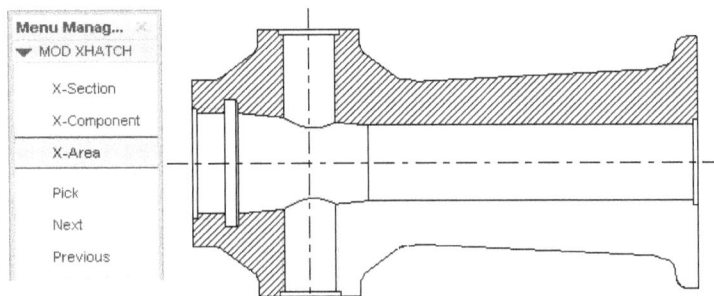

Figure 1–31

The drawing configuration options used in conjunction with cross-hatching in a drawing are described as follows:

Configuration Option	Value	Description
default_show_3d_ section_xhatch	**Yes**/No	Controls the default visibility of 3D sections in a drawing.
default_show_2d_ section_xhatch	**assembly_and_ part** assembly_only part_only No	Controls the default visibility of 2D sections in a drawing.

Shaded Views

Shaded views of models can be included in drawings. This capability improves the plotting of drawings with OLE objects and shaded views. Shaded drawing views display the color scheme from the part/assembly. This includes surface colors and textures. You can combine traditional views (such as wireframe, hidden line, etc.) and shaded views in one drawing, as shown in Figure 1–32.

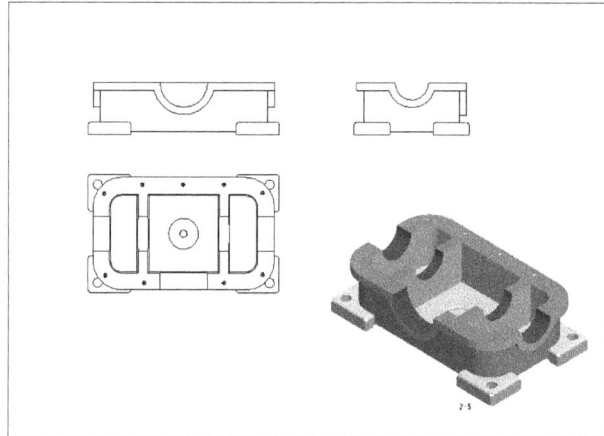

Figure 1–32

You define a view as shaded or shaded with edges in the *View Display options* area in the Drawing View dialog box. Select **Shading** or **Shading with Edges** in the **Display style** menu, as shown in Figure 1–33.

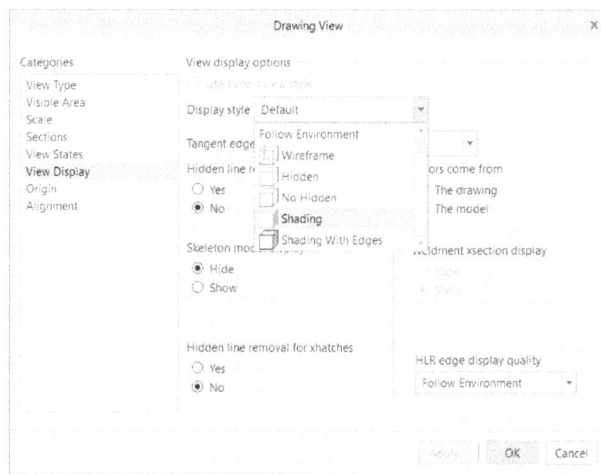

Figure 1–33

1.7 Drawing Options

The drawing setup file is a file that is stored with each drawing and controls specific characteristics of the drawing. For example, the drawing setup file values determine items, such as projection type (first or third angle), view scale format, drawing units, dimension, and note text height. All of the drawing setup file options can be reviewed using Creo Help Center.

To access the drawing setup file, select **File>Prepare>Drawing Properties**. The Drawing Properties dialog box opens. Select **change** in the *Detail Options* area as shown in Figure 1–34.

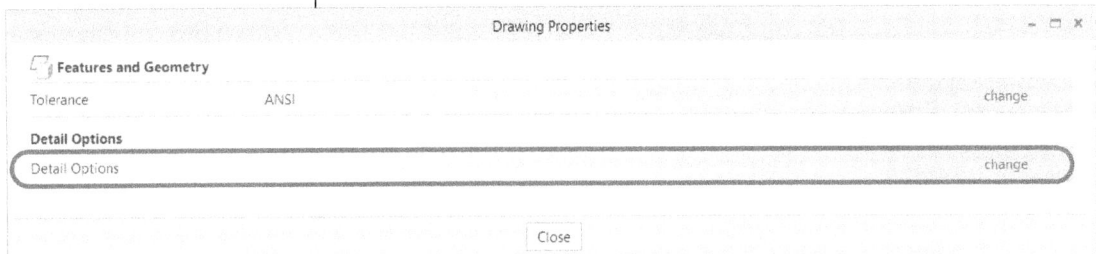

Figure 1–34

The Options dialog box opens as shown in Figure 1–35.

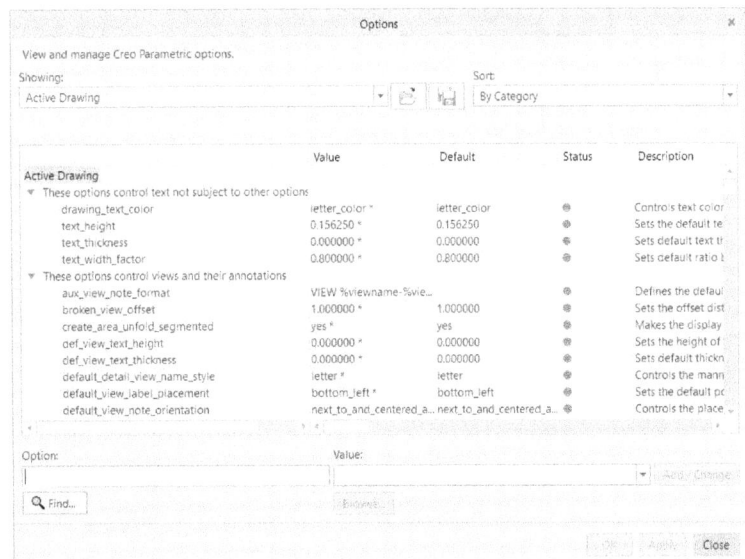

Figure 1–35

*Drawing setup files are saved with a .dtl extension. The **drawing_setup_file** configuration file option enables you to specify a drawing setup file to use for new drawings.*

Every drawing assigns default values to these setup file options. These values can be modified and saved for use in the same or other drawings. To save a drawing setup file for use in another drawing, click 🖫 (Save Configuration). To open a predefined setup, click 📂 (Open Configuration) and select the file.

Config.pro File

The config.pro is a configuration file that controls environment settings (e.g., drawing setup file, , etc.) in Creo Parametric. Select **File>Options>Configuration Editor** to access the config.pro file. The Options dialog box opens as shown in Figure 1–36.

*Click **Display Filters** and clear the **Show current session** option to display all of the options.*

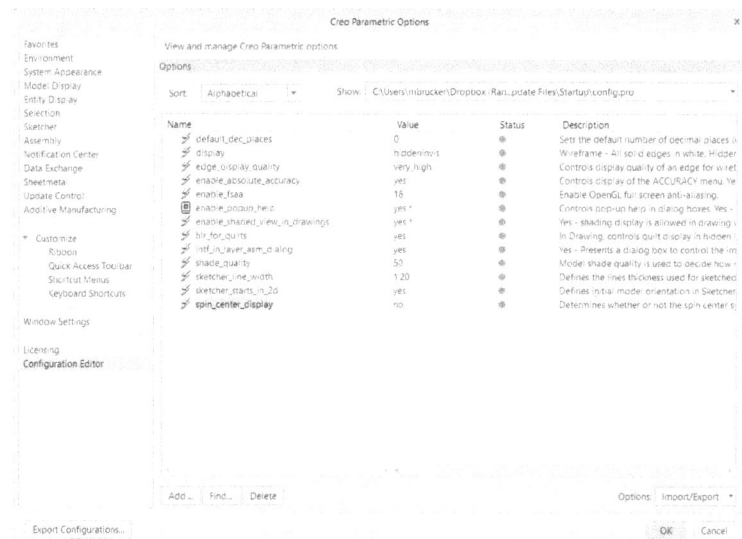

Figure 1–36

All of the configuration file options can be reviewed using Creo Help Center.

Many of the configuration file options are specific to Drawing mode. To access the specific drawing model options, select **By Category** in the **Sort** menu and scroll down to the Drawing list. All of the options in this section pertain to Drawing mode.

Unlike the drawing setup file, the config.pro is not automatically saved and stored with the drawing. Once the changes have been made, click **OK**. The PTC Creo Parametric Options dialog box opens in which you have the option of saving the settings, as shown in Figure 1–37.

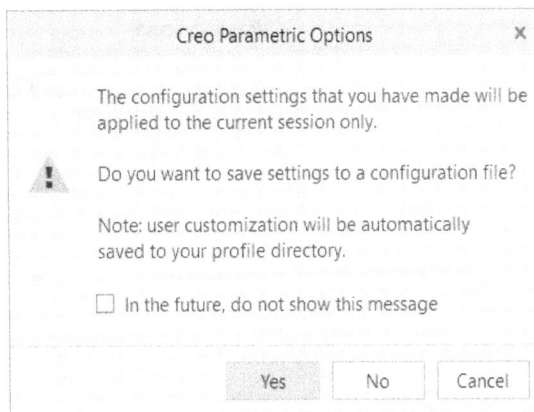

Figure 1–37

You can have the system save the settings by clicking **Yes**. Clicking **No** only changes the settings for the current session.

Creo Parametric reads the configuration file from several locations: the */loadpoint/text* directory, the user's home directory, and the startup directory. Additional configuration files can be stored in other locations, but must be explicitly loaded to affect the drawing. To import a config.pro, click **Import/Export**, select **Import** from the flyout, and select the file.

Practice 1a

Create a New Drawing

Practice Objectives

- Create a new drawing and assign a model to this drawing.
- Select the sheet size, place views on the drawing, and modify the drawing scale.

In this practice, you will create drawing views from a solid part. The drawing model is shown in Figure 1–38.

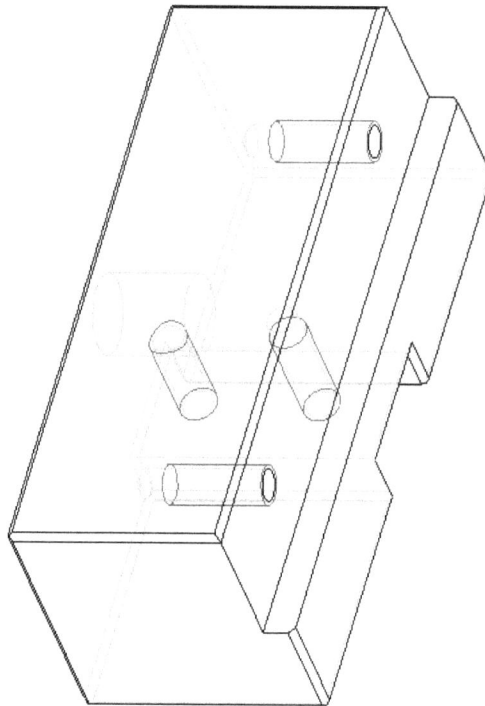

Figure 1–38

Task 1 - Create a new drawing and select the format and sheet size.

1. Set the working directory by clicking ⬎ (Select Working Directory). Select the *New_Drawing* folder.

2. Click ▢ (New) in the Quick Access Toolbar to create a new drawing. The New dialog box opens.

3. Select **Drawing**.

4. Clear the **Use default template** option and leave **Use drawing model file name** enabled. The New dialog box displays as shown in Figure 1–39.

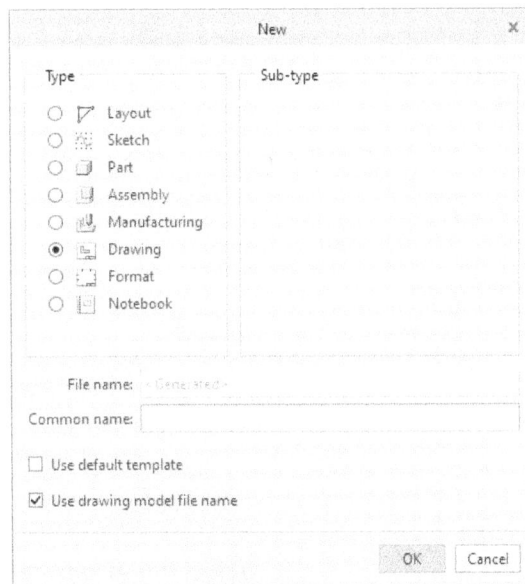

Figure 1–39

5. Click **OK**. The New Drawing dialog box opens.

6. Click **Browse** in the *Default Model* area in the New Drawing dialog box.

7. Select **support.prt** in the current working directory and click **Open**.

8. Select **Empty** in the *Specify Template* area.

9. Select **A** in the **Standard Size** menu. The New Drawing dialog box displays as shown in Figure 1–40.

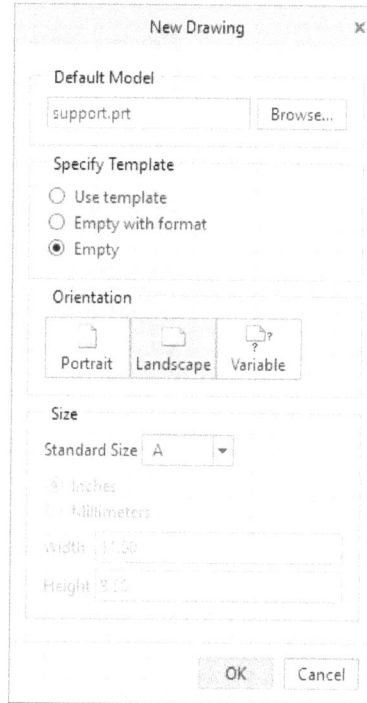

Figure 1–40

10. Click **OK** to create the drawing. The Drawing mode user-interface displays.

Task 2 - Define the drawing's projection type.

1. Select **File>Prepare>Drawing Properties**. In the Drawing Properties dialog box, click **change** next to **Detail Options**, as shown in Figure 1–41.

Click change

Figure 1–41

2. The Options dialog box opens. Select **By Category** in the **Sort** menu.

You can enter projection_type in the Option area in the dialog box to quickly find the config option.

3. Select **projection_type** and ensure that it is set to **third_angle**. This is the default option. The Options dialog box displays as shown in Figure 1–42.

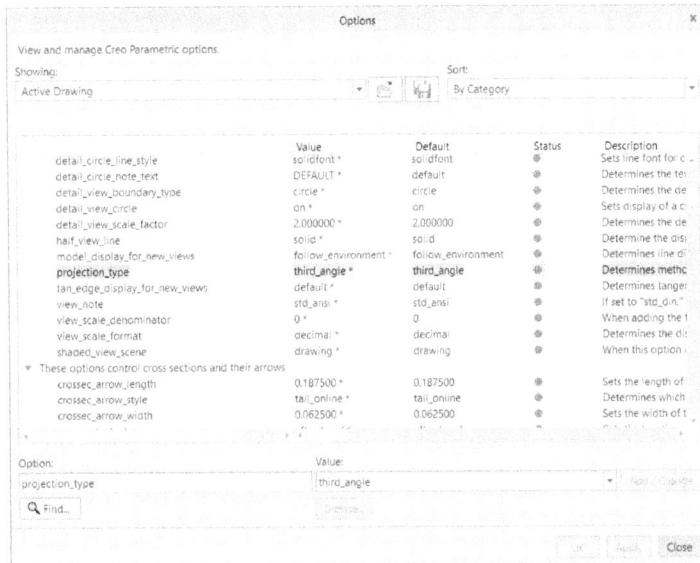

Figure 1–42

4. Close the Options dialog box and the Drawing Properties dialog box.

Task 3 - Place a General view in the default orientation.

You can also right-click and select Insert General View.

1. Set the model display as follows:

- (Datum Display Filters): All Off

- (Display Style): (Wireframe)

2. Ensure that the *Layout* tab is active.

3. Click (General View) in the Model Views group.

4. Ensure that **No Combined State** is selected and select **Do not prompt for Combined State**, as shown in Figure 1–43. Then, click **OK**.

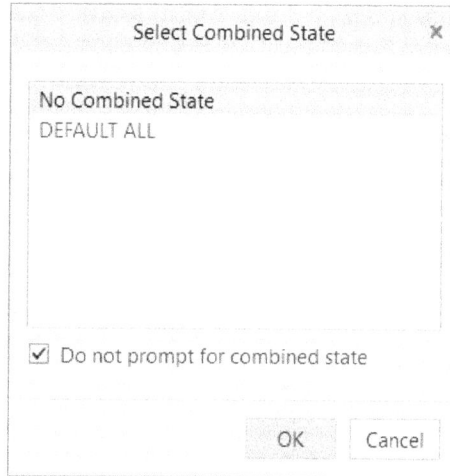

Select Combined State ✕

No Combined State
DEFAULT ALL

☑ Do not prompt for combined state

OK   Cancel

Figure 1–43

5. Select the top right corner of the drawing sheet to define the centerpoint for the drawing view. The Drawing View dialog box opens as shown in Figure 1–44.

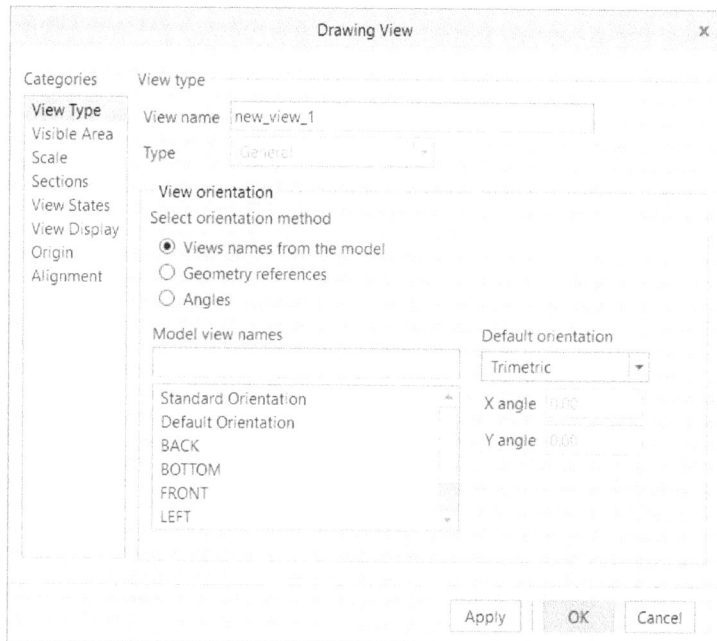

Drawing View ✕

Categories | View type

View Type
Visible Area
Scale
Sections
View States
View Display
Origin
Alignment

View name new_view_1
Type General

View orientation
Select orientation method
● Views names from the model
○ Geometry references
○ Angles

Model view names   Default orientation
                                     Trimetric
Standard Orientation   X angle 0.00
Default Orientation   Y angle 0.00
BACK
BOTTOM
FRONT
LEFT

Apply   OK   Cancel

Figure 1–44

6. Select **Default Orientation** in the *Model view names* area and click **OK**. The drawing model displays as shown in Figure 1–45 in its default orientation.

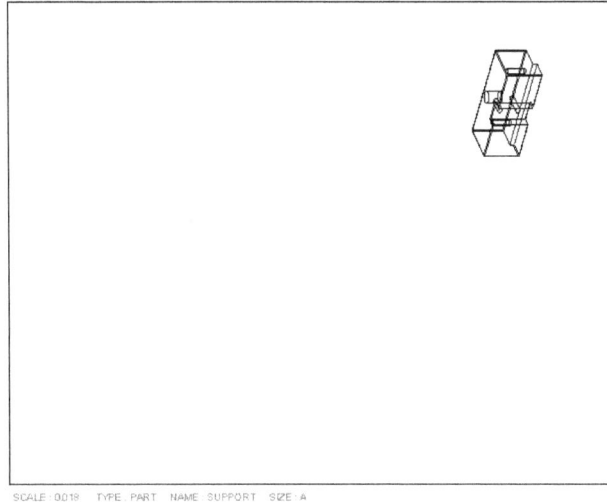

SCALE : 0.019   TYPE : PART   NAME : SUPPORT   SIZE : A

Figure 1–45

Task 4 - Place a General view.

1. Click on the screen so the view is no longer selected.

2. Right-click and select ⬚ (General View).

3. Select the bottom left corner of the drawing sheet using the left mouse button to define the centerpoint of the drawing view.

4. Select **RIGHT** from the model view names drop-down list, as shown in Figure 1–46.

While orienting a view, the drawing can be dynamically zoomed and panned. Dynamic rotation is not available in a 2D drawing.

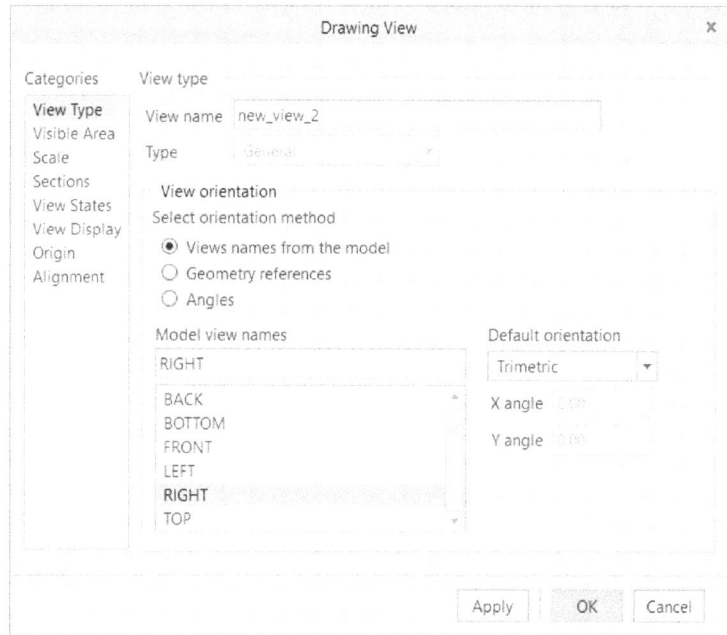

Figure 1–46

5. Click **OK**. The drawing updates as shown in Figure 1–47.

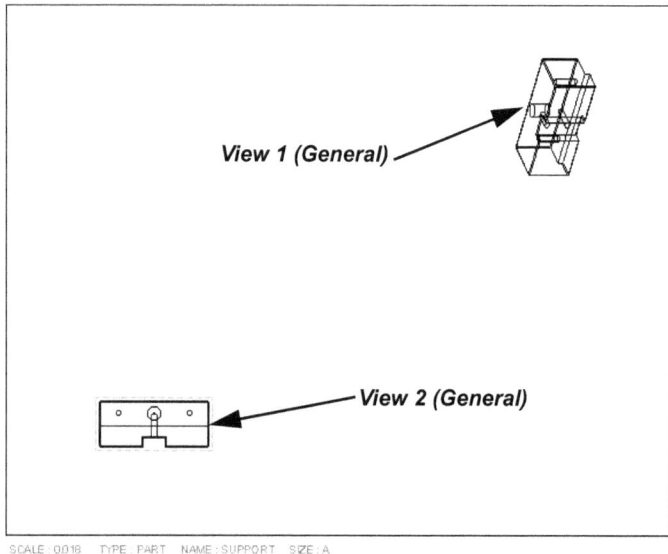

Figure 1–47

Task 5 - Modify the scale value for the drawing.

1. The *Scale* value is located in the lower left corner of the drawing. Double-click on it and modify it to **0.8**. The drawing and all of its views update, as shown in Figure 1–48.

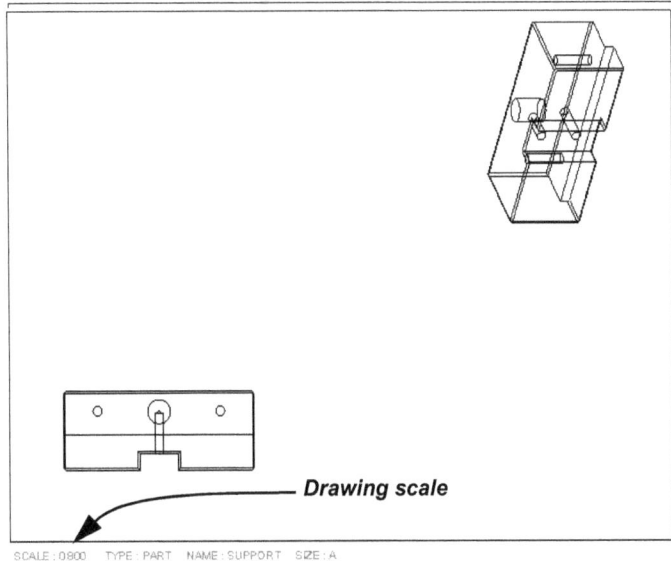

Drawing scale

SCALE : 0.800   TYPE : PART   NAME : SUPPORT   SIZE : A

Figure 1–48

Task 6 - Create projection views in the drawing.

1. Select the second General view that was created. This will be the parent view for the projection.

2. Click ⬚ (Projection View) in the mini toolbar.

3. Drag the cursor above its parent view.

4. Press the left mouse button to place the view. The drawing displays as shown in Figure 1–49.

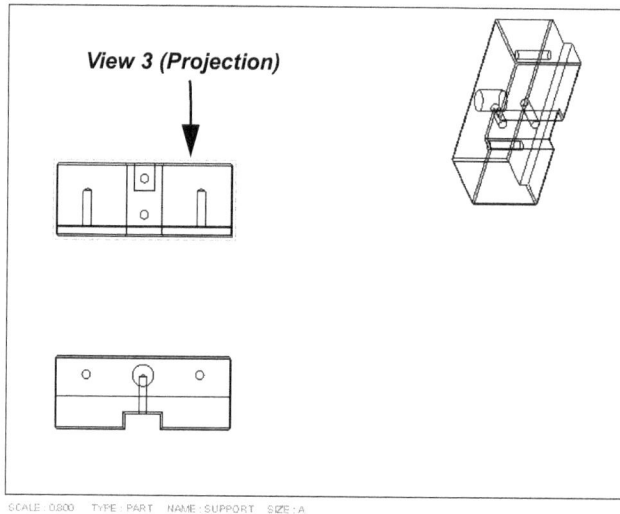

View 3 (Projection)

SCALE : 0.800   TYPE : PART   NAME : SUPPORT   SIZE : A

Figure 1–49

5. Repeat Steps 1 and 4 to place a Projected view to the right of View 2. The drawing displays as shown in Figure 1–50.

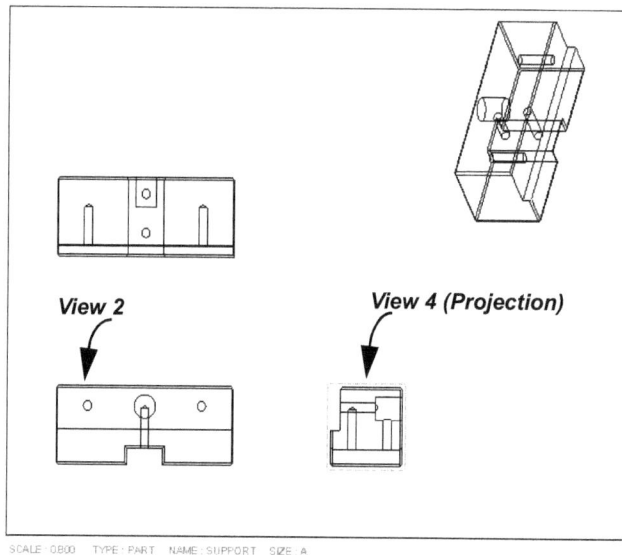

View 2

View 4 (Projection)

SCALE : 0.800   TYPE : PART   NAME : SUPPORT   SIZE : A

Figure 1–50

6. Click ⊟ (Save) to save the drawing and press <Enter>.

7. Close the window and erase all files from memory.

Practice 1b | Add a Drawing Format

Practice Objectives

- Create a new drawing and add a drawing format to it.
- Orient general views using saved views.
- Create cross-sectional and detailed views.

In this practice, you will create drawing views from a solid part. You will also assign a format to the drawing. The completed drawing is shown in Figure 1–51.

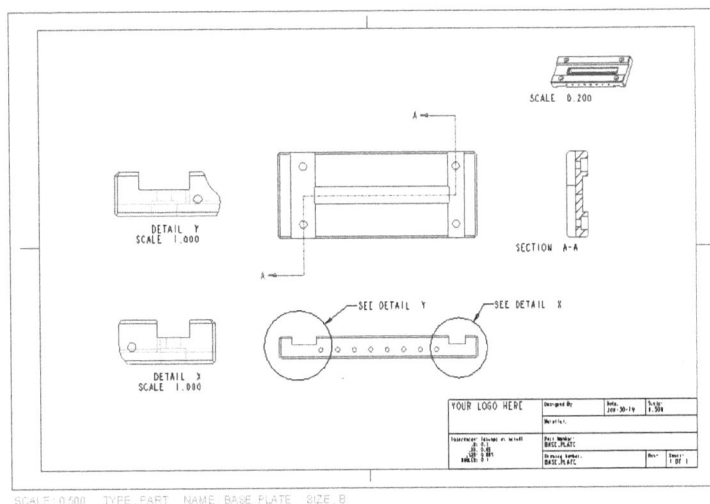

Figure 1–51

Task 1 - Create a new drawing.

1. Set the working directory to the *Add_Format* folder.

2. Click ⬜ (New) in the *Home* tab to create a new drawing. The New dialog box opens.

3. Select **Drawing**.

4. Set the drawing *Name* to **base_plate**.

5. Clear the **Use default template** option and leave **Use drawing model file name** enabled.

6. Click **OK**. The New Drawing dialog box opens.

7. Click **Browse** in the *Default Model* area in the New Drawing dialog box.

8. Select **base_plate.prt** in the current working directory and click **Open**.

9. Select **Empty with format**.

10. Click **Browse** in the *Format* area.

11. Click ⬚ (Working Directory) in the *Common Folders* area of the Open dialog box and double-click on **generic_b.frm**. The dialog box updates as shown in Figure 1–52.

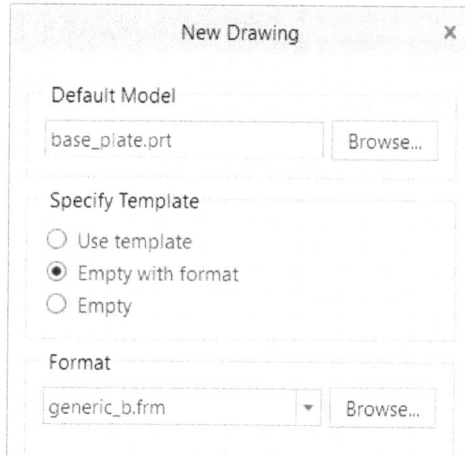

Figure 1–52

12. Click **OK** to create the drawing.

13. Set the model display as follows:

   - ⬚ *(Datum Display Filters)*: All Off

   - ⬚ *(Display Style)*: ⬚ (No Hidden)

Task 2 - Create a General view and orient it using a saved view.

---

1. Right-click and select ⬚ (General View).

2. If required, ensure that **No Combined State** is selected and select **Do not prompt for Combined State** as shown in Figure 1–53. Click **OK**.

Figure 1–53

3. Select the center of the drawing sheet as the centerpoint of the drawing view. The Drawing View dialog box opens.

4. Select **BOTTOM** in the *Model view names* area in the dialog box.

5. Click **Apply**. The view automatically orients itself as shown in Figure 1–54.

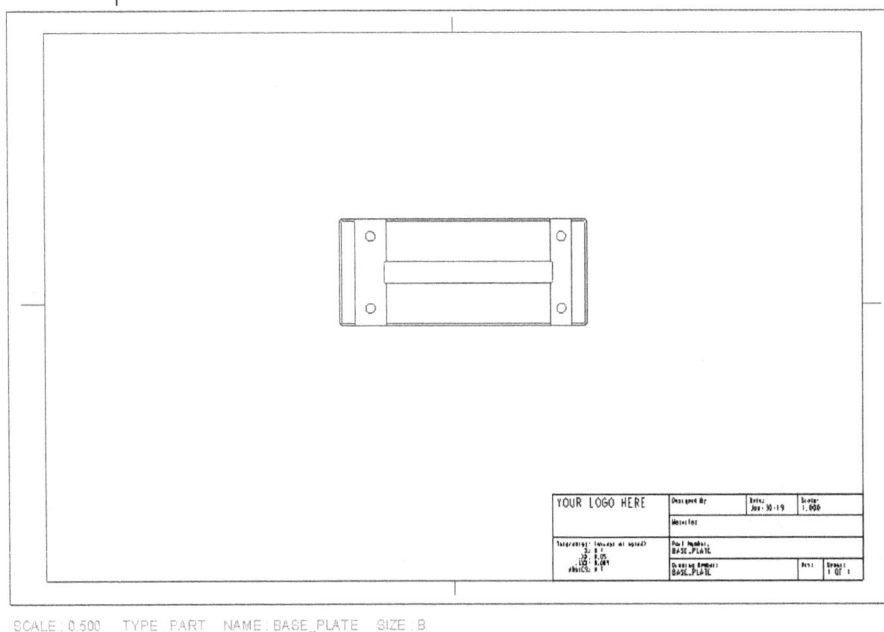

Figure 1–54

6. Click **OK** to complete view placement and close the Drawing View dialog box.

Task 3 - Create an offset cross-section view in the drawing.

1. Select the General view that was just added to the drawing and click ⬚₌ (Projection View) in the mini toolbar.

2. Drag the cursor to the right of the parent view and press the left mouse button to place the view.

3. Select the *View* tab. Display the datum axes and their tags by clicking ⁄ₒ (Axis Display) and ⬚ (Axis Tag Display).

4. Select the *Layout* tab.

You can also double-click on the Projection view to open the Drawing View dialog box.

5. Select the Projection view and click 🖌 (Properties) in the mini toolbar. The Drawing View dialog box opens. It enables you to further customize the drawing view so that it can be displayed as a section view.

6. Select the *Sections* category on the left side of the Drawing View dialog box.

7. Select **2D cross-section** to assign a cross-section to the view, but note that none are available, as shown in Figure 1–55.

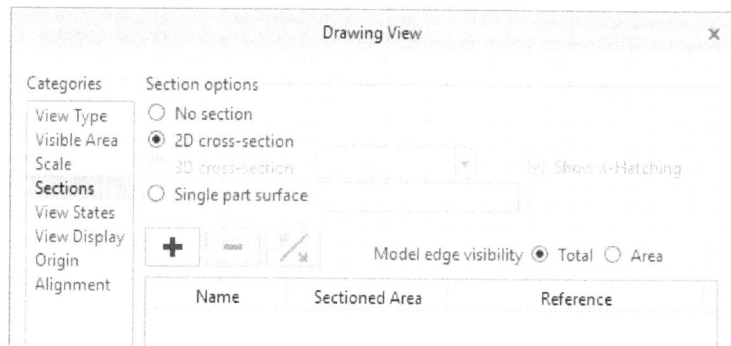

Figure 1–55

It is recommended that you create cross-sections in Part or Assembly mode, because the Sketcher environment is more flexible when working in these modes.

8. Click **Cancel** in the Drawing View dialog box.

9. In the Model Tree, right-click **BASE_PLATE.PRT** and click 📂 (Open) in the mini toolbar.

10. In the In-graphics toolbar, click 🔲 (View Manager).

11. In the View Manager, select the *Sections* tab.

12. Expand **New** and select **Offset**.

The cross-section sketch is created using Sketcher.

13. Enter **A** for the cross-section name and press <Enter>.

14. In the Model Tree, select **DTM2** as the sketching plane.

15. In the *Sketch* tab, click ⬚ (Sketch Setup).

16. In the Sketch dialog box, click **Flip** and click **Sketch**.

17. If the model is not oriented in 2D, in the In-graphics toolbar click ⬚ (Sketch View).

18. In the *Sketch* tab, click ⬚ (References).

19. Select **A_29** and **A_20** and the top and bottom surfaces as additional sketcher references. Close the References dialog box

20. Sketch the cross-section shown in Figure 1–56.

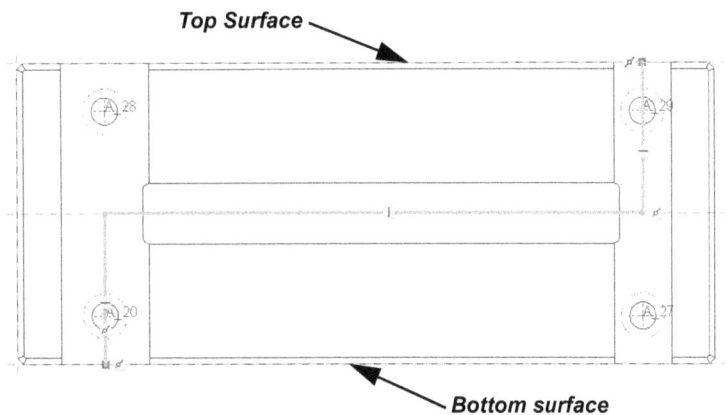

Figure 1–56

21. Click ✓ (OK) to complete the sketch.

22. Click ✓ (OK) to complete the section.

23. Close the View Manager, and then switch back to the drawing.

24. Select the Projection view and click 🖌 (Properties) in the mini toolbar.

25. Select the *Sections* category on the left side of the Drawing View dialog box.

26. Select **2D cross-section** to assign a cross-section to the view

27. Click ✚ (Add Section) to add a section to the view.

28. Ensure that **Full** displays in the *Sectioned Area* for the cross-section. This ensures that the full view is sectioned.

29. Scroll to the right of the information for section A and select the *Arrow Display* column, as shown in Figure 1–57.

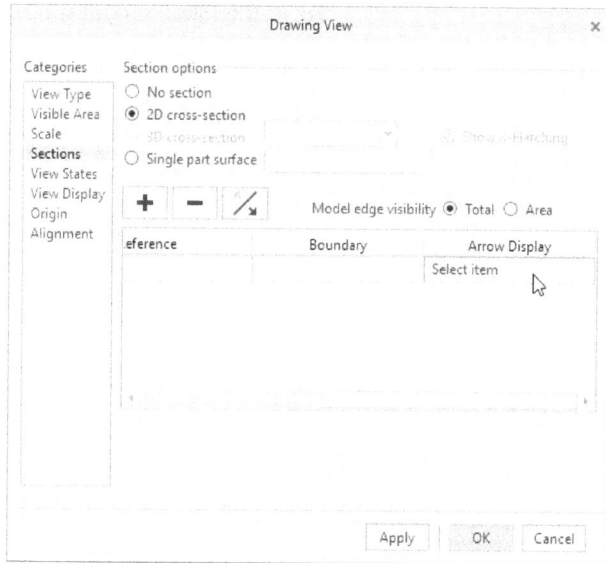

Figure 1–57

30. Select the General view in the drawing as the view to display the cutting plane arrows. Click **Apply**. The drawing displays as shown in Figure 1–58.

Flip the cutting plane arrows to point to the left if required.

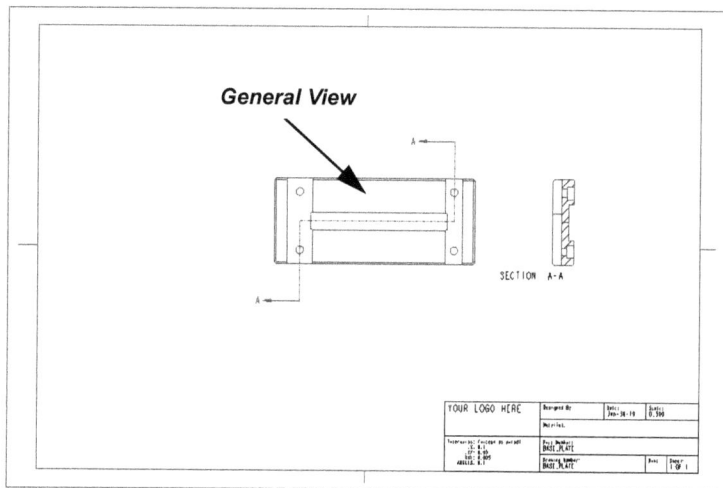

Figure 1–58

31. Click **OK** to complete the view placement and close the Drawing View dialog box.

32. Toggle off the display of the axes and their tags in the *View* tab.

Task 4 - Create a Projection view in the drawing.

1. Create the Projection view shown in Figure 1–59.

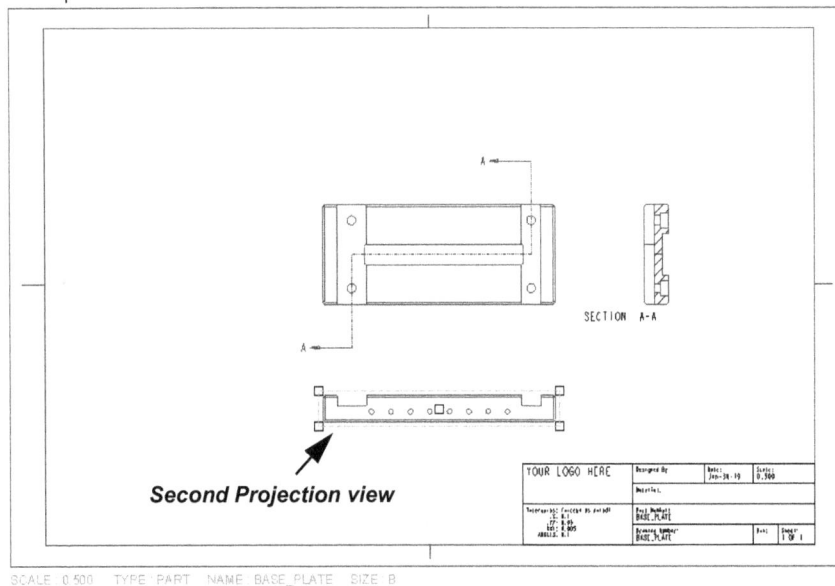

Figure 1–59

Task 5 - Create Detailed views in the drawing.

In this task, you will create the detailed view shown in Figure 1–60.

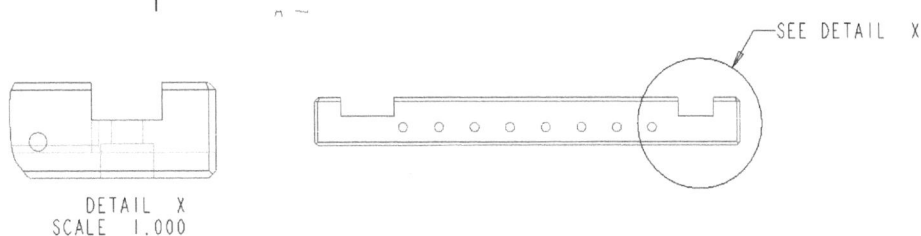

Figure 1–60

You can also click

⬚ (Detailed) in the Model Views group in the Layout tab.

1. Ensure that nothing is selected. Right-click and select
   ⬚ (Detailed View) as shown in Figure 1–61.

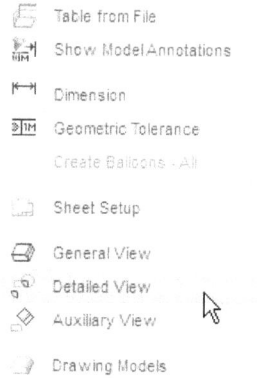

   ⬚ Table from File

   ⬚ Show Model Annotations

   ⟼ Dimension

   ⬚ Geometric Tolerance

   Create Balloons - All

   ⬚ Sheet Setup

   ⬚ General View

   ⬚ Detailed View

   ⬚ Auxiliary View

   ⬚ Drawing Models

   Figure 1–61

2. To define a Detailed view, you must select a centerpoint in an existing view. This centerpoint must be on the model geometry. Select the second Projection view, as shown in Figure 1–62.

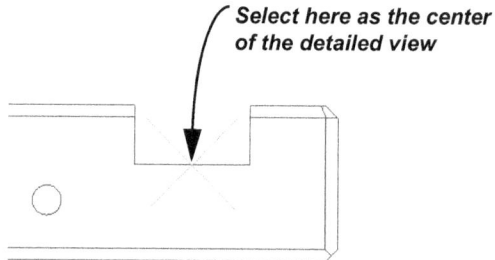

   Select here as the center of the detailed view

   Figure 1–62

3. Sketch a closed spline around the centerpoint as shown in Figure 1–63 using the left mouse button (Click the left button 10-15 times while moving around in an approximate circle). To complete the spline, press the middle mouse button. No entities should overlap.

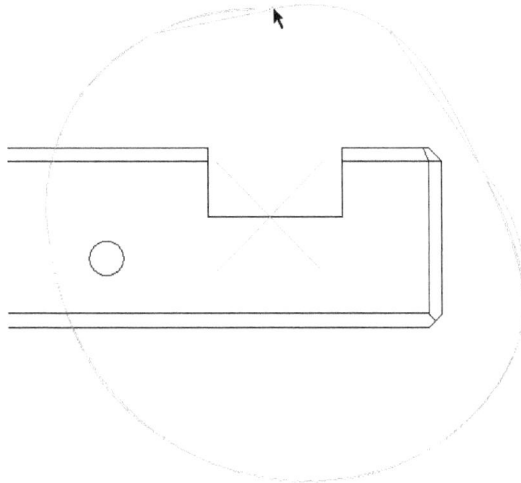

Figure 1–63

4. Select to the left side of the second Projection view as the centerpoint for placing this Detailed view, as shown in Figure 1–64.

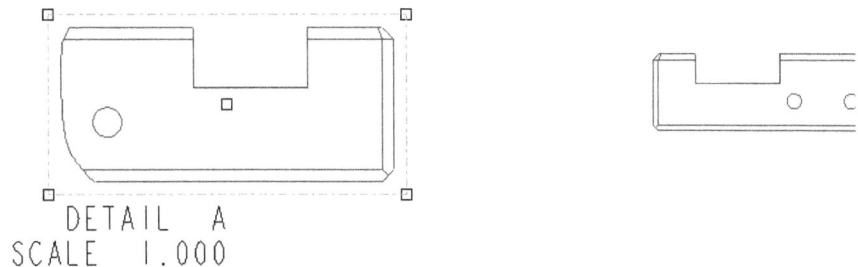

DETAIL A
SCALE 1.000

Figure 1–64

You can also double-click on the Detail view to open the Drawing View dialog box.

5. Select the new Detailed view and click 🥄 (Properties). The Drawing View dialog box opens.

6. Change the *View name* to **X** and click **Apply**.

7. Expand the **Boundary type on Parent view** menu in the *Detailed view properties* area. These options enable you to change the shape that identifies the detailed area. Keep **Circle** selected.

8. Select the *Scale* category. The default value is 1.000. Note how this value differs from the drawing scale. Maintain this value.

9. Select the *View Display* category.

10. Disable the **Use parent view style** option and select **Hidden** from the *Display style* drop-down list.

11. Click **OK** to complete the view.

12. The detailed view note is located by default. To change this location, select the note on the drawing and move it as required, as shown in Figure 1–65.

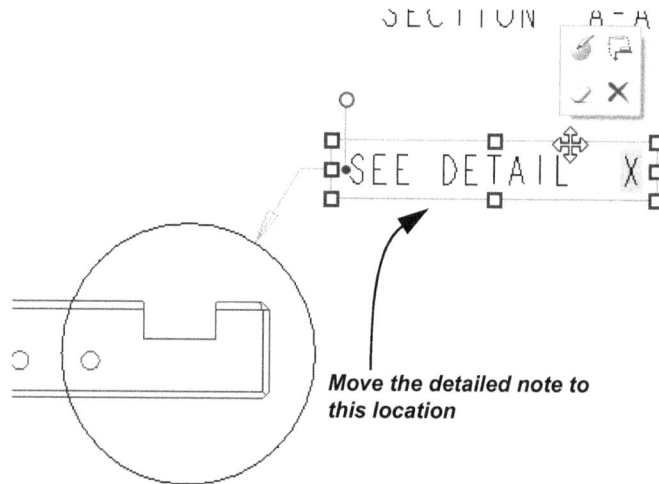

Move the detailed note to this location

Figure 1–65

13. Move the note below the detail view to center it.

The drawing updates after the successful creation of the Detailed view, as shown in Figure 1–66.

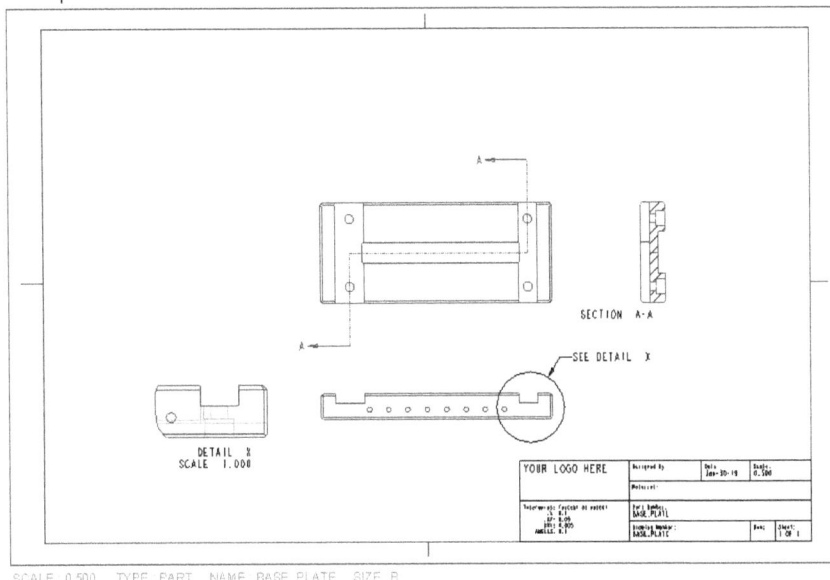

Figure 1–66

14. Repeat the steps in this task to create the Detailed view called **Y**, shown in Figure 1–67.

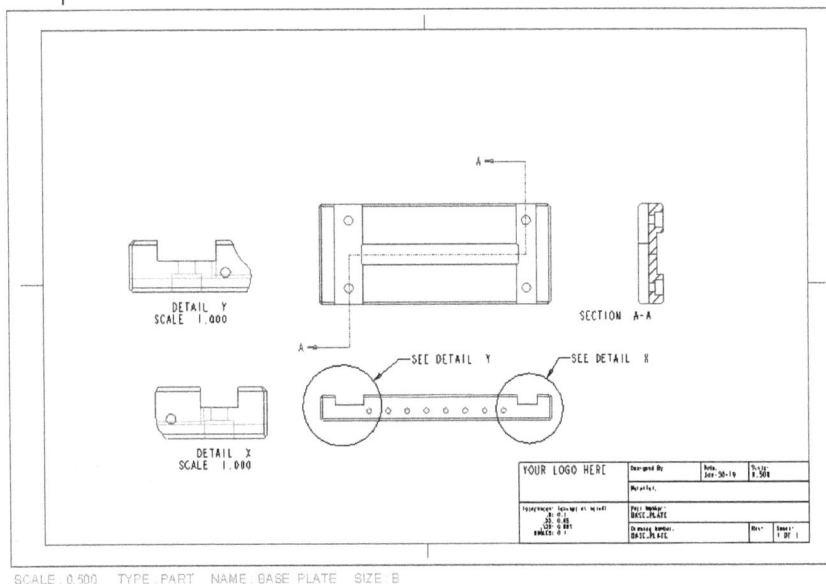

Figure 1–67

Task 6 - Create another General view using the default orientation.

1. Place an additional General view in the upper right corner of the drawing. Create the view with an independent *Scale* value of **0.2**. Use the model's default view to orient the model. The drawing updates as shown in Figure 1–68.

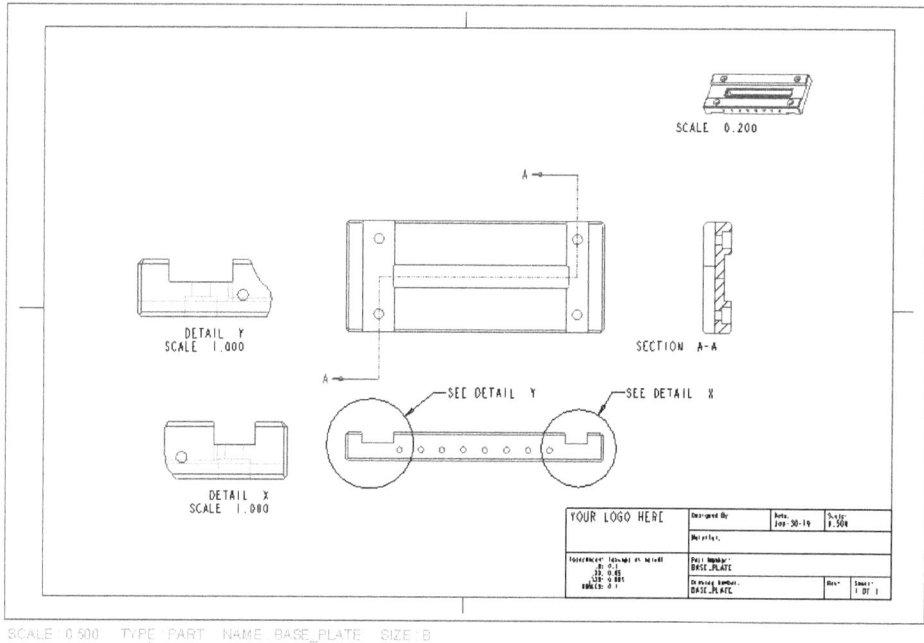

SCALE 0.500 TYPE PART NAME BASE_PLATE SIZE B

Figure 1–68

Task 7 - Move views as required.

*You can also select the view, right-click, and clear the **Lock View Movement** option.*

1. By default, all of the views are locked. To unlock them, click (Lock View Movement) in the *Layout* tab.

2. Once unlocked, you can select the view and drag it on the drawing sheet as required.

3. Relock the views once they have been moved (recommended).

4. Save and close the drawing. If required, close the part window, and erase all files from memory.

Practice 1c | Create Views

Practice Objectives

- Create a general view with partial sections
- Create a projection, a partial, and an auxiliary view.

In this practice, you will create partial, auxiliary, and partial section views of the spindle part shown in Figure 1–69. Note that this is a legacy part without any predefined views, so you will have to use the **Geometry references** option to orient the model on the sheet.

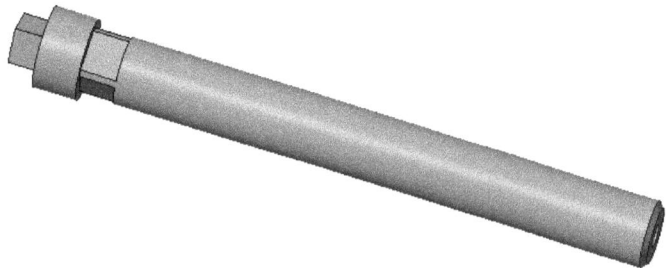

Figure 1–69

Task 1 - Create a new drawing.

1. Set the working directory to the *Create_Views* folder.

2. Create a new drawing, clear the **Use default template** option and leave **Use drawing model file name** enabled.

3. Click **Browse** and select **spindle.prt** as the default model.

4. Specify the template as **Empty with format** and select **generic_b.frm** (from the Working Directory).

5. Click **OK**.

6. Set the model display as follows:

   - ⅍ *(Datum Display Filters)*: All Off
   - ◻ *(Display Style)*: ▱ (Wireframe)

Ensure that the Layout tab is active.

Task 2 - Create a General view with a local cross-section.

1. Right-click and select ⬚ (General View).

2. Ensure that **No Combined State** is selected and select **Do not prompt for combined state**, as shown in Figure 1–70. Click **OK**.

```
Select Combined State          ✕

No Combined State
DEFAULT ALL

☑ Do not prompt for combined state

                        OK      Cancel
```

Figure 1–70

3. Place the view in the center of the drawing sheet. The Drawing View dialog box opens.

4. In the Drawing View dialog box, orient the view using **Geometry references**. Select **Right** for *Reference 1* and select **DTM1** from the Model Tree. Select **Top** for *Reference 2* and select **DTM2** from the Model Tree. The view displays as shown in Figure 1–71.

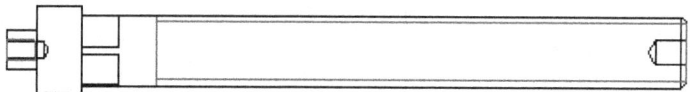

Figure 1–71

5. Select the *Sections* category in the left frame of the Drawing View dialog box.

6. Select **2D cross-section** to assign a cross-section to the view.

7. Maintain the **Total** option in the *Model edge visibility* area.

8. Click ✚ (Add Section).

9. Select cross-section **A** to add a section to the view.

Design Considerations

The section is predefined in the model. A cross-section defines a slice through a model. Cross-sections are created in a part by selecting the *Xsec* tab in the View Manager dialog box. The planar cross-section type was created for section A.

10. Expand the **Sectioned Area** drop-down list next to cross-section A in the dialog box.

11. Select **Local** as the sectioning area for this view. This enables you to define only the portion of the view that displays with cross-hatching.

12. Select the centerpoint for the Detailed view, as shown by the X in Figure 1–72. The reference displays in the *Reference* column.

13. Sketch a closed spline (click the left mouse button 10-15 times while moving around in an approximate circle as shown in Figure 1–72, then middle-click when complete). This area defines the boundary of the local section.

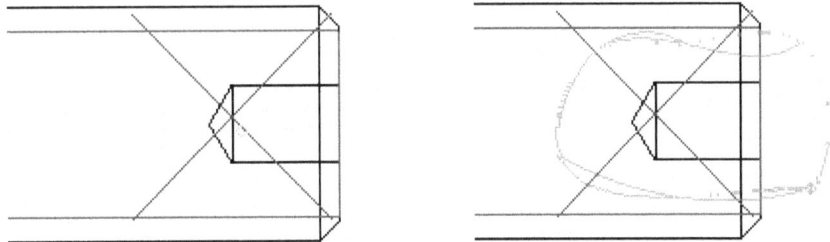

Figure 1–72

14. Click ✚ (Add Section). Select cross-section **A** to add another section to the view. This view is automatically assigned as **Local**. Keep this option selected.

15. Repeat Steps 12 and 13 to define the next local section on the opposite end of the spindle, as shown in Figure 1–73.

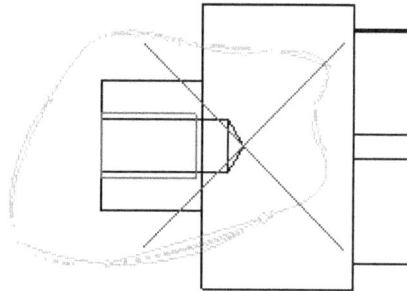

Figure 1–73

16. Click **Apply** to apply the changes. The Drawing View dialog box updates as shown in Figure 1–74.

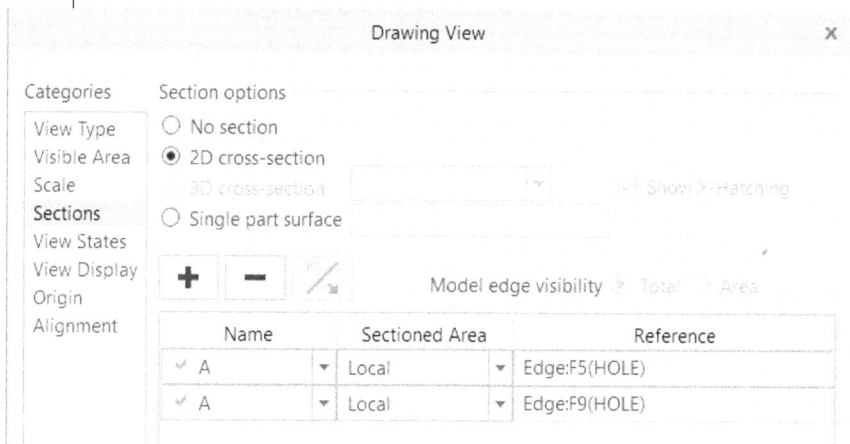

Figure 1–74

17. Click **OK** in the Drawing View dialog box to complete the view creation.

The partial sectioned view displays as shown in Figure 1–75.

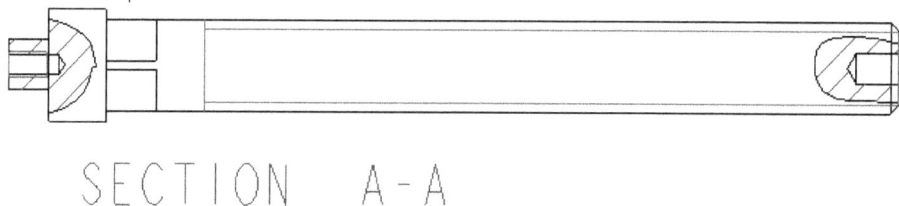

SECTION A-A

Figure 1–75

Task 3 - Modify the scale of the drawing.

1. Modify the drawing scale to **1**. The drawing displays as shown in Figure 1–76.

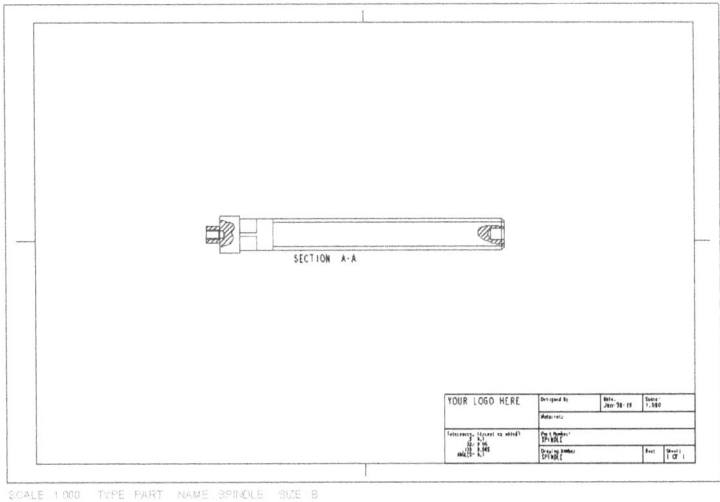

SCALE 1:000   TYPE: PART   NAME: SPINDLE   SIZE: B

Figure 1–76

Task 4 - Create Projection views in the drawing.

1. Place a Projected view to the left and right sides of the General view, as shown in Figure 1–77.

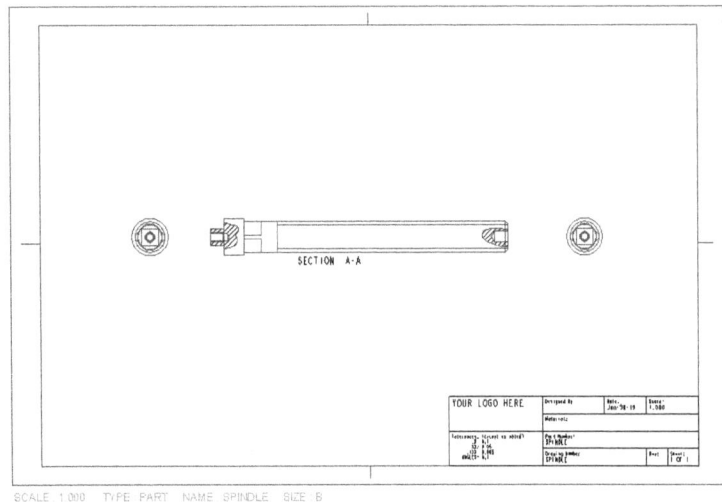

SCALE 1:000   TYPE: PART   NAME: SPINDLE   SIZE: B

Figure 1–77

Task 5 - Create an Auxiliary partial view in the drawing.

1. Ensure that no views are currently selected in the drawing.

2. Right-click and select ◇ (Auxiliary View).

When an edge, axis, surface, or datum plane is used as a reference, it must be parallel to the projection direction.

3. Read the message line. As a reference for the projection, select the edge of the view shown in Figure 1–78.

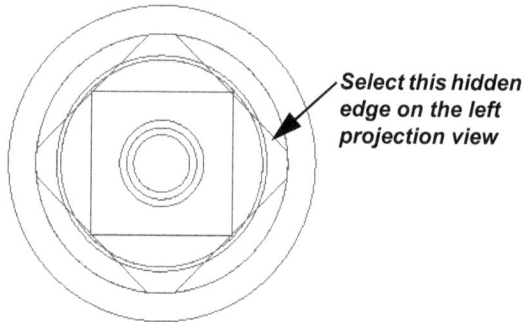

Select this hidden edge on the left projection view

Figure 1–78

4. Select the centerpoint to place the view, as shown in Figure 1–79.

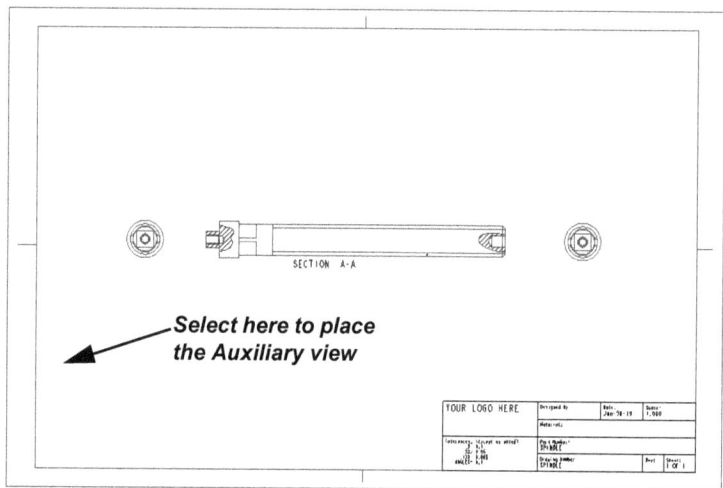

Select here to place the Auxiliary view

Figure 1–79

The auxiliary view displays as shown in Figure 1–80.

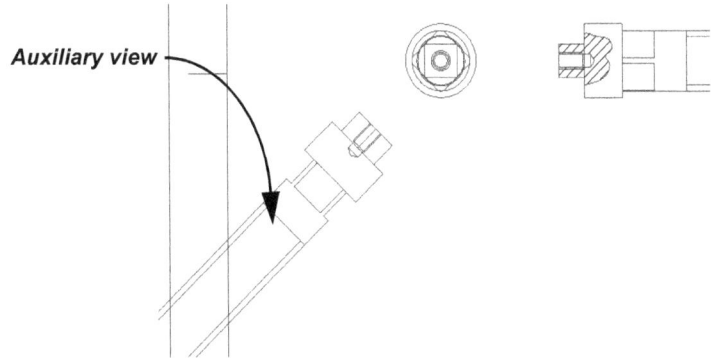

Auxiliary view

Figure 1–80

5. Double-click on the new Auxiliary view. The Drawing View dialog box opens.

6. Select the *Visible Area* category in the left column.

7. Select **Partial View** in the **View Visibility** menu.

8. Create the boundary for the Partial Auxiliary view by selecting the centerpoint and sketching a closed spline for the Partial view, as shown in Figure 1–81.

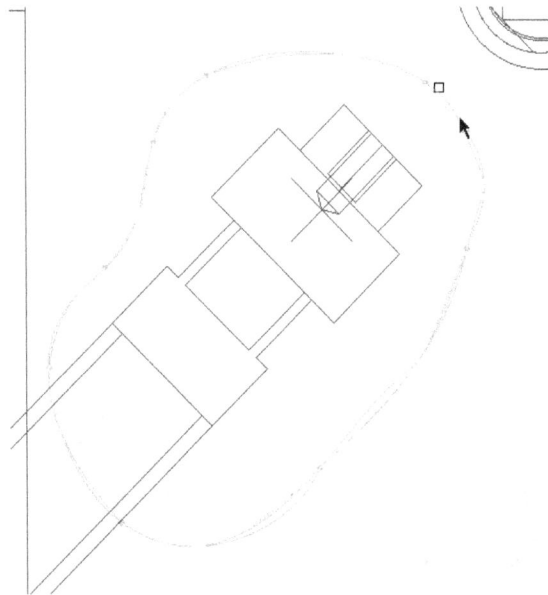

Figure 1–81

9. Click **Apply** to apply the changes. The Drawing View dialog box displays as shown in Figure 1–82.

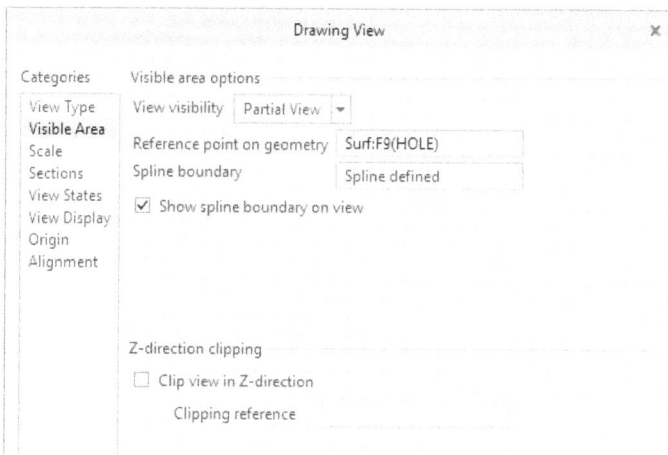

Figure 1–82

10. Click **OK** in the Drawing View dialog box. The partial view displays as shown in Figure 1–83.

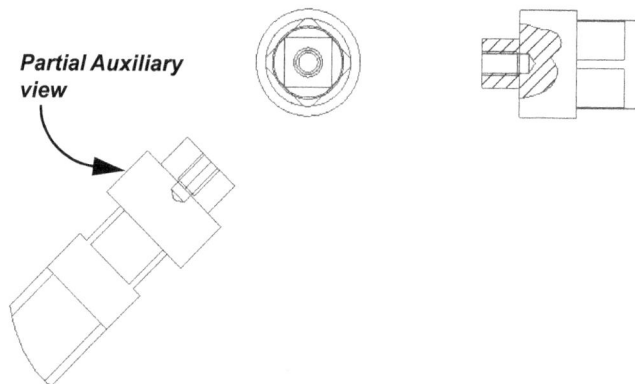

Partial Auxiliary view

Figure 1–83

Task 6 - Move the Auxiliary partial view.

*You can also select a view, right-click, and clear the **Lock View Movement** option to unlock it.*

1. If the views are locked, click ▯ (Lock View Movement) to unlock them.

2. Once unlocked, select the Auxiliary Partial view and drag the view to the location, as shown in Figure 1–84.

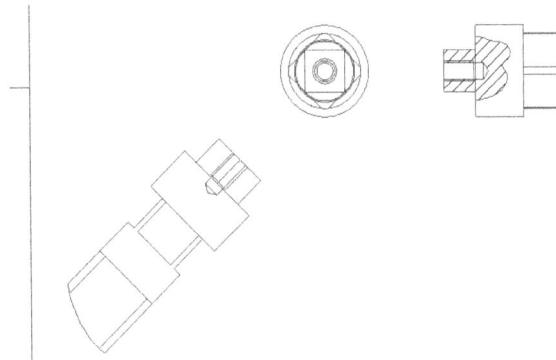

Figure 1–84

3. Relock the views once they have been moved.

Task 7 - Add additional Detailed views in the drawing.

1. Create the detailed views named **X** and **Y** (as shown in Figure 1–85) using a scale of **2.0**.

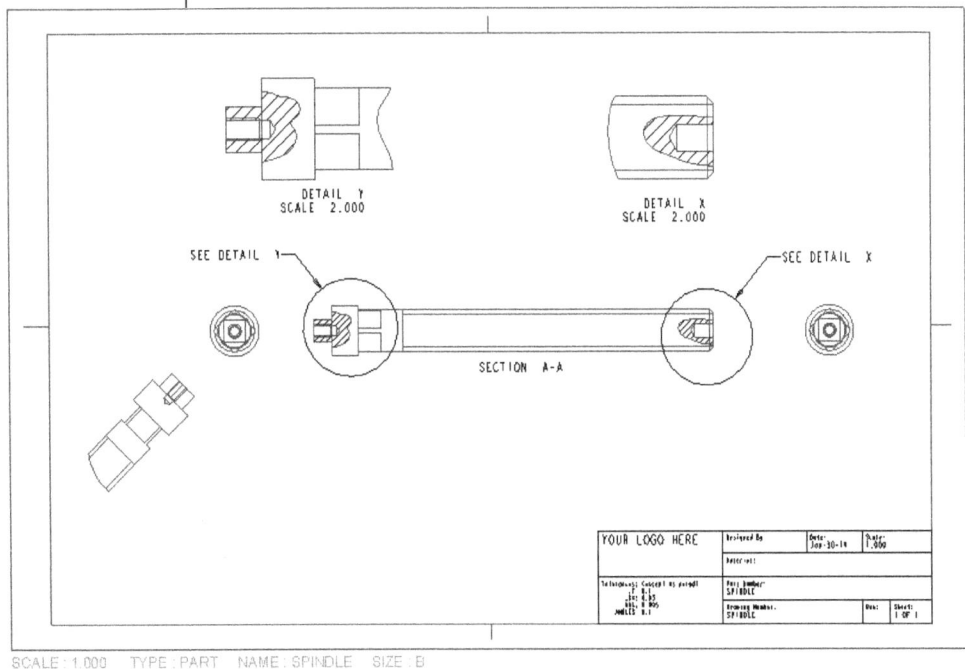

Figure 1–85

2. Save the drawing and close the working window.

Practice 1d

Create a Drawing

Practice Objectives

- Create a planar cross-section in a part.
- Create a new drawing and add a drawing format to it.
- Orient general views using saved views.
- Create a cross-sectional and a detailed view.
- Take specific measurements from a model.

In this practice, you will create drawing views from a Creo Parametric solid part. You will also assign a format to the drawing.

Task 1 - Open a part file.

1. Set the working directory to the *Broken_Views* folder.

2. Open **screw.prt**.

3. Set the model display as follows:

- ⚹ *(Datum Display Filters)*: All Off
- ⚬ *(Spin Center)*: Off
- ▱ (Annotation Display): Off
- ▯ *(Display Style)*: ▱ (Shading With Edges)

The model displays as shown in Figure 1–86.

Figure 1–86

Task 2 - Create the first planar cross-sections.

1. Select the *View* tab and enable 🔲 (Plane Display) and
   🔲 (Plane Tag Display). The model displays, as shown in
   Figure 1–87.

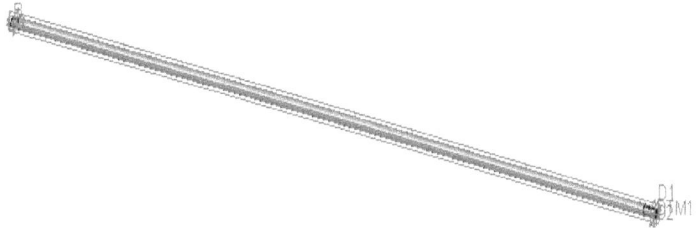

Figure 1–87

You can also click

🔲 *(View Manager) in
the In-graphics toolbar.*

2. Select the *View* tab. Expand 🔲 (Section) and select **Planar**
   to create a new cross-section.

3. Select the *Properties* panel and set the name to **A**.

4. Select datum plane **D3** and complete the cross-section. One
   side of the cross-section is removed from the display.

5. Disable 🔲 (Plane Display).

6. Click on the new cross-section in the Model Tree (in the
   Sections branch at the bottom of the tree) and select

   🔲 (Show Section) in the mini toolbar to display the
   cross-hatching for the section. The model displays as shown
   in Figure 1–88. Note that the hatching lines are far apart.

Figure 1–88

7. Right-click on the section in the Model Tree and select
   ▨ (Edit Hatching). The Edit Hatching dialog box opens as
   shown in Figure 1–89.

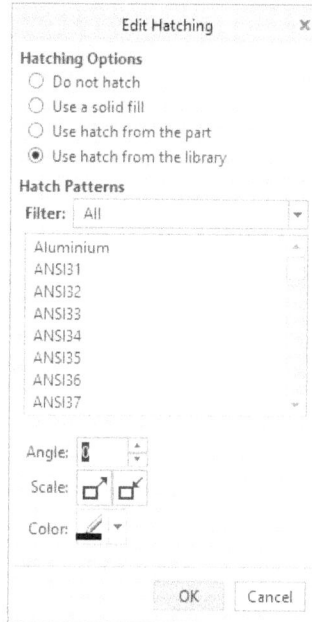

Edit Hatching ✕

Hatching Options
- ○ Do not hatch
- ○ Use a solid fill
- ○ Use hatch from the part
- ◉ Use hatch from the library

Hatch Patterns

Filter: All ▾

Aluminium
ANSI31
ANSI32
ANSI33
ANSI34
ANSI35
ANSI36
ANSI37

Angle: 0 ⬍

Scale: ◻ ◻

Color: ▱ ▾

OK   Cancel

Figure 1–89

8. Click ◻ (Halve Spacing) three times to change the line
   spacing as shown in Figure 1–90.

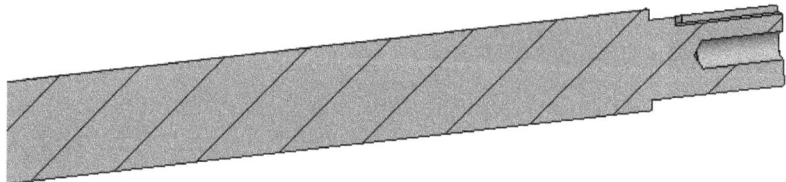

Figure 1–90

9. Click **OK** to close the dialog box.

10. Click on cross-section **A** in the Model Tree and click ▨ (Hide
    Section).

11. Click cross-section **A** in the Model Tree and select
    ▨ (Deactivate) in the mini toolbar.

Task 3 - Create the second planar cross-sections.

1. Create a new planar cross-section.

2. Select datum plane **B** in the Model Tree and name the section **B**.

3. Click ⟋ (Flip) in the dashboard to flip the arrow direction if required, to ensure the section displays as shown in Figure 1–91.

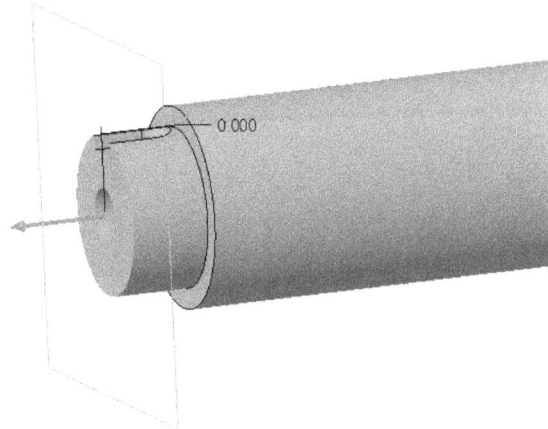

Figure 1–91

4. Complete the section. One side of the cross-section is removed from the display.

5. Display the cross-hatching for the section by clicking on it in the Model Tree and selecting ▨ (Show Section). The model displays as shown in Figure 1–92.

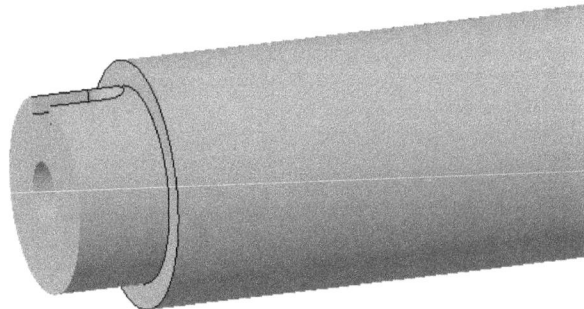

Figure 1–92

6. Right-click on cross-section B in the Model Tree and select ▨ (Edit Hatching).

7. Click ◻ four times to change the line spacing. The section displays as shown in Figure 1–93.

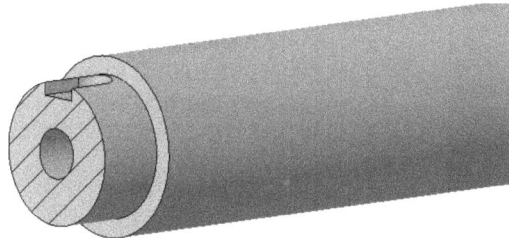

Figure 1–93

8. Click **OK**.

9. Click on cross-section **B** in the Model Tree and select ▨ (Hide Section).

10. Click cross-section **B** in the Model Tree and select ◈ (Deactivate) in the mini toolbar to return the display to normal.

Task 4 - Create the third planar cross-sections.

---

1. Create a new planar cross-section and set the name to **C**.

2. Select datum plane **C**. Flip the direction, if required. The cross-section displays as shown in Figure 1–94.

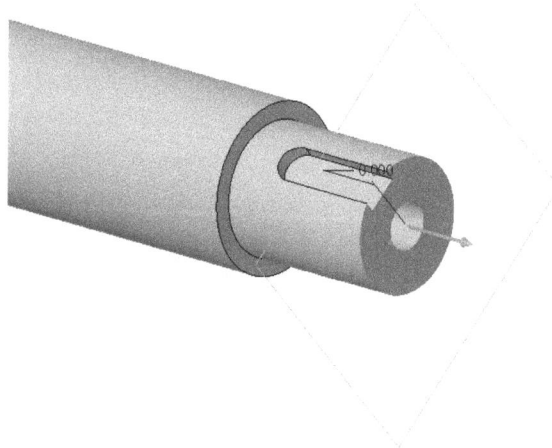

Figure 1–94

3. Complete the cross-section.

4. Display the cross-hatching for the section and change the hatching to display as shown in Figure 1–95.

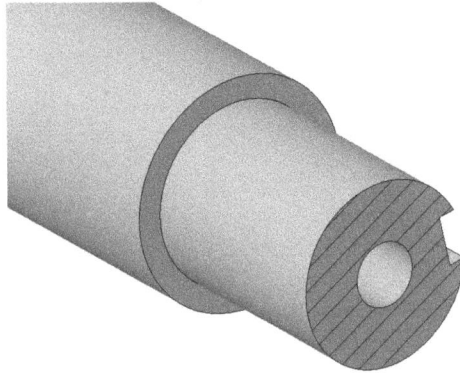

Figure 1–95

5. Remove the displayed cross-hatching and deactivate the cross-section to return the display to normal.

6. Save the part and close the window.

Task 5 - Create a new drawing called screw.

---

1. Click ☐ (New) in the Quick Access Toolbar to create a new drawing. The New dialog box opens.

2. Select **Drawing**.

3. Clear the **Use default template** option and leave **Use drawing model file name** enabled.

4. Click **OK**. The New Drawing dialog box opens.

5. If required, click **Browse** in the *Default Model* area in the New Drawing dialog box and select **screw.prt** in the current working directory. Click **Open**.

6. Select **Empty with format**.

7. Click **Browse** in the *Format* area and double-click on **generic_b.frm** in the working directory. If the **generic_b.frm** *format* is not listed in the Open dialog box, click ⬈ (Working Directory) to browse to the working directory. The dialog box opens as shown in Figure 1–96.

Figure 1–96

8. Click **OK** to create the drawing.

Task 6 - Create a Broken view and orient it using a saved view.

Ensure that the Layout tab is active.

1. In the In-graphics toolbar, click ⬚ (Wireframe).

2. Right-click on the drawing sheet and select ⬚ (General View).

3. Ensure that **No Combined State** is selected and select **Do not prompt for combined state**. Click **OK**.

4. Select the center of the drawing sheet as the centerpoint of the drawing view. The Drawing View dialog box opens.

5. Select **FRONT** in the *Model view names* area in the dialog box.

6. Click **Apply**. The view automatically orients itself as shown in Figure 1–97.

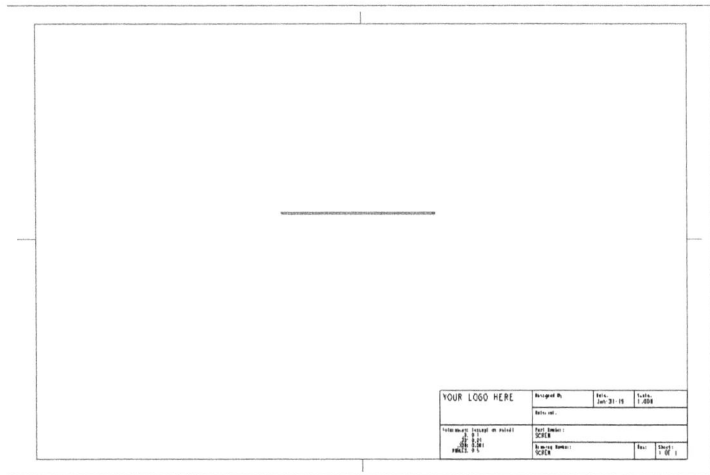

Figure 1–97

7. Click **OK** to complete the view placement and close the Drawing View dialog box.

Task 7 - Modify the scale value for the drawing.

1. Double-click on the *Scale* value at the bottom left of the view window to modify it to **0.1**. The drawing and view update, as shown in Figure 1–98.

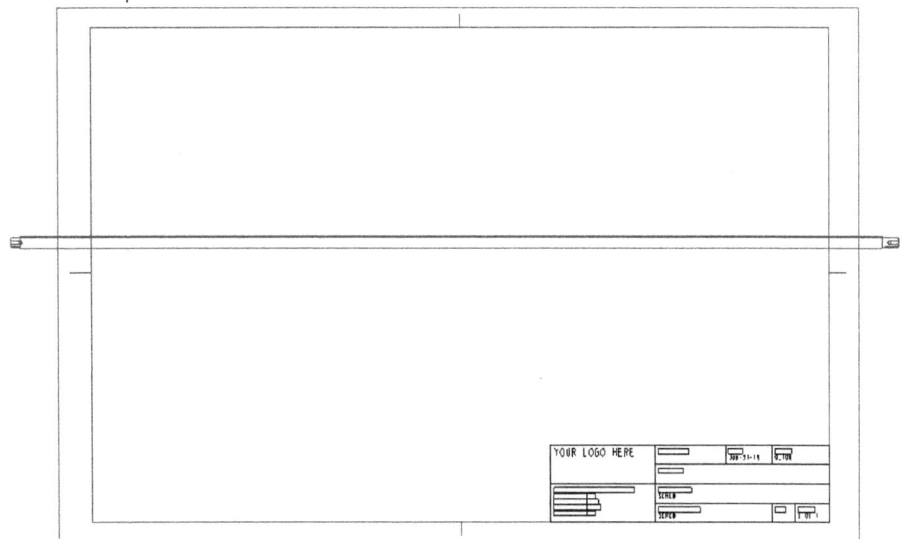

Figure 1–98

Task 8 - Modify a General view with a local cross-section.

1. Select the General view and click 🖌 (Properties). The Drawing View dialog box opens.

2. In the Drawing View dialog box, select the *Sections* category on the left side of the Drawing View dialog box.

3. Select **2D cross-section** to assign a cross-section to the view.

4. Maintain the **Total** option in the *Model edge visibility* area.

5. Click ➕ (Add Section).

6. Select cross-section **A** to add a section to the view. The section was predefined in the model.

7. Expand the **Sectioned Area** drop-down list next to cross-section **A** in the dialog box and select **Local** as shown in Figure 1–99.

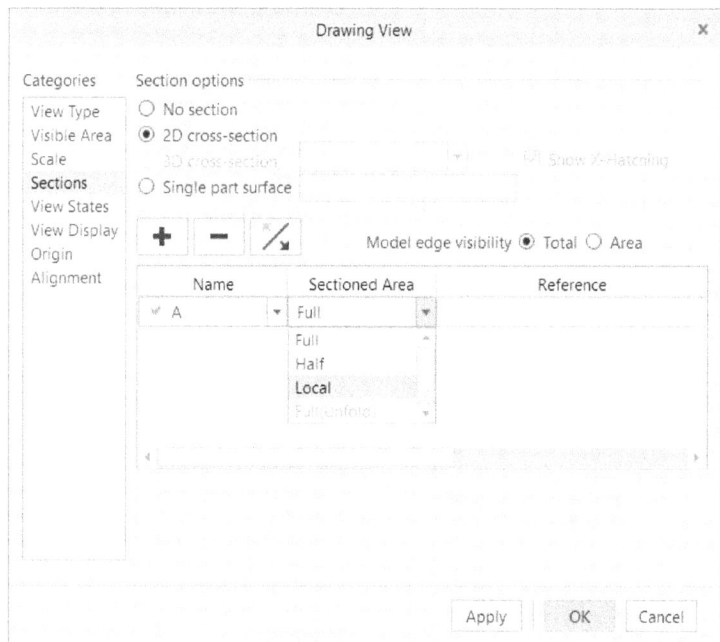

Figure 1–99

8. Select the centerpoint for the section view, as shown by the X in Figure 1–100. The reference displays in the *Reference* column.

9. Sketch a closed spline as shown in Figure 1–100. This area defines the boundary of the local section.

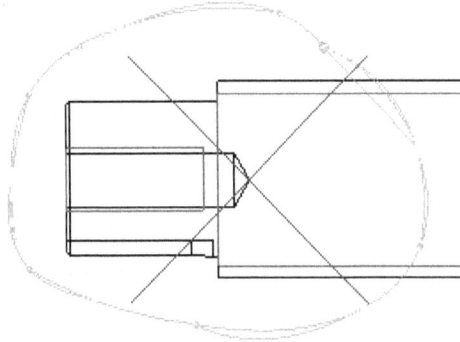

Figure 1–100

10. Click ✚ (Add Section). Select cross-section **A** to add another section to the view. The view is automatically assigned as **Local**. Keep this option selected.

11. Define the next local section on the opposite end of the screw, as shown in Figure 1–101.

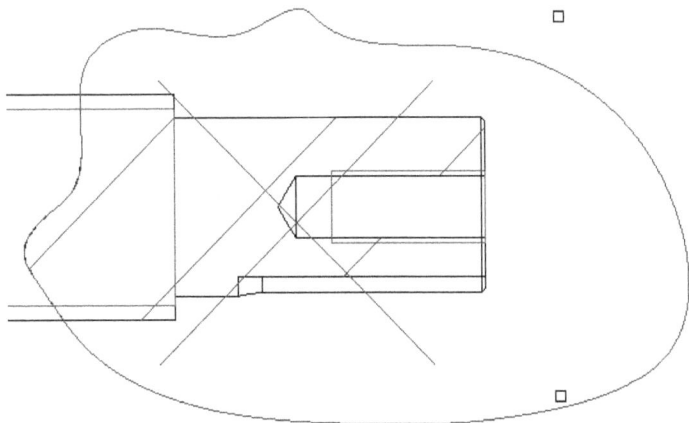

Figure 1–101

12. Click **Apply** in the Drawing View dialog box.

Task 9 - Define the break locations.

1. In the Drawing View dialog box, select the *Visible Area* category in the column on the left.

2. Select **Broken View** in the **View Visibility** drop-down list.

3. Click ✚ (Add Break) to add a breakout line to the view.

4. Select the horizontal edge of the view in the location shown in Figure 1–102.

Select the horizontal edge at this location

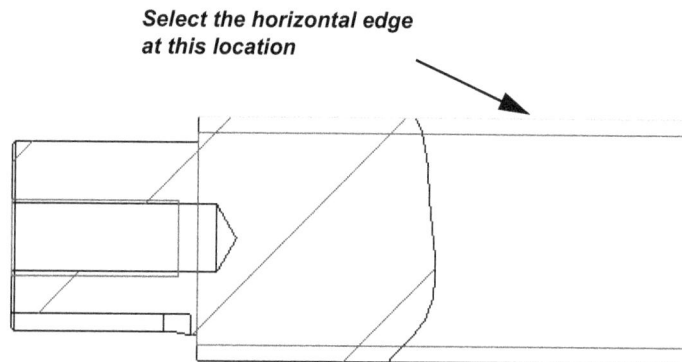

Figure 1–102

5. Move the cursor down and select again to draw the first vertical break line, as shown in Figure 1–103.

Drag to create this break line

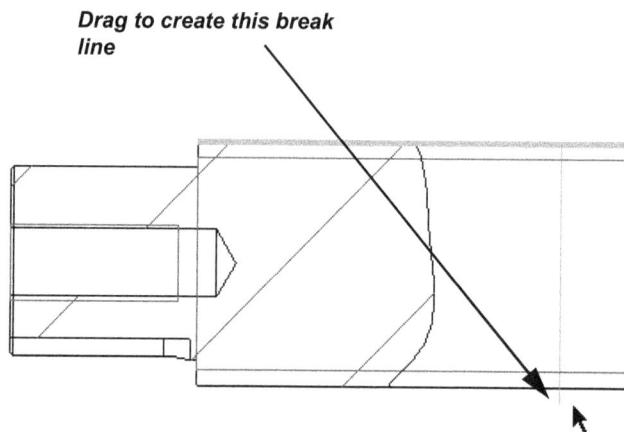

Figure 1–103

6. Select a second break line location, as shown in Figure 1–104.

Select the horizontal edge at this location

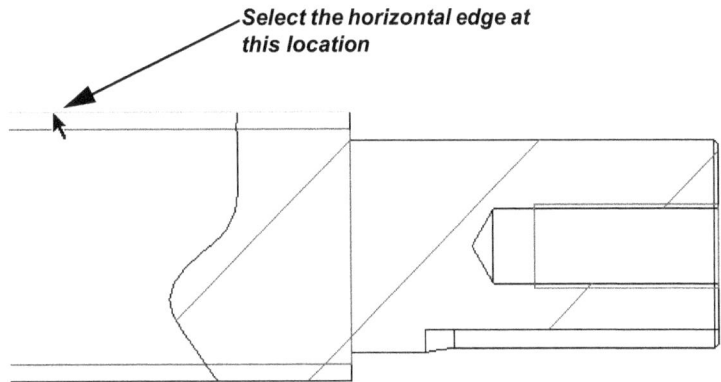

Figure 1–104

A second vertical break line displays as shown in Figure 1–105.

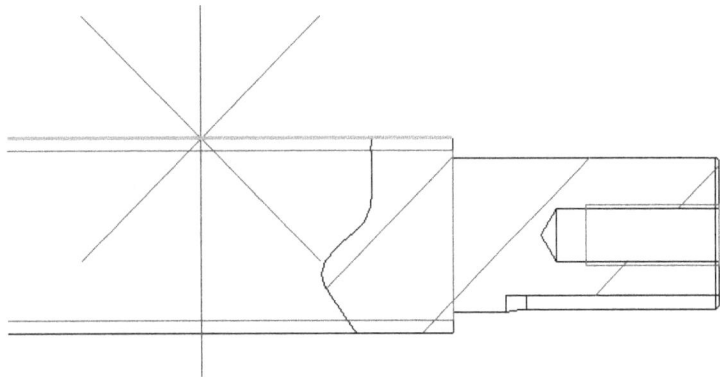

Figure 1–105

7. Scroll across to display the *Break Line Style* column in the Drawing View dialog box.

8. Select **Straight** in the *Break Line Style* column to expand the drop-down list and select **Sketch**. The Drawing View dialog box opens as shown in Figure 1–106.

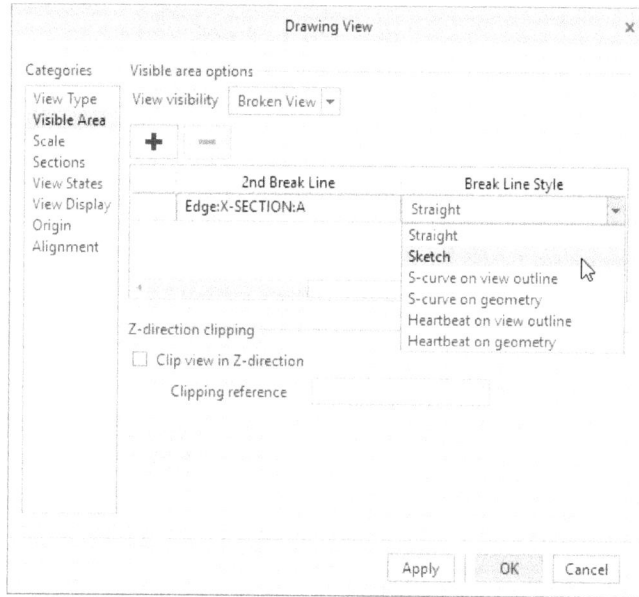

Figure 1–106

9. Sketch the spline shown in Figure 1–107 to represent the break line for the view. Press the middle mouse button to complete the spline.

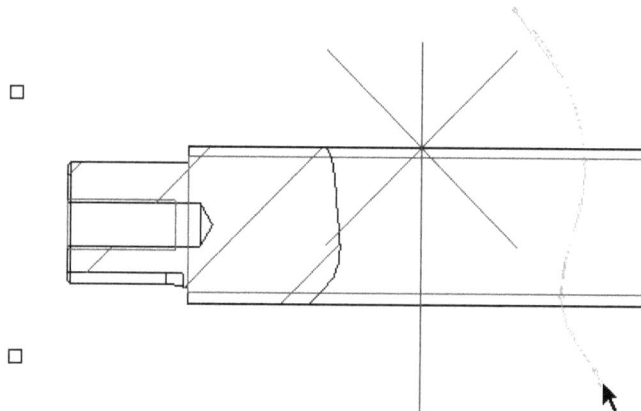

Figure 1–107

The break lines display as shown in Figure 1–108.

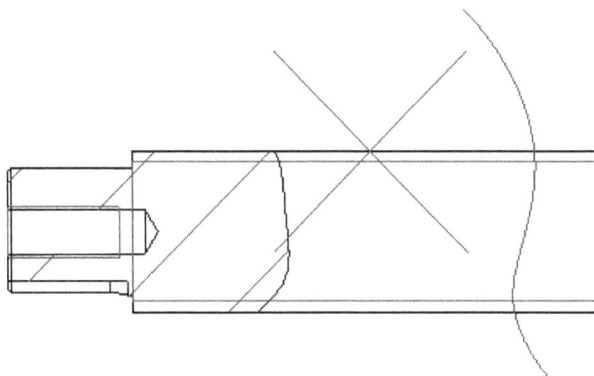

Figure 1–108

10. Click **Apply** and **OK** in the Drawing View dialog box. The Broken view displays as shown in Figure 1–109.

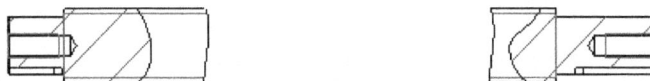

SECTION A-A

Figure 1–109

11. The view can now be centered in the drawing sheet.

Task 10 - Modify the scale value for the drawing.

1. Double-click on the *Scale* value in the lower left corner of your drawing and modify it to **0.5**. The drawing and view update, as shown in Figure 1–110.

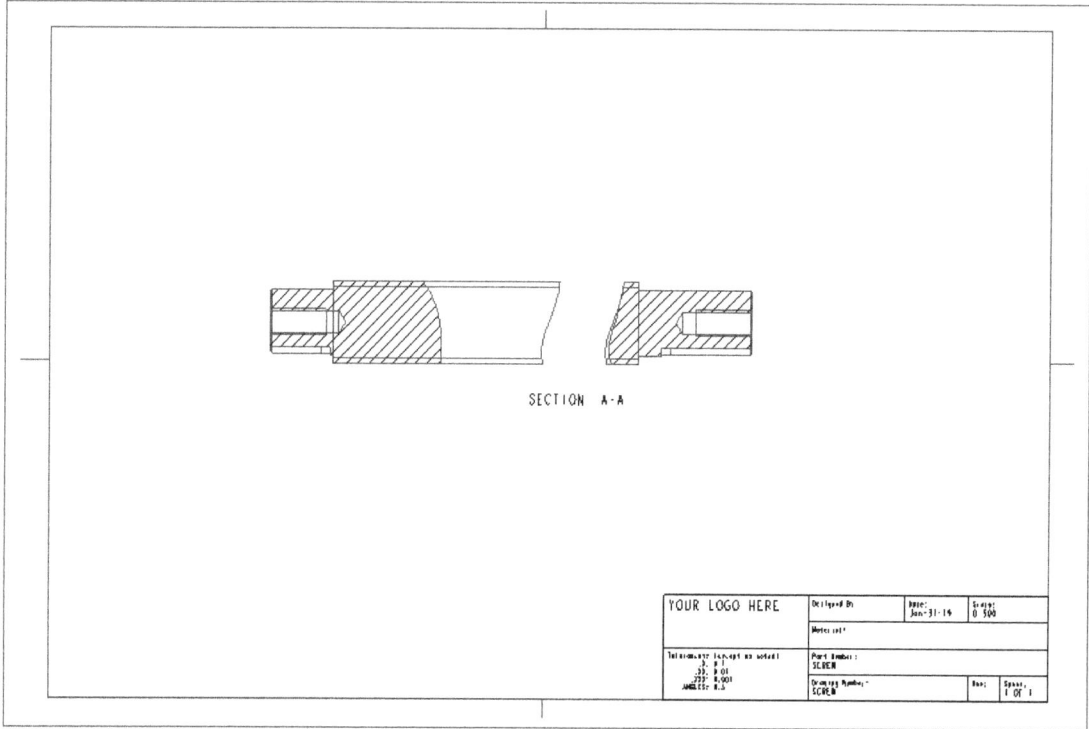

SECTION A-A

Figure 1–110

Task 11 - Create Projection views in the drawing.

1. Place a Projected view to the left and right sides of the General view with cross-sections **B** and **C**. The drawing displays as shown in Figure 1–111.

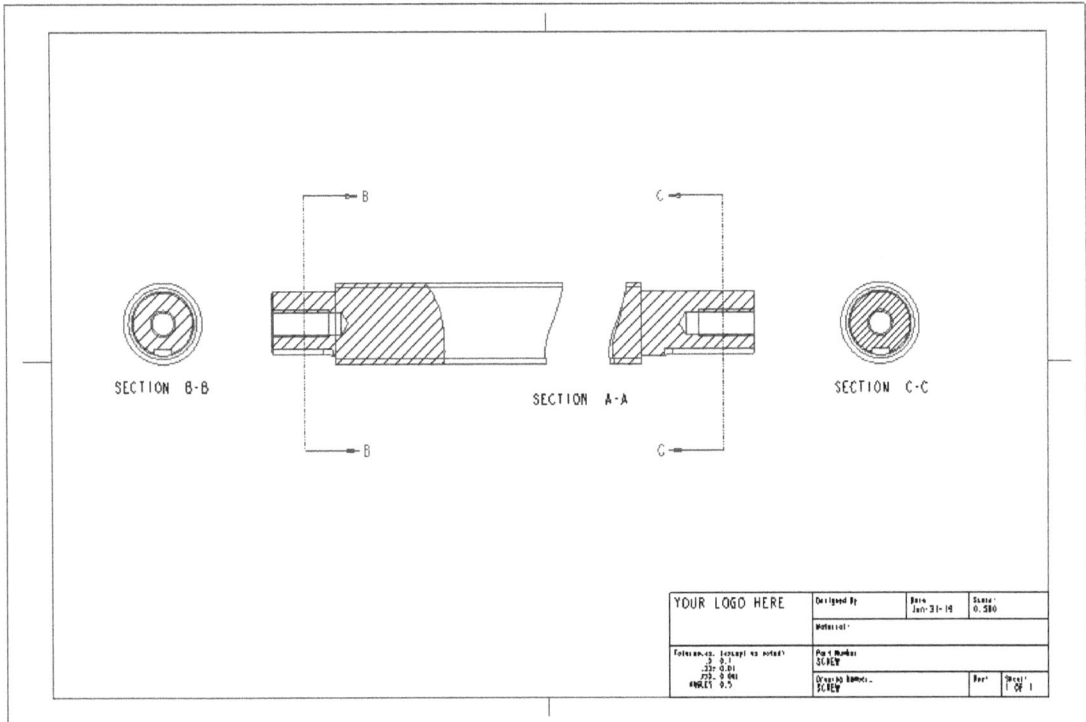

Figure 1–111

Task 12 - Create another General view using the default orientation.

1. Place an additional General view in the lower left corner of the drawing. Create the view with an independent *Scale* value of **0.05**. Use the model's default view to orient the model. The drawing updates as shown in Figure 1–112.

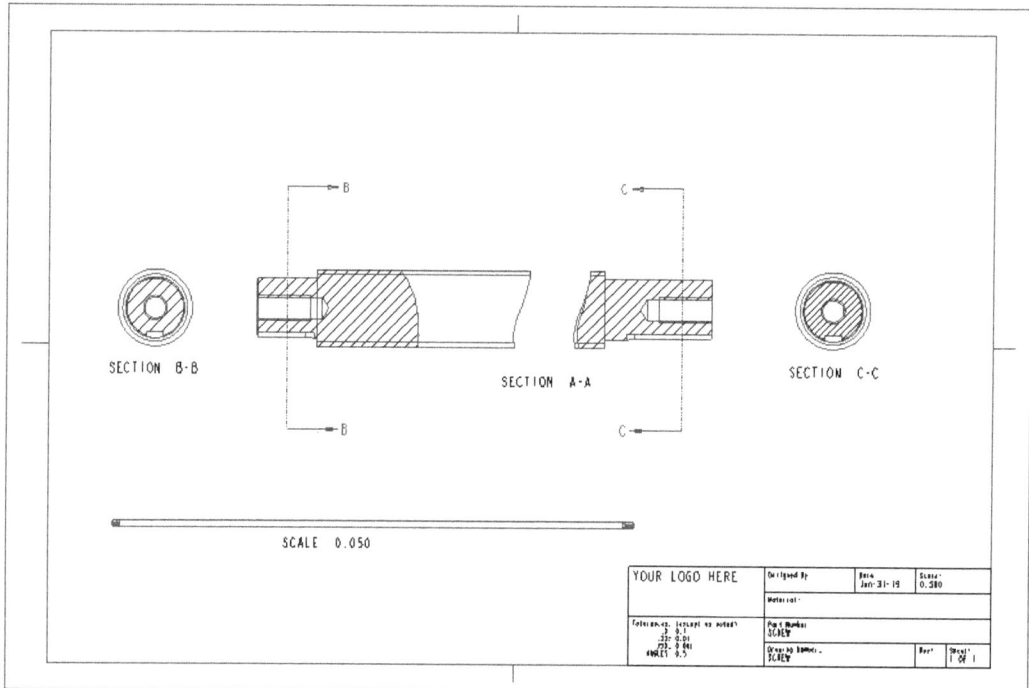

Figure 1–112

Task 13 - Move the views as required.

1. By default, all of the views are locked. To unlock them, click 🔒 (Lock View Movement) in the *Layout* tab.

2. Once unlocked, you can select the view and drag it on the drawing sheet as required.

3. It is recommended that you relock the views you have once moved them.

4. Save the drawing and close the window.

Chapter Review Questions

1. Which of the following **Specify Template** options enables you to define the orientation of the drawing sheet and set the sheet size for the drawing?

   a. Use template

   b. Empty with format

   c. Empty

2. Which of the following view types must be the first view in a drawing?

   a. Projection

   b. Auxiliary

   c. General

   d. Detailed

3. Which of the following view types enables you to create a 3D view in its default orientation?

   a. Projection

   b. Auxiliary

   c. General

   d. Detailed

4. An independent view scale enables you to ensure that a view maintains the same scale value as the drawing.

   a. True

   b. False

5. Which of the following references can be selected when orienting a view? (Select all that apply.)

   a. Datum planes

   b. Datum axis

   c. Planar surfaces

   d. Cylindrical surfaces

   e. Coordinate system axis

6. The Drawing Tree displays which of the following drawing items? (Select all that apply.)

   a. Sheets

   b. Views

   c. Tables

   d. Draft entities

   e. Datums

7. The *Layout* tab has be selected to create a General view.

   a. True

   b. False

8. Which cross-section option creates a cross-section that only displays the material in the cutting plane?

   a. Total

   b. Area

   c. Partial

   d. Local

9. Once arrows display in a view for a cross-section they cannot be removed.

   a. True

   b. False

10. Which of the following options can be changed in the drawing setup file? (Select all that apply.)

    a. Projection Type

    b. View scale format

    c. Drawing units

    d. Automatically Regenerate Views

    e. Note text height

Answers: 1c, 2c, 3b, 4b, 5ac, 6abcde, 7b, 8b, 9b, 10abce

View Manipulation

This chapter introduces additional categories in the Drawing View dialog box that can be used to customize the display of a drawing view. In addition, you learn view manipulation techniques to move and erase views in a drawing.

Learning Objectives in This Chapter

- Learn the general steps to modify the view type, view display, view origin, and alignment using the Drawing View dialog box.
- Understand how parent/child relationships can restrict view movement and how to remove the alignment restriction.
- Learn how to lock and unlock the view movements in a drawing.
- Learn the difference between erasing and deleting a view.
- Learn how to use the commands in the *Layout* tab to control the display of individual edges and the representations of individual components in an assembly drawing.
- Review the configuration and drawing setup file options that enable you to customize the modification of drawing views.

2.1 Modify View Properties II

The Visible Area, Scale, and Sections categories are available in the Drawing View dialog box to customize a view. Additional categories and options are also available to further refine views.

How To: Modify View Properties

1. If it is not already open, use one of the following techniques to open the Drawing View dialog box:
   - Double-click on the view that you are modifying.
   - Click on the view that you are modifying and select
     (🖑) Properties in the mini toolbar.

2. To modify a view property, you must select a category in the column on the left in the Drawing View dialog box. Once selected, the dialog box updates and displays the available options for the selected category.

   In this section you learn about the following additional options:
   - View Type
   - View Display
   - Origin
   - Alignment

3. To complete the modification to the drawing view, click **OK** in the Drawing View dialog box.

To review the name, type, parent/child information, etc., for a selected view, click

🖥 *(Drawing View). An Information Window opens displaying the information.*

You can also press the middle mouse button or press <Enter> to accept and close the Drawing View dialog box.

Additional Options

View Type

The *View Type* category is used when creating and orienting views. For General views, this category can be accessed at any time to reorient a view or to assign a new view name. If any existing views reference the General view, you must confirm the reorientation of the child views.

The information on the *View Type* category changes for the different view types that are created.

Projection and Auxiliary

For Projection views, the *View Type* information is straightforward and refers to its parent view, as shown in Figure 2–1.

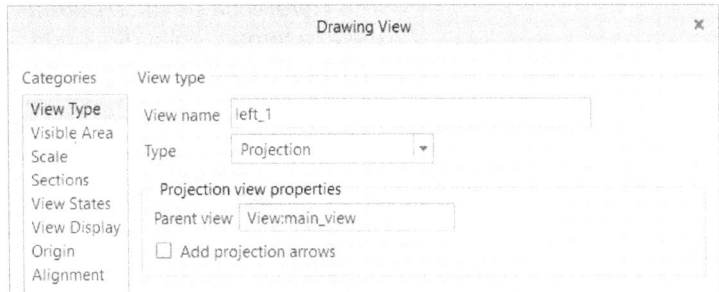

Figure 2–1

For Auxiliary views, the *View Type* information is shown in Figure 2–2.

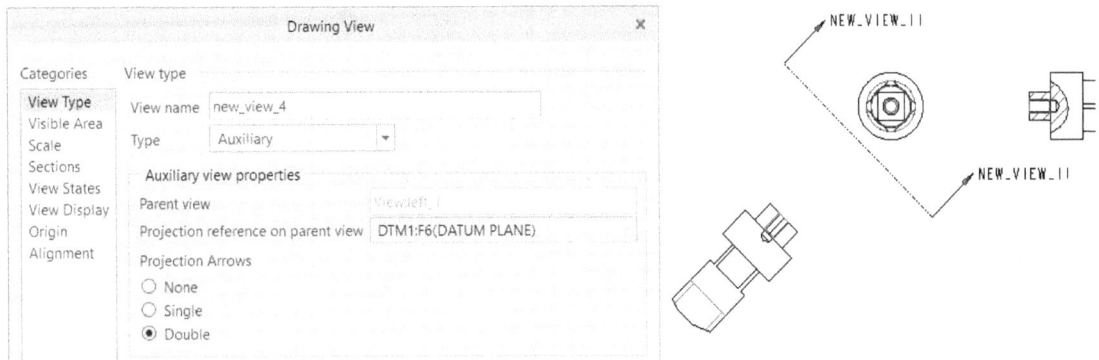

Figure 2–2

Detailed

For Detailed views, the *View Type* information displays as shown in Figure 2–3.

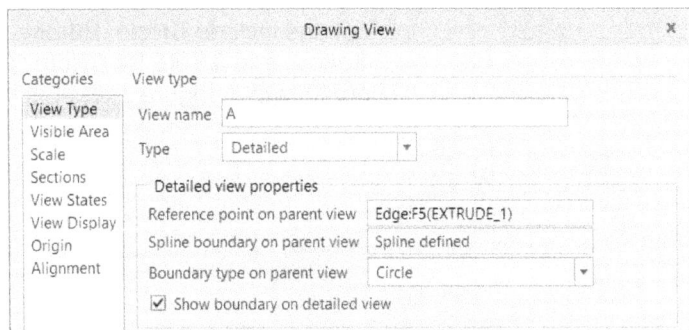

Figure 2–3

The *Reference point on parent view* field enables you to change the attachment point of a boundary spline. However, the shape of the spline remains the same, as shown in Figure 2–4.

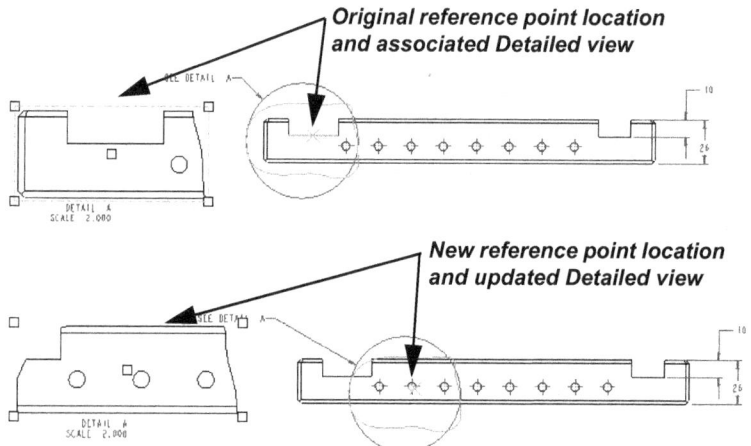

Original reference point location and associated Detailed view

New reference point location and updated Detailed view

Figure 2–4

The size of the callout for a Detailed view is determined by the overall size of the sketched boundary spline. To change the size of the callout, re-sketch the spline.

The *Spline boundary on parent view* field enables you to re-sketch the spline for the Detailed view, as shown in Figure 2–5.

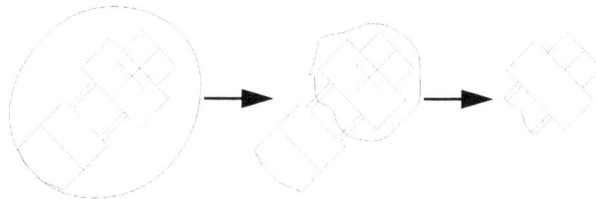

Figure 2–5

The **Boundary type in Parent View** menu enables you to select the boundary shape for the callout on the detailed view. The options include **Circle**, **Ellipse**, **Horizontal/Vertical Ellipse**, **Spline**, and **ASME 94 Circle**. The ellipse and spline boundaries are shown in Figure 2–6.

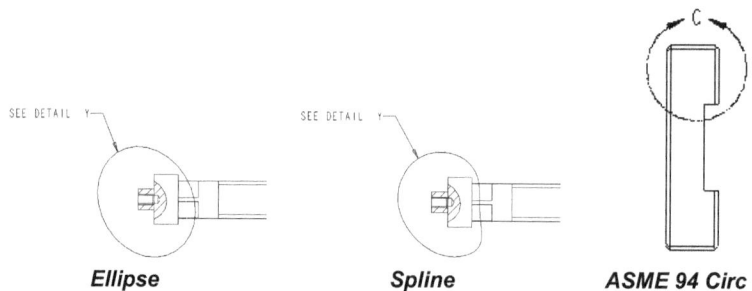

Ellipse   **Spline**   **ASME 94 Circ**

Figure 2–6

The **Show boundary on detailed view** option enables you to control whether or not the boundary of the detailed view displays, as shown in Figure 2–7.

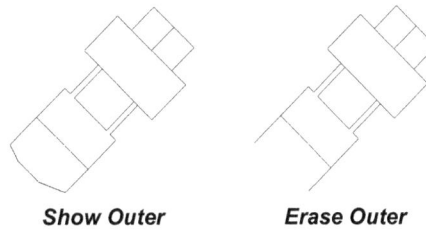

Show Outer   ***Erase Outer***

Figure 2–7

View Manager States

In View Manager, you can create a named combination of various graphical presentations of 3D geometry in Part or

Assembly modes by clicking (View Manager) and selecting **All**, as shown in Figure 2–8.

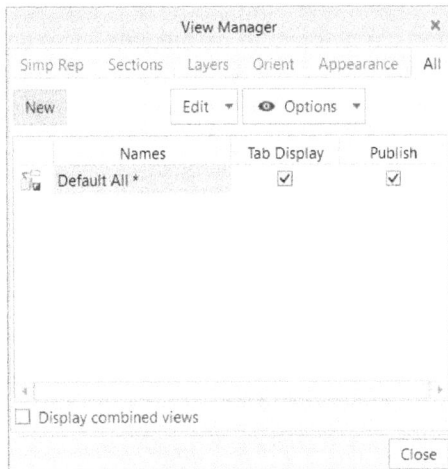

Part View Manager   ***Assembly View Manager***

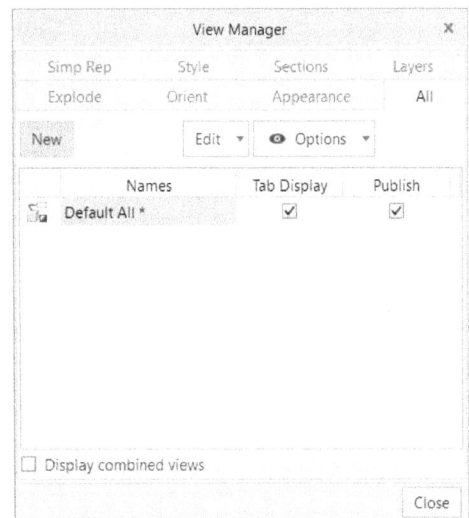

Figure 2–8

During the placement of the General View in the drawing, you are prompted to select one of the named combinations to be used for the view, as shown in Figure 2–9.

Figure 2–9

View Display

By default, the display for all of the drawing views is controlled by the display settings that are set using toolbar icons or options in the Environment dialog box. To manipulate the display of a view independent of these global environment settings, select the *View Display* category in the Drawing View dialog box and define the required display using the available options, as shown in Figure 2–10.

It is recommended that you set the view display for all views so that changes to the model's display do not affect your drawing.

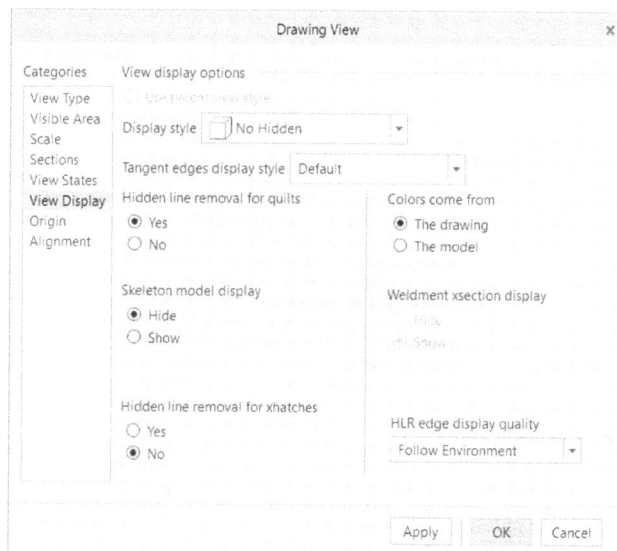

Figure 2–10

Examples of views using different combinations of display options are shown in Figure 2–11.

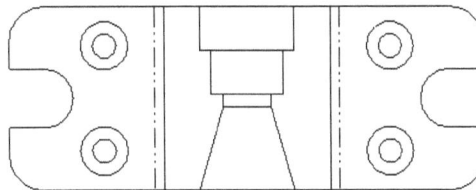

Wireframe, tangent edge Phantom

No Hidden,
tangent edge None

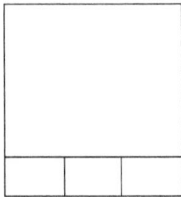

No Hidden, tangent
edge Solid

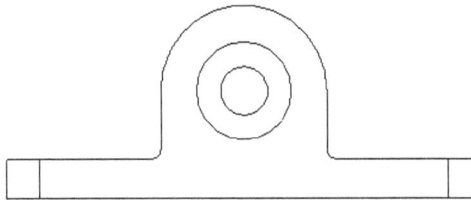

Hidden Line, tangent
edge Centerline

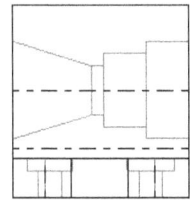

Figure 2–11

Shaded Views

Shaded views of models can be included in drawings. This capability can be used to improve the visualization of 3D models in the 2D drawing. The shaded views are plotted when they are sent to a capable, non-vector based printer.

Shaded views are one possible graphical representation of the model in a drawing. They use the colors defined in the part or assembly, including any individual surface colors and/or textures.

You can set a view's Display Style to be shaded or shaded with edges for most of the view types in the drawing (all except **Revolved** and **Of Flat Ply Views** and any view that has been customized using the *Section* category in the Drawing View dialog box). To set a view's Display Style to be shaded, right-click on the view and select **Properties**. Select **View Display** in the Drawing View dialog box and select **Shading** in the flyout, as shown in Figure 2–12.

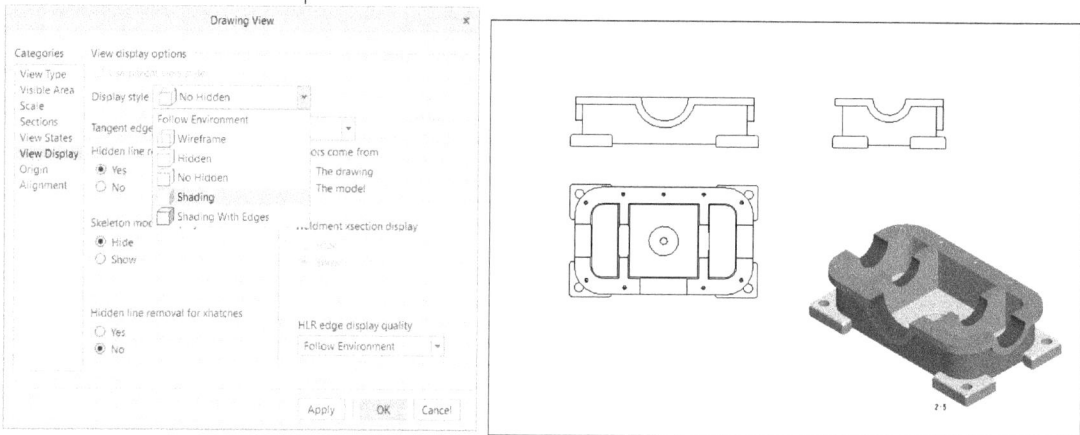

Figure 2–12

Origin

The default origin location of a view is the center of the view outline. To change this origin, select the *Origin* category in the Drawing View dialog box. The default option (**View center**) can be changed to **On Item** so that the origin references the model geometry, as shown in Figure 2–13.

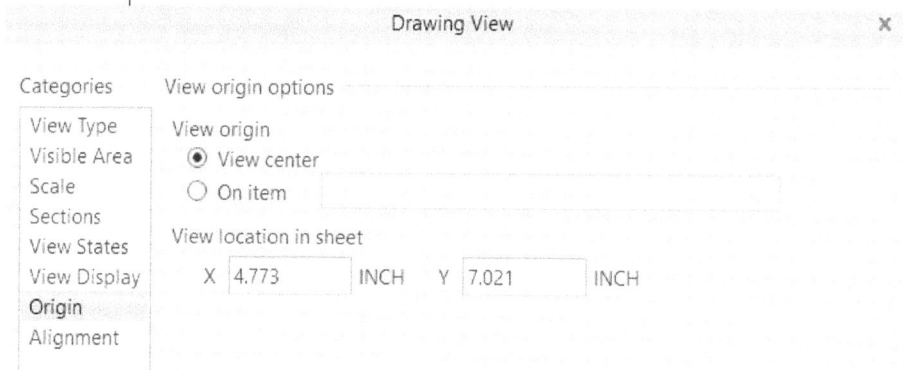

Figure 2–13

The origin can be changed for General, Auxiliary, and Broken views. It updates when changes are made to the model geometry. For example, the origin of the left view shown in Figure 2–14 is at its default location.

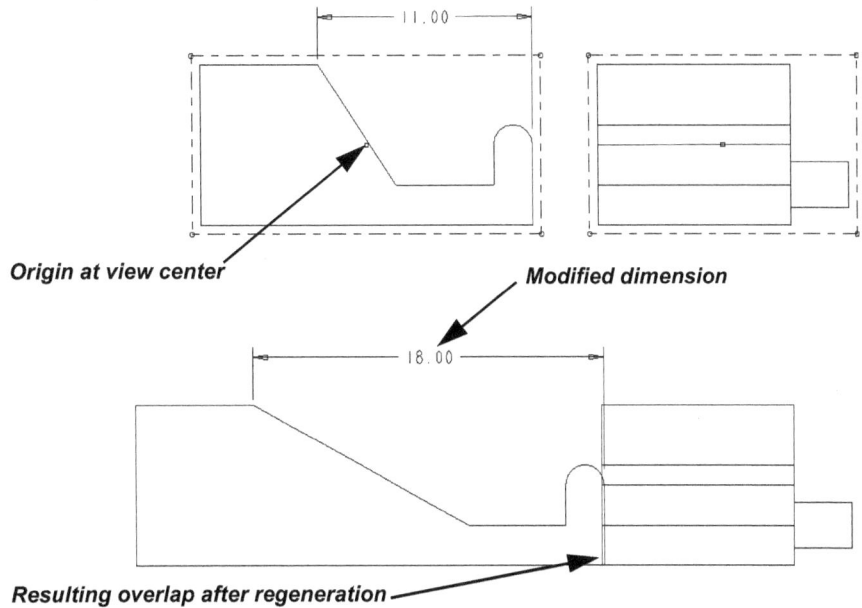

Figure 2–14

Modifying this view causes it to overlap with the right view. To ensure that the views do not overlap when additional modifications are made, the origin relocates for the left view, as shown in Figure 2–15.

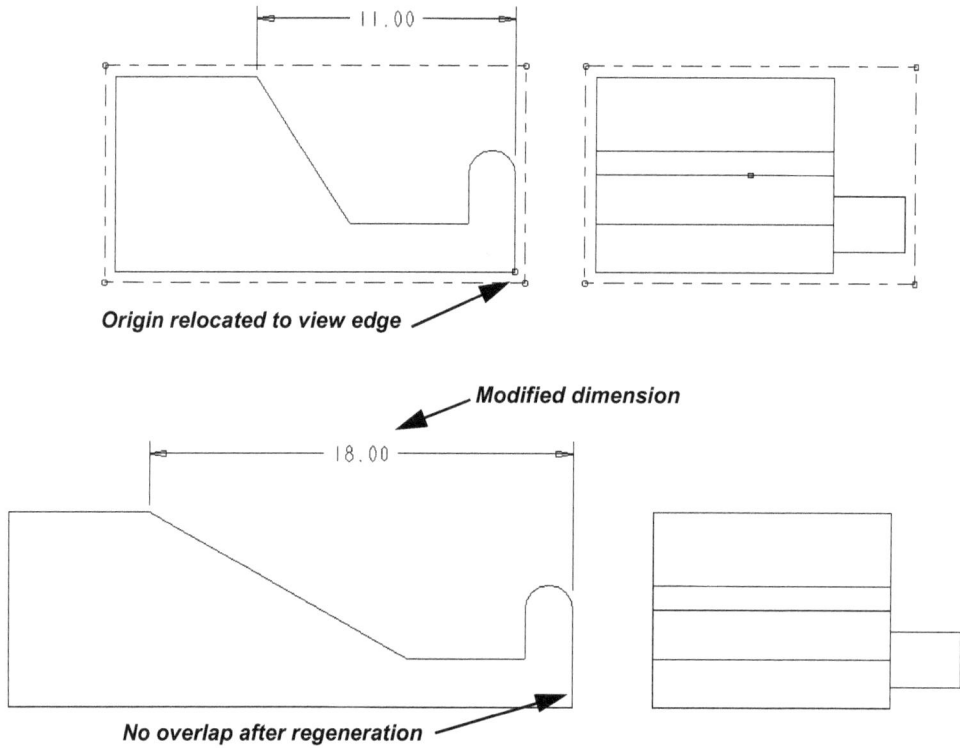

Origin relocated to view edge

Modified dimension

No overlap after regeneration

Figure 2–15

Alignment

The *Alignment* category in the Drawing View dialog box enables you to align and unalign views using the options shown in Figure 2–16. Aligning establishes a parent/child relationship between views. Therefore, when the parent view is moved, the aligned child view also moves (e.g., you can align two General views horizontally or vertically).

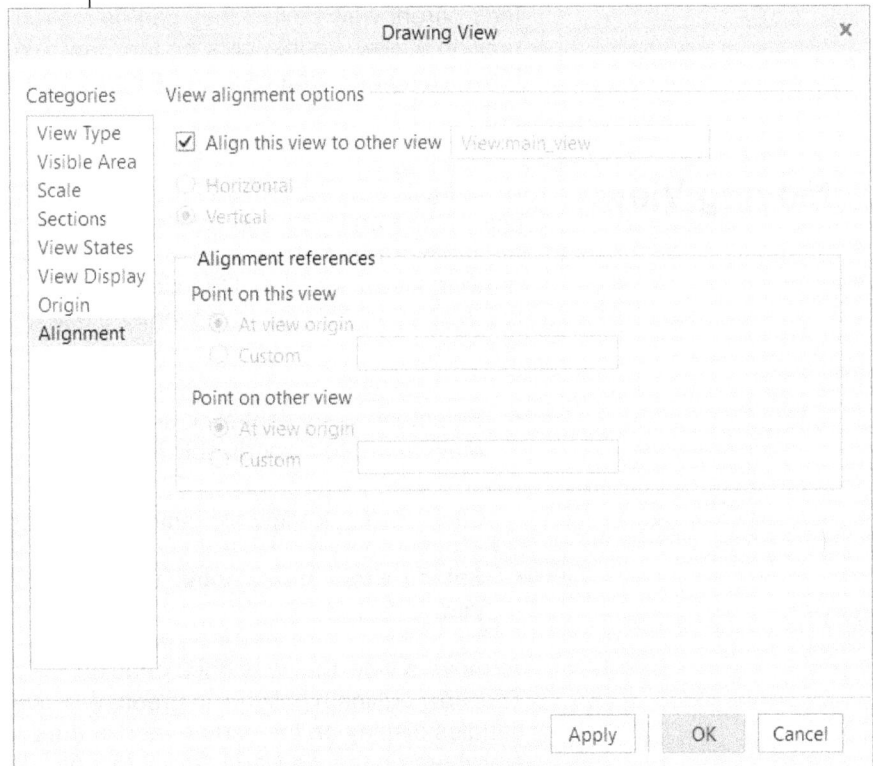

Figure 2–16

2.2 Manipulate Drawing Views

View Alignment

Parent/child relationships are established during view creation, which can limit view movement. For example, if a General view is moved, all of the dependent views (Projected or Auxiliary) move with it.

Projected and Auxiliary views can be unaligned, if required, from their parent view so that they can be moved independently. To unalign a view, double-click on the view to open the Drawing View dialog box, and clear the **Align this view to other view** option

Moving Views

By default, view movement functionality is disabled when you start Creo Parametic and create or open a drawing. This prevents drawing views from accidentally being moved. Locking drawing views is a global function applying to all of the drawings in the session. To enable movement, use one of the following methods:

- Select the view, right-click and select ▣ (Lock View Movement) to clear disable it.

- Click ▣ (Lock View Movement) in the *Layout* tab.

- Set the **allow_move_view_with_move** config.pro option to **yes**.

To move a view that was once enabled, select it on the screen. The view outline highlights in green, and five square drag handles display on the corners and in the center. Select anywhere on the view and drag it to a new location. If you move a view accidentally, you can press <Esc> while the move is in progress to snap the view back to its original position. You can also use the **Undo** function after the view has been placed.

Delete Views

Deleting a view permanently removes it from a drawing. Any view that does not have an associated child view or detail items that reference it can be deleted. If a child references exists, it must also be deleted.

How To: Delete a View

1. Select the view to be deleted.
2. Right-click and select **Delete** or press <Delete>.
3. Confirm the deletion by clicking **Yes** in the **Confirm** menu (you are only prompted if a child entity exists).

You can also click

✕ *(Delete) in the Annotate tab.*

Until an operation is completed that clears the Undo memory, you can click ↶ (Undo) to undo the view deletion.

Erasing Views

Erasing views temporarily removes them from the drawing. Since erasing does not permanently remove them, all of the children remain displayed on the drawing. Once erased, a view can be restored to the drawing.

*After erasing a view, a green rectangle displays in place of the view. To toggle this rectangle off, set the config.pro option **highlight_erased_dwg _ view** to **no**.*

How To: Erase a View

1. Click ⬚ (Erase View) in the Display group in the *Layout* tab.
2. Select the view to be erased.

You can also use the Drawing Tree to resume the view.

How To: Resume a View

1. Click ⬚ (Resume View) in the Display group in the *Layout* tab or right-click and select **Resume View**.
2. Select the view to be resumed in the Graphics window.

Drawing Display

Click ⬚ (Edge Display) in the Edit group in the *Layout* tab to access options for controlling the display of individual edges and the representation of individual components (for assembly drawings).

Click (Show Modified Edges) to highlight any edges that have custom display settings applied.

The drawing display options are described as follows:

Option	Description
Component Display	Controls the Display mode of assembly components.
Process Display	Controls the Display mode for the steps in a process assembly.
Edge Display	Controls the display of edges in a drawing. The available options are shown on the left in . Different edge displays for three edges in a General view are shown on the right.

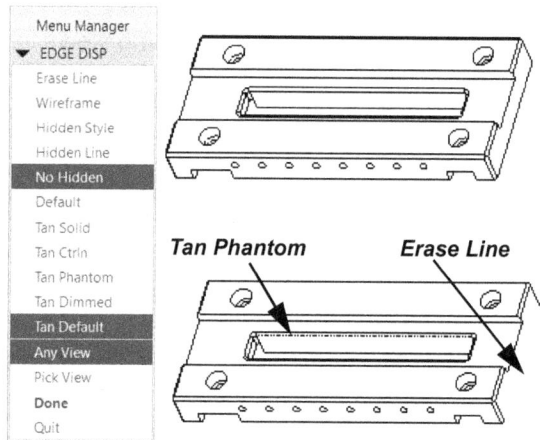

Tan Phantom   *Erase Line*

Model Edge Display

As an alternative to converting model edges to draft entities to manipulate their display state, you can now modify color, thickness, and line style (font) directly in the drawing view. To do so, select the **Edge** option in Filter drop-down list (as shown in Figure 2–17), and select the edge.

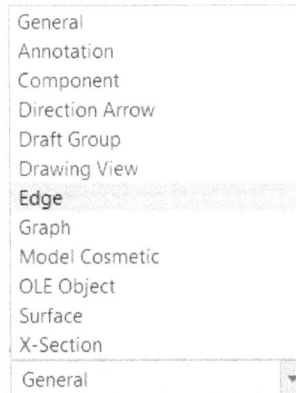

General
Annotation
Component
Direction Arrow
Draft Group
Drawing View
Edge
Graph
Model Cosmetic
OLE Object
Surface
X-Section

General

Figure 2–17

Right-click on the edge and select **Line Style** or click ✎ (Line Style) in the Format group in the *Layout* tab. You can change all of the instances or a single instance if the selected edge displays in multiple views. Figure 2–18 shows the menu options that are available if a model edge is to be modified.

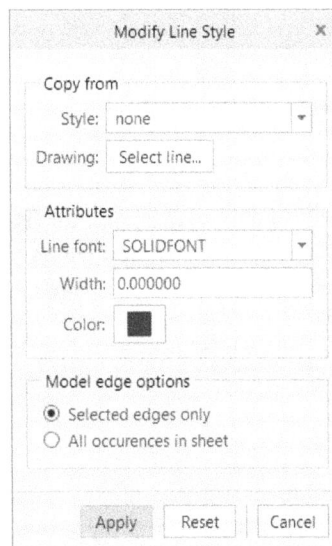

Modify Line Style ✕

Copy from
Style: none
Drawing: Select line...

Attributes
Line font: SOLIDFONT
Width: 0.000000
Color: ■

Model edge options
◉ Selected edges only
○ All occurences in sheet

Apply   Reset   Cancel

Figure 2–18

2.3 Configuration Options

The following configuration file options enable you to customize the modification of drawing views.

Option	Values	Description
auto_show_3D_detail_items	no **yes**	By default, 3D detail items with defined annotation planes are automatically displayed in drawing views.
highlight_erased_dwg_views	**yes** no	By default, a green rectangle displays in place of an erased view. If this option is set to **no**, the green rectangle is not displayed.
allow_move_view_with_move	**no** yes	Prevents the movement of drawing views with the mouse.
make_proj_view_notes	**no** yes	Automatically adds view names to projection views in the following format: VIEW viewname-viewname.

The following drawing setup file options enable you to customize the modification of drawing views.

Option	Values	Description
model_display_for_new_views	**follow_environment** wireframe hidden_line no_hidden save_environment shading	Determines the line display style of models when creating views.
tan_edge_display_for_new_views	**default** tan_solid no_disp_tan tan_ctrln tan_phantom tan_dimmed save_environment	Determines the tangent edge display for models when creating views.

hidden_tangent_ edges	**default** dimmed erased	Controls the display of hidden tangent edges in drawing views.
default_view_label_ placement	**bottom_left** bottom_center bottom_right top_left top_center top_right	Sets the default position and justification for the view label.

Practice 2a

Move Drawing Views

Practice Objectives

- Move views.
- Modify view scale and display.

In this practice, you will move views and modify their view display. The final drawing is shown in Figure 2–19.

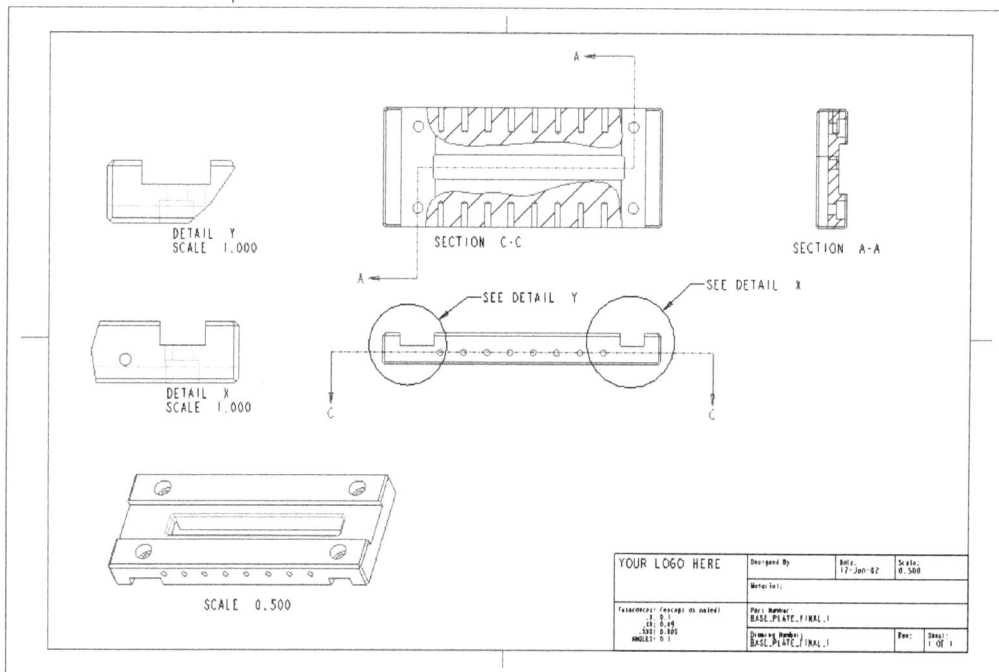

Figure 2–19

Task 1 - Open a drawing file.

Base_plate_ final_1.drw references the model base_plate_final_1.prt and the format generic_b.frm.

1. Set the working directory to the *Move_Views* folder.

2. Open **base_plate_final_1.drw**.

3. Set the model display as follows:

- (Datum Display Filters): All Off

- (Display Style): (Wireframe)

Task 2 - Move the views.

1. Ensure that the *Layout* tab is selected.

*You can also select the view, right-click, and ensure that **Lock View Movement** is not selected.*

2. Click 🔓 (Lock View Movement) to unlock the drawing views if the icon is not already toggled off.

3. Select a drawing view and place it in its new position using the view drag handles and the left mouse button. Move all of the views to their new positions, as shown in Figure 2–20.

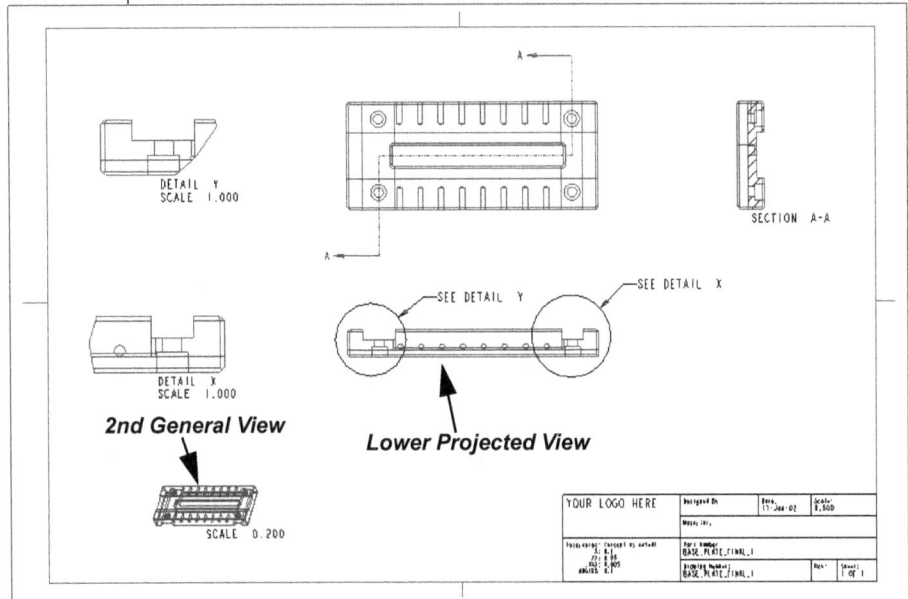

2nd General View

Lower Projected View

Figure 2–20

Task 3 - Modify a view scale in the drawing.

Alternatively, you can set the scale in the Drawing View dialog box.

1. Select the scale text under the second General view as shown in Figure 2–21.

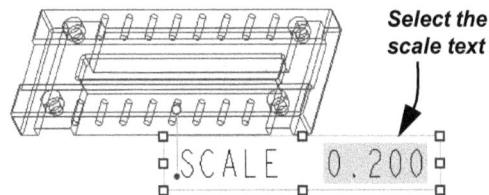

Select the scale text

SCALE 0.200

Figure 2–21

2. **SCALE 0.200** will highlight. Once the text has been highlighted, double-click on **0.200** under the second General view.

3. Set the new *Scale* value for this view to **0.5** and press <Enter>. The second General view updates with the new scale value. Move the text if required so that the view displays as shown in Figure 2–22.

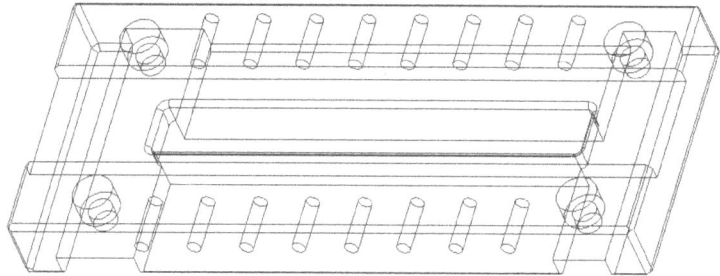

SCALE   0.500

Figure 2–22

Task 4 - Modify the view display.

You can also click the view and select

 (Properties) in the mini toolbar.

1. Double-click on the lower Projected view as shown in Figure 2–23. The Drawing View dialog box opens.

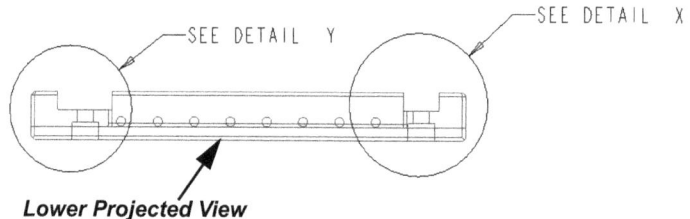

SEE DETAIL   Y   SEE DETAIL   X

Lower Projected View

Figure 2–23

2. Select the *View Display* category.

3. Select **No Hidden** in the **Display style** menu.

4. Select **None** in the **Tangent edges display style** menu.

5. Maintain the remaining default options for the view display. The Drawing View dialog box displays as shown in Figure 2–24.

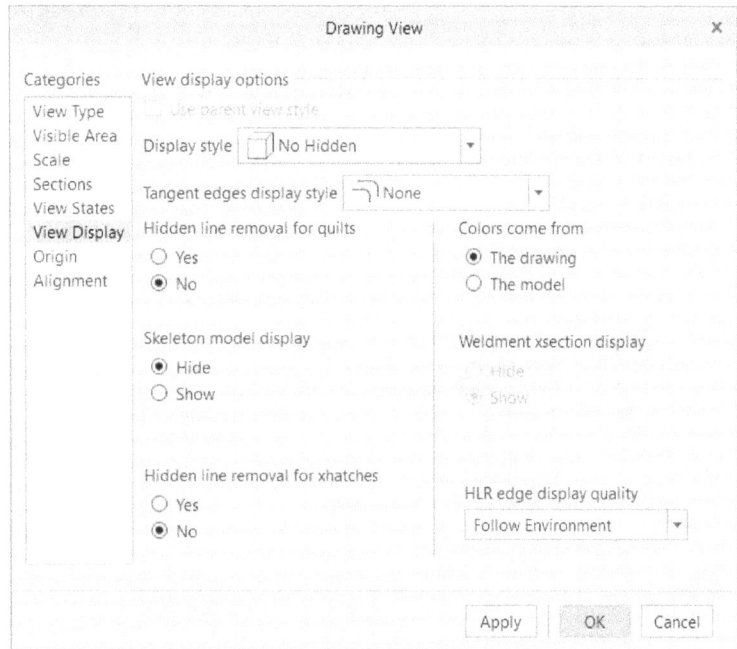

Figure 2–24

6. Apply the changes and click **OK** in the Drawing View dialog box. The drawing displays as shown in Figure 2–25. Note that views X and Y share the same display as the lower Projected view.

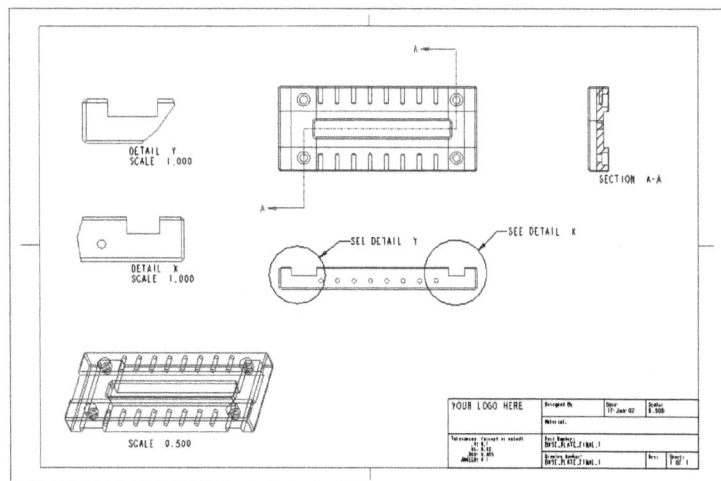

Figure 2–25

Task 5 - Modify the Display style so that views X and Y are independent of their parent view.

1. Double-click on the DETAIL X view. The Drawing View dialog box opens.

2. Select the *View Display* category.

3. Clear the **Use parent view style** option at the top of the dialog box. All of the remaining view display options are now available so that you can set the view display independent of the parent view.

4. Select **Hidden** in the **Display Style** menu.

5. Maintain the remaining default options, as shown in Figure 2–26.

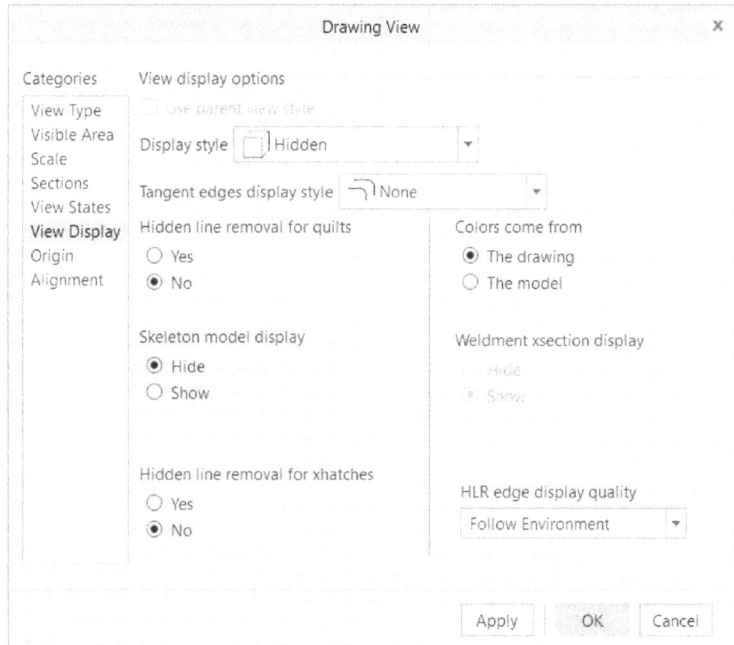

Figure 2–26

6. Click **OK**.

7. Double-click on the DETAIL Y view and set the View Display as was done for the DETAIL X view. The views display as shown in Figure 2–27.

When plotted, hidden lines display as a dashed font. Depending on the size of the entity, they could display as a solid line.

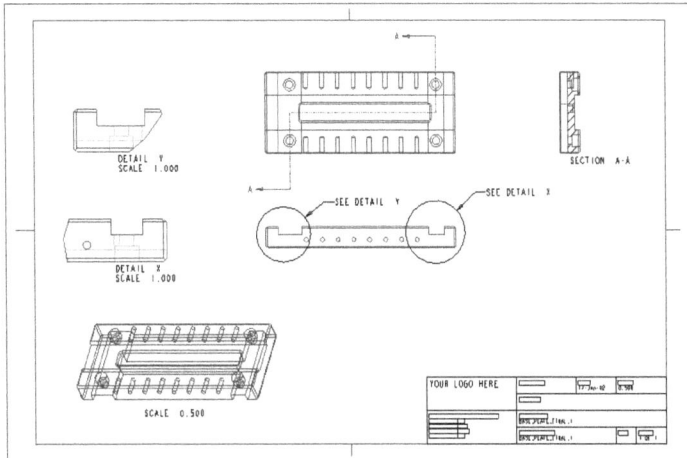

Figure 2–27

8. Change the view display for the two General views and the section view A-A, as shown in Figure 2–28.

- **1st General & section view: No Hidden** and tangent lines are **None**. Move SECTION A-A note.
- **2nd General view: No Hidden** and tangent lines are **Dimmed**.

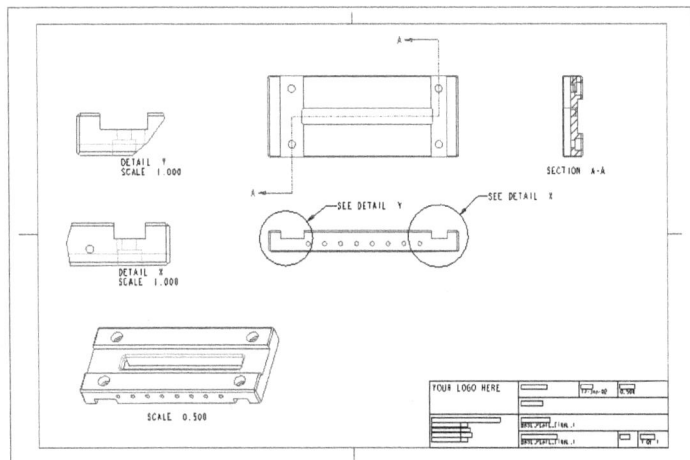

Figure 2–28

Task 6 - Redefine the General view as a cross-sectional view.

1. In the Model Tree, right-click on
   BASE_PLATE_FINAL_1.PRT and select 📂 (Open).

2. In the In-graphics toolbar, click 🔳 (View Manager).

3. Click the *Sections* tab.

4. Select **New>Planar**.

5. Enter **C** as the cross-section name and press <Enter>.

6. On the far-right of the *Sections* tab, expand ▦ (Datum) and
   select ▱ (Plane).

7. Select the hole shown in Figure 2–29 by placing the cursor
   over the hole, right-clicking until it highlights, and then
   selecting it.

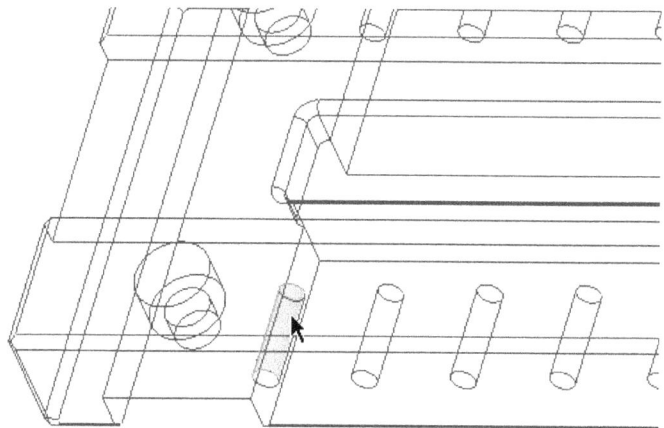

Figure 2–29

8. Press <Ctrl> and select datum plane **DTM2** in the Model
   Tree.

9. In the Datum Plane dialog box, select **Parallel**, as shown in Figure 2–30.

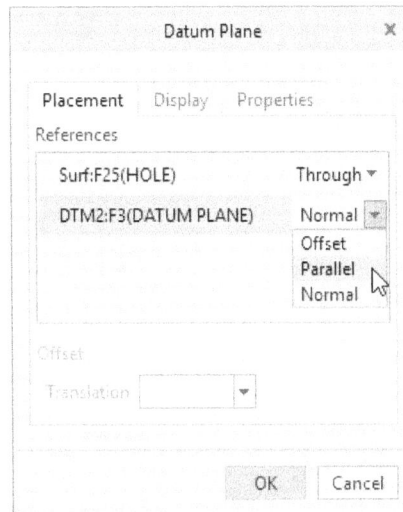

Figure 2–30

10. Click **OK**.

11. In the *Section* tab, click ▶ (Resume), and then click ✔ (OK).

12. Close the View Manager and return to the drawing window.

13. Double-click on the 2D General view (i.e., the view with section arrows). The Drawing View dialog box opens.

14. Select the *Sections* category.

15. Select **2D cross-section** to assign a cross-section to the view.

16. Click ✚ (Add Section) to add a section to the view.

17. Select section **C**.

18. Scroll to the right side of the information for section **C** and select the *Arrow Display* collector.

19. Select the bottom Projected view as the one in which to display the cross-section arrows.

20. Click **OK** in the Drawing View dialog box. The drawing displays as shown in Figure 2–31.

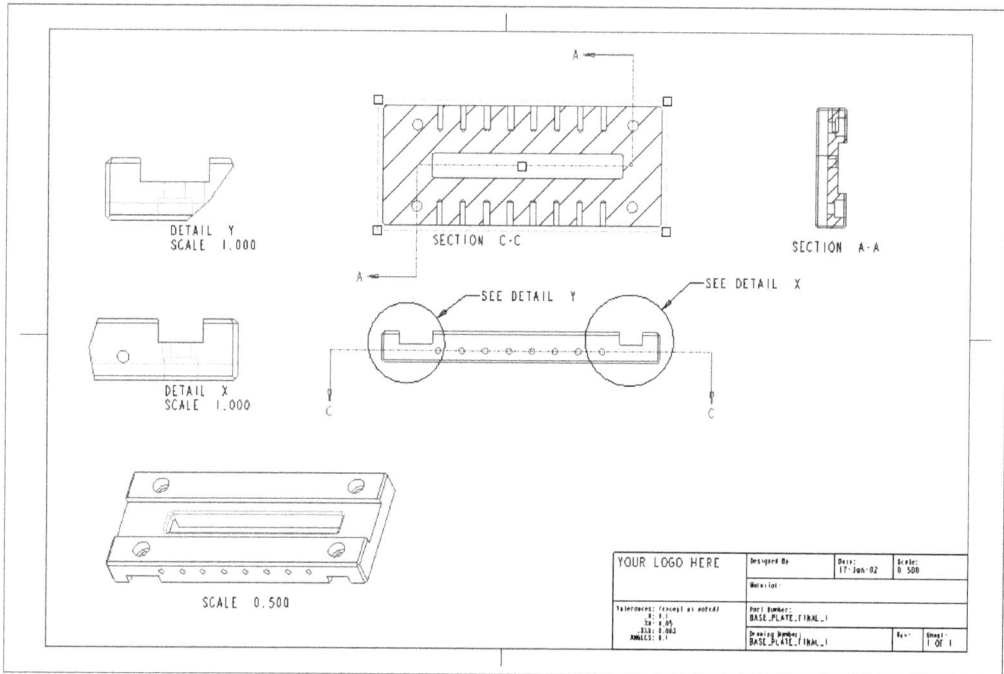

DETAIL Y
SCALE 1.000

SECTION C-C

SECTION A-A

SEE DETAIL Y

SEE DETAIL X

DETAIL X
SCALE 1.000

SCALE 0.500

YOUR LOGO HERE

Figure 2–31

Task 7 - Redefine the General view as a local sectional view.

Double click near the edge of the view, otherwise Creo Parametric may select the cross hatching instead.

1. Double-click on the General view now labeled **SECTION C-C**.

2. When the Drawing View dialog box opens, select the *Sections* category.

3. Select **Local** in the Sectioned Area drop-down list.

4. Select a centerpoint for the first break-out and sketch a spline, as shown in Figure 2–32.

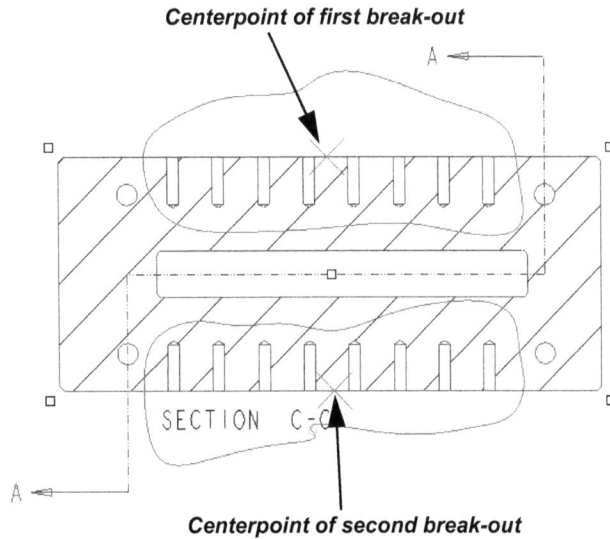

Centerpoint of first break-out
Centerpoint of second break-out

Figure 2–32

5. Add another cross-section to create a second local section in the same view. Click ✚ (Add Section) to add a section to the view.

6. Select section **C**. By default, the sectioned area displays as **Local**.

7. Select a centerpoint for the second breakout and sketch a spline.

8. Apply the changes. The Drawing View dialog box updates as shown on in Figure 2–33.

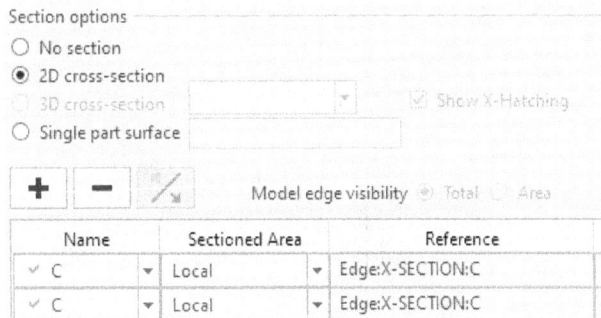

Figure 2–33

9. Click **OK** in the Drawing View dialog box. The drawing displays as shown in Figure 2–34.

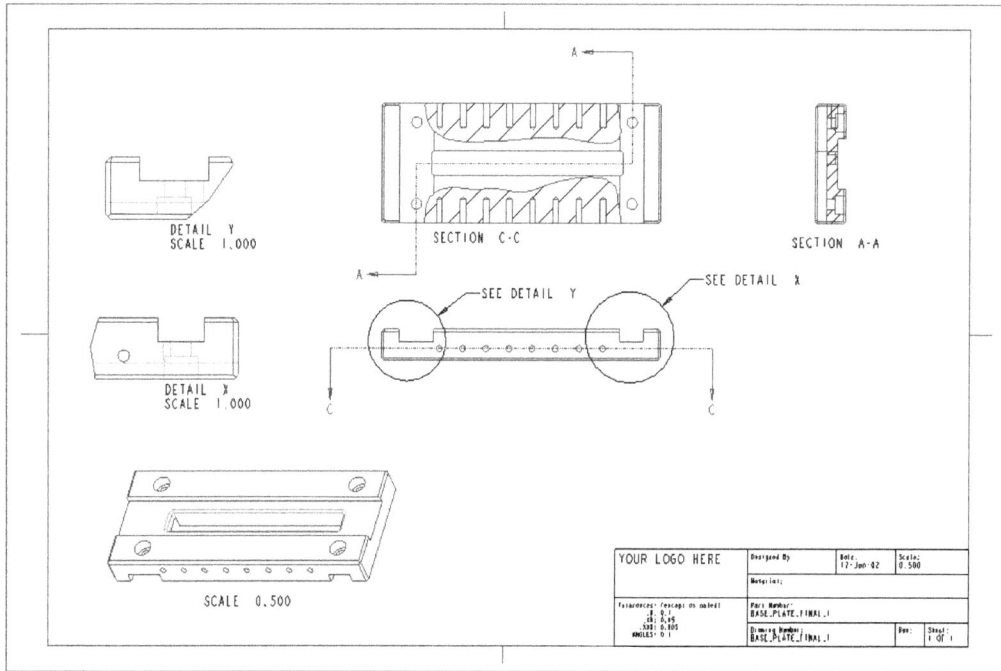

Figure 2–34

10. Save the drawing and close the window.

Practice 2b | Move Broken Views

Practice Objective

- Change the position of Broken views.

In this practice, you will move a Broken view. The final drawing displays as shown in Figure 2–35.

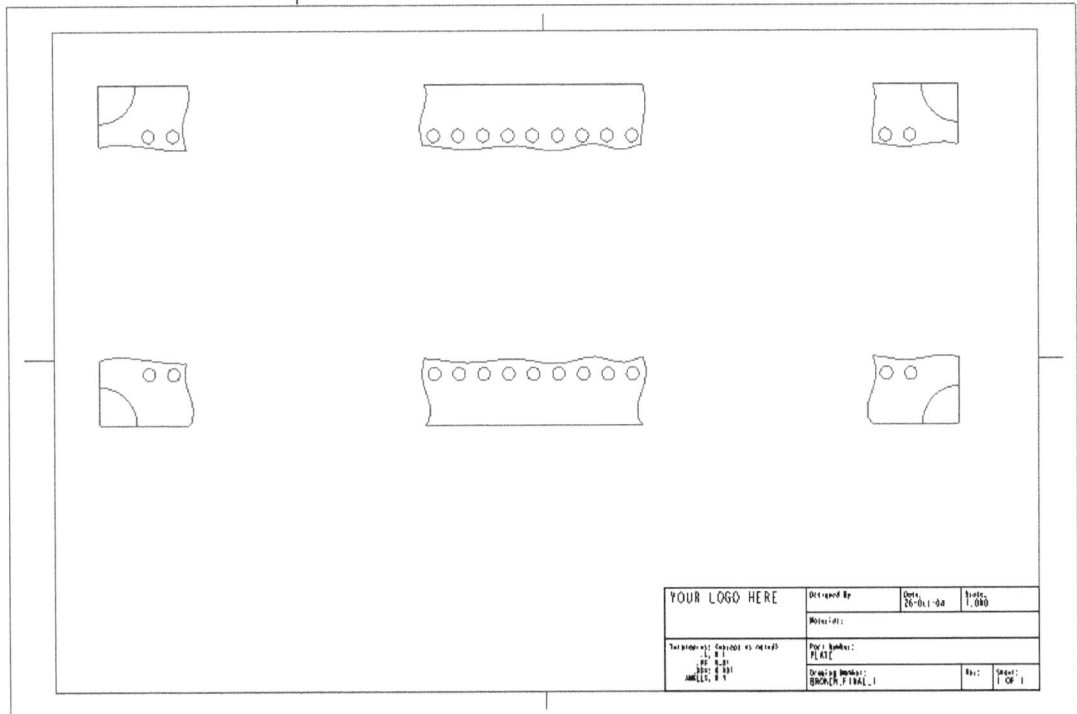

Figure 2–35

Task 1 - Open the broken drawing.

Broken_final_1.drw references the model plate.prt and the format generic_b.frm.

1. Set the working directory to the *Move_Broken_Views* folder.

2. Open **broken_final_1.drw**.

3. Set the model display as follows:

    - *(Datum Display Filters)*: All Off

Task 2 - Move the Broken view.

1. Ensure that the *Layout* tab is active and that the view lock has been disabled.

2. Select the upper left section of the Broken view.

3. Select on the drag handle and drag the view to the location shown in Figure 2–36. Place the view by pressing the left mouse button.

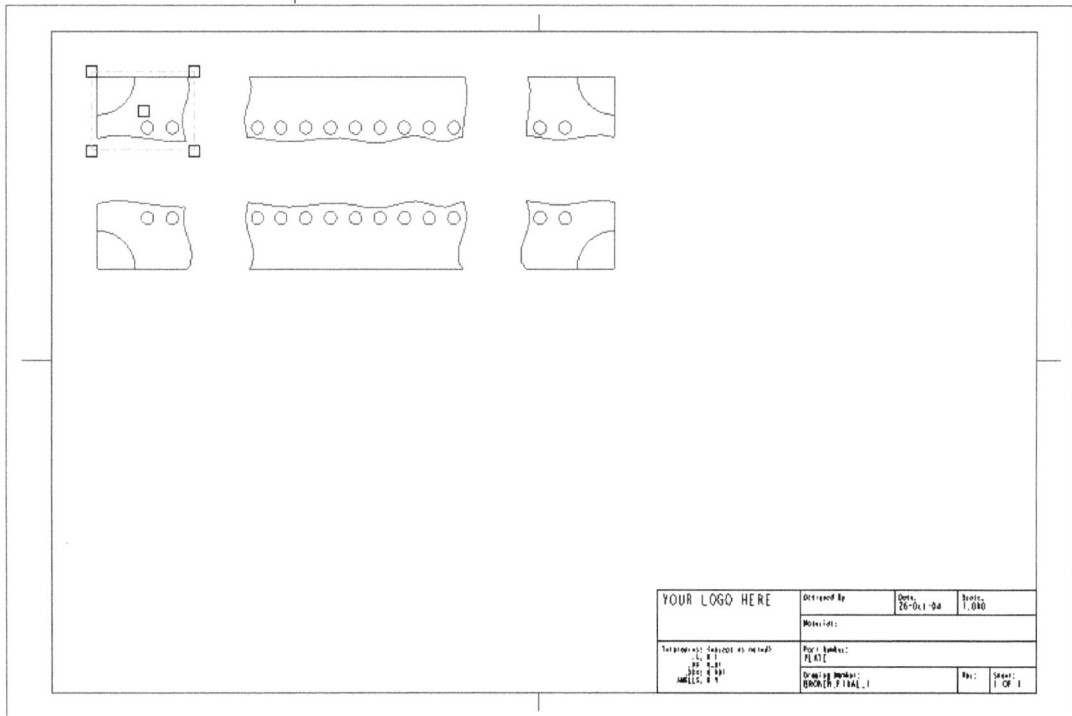

Figure 2–36

Task 3 - Move the children areas of the Broken view.

1. Select the lower right section of the view.

2. Select the drag handle and move the section to the lower right side of the drawing as shown in Figure 2–37. Note that selecting this section of the broken view separates the breaks.

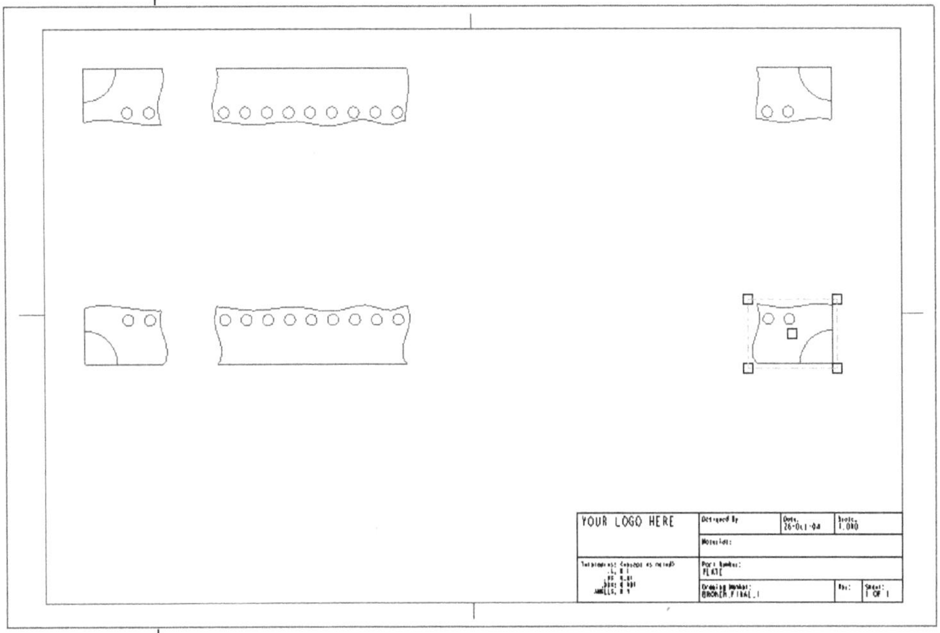

Figure 2–37

3. Continue to move the breaks as shown in Figure 2–38. Note the relationships between the sections of the Broken view.

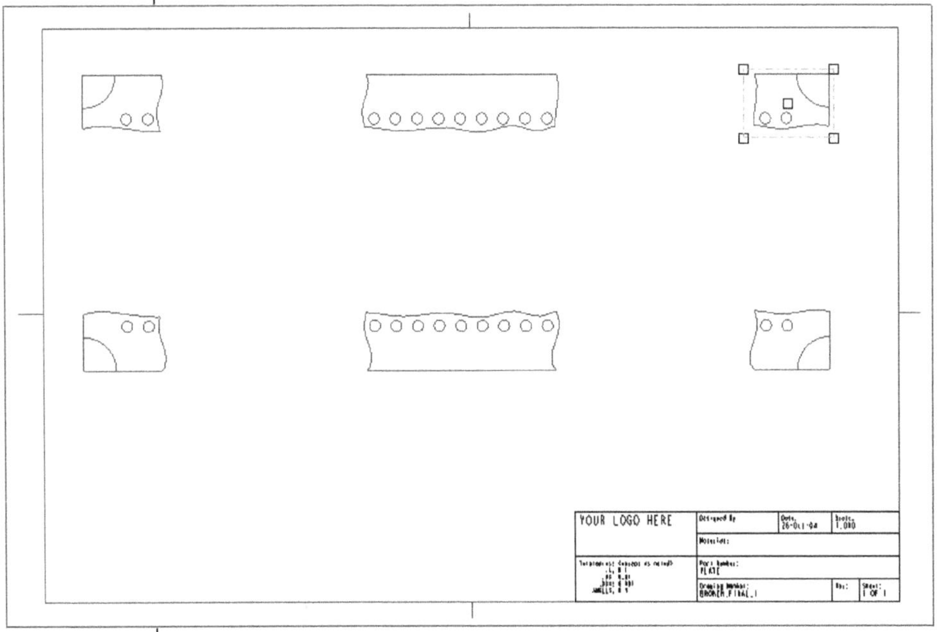

Figure 2–38

4. Save the drawing and close the window.

Practice 2c | Modify Drawing Views

Practice Objective

- Modify the type of view.

In this practice, you will change the view types in the drawing using the Drawing View dialog box. The final drawing displays as shown in Figure 2–39.

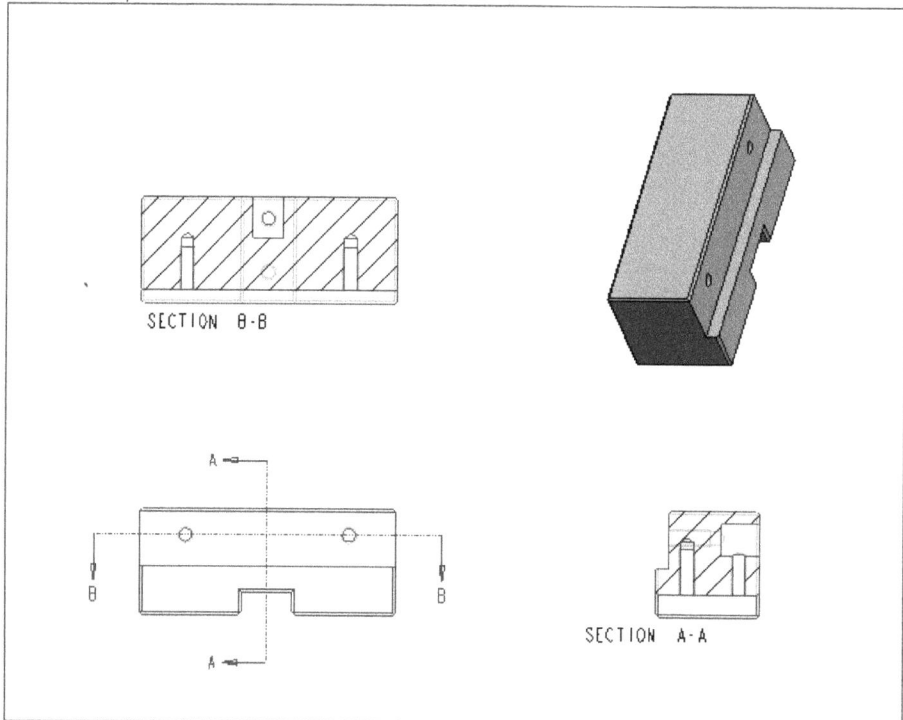

Figure 2–39

Task 1 - Open a drawing file.

Support_final_1.drw *references the model* **support_final_1.prt**.

1. Set the working directory to the *Modify_Views* folder.

2. Open **support_final_1.drw**.

3. Set the model display as follows:

- *(Datum Display Filters)*: All Off
- *(Display Style)*: (Wireframe)

Task 2 - Modify the type of views used for creating the projected views.

1. Double-click on the projected right view as shown in Figure 2–40.

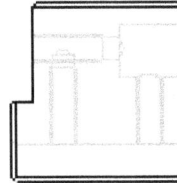

Figure 2–40

*Projected views can be relocated so they are not aligned with parent views. Open the Drawing View dialog box and select the Alignment category. Clear the **Align this view to other view** option. Once unaligned, the views can be moved.*

2. Select the *Sections* category.

3. Select **2D cross-section** to assign a cross-section to the view.

4. Keep the **Total** option selected in the *Model edge visibility* area to ensure that all of the edges are visible throughout the model, and not only for the 2D area of the section.

5. Click ✚ (Add Section).

6. Select cross-section **A** to add a section to the view. This section was predefined in the model.

7. Scroll to the right of the information for section A and select the *Arrow Display* field.

8. Select the parent 2D General view (the lower left view) as the view to display the cutting plane arrows. The Drawing View dialog box displays as shown in Figure 2–41.

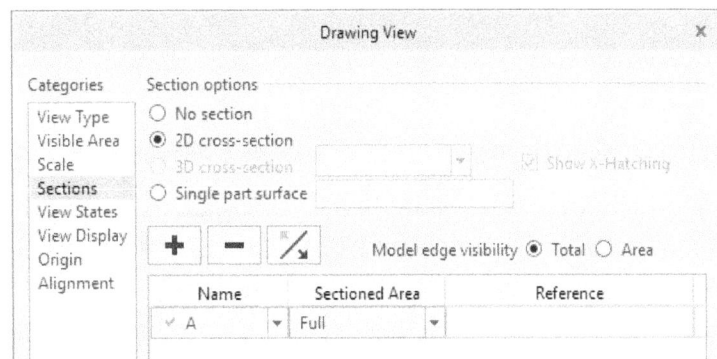

Figure 2–41

9. Click **OK** in the Drawing View dialog box. The drawing displays as shown in Figure 2–42.

Place all cross-section arrows in this General view

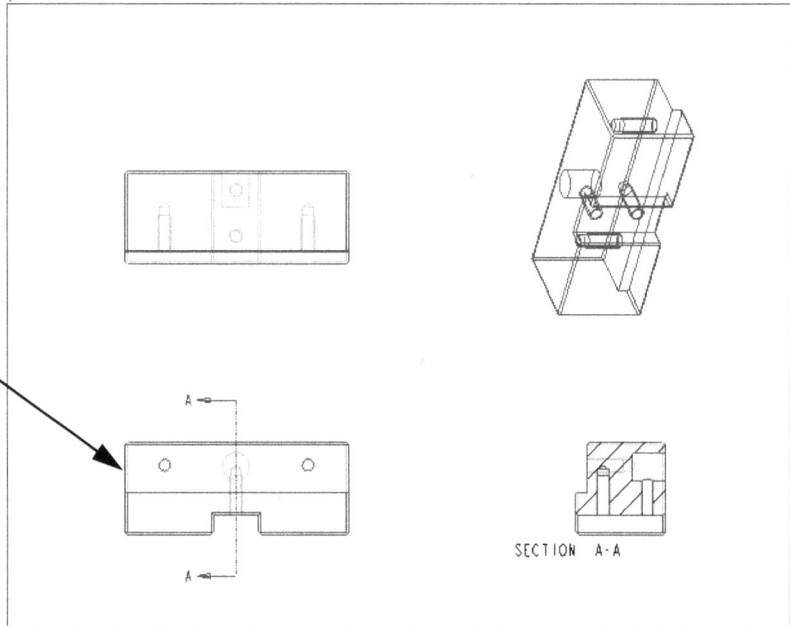

Figure 2–42

10. Change the top Projection view to display cross-section B. Place the cross-section arrows in the lower left General view, as shown in Figure 2–43.

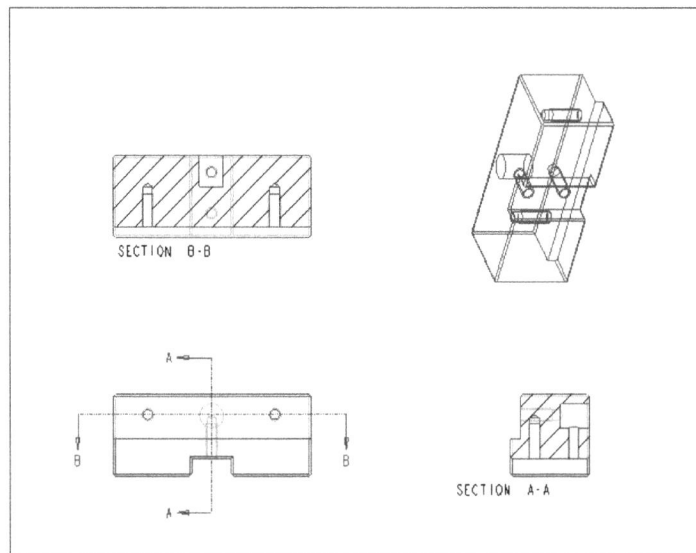

Figure 2–43

Task 3 - Modify the Display mode of the views

1. Double-click on the 2D General view (the lower left view).

2. Select the *View Display* category.

3. Select **No Hidden** in the **Display Style** menu.

4. Select **None** in the **Tangent Edges Display Style** menu.

5. Click **OK** in the Drawing View dialog box.

6. Change the View Display settings for both of the projected views (top and right views) using the same options. The drawing displays as shown in Figure 2–44.

To open the Drawing View dialog box for a sectioned view, verify that the view outline is highlighted when double-clicking and not the cross-hatching. If you just double-click on the view, you can access the cross-hatching menus.

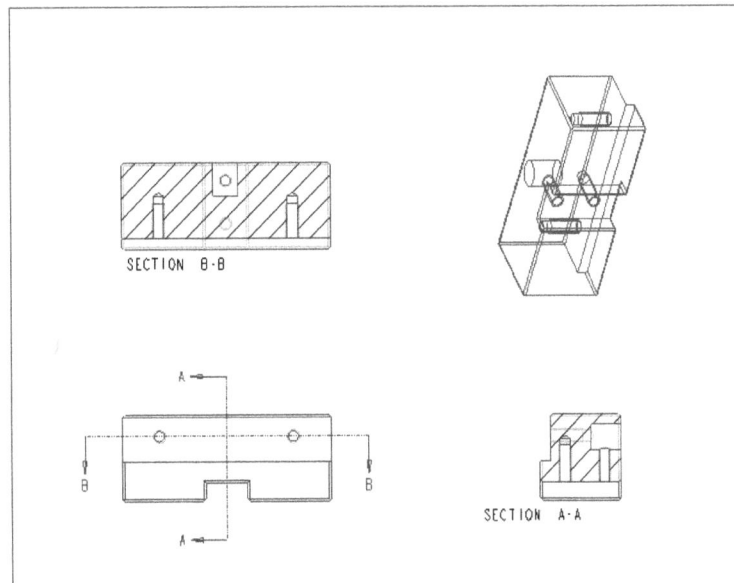

Figure 2–44

Task 4 - Modify the Display mode of the 3D General view

1. Double-click on the 3D General view (upper right view). The Drawing View dialog box opens.

2. Select the *View Display* category.

3. Select **Shading With Edges** in the **Display Style** drop-down list.

4. Click **OK**. The drawing displays as shown in Figure 2–45.

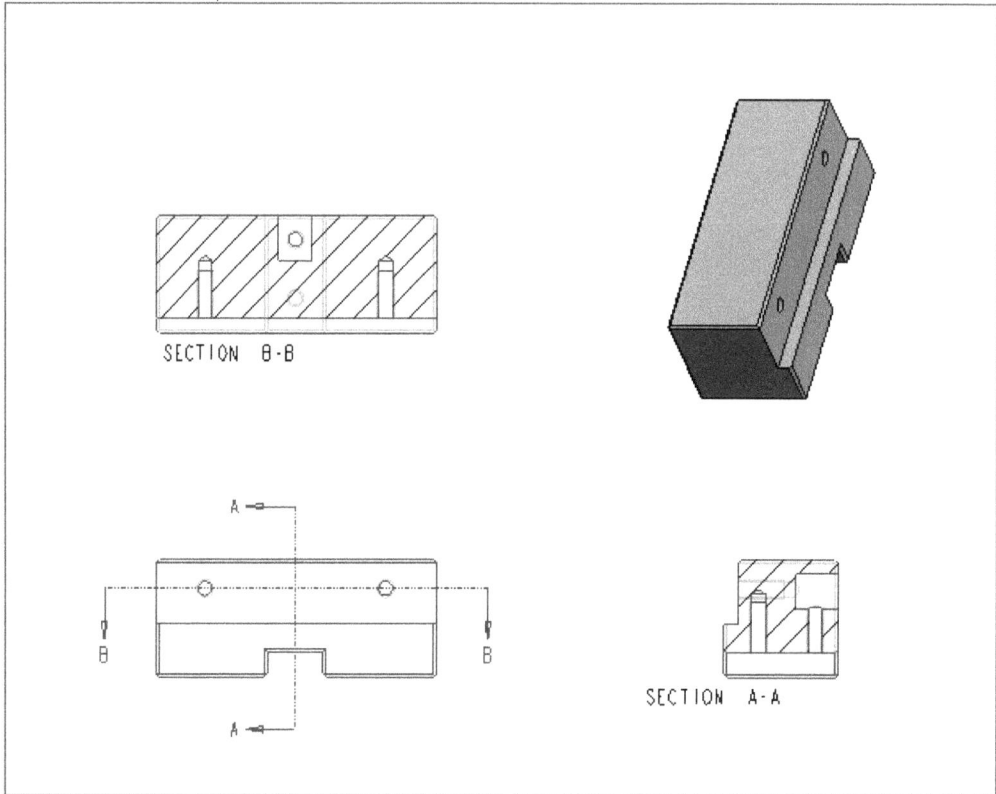

Figure 2–45

5. Save the drawing and close the window.

Practice 2d | Modify View Boundaries

Practice Objective

- Redefine the boundary of a Detailed view.

In this practice, you will modify the boundary of Detailed view Y. The final drawing displays as shown in Figure 2–46.

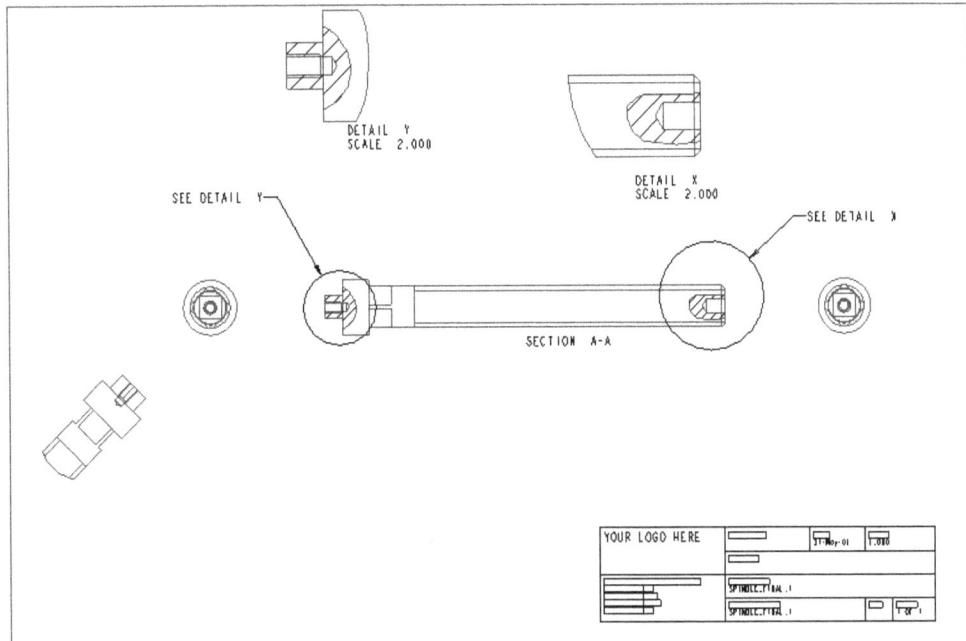

Figure 2–46

Task 1 - Open a drawing file.

Spindle_final_1.drw references the model spindle_final_1.prt and the format generic_b.frm.

1. Set the working directory to the *Modify_View_Boundaries* folder.

2. Open **spindle_final_1.drw**.

3. Set the model display as follows:

- 🏷️ *(Datum Display Filters)*: All Off

- 🔲 *(Display Style)*: 🔳 (Wireframe)

Task 2 - Modify the boundary of a Detail view.

To open the Drawing View dialog box on a sectioned view, verify that the view outline is highlighted when double-clicking and not the cross-hatching. If you just double-click on the view, you can access the cross-hatching menus.

1. Double-click on the Detailed Y view.

2. In the *View Type* category, the *Reference point on parent view* field is active. Select the new reference point as shown in Figure 2–47. The *Spline boundary on parent view* field now becomes active. Sketch the spline shown in Figure 2–47.

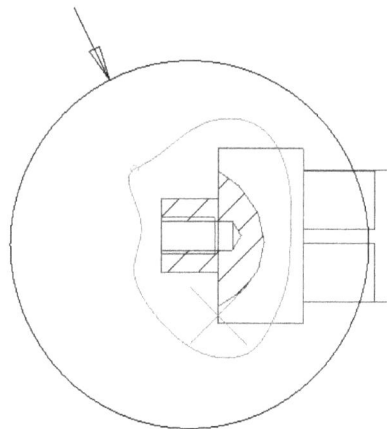

Figure 2–47

3. Click **OK** in the Drawing View dialog box. The drawing displays as shown in Figure 2–48.

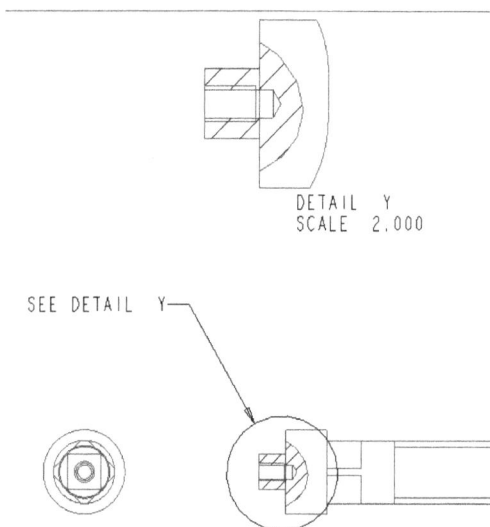

Figure 2–48

4. Save the drawing and close the window.

Chapter Review Questions

1. By default, the display for all of the drawing views is wireframe.

   a. True

   b. False

2. The *View Type* category is used when creating and orienting General views. For General views, this category can be accessed at any time to reorient it or to assign a new view name. If any existing views reference the General view, you must confirm the reorientation of the child views.

   a. True

   b. False

3. The default origin location of a view is the center of the view outline and cannot be changed.

   a. True

   b. False

4. When a parent view is erased, all of the children are removed from the display on the drawing.

   a. True

   b. False

Answers: 1b, 2a, 3b, 4d

Detailing a Drawing

Detailing a drawing involves adding information from the model to the drawing so that all of the design information is effectively communicated. Detail items can include dimensions, notes, and tolerances.

Learning Objectives in This Chapter

- Learn how to display detailed items on drawing views using the **Show Model Annotations** command.
- Learn how to Erase and Unerase detailed items on drawing views.
- Learn how to create dimensions, ordinate dimensions, and coordinate dimensions in a drawing using the *Annotate* tab.
- Learn how to erase and delete created dimensions.
- Learn to move and manipulate detail items in the drawing view using the *Annotate* tab or contextual menu.
- Learn to manipulate the attributes of a cross-hatching pattern.
- Review the configuration file and drawing file options to customize the drawing environment.

3.1 Show Detail Items

Detail items can be shown or created in a drawing. Shown information is associative with the model and any changes made in the model reflect in the drawing. The same is true if changes are made to the drawing. The model updates accordingly. Detail items that are created in the drawing are not associative with the model. However, they update if the geometry they reference changes.

Showing detail items is the preferred method of maintaining associativity between the drawing and the model. The following are some of the benefits of showing detail items:

- Avoid repetitions.

- Save time.

- Preserve the associativity between models and drawings (model dimensions can be modified in the model or drawing and the change is reflected in all of the modes).

How To: Show Detail Items in a Drawing

1. Select the *Annotate* tab to activate the annotation options, as shown in Figure 3–1. Annotations can be moved with any tab active.

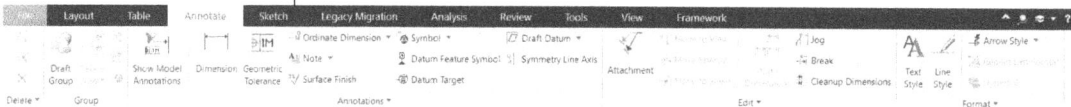

Figure 3–1

2. You can display detail items using the Show Model Annotations dialog box, as shown in Figure 3–2. To open this dialog box, click ⬚ (Show Model Annotations) in the Annotations group in the *Annotate* tab or mini toolbar. This dialog box enables you to select the type of detail item(s) to be shown using the tabs across the top shown in Figure 3–2.

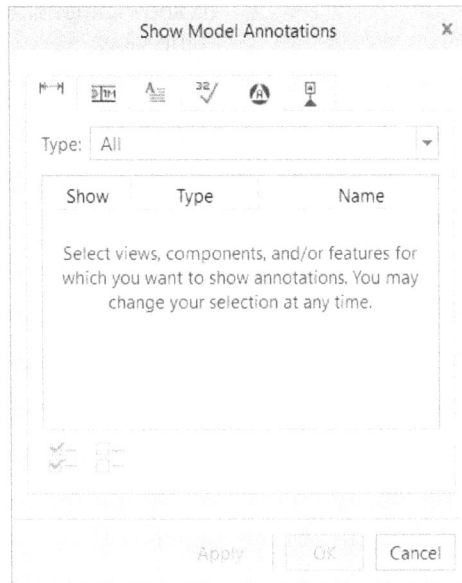

Figure 3–2

3. To show a detail item, select the appropriate annotation type tab at the top of the dialog box. The types of items and their associated icons are described as follows:

Option	Description
⊢⟶⊣	Shows model dimensions.
ⓓⓘM	Shows geometric tolerances.
A≡	Shows notes.
³²√	Shows surface finishes.
Ⓐ	Shows symbols.
▯⟂	Shows datums.

Once you select a tab, select a view, component, or feature to show the annotations.

- To show all of the annotations, select the model in the Model Tree.

- To show all of the annotations for a view, select the view in the Drawing Tree or Graphics window.

- To show dimensions for a feature in a view, select the feature in the view.

- To show dimensions for a feature, select the feature in the Model Tree.

Annotations display as shown in Figure 3–3.

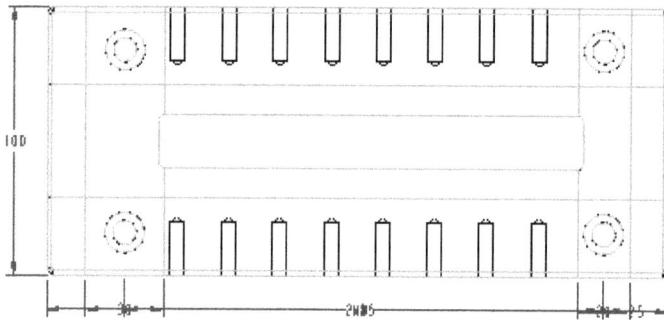

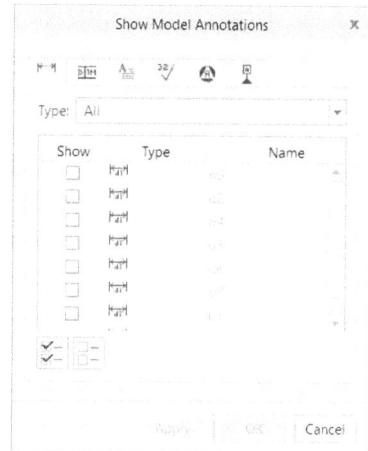

Figure 3–3

You can specify the type for the dimension and datum tabs in the menu, as shown in Figure 3–4.

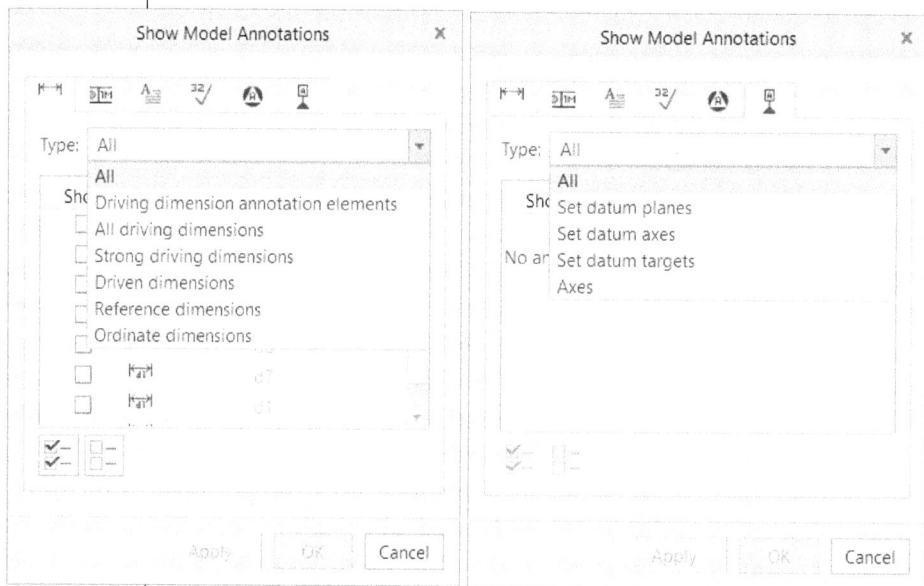

Figure 3–4

4. Once all of the dimensions display in the Show Model Annotation dialog box, select the dimensions you want to keep.

5. Place a checkmark next to the annotations that you want to keep, as shown in Figure 3–5. You can select the dimensions in the dialog box or from in the view. When you select in the view, a checkmark displays next to the related annotations in the Show Model Annotation dialog box.

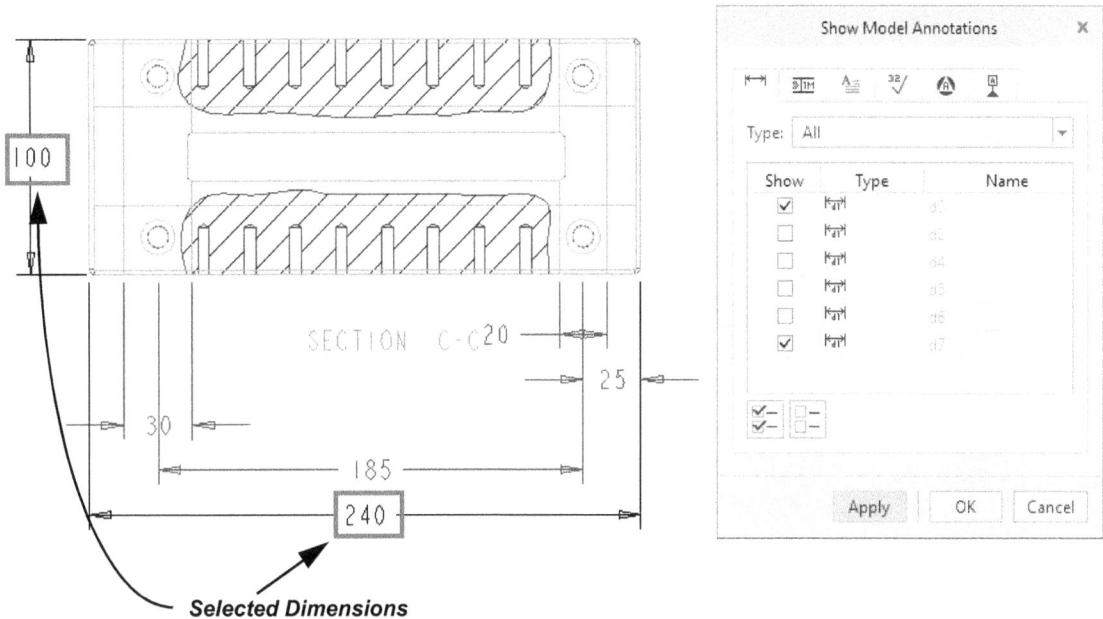

Selected Dimensions

Figure 3–5

- (Select All) places a check next to all of the annotation items in the dialog box.

- (Deselect All) removes the checkmarks from all of the annotation items in the dialog box.

6. Click **OK** to show the annotations on the drawing and close the dialog box. Click **Apply** to show the selected annotations and keep the Show Model Annotation dialog box open.

To remove the detail items you must use the **Delete** *option.*

To erase previously shown detail items, select the item and click ⟋ (Erase) in the mini toolbar. You can also use the selection filter to quickly erase multiple detailed items. Undo the operation by selecting the item in the Drawing Tree and clicking ⤬ (Unerase), as shown in Figure 3–6.

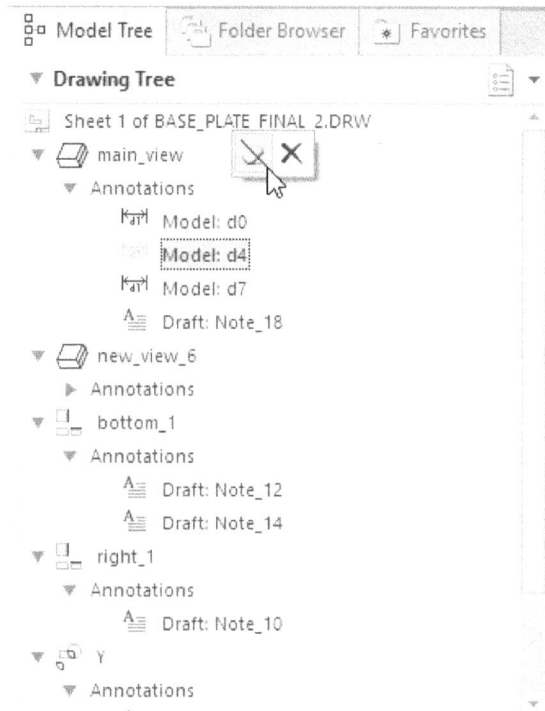

Figure 3–6

3.2 Create Dimensions

If a required dimension does not exist in the model and therefore cannot be shown, it can be created. Since created dimensions are driven by the model geometry (and are not associative with the model), their values cannot be directly modified. Only shown dimension values can be modified to change the model. Showing detail items is preferred to maintain the associativity between the model and the drawing. This ensures that a change in one mode reflects in all other modes.

How To: Create a Dimension in a Drawing

1. Select the *Annotate* tab to activate the annotation options. This tab must be active to show, create, and move annotations.
2. To create dimensions, click the appropriate icon in the Annotations group:

   - ⊢⊣ (Dimension)

   - ⁼₁₂⁰ (Ordinate Dimension)

   - Select **Annotations>** ▦ (Coordinate Dimension)

   - Select **Annotations>** ⊢⊣ (Reference Dimension)

Reference dimensions are created to only display information. These dimensions are not required to manufacture the model. They are read-only and therefore not parametric with the model. However, reference dimensions update accordingly if changes are made to the model's geometry. By default, reference dimensions are distinguished from standard dimensions by appending the letters **REF** to the end of the dimension value, as shown in Figure 3–7.

*To display reference dimensions surrounded by parentheses, set the **parenthesize_ref_ dims** option to **yes**.*

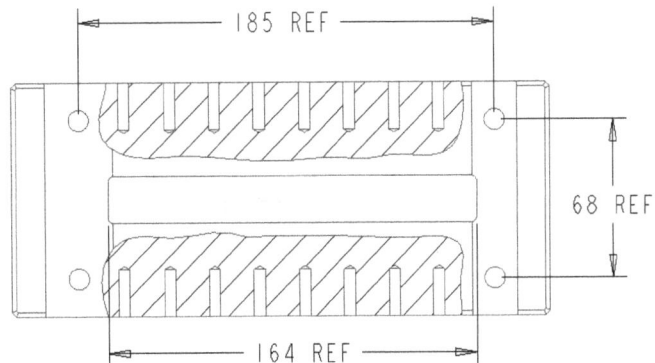

Figure 3–7

3. Create a dimension using the methods described in the following sections.

4. As with shown dimensions, created dimensions can be erased from a drawing. You can erase created dimensions by selecting them and clicking ∠ (Erase) in the mini toolbar.

   You can delete created dimensions by clicking on them and selecting ✕ (Delete) in the mini toolbar or *Annotate* tab.

   Created drawing items that have been erased can be shown again using the shortcut menu. Items that have been deleted need to be recreated if required again.

Creating Dimensions

Standard and Reference Dimensions

When you click ↦ (Dimension) or ↦ (Reference Dimension), the Select Reference dialog box displays with the available reference selection options, as shown in Figure 3–8.

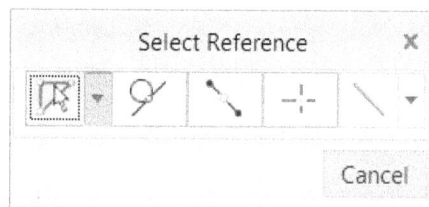

Figure 3–8

The options are described as follows:

Attach Type	Description
▱ (Entity)	Creates the dimension using the selected reference, such as an edge or point.
⌐ (Surface)	Creates the dimension using the selected surface.
▹ (Reference)	Creates a dimension by selecting any appropriate references.
♀ (Tangent)	Creates the dimension tangent to a selected arc or circle.
⬀ (Midpoint)	Creates the dimension using the midpoint of the selected entity.
⊣⊢ (Intersection)	Creates the dimension using the closest intersection point of two selected entities. Press and hold <Ctrl> while selecting each set of intersecting entities.

╲ (Line)	Creates a two-point line for the dimension reference.
— (Horizontal Line)	Creates a horizontal line for the dimension reference.
│ (Vertical Line)	Creates a vertical line for the dimension reference.

It is recommended to reference surfaces when creating dimensions, just as when you create solid models.

To dimension between entities, select the first entity, hold <Ctrl>, and select the second entity. Depending on the selected references, you can right-click to access additional options. For example, if an arc or circle is selected, you can set the dimension type as shown in Figure 3–9.

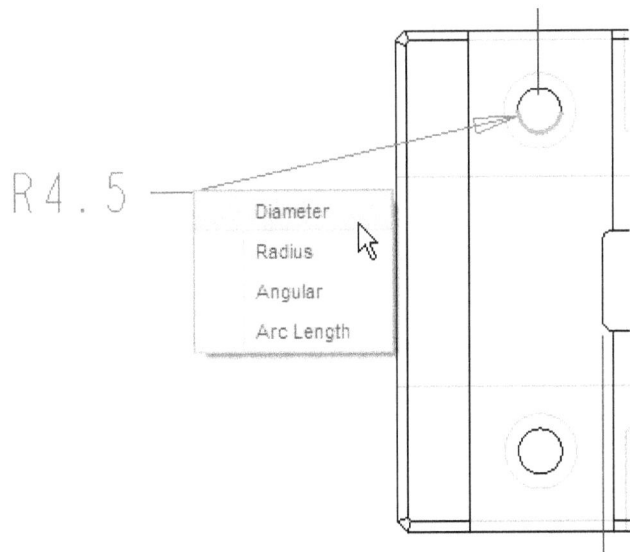

Figure 3–9

If two arcs or circles are selected, the options in the shortcut menu change as shown in Figure 3–10.

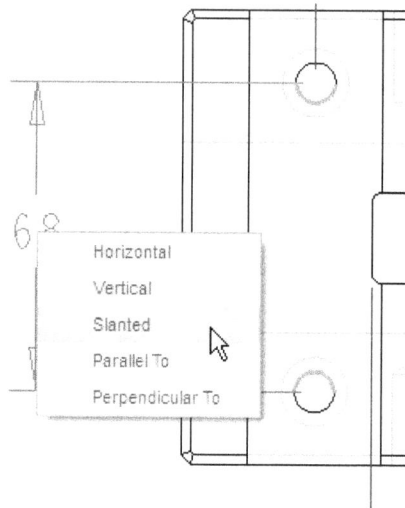

Figure 3–10

Move the cursor to the appropriate location for the dimension, and click the middle mouse button to place it.

Additionally, once a dimension is placed, you can change the options by clicking **Orientation** in the Display Group of the *Dimension* tab, as shown in Figure 3–11.

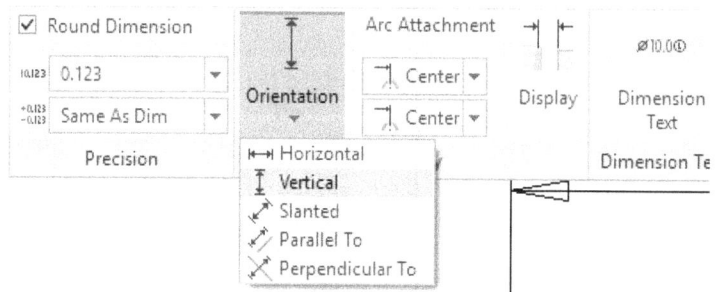

Figure 3–11

Ordinate

Ordinate dimensions are a useful way to save space in a drawing. The $\equiv_{1}^{0}$ (Ordinate Dimension) option enables you to create dimensions in an ordinate format from either a baseline dimension or geometry.

How To: Convert Linear Dimensions to Ordinate

1. Create or show an initial standard format dimension to represent the required baseline, as shown in Figure 3–12.

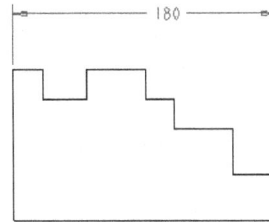

Figure 3–12

2. Select the dimension that was created/shown in Step 1, right-click and select **Toggle Ordinate/Linear**. Once toggled, select the witness line that represents the baseline. The ordinate dimension displays similar to that shown in Figure 3–13.

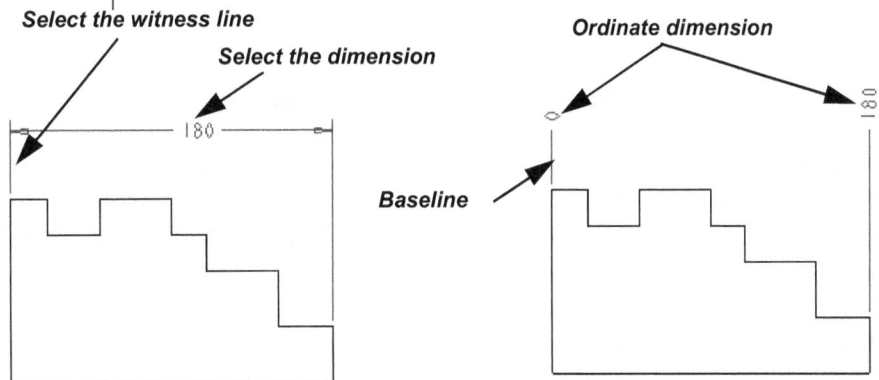

Figure 3–13

How To: Create New Ordinate Dimensions

You might need to click

▾ *next to* ⁻⁴⁄₁₂ *(Ordinate Dimension) to expand the flyout and click* ⁼⁰⁄₁₂ *(Ordinate Dimension). The last used icon displays on top.*

1. Select the *Annotate* tab.
2. Click ⁼⁰⁄₁₂ (Ordinate Dimension) in the Annotations group in the *Annotate* tab.
3. Select either the zero baseline in an existing ordinate dimension or linear model geometry to act as a baseline.

4. Press <Ctrl> and select any additional entities. Place the dimensions using the middle mouse button, as shown in Figure 3–14.

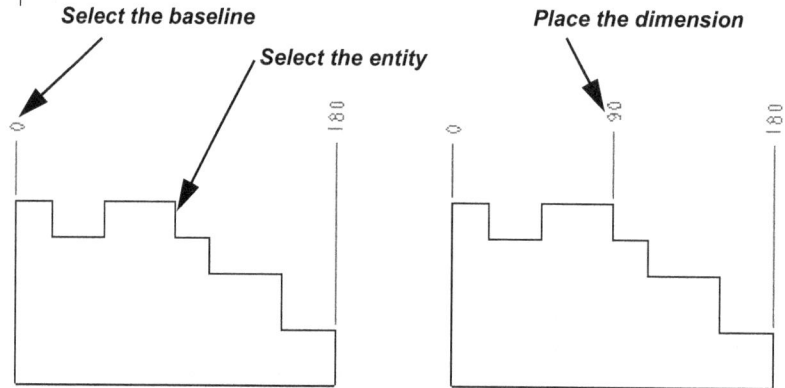

Figure 3–14

If the detail option **ord_dim_standard** is set to *std_ansi*, then the option **default_ansi_ord_dim_aligned** can be set to specify the alignment of the ordinate dimension. If it is set to **yes** (default option), ordinate dimensions align with the baseline dimension. If it is set to **no**, the ordinate dimensions remain in the position selected on screen.

The dimension arrow style shown in Figure 3–15 can be set by changing the **ord_dim_standard** drawing option from *std_ansi* to **std_iso**.

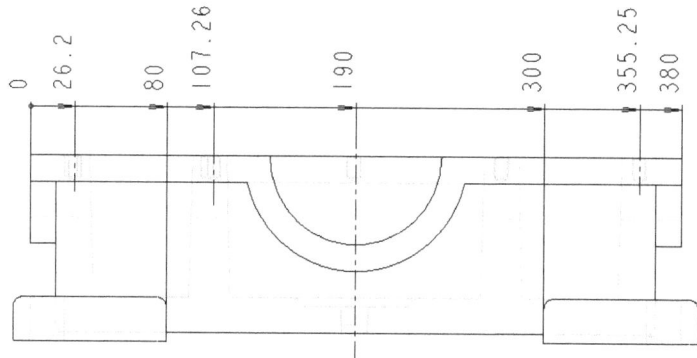

Figure 3–15

Auto Ordinate

This option enables you to automatically create an ordinate dimensioning format for a surface or collection of surfaces. This is very useful when you are producing documentation for molds or sheet metal flat patterns.

Expand ⁻₁⁰̣₂ (Ordinate Dimension) and click ⁻⁴̣₂ (Auto Ordinate Dimension) in the *Annotate* tab. Select a surface on which to create ordinate dimensions. Press the middle mouse button, then select **Select Base Line** in the Menu Manager and select a reference to use as the baseline. The ordinate dimensions for the surface are created automatically.

Coordinate Dimensions

Select **Annotations>** ▦ (Coordinate Dimension) in the *Annotate* tab to create a Coordinate Dimension. Next, select the following items to create the dimension using the coordinate dimension style: an edge on a view to place the arrow head, a location for the coordinate dimension symbol, a dimension for xdim, and a dimension for ydim. The coordinate dimension displays as shown in Figure 3–16.

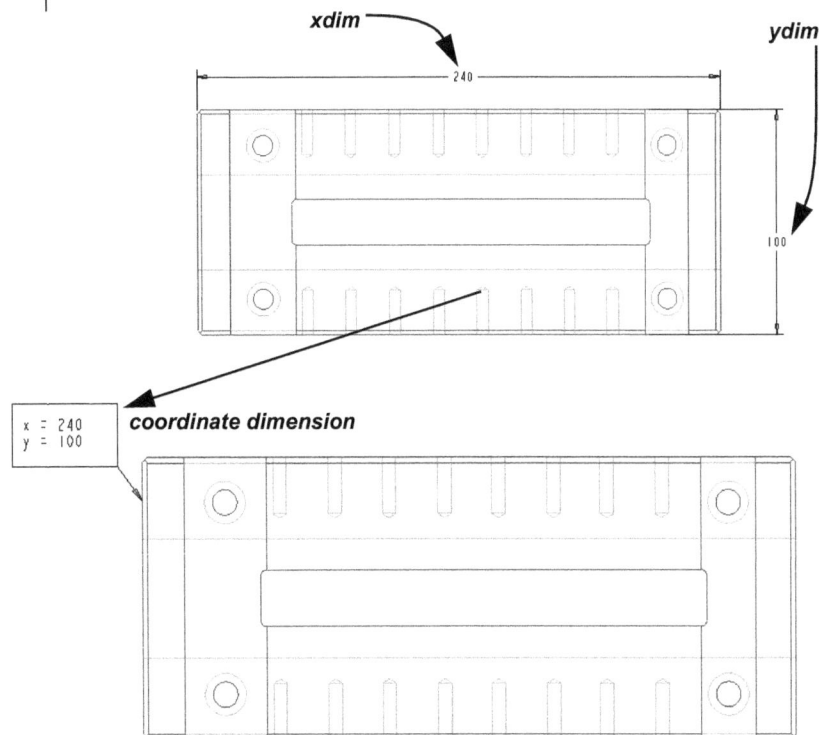

Figure 3–16

3.3 Manipulate Detail Items

Shown and created detail items can be manipulated using the *Annotate* tab and contextual menu.

How To: Manipulate Detail Items from a Drawing

1. Select the *Annotate* tab to activate the annotation options.
2. When manipulating detail items, you can select and manipulate them individually, or to be more efficient you can select multiple entities using one of the following techniques:

    - Press and hold <Ctrl> as you select items. <Ctrl> can also be used to clear items from the current selection set.

    - The ⬚ ⁓ (Selection) option in the Quick Access Toolbar provides you with various options for selecting items in a drawing. The default option, ⬚ (Inside/Across Box), enables you to draw a rectangular box. All of the items specified by the filter that lie entirely in the rectangular box are selected if you drag the box toward the right. To select items that lie across the sketched boundary, drag the box toward the left.

    - ⬡ (Inside Polygon) enables you to sketch a spline that defines the selection area. The remaining selection options in this menu are available for facet surfaces and do not apply to Drawing mode.
    - Use the Selection Filter in conjunction with the **Selection** tool to more accurately and efficiently select items.

3. Use one of the various manipulation options for detail item(s) described.

Modify Dimensions

To modify shown dimension or tolerance values in a drawing, use one of the following techniques once the dimension or tolerance has been selected:

- Right-click and select **Modify Nominal Value**.

- Double-click on the dimension value when selecting it.

To modify dimension items (i.e., Tolerance mode, dimension format, dual dimensioning, text, etc.) select the dimension to open the *Dimension* tab in the ribbon.

When modifying dimension items, the *Dimension* tab opens as shown in Figure 3–17. The *Dimension* tab controls the value of the dimension, its Tolerance mode, dimension format (e.g., decimal and number of decimal places), dual dimensioning, display type, and witness line display.

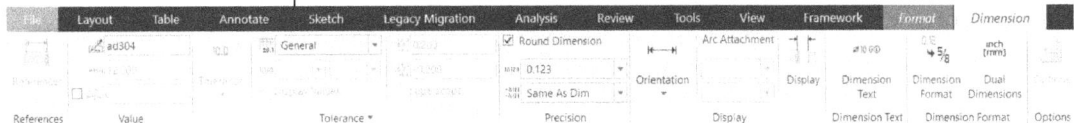

Figure 3–17

The **Dimension Text** option shown in Figure 3–18 controls the dimension text. You can add and edit the text that is associated with the dimension. You can also enter text in the *Prefix* and/or *Suffix* fields.

If you replace @D with @S in the Dimension Text field, the dimension displays the dimension symbol (e.g., d7) rather than the dimension value (e.g., 50.00).

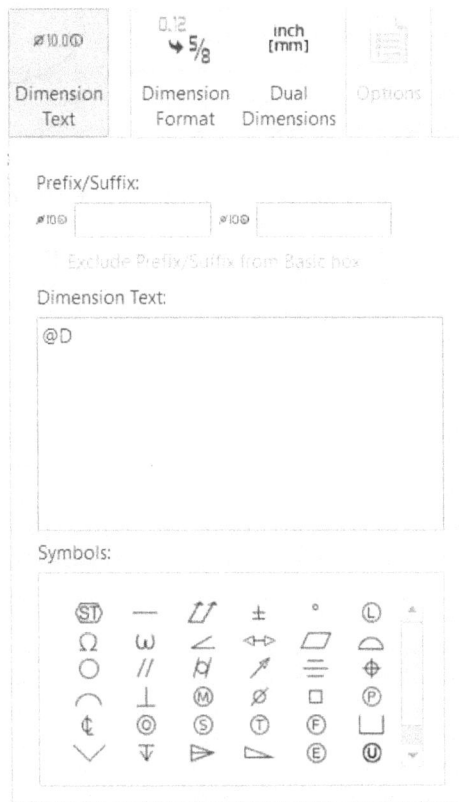

Figure 3–18

The *Format* tab shown in Figure 3–19 controls the text style, text character (e.g., font), and text justification (e.g., line spacing, position, and color).

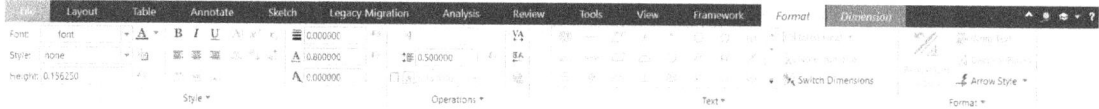

Figure 3–19

If you make a text style change to a dimension, consider using

 to repeat this formatting on other dimensions. If you expand the Style group and select **Text Style**, the Text Style dialog box opens, as shown in Figure 3–20.

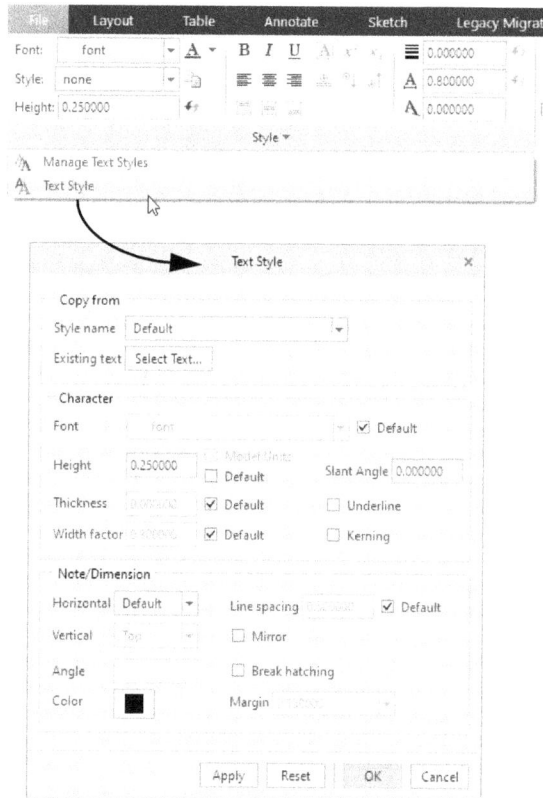

Figure 3–20

Delete

The **Delete** option removes a created or shown detail item from the drawing. To delete a detail item, use one of the following techniques once the item has been selected:

- Press <Delete>.

- Click ✕ (Delete) in the mini toolbar or **Delete** group in the *Annotate* tab.

Move

To move a detail item, use one of the following techniques once the item has been selected:

- When a dimension is selected, the cursor changes to a **Move** cursor, as shown in Figure 3–21, and enables you to move the dimension.

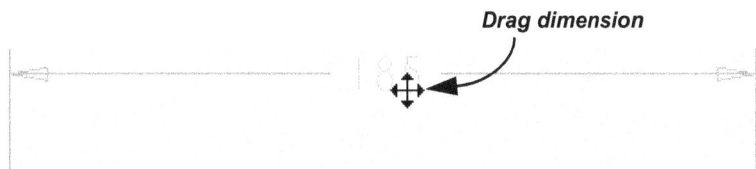

Drag dimension

Figure 3–21

- To move the text, hold <Shift>. The cursor changes to a **Move** text cursor as shown in Figure 3–22. The text can also snap to the center using <Shift>.

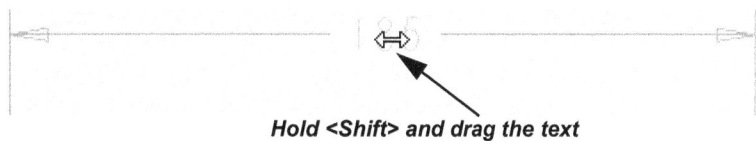

Hold <Shift> and drag the text

Figure 3–22

- You can also move a dimension line. Move the cursor to the dimension line and drag it right, left, up, or down as shown in Figure 3–23.

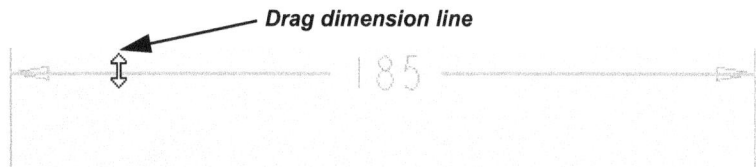

Drag dimension line

Figure 3–23

- Extension lines can also be moved. When you move the cursor to an extension line a drag box displays, as shown in Figure 3–24. Drag the box to a new location.

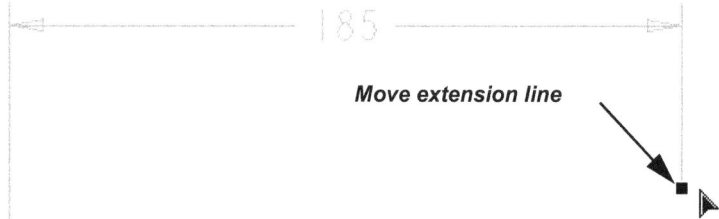

Figure 3–24

- Click ⬚⊹ (Move Special) in the Edit group in the *Annotate* tab to move items to specific coordinates or points.

Edit Attachment

The ⍫ (Attachment) option modifies the attachment type for an annotation's leader. To modify the attachment, and use one of the following techniques once the item has been selected:

- Click ⍫ (Attachment) in the Edit group in the *Annotate* tab.

- Click ⟋ (Edit Attachment) in the mini toolbar.

You can use ⍫ (Attachment) or ⟋ (Edit Attachment) to attach dimension leaders that might reference various entities for features, such as rounds, chamfers, or patterned entities. The default position of a chamfer dimension is shown in Figure 3–25.

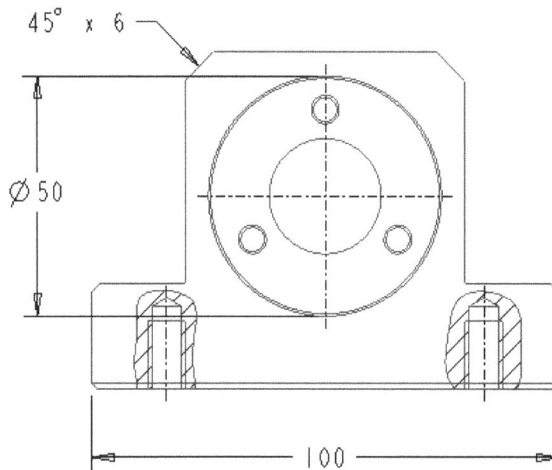

Figure 3–25

To move the dimension to the opposite edge, select the chamfer dimension and click in the mini toolbar. Select the new attachment edge of the chamfer feature, as shown in Figure 3–26.

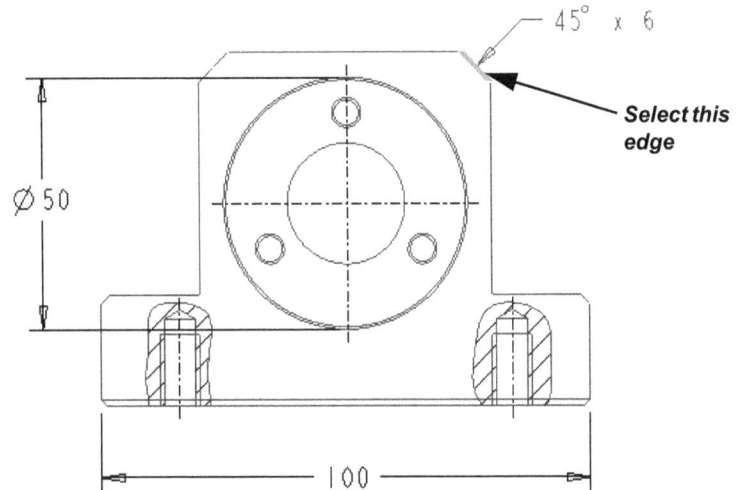

Figure 3–26

Cross-Hatching Attributes

To manipulate the attributes of a cross-hatching pattern, select the *Layout* tab and use one of the following techniques:

- Double-click on the hatching.
- Select the hatching, right-click, and select **Properties**.

The **MOD XHATCH** menu displays as shown in Figure 3–27.

Figure 3–27

Modify the detail item(s) using the options in the **MOD XHATCH** menu. These are described as follows:

Option	Description
Spacing	Changes the spacing between lines in the hatch pattern. The spacing options are shown below.

Angle	Changes the angle of an individual or all cross-hatch lines. You can enter a specific value (zero is horizontal) or select from a predefined list, as shown below.

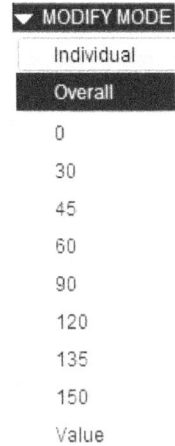

Offset	Changes the offset distance of a selected set of hatch pattern lines, as shown below. The offset distance is measured in drawing units.

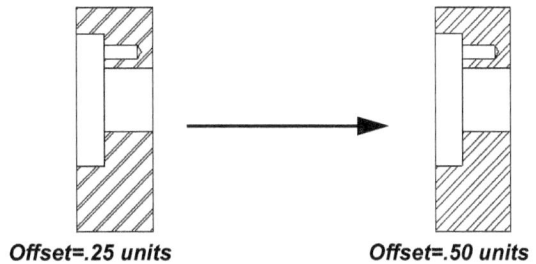

Offset=.25 units *Offset=.50 units*

Line Style	Changes the line font, width, and color of a selected set of hatch pattern lines. The Modify Line Style dialog box is shown below.
	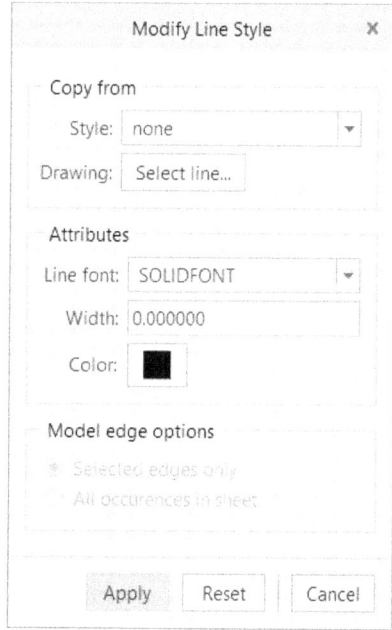
Add Line	Adds a set of lines to an existing hatch pattern. Angle, offset, and spacing parameters are required. Offset and spacing distances are measured in drawing units as shown below.
	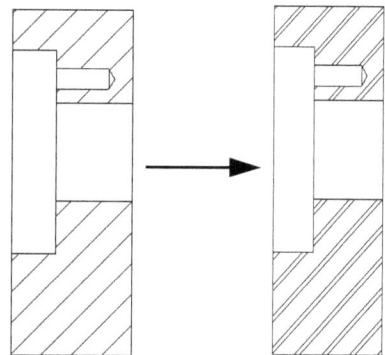
Delete Line	Removes a set of lines from an existing hatch pattern.
Next Line, Prev Line	Enables you to select a set of lines in a hatch pattern. Once selected, it can be modified or deleted.
Save	Enables you to save a user-defined hatch pattern. The pattern is saved to the directory set by the **pro_ crosshatch_dir** config option. If a crosshatch directory is not specified, it is saved to the working directory.

Retrieve	Enables you to replace an existing hatch pattern with a system- or user-defined hatch pattern.
Copy	Copies a cross-hatch style.
Det Indep	Sets the hatch pattern of a Detailed view as independent of the hatch pattern of its parent view. This option is only available for Detailed views as shown below. 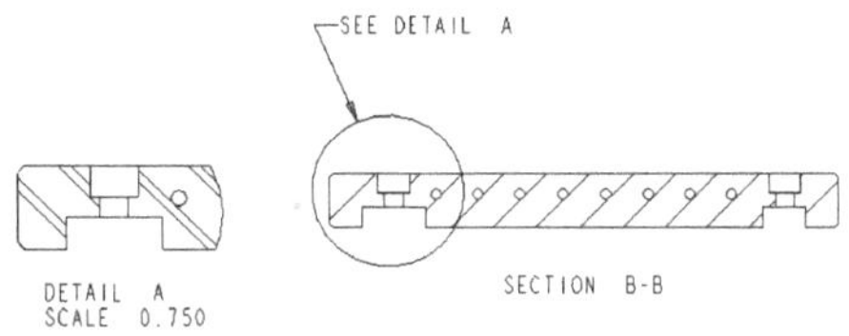
From Parent	Sets the hatch pattern of a Detailed view to be dependent on the hatch pattern of its parent view.
Hatch	Hatches the cross-section.
Fill	Fills the cross-section with a solid fill.

Once you have modified your section hatch, select **Done** in the **MOD XHATCH** menu to finish.

Breaking Cross-Hatch Lines

The cross-hatching that displays in section views can be broken around dimension text and notes, as shown in Figure 3–28. This is not done by default. To break the cross-hatching, click on the dimension or note and select the *Format* tab, then expand the Style group and click **Text Style**. In the Note/Dimension area of the Text Style dialog box, select **Break hatching**. You can also enter a Margin value to determine the area around the text where the hatching is broken.

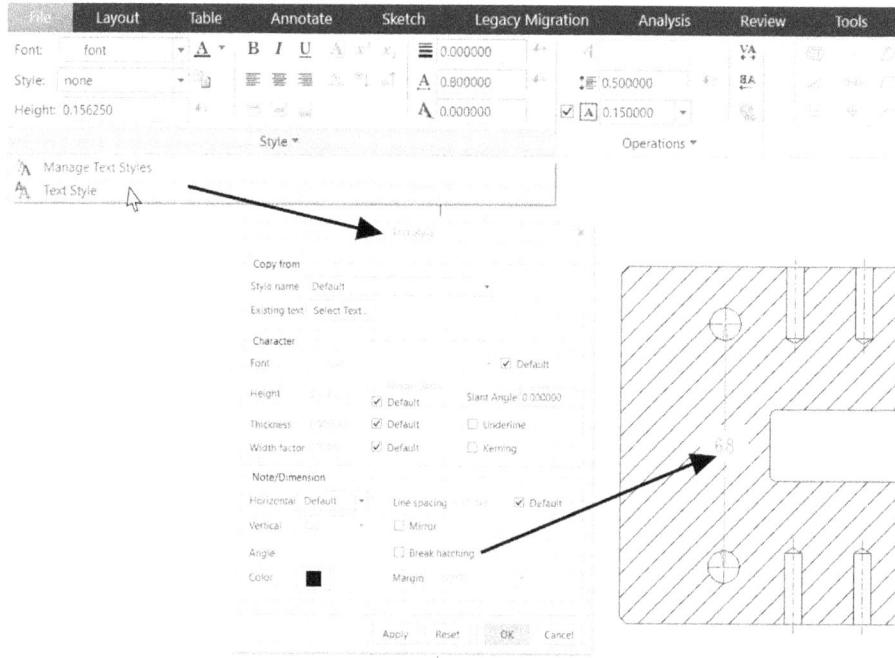

Figure 3–28

Break

The **Break** option can be used to break witness lines. You can create a Parametric or Simple break. A Simple break is not associated with any other entity, you select the break start and end points.

How To: Create a Simple Break

1. In the Annotate tab, click -¦ (Break).
2. Select the witness line to break at the point at which you want the break to start.
3. The **BREAK TYPE** menu displays.
4. Select the break end point on the same dimension witness line.

5. Press the middle mouse button or select another witness line to break.

Figure 3–29 shows an example of a Simple break.

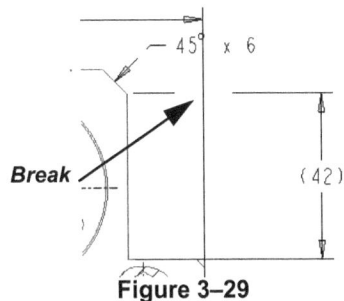

Figure 3–29

A parametric break prompts you to select a reference (witness line or snap line) to break around. You are also prompted for a break size. The break moves with the reference line if you move it, because the reference line is parametric.

How To: Create a Parametric Break

1. Click ⫶ (Break) in the Annotations group in the *Annotate* tab.
2. Select the witness line to break. The **BREAK TYPE** menu displays.
3. Clear the **Simple** option.
4. Select the intersecting witness or snap line to break around.
5. Select the intersecting witness or snap line to define the break.
6. Press the middle mouse button to finish or select another witness line to break.

Use one of the following methods to remove breaks:

• Select the dimension and move one break drag handle until it overlaps the second break drag handle to close the gap. The break disappears.

• Select the dimension and move the cursor near the end point of the break. Right-click and select **Remove All Breaks**.

Clip

You can change the length of extension lines or axes. To clip an extension line or axis, select the item and change its length using the drag handles as shown in Figure 3–30.

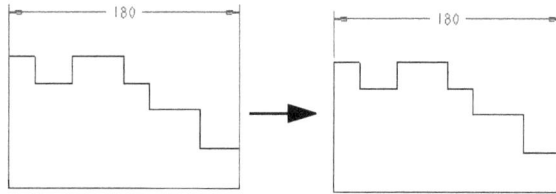

Figure 3–30

Move Item to View

The **Move Item to View** option moves detail items between views. To move an item to another view, select an item and click ⌐ (Move To View) in the mini toolbar or Edit group in the *Annotate* tab.

Flip Arrows

The ⊣⊢ (Flip Arrows) option changes the arrow direction for a dimension. To flip the dimension arrows, use one of the following techniques once the item has been selected:

- In the mini toolbar, click ⊣⊢ (Flip Arrows).

- In the *Dimension* tab, click ⌐⌐ (Display) and click ⊣⊢ (Flip Arrows).

- While dynamically moving a dimension, you can right-click and the arrows will automatically flip. This enables you to toggle through the available configurations.

Make Jog

The ⌐ (Jog) option adjusts the witness lines of a detail dimension (as shown in Figure 3–31), or the leader lines of notes.

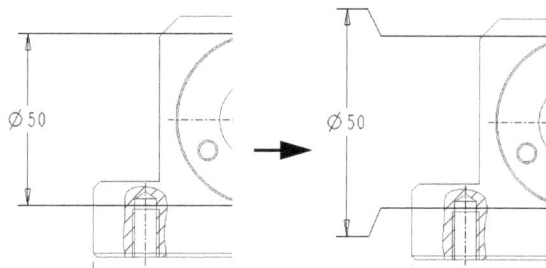

Figure 3–31

To create a jog, use one of the following techniques once the item has been selected:

- Click ⌐ (Jog) in the Edit group in the *Annotate* tab. Select the dimension/note and select a point on witness/leader line to jog and drag as required. Place the jog with the left mouse button.

- Right-click on a note leader line and select **Insert Jog**. Select a point on leader line to jog and drag as required. Place the jog with the left mouse button.

To remove a jog, right-click and select **Remove All Jogs** once the item has been selected.

Align Dimensions

The **Align** option aligns multiple detail items horizontally or vertically. To align detail items, use one of the following techniques once the items are selected:

- Click ⊶ (Align Dimensions) in the Edit group in the *Annotate* tab.

- Right-click and select **Align Dimensions**.

Aligned dimensions are shown in Figure 3–32.

Once aligned, you can independently move aligned items to unalign them.

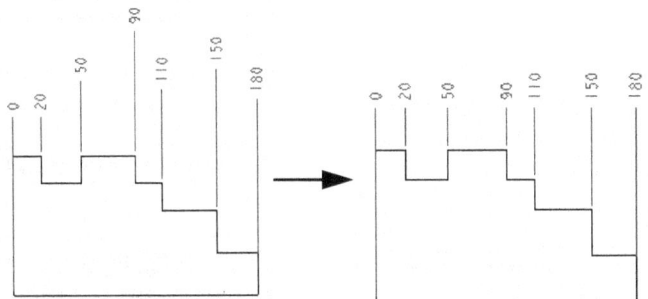

Figure 3–32

Snap Lines

Snap lines are 2D construction entities that can be created in drawing views to help organize detail items. For example, when moving detail items, they attach to (snap to) nearby snap lines.

To create a snap line, select **Edit>Create Snap Line** in the *Annotate* tab. The **CR SN LINE** menu displays as shown in Figure 3–33.

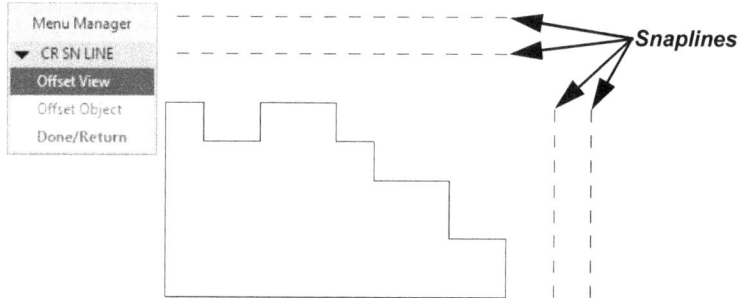

Figure 3–33

*To remove the display of snap lines, change the display filter to **Snap Line** and select the snap lines using a selection box. Once the snap lines have been selected, right-click and select **Erase**.*

Offset the new snap line(s) from a selected view outline (**Offset View**), a view edge, or another snap line (**Offset Object**). The message window prompts you to enter three parameters: the offset distance of the first snap line from the selected entity, how many snap lines to create, and the spacing between the snap lines (if applicable).

To change the location of snap lines, use one of the following techniques once the item has been selected:

Snap lines are not included when printed.

- Right-click and select **Properties**. Enter a new offset and/or increment value.

- Select and drag the snap line.

You can also double-click on the snap line to change the spacing.

Cleaning Dimensions

The ⇥ (Cleanup Dimensions) option enables you to quickly organize the display of the linear dimensions in a drawing. To clean up the dimension display, use one of the following techniques once the dimension has been selected:

- Click ⇥ (Cleanup Dimensions) in the Edit group in the *Annotate* tab.
- Right-click and select **Cleanup Dimensions**.

The Clean Dimensions dialog box opens as shown in Figure 3–34.

You can also select additional dimensions to clean in the Clean Dimensions dialog box by clicking 🔍 *.*

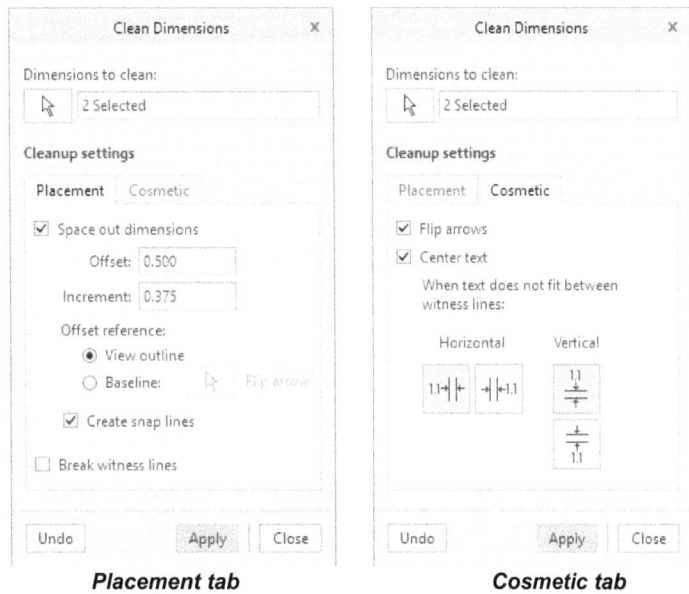

Placement tab   Cosmetic tab

Figure 3–34

Specify the Placement and Cosmetic settings and click **Apply** to arrange the dimensions.

Erase Witness Lines

To erase the display of dimension witness lines, select the dimension, right-click on a witness line and select **Erase Witness Line**. Figure 3–35 shows that a witness line has been erased.

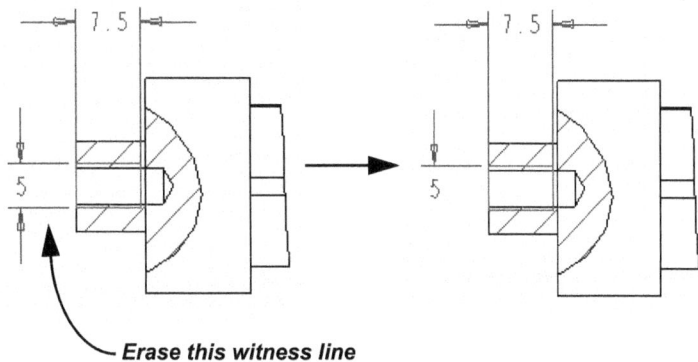

Erase this witness line

Figure 3–35

Diameter/Linear Format

To change a diameter dimension to a linear format, select the dimension and click ⫟⊦ (Display) in the *Dimension* tab. To change the dimension format, select **Linear** in the *Configuration* drop-down list. Figure 3–36 shows two diameter dimensions that were converted to linear dimensions.

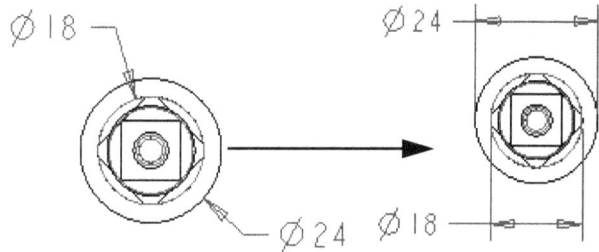

Figure 3–36

Radial and Diameter Dimensions

The ⌐⌐ (Display) panel has a **Text Orientation** option for radial and diameter dimensions. This option enables you to control the text position relative to its witness line, as shown in Figure 3–37.

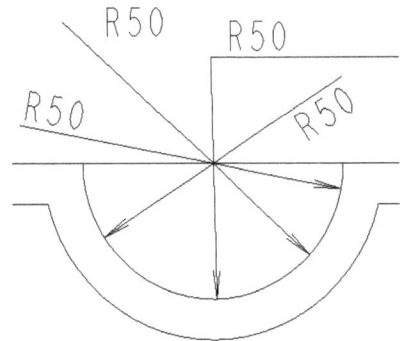

Figure 3–37

The ⌐⌐ (Display) panel enables you to toggle between diameter and linear formats, using the **Configuration** option (as shown in Figure 3–38), and **Flip** to flip arrows.

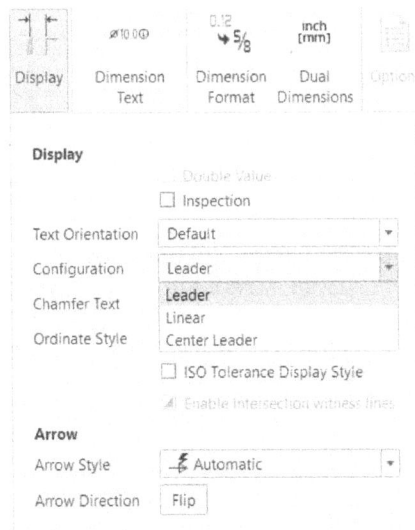

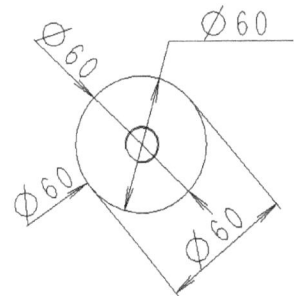

Figure 3–38

Automatic Clipped Dimensions

Clipped dimensions are used when you want to report twice the distance between selected entities, such as when dimensioning symmetrical or mirrored geometry.

How To: Create a Clipped Linear Dimension

1. Click ⊢⊣ (Dimension) and select the first reference (this can be an edge, straight entity, datum plane, axis, or silhouette).
2. Press and hold <Ctrl> and select another edge, straight entity, datum plane, axis, or silhouette as the second reference.
3. In the ⁱ⊦ (Display) panel, select **Double Value**.
4. Press the middle mouse button at the required location to place the dimension. A clipped linear dimension, equal to twice the distance between the selected entities, is created as shown in Figure 3–39.

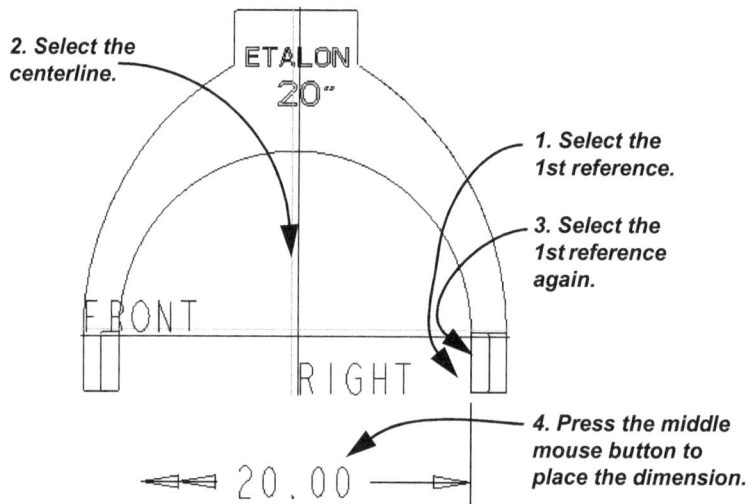

Figure 3–39

5. To change the appearance of the arrow, in the ⁱ⊦ (Display) panel, select the Arrow Style drop-down list.
6. The missing witness line can be added by right-clicking and selecting **Show Witness Line**.

3.4 Customizing Options

Use the configuration file options in to customize how Creo Parametric handles dimension creation.

Option	Values	Description
create_fraction_dim	**no** yes	Displays all created dimensions as fractions.
default_ang_dec_ places	**1** value	Specifies the number of decimal places shown in angular dimensions.
draw_models_read_ only	**no** yes	Sets drawing models to read-only (dimensions cannot be modified in a drawing if set to **yes**).
highlight_new_dims	**no** yes	Highlights all newly added dimensions in red, until they are moved or the screen is repainted.
parenthesize_ref_ dims	**no** yes	Encloses reference dimensions in parentheses.
show_preview_ default	**remove** keep	Sets the default behavior for preview in the Show/Erase dialog box (**Sel to Keep** or **Sel to Remove**).

Use the drawing setup file options in to customize how Creo Parametric handles dimension creation. Additional options are available that should also be reviewed in the drawing setup file.

Option	Values	Description
allow_3d_dimensions	**no** yes	Determines whether or not dimensions are shown in isometric views.
dual_dimensioning	**no** primary [secondary] secondary	Controls the formatting of the dimension display.

dual_secondary_units	**mm** inch foot cm m	Specifies the type of units displayed for secondary dimensions in dual dimension schemes.
lead_trail_zeros	**no** yes	Controls the display of leading and trailing zeros in dimensions.
witness_line_delta	**.125** value	Controls how far the witness line extends beyond the leader arrows.
witness_line_offset	**.0625** value	Controls the offset between the witness line and the object being dimensioned.

Practice 3a

Detailing a Drawing I

Practice Objectives

- Show dimensions.
- Show axes.
- Move dimensions and detail items.

In this practice, you will create the spindle drawing, which involves showing and arranging dimensions, modifying dimensions and dimension parameters, and showing datum axes. The final drawing displays as shown in Figure 3–40.

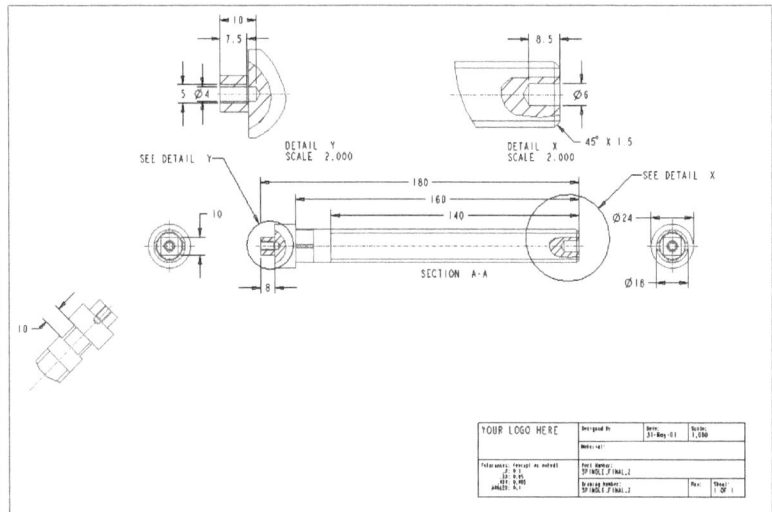

Figure 3–40

Task 1 - Open a drawing file.

Spindle_final_2.drw references the model spindle_final_2.prt.

1. Set the working directory to the *Detailing_I* folder.

2. Open **spindle_final_2.drw**.

3. Set the model display as follows:

   - ⚙ *(Datum Display Filters)*: All Off

   - ▱ *(Display Style)*: ▱ (Wireframe)

Task 2 - Display dimensions for selected drawing features.

1. Select the *Annotate* tab.

2. Click 📋 (Show Model Annotations) in the Annotations group in the *Annotate* tab. The Show Model Annotations dialog box opens as shown in Figure 3–41.

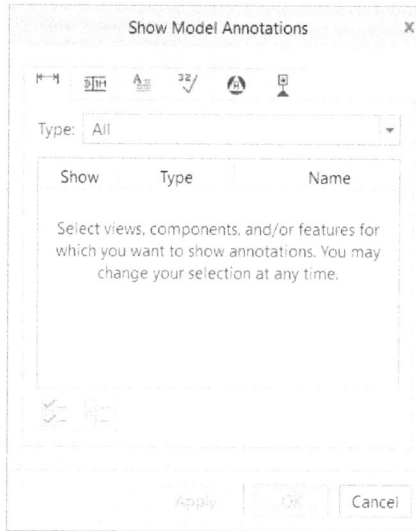

Figure 3–41

3. Ensure that the ⊢⊣ *(Dimension)* tab is selected.

4. Place the cursor on the SECTION A-A view, right-click, and select **Pick From List**.

5. Select **F1 (FIRST FEATURE)** in the Pick From List dialog box as shown in Figure 3–42, and press the middle mouse button to accept the selection.

You can also select ***First Feature id33*** *in the Model Tree to show the dimensions.*

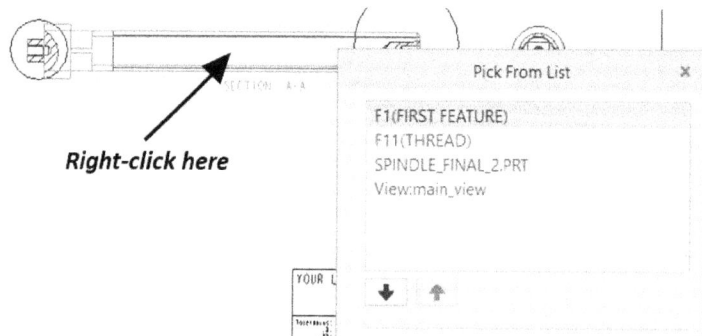

Figure 3–42

6. Click **OK**.

The General view displays as shown in Figure 3–43.

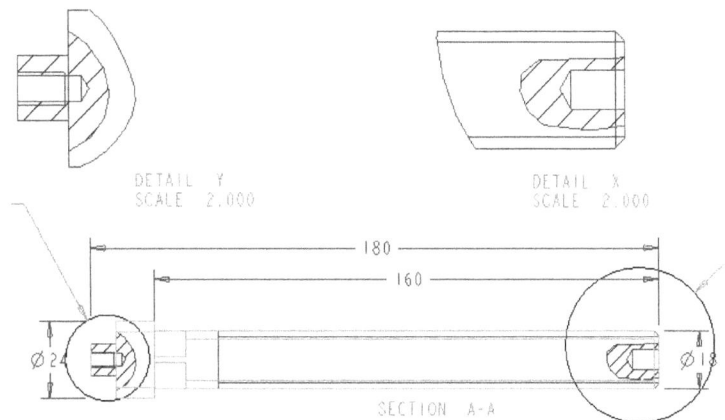

Figure 3–43

7. Click ☑ (Select All) to place a check next to all of the dimensions, as shown in Figure 3–44. Click **Apply**.

Figure 3–44

8. Place the cursor in the DETAIL X view, right-click, and select **Pick From List**. Select **F5(HOLE)** in the Pick From List dialog box, as shown in Figure 3–45.

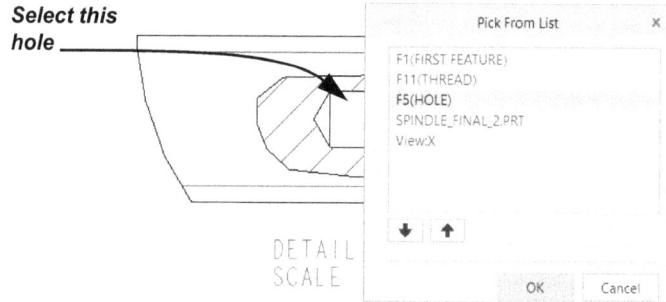

Figure 3–45

9. Click **OK**.

10. Place a checkmark next to all of the dimensions, except the 59° (d66) angle dimension. The dimensions highlight in green as you place the cursor over them in the dialog box. Click **Apply**. The (d66) dimension will disappear when you select another feature.

11. Move the cursor into the DETAIL Y view, select **F9(HOLE)** in the Pick From List dialog box as shown in Figure 3–46.

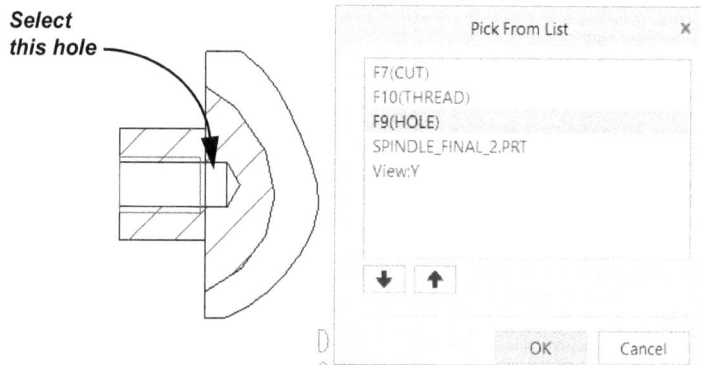

Figure 3–46

12. Click **OK**.

13. Place a checkmark next to all of the dimensions, except the 59° (d288) angle dimension. Click **Apply**.

14. Move the cursor to the DETAIL Y view, select **F10(THREAD)** in the Pick From List dialog box and click **OK**.

15. Select both of the dimensions and click **Apply**.

16. Click **Cancel** to close the dialog box, and the drawing displays as shown in Figure 3–47.

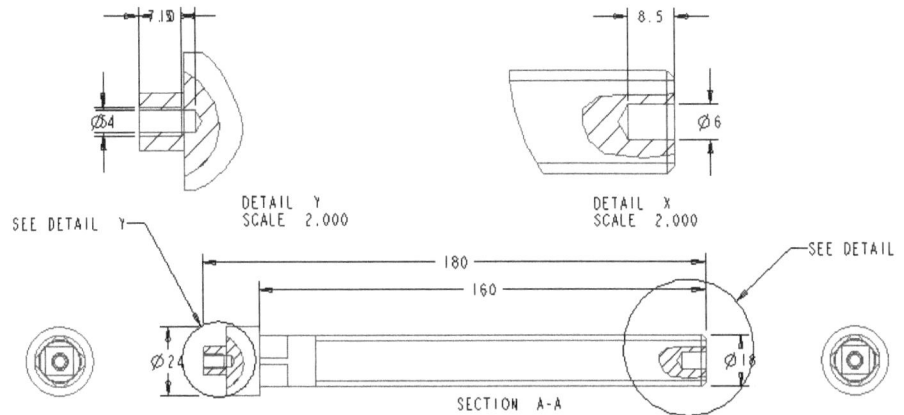

DETAIL Y
SCALE 2.000

DETAIL X
SCALE 2.000

SEE DETAIL Y

SEE DETAIL

SECTION A-A

Figure 3–47

Task 3 - Arrange the dimensions.

1. Select **Dimension** from the selection filter in the bottom right corner of the main window.

2. Select all of the dimensions using the left mouse button bounding box.

3. Select the *Annotate* tab.

4. Click ⧕ (Cleanup Dimensions) in the Edit group. The Clean Dimensions dialog box opens. Set the following properties:
   - *Offset:* **0.25**
   - *Increment:* **0.4**
   - Select **View Outline**.
   - Clear the **Create Snap lines** option.

The Clean Dimensions dialog box opens as shown in Figure 3–48.

Clear this option

Figure 3–48

5. Click **Apply** and **Close**. The drawing displays as shown in Figure 3–49.

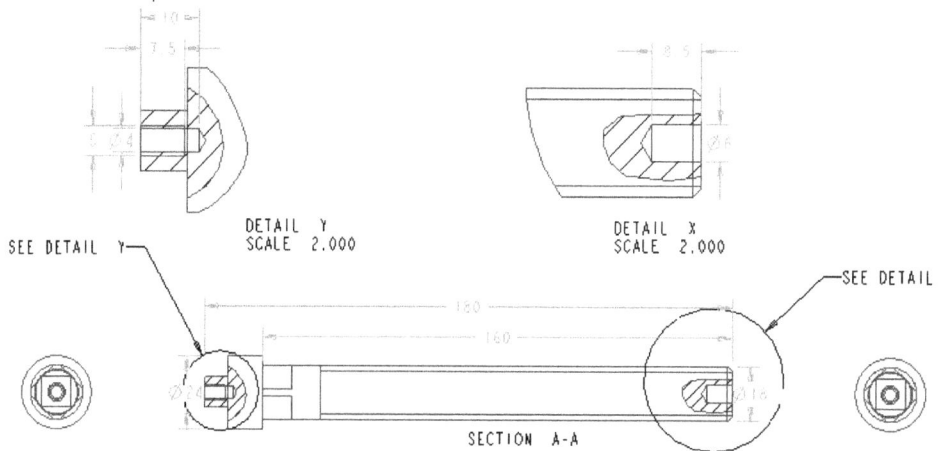

DETAIL Y
SCALE 2.000

DETAIL X
SCALE 2.000

SEE DETAIL Y

SEE DETAIL

SECTION A-A

Figure 3–49

Task 4 - Show additional dimensions in the drawing.

1. Click ⊞ (Show Model Annotations). The Show Model Annotations dialog box opens.

2. Select the **F7(CUT)** in the General view and the **F8(CUT)** in the Auxiliary view and apply the dimensions, as shown in Figure 3–50. Use **Pick From List** to select the features if required.

3. Accept all of the dimensions as shown in Figure 3–50.

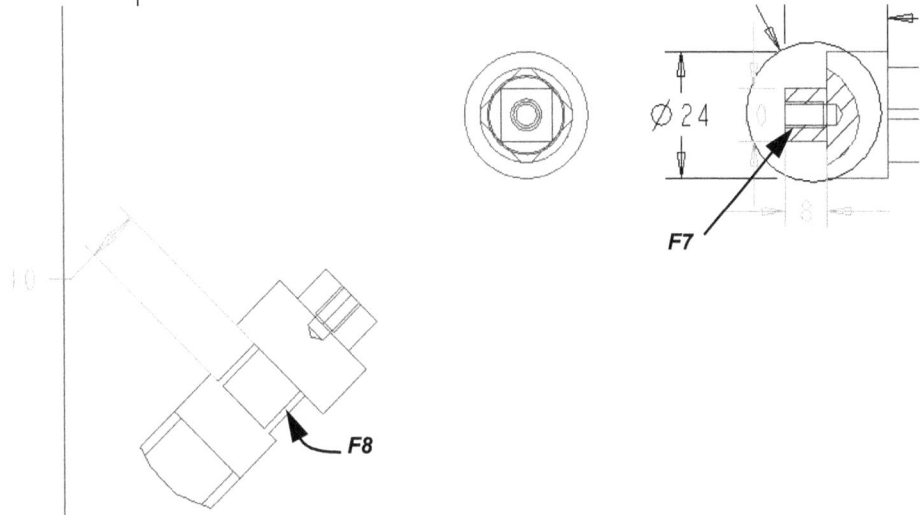

Figure 3–50

4. Close the Show Model Annotation dialog box.

Task 5 - Move dimensions to other views.

1. Select the **Ø18** dimension in the General view.

You can also click

⊏ (Move to View) in the Edit group in the Annotate tab.

2. Select ⊏ (Move to View) in the mini toolbar.

3. Select the right Projected view. The dimension moves to that view.

4. Select the **Ø24** dimension in the General view and move it to the right Projected view.

5. Select the **10** dimension in the General view and move it to the left Projection view.

6. Position the moved dimensions in new locations, as shown in Figure 3–51.

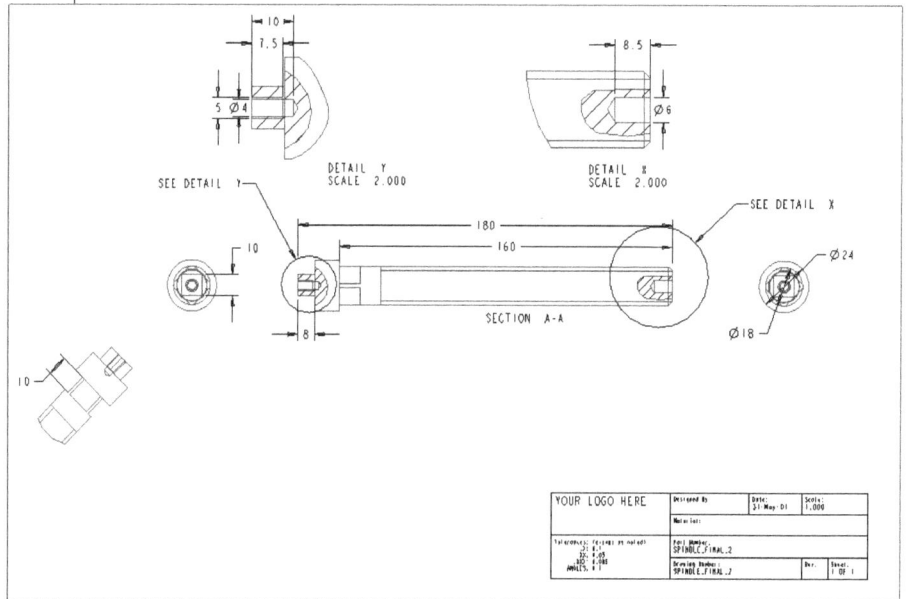

Figure 3–51

Task 6 - Modify dimension parameters.

1. Right-click on the **Ø18** dimension and select **Show as linear**.

2. Change the **Ø24** dimension to a linear dimension using the same method.

3. Move the dimensions as shown in Figure 3–52. To move rotationally, select the dimension and click ✎ (Edit Attachment) in the mini toolbar.

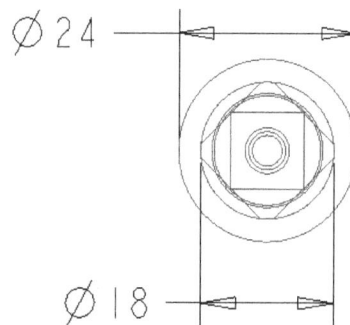

Figure 3–52

Task 7 - Show additional dimensions.

1. Show the dimensions for feature **F6(CHAMFER)** in the X view, as shown in Figure 3–53.

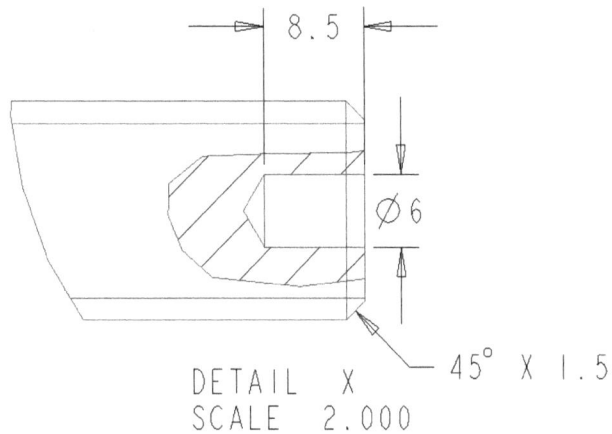

Figure 3–53

Task 8 - Show axes in the drawing.

1. Click ⊞ (Show Model Annotations).

2. Click ⊥ (Show Model Datums) to display the tab.

3. Select **First Feature is 33** from the Model Tree (the First Feature in the Model Tree). The axis displays in the Show Model Annotations dialog box as shown in Figure 3–54.

Figure 3–54

4. Click ⚙ (Select All) to accept all of the displayed axes. The drawing displays as shown in Figure 3–55.

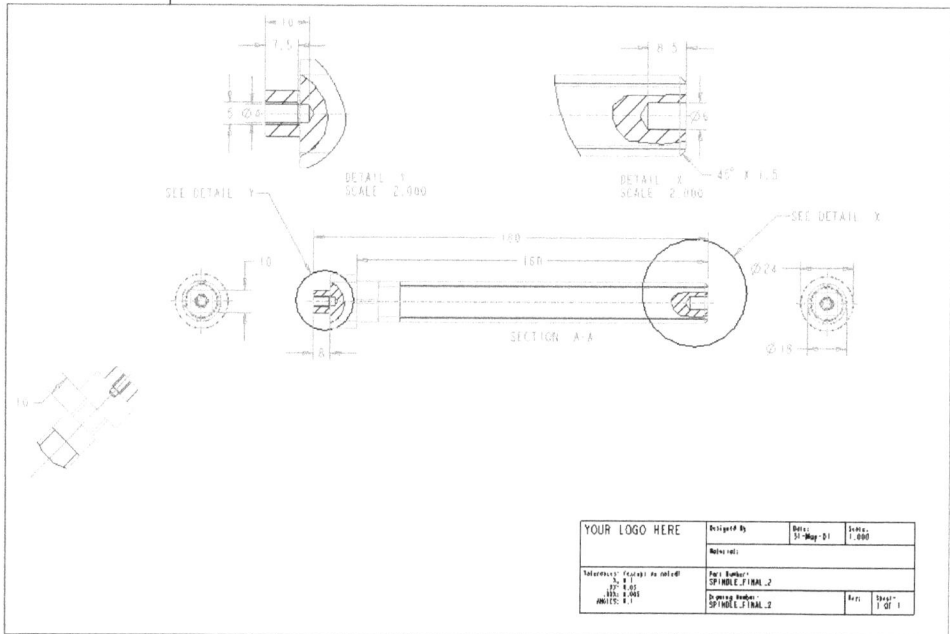

Figure 3–55

5. Click **OK** to accept the axis and close the dialog box.

Task 9 - Manually arrange the location of the dimensions.

1. Select the **10** dimension in the left Projected view. The dimension highlights in green. Hover the cursor over different parts of the dimension and note how the cursor changes.

   • When the cursor is over the dimension text, the cursor displays as a four way arrow and indicates that the dimension can be moved.

- To only move the text, hold <Shift> and move the cursor. Several examples of how the cursor changes and what the symbol means are shown in Figure 3–56.
- By selecting and moving the cursor, you can modify the position of the dimension, witness lines, and dimension text.

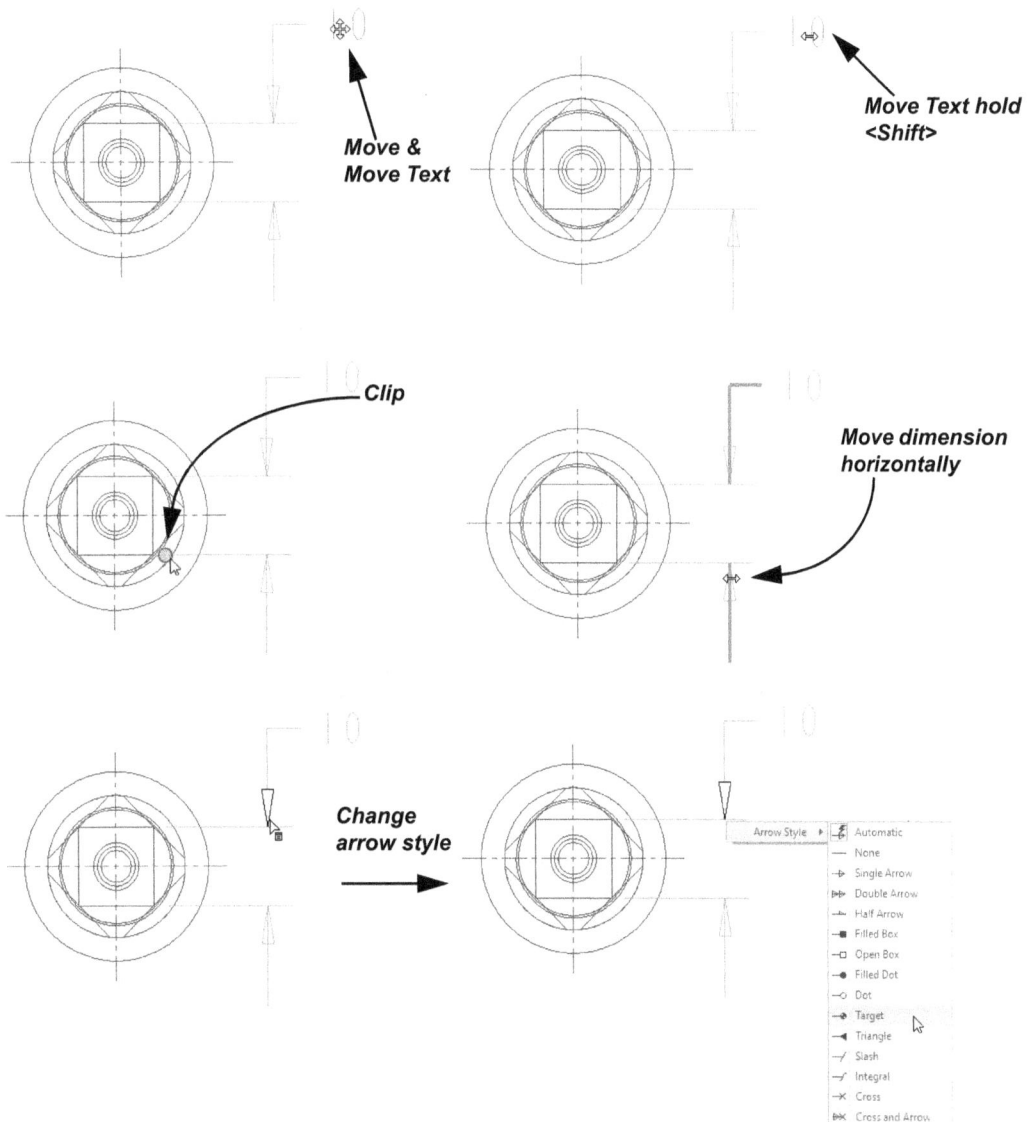

Move & Move Text

Move Text hold <Shift>

Clip

Move dimension horizontally

Change arrow style

Figure 3–56

2. Return the dimension to its original display.

Ensure that the

⊢⊣ *(Dimension) tab in the Show Model Annotation dialog box is selected to show dimensions.*

3. Show the **140** dimension established by the length of the cosmetic thread feature on the spindle in the General view.

4. Arrange the drawing as shown in Figure 3–57. To flip the arrows, click ⊬⊩ (Flip Arrows) in the mini toolbar.

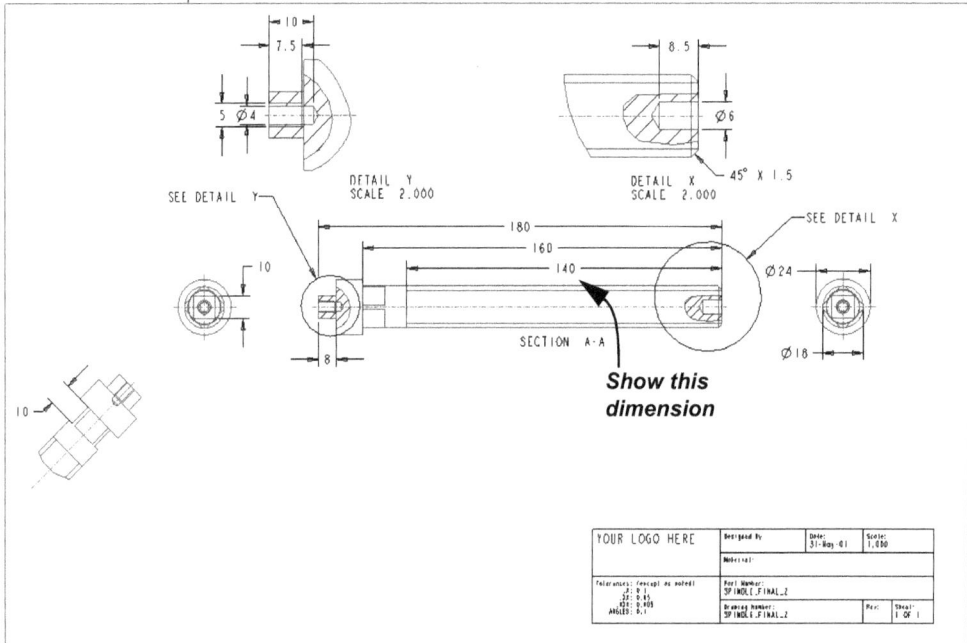

Figure 3–57

5. Save the drawing and close the window.

Practice 3b

Detailing a Drawing II

Practice Objectives

- Redefine a drawing view type.
- Show and modify detail items.
- Modify the drawing scale.
- Break witness lines.
- Create centerlines.
- Modify the dimension text.

In this practice, you will redefine drawing views, show and modify drawing dimensions, and create a centerline. The final drawing displays as shown in Figure 3–58.

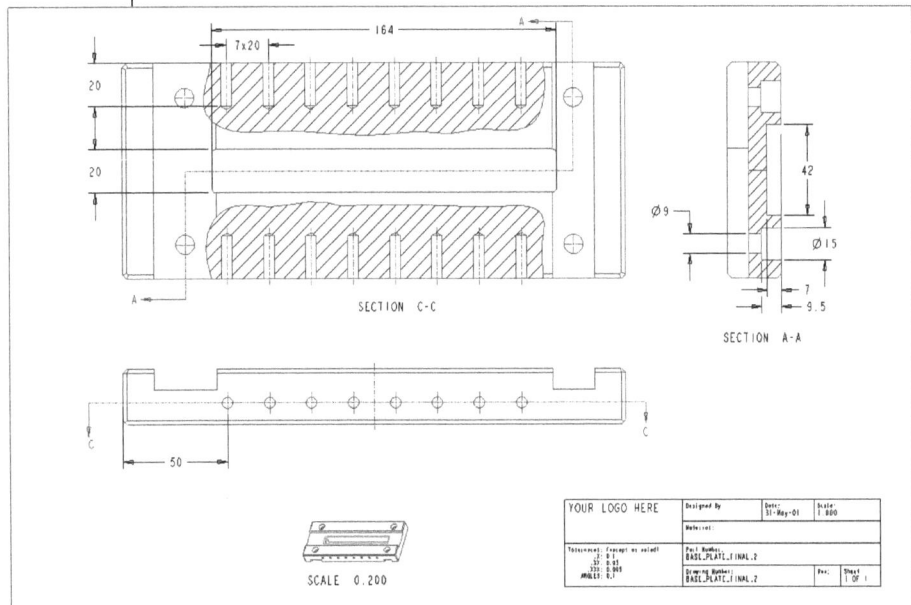

Figure 3–58

Task 1 - Open a drawing file.

1. Set the working directory to the *Detailing_II* folder.

2. Open **base_plate_final_2.drw**.

3. Set the model display as follows:

   - ⠿ *(Datum Display Filters)*: All Off

   - ▱ *(Display Style)*: ⊞ (Wireframe)

Task 2 - Show the dimensions in the drawing.

1. Select the *Annotate* tab.

2. Click ⬚ (Show Model Annotations).

3. Click ⊢⊣ (Dimension) to display the tab.

*You can also select **Cut id 1221** in the Model Tree.*

4. Select feature **F9 (CUT)** in the General section view, as shown in Figure 3–59.

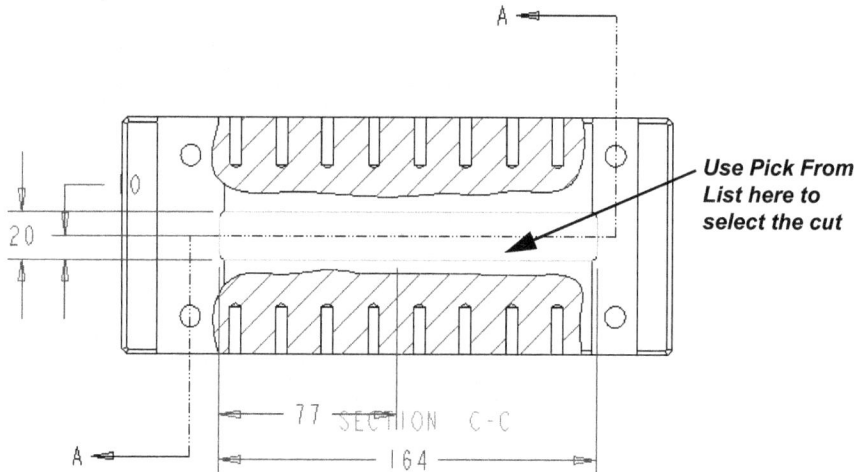

Use Pick From List here to select the cut

Figure 3–59

5. Select **d91 (164)** and **d92 (20)** in the Show Model Annotation dialog box, as shown in Figure 3–60.

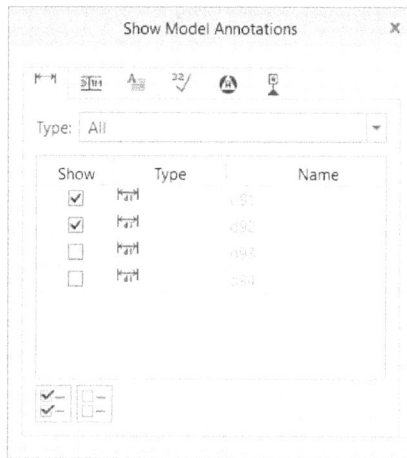

Figure 3–60

6. Click **Apply**.

7. Show the **50** and **20** dimensions for the last hole (upper left) in the General section view as shown in Figure 3–61.

8. Click **Apply** and close the dialog box.

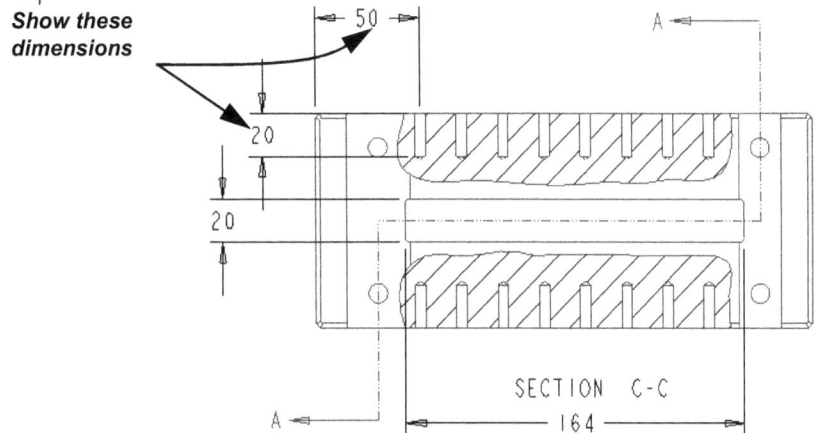

Show these dimensions

SECTION C-C

Figure 3–61

9. Select the **50** dimension and click ⌒ (Erase). Click anywhere on the screen. The dimension disappears.

10. Click ▶ in the Drawing Tree next to Annotations under the **main_view**, as shown in Figure 3–62.

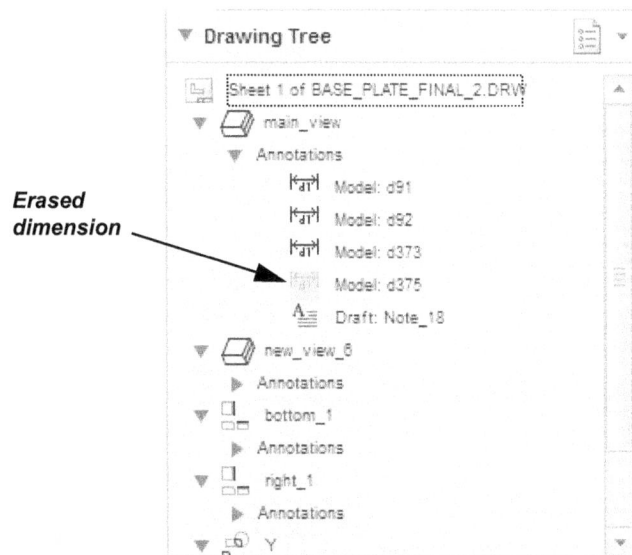

Erased dimension

Figure 3–62

11. Note that the **d375** dimension is still in the Model Tree. Select it and **click** ✕ (Unerase) in the mini toolbar, as shown in Figure 3–63.

If a shown dimension is erased, it will not display in the Show Model Annotation dialog box when that feature is selected. If a shown dimension is deleted, it will display in the Model Annotation dialog box.

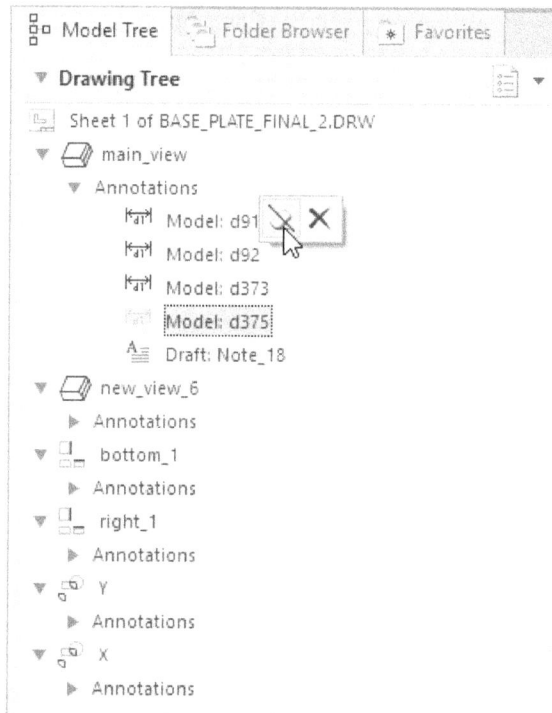

Figure 3–63

Task 3 - Arrange the newly placed dimensions in the General view.

1. Select the four dimensions that you just added to the drawing.

2. Click ⬚ (Cleanup Dimensions) in the Edit group in the *Annotate* tab. Set the following properties in the Clean Dimensions dialog box:

   - *Offset:* 0.5
   - *Increment:* 0
   - Select **View Outline**.
   - Clear the **Create Snap Lines** option.

3. Apply the changes and close the Clean Dimensions dialog box.

4. Move the Section view name, if required. The drawing displays as shown in Figure 3–64.

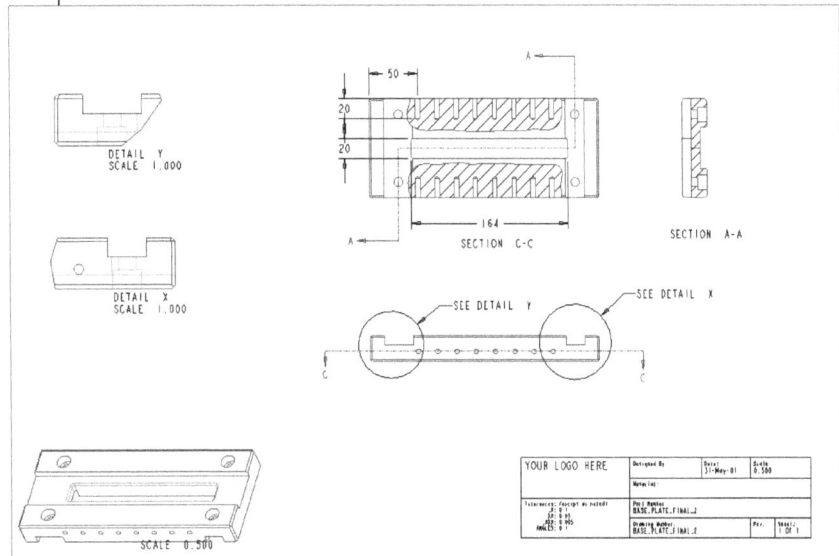

Figure 3–64

Task 4 - Show the dimensions in the SECTION A-A view.

1. Show the dimensions for the following features in the SECTION A-A view:

- **F8(CUT)**
- **F15(HOLE)**

2. Keep only the dimensions shown in Figure 3–65.

You can select the dimensions in the Graphics window and a checkmark will be placed next to them in the Show Model Annotations dialog box.

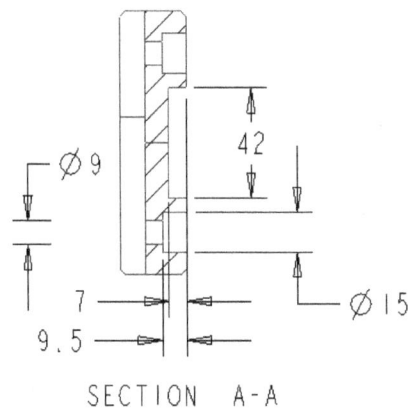

Figure 3–65

Task 5 - Move a dimension to another view.

To move dimensions between drawing views, select the dimension and click ⤤ (Move to View) in the Edit group in the Annotate tab.

1. Select the **50** dimension displayed in the sectioned General view.

2. Select ⤤ (Move to View) in the mini toolbar.

3. Select the projected view below the sectioned General view. The drawing displays as shown in Figure 3–66.

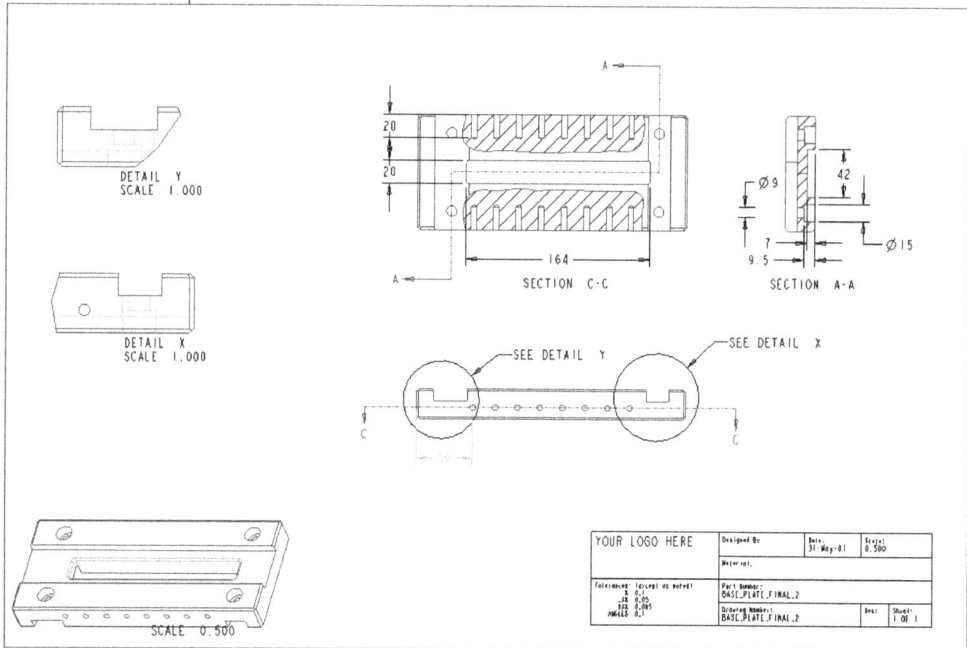

Figure 3–66

Task 6 - Delete the X and Y views.

If you need to remove a view that has a child, you can use ▭ (Erase View) in the mini toolbar. However, if you delete it all of its children are also deleted.

1. Select the DETAIL X view and click ✕ (Delete) in the mini toolbar.

2. Select the DETAIL Y view and click ✕ (Delete) in the mini toolbar.

Task 7 - Modify the drawing scale.

1. Double-click on the drawing scale value in the lower left corner of the drawing window.

2. Enter **1** in the message window prompt.

3. Modify the *Scale* value for the 3D General view to **0.2**.

4. Move the drawing views as shown in Figure 3–67. Unlock the view movement, if required.

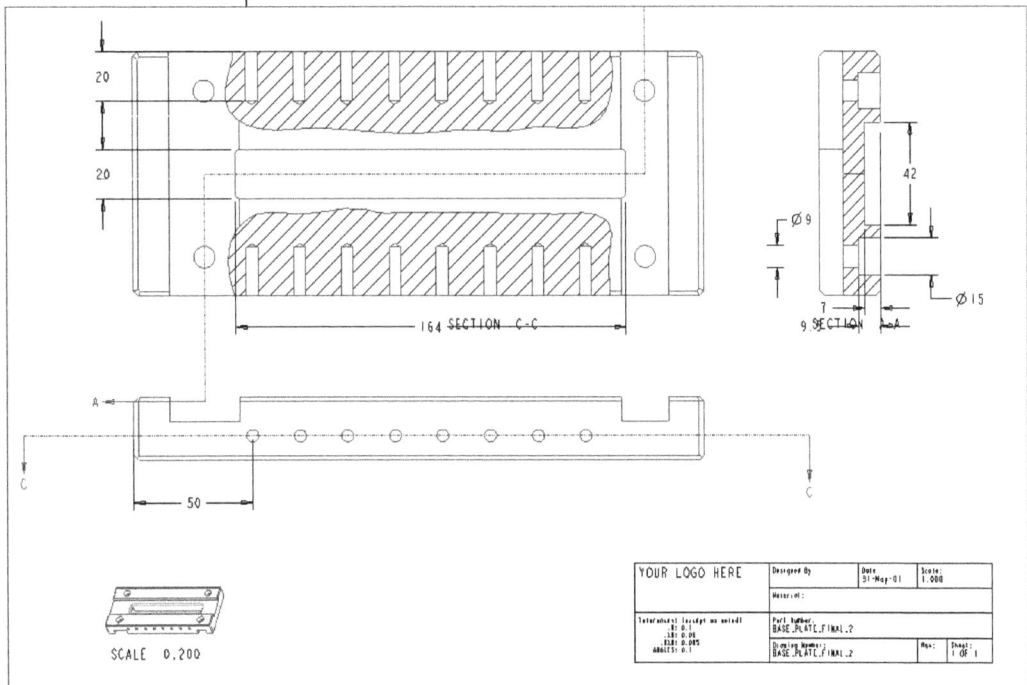

Figure 3–67

Task 8 - Arrange the dimensions.

1. Rearrange the dimensions as shown in Figure 3–68. Ensure that you move both the dimension text and arrows.

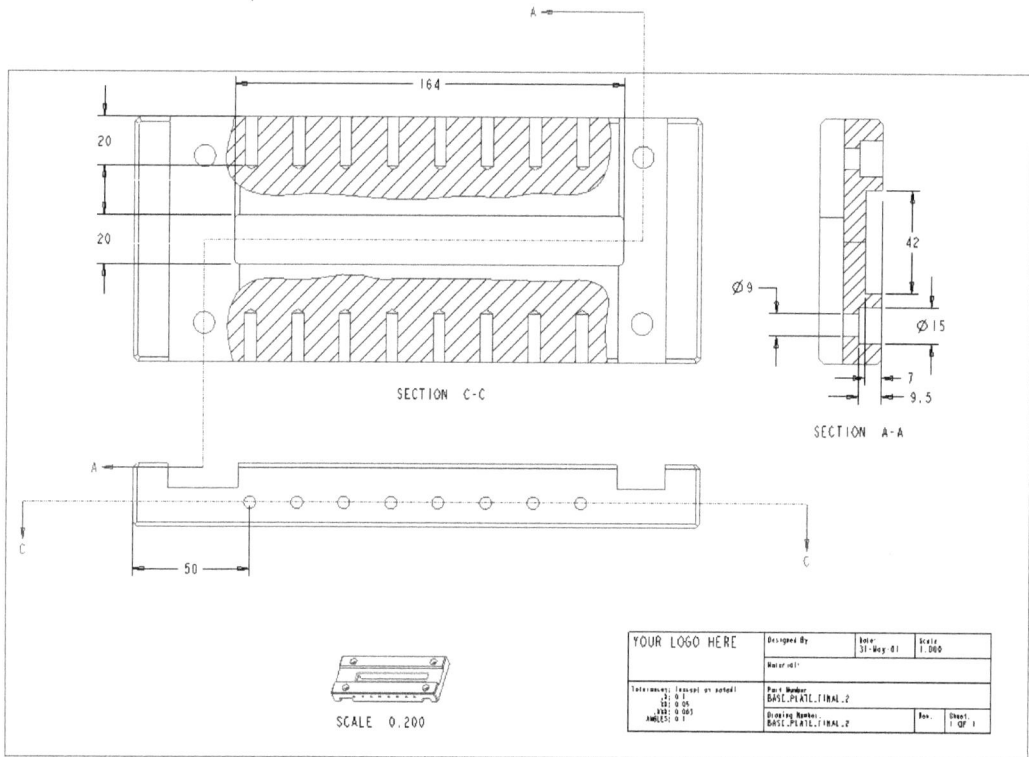

Figure 3–68

Task 9 - Move the cross-sectional arrows and view notes.

1. Select the Section C-C arrows and move them closer to the view.

2. Select the Section A-A arrows and move them closer to the view.

3. Select the view note for Section A-A and move the view note below the appropriate view.

4. Select the view note for Section C-C and move the view note, as shown in Figure 3–69.

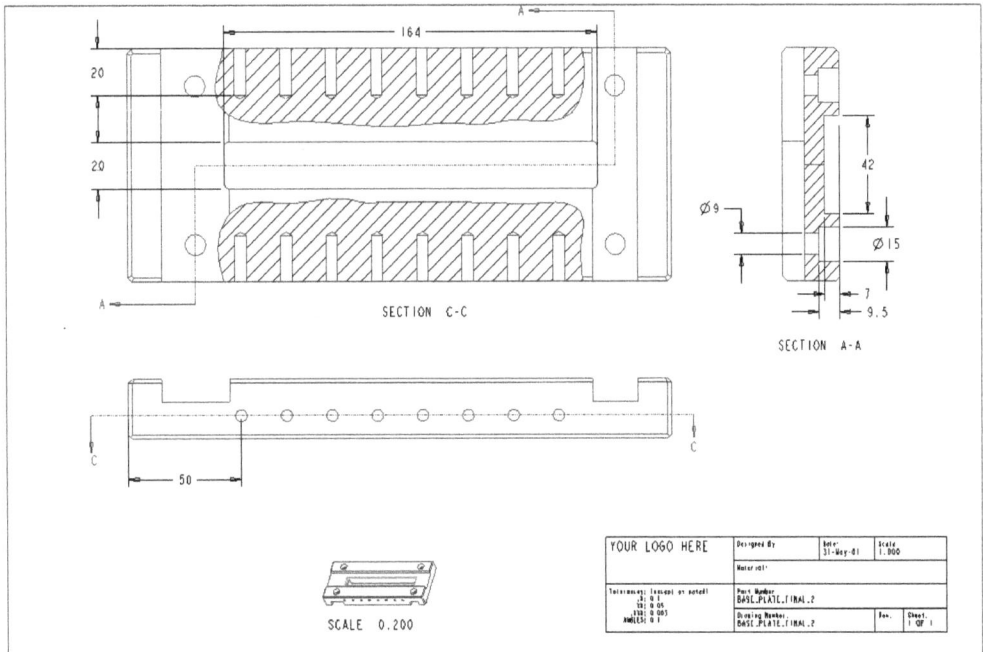

Figure 3–69

Task 10 - Show additional drawing items.

1. Click ⬛ (Show Model Annotations).

2. Click ⬛ (Show Model Datums) to display the tab.

You can show the axis in more than one view at a time by selecting the feature in the Model Tree. You can also use <Ctrl> to select multiple features.

3. Do the following, as shown in Figure 3–70:

   - Show the axes in the General view and bottom Projected.
   - Show the remaining dimensions.
   - Arrange the dimensions and any additional detail items.

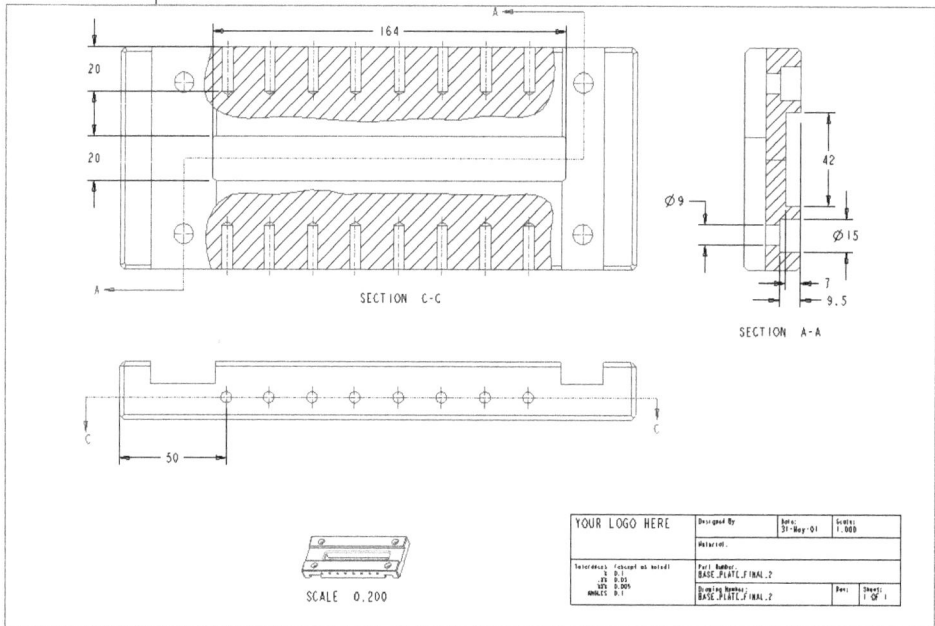

Figure 3–70

Task 11 - Break the witness line of the 9.5 dimension in the right Projected view.

1. Click ⊣̵ (Break) in the Edit group in the *Annotate* tab.

To remove the break for the specific dimension, right-click on the dimension and select Remove All Breaks.

2. Select the witness line shown in Figure 3–71 as the line to break. Where you select along the witness line defines the start point of the simple break. Accept the default settings in the **BREAK TYPE** menu.

3. Select the witness line at the location shown in Figure 3–71 to end the break, then middle-click to finish. The break displays.

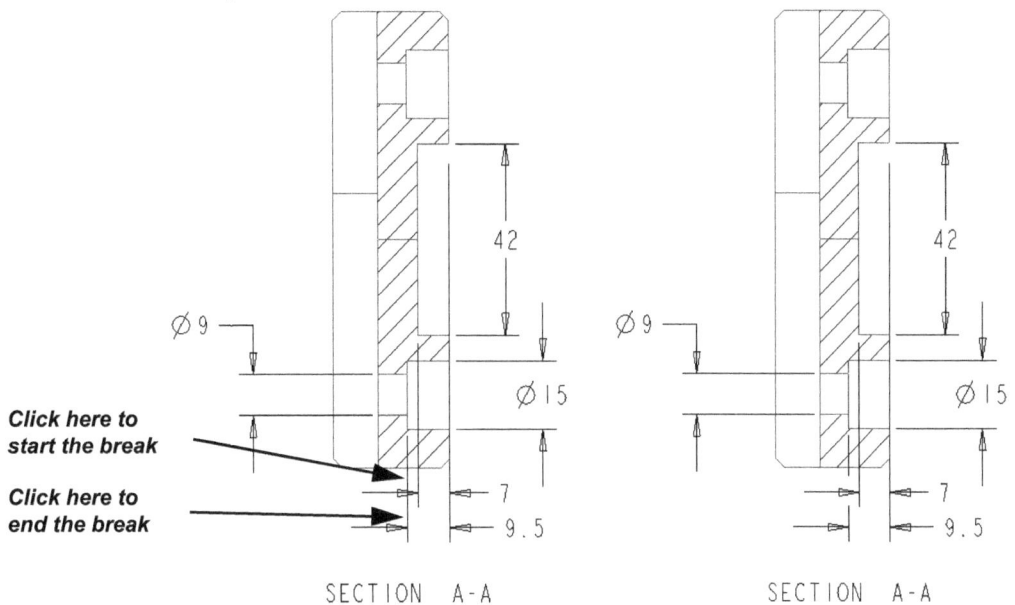

Figure 3–71

Task 12 - Create a centerline on the right Projected view.

1. In the Model Tree, right-click on
   BASE_PLATE_FINAL_2.PRT and click **Open**, as shown in
   Figure 3–72.

Figure 3–72

2. In the *Model* tab, in the Datum group, click / (Axis) to create
   a datum axis in the part.

3. While holding <Ctrl>, select **DTM3** and **DTM7** in the Model
   tree. The Datum Axis dialog box updates as shown in
   Figure 3–73.

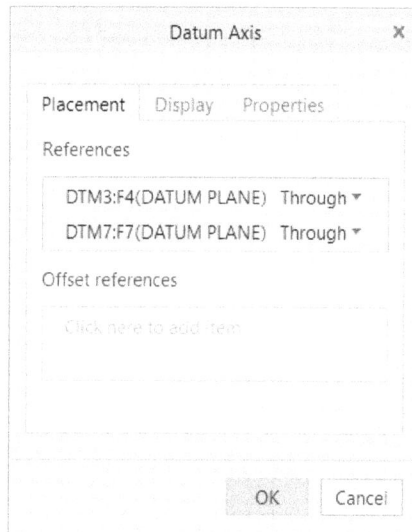

Figure 3–73

4. Click the *Properties* tab and enter **Center1** as the name of the axis, as shown in Figure 3–74.

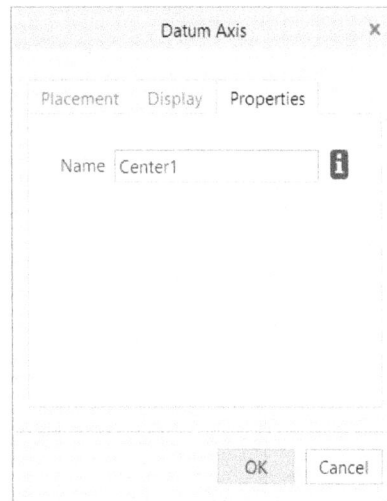

Figure 3–74

5. Click **OK** to complete the feature.

6. Save the model and change back to the drawing window.

7. In the Model Tree, right click on **Center1** and select (Show Model Annotations), as shown in Figure 3–75.

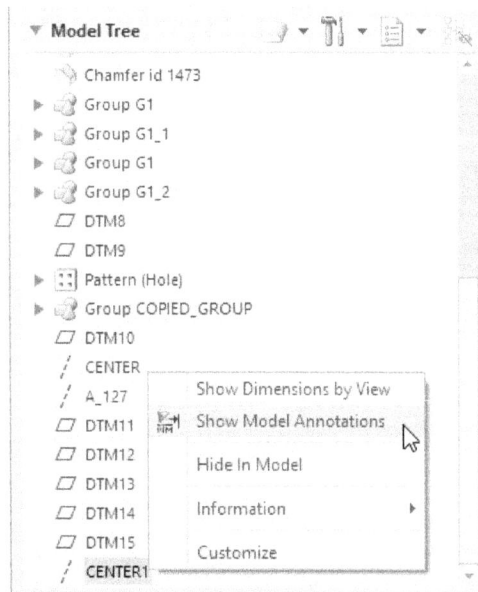

Figure 3–75

8. In the Show Model Annotations dialog box, select the ⊼ (Show the Model Datums) tab, as shown in Figure 3–76.

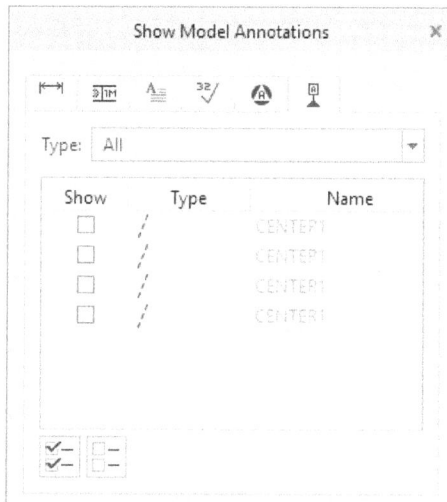

Figure 3–76

9. Click ✓– (Select All).

10. Click **OK**.

Task 13 - Erase the created axes.

1. Select the axes you just displayed in the scaled General view and right Projected view, and click ✓ (Erase) from the mini toolbar.

2. Click anywhere in the drawing to complete the erase operation.

Task 14 - Add text to a dimension.

1. In the General section view (Section C-C), show the **20** dimension for the spacing between the holes, as shown in Figure 3–77. Note that **7x** displays in front of the dimension.

2. Move the dimension, if required. The drawing displays as shown in Figure 3–77.

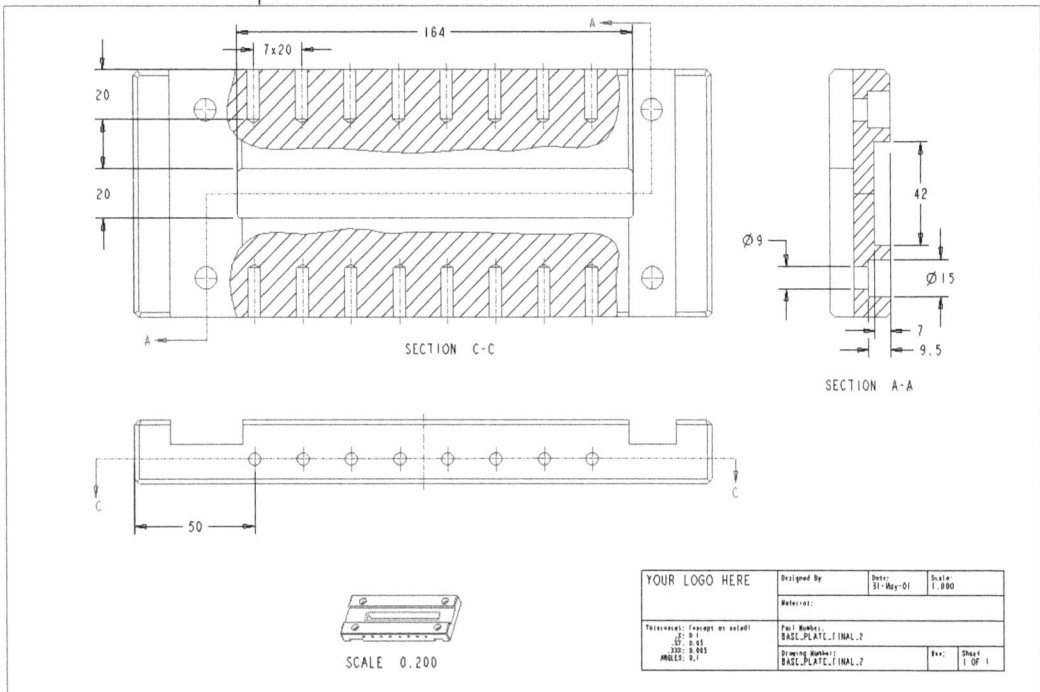

Figure 3–77

3. Save the drawing and close the window.

Practice 3c | Creating Dimensions

Practice Objectives

- Create dimensions in the drawing.
- Create a Detail view.
- Modify section hatching.

In this practice, you will show and create dimensions, add a detailed view, and modify the section hatching on a cross-sectional view. The final drawing displays as shown in Figure 3–78.

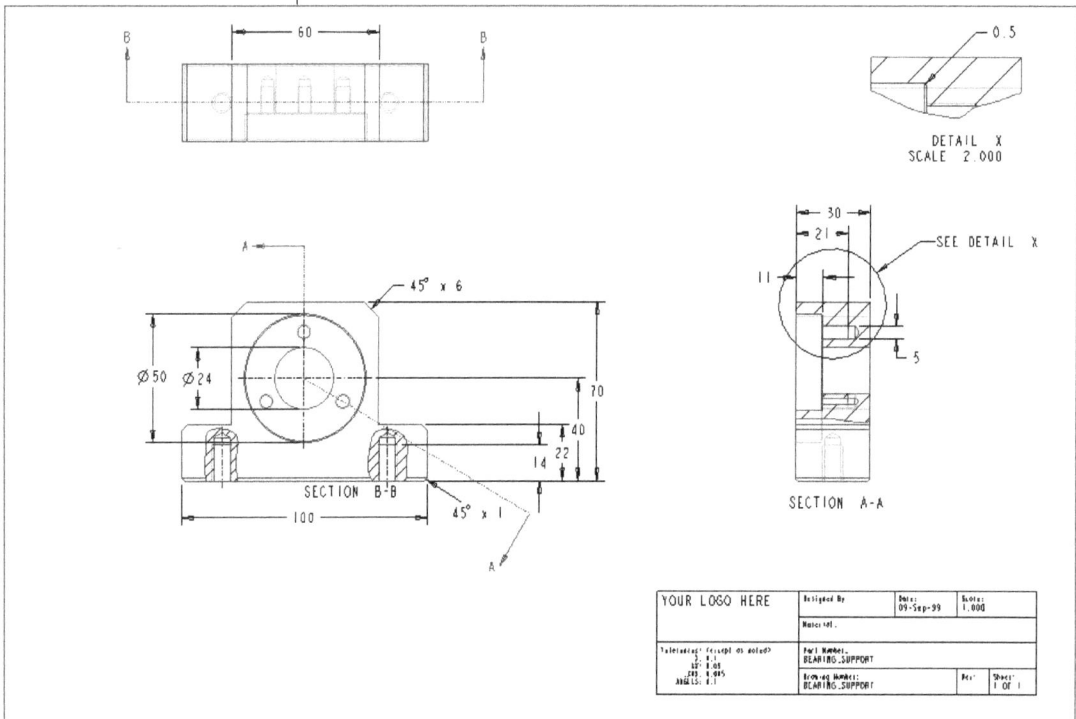

Figure 3–78

Task 1 - Open a drawing file.

Bearing_support.drw references the model bearing_support.prt.

1. Set the working directory to the *Creating_Drawing_Dimensions* folder.

2. Open **bearing_support.drw**.

3. Set the model display as follows:

- ⁺ᵡₐ (*Datum Display Filters*): All Off

- ⬚ (*Display Style*): ⬚ (Wireframe)

Task 2 - Create dimensions.

*Use **Pick From List** to select items more easily and quickly.*

1. Select the *Annotate* tab and click ⊢⊣ (Dimension) in the Annotations group.

2. Create the dimension shown in Figure 3–79, Click one vertical line, press and hold <Ctrl> and select the other line. Click the middle mouse button to place the dimension.

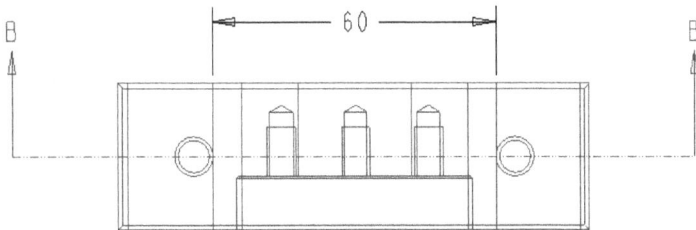

Figure 3–79

3. Create the dimension shown in Figure 3–80. Select the arc, right-click and select **Diameter**. Then, press the middle mouse button to place the dimension.

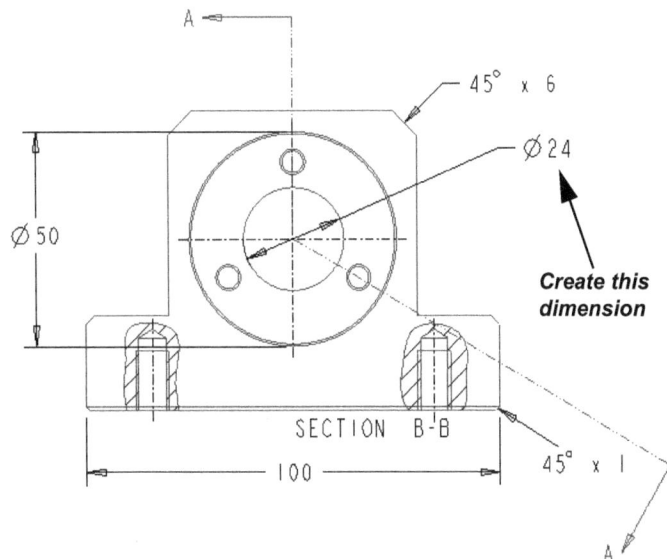

Figure 3–80

4. Click **Cancel** in the Select Reference dialog box.

5. Select the **Ø24** dimension.

You can also use the Dimension Properties dialog box and the Display tab.

6. Right-click and select **Show as linear**.

7. Select the **Ø24** dimension and click ✐ (Edit Attachment) in the mini toolbar. You need to reselect the references.

8. In the Select References dialog box, click ✐ (Tangent).

9. Press <Ctrl> and select the two halves of the arcs.

10. Move the ⌀24 dimension to the position shown in Figure 3–81 and press the middle mouse button.

To add additional information to a dimension, click

⌀¹⁰⁰ *(Dimension Text) in the Dimension tab to create the required dimension notation (e.g., to add the Ø symbol to a dimension).*

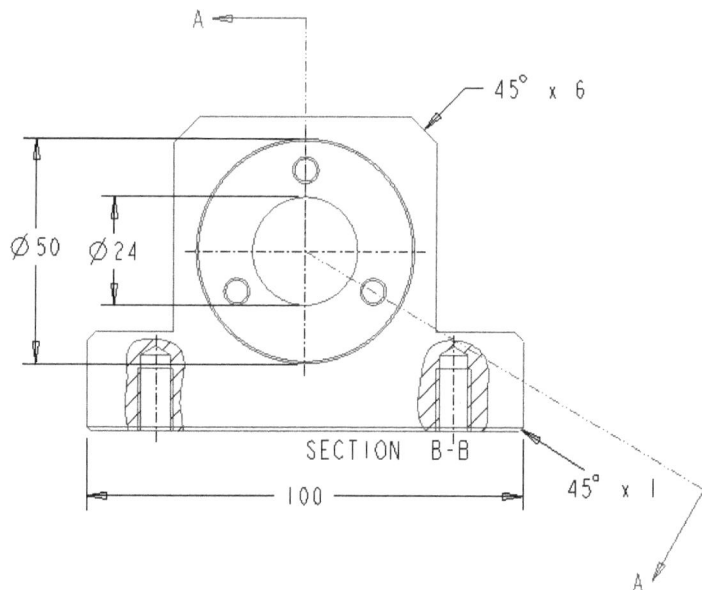

Figure 3–81

11. Create the dimensions shown in Figure 3–82.

Use ✐ *(Edit Attachment) and*

✛ *(Flip Arrows) to rearrange the dimensions.*

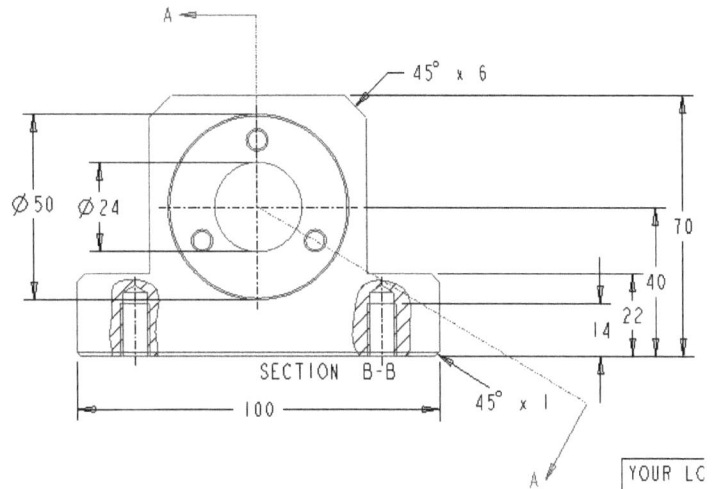

Figure 3–82

12. Create the dimensions shown in Figure 3–83.

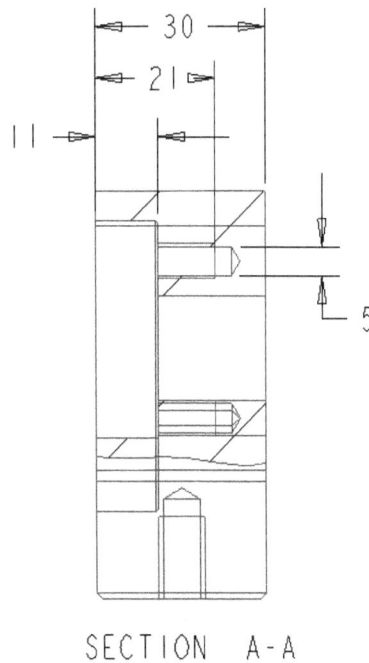

SECTION A-A

Figure 3–83

Task 3 - Add the detailed view.

1. Add the DETAIL X view as shown in Figure 3–84. Create the view with a **2.0** scale.

2. Show the **0.5** dimension of the chamfer in the Detailed view.

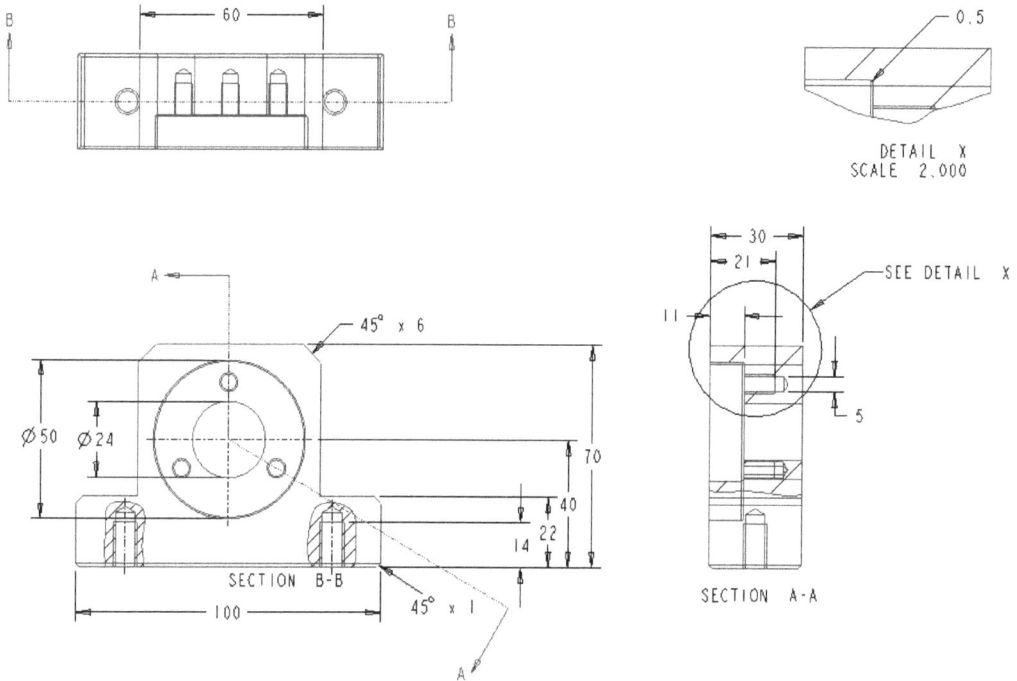

Figure 3–84

Task 4 - Modify the cross-hatching in the drawing views.

*You can also right-click and select **Properties** to open the **MOD XHATCH** menu.*

1. Select the *Layout* tab. Double-click on the cross-hatching in the Projected view on the right side.

2. Select **Spacing** in the **MOD XHATCH** menu.

3. Select **Overall>Value** in the **MODIFY MODE** menu and enter **.25**.

4. Select **Done** in the **MOD XHATCH** menu. The drawing updates.

Task 5 - Modify the display of the drawing views.

1. Modify the Display mode of the views so that the drawing displays as shown in Figure 3–85.

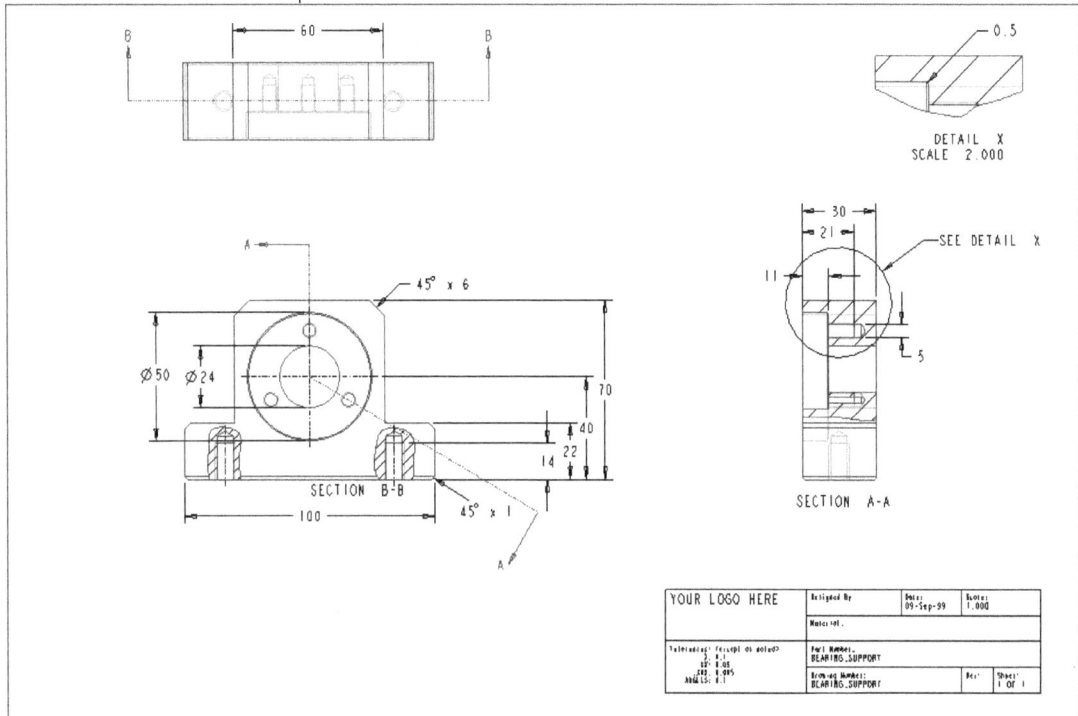

Figure 3–85

2. Save the drawing and close the window.

Practice 3d

Ordinate Dimensions

Practice Objective

- Switch linear dimensioning to ordinate dimensioning,

In this practice, you will convert drawing dimensions to the ordinate type. The final drawing displays as shown in Figure 3–86.

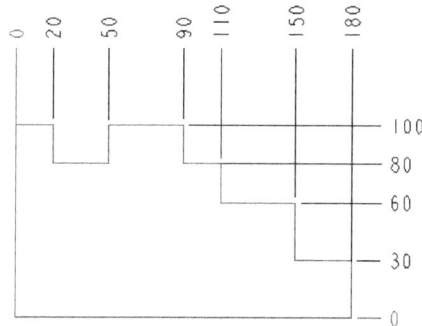

Figure 3–86

Task 1 - Open a drawing file.

1. Set the working directory to the *Ordinate_Dimensions* folder.

2. Open **ordinate_dim.drw**.

3. Set the model display as follows:

- ✗̇ᵢ (*Datum Display Filters*): All Off

- ⬚, (*Display Style*): ⬚ (Wireframe)

Ordinate_dim.drw references the ordinate_dim.prt.

Task 2 - Switch linear dimensions to ordinate dimensions.

1. Select all of the horizontal dimensions.

2. Select the *Annotate* tab.

3. Right-click and select **Toggle Ordinate/Linear**. All of the selected linear dimensions toggle to ordinate ones.

4. Repeat the process for the vertical dimensions. The drawing displays as shown in Figure 3–87.

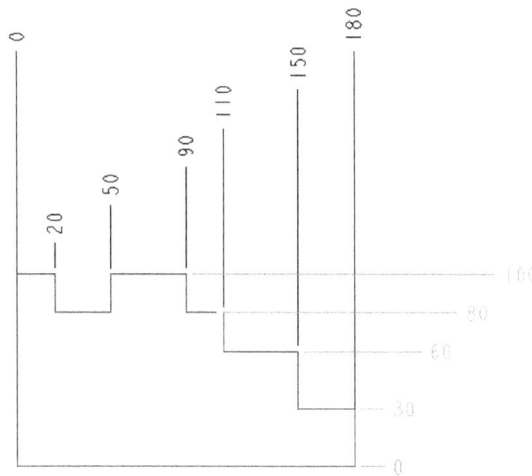

Figure 3–87

5. Use ⊞ (Align Dimension) and move the dimensions to rearrange the drawing dimensions, as shown in Figure 3–88.

Select all of the horizontal or vertical dimensions, right-click, and select ⊞ (Align Dimension).

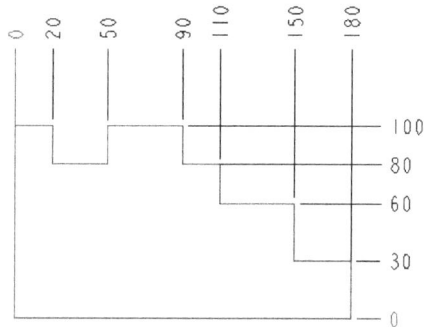

YOUR LOGO HERE	Designed By	Date: 09-Sep-99	Scale: 0.500		
	Material:				
Tolerances: (except as noted) .X: 0.1 .XX: 0.05 .XXX: 0.005 ANGLES: 0.1	Part Number: ORDINATE_DIM				
	Drawing Number: ORDINATE_DIM			Rev:	Sheet: 1 OF 1

Figure 3–88

6. Save the drawing and close the window.

Chapter Review Questions

1. Showing detail items is the preferred method of maintaining associativity between the drawing and the model. Which of the following are some of the benefits of showing detail items? (Select all that apply.)

   a. Avoid repetitions.

   b. Saves time.

   c. Preserve the associativity between models and drawings.

   d. The dimensions are a different color than draft dimensions.

2. The *Annotate* tab must be active to show detail items.

   a. True

   b. False

3. Which of the following are valid statements related to showing dimensions? (Select all that apply.)

   a. To show all of the annotations, select the model in the Model Tree.

   b. To show all of the annotations for a view, select the view in the Drawing Tree or Graphics window.

   c. To show dimensions for a feature in a view, select the feature in the view.

   d. To show dimensions for a feature, select the feature in the Model Tree.

4. The *Annotate* tab must be active to display the shown and created dimensions in the Drawing Tree.

   a. True

   b. False

5. Which of the following icons enables you to display model dimensions in a drawing?

   a.

   b.

   c.

   d.

6. To modify a created dimension value, select the dimension and right-click and select **Edit Value**.

   a. True

   b. False

7. What command can be used to move a dimension for a round to the opposite edge?

   a. **Switch Item to View**

   b. **Flip Arrow**

   c. **Edit Attachment**

   d. **Select** tool

Project Labs 1 & 2

This chapter contains two projects. These projects cover the material learned in Chapters 1, 2, and 3.

Learning Objectives in This Chapter

- Create and detail a drawing.
- Show dimensions on a 3D view.

Practice 4a

Creating a Detailed Drawing

Practice Objective

- Create and detail a drawing.

In this project, you will create a detail drawing from a part that has been provided for you. When creating this drawing, consider the following:

Before releasing a drawing, it is important to ask: **Can this model be manufactured from the information provided in the drawing?**

- The drawing units, projection angle, and scale are important for communicating the correct information.

- You might need to show and create dimensions to represent the model.

You will create the drawing shown in Figure 4–1.

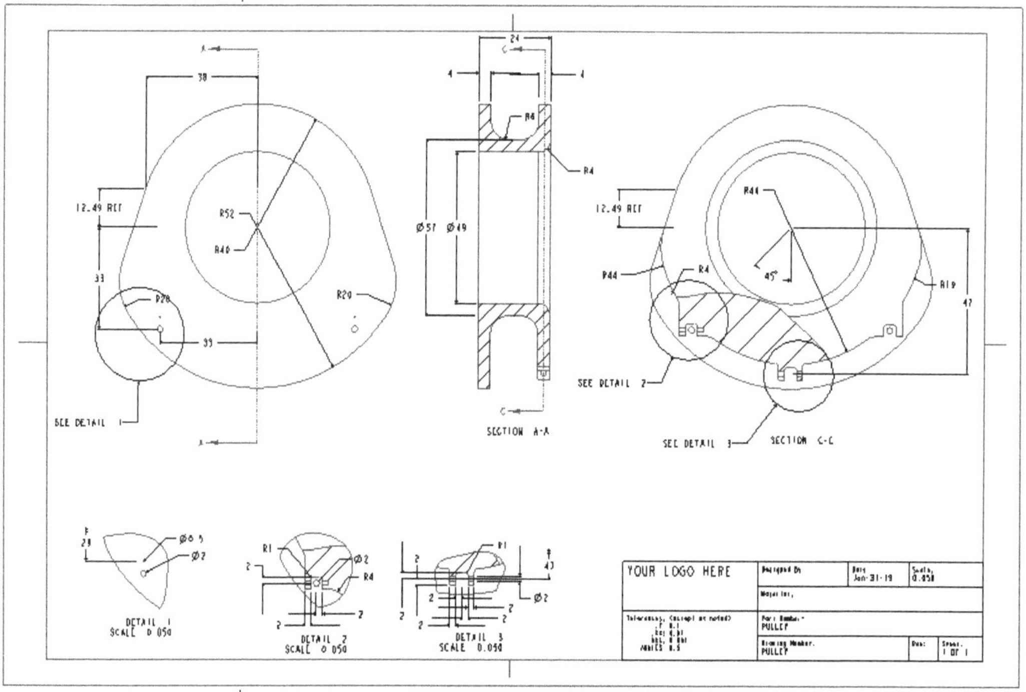

Figure 4–1

Task 1 - Open a part file.

1. Set the working directory to *Create_Detailed_Drawing*.

2. Open **pulley.prt**.

3. Set the model display as follows:

- ⚘ *(Datum Display Filters)*: All Off
- ⤴ *(Spin Center)*: Off
- ⬛ *(Display Style)*: ⬛ (Shading With Edges)

The part displays as shown in Figure 4–2.

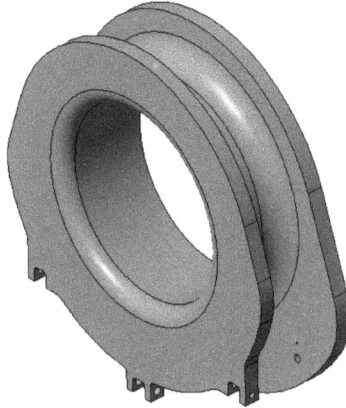

Figure 4–2

4. Create two cross-sections, one through datum plane **RIGHT** and another through datum plane **TOP**. Name the cross-sections **A** and **B**, respectively.

   To create a cross-section in a model, select the *View* tab, expand ⬛ (Section) and select **Planar**. Select the planar surface or datum plane through which you want the cross-section to pass. Click the *Properties* tab in the *Section* dashboard and change the name as required, then complete the section.

5. Select **File>Prepare>Model Properties**. The Model Properties dialog box opens. Note the Units listed (Inch Ibm Second).

6. Save the model.

Task 2 - Create a new drawing.

1. Create a new drawing. Enable the **Use drawing model file name** option and assign **generic_b.frm** as the format (browse to the ⬛ (Working Directory), if required).

2. In the In-Graphics toolbar, enable ⬛ (No Hidden).

3. Select **File>Prepare>Drawing Properties**. Select **change** next to Detail Options. The Options dialog box opens as shown in Figure 4–3.

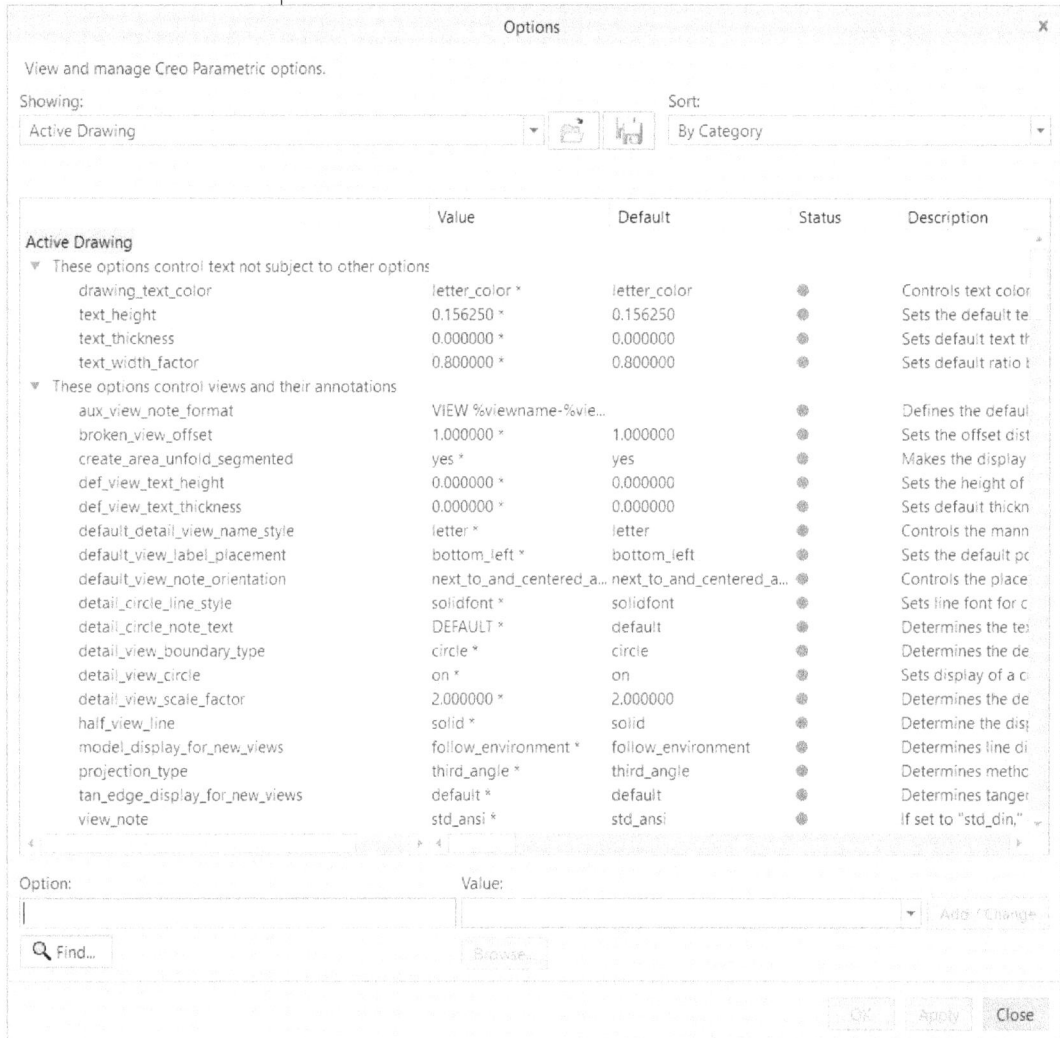

	Value	Default	Status	Description
Active Drawing				
▼ These options control text not subject to other options				
drawing_text_color	letter_color *	letter_color	●	Controls text color
text_height	0.156250 *	0.156250	●	Sets the default te
text_thickness	0.000000 *	0.000000	●	Sets default text th
text_width_factor	0.800000 *	0.800000	●	Sets default ratio b
▼ These options control views and their annotations				
aux_view_note_format	VIEW %viewname-%vie...		●	Defines the defaul
broken_view_offset	1.000000 *	1.000000	●	Sets the offset dist
create_area_unfold_segmented	yes *	yes	●	Makes the display
def_view_text_height	0.000000 *	0.000000	●	Sets the height of
def_view_text_thickness	0.000000 *	0.000000	●	Sets default thickn
default_detail_view_name_style	letter *	letter	●	Controls the mann
default_view_label_placement	bottom_left *	bottom_left	●	Sets the default po
default_view_note_orientation	next_to_and_centered_a...	next_to_and_centered_a...	●	Controls the place
detail_circle_line_style	solidfont *	solidfont	●	Sets line font for c
detail_circle_note_text	DEFAULT *	default	●	Determines the tex
detail_view_boundary_type	circle *	circle	●	Determines the de
detail_view_circle	on *	on	●	Sets display of a c
detail_view_scale_factor	2.000000 *	2.000000	●	Determines the de
half_view_line	solid *	solid	●	Determine the disp
model_display_for_new_views	follow_environment *	follow_environment	●	Determines line di
projection_type	third_angle *	third_angle	●	Determines metho
tan_edge_display_for_new_views	default *	default	●	Determines tanger
view_note	std_ansi *	std_ansi	●	If set to "std_din,"

Figure 4–3

4. Verify that your **drawing_units** drawing setup file option is the same as the units in the model. If not, select the value in the **Value** menu and apply the changes.

5. Sort the options alphabetically and assign the following new values to the options. Apply the changes and close the Options dialog box.

Option	Value
arrow_style	filled
crossec_arrow_length	0.2
crossec_arrow_width	0.08
draw_arrow_length	0.1
draw_arrow_width	0.04
lead_trail_zeros	std_metric(both)
text_height	0.11
witness_line_delta	0.0325
witness_line_offset	0.0425

6. Add views and modify their view display, as shown in Figure 4–4.

7. Change the drawing scale to **0.05**. The drawing displays as shown in Figure 4–4.

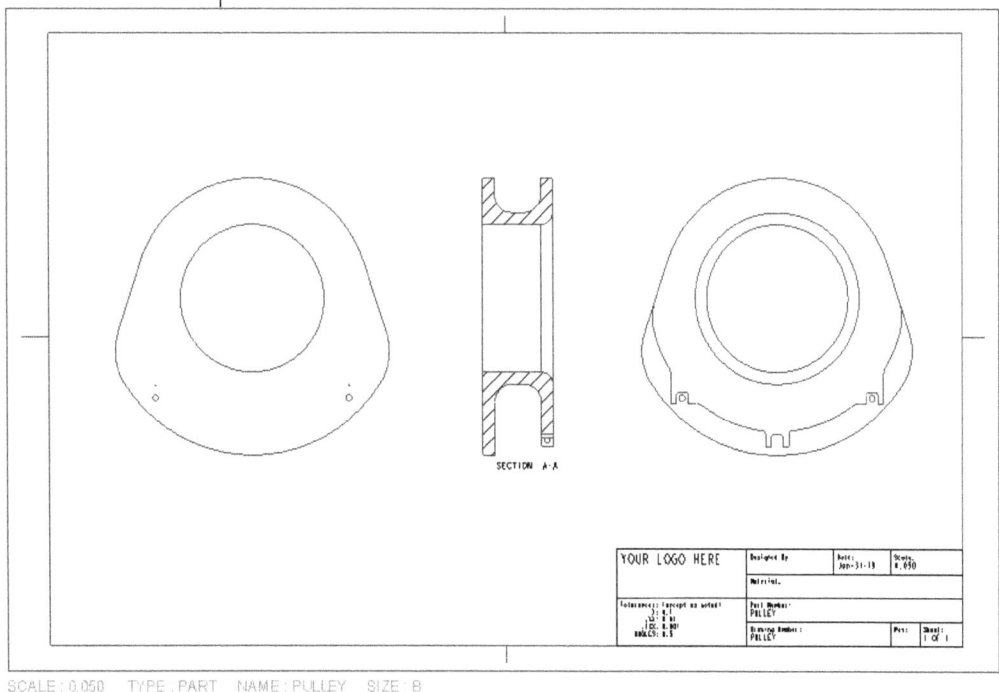

SCALE : 0.050   TYPE : PART   NAME : PULLEY   SIZE : B

Figure 4–4

8. Show, move, and rearrange the dimensions as shown in Figure 4–5.

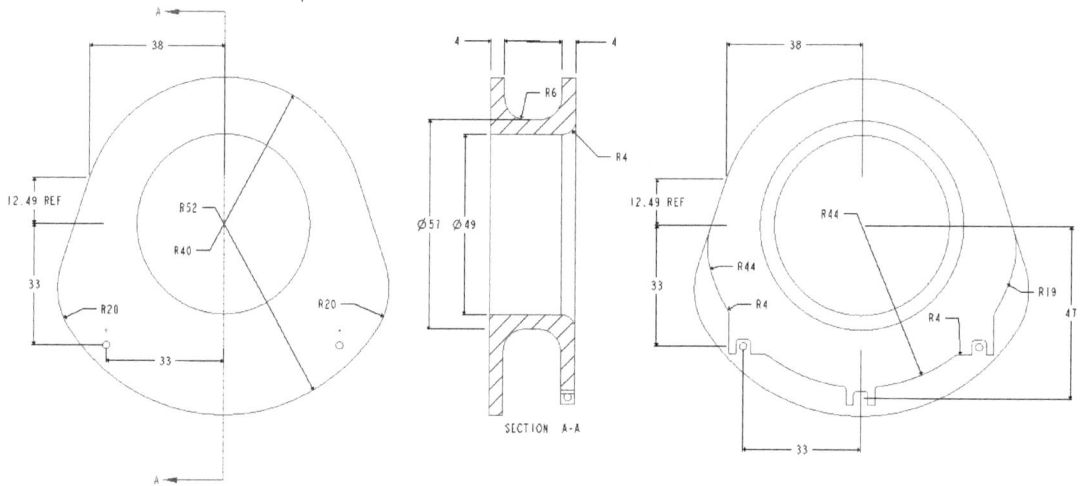

Figure 4–5

9. Modify the right projection view to a local section view, as shown in Figure 4–6.

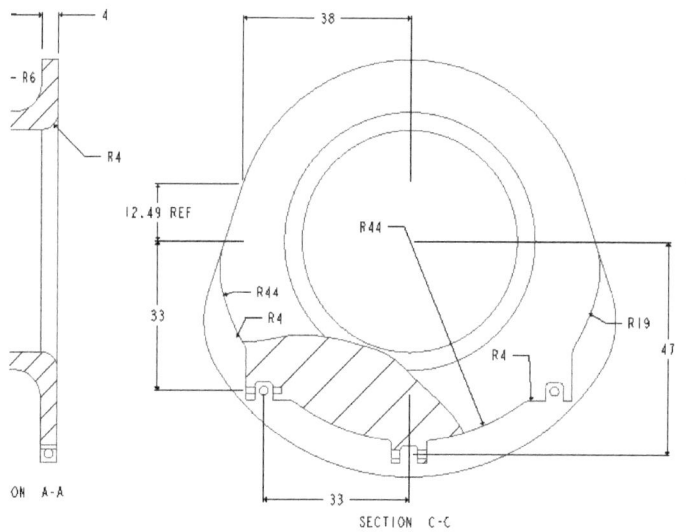

Figure 4–6

10. Add detail views 1, 2, and 3 to the drawing, as shown in Figure 4–7.

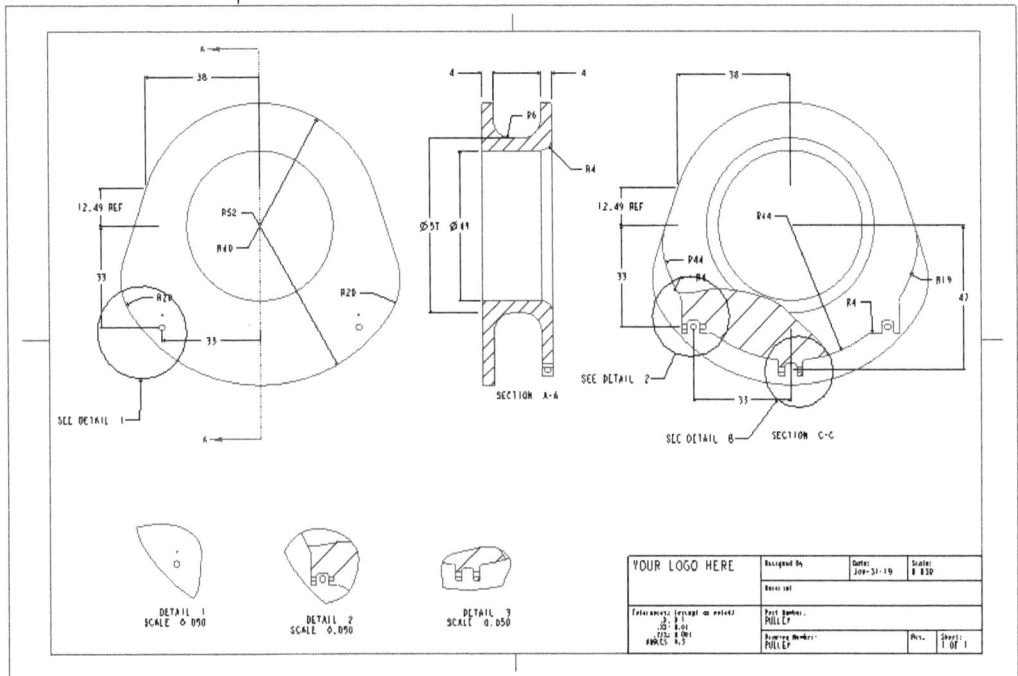

Figure 4–7

11. Show dimensions for detail views 1, 2, and 3, as shown in Figure 4–8.

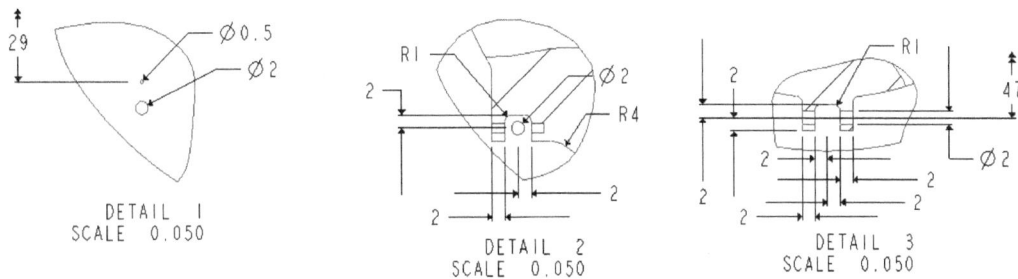

Figure 4–8

12. Create and erase the dimensions shown in Figure 4–9 and then flip the dimension arrows as required to complete the drawing.

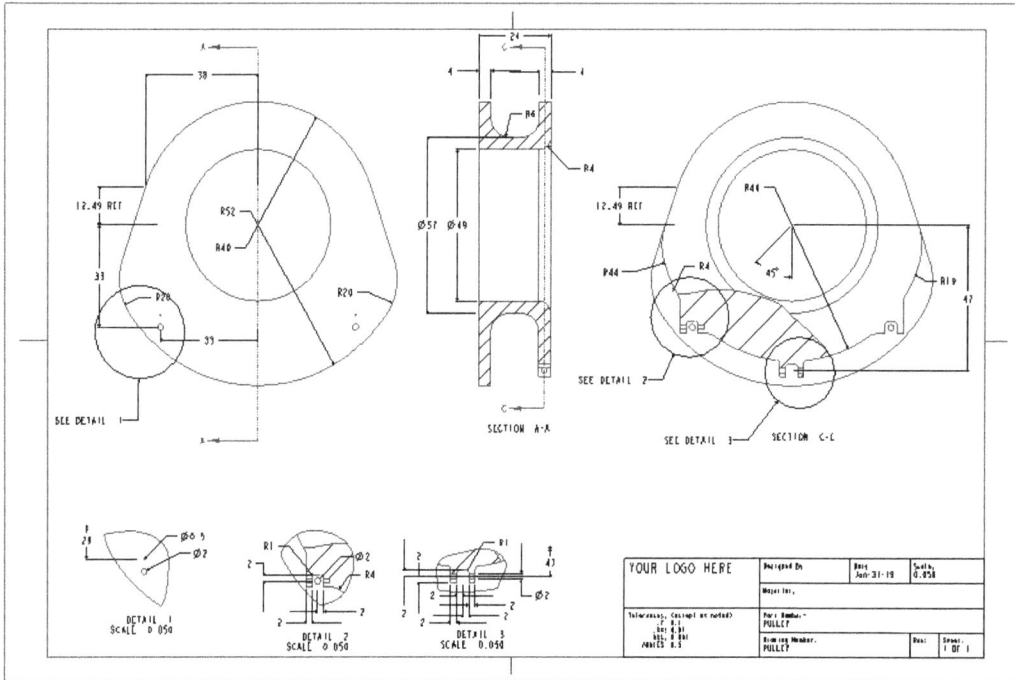

Figure 4–9

13. Save the drawing and close the window.

Practice 4b | Creating 3D Drawings

Practice Objective

- Show dimensions on a 3D view.

In this project, you will show dimensions on a 3D view. The final drawing displays as shown in Figure 4–10.

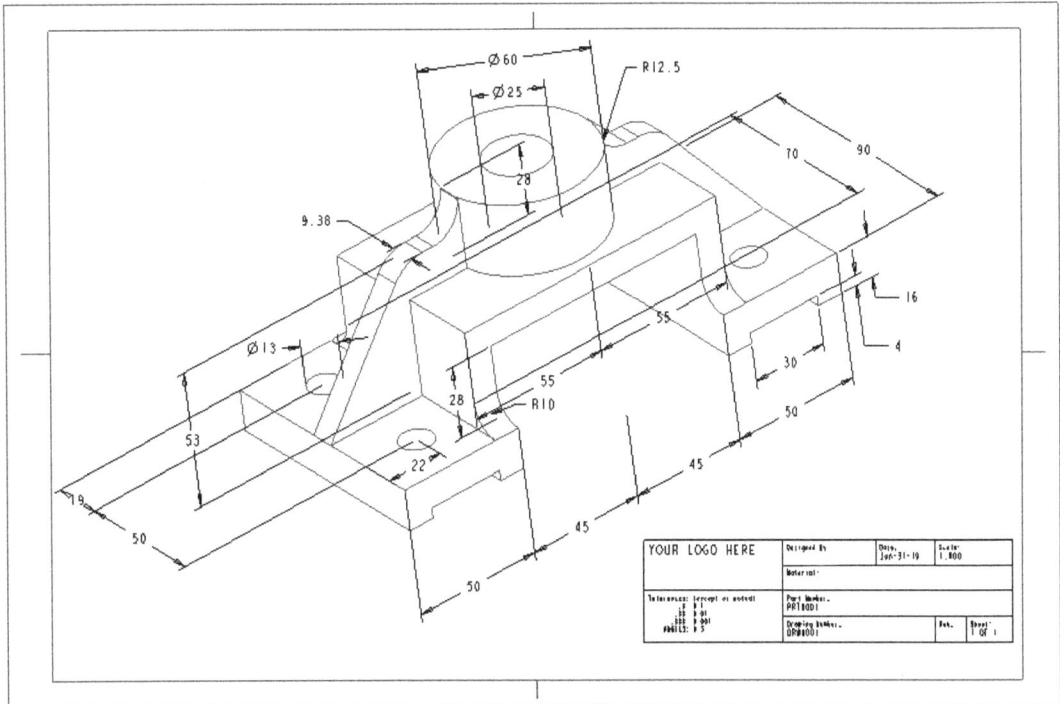

Figure 4–10

Task 1 - Open a part file.

1. Set the working directory to *Create_3D_Drawing*.

2. Open **spindle_bearing.prt**.

3. Set the model display as follows:

- ⚡ *(Datum Display Filters)*: All Off
- ⚙ (Spin Center): Off
- ⬛ *(Display Style)*: ⬜ (Shading With Edges)

The part displays as shown in Figure 4–11.

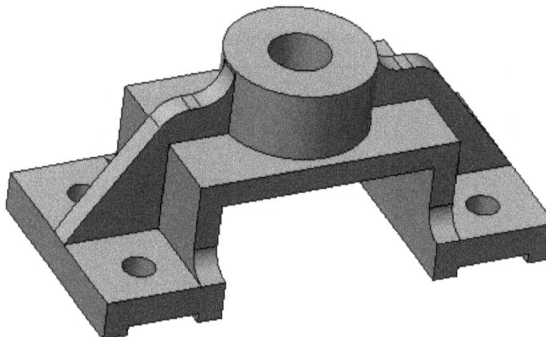

Figure 4–11

*Clear the **Spin Center** option to clean up the display of the model.*

Task 2 - Create a new drawing called spindle_bearing.drw.

1. Create a new drawing. Enable the **Use drawing model file name** option and assign **generic_b.frm** as the format.

2. Select **File>Prepare>Drawing Properties**. Select **change** next to **Detail Options**. The Options dialog box opens.

3. Change the **allow_3d_dimensions** drawing setup file option to **yes**. Apply the changes and close the dialog box.

4. Select **File>Options>Configuration Editor**. Assign new values to the configuration file options as follows:

These options set the drawing line thicknesses for printing. Changing this value does not affect the display of lines in Drawing mode.

Option	Value
pen1_line_weight	9 (pen1 color is white)
pen2_line_weight	5 (pen2 color is yellow)

5. Apply the changes and close the dialog box.

6. Add the view as shown in Figure 4–12. This orientation is a previously saved orientation in the 3D model called **spindle_bearing**.

7. Change the drawing scale to **1.2**. The drawing displays as shown in Figure 4–12.

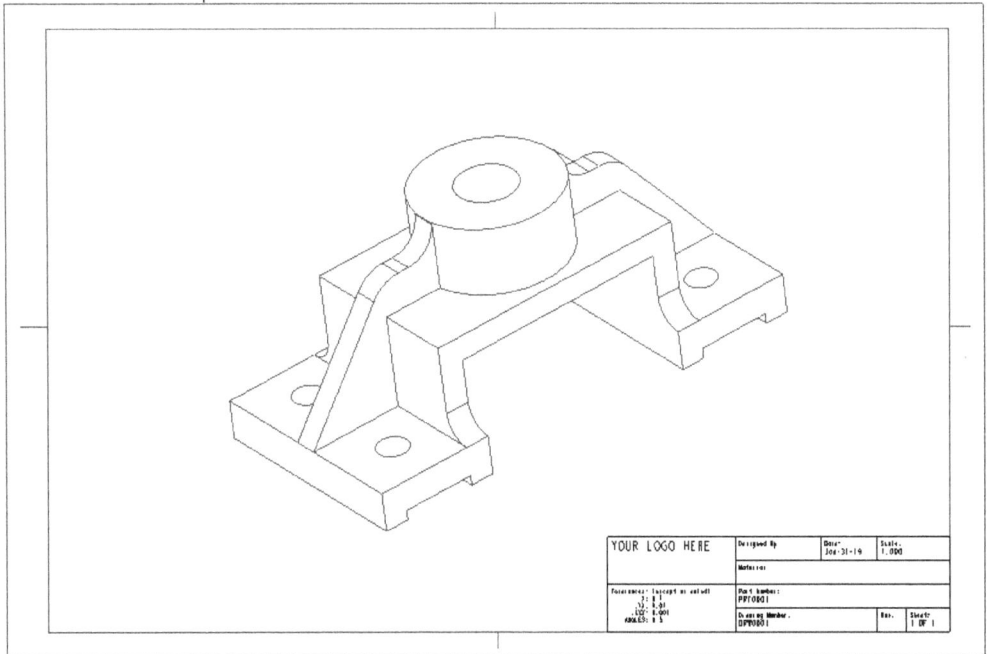

Figure 4–12

8. Show, move, and rearrange the dimensions on the view as shown in Figure 4–13.

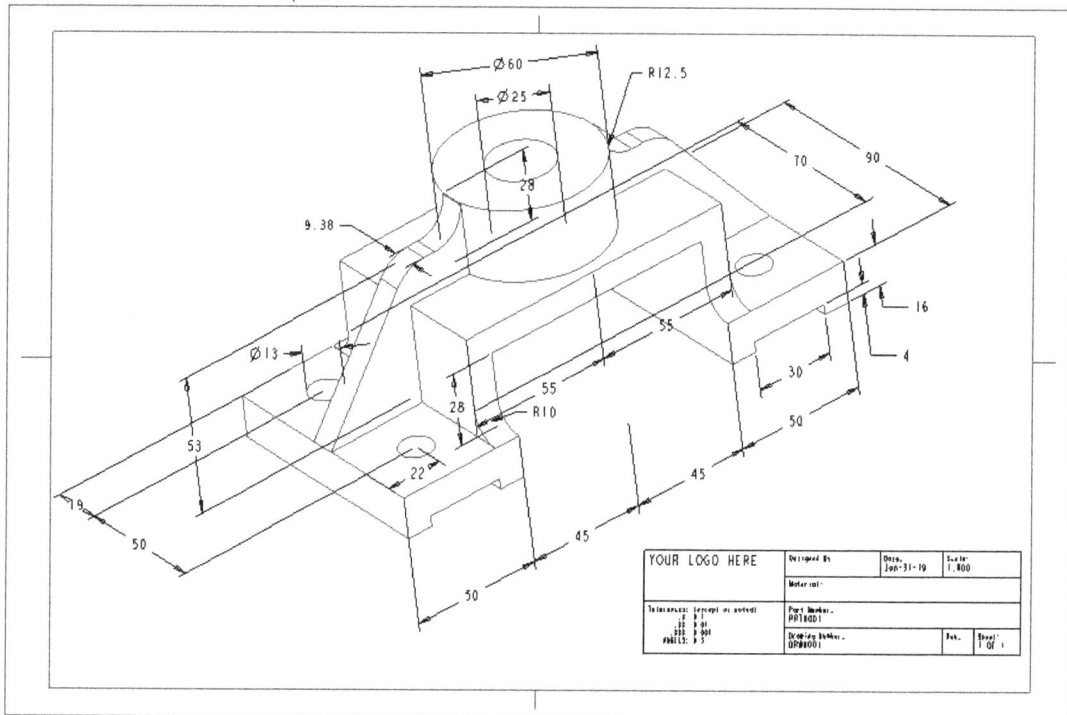

Figure 4–13

9. Save the drawing and close the window.

Drawing Notes

Notes are added to drawings to provide a more detailed description of the model being represented in the drawing. Notes can be displayed directly on the model or created in the drawing.

Learning Objectives in This Chapter

- Learn to create a note with or without a leader using the *Annotate* tab.
- Learn to enter system-defined parameters, user-defined parameters, special characters, and symbols to define a note.
- Use manipulation tools to move, edit, and save notes in a drawing.
- Review configuration file and drawing file options to customize notes in the drawing environment.

5.1 Create and Modify Notes

Drawing notes can contain user-defined text or parametric information regarding the drawing model. Parametric information can be transferred between the model and the drawing. Therefore, if a parameter value is changed in a note it can automatically change in the model and vice-versa.

How To: Create a Drawing Note

1. Select the *Annotate* tab, to activate the annotation options.

2. To create a new note in a drawing, expand ᴬ≣ (Note) in the Annotations group in the *Annotate* tab. The various note types are available as shown in Figure 5–1.

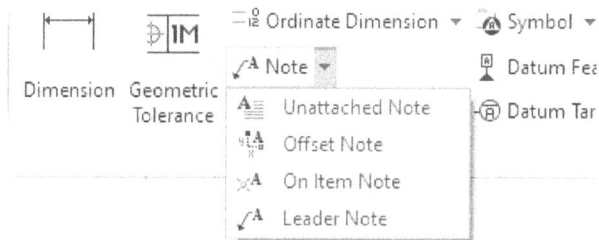

Figure 5–1

The following options are available:

Option	Description
ᴬ≣ (Unattached Note)	Free placement in the annotation plane.
⁺ᴬ (Offset Note)	Attach note offset from a dimension, arrow, other note, gtol, and so on.
⤳ᴬ (On Item Note)	Attach note to another entity.
⟋ᴬ (Leader Note)	Attach note with a standard leader.

After selecting the note type, select the appropriate attachment reference. If you select the $A\equiv$ (Unattached Note) type, the Select Point dialog box opens, as shown in Figure 5–2.

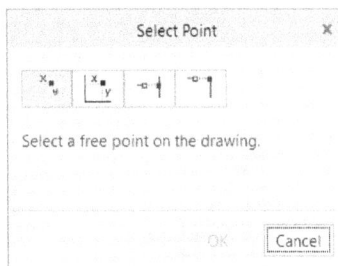

Figure 5–2

The following placement options are available:

Option	Description
$^{x}\!\!_{y}$ (Free Point)	Select a free point on the drawing.
$\boxed{^{x}\!\!_{y}}$ (Absolute Coordinates)	Select a point using absolute coordinates.
(On Object)	Select a point on a drawing object or entity.
(On Vertex)	Select a vertex.

If you select the $\nearrow^{A}$ (Leader Note) type, the Select Reference dialog box opens, as shown in Figure 5–3.

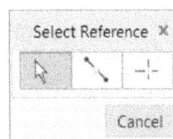

Figure 5–3

The following selection options are available:

Option	Description
(Reference)	Select an entity or free point on the drawing.
(Midpoint)	Select the midpoint of an edge or entity.
(Intersection)	Select an intersection defined by two objects.

When you place a leader note on an edge, you can move the note so that it is in a tangent or normal position and an icon displays as the note snaps to either position, as shown in Figure 5–4.

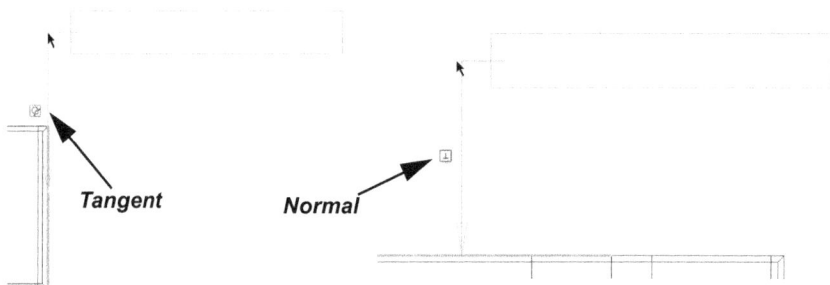

Tangent   *Normal*

Figure 5–4

Multiple arrows can be added by pressing <Ctrl> while selecting attachment locations, as shown in Figure 5–5.

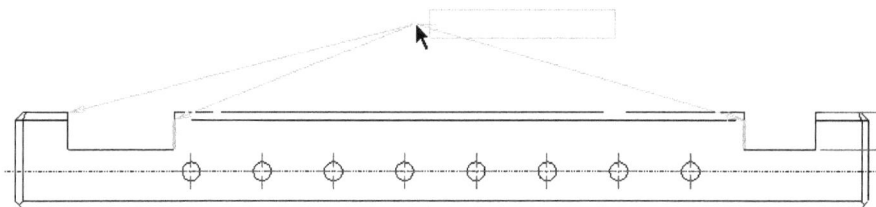

Figure 5–5

3. Once the leader references have been defined, select the note location on the model by pressing the middle mouse button in the appropriate location. Enter the note information directly into the text field, as shown in Figure 5–6.

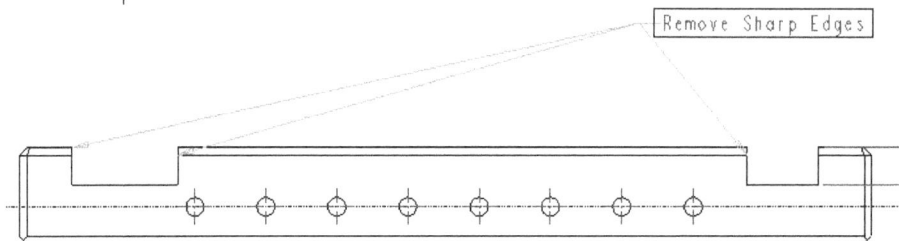

Remove Sharp Edges

Figure 5–6

When a note is active, Creo Parametric displays the *Format* tab, which provides various tools for formatting your notes, as shown in Figure 5–7.

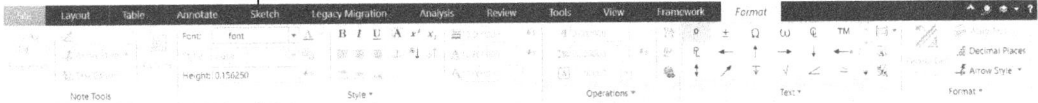

Figure 5–7

In addition to user-defined text, the following information can be included in drawing notes:

- Dimensions
- System-defined parameters
- User-defined parameters
- Special characters
- User-defined symbols

4. Once a drawing note has been created, it can be manipulated using various methods.

Dimensions

Parametric dimension values can be displayed in notes, but the same dimension cannot be shown more than once in a drawing. Once a dimension has been written to a note, the duplicate dimension is removed from the drawing.

Symbolic names of dimensions can be displayed by selecting **Format>Switch Dimensions** *in the Annotate tab.*

To add a dimension value to a note, you must enter the symbolic name for the dimension preceded by the ampersand (&) symbol. The symbolic names for the drawing dimensions displayed by clicking 🔣 (Switch Dimensions) in the *Format* tab when you create a note, as shown in Figure 5–8.

Text entered for note:
ALL CHAMFERS 45° x &d102

Resulting note

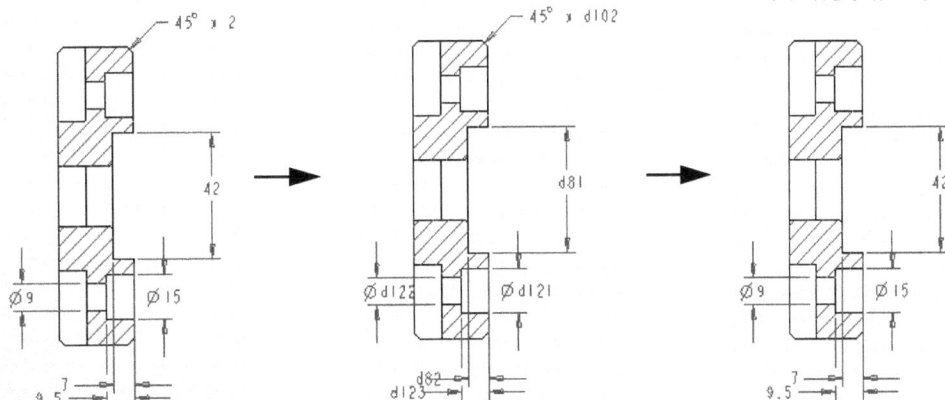

Figure 5–8

Once a model dimension displays in a note, it can be modified directly in the note to change the model geometry. If the model dimension is removed from the note, the duplicate dimension that was removed returns to its original position.

The following symbolic names can be displayed in drawing notes:

- **d#:** Shown model dimensions.

- **ad#:** Created drawing dimensions.

- **p#:** Pattern dimensions.

- **rd#:** Reference dimensions.

System-defined Parameters

System-defined parameters can be included in drawing notes. These parameters supply helpful information about the model and drawing.

Several common parameters are available in the ⊟ (Insert Field) drop-down list, as shown in Figure 5–9.

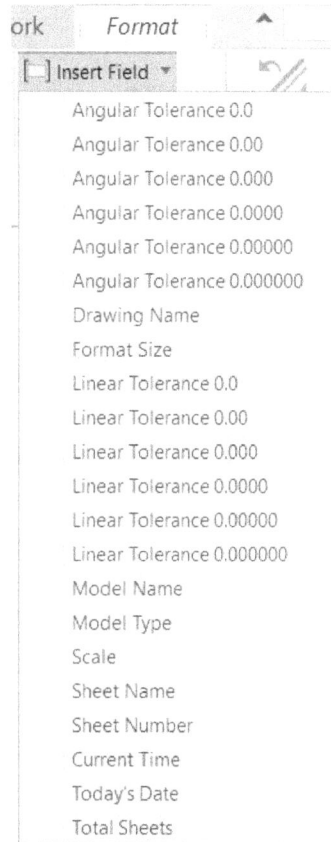

ork   *Format*   ∧

[⊟] Insert Field ▼

Angular Tolerance 0.0
Angular Tolerance 0.00
Angular Tolerance 0.000
Angular Tolerance 0.0000
Angular Tolerance 0.00000
Angular Tolerance 0.000000
Drawing Name
Format Size
Linear Tolerance 0.0
Linear Tolerance 0.00
Linear Tolerance 0.000
Linear Tolerance 0.0000
Linear Tolerance 0.00000
Linear Tolerance 0.000000
Model Name
Model Type
Scale
Sheet Name
Sheet Number
Current Time
Today's Date
Total Sheets

Figure 5–9

Simply select the parameter from the list, and it is added to the note. Additionally, you can manually enter other system-defined parameters, which can be found in the Creo Parametric Help Center.

Some of the system-defined parameters that are available are described as follows:

Field Name	Parameter	Description
Today's Date	&todays_date	Adds the date of the note creation to the drawing. The format can be modified in the configuration file (e.g., DDMMYY 24-06-01).
Model Name	&model_name	Adds the name of the model used in the drawing.
Drawing Name	&dwg_name	Adds the name of the drawing.
Scale	&scale	Adds the scale of the drawing.
Model Type	&type	Adds the type of drawing model (e.g., part, assembly).
Format Size	&format	Adds the size of the drawing format.
Linear Tolerance 0.0...	&linear_tol_#_#	Adds the linear tolerance values from 1 to 6 decimal places.
Angular Tolerance 0.0...	&angular_tol_#_#	Adds the angular tolerance values from 1 to 6 decimal places.
Sheet Number	&current_sheet	Adds the current number of the drawing sheet in which the note is located.
Total Sheets	&total_sheets	Adds the total number of sheets in the drawing.

If you manually enter parameters into notes, always precede the parameter name with the ampersand (&) symbol. Once the note has been completed, the value of the system-defined parameter is automatically entered into the note.

User-defined Parameters

User-defined model or drawing parameters can be displayed in notes using the following notation:

&parametername

Special Characters

To display radius and diameter dimensions in a note, you must manually insert the R or Ø symbols in front of the dimension using the symbol palette, as shown in Figure 5–10 or the keyboard.

The *Format* tab has a palette of special characters. You can expand the palette to see all of the available characters, as shown in Figure 5–10.

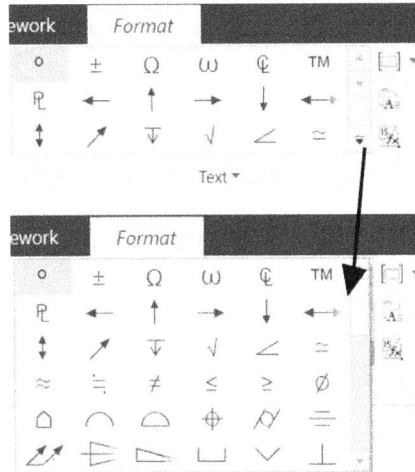

Figure 5–10

Click an icon in the palette and the corresponding character is inserted into the note.

User-defined Symbols

*It is recommended that you set the config.pro option **pro_symbol_dir** to a specific directory so that all of the user-defined and system-defined symbols are in one location.*

If a note requires a symbol that does not exist in the Special Characters symbol palette, you can insert a user-defined symbol into the note. To place a user-defined symbol into a note, use the following notation:

&sym(symbolname)

The example shown in Figure 5–11 is of a note that incorporates a user-defined symbol called **square**. This symbol already exists and is stored in the **pro_symbol_dir** directory.

Text entered from Message Window: TEXT &SYM(SQUARE) TEXT

Resulting drawing note: TEXT ☐ TEXT

Figure 5–11

Many options for manipulating a note are available in the *Annotate* tab, as shown in Figure 5–12.

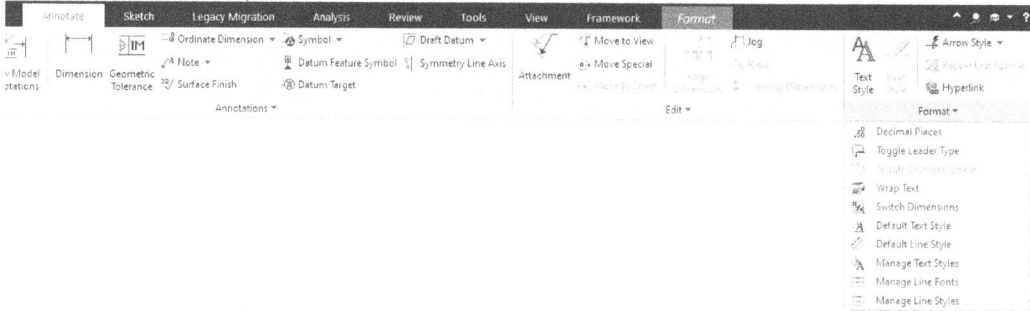

Figure 5–12

Note Handles

When a note is selected, several handles and the mini toolbar display with various functions. To move a note, select an edge of the box that surrounds the note, as shown in Figure 5–13 and drag the note to a new location.

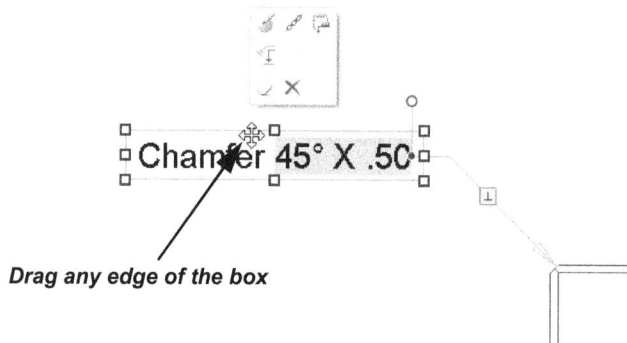

Drag any edge of the box

Figure 5–13

To rotate the note, select the green handle and move the cursor. The note rotates as shown in Figure 5–14.

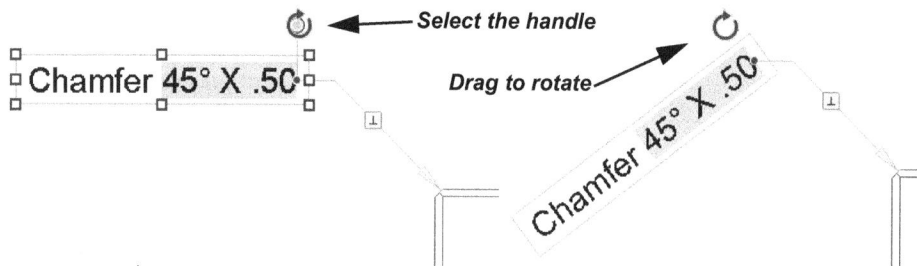

Select the handle

Drag to rotate

Figure 5–14

The following mini toolbar options are available when selecting a note:

Option	Description
(Properties)	Access the Note Properties dialog box.
(Change Reference)	Change leader attachment reference.
(Toggle Leader Type)	Change the type of leader used for the note.
(Move to View)	Move the note to another view.
(Erase)	Erase the note.
(Delete)	Delete the note.

Editing Attachments

To move the attachment point of a note along the current reference, select the note and use the handle shown in

Figure 5–15 or on the angular leader line segment. The symbol displays when you place the cursor over these locations.

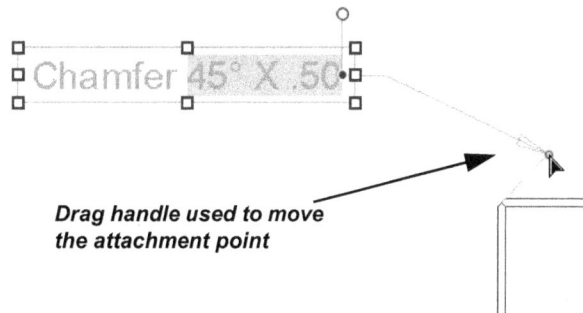

Drag handle used to move the attachment point

Figure 5–15

If you right-click on the handle at the end of the arrow, you can access the various arrow head styles, as shown in Figure 5–16.

You can also use the 🎵 (Arrow Style) option in the Annotate or Format tabs.

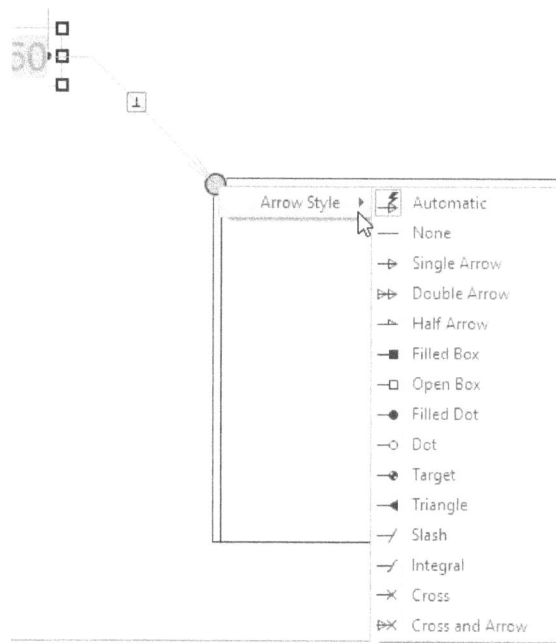

Figure 5–16

If you select the note leader and right-click, you can insert a jog, change the reference, change the arrow style, or delete the leader, as shown in Figure 5–17.

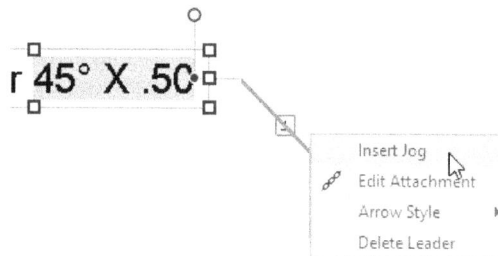

Figure 5–17

Modifying Text

To edit the text of a note, select the note to activate it, then click in the text field and make edits as required.

While editing a note, select text to access various formatting tools, as shown in Figure 5–18.

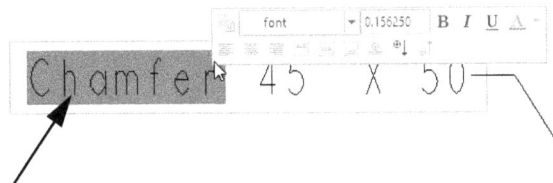

Select text to access the formatting options

Figure 5–18

Hyperlinks

To assign a hyperlink to a note, right-click the note and select **Add Hyperlink**. Alternatively, use 🔗 (Hyperlink) in the Operations group of the *Format* tab. The Edit Hyperlink dialog box opens as shown in Figure 5–19. You can enter the URL link and assign a screen tip that is visible when you move the cursor over the note.

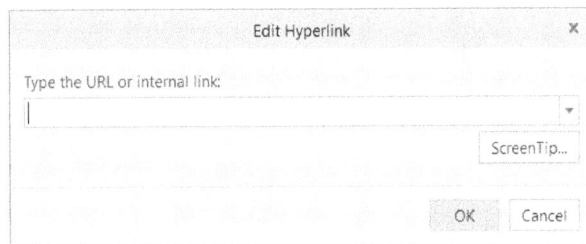

Figure 5–19

To activate a hyperlink, hold <Ctrl> while selecting the note in the drawing. The website displays in the Creo Parametric browser.

Superscript and Subscript Text

To create superscripts or subscripts in a note, use the x^2 (Superscript) and x_2 (Subscript) options in the Style group of the *Format* tab, as shown in Figure 5–20.

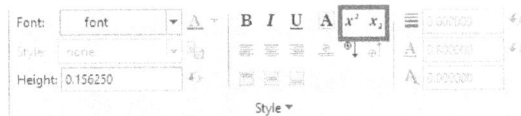

Figure 5–20

Outlining a Note

To enclose a note in a box, use the A (Box) option while entering or editing the note.

Modifying Text Styles

How To: Change the Text Style of a Note (or Other Text Entity)

1. Use the options in the Style group in the *Format* tab. For additional options, click the arrow in the Style group to open the Text Style dialog box.

2. Alternatively, click $\triangle$ (Text Style) in the Format group in the *Annotate* tab.

You can also preselect the items in the drawing and click $\triangle$ (Text Style) to open the Text Style dialog box.

3. Select the notes to edit. You can select individual items or multiple items using either <Ctrl> or the **Selection** tool.

4. Press the middle mouse button to complete the selection or click **OK**.

The Text Style dialog box opens as shown in Figure 5–21.

You can also open the Text Style dialog box by right-clicking on the item and selecting the Text Style tab in the Note Properties dialog box.

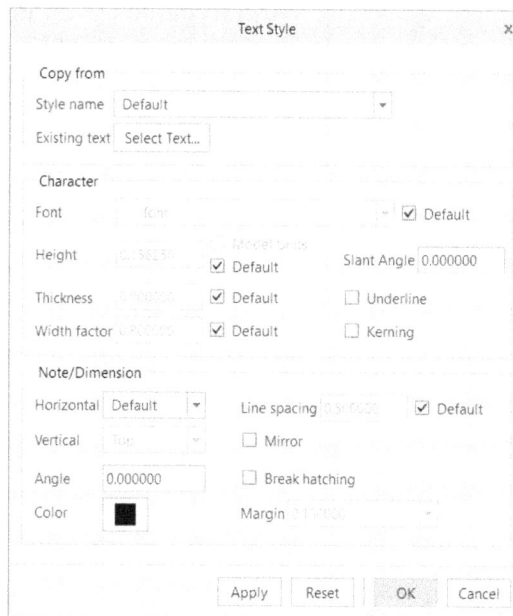

Figure 5–21

- To assign a style, select it in the **Style name** menu.

- To copy the style assigned to an existing note, click **Select Text** and select the note on the drawing.

- Changes to the *Character* area affect the selected text. You can select a portion of a text note (enclosed with {n:} brackets) and change it without affecting the rest of the note.

- Changes made in the *Note/Dimension* area affect the entire note, whether you select the whole note or a portion of it or not.

5. Click **Apply** to apply the changes to the drawing.
6. To apply this formatting change to another item in the drawing, select it and click ⚎ (Repeat Last Format) in the *Annotate* or *Format* tabs.

Text Editor

Once a note is created or exiting text is selected, you can click

⚎ (Text Editor) in the Note Tools group, in the *Format* tab of the ribbon. This opens the Text Editor dialog box, as shown in Figure 5–22.

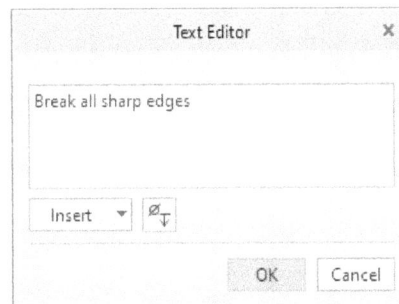

Figure 5–22

You can edit the text, or use the Insert drop-down list and select **From File** or **From Note** to add text from an existing text file or another note in the drawing respectively.

Use ⚎ (Select Symbol) to select a symbol from the palette. Any recently selected symbols are added to the upper portion of the Symbols dialog box, as shown in Figure 5–23.

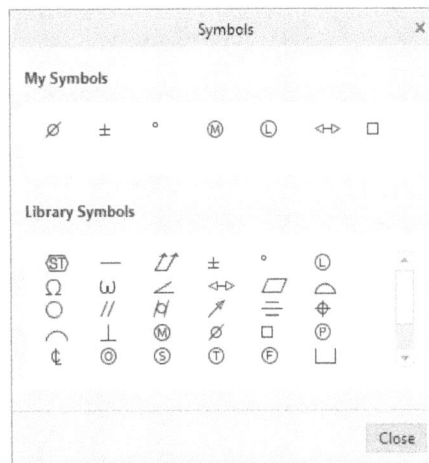

Figure 5–23

Creating a Style Library

The Text Style Gallery dialog box enables you to create a library of predefined text styles. Each text style has its own set of text attributes that are defined by the Text Style dialog box.

To create a style library, select **Format>Manage Text Styles** in the *Annotate* tab. The Text Style Gallery dialog box opens as shown in Figure 5–24.

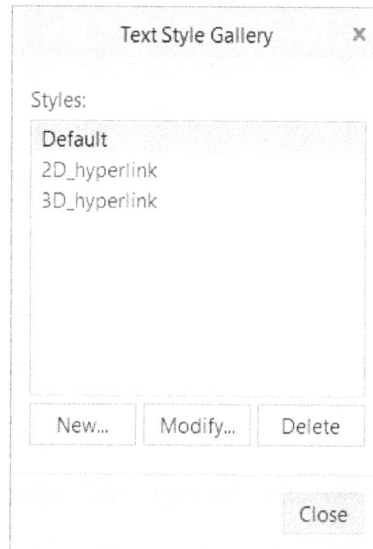

Text Style Gallery ✕

Styles:

Default
2D_hyperlink
3D_hyperlink

New...   Modify...   Delete

Close

Figure 5–24

Click **New**. The New Text Style dialog box opens as shown in Figure 5–25.

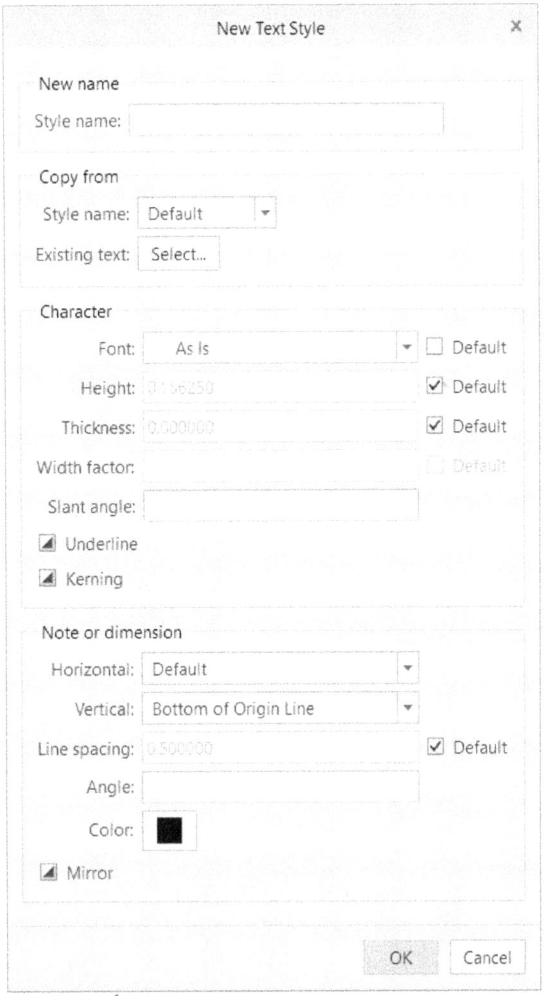

Figure 5–25

To use the same style library in multiple drawings, use a drawing template with a predefined style library.

Enter a name in the *Style name* field and define the text style attributes. Click **OK** to complete the definition of the style. The Text Style Gallery dialog box updates and lists all of the new styles.

When a style library is created, it is only saved in the active drawing. A new style library must be created for each subsequently created or opened drawing file.

Saving Notes

Notes can be saved for later reuse. To save a note, right-click on the note that you want to save and select **Save Note**. Enter the *File name*.

The note is always stored in the current working directory with a .txt.# file extension, where # is an integrating integer extension number.

Common notes can be placed in a specific directory. The **pro_note_dir** configuration option can be set to enable quick access to these notes. You can then browse to the *Note Text Directory* folder using the Open dialog box, as shown in Figure 5–26.

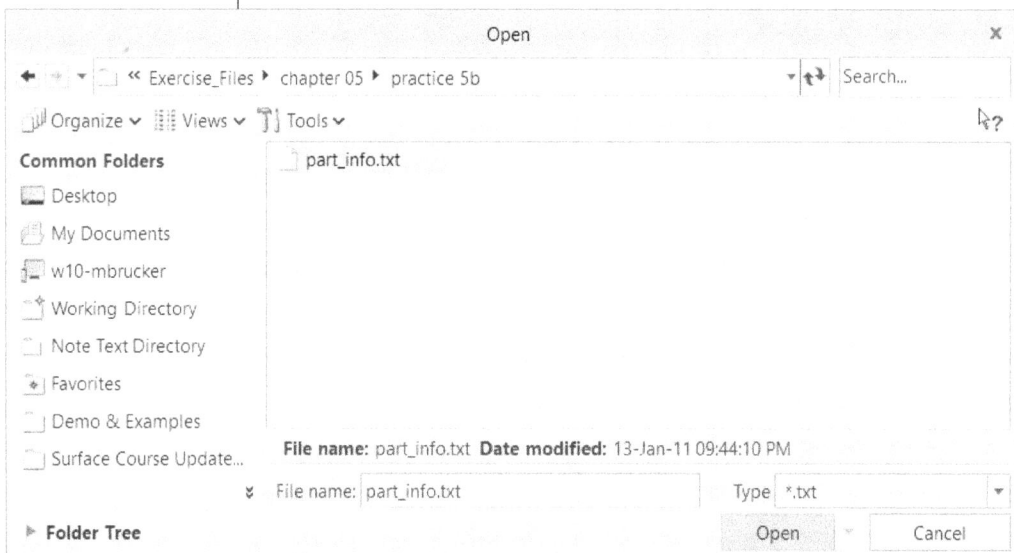

Figure 5–26

To place a note from a file, select the placement option as you would for a standard note, select the placement references, then press the middle mouse button to place the note. Instead of typing the note however, click ⒜ (Note From File) in the *Format* tab. Open the text file and it is imported into your note.

Model notes that have been created in a part or assembly model must be shown to be displayed in the drawing.

To show the note, click 🖹 (Show Model Annotations) and the ⒜ tab in the Show Model Annotation dialog box. Showing a model note uses the same techniques as those used to show model dimensions.

*To create notes in Part or Assembly mode, select the Annotate tab and click ⒜ in the Annotations group. Select **New** and add the note using the Note dialog box.*

5.2 Customizing Options

The configuration file options that enable you to customize how Creo Parametric handles note creation are described as follows:

Option	Values	Description
pro_note_dir	N/A	Sets a directory for saved notes (e.g., *c:\drawing\notes*).
switch_dims_for_notes	yes no	Sets the display of dimensions during note creation as symbolic.
symbol_palette_input	yes no	Displays the symbol palette during note creation.
todays_date_note_format	N/A	Sets the initial format of the **todays_date** parameter value (e.g., %Mmm. %dd, %yyyy = Jan. 01, 2012).

The drawing setup file options that enable you to customize how Creo Parametric handles note creation are described as follows:

Option	Values	Description
text_height	number	Sets the height of all of the text in the drawing (including notes). To control the height of individual notes, use the Text Style editor.
draw_arrow_length	number	Sets the length of the leader line arrow.
arrow_style	closed open filled	Controls the style of the arrow head for all of the detail items that use arrows.
dim_dot_box_style	default hollow filled	Controls the arrow style display of dots and boxes for leaders. When set to **default**, it uses the **draw_arrow_style** setting.
draw_arrow_width	default number	Sets the width of the leader line arrows.
draw_attach_sym_ height	default number	Sets the height of the leader line slashes, integral signs, and boxes. When set to **default** it uses the **draw_arrow_width** setting.

draw_attach_sym_width	default number	Sets the width of the leader line slashes, integral signs, and boxes. When set to **default**, it uses the **draw_arrow_width** setting.
draw_dot_diameter	default number	Sets the diameter of the leader line dots. When set to **default**, it uses the **draw_arrow_width** setting.
leader_elbow_length	number	Sets the length of the leader elbow (the horizontal leg attached to the text).
leader_extension_font	Dashfont Solidfont	Sets the font for the leader extension lines.

Practice 5a

Creating Notes

Practice Objectives

- Redefine an offset cross-section.
- Create notes as simple text.
- Create notes with user-defined parameters and process them.

In this practice, you will modify Section A-A and create notes. The final drawing displays as shown in Figure 5–27.

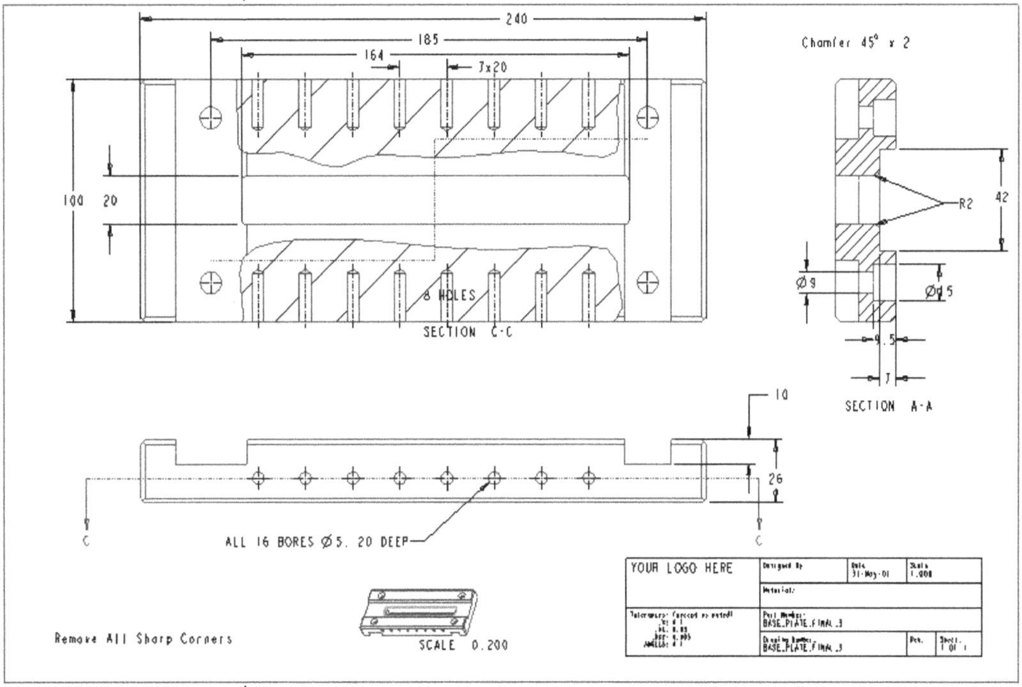

Figure 5–27

Task 1 - Open a drawing file.

*Base_plate_
final_3.drw references
the model **base_plate_
final_3.prt**.*

1. Set the working directory to the *Creating_Drawing_Notes* folder.

2. Open **base_plate_final_3.drw**.

3. Set the model display as follows:

   - (Datum Display Filters): All Off

   - (Display Style): (No Hidden)

Task 2 - Redefine cross-section A in the model.

1. Open the base plate model by right-clicking on the part name at the top of the Model Tree.

2. Scroll down to the bottom of the Model Tree. Sections **A**, **B**, and **C** are listed.

3. Expand section **A** to display the curve used to create the offset cross-section as shown in Figure 5–28.

Figure 5–28

4. Click **Curve id 8839** and select 🖌 (Edit Definition). The *Sketch* tab becomes active.

5. Click 🔲 (Sketch View) to orient the view.

6. Edit the cross-section as shown in Figure 5–29.

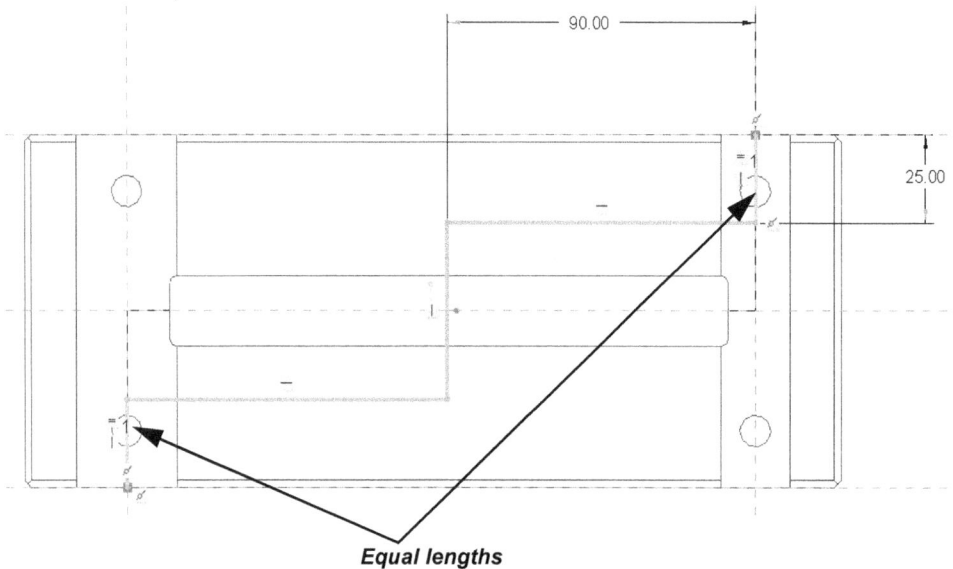

Figure 5–29

7. Click ✓ (OK) to complete the sketch.

8. Click cross-section **A** in the Model Tree and select ⛶ (Show Section) in the mini toolbar.

9. Save the model and close the model window.

Task 3 - Update the drawing.

---

1. If the **auto_regen_view** option is set to **yes**, the views are automatically regenerated. If set to **no**, you must manually regenerate the views by clicking ⟲ (Regenerate). You can also regenerate the sheet by right-clicking on the *Sheet 1* tab at the bottom of the window, and selecting **Update**.

Task 4 - Show the dimension for a chamfer and create a parametric note.

---

1. Select the *Annotate* tab.

2. Show the 45° x 2 dimension by selecting **Chamfer 1** in the Model Tree and selecting **Show Model Annotations** as shown in Figure 5–30.

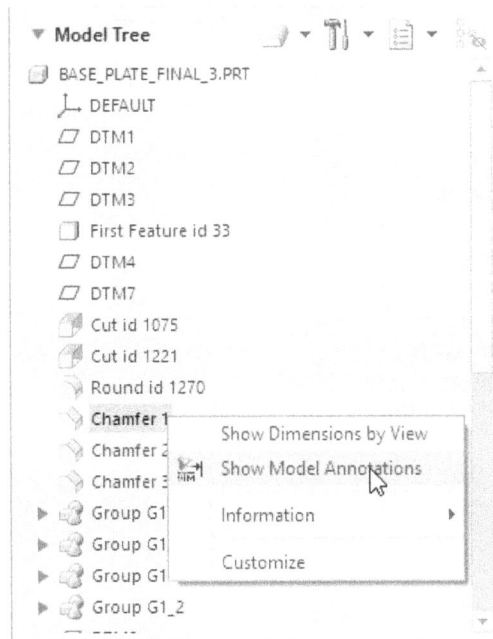

Figure 5–30

3. Accept the chamfer dimension as shown in Figure 5–31 and click **Apply**. Close the Show Model Annotations dialog box.

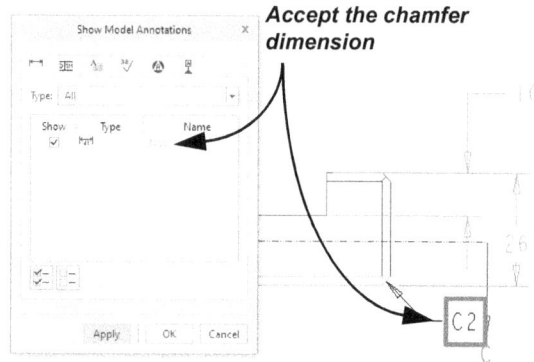

Figure 5–31

4. Expand A≣ (Note) in the *Annotate* tab and select A≣ (Unattached Note).

5. Select a location in the upper right corner of the drawing (as shown in Figure 5–32) to locate the note.

6. Click 15⁄ (Switch Dimensions) from the *Format* tab.

7. Enter **Chamfer 45° x &d455**. To enter the ° symbol, select it in the symbol palette in the *Format* tab.

8. Click on the screen to complete the note. The note displays as shown in Figure 5–32.

The previously displayed chamfer dimensions disappear. Shown dimensions can only be displayed once in a drawing. If the dimension displays parametrically in a note, it is removed from the drawing.

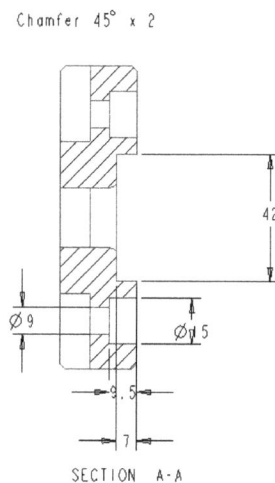

Figure 5–32

Task 5 - Show the dimension for the round.

1. Click 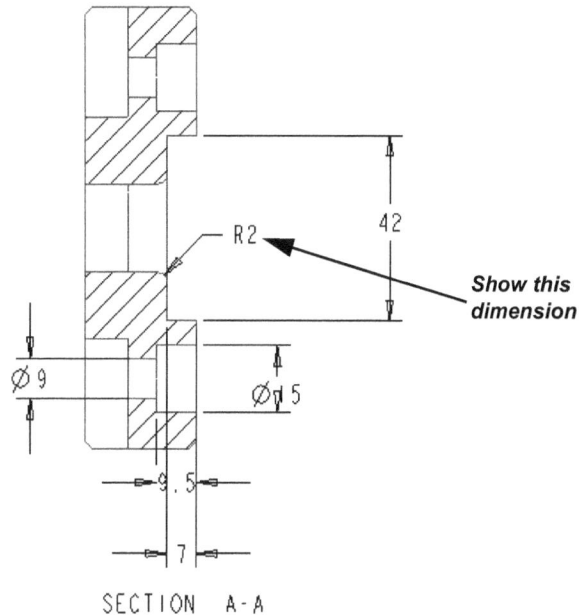 (Show Model Annotations). Show dimension **R2** (Round **id 1270**, dimension **d95**) in section view A-A, as shown in Figure 5–33.

Chamfer 45° x 2

R2

42

Show this dimension

Ø 9

Ø 15

9.5

7

SECTION A-A

Figure 5–33

2. Close the Show Model Annotations dialog box.

To display the numerical value of a dimension in a note, you must know its symbolic name.

Task 6 - Add a parametric note displaying the round's dimension value.

1. Expand ^A (Note) and select ✓^A (Leader Note).

2. Hold <Ctrl> and select the two edges of feature **F10(ROUND)**, as shown in Figure 5–34.

3. Press the middle mouse button to place the note in the location shown in Figure 5–34.

4. Enter **R&d95** in the text field. Click anywhere on the screen.

5. The note displays as shown in Figure 5–34. The original dimension value is removed because a shown dimension can only be shown once in a drawing.

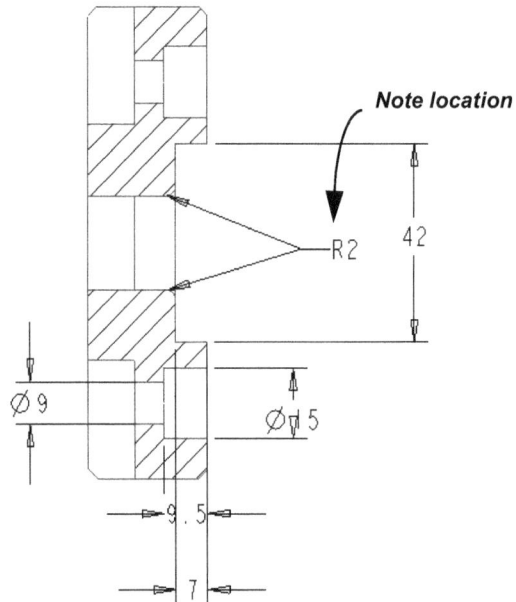

Figure 5–34

Task 7 - Create a note with a user-defined parameter and dimension.

The Note icon changes to match the last used option.

1. Click $\nwarrow^{\text{A}}$ (Note).

2. Select the edge shown Figure 5–35 as the attachment in the lower projected view. If required, use the **Pick From List** to select the feature **F40 (HOLE)**.

3. Press the middle mouse button to place the note.

Bores is a user-defined parameter. The value .0 forces the Bores parameter value to display no decimal places. The dimensions d374 and d373 were used to create the feature.

4. Select the note placement and enter **ALL &BORES[.0] BORES Ø&d374, &d373 DEEP** as the note. Click on the screen to complete the note, which displays as shown in Figure 5–35.

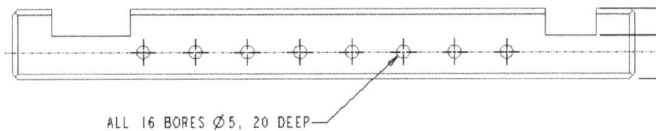

ALL 16 BORES Ø5, 20 DEEP

Figure 5–35

Task 8 - Create a new note.

1. Create a note in the lower left corner of the drawing that says, **Remove all Sharp Corners**. Use $^{\text{A}}\equiv$ (Unattached Note). The note displays as shown in Figure 5–36.

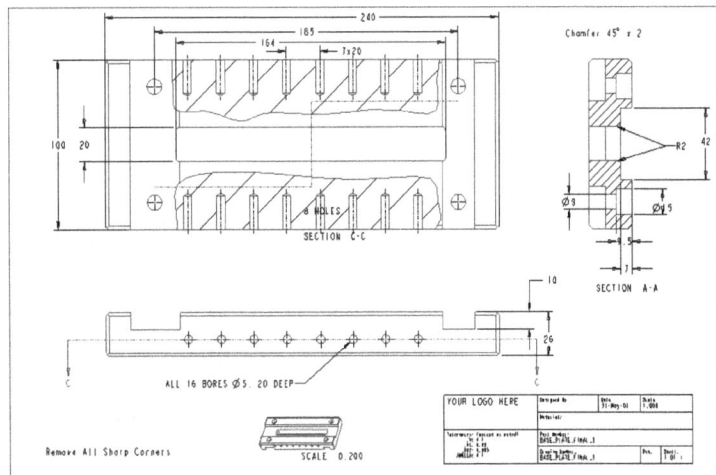

Figure 5–36

2. Save the drawing and close the window.

Practice 5b | Read a Note From File

Practice Objective

- Read a note from file.

In this practice, you will import a text file to create a note in the flywheel drawing. You will also edit the note and modify the text style. The final drawing displays as shown in Figure 5–37.

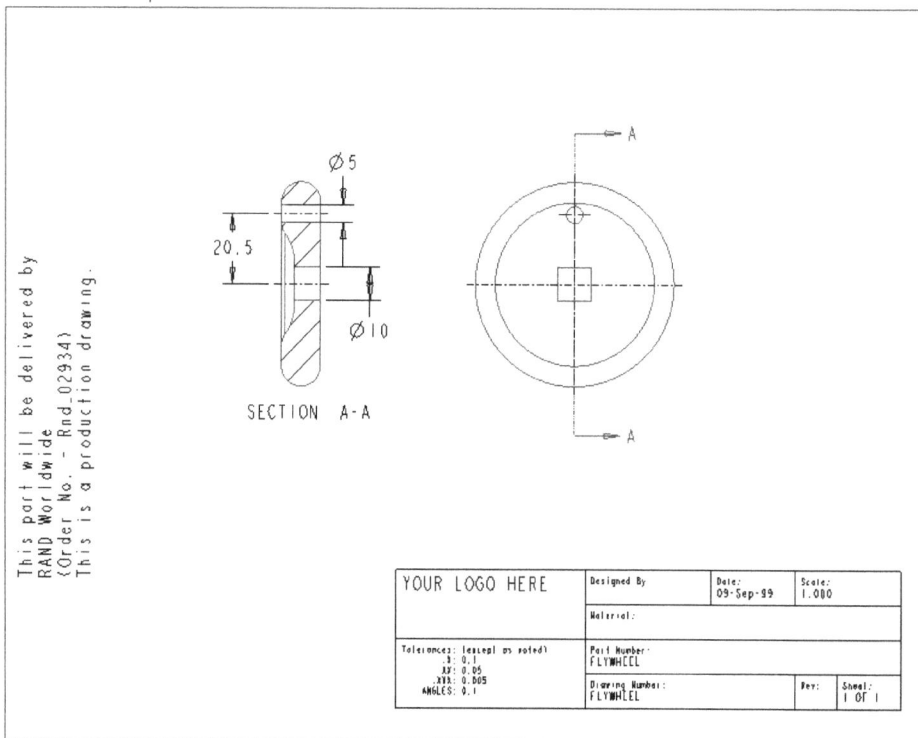

Figure 5–37

Task 1 - Open a drawing file.

1. Set the working directory to the *Note_From_File* folder.

2. Open **flywheel.drw**.

3. Set the model display as follows:

   - ⚒ *(Datum Display Filters)*: All Off

   - ⬜ *(Display Style)*: ⬜ (No Hidden)

Task 2 - Read a note from an existing file.

Ensure that the Annotate tab is selected.

1. Select the *Annotate* tab.

2. Click $\overset{A}{\equiv}$ (Note).

3. Select a location on the lower left corner (as shown in Figure 5–38) to place the note.

4. Click $\overset{A}{\equiv}$ (Note From File) in the *Format* tab.

5. Double-click on the file **part_info.txt**.

6. Click on the screen to complete the note. The note displays as shown in Figure 5–38.

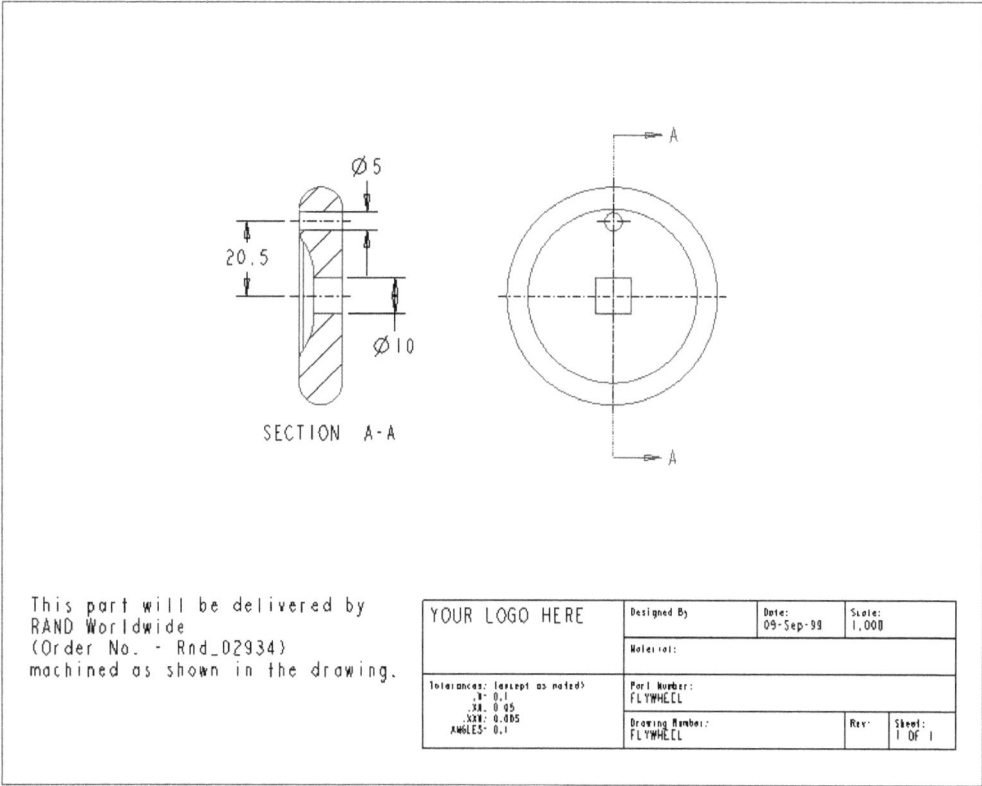

Figure 5–38

Task 3 - Modify the note text and its font.

1. Select the note and highlight the last line of text.

2. Edit the last line of the note by entering **This is a production drawing**, as shown in Figure 5–39.

Figure 5–39

3. Select the note, then click on any text in the note and select **isofont** from the Font drop-down list in the *Format* tab, as shown in Figure 5–40.

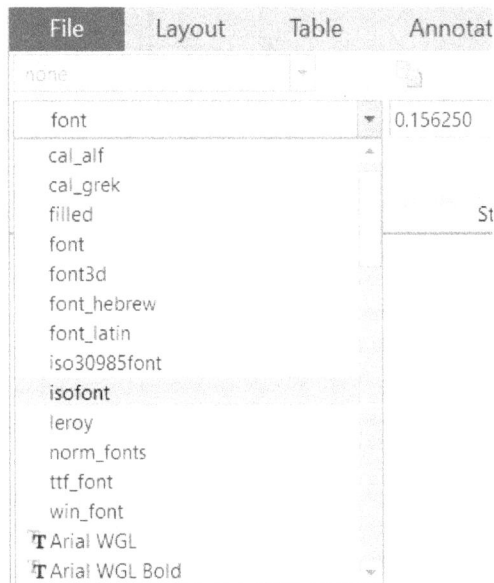

Figure 5–40

4. Select the drag handle and rotate the text, as shown in Figure 5–41.

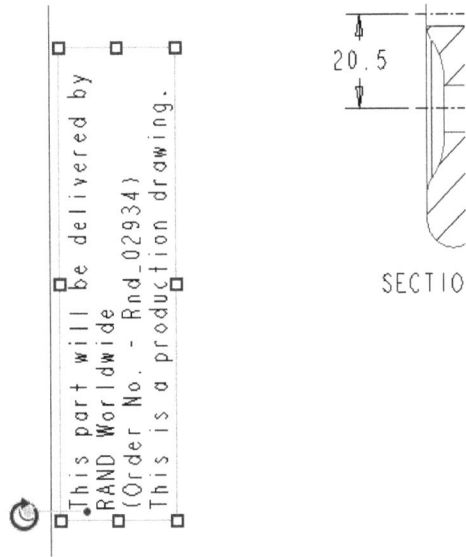

Figure 5–41

5. Select on the screen to complete the edits. The drawing displays as shown in Figure 5–42.

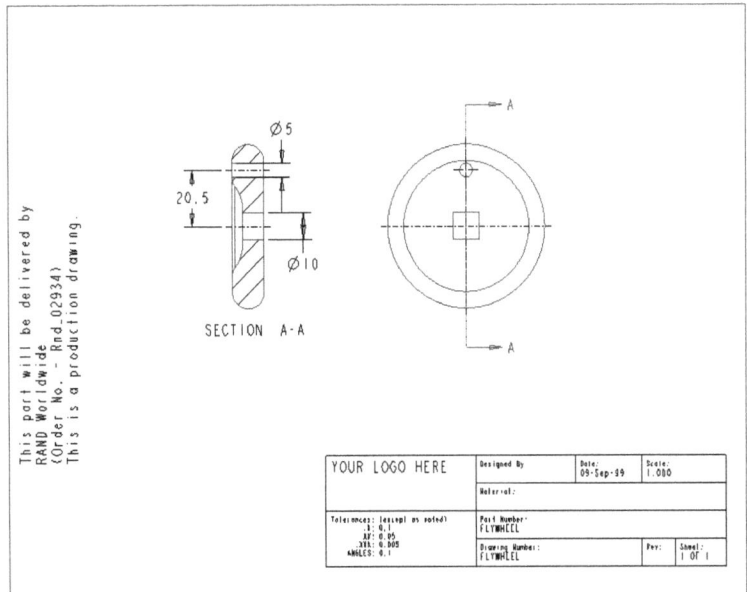

Figure 5–42

6. Save the drawing and close the window.

Chapter Review Questions

1. In addition to user-defined text, which of the following information can be included in drawing notes? (Select all that apply.)

    a. Dimensions

    b. System-defined parameters

    c. User-defined parameters

    d. Special characters

2. To add a dimension value to a note, you must enter the symbolic name for the dimension preceded which symbol.

    a. *

    b. &

    c. #

    d. No symbol is required.

3. Which of the following methods enables you to modify the text in a note? (Select all that apply.)

    a. Right-click on the note and select **Modify**.

    b. Right-click on the note and select **Properties**.

    c. Select the note to activate it.

    d. Select the note and select **Annotations>Modify**.

4. Which of the following options enable you to enclose a note in a box?

    a. ⊟

    b. A

    c. ⬚

    d. ▱

Tolerances

Creo Parametric enables you to assign both dimensional and geometric tolerances in a drawing. It also enables you to set tolerances for part and assembly dimensions using ISO or ANSI standards. Specifying geometric tolerances in Creo Parametric enables you to set critical surfaces, explain how they relate to one another, and set inspection criteria.

Learning Objectives in This Chapter

- Set the tolerance display configuration option and learn the different formats to display tolerances in the drawing.
- Change the tolerance setup options in the Model Properties dialog box.
- Use the Properties dialog box to modify tolerances individually in the drawing.
- Learn to set or create datum references for geometrical tolerances.
- Create a geometrical tolerance by selecting the type, references, datum references, value, and symbols in the dialog box.
- Learn to display and copy geometric tolerances in the drawing.
- Review configuration file options to customize dimensional and geometrical tolerances in the Creo Parametric environment.
- Review drawing setup file options to customize dimensional and geometric tolerances in the drawing environment.

6.1 Showing Dimensional Tolerances

Dimensional tolerances can be displayed in Part or Assembly mode by setting the **tol_display** option to **yes** in the configuration file(config.pro). To display dimensional tolerances in Drawing mode, set **tol_display** in the Detail Options file (stored in the part or assembly) to **yes**.

The format (e.g., limits or plusminus) for tolerances in all modes is controlled by the **default_tolerance_mode** configuration option in the Options dialog box.

In part or assembly mode, you access the Options dialog box by selecting **File>Prepare>Model Properties>Detail Options**. In Drawing mode, select **File>Prepare>Drawing Properties> Detail Options**.

Once enabled, the format can be changed individually using the Dimension Properties dialog box, which is available in the Part, Assembly, and Drawing modes. The format options are as follows.

Option	Format	Description
nominal (default)	99.7 100.3	Displays the dimension tolerance with upper and lower limits.
limits	100	Displays the dimension without tolerances.
plusminus	+0.3 100 -0.3	Displays the dimension with independent plus and minus values.
plusminussym	100±0.3	Displays the dimension with a single ± value.
plusminussym _super	$100\pm^{0.3}$	Displays the dimension with a single ± value, but displayed as a superscript.

The **default_tolerance_mode** configuration option only affects newly created dimensions. When working with dimensions that were created before setting the configuration option, you must manually set the Tolerance modes using the Dimension Properties dialog box.

6.2 Set Tolerance Standards

Creo Parametric enables you to set tolerances for part and assembly dimensions using ISO or ANSI standards. ISO tolerances are based on a set of tolerance tables, while ANSI tolerances are based on the number of digits in the nominal dimension.

How To: Set the Tolerance Standard for Part/Assembly Dimensions

1. While in Part or Assembly mode, select **File>Prepare>Model Properties** to open the Model Properties dialog box. Select **change** for the Tolerance property, as shown in Figure 6–1.

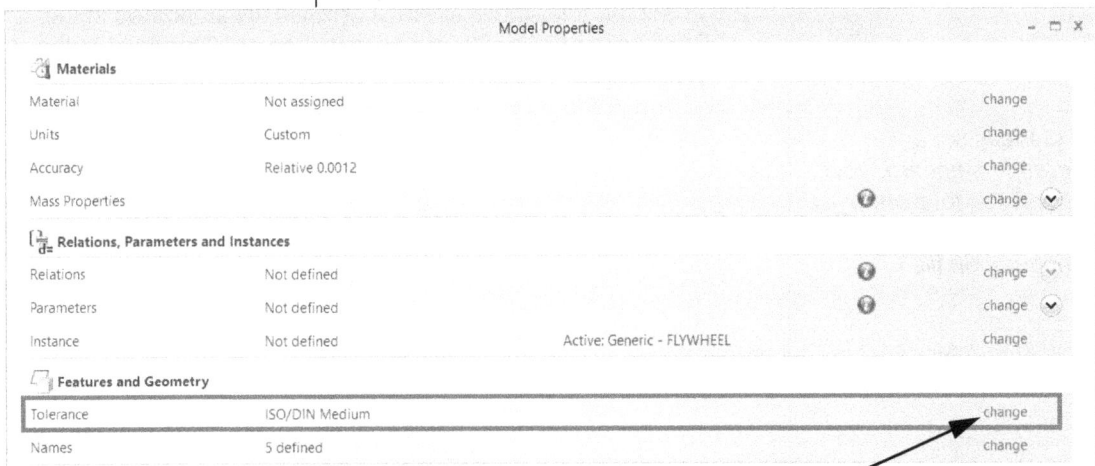

Select this option

Figure 6–1

The **TOL SETUP** menu displays. The options set for part/assembly dimensions are automatically recognized while you are creating a drawing of a part or assembly. Setting the tolerance standard only affects those dimensions, which are shown on the model or created using model geometry.

While in Drawing mode, you can set the tolerance standard for drawing dimensions created using 2D draft geometry. Select **File>Prepare>Drawing Properties**. Select **change** next to Tolerance. You can then use the options in the **TOL SETUP** menu, as shown in Figure 6–2.

Figure 6–2

2. To set the tolerances to ANSI or ISO/DIN standards in the Part, Assembly, or Drawing modes, select **Standard** in the **TOL SETUP** menu. The **TOL STANDARD** menu displays as shown in Figure 6–3.

Figure 6–3

*To globally set a tolerance standard, you can set the **tolerance_ standard** option in the configuration file.*

ISO Standards

ISO tolerances are based on a set of tolerance tables. A tolerance table contains a specific tolerance value for a range of values. Each range can have different tolerance values for each class (e.g., fine or medium). A standard tolerance table is shown in Figure 6–4.

Figure 6–4

Select **File>Prepare>Model properties**. Select **change** in the Tolerance line to open the **TOL SETUP** menu. To set the tolerance standard to ISO, select **ISO/DIN** in the **TOL STANDARD** menu. The **Model Class** and **Tol Tables** options in the **TOL SETUP** menu are now activated, as shown in Figure 6–5.

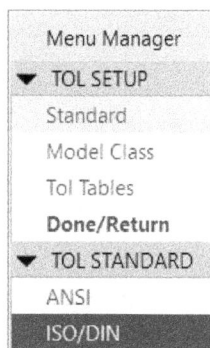

Figure 6–5

The **Model Class** option enables you to define the level of tolerance values that are used. A more coarse level results in a wider tolerance standard. The **TOL CLASSES** menu displays as shown in Figure 6–6.

*To globally set a tolerance class, you can set the **tolerance_class** option in the configuration file.*

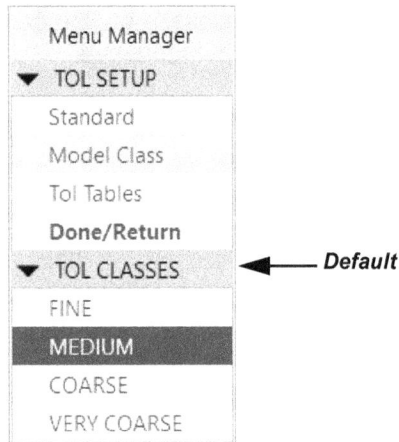

Figure 6–6

To modify, open, show, or save a tolerance table, select **Tol Tables**. The **TOL TBL ACT** menu displays as shown in Figure 6–7.

Figure 6–7

Creo Parametric contains four default tolerance tables: General Dims, Broken Edges, Shafts, and Holes. To create and assign a new tolerance table based on one of these default tables, select **Modify Value** and select the table. When you are finished editing the table, save it with a new name and open it.

ANSI Standards

ANSI tolerances are based on the number of digits in the nominal dimension. To switch to ANSI standards, select **ANSI** in the **TOL STANDARD** menu.

3. Changes made to tolerance values or their formats in any one of the three modes (Part, Assembly, or Drawing) are reflected in the other modes. Use one of the following methods to change the tolerances in Drawing mode:

   • Double-click on the tolerance and enter a new value.

   • Select the dimension to open the *Dimension* tab in the ribbon. Click an option in the **Tolerance** menu to set the tolerance type, or enter a value for the tolerance, as shown in Figure 6-8.

The options in the Value and tolerance areas in the dialog box vary depending on the Tolerance mode.

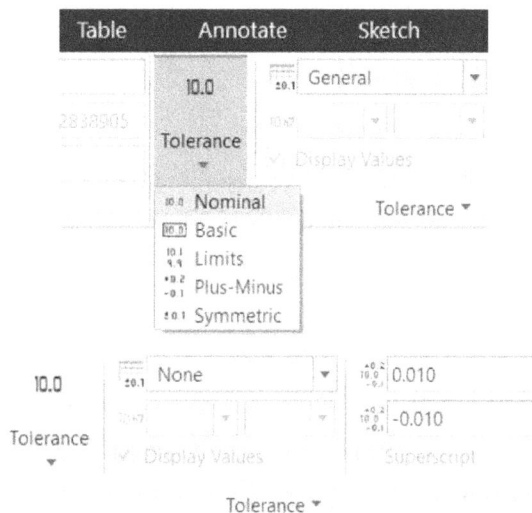

Figure 6–8

6.3 Datum Feature Symbols

To create a datum feature symbol, click ⍑ (Datum Feature Symbol) in the *Annotate* tab and a preview is immediately attached to the cursor. Drag the preview to the attachment reference, then press the middle mouse button to place it, as shown in Figure 6–9.

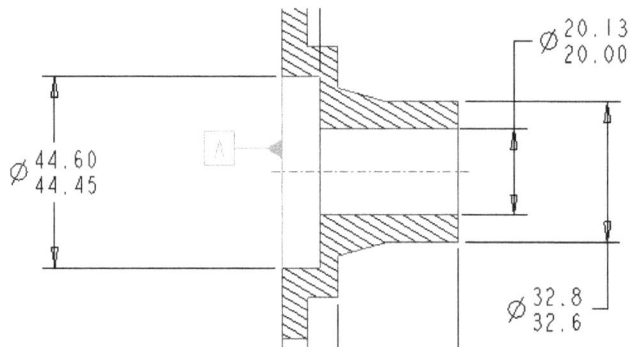

Figure 6–9

The datum feature options are available in the *Datum Feature* tab, as shown in Figure 6–10. This tab displays after the datum is placed on the screen. To close the tab, click anywhere on the screen. If you select a datum from the screen, the tab opens.

Figure 6–10

You can change the attachment reference by clicking the Datum Feature Symbol and selecting 🔗 (Change Reference) in the mini toolbar, as shown in Figure 6–11.

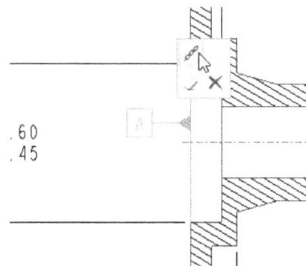

Figure 6–11

Automatic Naming

When you create a datum feature symbol, the next available name in the standard sequence (A, B, C, etc.) is automatically assigned. You can manually enter a label at any time using the field in the *Datum Feature* tab. If a datum label in the sequence is missing, the next datum created will have the missing label. For example, if datum A and datum C exist on the drawing, the next label will automatically be assigned to B.

Additional Text

You can include additional text with a datum feature symbol using the *Additional text* field. If you click 🔲ᴬ¹ (Rotate Text Position), the text will move around the datum label, as shown in Figure 6–12.

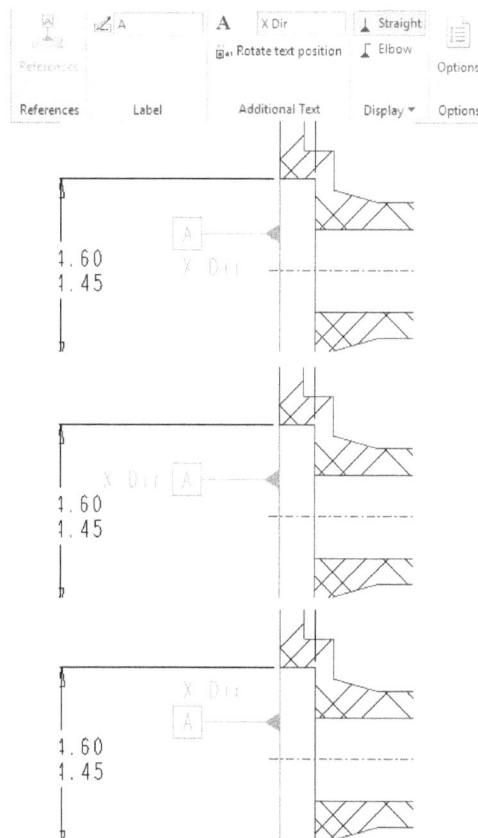

Figure 6–12

Adding Elbows

You can click ⊥ (Elbow) to add an elbow to the datum feature symbol. You can adjust the length of the elbow by pressing <Shift> when you drag the label.

6.4 Create Geometric Tolerances

Specifying geometric tolerances in Creo Parametric enables you to set critical surfaces, explain how they relate to one another, and set inspection criteria. Unlike dimensional tolerances, geometric tolerances do not have an effect on geometry.

How To: Create a Geometric Tolerance

1. Select the *Annotate* tab to activate the annotation options.
2. Geometric tolerances are created based on reference entities and can be created in the model or drawing. The reference entities are called Datum Feature Symbols.
3. Click ⊞⊤ₘ (Geometric Tolerance) in the Annotations group or right-click and select ⊞⊤ₘ (Geometric Tolerance) to start the creation of a geometric tolerance. The Geometric Tolerance dialog box opens as shown in Figure 6–13.

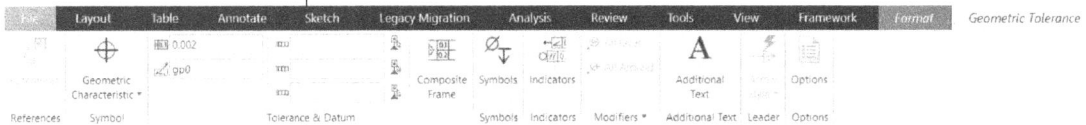

Figure 6–13

4. Select the entity that you want to attach the geometric tolerance to. The geometric tolerance will display as shown in Figure 6–14.

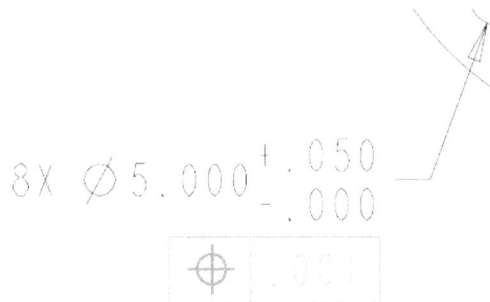

Figure 6–14

5. If attaching the geometric tolerance with a leader, move the geometric tolerance to the required position and click the middle mouse button to place the geometric tolerance.

6. Select the type of geometric tolerance by choosing an option from the Geometric Characteristic menu, as shown in Figure 6–15.

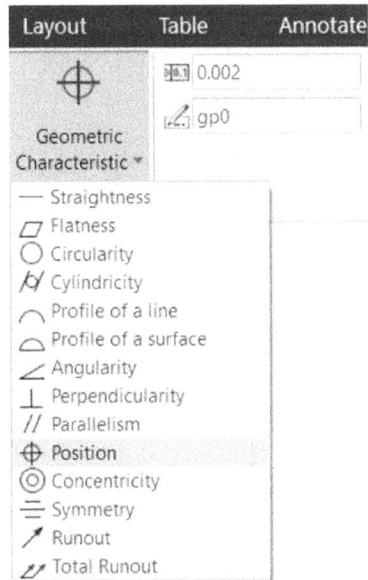

Figure 6–15

7. In the Tolerance & Datum group, enter a value for the tolerance, as show in Figure 6–16.

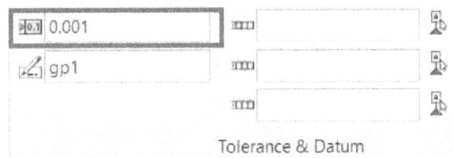

Figure 6–16

8. In the Tolerance & Datum group, enter a value for the tolerance *Name*, as show in Figure 6–17.

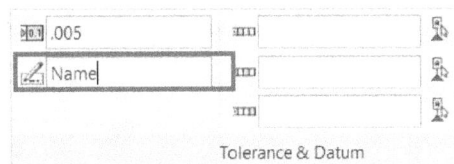

Figure 6–17

9. Set the Datums to be referenced in the Geometric Tolerance. You can select an existing Datum Feature Symbol from the drawing by first selecting ⬚ (Datum Reference) in the Tolerance & Datum group, next to the *Primary, Secondary,* or *Tertiary* datum fields, as shown in Figure 6–18.

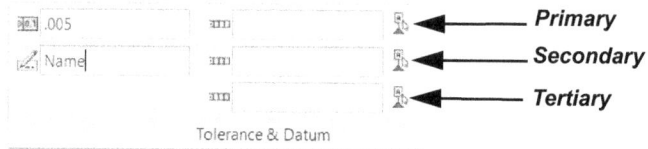

Figure 6–18

You may also type in the Datum Reference fields instead of selecting a datum from the drawing.

If you type the name of a datum that is already in the model or drawing, it will display in green text in the dashboard. If not, it will display in black text.

10. Select the datum feature symbol (in this case Datum A) from the drawing as the Primary datum reference. The GTOL updates as shown in Figure 6–19.

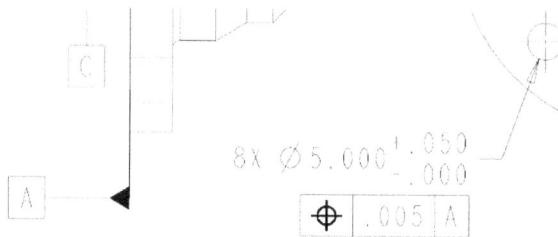

Figure 6–19

11. Select the Secondary and Tertiary datums, as required. The geometric tolerance updates as shown in Figure 6–20 with datum C selected as the Secondary datum reference.

Figure 6–20

12. Additional symbols may now be added to the geometric tolerance. First, click in the field in which you want to add the text or symbol. Then, add a maximum material condition symbol after the tolerance value, as shown in Figure 6–21.

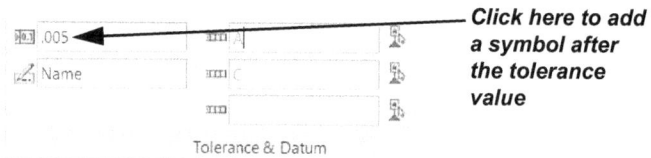

Figure 6–21

You can type spaces as required, to separate symbols and text.

13. In the *Geometric Tolerance* tab, expand (Symbols) and select a symbol, as shown in Figure 6–22.

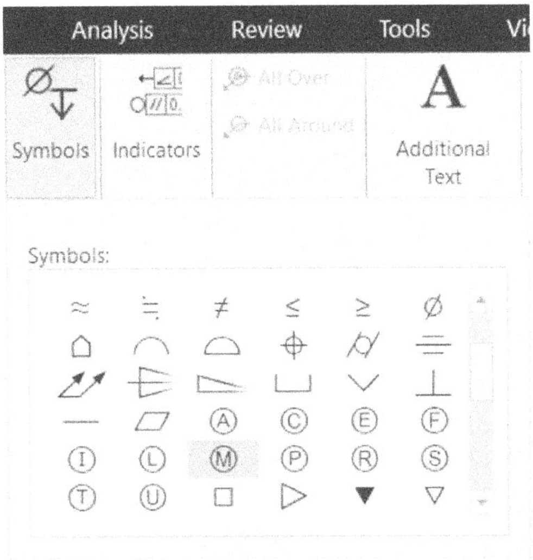

Figure 6–22

- The geometric tolerance updates to show the maximum material condition symbol, as shown in Figure 6–23.

Figure 6–23

- You can add additional symbols in other locations, such as maximum material condition after datum C, as shown in Figure 6–24.

Figure 6–24

14. Additional text may also be added above, below, to the left or to the right of the geometric tolerance. Enter text in the appropriate filed in the Additional Text panel, as shown in Figure 6–25.

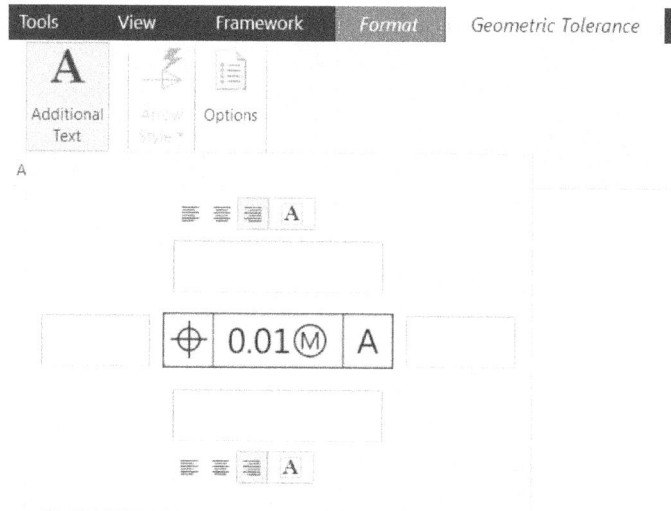

Figure 6–25

Symbols may also be included in the additional text fields.

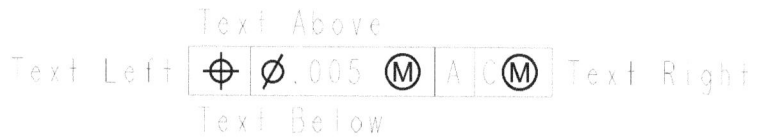

The geometric tolerance updates with the additional text, as shown in Figure 6–26.

Figure 6–26

Showing Geometric Tolerances

Geometric tolerances created in the model can be displayed in the drawing by clicking ⬛ (Geometric Tolerance) in the Show Model Annotations dialog box, as shown in Figure 6–27.

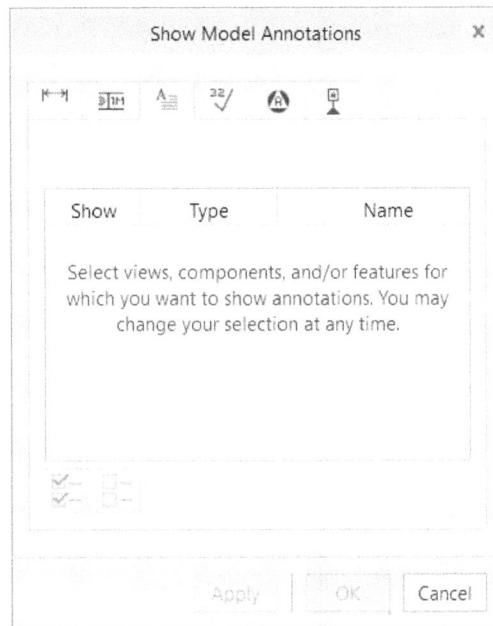

Figure 6–27

Composite Geometric Tolerances

You can create composite tolerance frames by clicking ⬛ (Composite Frame). The Composite Frame panel that expands enables you to edit the tolerances and datums, as shown in Figure 6–28.

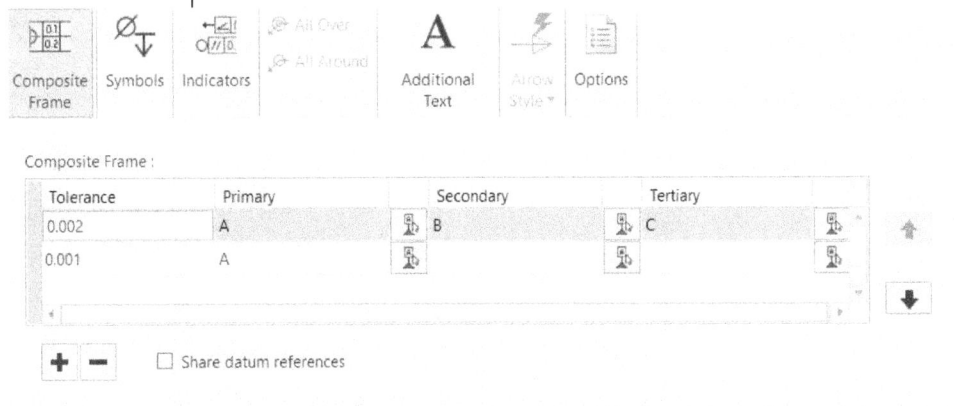

Figure 6–28

ISO GPS Indicators

You can use ⬚ (Indicators) to add indicators to your Geometric Tolerance to comply with ISO GPS standards. You can click

⬚ (Indicators) to expand the Indicators Frame, as shown in Figure 6–29.

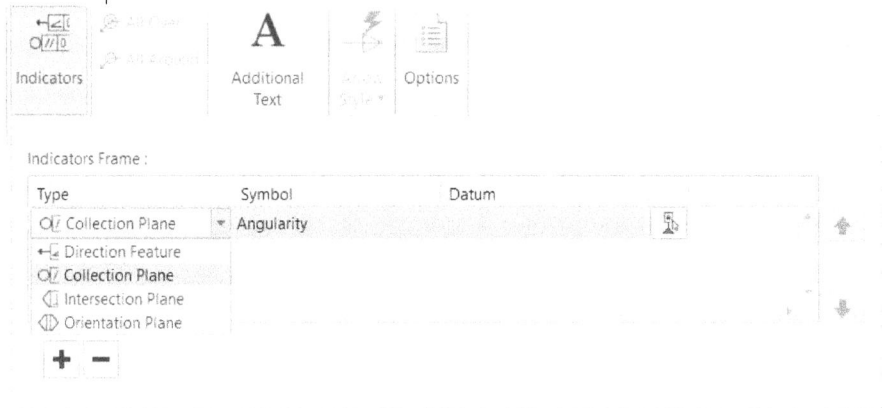

Figure 6–29

6.5 Syntax Checking

Datum target and Geometric tolerance annotations have built-in syntax checking. This ensures that the following comply with ASME and ISO GD&T standards:

- Datum names.

- The datum reference for Datum targets.

- The specified tolerance value and datum references, including modifiers, for Geometric tolerances.

Datum and Datum Target

For datum feature symbols, if you enter a value for the datum label that does not comply with standards, you will receive a notification. The datum labels are checked to ensure that they conform to the conventions specified by the ASME Y14.5 standard. To comply with the standard, the label must be either one or two uppercase letters, where the letters O, Q, and I are not permitted. In the example shown in Figure 6–30, the datum name was entered in lowercase, which does not meet the standard requirement that it should be uppercase. The system highlights it in the dashboard as well as on the drawing.

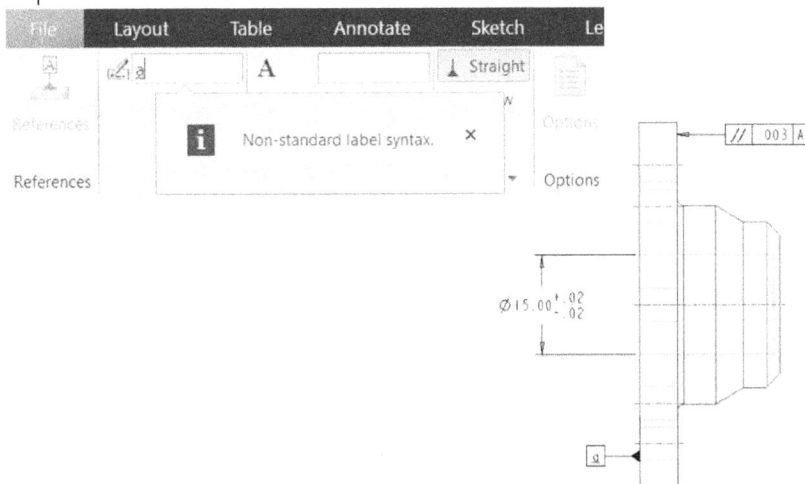

Figure 6–30

Datum features follow the convention of a letter proceeded by a number. For datum targets, if the text typed into the datum reference field does not meet the standard convention, it is identified in the ribbon as well as in the graphics area, as shown in Figure 6–31.

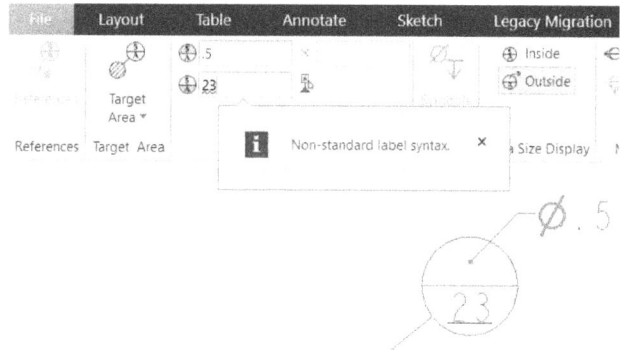

Figure 6–31

In either case, fixing the datum feature reference to comply with the convention clears the syntax check error.

Geometric Tolerance

For geometric tolerance annotations, if the text or symbols entered in the value or datum reference fields do not meet the standard, the issue is highlighted in the *Geometric Tolerance* tab and the graphics area, as shown in Figure 6–32.

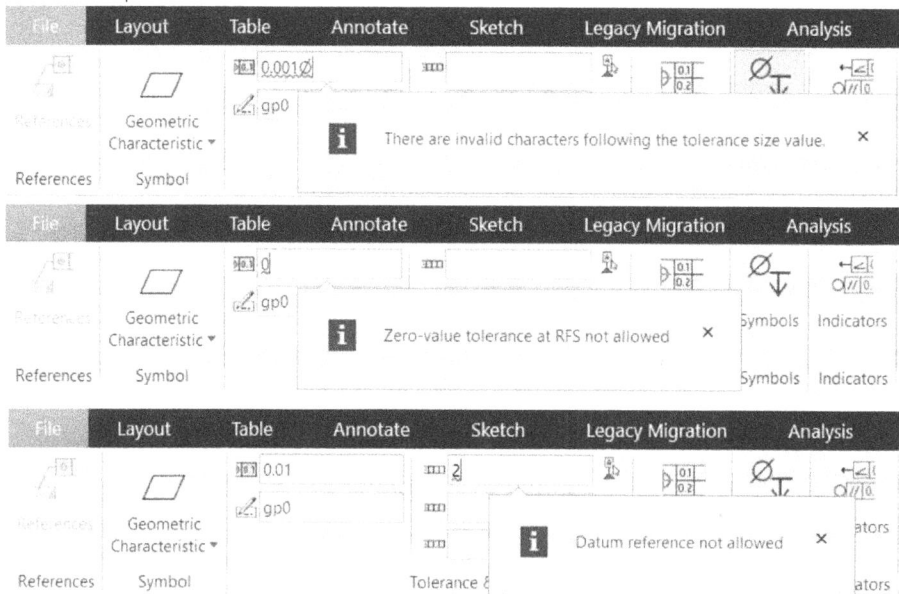

Figure 6–32

6.6 Handling Legacy Datums

In previous releases of Creo Parametric, a Set Datum was created as a property of a plane or axis feature. Now, a Datum Feature Symbol is created as either a standalone annotation, or inside of an annotation feature, and can only be placed on a surface, dimension, witness line, or GTOL.

In Creo Parametric 3.0 and earlier, Set Datum Tags could be created in one of two ways:

1. Using the ◁⊣ (Set Datum Tag annotation) option in the Datum dialog box (as shown in Figure 6–33), or the ⌐ (Set Datum Tag annotation element) option from inside an annotation feature.

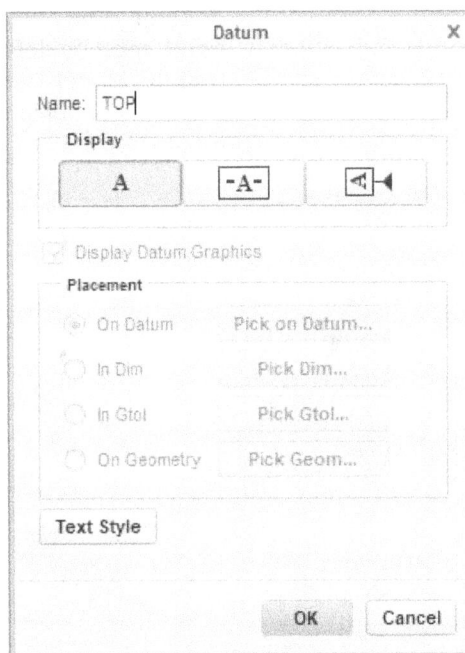

Figure 6–33

2. Using the -A- (Set) option in the Datum dialog box.

Prior to Creo Parametric 4.0, Set Datums were derived from existing datum planes or axes. Now, Datum Feature Symbols must be associated with model geometry. This means that when you open a model that was created in Creo Parametric 3.0 or earlier, you have to update any existing Set Datums to Datum Feature Symbols if you need to make any changes to dimensions, Geometric Tolerances, and so on. It is important to note that the Set Datums might also be connected to geometric tolerances, so you must manage that circumstance as well.

As of Creo Parametric 4.0 M060, a Legacy Datum Annotations Conversion tool is available to help convert legacy datums to datum feature symbol annotations.

The following steps should be followed:

1. Set the configuration option **combined_state_type** to **mbd** or **semi_mbd**. Note that Creo Parametric 5.0 uses **semi_mbd** by default.
2. Use the Model Tree Items dialog box to ensure **Annotations** display is enabled in the Model Tree, as shown in Figure 6–34.

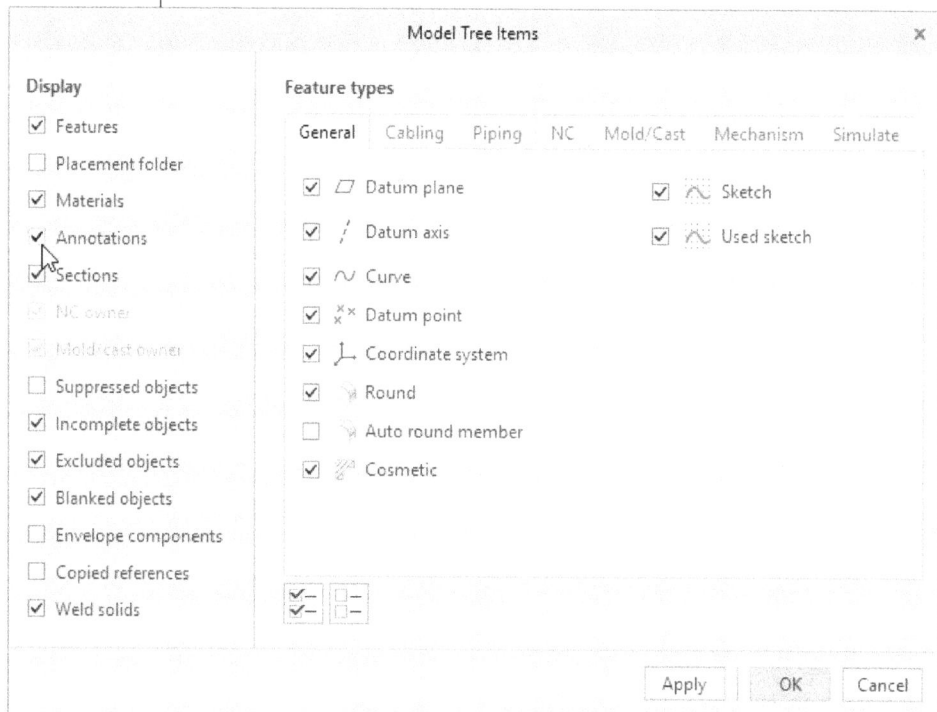

Figure 6–34

3. Right-click an annotation in the Detail Tree or Annotations group in the Model Tree and click **Convert All**, as shown in Figure 6–35.

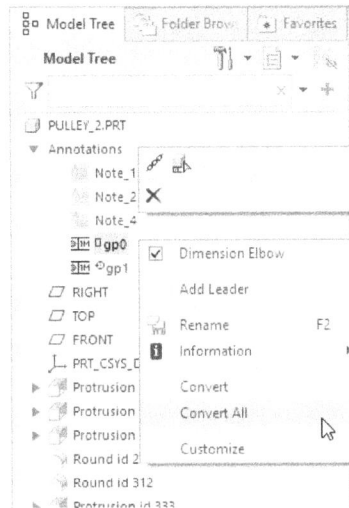

Figure 6–35

4. In the ribbon, select the *Annotate* tab and click **Annotations>Legacy Datum Annotations Conversion** to open the Legacy Datum Annotations Conversion dialog box, as shown in Figure 6–36.

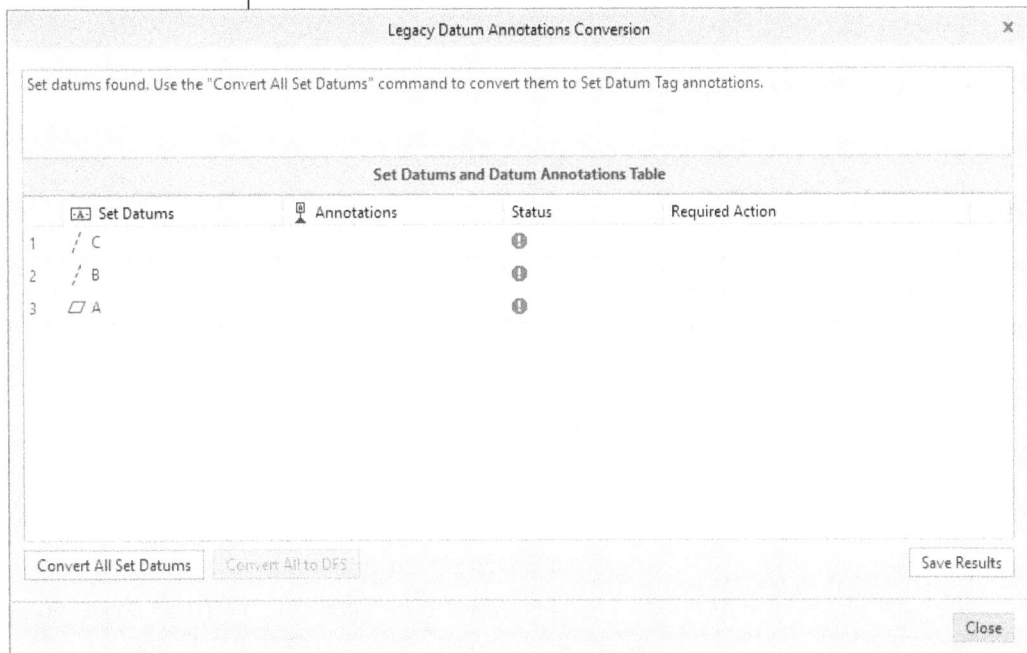

Figure 6–36

Note the following:

- If you are working in Drawing mode, you must open the model and access the Legacy Datum Annotations Conversion dialog box from there.

- If you are working in Assembly mode, you must access the Legacy Datum Annotations Conversion dialog box from the top model.

- For annotations assigned from an inheritance feature, the Legacy Datum Annotations Conversion dialog box must be accessed from the source model.

5. All legacy Set Datums must be converted to Set Datum Tag annotations. Click **Convert All Set Datums** to complete that conversion. The results of the conversion display in the Set Datums and Datum Annotations Table of the Legacy Datum Annotations Conversion dialog box, as shown in Figure 6–37.

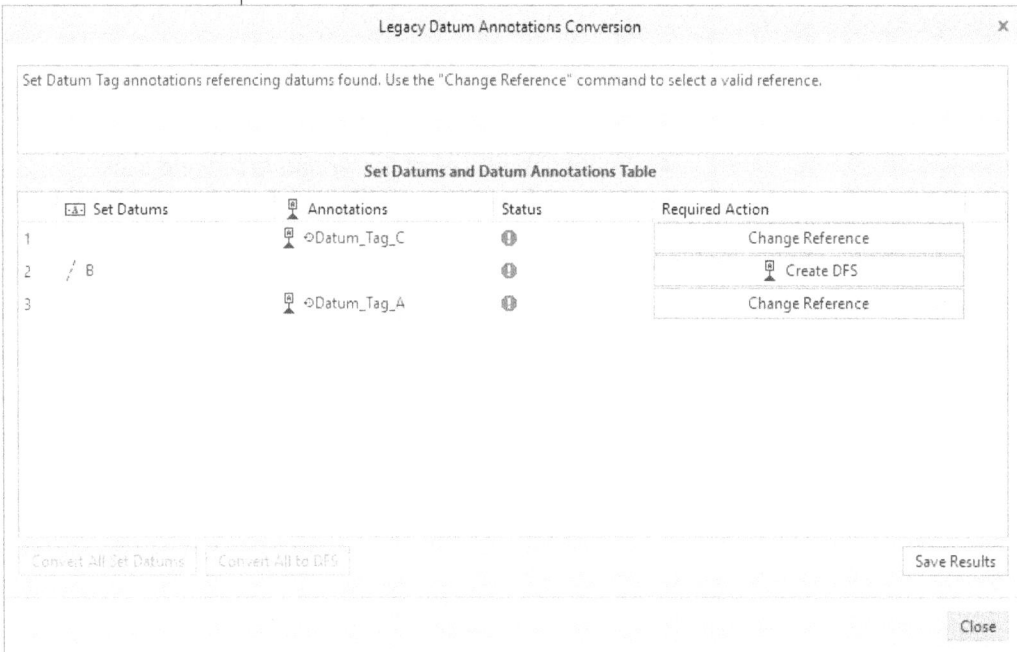

Figure 6–37

- If the conversion is successful, the datum is moved from the Set Datums column to the Annotations column and the Status column is empty.

- When a conflict is encountered, the datum is moved from the Set Datums column to the Annotations column, and

   displays in the Status column. **Change Reference** displays in the Required Actions column.

- When a failure is encountered, the datum stays in the Set Datums column and 🔴 displays in the Status column. **Create DFS** displays in the Required Actions column.

- Hover the cursor over 🔴 to display additional information related to a conflict or failure, as shown in Figure 6–38.

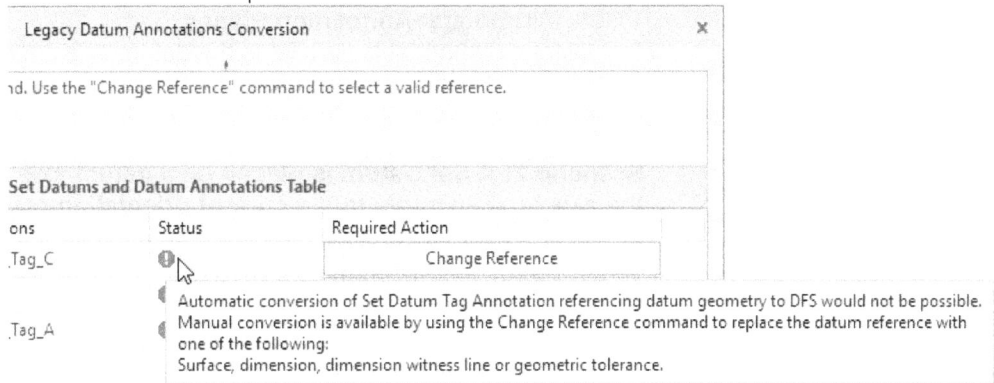

Legacy Datum Annotations Conversion ✕

nd. Use the "Change Reference" command to select a valid reference.

Set Datums and Datum Annotations Table

ons	Status	Required Action
.Tag_C	🔴	Change Reference
.Tag_A		

Automatic conversion of Set Datum Tag Annotation referencing datum geometry to DFS would not be possible. Manual conversion is available by using the Change Reference command to replace the datum reference with one of the following:
Surface, dimension, dimension witness line or geometric tolerance.

Figure 6–38

6. Resolve the conversion conflicts by clicking **Change Reference** and selecting a reference on the model. The legacy Set Datum Tag annotation converts to a Datum Feature Symbol annotation. This must be repeated for all conflicts. Once corrected, the Annotations turn green, as shown in Figure 6–39.

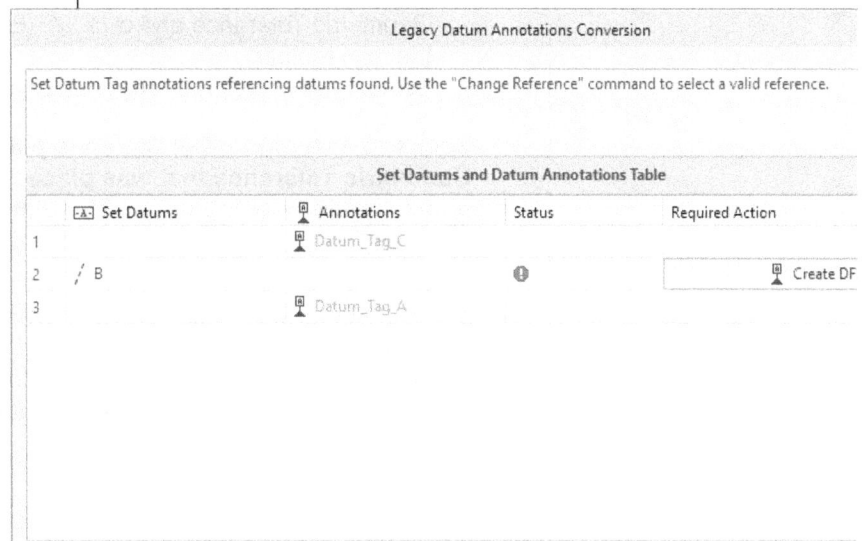

Legacy Datum Annotations Conversion

Set Datum Tag annotations referencing datums found. Use the "Change Reference" command to select a valid reference.

Set Datums and Datum Annotations Table

	Set Datums	Annotations	Status	Required Action
1		Datum_Tag_C		
2	∕ B		🔴	Create DF
3		Datum_Tag_A		

Figure 6–39

7. When Creo Parametric cannot convert a legacy Set Datum, **Create DFS** displays in the Required Action column, indicating a failure. Review each failure and match it to one of the following scenarios. Use the indicated steps to correct it:

Scenario 1: A Set Datum is placed on a datum axis and the axis is normal to the current orientation plane.

1. Click **Annotate>Annotation Planes**.
2. Select a plane that is parallel to the datum axis such that the datum axis becomes parallel to the current orientation plane.

Scenario 2: A Set Datum is placed on a datum axis and the axis is at an angle to the current orientation plane.

1. Create a datum plane passing through the datum axis.
2. Click **Annotate>Annotation Planes** and select the new datum plane.
3. Click **Active Annotation Plane** so that the datum axis becomes parallel to the current orientation plane.

Scenario 3: A model Set Datum is placed on a Geometric Tolerance that was created in Drawing mode with the As Free Note placement type.

Since the Geometric Tolerance was created as a free note in Drawing mode, it fails to convert because it does not have any reference in the model and is treated as a draft Geometric Tolerance in Part mode.

1. In the Drawing Tree or the Model Tree, select the draft Geometric Tolerance and click ✐ (Edit References) from the mini toolbar.
2. Select the appropriate reference on the model.

Scenario 4: A model Set Datum is placed on a model Geometric Tolerance that was placed on a model dimension in Drawing mode. The dimension was created with the Dimension Elbow placement type and an Edge reference.

The Geometric Tolerance fails to convert because it was created with an edge reference in Drawing mode and so does not have any reference in the model. Creo Parametric treats It as a draft Geometric Tolerance in Part mode.

1. In the Model Tree, select the draft Geometric Tolerance and click ✎ (Edit References) from the mini toolbar.
2. Select an edge on the model to temporarily place the Geometric Tolerance.
3. Again select the Geometric Tolerance and click ✎ (Edit References) from the mini toolbar.
4. Select the dimension on which to place the Geometric Tolerance.
5. Right-click the Geometric Tolerance and select **Dimension Elbow**.

Scenario 5: A model Set Datum is placed on a model Geometric Tolerance that was placed on a model leader note in Drawing mode. The note was placed with the Note Elbow placement type.

The Geometric Tolerance fails to convert because it was created with a model leader note in Drawing mode and so does not have any reference in the model. Creo Parametric treats It as a draft Geometric Tolerance in Part mode.

1. In the Model Tree, select the draft Geometric Tolerance and click ✎ (Edit References) from the mini toolbar.
2. Select the leader note as a reference on the model.

8. Repeat the previous step for all of the failures that have a workaround, and then click **Convert All Set Datums** to convert the legacy Set Datums to Set Datum Tag annotations.

9. If no workaround (from Step 7) is available for the failure, click **Create DFS** to create a new Datum Feature Symbol annotation. The datum feature symbol annotation displays in green with the same name as the set datum. Repeat this step for all failures that do not otherwise have a workaround. Once complete, the Annotations display in green, as shown in Figure 6–40.

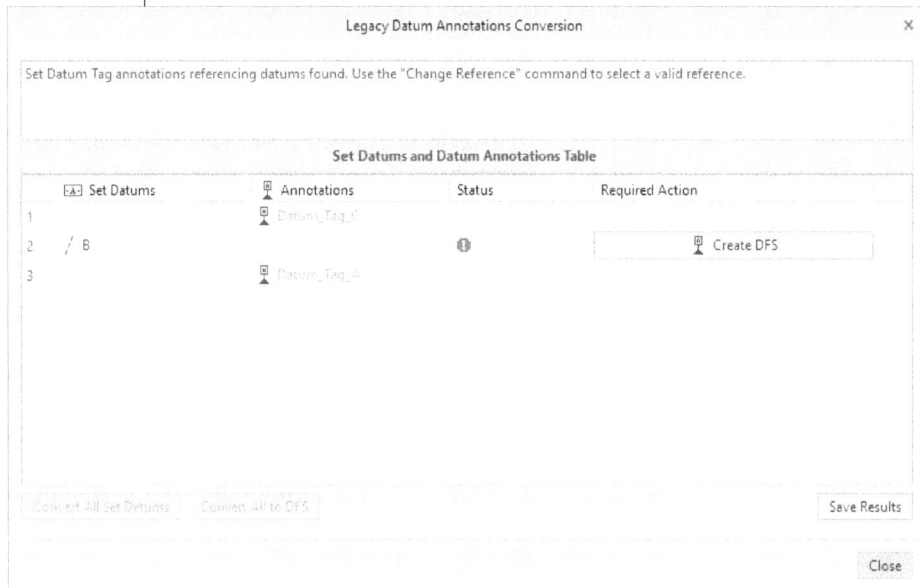

Figure 6–40

10. If any legacy Set Datum Tag annotations remain, click **Convert All to DFS** to convert all them to Datum Feature Symbol annotations, which will display in green.
Note that you can use the **Save Results** option to save the current state of Set Datums and the Datum Annotations Table to an information file.

If you are working in a drawing, you have to open the part to perform the conversion operations. Once you have finished, return to the drawing and update all sheets using the following steps:

1. If there are multiple sheets, right-click a sheet and click **Select All**.
2. Select the Review tab and click Update Sheets from the Update group. This will update all of the drawing sheets.

Select the *Annotate* tab and click ⬚ (Show Model Annotations) to display the new Datum Feature Symbols.

6.7 Datum Targets

To create a datum target, click ⊕ (Datum Target) in the *Annotate* tab in the ribbon. The target preview is attached to the cursor. To place the target, select the reference, and then press the middle mouse button to the placement location, as shown in Figure 6–41.

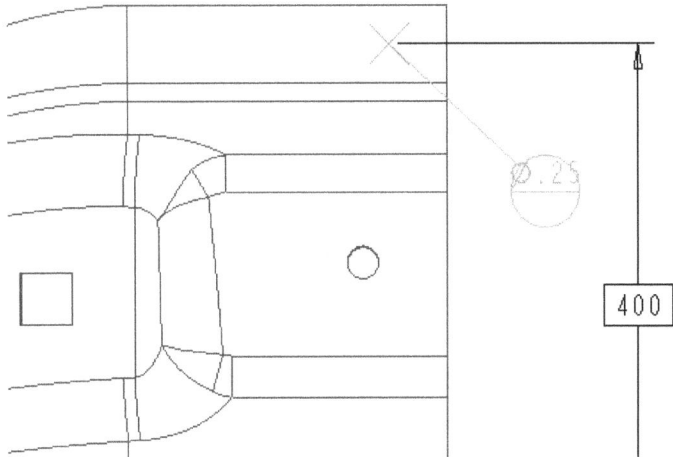

Figure 6–41

You can pick a location on a surface or edge or you can pick a datum point. You can modify the placement of the datum target annotation by dragging it along the current reference, or by right-clicking and selecting **Change Reference** to choose a new reference.

Specifying Datum References

You can type the datum reference letter and number in the datum reference field, or you can click 🔧 (Select Datum) and select an existing datum from the drawing. When you select an existing datum, the letter of the datum is automatically used and for each target added, the number is automatically incremented.

If the datum feature symbol exists in the model or drawing, a connection is then established between the datum feature symbol and the datum target, The label displays as green text in the *Datum Target* tab, as shown in Figure 6–42.

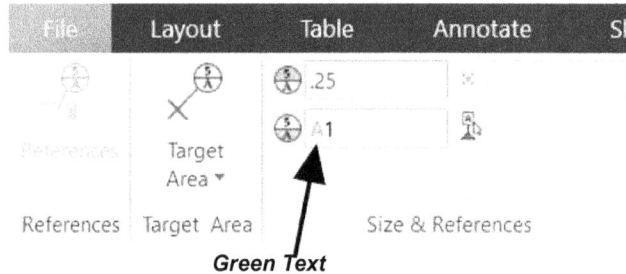

Green Text

Figure 6–42

If the datum feature symbol does not exist in the model or the drawing, the datum reference box is populated with plain text. Note that a datum does not have to exist in the drawing when you create the target.

Intelligent Target Areas

You can choose the type of target area using the **Target Area** options in the ribbon, as shown in Figure 6–43.

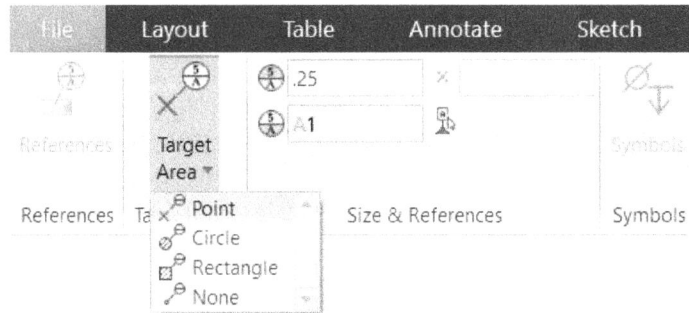

Figure 6–43

Both the **Circle** and **Rectangle** options require size parameters to control the shape on the model. If you use the circle target area, a diameter symbol prefix is applied, along with the size parameter, as shown in Figure 6–44.

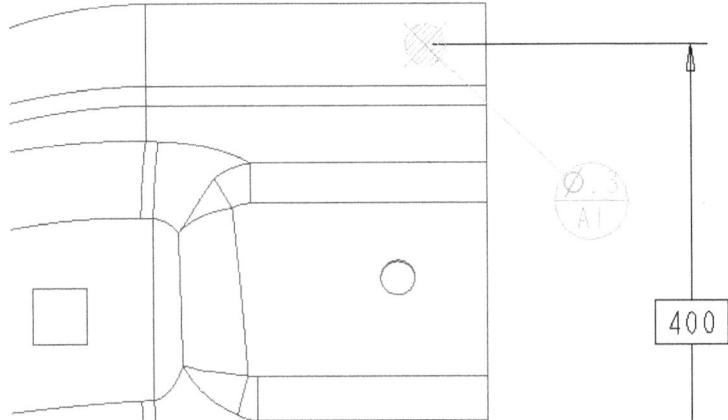

Figure 6–44

If you use the rectangle target area, the length and width dimensions are separated by an X. If the same value is used for length and width, the box symbol prefix is used to indicate a square dimension.

Datum Target Annotations

By default, the dimension for the target area size is placed inside the upper half of the target circle. You can move it outside the target circle with a leader by clicking ⌖ (Outside), as shown in Figure 6–45.

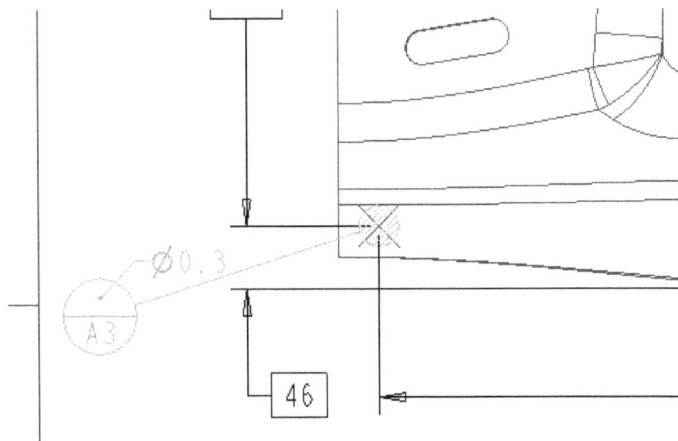

Figure 6–45

You can use the movable datum target symbol, as shown in Figure 6–46.

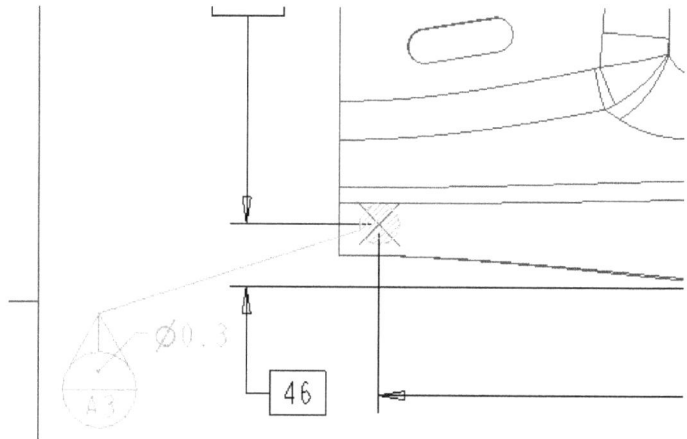

Figure 6–46

To set the datum target annotation to be movable, click ⊖ (Movable Datum Target). To change the orientation, click ⍙ (Rotate Symbol).

Finally, you can click ⤺ (Far Side) to indicate placement of the datum target on a surface on the far side of the drawing view, as shown in Figure 6–47.

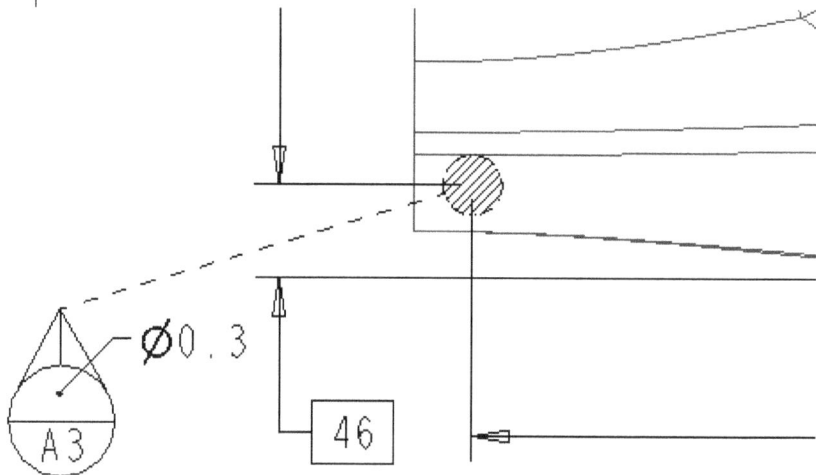

Figure 6–47

6.8 Drawing Configuration Options

The drawing configuration options that enable you to customize dimensional and geometric tolerances are described as follows (values in bold indicate the default value).

Option	Values	Description
tol_display	**no** yes	Displays dimensions with or without tolerances.
linear_tol	#tolerance	Sets the tolerance value for linear dimensions. The # symbol defines the number of decimal places and the tolerance defines the actual tolerance value.
angular_tol	#tolerance	Sets the tolerance value for angular dimensions. The # symbol defines the number of decimal places and tolerance defines the actual tolerance value.
tolerance_standard	**ANSI** ISO	Determines the tolerance standard when creating the mode.
display_dwg_tol_tags	**yes** no	Controls the display of geometric tolerances.
tolerance_class	**medium** fine coarse very_coarse	Determines the tolerance class for ISO models.
tolerance_table_dir	directory path	Sets the directory for user-defined tolerance tables.
gtol_dim_placement	**on_bottom** under_value	Determines the location of geometric tolerance when it is attached to a dimension to which additional text has been added.
maintain_limit_tol_nominal	**no** yes	Maintains the nominal value of a dimension regardless of the change you make to the tolerance values.
restricted_gtol_dialog	**yes** no	Determines whether the Geometric Tolerance dialog box restricts the users by graying out elements that are considered illegal.

allow_rfs_default_gtols_always	no yes	If set to **yes**, enables RFS/Default gtols to be created even when not permitted by ANSI standard.
display_tol_by_1000	no yes	If set to **yes**, tolerances for non-angular dimensions display multiplied by 1000.

6.9 Drawing Setup File Options

The drawing setup file options that enable you to customize dimensional and geometric tolerances are described as follows (values in bold indicate the default value).

Option	Value	Description
asme_dtm_on_dia_dim_ gtol	**on_gtol** on_dim	Controls the display of a set datum placed in a diameter dimension.
blank_zero_tolerance	**no** yes	Determines whether tolerances with values of 0 display.
gtol_datums	**std_ansi** std_iso std_asme std_jis std_din	Sets the drawing standard for the display of set datums.
gtol_dim_placement	**on_bottom** under_value	Determines the location of geometric tolerance when it is attached to a dimension to which additional text has been added.
tol_display	**no** yes	Displays dimensions with or without tolerance in the drawing.
new_iso_set_datums	**yes** no	Controls the display of set datums if accordance with ISO standards.
dim_trail_zero_max_ placestol	**same_as_ dim**	Sets the maximum number of decimal places that trailing zeros are extended to in the dimension primary value, when dimension trailing zeros are used.
default_tolerance_mode	**nominal** limits plusminus plusminussym plusminussym _super	Defines the format of the tolerance.

Practice 6a | Dimensional Tolerances

Practice Objectives

- Set the tolerance display in the model.
- Set the tolerance display in the drawing.
- Change the display of dimensional tolerances in the drawing.
- Modify dimensional tolerances in the drawing.

In this practice, you will set, change, and modify the dimensional tolerances for the base_plate drawing. The final drawing displays as shown in Figure 6–48.

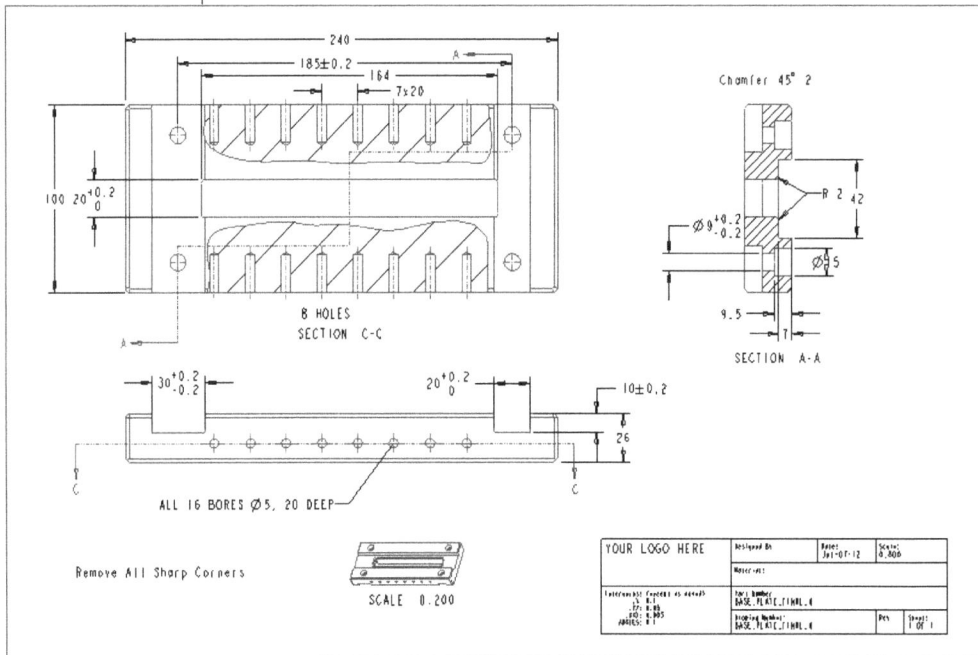

Figure 6–48

Task 1 - Open the base_plate part.

1. Set the working directory to the *Dimensional_Tolerances* folder.

2. Open **base_plate_final_4.drw**.

3. Set the model display as follows:

   - ✖ *(Datum Display Filters)*: All Off

   - ▱ *(Display Style)*: ▱ (No Hidden)

4. Select **File>Prepare>Drawing Properties**. Select **change** next to *Detail Options* to access the drawing options.

5. Set the **tol_display** option value to **yes**.

6. Click **Add/Change** then click **OK** to close the dialog box.

7. Click **Close** in the Drawing Properties dialog box.

8. Click **File>Options>Configuration Editor** and ensure that the configuration option **tol_display** is set to **yes**. If it is not, set it.

Task 2 - Show dimensions.

1. Select the *Annotate* tab.

2. Show the 20 and 30 dimensions in the Projected view below section view C-C, as shown in Figure 6–49.

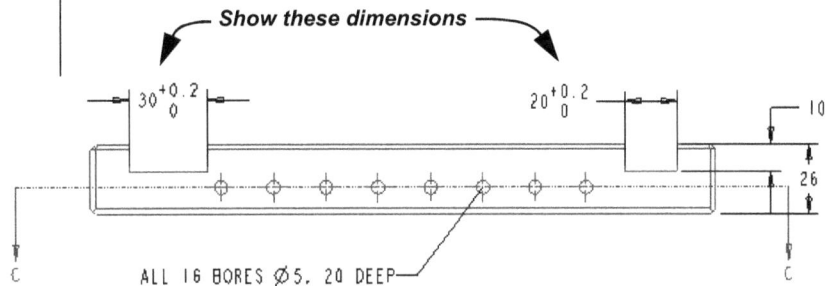

Figure 6–49

Task 3 - Assign dimensional tolerances in the drawing.

1. Set the selection filter to **Dimension** and select all of the dimensions in the drawing by dragging a selection box around the entire drawing.

2. The *Dimension* tab opens. Set the tolerance type for all dimension to **Nominal**. The **Tolerance Mode** menu as shown in Figure 6–50.

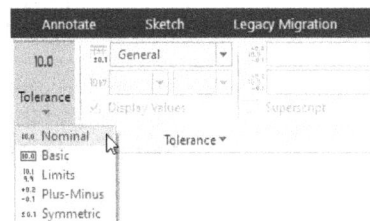

Figure 6–50

3. Select the **20** dimension in the bottom Projection view.

4. In the **Tolerance Mode** menu, select **Plus-Minus**.

5. Enter **0.2** in the *Upper tolerance* field and **-0.2** in the *Lower tolerance* field.

6. Click on the screen to complete the edit. The dimension displays as shown in Figure 6–51.

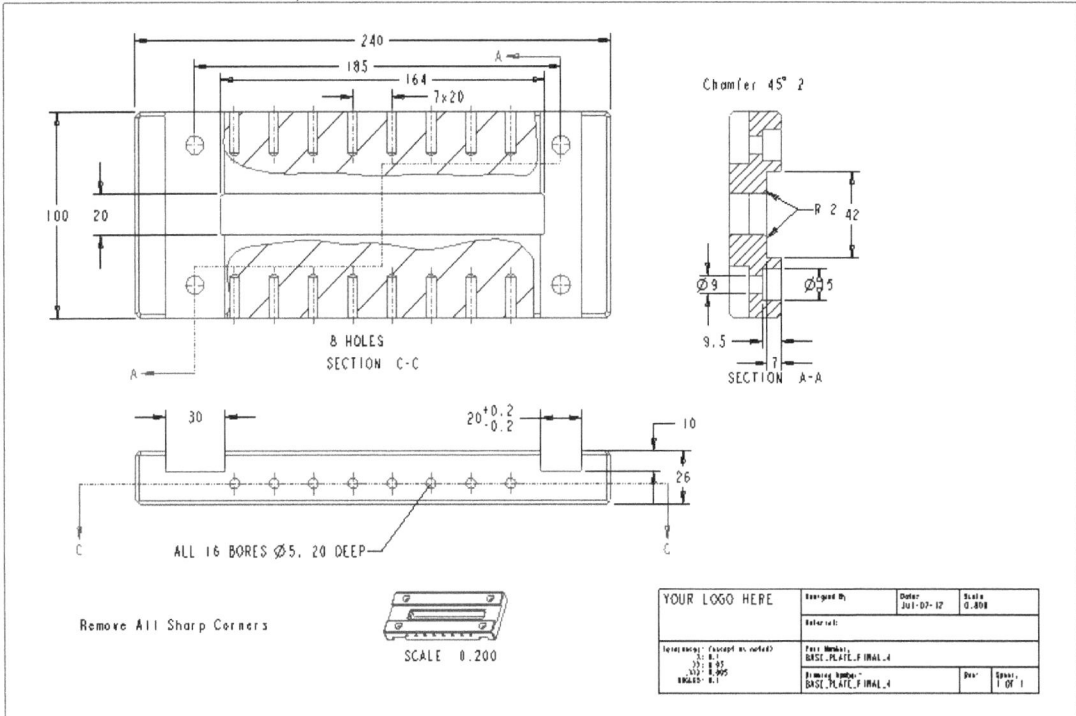

Figure 6–51

Task 4 - Modify the tolerance values for multiple dimensions in the drawing.

1. Select the **20** dimension associated with the two tolerance values in the bottom Projected view. Modify the **-0.2** tolerance value back to **0**.

2. Modify the **30** dimension to display a **Plus-Minus** tolerance. Enter **0.2** in the *Upper tolerance* field and **-0.2** in the *Lower tolerance* field.

3. Add dimensional tolerances to the other dimensions shown in Figure 6–52 using **Plus-Minus** and **+-Symmetric**. Create a dimension between the two holes, as shown in Figure 6–52.

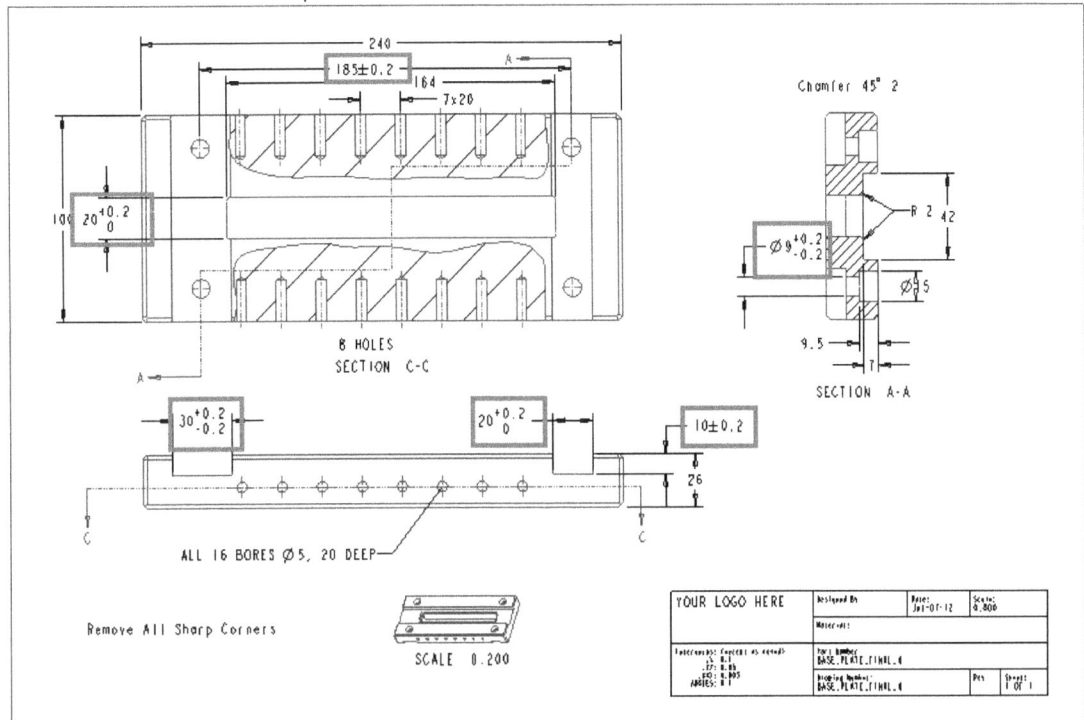

Figure 6–52

4. Save the drawing and close the window.

Practice 6b | Geometric Tolerances

Practice Objective

- Create geometric tolerances.

In this practice, you will create a Geometric Tolerances, Datum Feature symbols, and Datum Target symbols. The final drawing displays as shown in Figure 6–53.

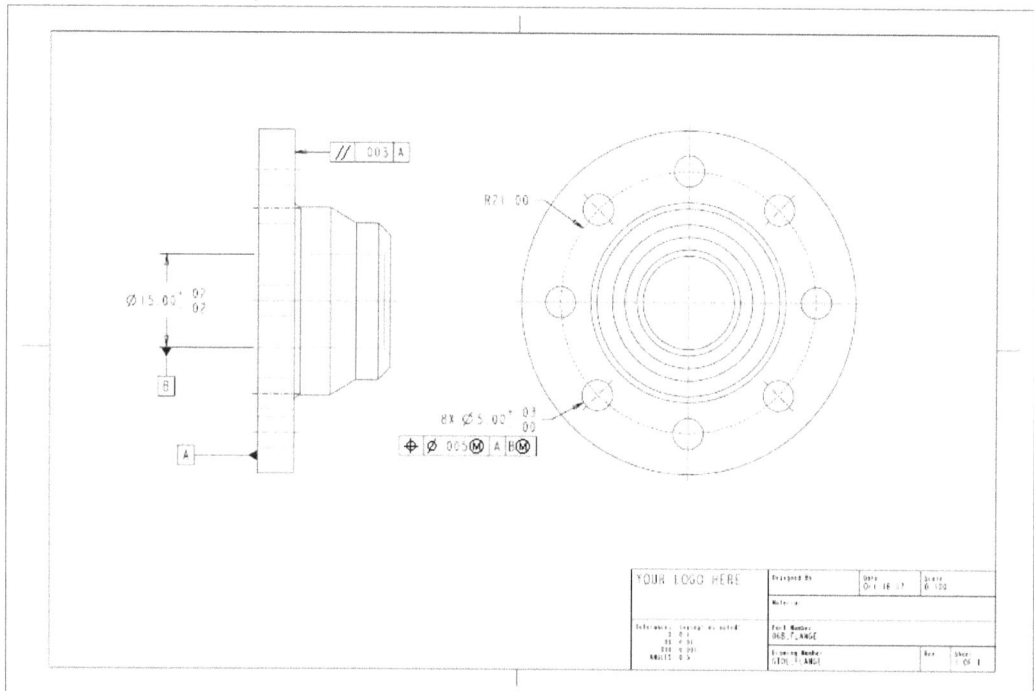

Figure 6–53

Task 1 - Open a drawing file.

1. Set the working directory to the *Geometrical_Tolerances* folder.

2. Open **gtol_flange.drw**.

3. Set the model display as follows:

   - *(Datum Display Filters)*: All Off

   - *(Display Style)*: (No Hidden)

The drawing displays as shown in Figure 6–54.

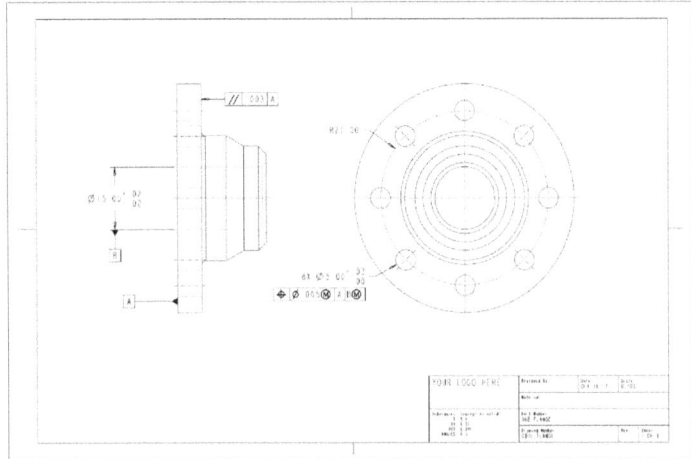

Figure 6–54

Task 2 - Create Datum Target Symbols

1. Select the *Annotate* tab.

2. In the Annotations group, click 🔲 (Datum Feature Symbol).

3. Select the edge show in Figure 6–55.

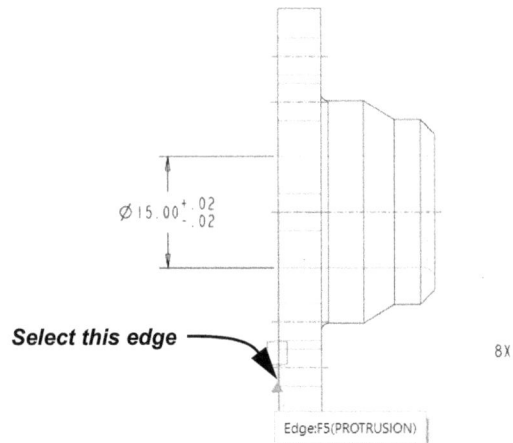

Figure 6–55

4. Move the Datum Feature Symbol to the location show in Figure 6–56 and click the middle mouse button.

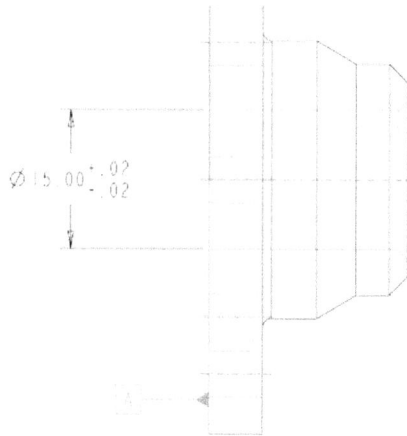

Figure 6–56

5. Note that the name defaults to A, as shown in Figure 6–57. Click the left mouse button to complete the Datum Feature Symbol.

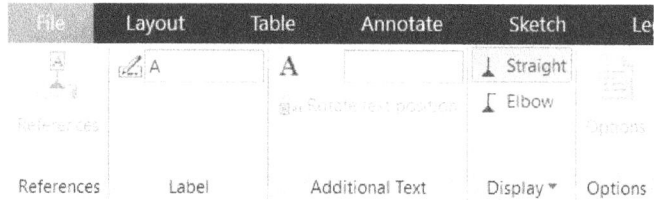

Figure 6–57

6. Click on the screen to complete the placement.

7. In the Annotations group, click ⊥ (Datum Feature Symbol).

8. Click on the lower witness line of the 15.00 dimension, as shown in Figure 6–58.

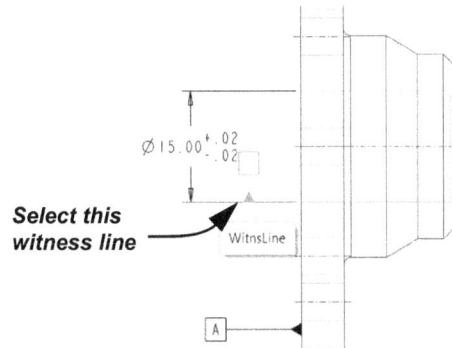

Figure 6–58

9. Move the Datum Feature Symbol to the location shown in Figure 6–59 and click the middle mouse button.

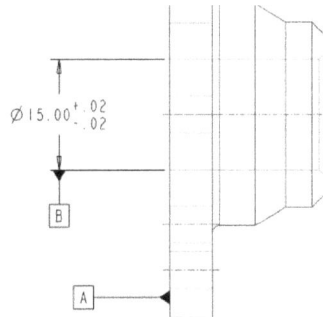

Figure 6–59

10. Click on the screen to complete the placement.

Task 3 - Create Geometric Tolerances

1. In the Annotations group, click ⊕⏢ (Geometric Tolerance), as shown in Figure 6–60.

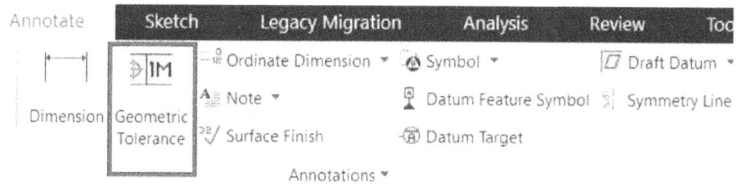

Figure 6–60

2. Click on the **5.00** dimension, as shown in Figure 6–61.

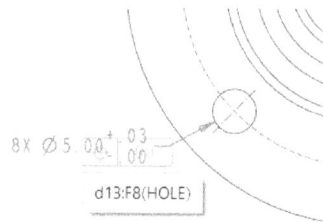

8X Ø 5.00 +.03 / 00

d13:F8(HOLE)

Figure 6–61

3. Select ⊕ (Position) as the Geometric Characteristic, as shown in Figure 6–62.

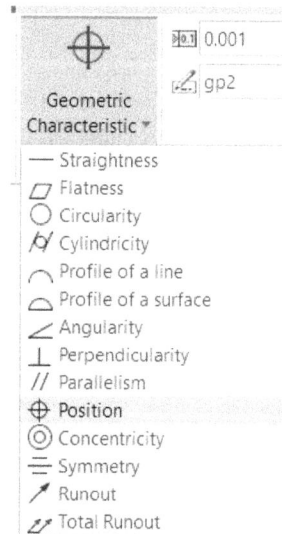

Figure 6–62

4. Enter **0.005** as the tolerance value, as shown in Figure 6–63.

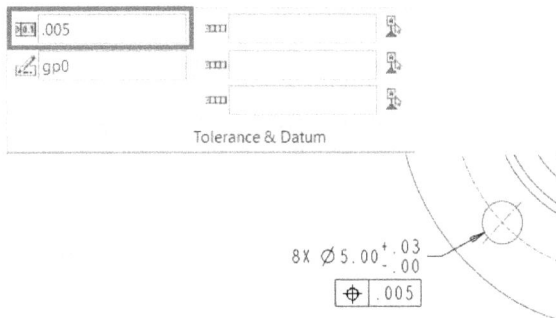

Figure 6–63

5. In the Primary Datum Reference field, type **A** as shown in Figure 6–64.

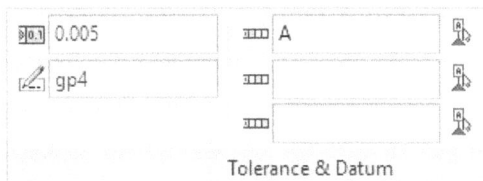

Figure 6–64

6. The Geometric Tolerance updates as shown in Figure 6–65.

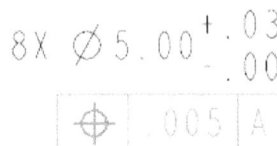

Figure 6–65

7. In the Secondary Datum Reference, type **B**, as shown in Figure 6–66.

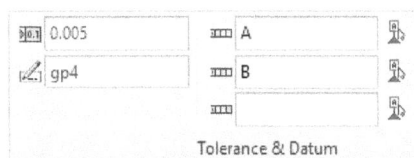

Figure 6–66

8. The Geometric Tolerance updates as shown in Figure 6–67.

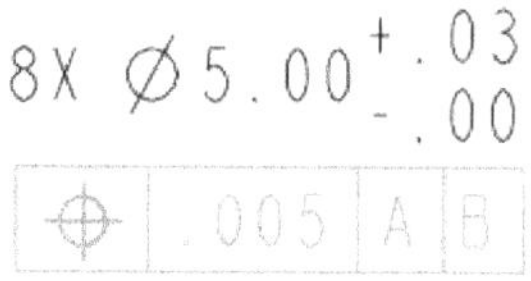

$$8X \ \varnothing 5.00 ^{+.03} _{-.00}$$

$$\oplus \ | \ .005 \ | \ A \ | \ B$$

Figure 6–67

9. Click after the 5 in the *Tolerance Value* field as shown in Figure 6–68.

— **Select here**

Figure 6–68

10. Expand $\varnothing_{\top}$ (Symbols) and select maximum material condition (you may need to scroll down in the symbol list), as shown in Figure 6–69.

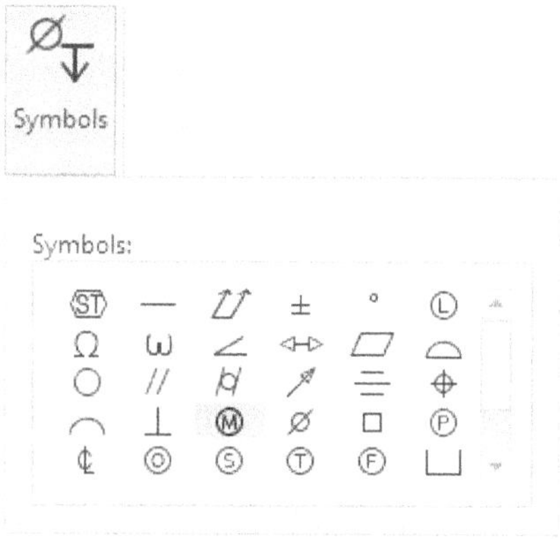

Figure 6–69

11. Click after the B in the Secondary Datum Reference field, as shown in Figure 6–70.

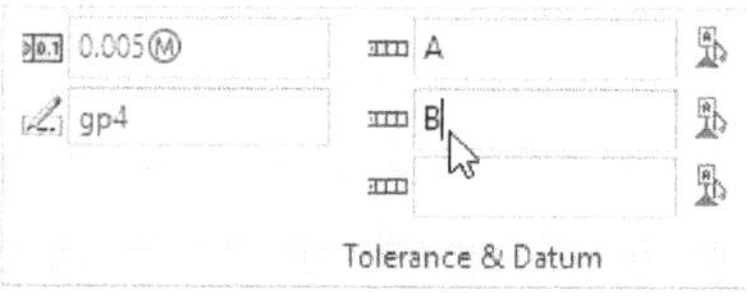

Figure 6–70

12. Expand $^{\varnothing}_{\top}$ (Symbols) and maximum material condition, as shown in Figure 6–71.

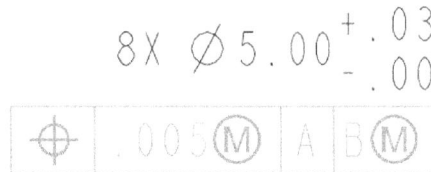

$$8X \ \varnothing 5.00^{+.03}_{-.00}$$

$$\oplus \ | \ .005 \ \text{M} \ | \ A \ | \ B \ \text{M} \ |$$

Figure 6–71

13. To add a diameter symbol before the tolerance value, click before the tolerance value, as shown in Figure 6–72.

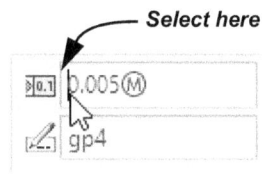

Figure 6–72

14. Select the diameter symbol as shown in Figure 6–73.

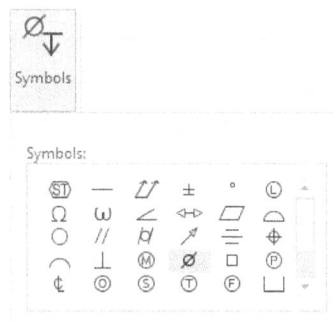

Figure 6–73

15. Click the left mouse button on the drawing to complete the Geometric Tolerance, as shown in Figure 6–74.

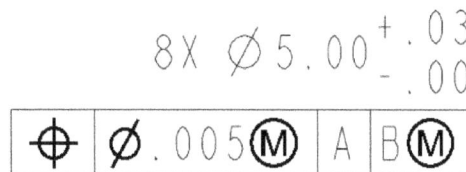

$$8X \ \varnothing 5.00^{+.03}_{-.00}$$

$$\oplus \ | \ \varnothing.005 \ \text{M} \ | \ A \ | \ B \ \text{M} \ |$$

Figure 6–74

16. In the Annotations group, select ▓▀ (Geometric Tolerance).

17. Select the edge shown in Figure 6–75.

Select here

5.00$^{+.02}_{-.02}$

Figure 6–75

18. Move the geometric tolerance until the leader is perpendicular to the edge and the Perpendicular constraint icon displays as shown in Figure 6–76. Then, click the middle mouse button.

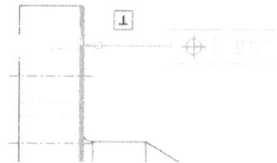

Figure 6–76

19. Select // (Parallelism) as the Geometric Characteristic as shown in Figure 6–77.

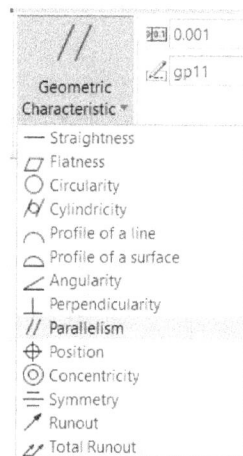

Figure 6–77

20. Enter **0.003** as the tolerance value and **Parrallel1** as the name, as shown in Figure 6–78.

Tolerance & Datum

Figure 6–78

21. Click 🔩 (Select Datum Reference) next to the Primary Datum Reference.

22. In the drawing, select datum A and click **OK**. The geometric tolerance updates as shown if Figure 6–79.

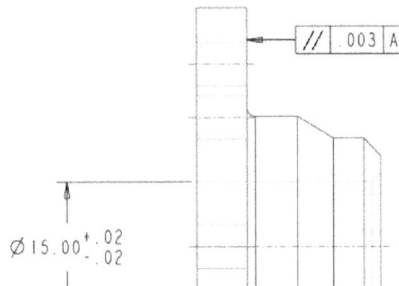

Figure 6–79

23. Save and close the drawing.

Task 4 - Create Datum Target Symbol

In this task, you will create three datum targets to define a primary datum.

1. Open **datum_target.drw**. The drawing displays as shown in Figure 6–80.

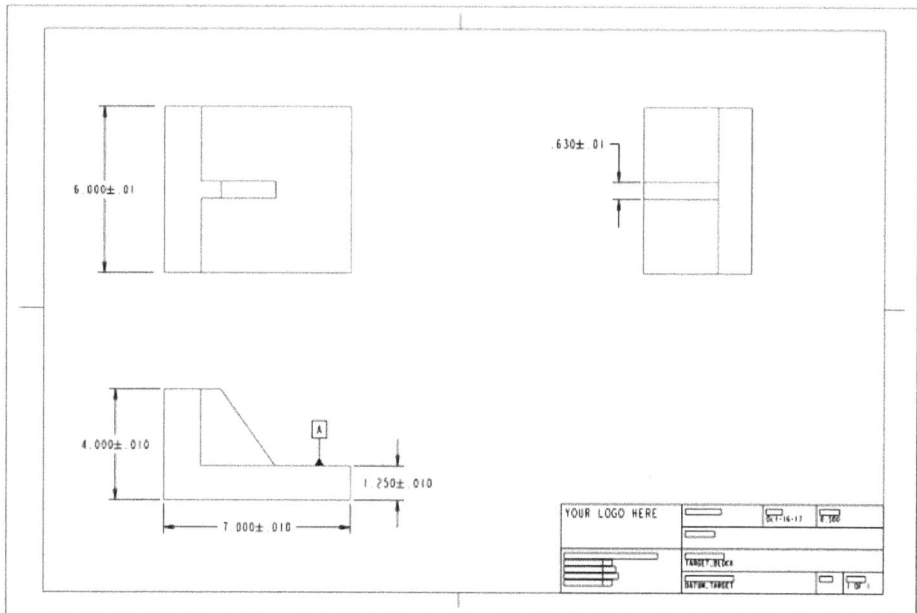

Figure 6–80

2. Select the *Annotate* tab.

3. In the Annotations group, click ⊕ (Datum Target).

4. In the top view, select the location shown in Figure 6–81.

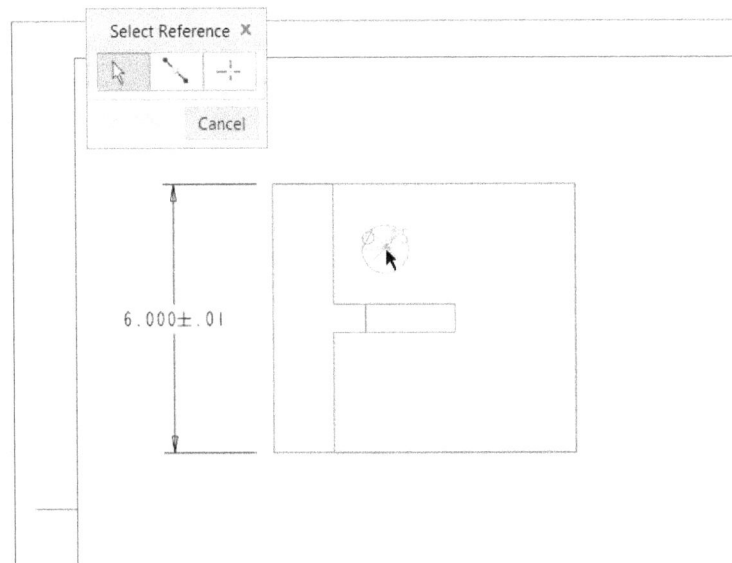

Figure 6–81

5. Move the datum target to the location shown in Figure 6–82, and click the middle mouse button.

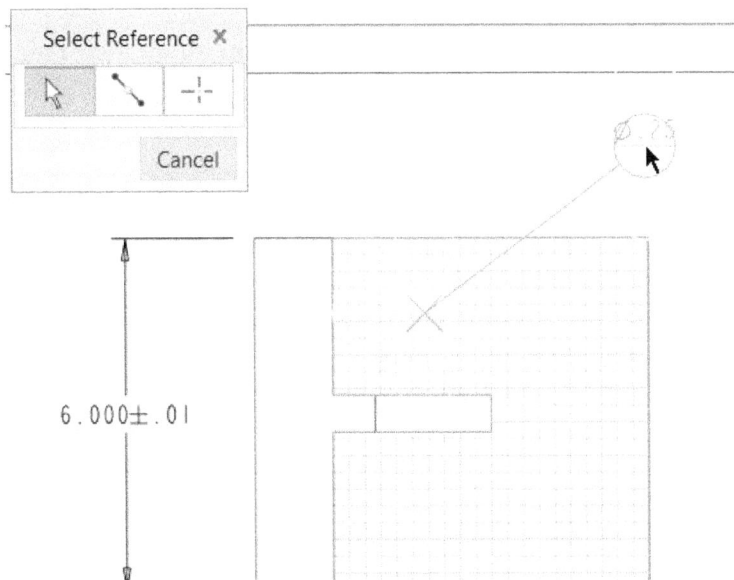

Figure 6–82

6. Enter **0.5** as the width of the datum target, as shown in Figure 6–83.

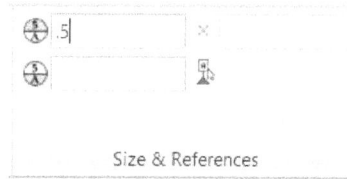

Figure 6–83

7. In the Size & References group, click 🔧 (Select Datum Reference).

8. In the lower view, click on datum A, as shown in Figure 6–84.

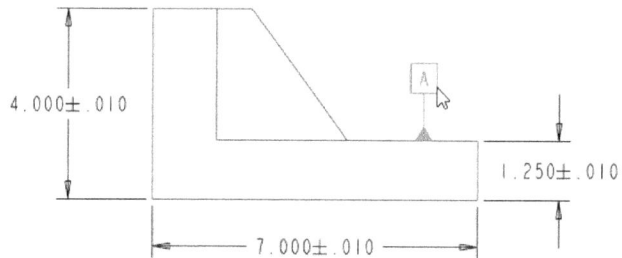

Figure 6–84

9. Click **OK**. The datum target updates as shown in Figure 6–85.

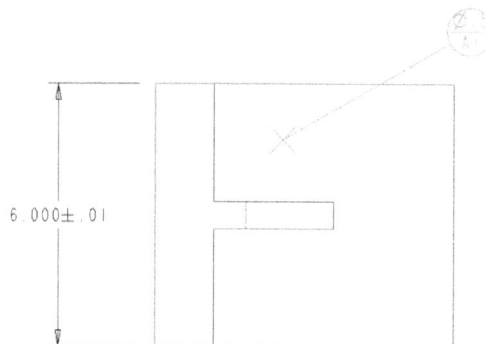

Figure 6–85

10. Select **Circle** as the Target Area type, as shown in Figure 6–86.

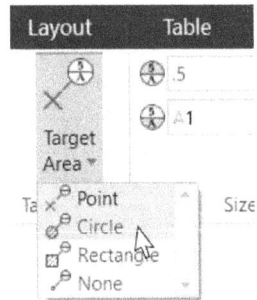

Figure 6–86

11. In the Area Size Display group, click ⟲ (Outside), as shown in Figure 6–87.

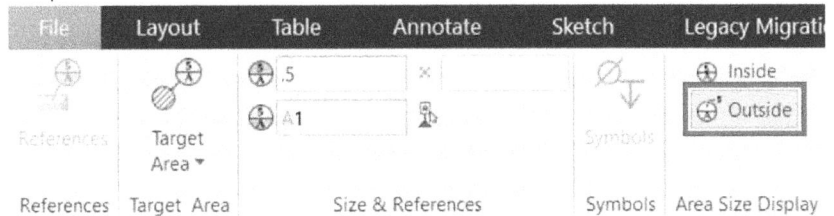

Figure 6–87

12. The datum target updates as shown in Figure 6–88.

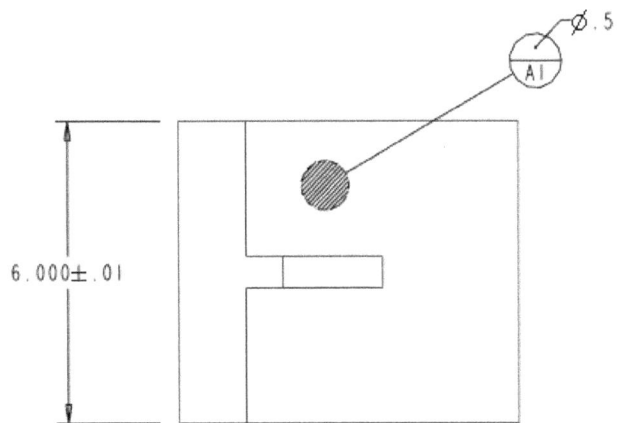

6.000±.01

Figure 6–88

13. Repeat steps 3-12 to create the two additional datum targets shown in Figure 6–89.

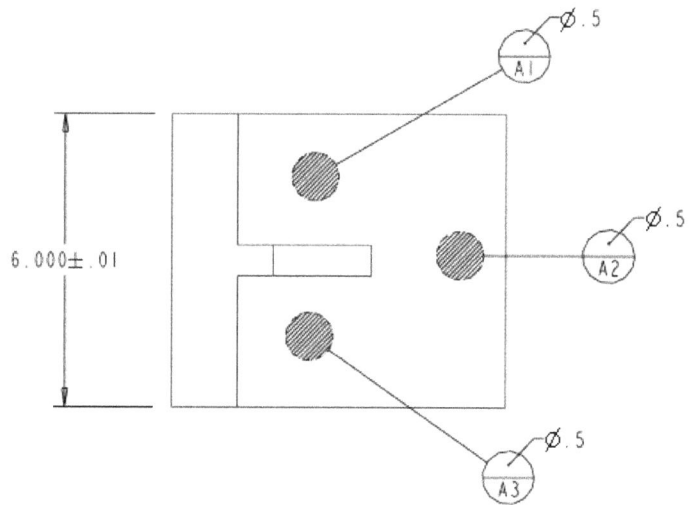

Figure 6–89

14. Save and close the drawing.

Practice 6c

Handling Legacy Datums

Practice Objectives

- Open a drawing created in a previous release of Creo Parametric.
- Investigate the legacy datums using the Legacy Datum Annotation Conversion tool.
- Update legacy datums to Datum Feature Symbols.

In this practice, you will open a drawing started in an older release of Creo Parametric, and will update the legacy set datums using the Legacy Datum Annotation Conversion tool.

Task 1 - Open the pulley.drw drawing.

1. Set the Working Directory to *Legacy_Datums*, if required.

2. Open **pulley_legacy.drw**.

3. A warning temporarily displays, indicating that there are legacy annotations, as shown in Figure 6–90.

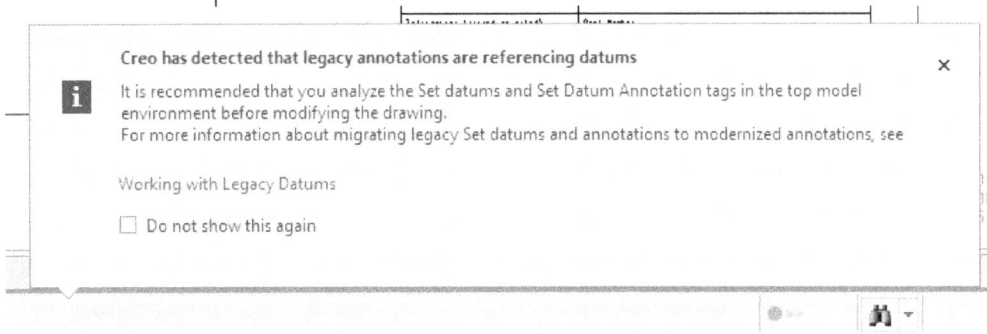

Creo has detected that legacy annotations are referencing datums

It is recommended that you analyze the Set datums and Set Datum Annotation tags in the top model environment before modifying the drawing.
For more information about migrating legacy Set datums and annotations to modernized annotations, see

Working with Legacy Datums

☐ Do not show this again

Figure 6–90

4. Set the model display as follows:

- *(Datum Display Filters)*: All Off

The drawing displays as shown in Figure 6–91.

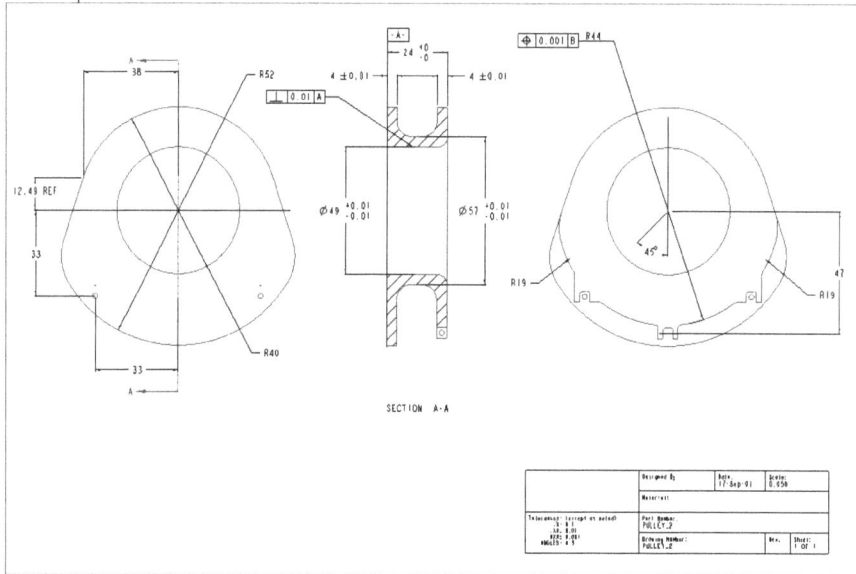

Figure 6–91

Task 2 - Investigate the two geometric tolerances.

1. Select the *Annotate* tab.

2. Select the geometric tolerance shown in Figure 6–92. In the ribbon, in the *Geometric Tolerance* tab, note that the primary datum A displays in black, indicating that a Datum Feature Symbol has not been defined.

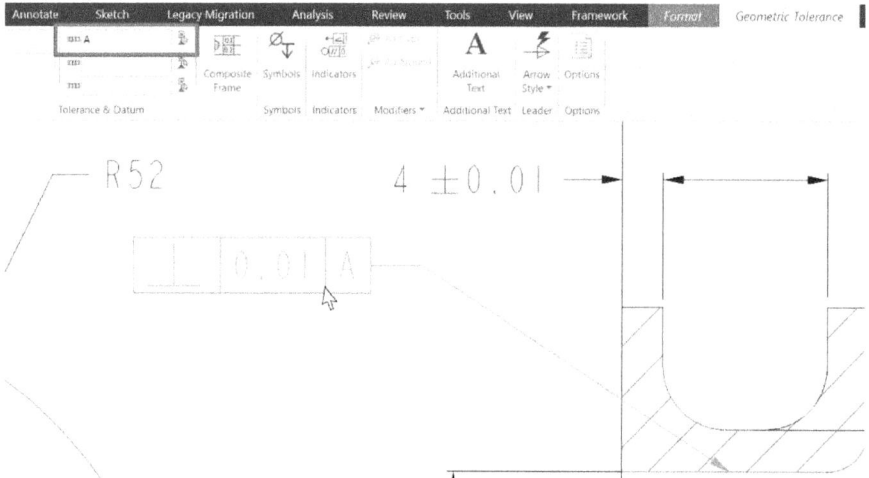

Figure 6–92

3. Select the other geometric tolerance and note that datum B has not been defined as a Datum Feature Symbol.

4. In the Model Tree, right-click **PULLEY_2.PRT** and select 🗁 (Open).

Task 3 - Use the Legacy Datum Annotation Conversion tool to update the datums.

---

1. If the annotation node does not display in the Model Tree, select 🗍 ˅ (Settings)>**Tree Filters** and enable Annotations.

2. Expand the Annotation node in the Model Tree.

3. Note the icon next to gp0 and gp1, as shown in Figure 6–93.

The icon next to gp0 indicates a missing reference and the icon next to gp1 indicates a legacy annotation.

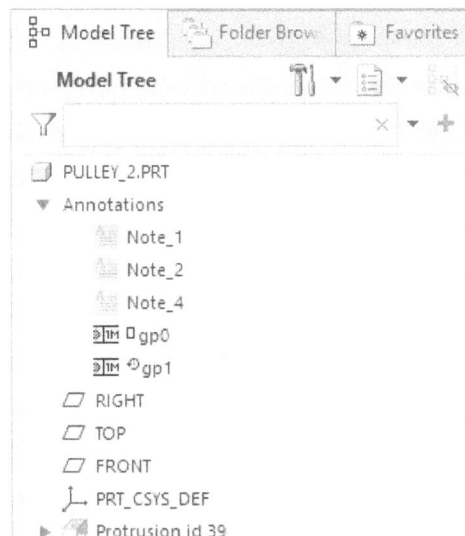

Figure 6–93

4. Select either geometric tolerance in the Model Tree, then right-click and select **Convert All**, as shown in Figure 6–94.

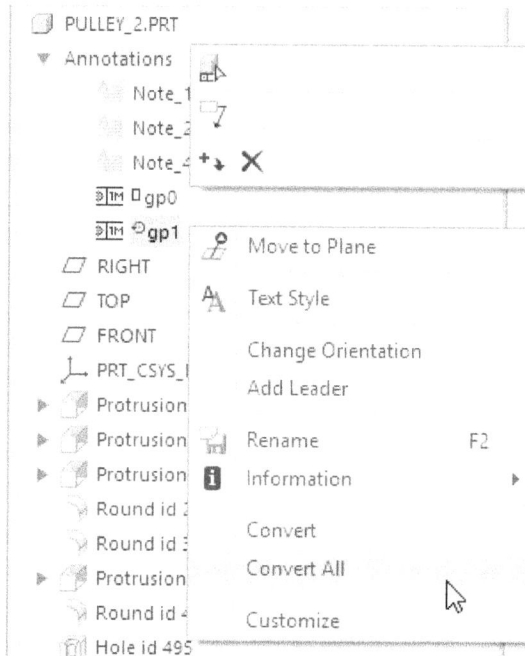

Figure 6–94

5. Click **Close** in the Conversion Warning dialog box, shown in Figure 6–95.

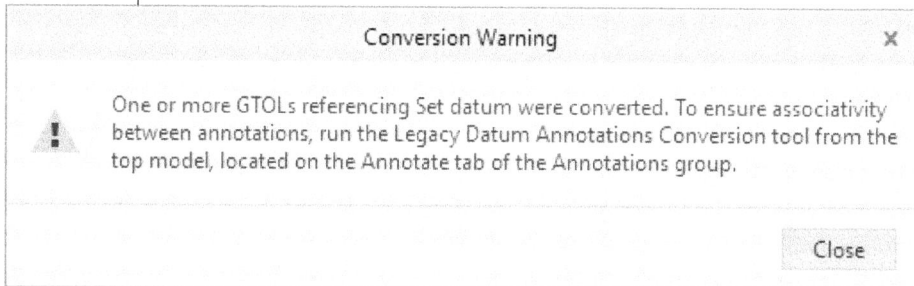

Figure 6–95

6. Select the *Annotate* tab.

7. Click **Annotations>Legacy Datum Annotation Conversion** to open the Legacy Datum Annotation Conversion tool, as shown in Figure 6–96.

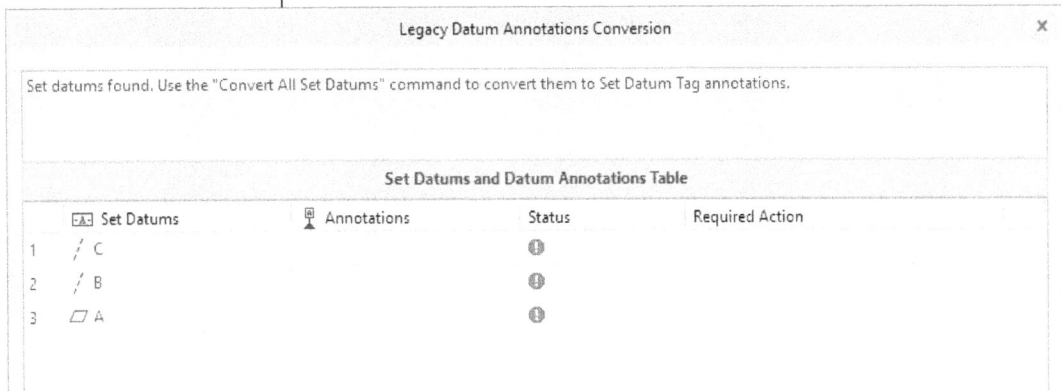

Legacy Datum Annotations Conversion   ✕

Set datums found. Use the "Convert All Set Datums" command to convert them to Set Datum Tag annotations.

Set Datums and Datum Annotations Table

	Set Datums	Annotations	Status	Required Action
1	C		ⓘ	
2	B		ⓘ	
3	A		ⓘ	

Figure 6–96

8. Click **Convert All Set Datums**.

9. Two datums have been converted, but require updated references. The third cannot be converted and requires that a Datum Feature Symbol be created, as shown in Figure 6–97.

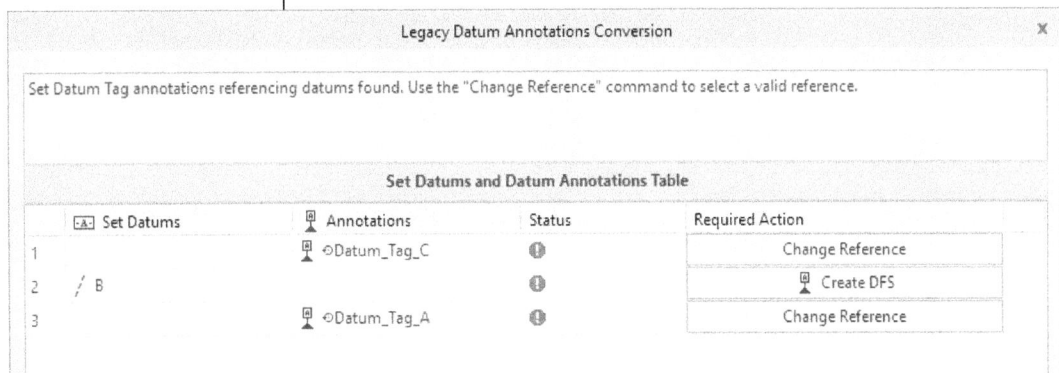

Legacy Datum Annotations Conversion   ✕

Set Datum Tag annotations referencing datums found. Use the "Change Reference" command to select a valid reference.

Set Datums and Datum Annotations Table

	Set Datums	Annotations	Status	Required Action
1		⊙Datum_Tag_C	ⓘ	Change Reference
2	B		ⓘ	Create DFS
3		⊙Datum_Tag_A	ⓘ	Change Reference

Figure 6–97

10. Place your cursor over each ⊕ icon in the status column to display a description of the issues, as shown in Figure 6–98.

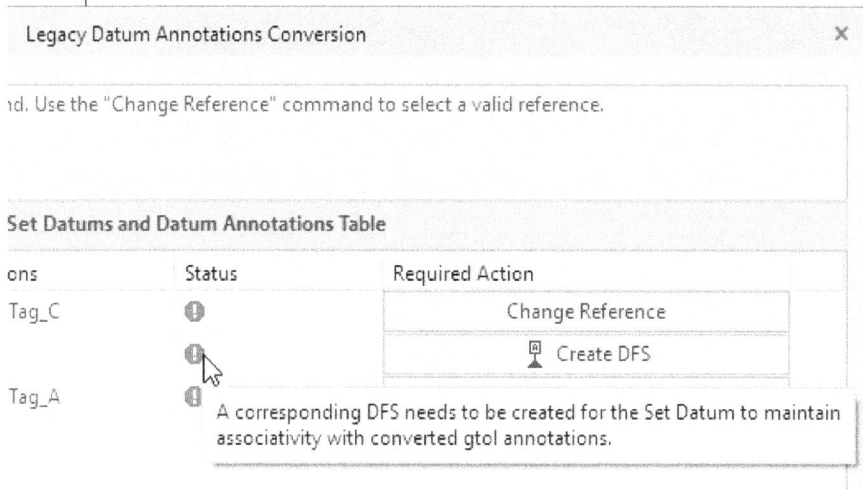

Figure 6–98

11. Click **Create DFS** for datum Set Datum B.

12. Select the **49.00** diameter dimension.

13. Middle-click to place the dimension as shown in Figure 6–99.

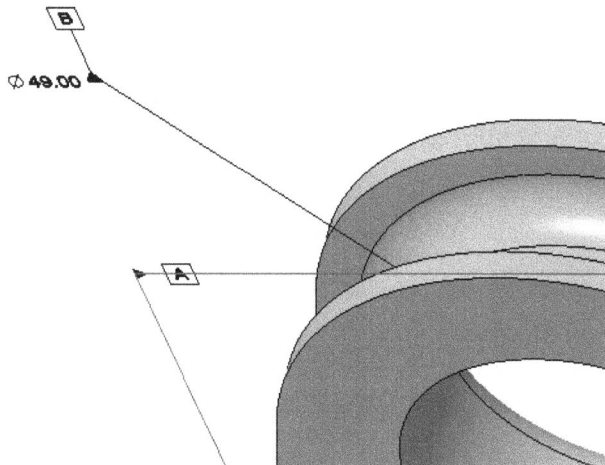

Figure 6–99

14. Note that Datum_Tag_B is added to the Annotations column, and is displayed in green, as shown in Figure 6–100.

Set Datums and Datum Annotations Table

Annotations	Status	Required Action
⊙Datum_Tag_C	❶	Change Reference
Datum_Tag_B		Create DFS
⊙Datum_Tag_A	❶	Change Reference

Figure 6–100

15. Click **Change Reference** for Datum_Tag_C.

16. Select the surface shown in Figure 6–101.

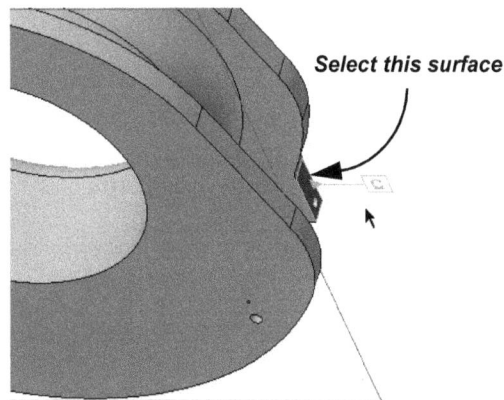

Select this surface

Figure 6–101

17. Middle-click to place the Datum Feature Symbol.

18. Note that Datum_Tag_C turns green in the Annotations column, and the Status and Required Action columns clear, as shown in Figure 6–102.

Set Datums and Datum Annotations Table

Annotations	Status	Required Action
Datum_Tag_C		
Datum_Tag_B		Create DFS
⊙Datum_Tag_A	❶	Change Reference

Figure 6–102

19. Click **Change Reference** for Datum_Tag_A.

20. In the *Annotate* tab, select ⬧ (RIGHT) for the annotation plane.

21. Select the surface shown in Figure 6–103.

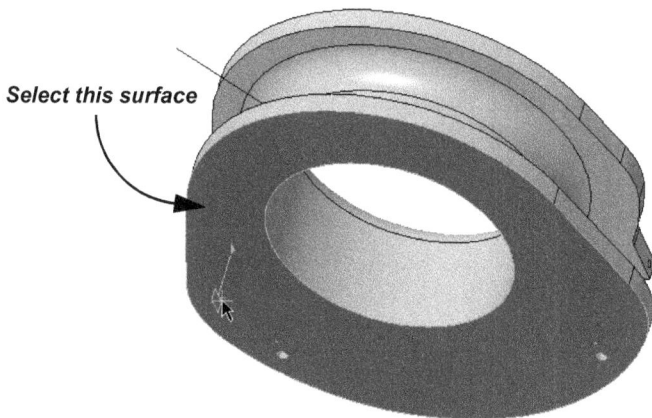

Select this surface

Figure 6–103

22. Middle click to place the Datum Feature Symbol, as shown in Figure 6–104.

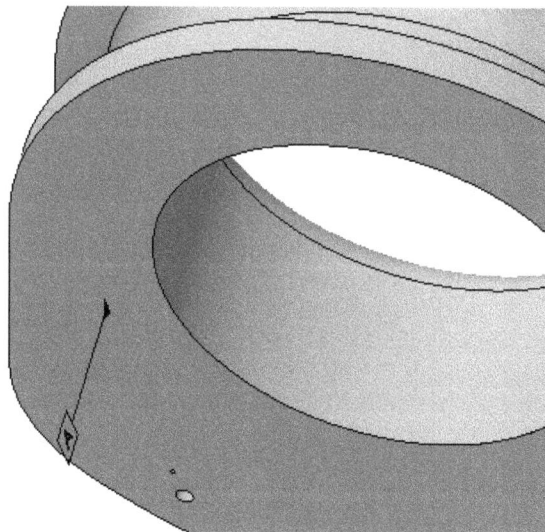

Figure 6–104

23. Datum_Tag_A turns green in the Annotations column, and the Status and Required Action columns clear.

24. Click **Close** in the Legacy Datum Annotation Conversion dialog box.

Task 4 - Return to the drawing to clean up the annotations.

1. In the Quick Access toolbar, expand ⬚ ▾ (Windows) and select **PULLEY_2.DRW**.

2. Select the *Review* tab.

3. Click ⬚ (Update Sheets).

4. Select Datum Feature Symbol **A**, select the attachment and drag it to the position shown in Figure 6–105.

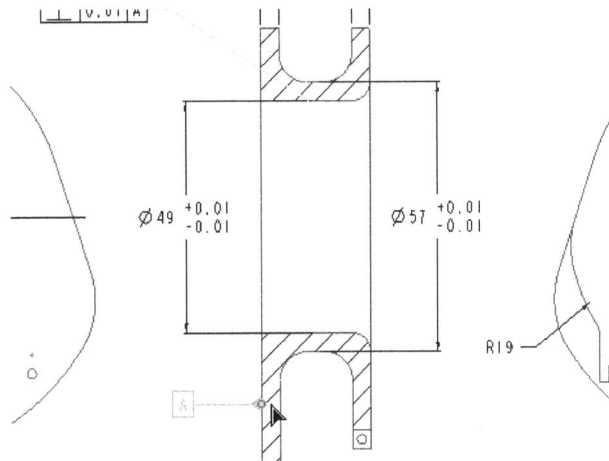

Figure 6–105

5. Select the *Annotate* tab.

6. Click ⬚ (Show Model Annotations).

7. In the Show Model Annotations dialog box, select the Datum tab.

8. Select the section view.

9. Select Datum_Tag_B, as shown in Figure 6–106.

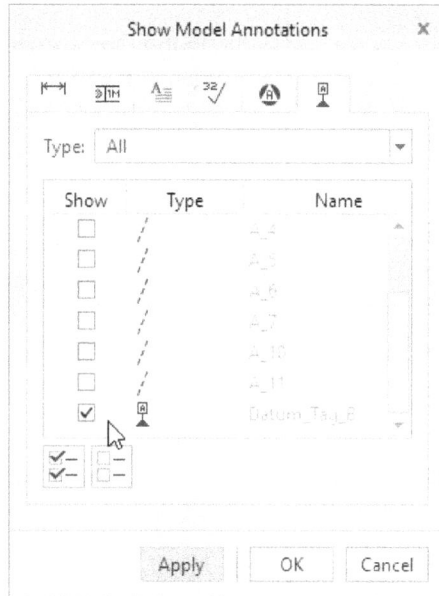

Figure 6–106

10. Click **Apply**.

11. Click **Cancel** to close the Show Model Annotations dialog box.

12. Adjust the location of the datums as shown in Figure 6–107.

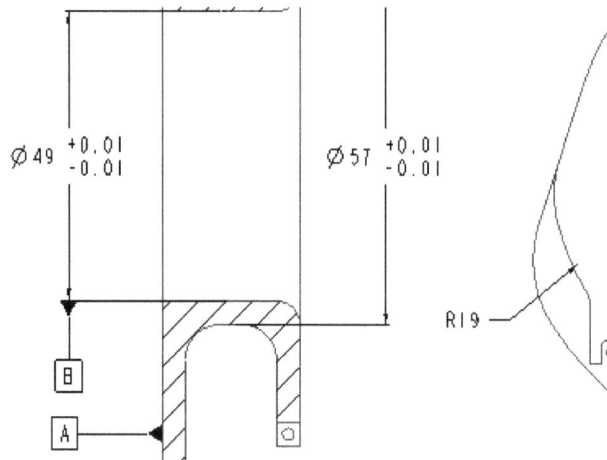

Figure 6–107

13. Select the perpendicularity geometric tolerance, and note that the primary datum A is now shown in green in the Geometric Tolerance tab of the ribbon, indicating that the Datum Feature Symbol has been created, as shown in Figure 6–108.

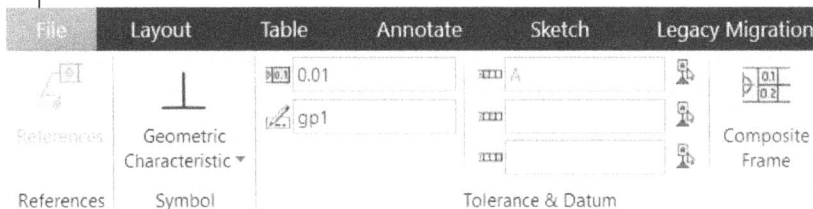

Figure 6–108

14. Note however that the leader is not defined, indicated by the orange leader. Select the geometric tolerance and click

   🔗 (Change Reference).

15. Select the silhouette edge and click the middle mouse button to place the Geometric Tolerance as shown in Figure 6–109.

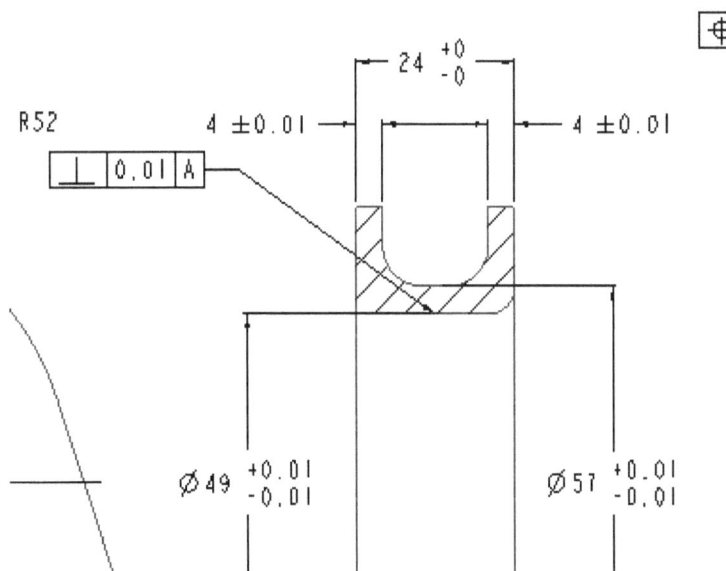

Figure 6–109

16. The updated drawing displays as shown in Figure 6–110.

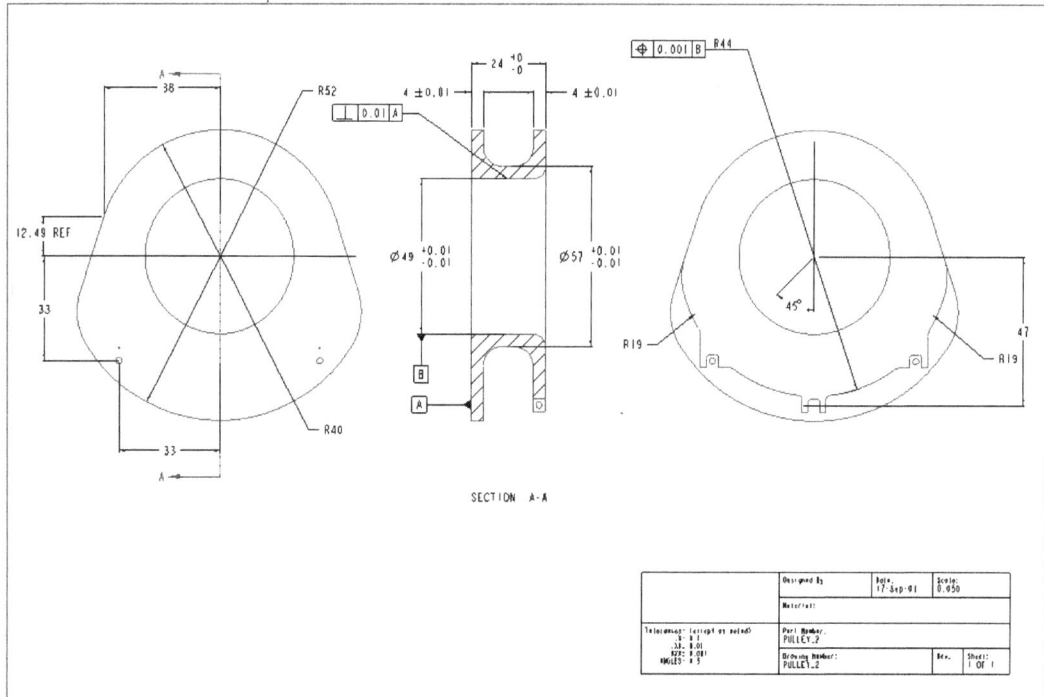

Figure 6–110

17. The drawing would now be ready to continue working on it. Close all files and erase them.

Chapter Review Questions

1. The **default_tol_mode** drawing option only affects newly created dimensions. When working with dimensions that were created before setting the option, you must manually set the Tolerance modes using the Dimension Properties dialog box.

   a. True

   b. False

2. Set datum references are not displayed if the datum display is toggled off.

   a. True

   b. False

3. Which of the following additional symbols can be added to the tolerance using the *Symbols* tab. (Select all that apply.)

   a. Statistical Tolerance

   b. Diameter Symbol

   c. Free State

   d. All Around Symbol

   e. Tangent Plane

4. Geometrical tolerances in assemblies and sub-assemblies only affect their specific level.

   a. True

   b. False

5. Which tolerance standard is based on a set of tolerance tables?

   a. ISO

   b. ANSI

6. Which tolerance standard is based on the number of digits in the nominal dimension?

   a. ISO

   b. ANSI

Answers: 1a, 2b, 3abcde, 4a, 5a, 6b

Chapter 7

Project Lab 3

This chapter contains one project. This project covers the material learned in Chapters 5 and 6.

Learning Objective in This Chapter

- Add notes and tolerances to a drawing.

Practice 7a | Tolerancing a Drawing

Practice Objective

- Add notes and tolerances to a drawing.

In this project, you will add notes and tolerances to the pulley drawing. Figure 7–1 shows the final drawing that you will be creating.

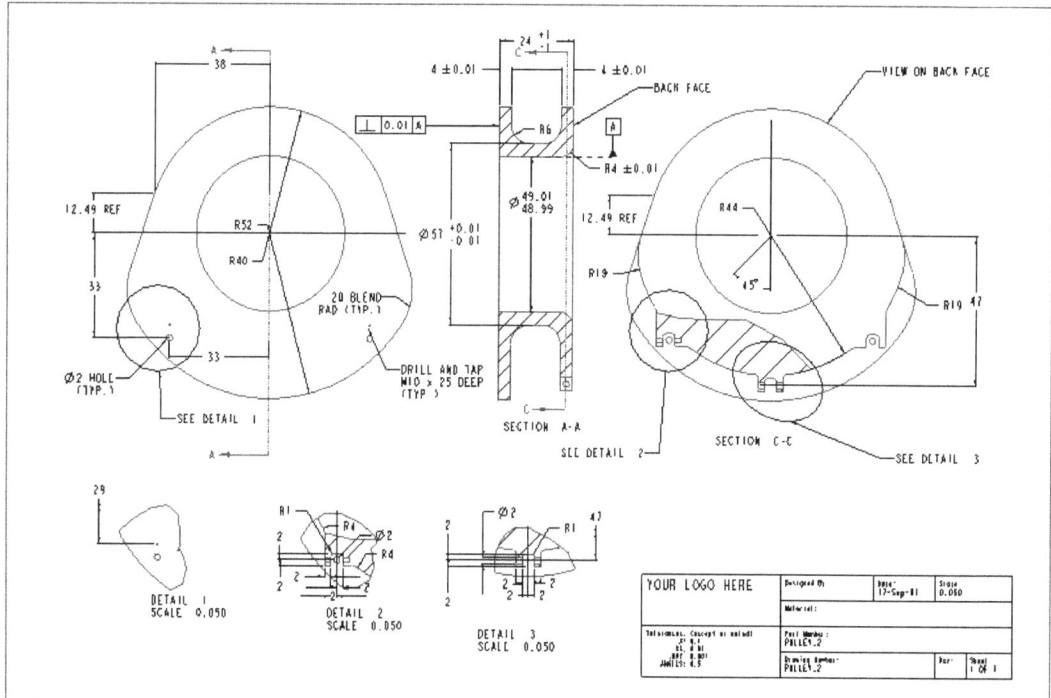

Figure 7–1

Pulley_2.drw references the model pulley_2.prt.

1. Set the working directory to the *Tolerancing_A_Drawing* folder.

2. Open **pulley_2.drw**.

3. Set the model display as follows:

   - ⬚ *(Datum Display Filters)*: All Off

   - ⬚ *(Display Style)*: ⬚ (No Hidden)

The drawing displays as shown in Figure 7–2.

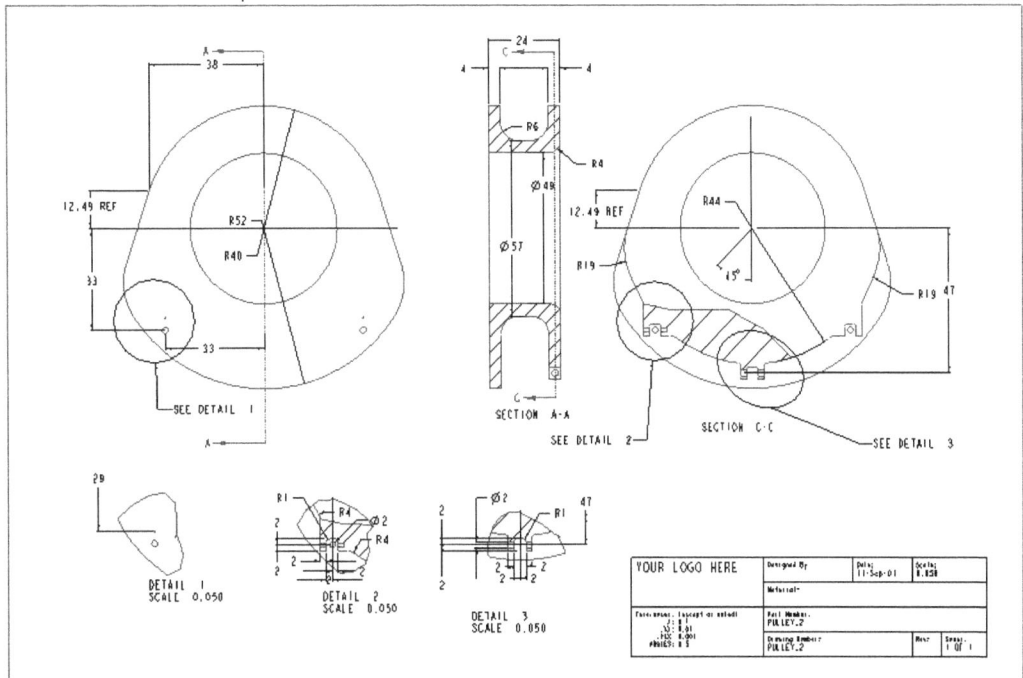

Figure 7–2

4. Display the model notes on the left projection view, as shown in Figure 7–3.

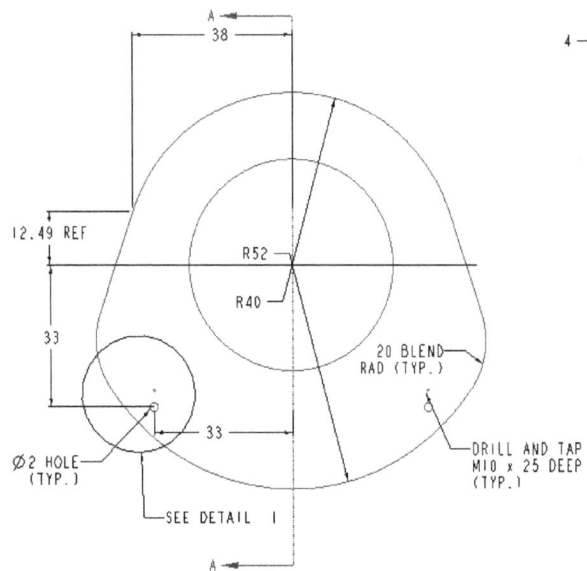

Figure 7–3

5. Create the notes shown in Figure 7–4.

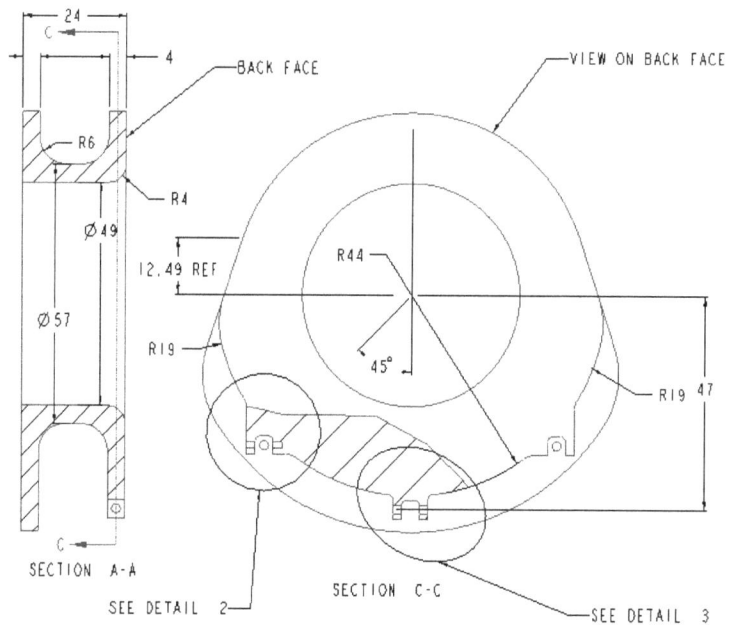

Figure 7–4

6. Open the drawing options file and set the **tol_display** option value to **yes**. Apply the change and close the dialog box.

7. Repaint the drawing.

8. Set the selection filter in the lower right corner of the Creo Parametric window to **Dimension**.

9. Select all of the dimensions using the **Selection Box** in the toolbar.

10. Change the Tolerance mode for all of the dimensions to **Nominal**.

11. Regenerate the drawing.

12. Modify the tolerance display for the dimensions shown in Section A-A in Figure 7–5.

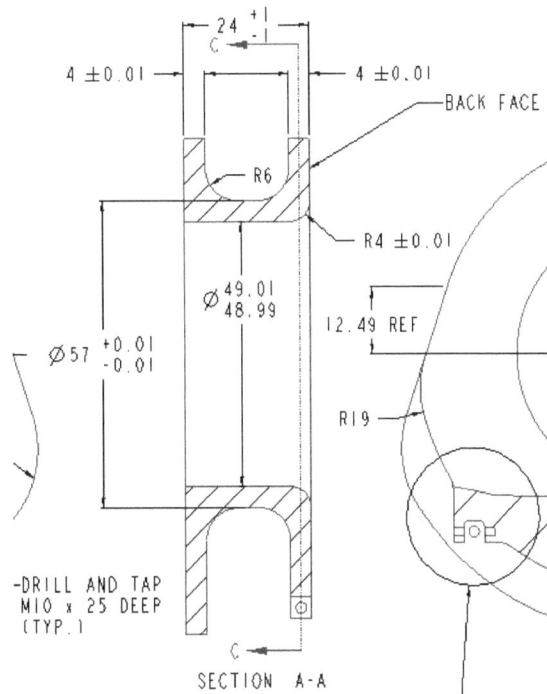

Figure 7–5

13. Create the perpendicular geometric tolerances shown in Figure 7–6.

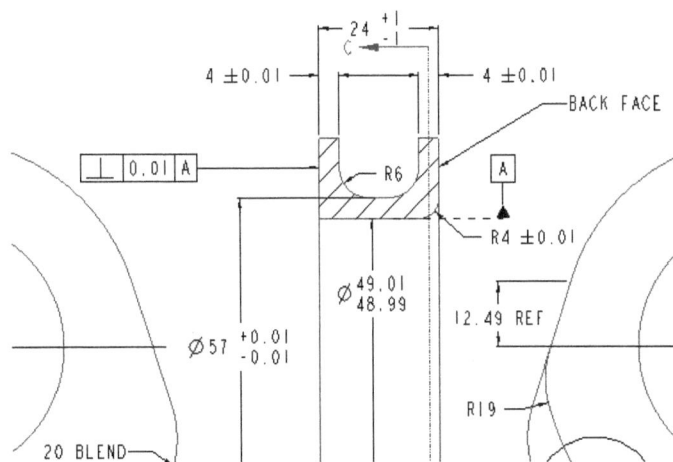

Figure 7–6

14. Save the drawing and close the window.

Assembly Drawings

Creating assembly drawings is similar to creating part drawings, but additional options are available to help you create a drawing that fully communicates the assembly model's information. This chapter describes these options in more detail.

Learning Objectives in This Chapter

- Add, activate, and delete models to fully document the assembly model in the drawing.
- Learn to change the display of a view to its exploded state and modify the position of the components, if required.
- Customize the display of individual components in an assembly view using the **Component Display** option.
- Learn to independently modify the spacing, angle, offset, and line style of each component in a section view using the MOD XHATCH menu.
- Learn to create a zone and a 3D cross-section in the drawing using the newly created zone.

8.1 Add Models

Only one model is assigned when a drawing is initially created. Additional models can be assigned to the drawing to fully document the assembly model.

How To: Add Models to a Drawing

1. Use one of the following steps to add a model:

   - Click ⟋ (Drawing Models) in the *Layout* tab.
   - Select the *Layout* tab, right-click and select **Drawing Models**.

   The **DWG MODELS** menu displays as shown in Figure 8–1.

*The **Replace** option in the **DWG MODELS** menu enables you to replace a model with one of its family table instances, or add several instances to the same drawing.*

Menu Manager
▼ DWG MODELS
Add Model
Del Model
Set Model
Remove Rep
Set/Add Rep
Replace
Model Disp
Done/Return

Figure 8–1

2. Select **Add Model** in the **DWG MODELS** menu. The Open dialog box opens. Select the model and open it.
3. The last model added to the drawing is considered the current active model. To set an alternate model as the active model, use one of the following techniques:

   - Expand ⟋ ▾ (Set Active Model) in the Model Tree and select a model from the list.
   - Double-click on the model name in the bottom border of the drawing in the Graphics window and select a model from the shortcut menu.
   - Select **Set Model** in the **DWG MODELS** menu and select a model.

The Model Tree identifies the current active model. You can also select **Model Disp>Hilite Cur** in the **DWG MODELS** menu to highlight any view containing the currently active model. Select **Model Disp>Normal** to disable the highlighted views.

4. Adding models increases a drawing's retrieval time because all of the associated models are retrieved into RAM with the drawing. Therefore, it is important to delete any models that are not required in the drawing.

   Deleting all of the views in a model does not remove its association to the drawing. To break associativity between a model and the drawing, delete all of the model's views, select **Del Model** in the **DWG MODELS** menu, and select the model to remove from the drawing.

   An example of a multi-model drawing is shown in Figure 8–2. Three models (**SPINDLE.ASM**, **SPINDLE.PRT**, and **PIN.PRT**) have been added to the drawing.

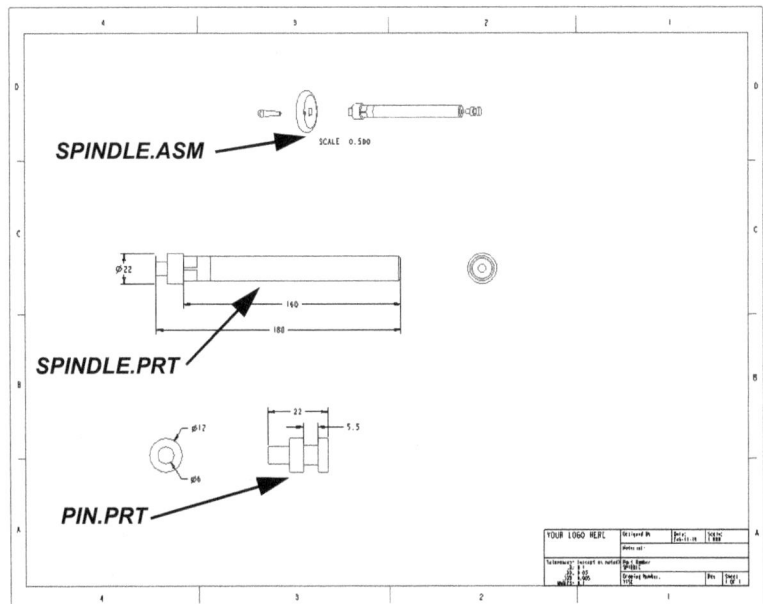

Figure 8–2

8.2 Explode Assembly Views

In some cases, assembly drawings are best displayed in their exploded state. This option is only available if the current model is an assembly.

How To: Explode an Assembly View in a Drawing

1. Once a view has been added to a drawing, you can change its display to exploded using the **View State** category in the Drawing View dialog box. To explode an assembly view, select the **Explode components in view** option and select an Assembly Explode State from the menu, as shown in Figure 8–3.

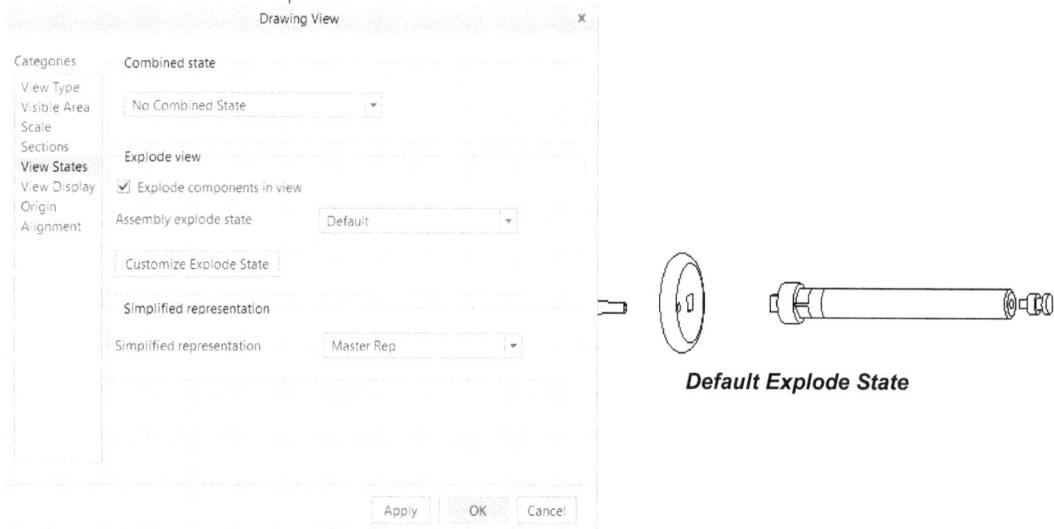

Default Explode State

Figure 8–3

2. All assemblies have a default explode state that is automatically defined. You can customize the location of the components in this default state by editing the explosion distances between components.

If an exploded state is modified in the drawing, it becomes independent of the exploded state in the assembly (i.e., if the exploded state changes in the assembly, that change is no longer reflected in the drawing). Therefore, it is highly recommended that you modify the explode positions in the assembly.

How To: Customize the Default Explode State

1. Click **Customize Explode State** in the *View State* category in the Drawing View dialog box. The Explode Position dialog box opens as shown in Figure 8–4.

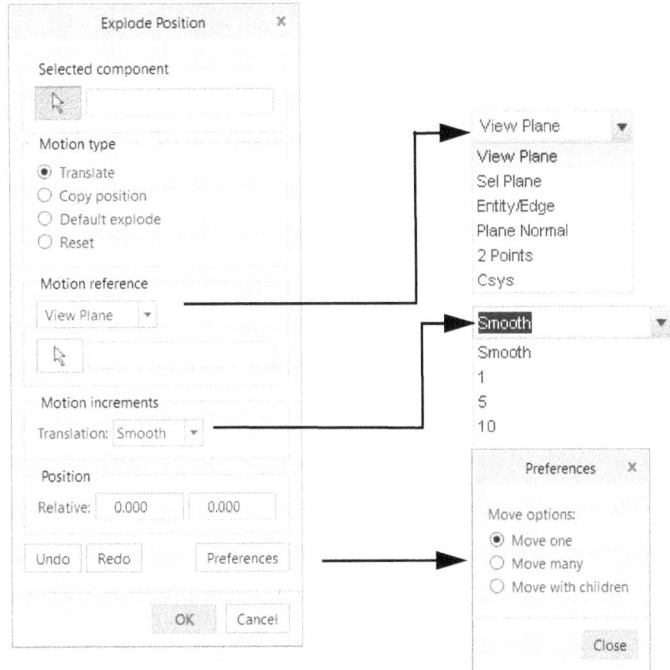

Figure 8–4

2. Select a component in the assembly to edit and select a Motion Type to customize the movement for the position change. Use the cursor to drag the component to a new position.
3. Continue to move components as required. Click **OK** to complete the change.
4. The **MOD EXPLODE** menu displays. It contains options for modifying the position of the components and the Explode Status. **Position** is the default and it opens the Explode Position dialog box. **Expld Status** enables you to toggle the status of components in an exploded view.
5. To complete customization and return to the Drawing View dialog box, select **Done/Return** in the **MOD EXPLODE** menu.

8.3 Change Component Display

When an assembly view is added to a drawing, you can customize the view display in the Drawing View dialog box. This setting determines the display for all of the components in the entire view. Alternatively, you can customize the display of individual components in an assembly view using the **Component Display** option. This option enables you to independently set the following items:

- Hidden line display of assembly members in the drawing.

- Line style of assembly members in the drawing.

The functionality of setting the component display for a drawing view is similar to setting the component display using the View Manager in Assembly mode. However, the two are independent of each other and cannot be accessed in other views.

How To: Change the Component Display

1. The *Layout* tab only displays the commands relevant to that function. This tab must be active to create and modify views.

2. Click ⬚ (Component Display) in the Edit group in the *Layout* tab. The **MEMB DISP** menu displays as shown in Figure 8–5.

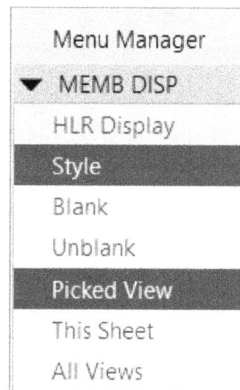

Figure 8–5

3. Once you have selected an option, select the assembly components to apply the change. Click **OK** in the SELECT dialog box to finish the selection.

4. Select the appropriate options to change the component display. The **MEMB DISP** menu options are as follows.

Option	Description
HLR Display	Changes the hidden line removal setting for individually selected components. The available options are **Hidden Line**, **No Hidden**, or **Default**. The **Default** option enables you to set components so that they maintain the view display that was set when the view was placed in the drawing as shown below.

Base_plate.prt set to No Hidden

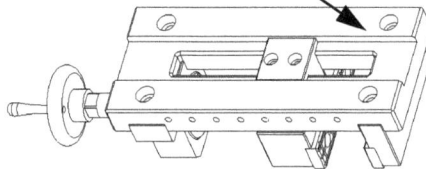

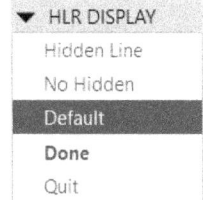

Base_plate.prt set to Hidden Line

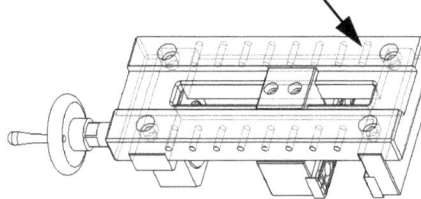

Option	Description
Style	Changes the edge display line style for a selected component or assigns a user-defined color to a selected component. These changes display in the drawing and do not affect the model as shown below.

base_plate.prt set to Phantom Opque

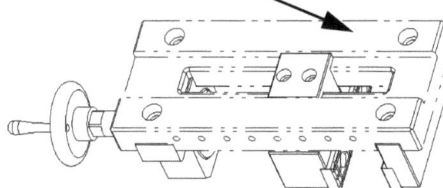

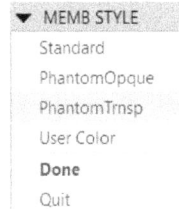

base_plate.prt set to Phantom Trnsp

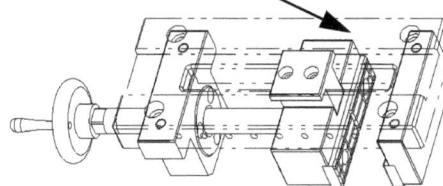

Blank	Blanks a component from a drawing.
Unblank	Resumes a blanked component. All of the views containing blanked components highlight in cyan. When you select a view, the system highlights its blanked components. You can then select the components that you want to resume.

The **Picked View**, **This Sheet**, and **All Views** options in the **MEMB DISP** menu enable you to specify the extent of the changes to the assembly component.

8.4 Display Cross-Sections

As in part drawings, cross-sectional views can be displayed for assembly drawings using the *Sections* category in the Drawing View dialog box. By default, all of the components that intersect the cutting plane display using the default cross-hatching.

How To: Modify the Default Cross-hatching

1. The *Layout* tab only displays commands relevant to that function.
2. To modify the default cross-hatching for individual components in an assembly view, double-click on the cross-section in the drawing view. The **MOD XHATCH** menu displays as shown in Figure 8–6.

*You can also select the cross-section, right-click and select **Properties**.*

Menu Manager
▼ MOD XHATCH
X-Section
X-Component
X-Area
Pick
Next
Previous
Spacing
Angle
Offset
Line Style
Color
Scale
Add line
Delete line
Next line
Prev line
Save
Retrieve
Copy
Erase
Show
Exclude
Restore
Hatch
Fill
Done
Quit

Figure 8–6

3. Select **Next** and **Previous** to scroll through the hatching of each component in the sectioned view. As each component's hatching is selected, it highlights. Select **Pick** to select a specific component's hatching.
4. Once the required component's hatching has been highlighted, you can independently modify the spacing, angle, offset, and line style of its hatching using the options in the **MOD XHATCH** menu.

To remove a component from the cross-sectional display, select **Exclude**. Select **Restore** to restore the cross-sectional display of the component.

Cross-Section Material Files

When you create a cross-section in Part or Assembly mode, the system automatically checks whether the parts intersected by the cross-section have assigned materials. If the material name matches the name of a saved cross-hatching pattern file (e.g., **copper.xch**), the cross-hatching pattern is automatically applied. The **pro_crosshatch_dir** config.pro option is used to point to a directory containing user-defined cross-hatching pattern files.

In Figure 8–7, the assembly drawing contains a section view. The materials assigned to the two components (i.e., aluminum and steel) match the names of saved cross-hatching files (i.e., **aluminum.xch** and **steel.xch**). When the section view is created and placed, these cross-hatching patterns are automatically applied.

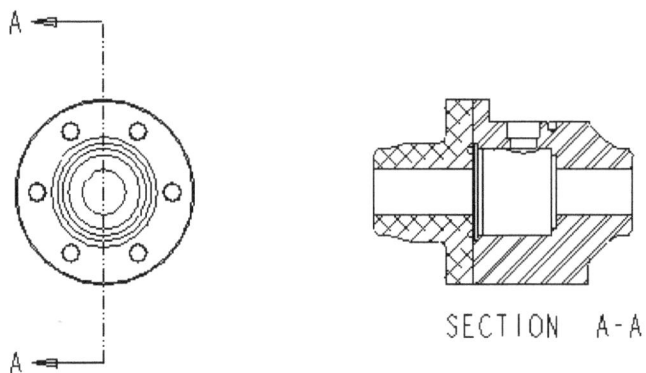

SECTION A-A

Figure 8–7

3D Cross-Sections

To show a 3D cross-section in a view, you first need to define a zone in the 3D object.

Creation of Zones

Zones can be used to help define Simplified Representations. You can also use them to display 3D cross-sections in a drawing. Zones are created in a similar way to cross-sections in parts and assemblies.

How To: Create and Use a Zone

You can also click

*(View Manager), select the Sections tab, expand **New**, and select **Zone**.*

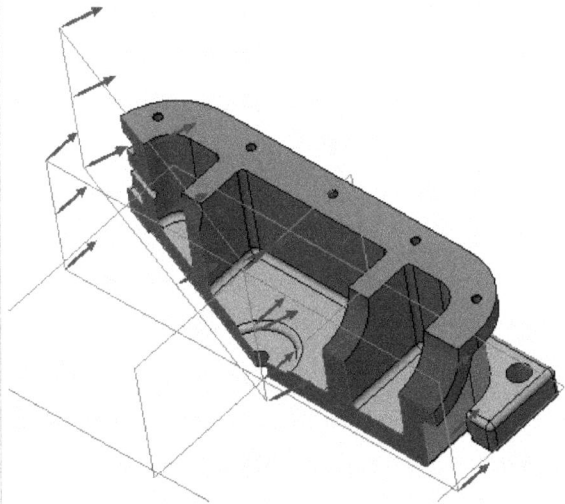

1. In the model (part or assembly), in the *View* tab, expand

    (Section) and select **Zone**. In assembly mode,

    (Section) is also available in the *Model* tab.
2. Select datum planes and/or planar surfaces to create the zone. These zones can then be used in the drawing to display 3D cross-sections, as shown in Figure 8–8.

Figure 8–8

You can control the zone's clipping direction using

 (Change Orientation).

Using Zones in the Drawing View

Zones can be used in the Drawing mode to display 3D cross-sections. The differences in the use of 3D and 2D cross-sections are as follows:

- In a 2D cross-section you cannot switch off X-hatching.

- Any projection and auxiliary views of a 3D cross-sectioned view also include the section by default.

- 3D cross-section hatching is switched off by default; it can be enabled although the hatching cannot be modified.

- A 3D cross-section cannot display section arrows.

To display a 3D cross-section in the drawing, you first create or select the appropriate view and open its Drawing View dialog box. Select the *Sections* category and the **3D cross-section** option, as shown in Figure 8–9. This enables you to select a previously created zone.

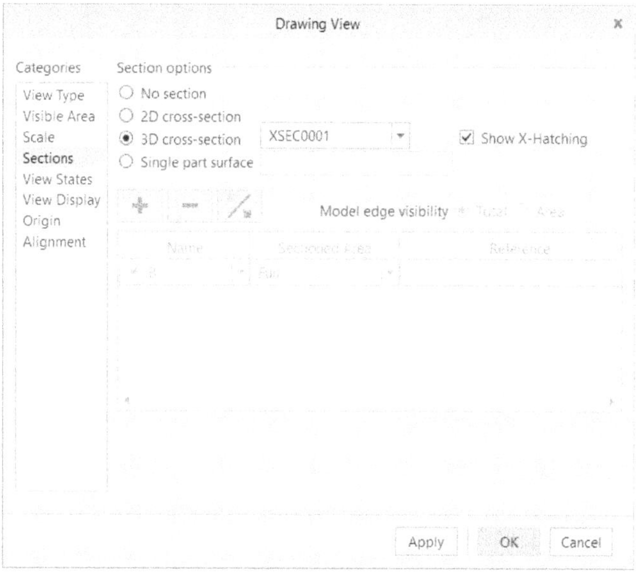

Figure 8–9

You can enable hatching by selecting **Show X-Hatching**. The 3D cross-section displays the X-Hatching as shown in Figure 8–10.

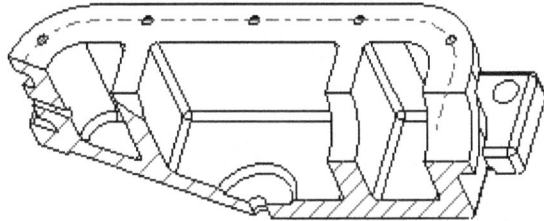

Figure 8–10

Any projection or auxiliary views that reference a view displaying a 3D cross-section also display the section as shown in Figure 8–11. This can be over-ridden using the **No Section** option in the *Sections* area in the appropriate Drawing View dialog box.

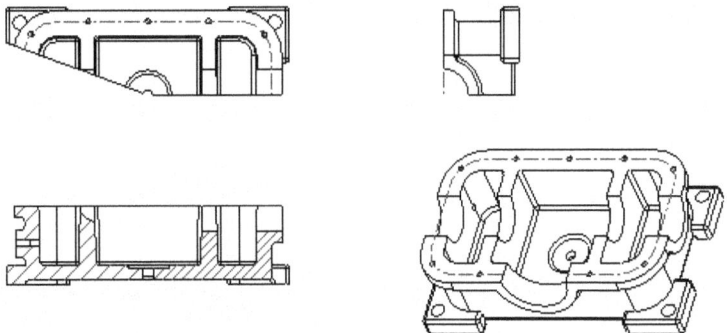

Figure 8–11

8.5 Modify Assembly Views

To modify an assembly view, double-click on the view you want to modify. The Drawing View dialog box opens. The *Visible Area* and *View States* categories are specific to assembly drawings, as shown in Figure 8–12.

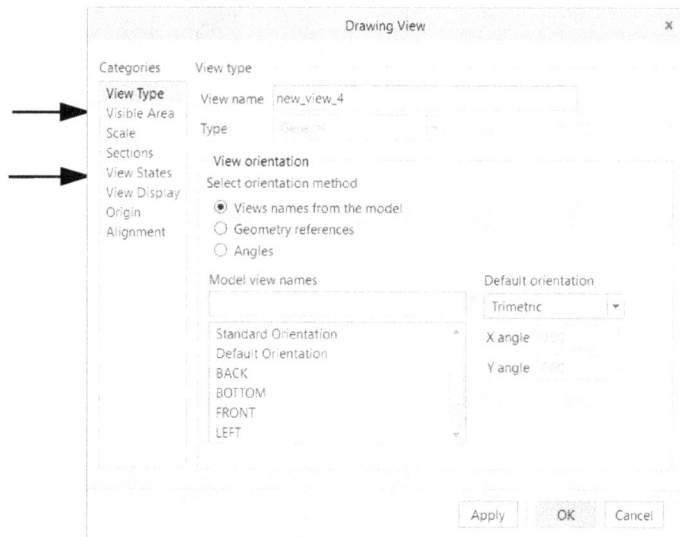

Figure 8–12

View State

To change the simplified representation displayed in an assembly drawing, select the *View States* category in the Drawing View dialog box. Select the required simplified representation from the **Assembly Simplified Representation** menu. Once selected, the modified view and all parent/child views update. Simplified representations must be created in the assembly model to be available in the Drawing View dialog box.

Combined States

In the View Manager, you can create a named combination of various graphic representations of the 3D geometry in the part or assembly by clicking ⬚ (View Manager) and selecting the *All* tab as shown in Figure 8–13.

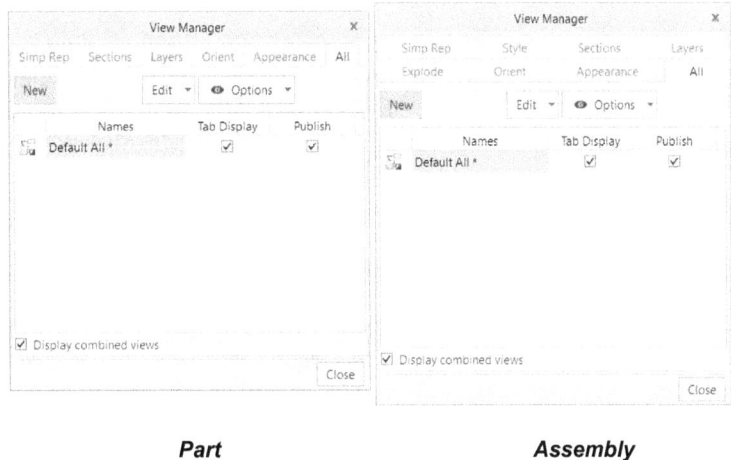

| Part | Assembly |

Figure 8–13

During the placement of the General View in the drawing, the system prompts you to select one of the named combinations to be used for the view, as shown in Figure 8–14.

Figure 8–14

Z-Clipping

Z-clipping enables you to customize the display of a drawing view so that all of the geometry behind a selected plane or the selected point along an edge is removed, as shown in Figure 8–15. Z-clipping can significantly improve performance by reducing the amount of hidden line calculations, especially when working with complex parts or assemblies.

To assign Z-Clipping to a drawing view, select the *Visible Area* category in the Drawing View dialog box and enable **Clip view in Z-direction**. Once enabled, you can select the clipping reference to define the plane beyond which geometry is clipped. The reference can be selected in any of the drawing views.

Z-Clipping is available for part drawings and assembly drawings.

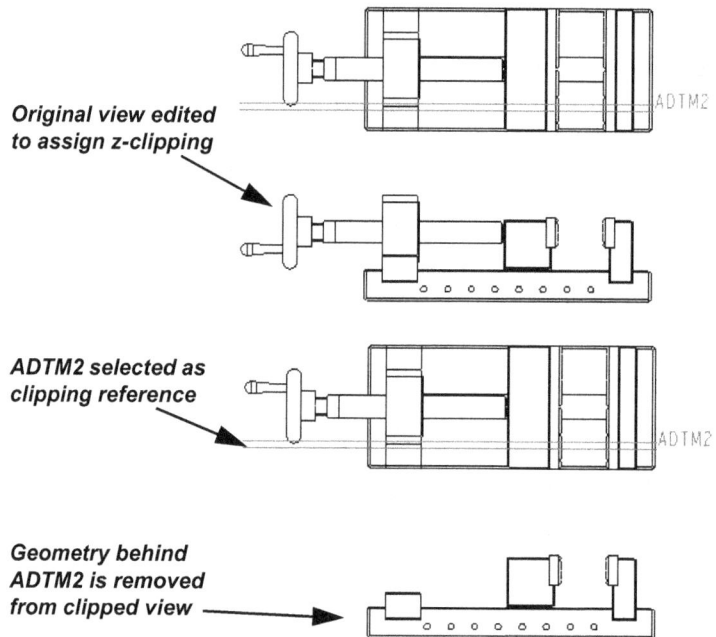

Original view edited to assign z-clipping

ADTM2 selected as clipping reference

Geometry behind ADTM2 is removed from clipped view

Figure 8–15

Practice 8a | Assembly Drawing

Practice Objectives

- Add cross-sectional views of assemblies.
- Modify cross-hatching.
- Add a model to the drawing.
- Explode assembly views.
- Reposition components of exploded assembly views.
- Modify the component display of assembly views.
- Reduce the geometry display in a view.

In this practice, you will create an assembly drawing with cross-section and exploded views. You will then reposition components in views and redefine the component display to create the final drawing shown in Figure 8–16.

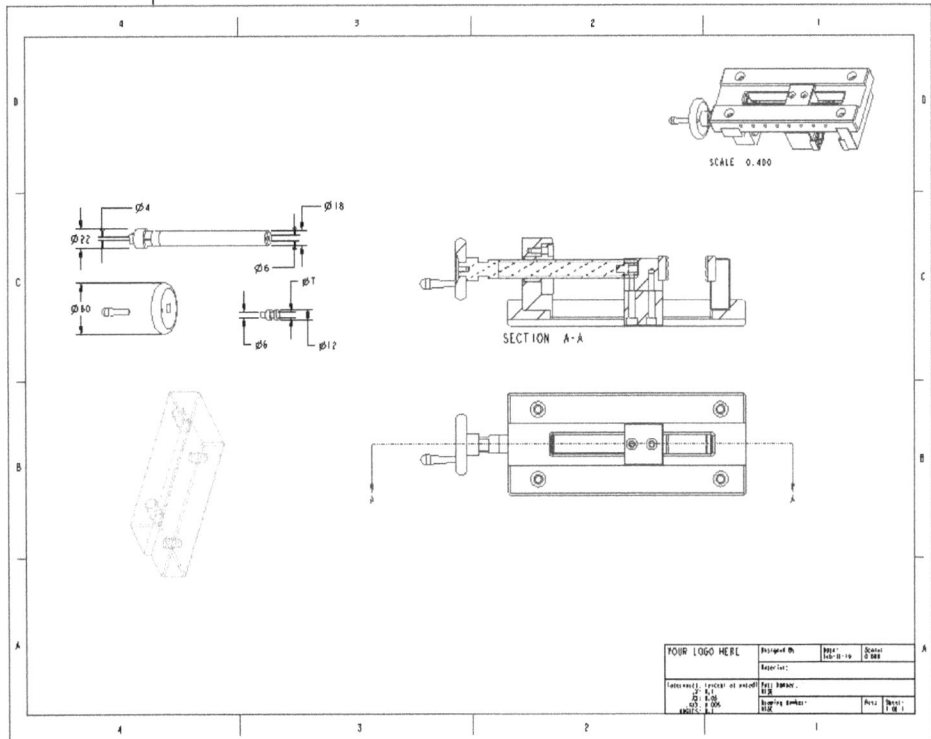

Figure 8–16

Task 1 - Create a new drawing.

1. Set the working directory to the *Assembly_Drawing* folder.

2. Create a new drawing. Enable the **Use drawing model file name** option and clear the **Use default template** option.

You may need to click

⌐ *(Working Directory) in the Open dialog box to show the working directory contents.*

3. Click **Browse** and open **vise.asm** as the default model.

4. Select the **Empty with format** option as the template and select the **generic_c** format.

5. Set the model display as follows:

   - ⅍ *(Datum Display Filters)*: All Off

   - ⎗ *(Display Style)*: ⬚ (No Hidden)

Add the Section A-A view using the existing cross-section A that was created in the assembly. This cross-section passes through ADTM1.

6. Add the three drawing views shown in Figure 8–17. Accept the **No Combined State**. Begin with the **TOP** view, then project the Section view. After that, add the upper right General view with custom scale.

7. Make the following changes:

   - Set the drawing scale value to **0.6**.
   - Set the reference general view (upper right) scale value to **0.4**.

   The drawing displays as shown in Figure 8–17.

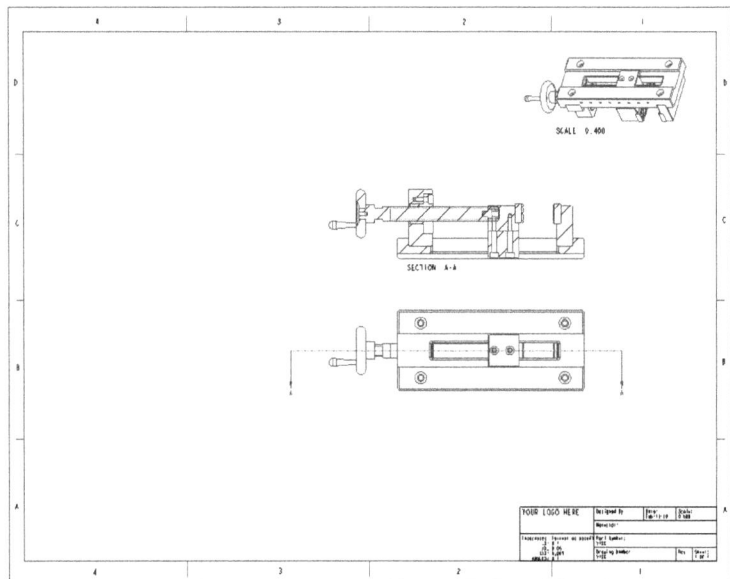

Figure 8–17

Task 2 - Modify the text height of the SECTION A-A view label.

1. Ensure that no drawing entity is selected.

2. Select the **SECTION A-A** label.

3. Select the *Format* tab, and in the *Height* field and enter **0.2** as the new text height, as shown in Figure 8–18.

Figure 8–18

4. Click on the screen.

Task 3 - Modify the SECTION A-A cross-hatching.

1. In the SECTION A-A view, hover the cursor over the cross-hatching and double-click on it. The **MOD XHATCH** menu displays as shown in Figure 8–19.

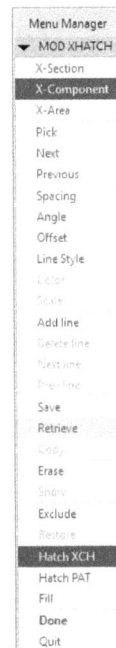

Figure 8–19

2. Select **Next** until the component's hatching is highlighted as shown in Figure 8–20.

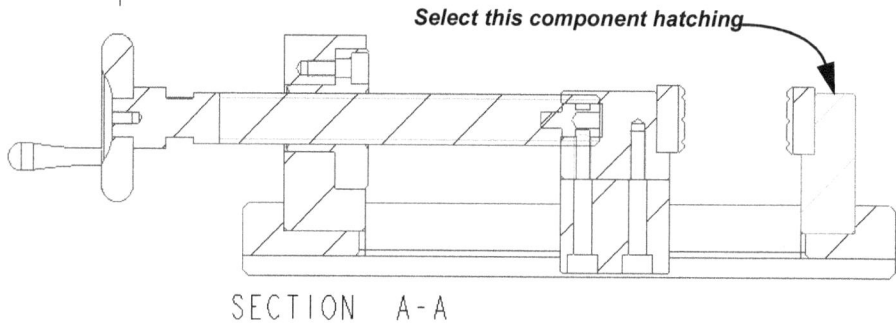

Select this component hatching

SECTION   A-A

Figure 8–20

3. Select **Spacing>Half**. Continue to select **Half** until the component hatching displays as shown in Figure 8–21.

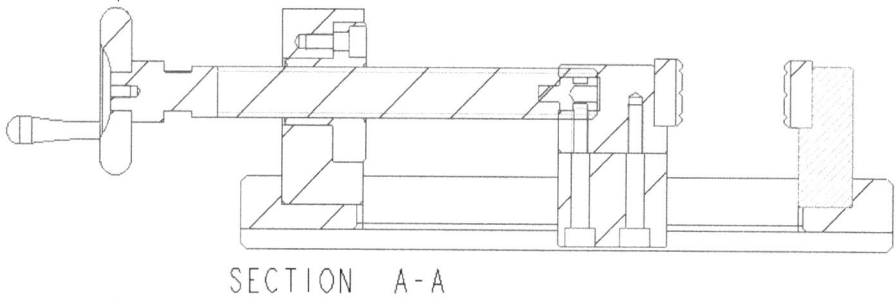

SECTION   A-A

Figure 8–21

*Alternatively, you can select **Prev Xsec** or **Pick Xsec**.*

4. Select **Next** until the component shown in Figure 8–22 is highlighted.

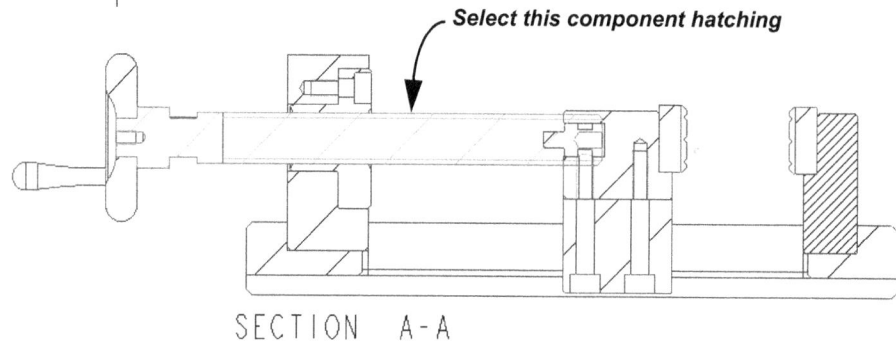

Select this component hatching

SECTION   A-A

Figure 8–22

5. Select **Spacing>Half** and modify the component hatching similar to the spacing shown in Figure 8–23. You will adjust the line style later in the task.

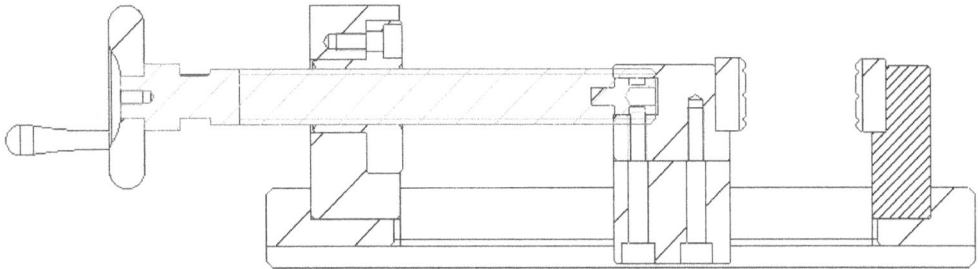

SECTION A-A

Figure 8–23

6. Select **Angle** and change the line angle for the hatching to **30°**.

7. Select **Line Style**. The Modify Line Style dialog box opens as shown in Figure 8–24.

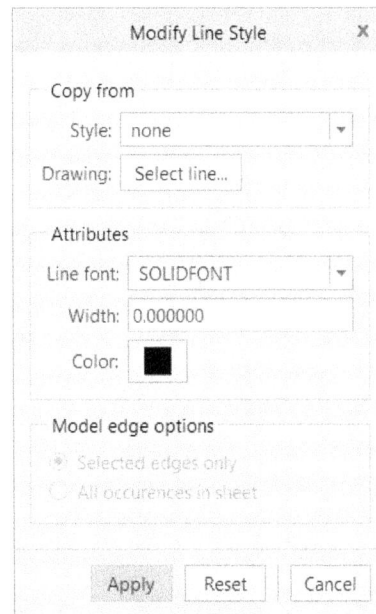

Figure 8–24

8. Select **DASHFONT_S_S** in the **Line Font** menu and click **Apply**. The component displays as shown in Figure 8–25.

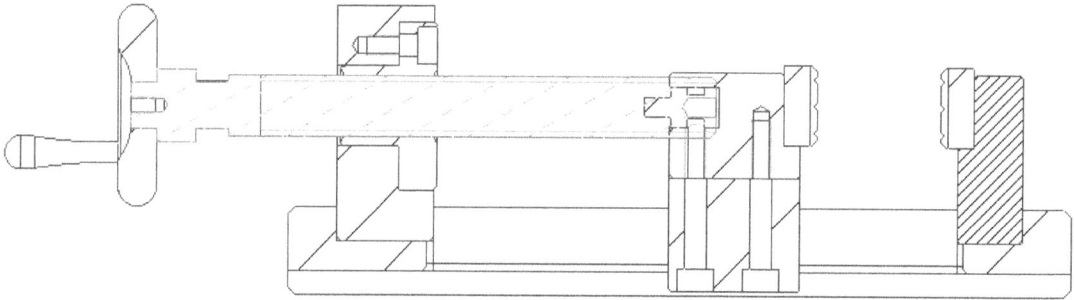

SECTION   A-A

Figure 8–25

9. Close the Modify Line Style dialog box.

10. Highlight the component hatching as shown in Figure 8–26.

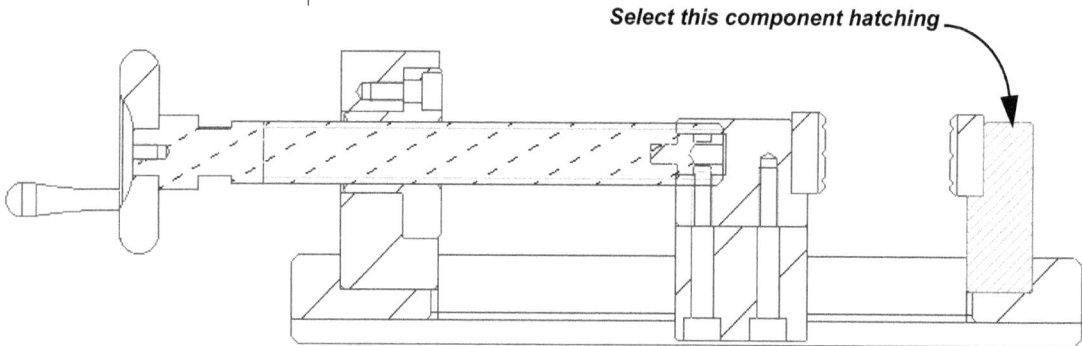

Select this component hatching

SECTION   A-A

Figure 8–26

11. Select **Exclude** to exclude the cross-sectional display from this component. **SECTION A-A** displays as shown in Figure 8–27.

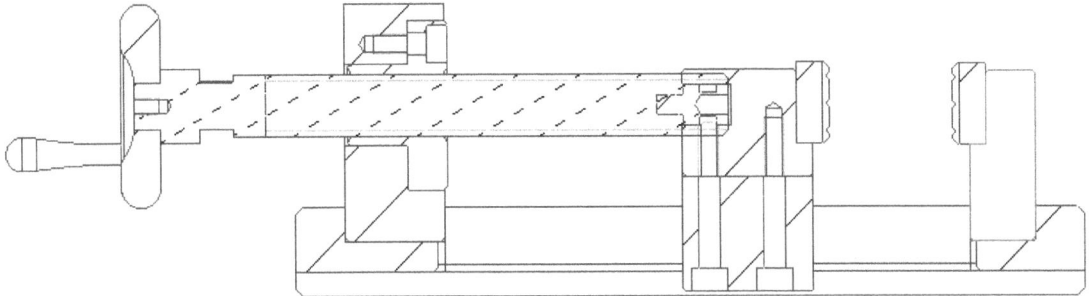

SECTION   A-A

Figure 8–27

12. Select **Done** in the **MOD XHATCH** menu.

Task 4 - Add a new model to the drawing.

---

*You can also right-click and select **Drawing Models**.*

1. Ensure that the Layout tab is selected. Click ⌐ (Drawing Models). The **DWG MODELS** menu displays.

2. Select **Add Model**. The Open dialog box opens.

   - **Note:** To change the active model, select **Set Model** in the **DWG MODELS** menu and select an appropriate model. You can also double-click on the part name at the bottom of the view window to set the current active model, as shown in Figure 8–28.

SPINDLE
VISE

E : ASSEM   NAME : VISE   SIZE : C

Figure 8–28

3. Double-click on **spindle.asm**.

4. Select **Done/Return**. The **spindle.asm** is now the current active model.

5. Add a default General view of the spindle assembly to the drawing and modify the view display, as shown in Figure 8–29. If required, accept the **No Combined State** for the general view.

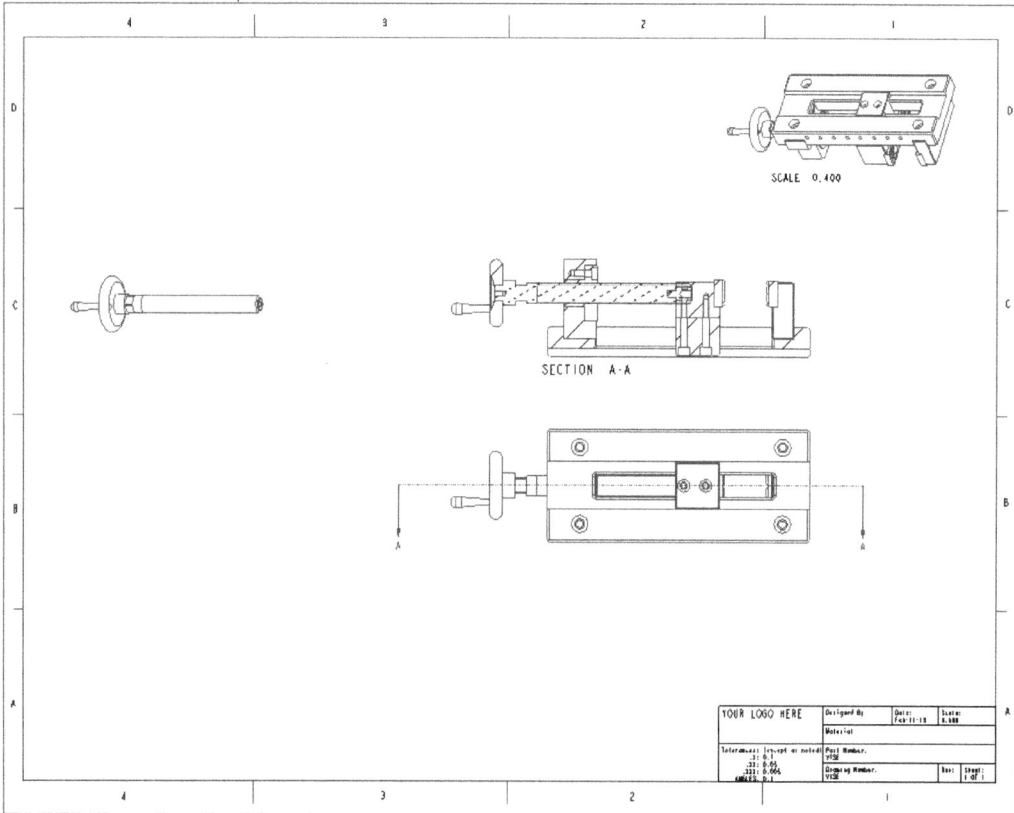

Figure 8–29

Task 5 - Redefine an existing view so that it displays in its exploded state.

1. Double-click on the new view of the spindle assembly that you just created. The Drawing View dialog box opens.

2. Select the *View States* category and select the **Explode components in view** option. The Drawing View dialog box opens as shown in Figure 8–30.

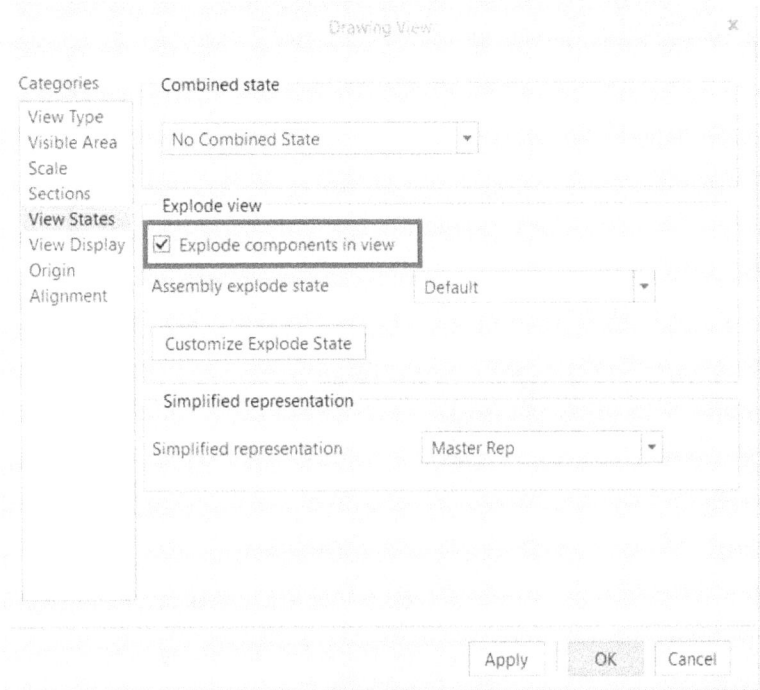

Figure 8–30

3. Apply the change. The view displays as shown in Figure 8–31.

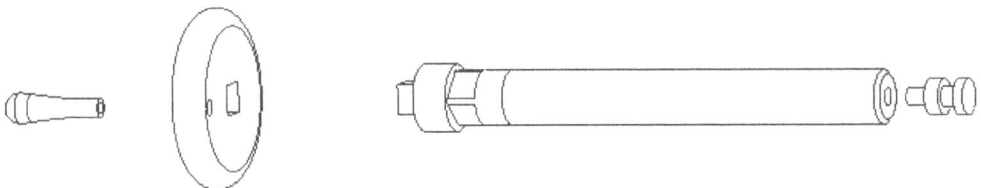

Figure 8–31

Task 6 - Reposition the exploded assembly view.

1. Click **Customize Explode State** in the *View States* category.

The *Expld Status* option in the **MOD EXPLODE** menu toggles the status of components in an exploded view.

2. The Explode Position dialog box opens. Individually select each component and reposition them, as shown in Figure 8–32.

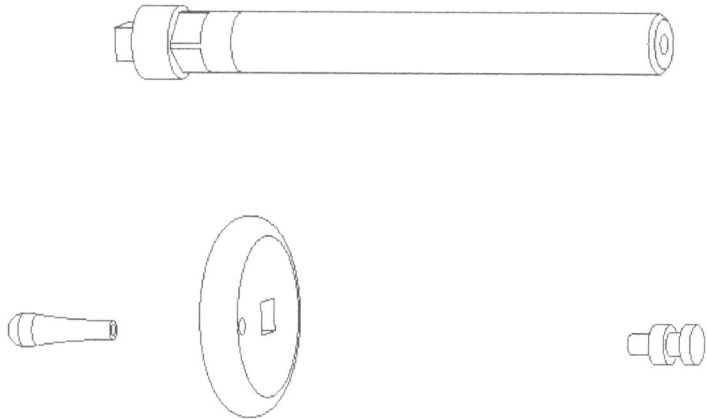

Figure 8–32

3. Click **OK** in the Explode Position dialog box to complete the modification.

4. Select **Done/Return** in the **MOD EXPLODE** menu.

5. Click **OK** in the Drawing View dialog box.

Task 7 - Add a new model and modify its display in the new view.

1. Add **support_end.asm** assembly to the drawing.

You might need to adjust the drawing scale as you add new models.

2. Add a default general view to the drawing and modify the view display, as shown in Figure 8–33.

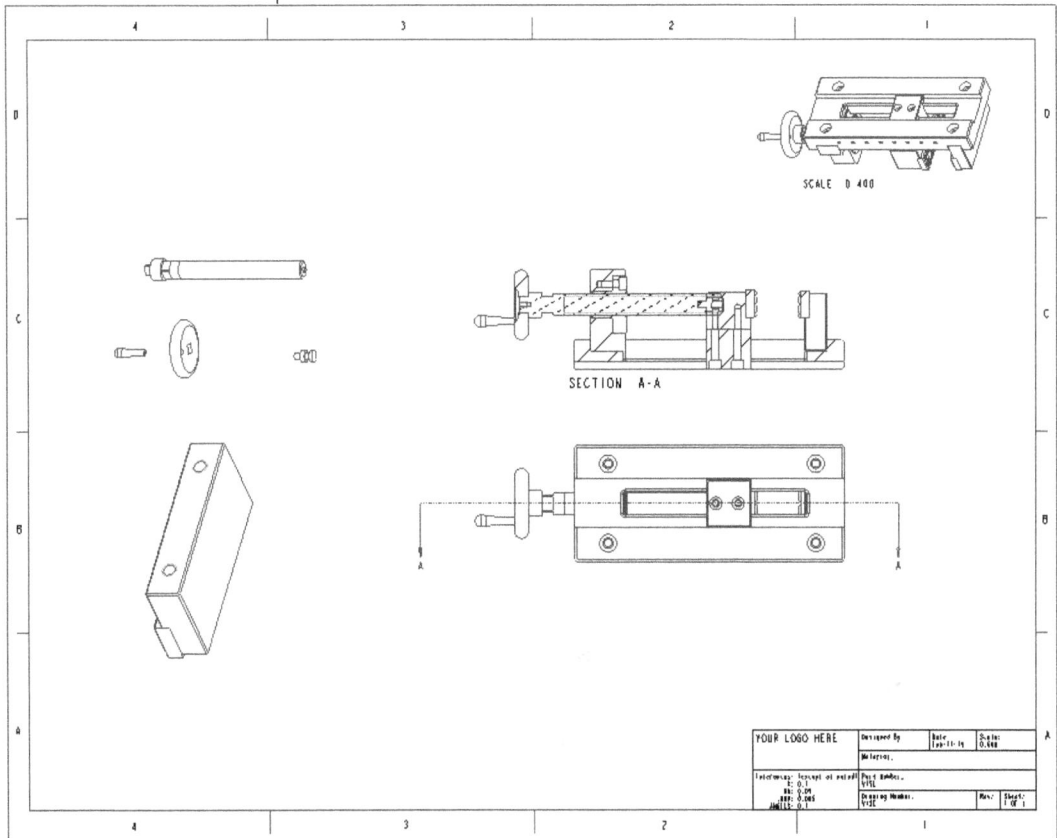

Figure 8–33

3. Click (Component Display) in the Edit group in the *Layout* tab. The **MEMB DISP** menu displays.

4. Select **HLR Display**.

5. Select the component shown in Figure 8–34 and click **OK** in the SELECT dialog box.

6. Select **Hidden Line>Done**. The view displays as shown in Figure 8–34.

Select this component and change its component display to Hidden Line.

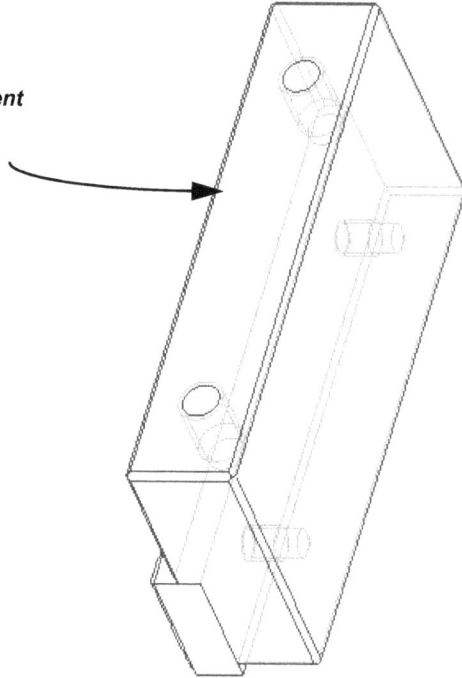

Figure 8–34

*Use **Unblank** to display the components that have been blanked, which display in red. Select the components that you want to unblank.*

7. Select **Style** in the **MEMB DISP** menu.

8. Select the component used in Step 5 and click **OK** in the SELECT dialog box.

9. Select **PhantomTrnsp>Done** in the **MEMB STYLE** menu.

10. Select **Blank** in the **MEMB DISP** menu.

11. Select the component shown on the left in Figure 8–35 and click **OK** in the SELECT dialog box. The view displays as shown on the right in Figure 8–35.

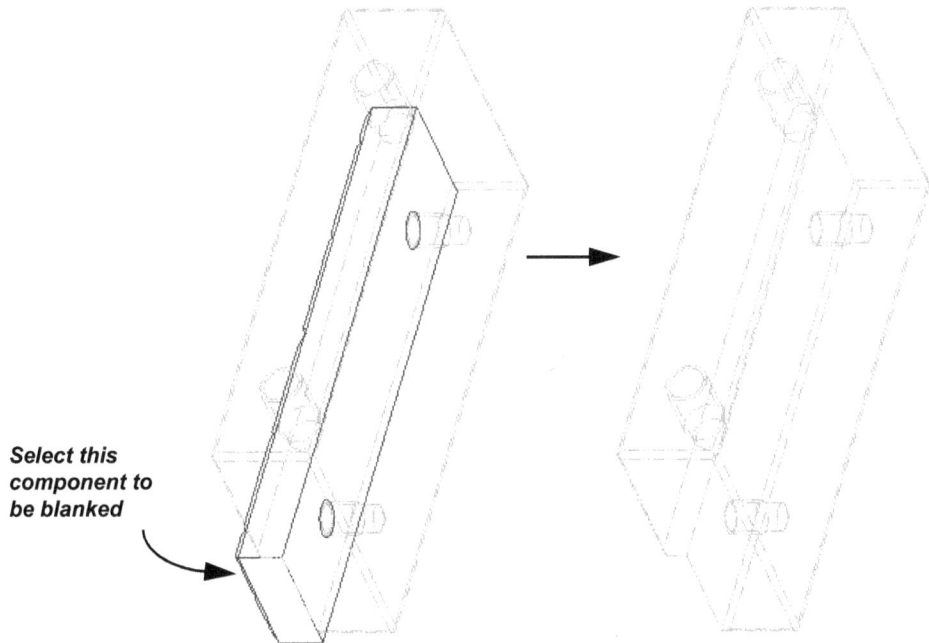

Select this component to be blanked

Figure 8–35

12. Press the middle mouse button twice to close the **MEMB DISP** menu.

Task 8 - Reduce geometry that displays in a view.

You can also click

in the Model Tree and select VICE.ASM and Master Rep.

1. Set **vise.asm** as your current active model. Double-click on the part name (**SUPPORT_END**) in the bottom border of the drawing in the Graphics window (as shown in Figure 8–36), and select **VISE**.

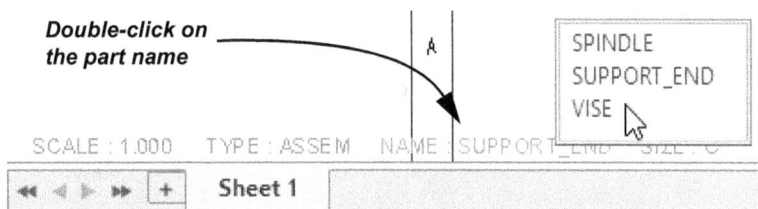

Double-click on the part name

A

SPINDLE
SUPPORT_END
VISE

SCALE : 1.000   TYPE : ASSEM   NAME : SUPPORT_END   SIZE : C

◀◀ ◀ ▶ ▶▶ +   Sheet 1

Figure 8–36

2. Double-click on the Section A-A view (do not click on the cross hatching) shown in Figure 8–37. The Drawing View dialog box opens.

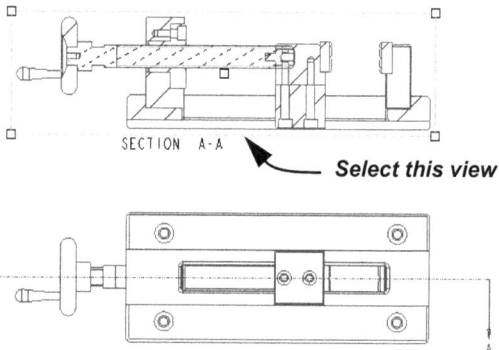

Figure 8–37

You can select an edge, datum, or point on a surface as a clipping plane.

3. Select the *Visible Area* category and **Clip view in Z-direction**.

To display features in the Model Tree, click

⊤ ⌄ *(Settings)>Tree Filters and select Features.*

4. Select datum plane **ADTM1** as your clipping plane. You can select datum plane **ADTM1** in the Model Tree. Datum plane **ADTM1** is the reference plane of cross-section A. Note the magenta arrow in the bottom view pointing to the area that to be removed. The Drawing View dialog box opens as shown in Figure 8–38.

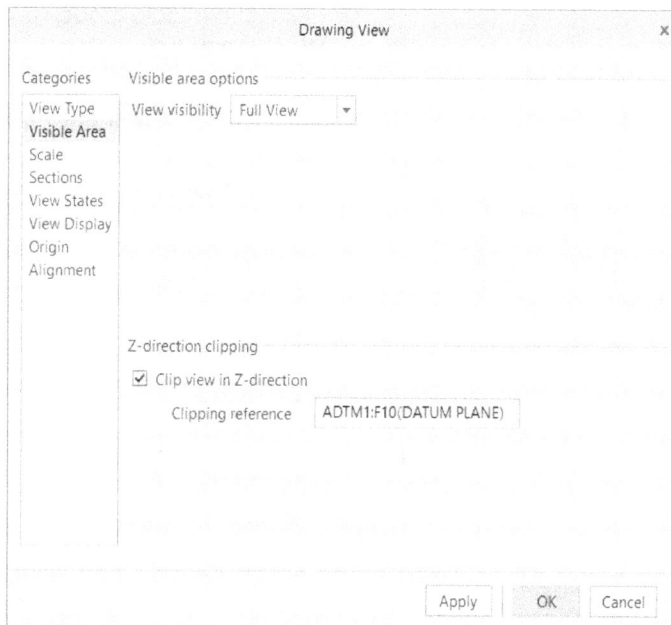

Figure 8–38

5. Apply the change and close the Drawing View dialog box. The view displays as shown in Figure 8–39.

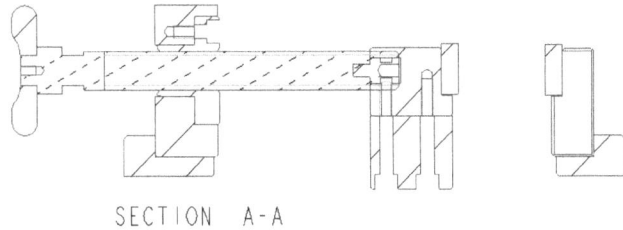

SECTION A-A

Figure 8–39

6. To remove the clipping display, open the Drawing View dialog box again and clear the **Clip view in Z-direction** option in the *Visible Area* area.

7. Click **OK** in the Drawing View dialog box.

Task 9 - Show dimensions for the components in the spindle assembly.

---

1. Set **spindle.asm** as your current active model.

2. Regenerate the drawing.

3. Show the dimensions for the view shown in Figure 8–40. Move the dimensions and break dimension witness lines as required.

*To show the dimensions ensure that the Annotate tab is selected. To quickly show dimensions, right-click on the model in the Model Tree and select **Show Model Annotations**.*

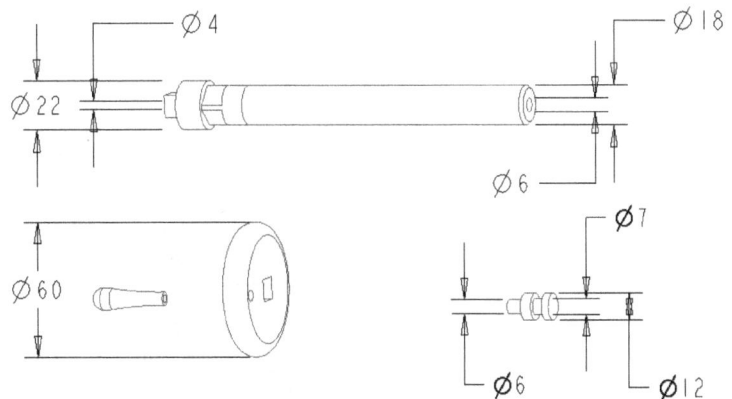

Figure 8–40

4. Save the drawing and close the window.

Practice 8b

Model Configurations on Drawings

Practice Objectives

- Create and use 3D Cross-sections.
- Use Simplified Representation in a drawing.
- Use a Combined State of a model in a drawing.

In this practice you will use a zone to create a 3D Cross-section. You will also use a Simplified Representation and Combined State of a model in the drawing as shown in Figure 8–41.

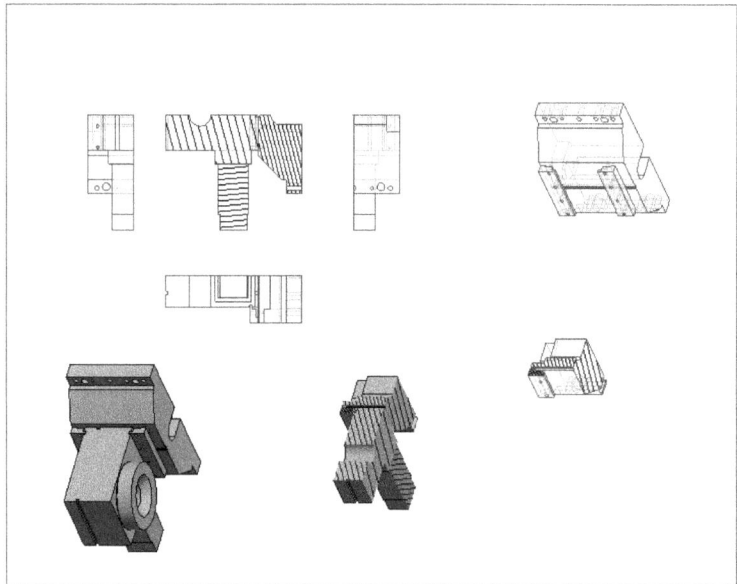

Figure 8–41

Task 1 - Create a zone in the model and use it to create a 3D cross-section in a drawing view.

1. Set the working directory to the Model_Configurations_Drawings folder.

2. Open **08_holder.asm**.

3. Set the model display as follows:

- ⁒ *(Datum Display Filters)*: All Off
- ⋟ *(Spin Center): Off*
- ⃗ *(Annotation Display): Off*
- ⬚ *(Display Style)*: ⬚ (Shading With Edges)

4. In the In-graphics toolbar, click ◉ (View Manager).

5. Select the *Sections* tab.

6. Expand **New** and select **Zone**.

7. Edit the name to **Z1** and then press <Enter>.

When defining Zones the arrows point in the direction in which the geometry is shown.

8. Select datum plane **SECOND_Z1** in the Model Tree. Change the arrow direction using ↻ (Change Orientation), as shown in Figure 8–42.

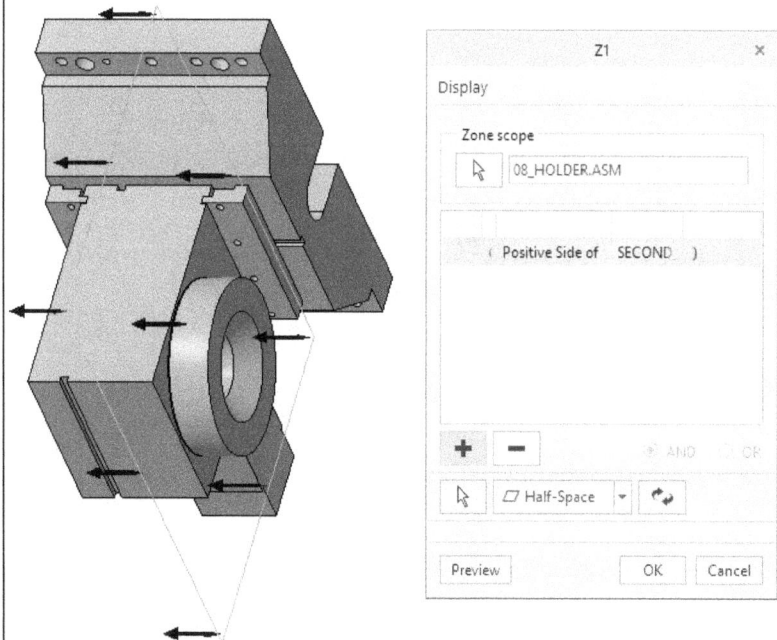

Figure 8–42

9. Add datum plane **FIRST_Z1** using ✚ (Add Reference). Click
   ↻ (Change Orientation), as shown in Figure 8–43.

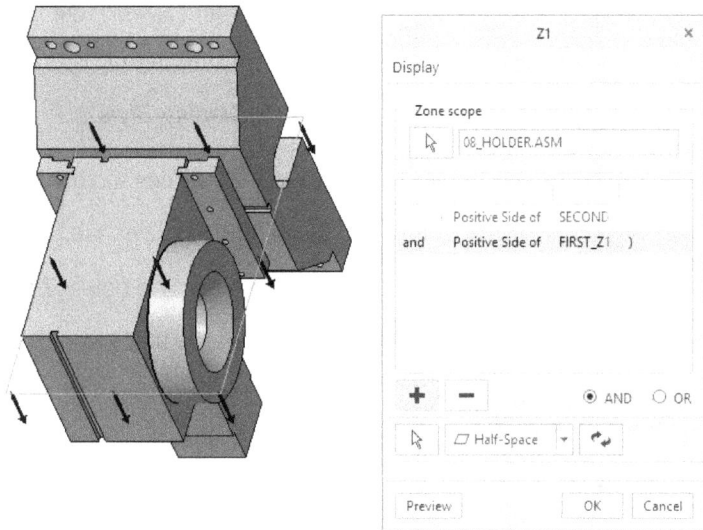

Figure 8–43

10. Click **OK** to complete the zone.

11. Double-click on the text **Z1** in the View Manager dialog box to
    set the zone to be active, as shown in Figure 8–44.

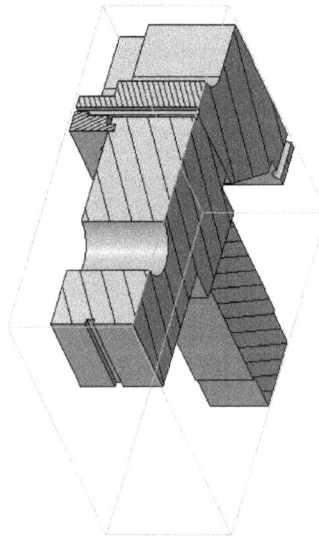

Figure 8–44

12. Double-click on **No Cross Section** to toggle off the zones display.

13. Click **Close**.

14. Save the model and close the window.

Task 2 - Create a new drawing.

---

1. Create a new drawing. Enable the **Use drawing model file name** option and disable the **Use default template** option. Use **08_holder.asm** as the default model. Use an empty A-size sheet as the template.

2. Click **Open** to accept the **Master Rep** in the Open Representation dialog box.

3. Set the model display as follows:

   - $\overset{\times}{/}\!\!*$ *(Datum Display Filters)*: All Off

   - $\square$ *(Display Style)*: $\square$ (Hidden Line)

4. Create a general view in the upper middle section of the page. Verify that the **Do not prompt for Combined State** option is not selected and accept the **No Combined State**. Use view name **RIGHT** for the model orientation and apply the change.

5. In the View Display category, select $\square$ (Hidden) from the *Display style* drop-down list.

6. Specify a 3D cross-section for the view by selecting the **3D cross-section** option. Select **Z1** in the list. Enable **Show X-Hatching,** as shown in Figure 8–45.

If you use a 3D Cross-section in a drawing, all of the dependent views automatically use the 3D Cross-section from the parent view.

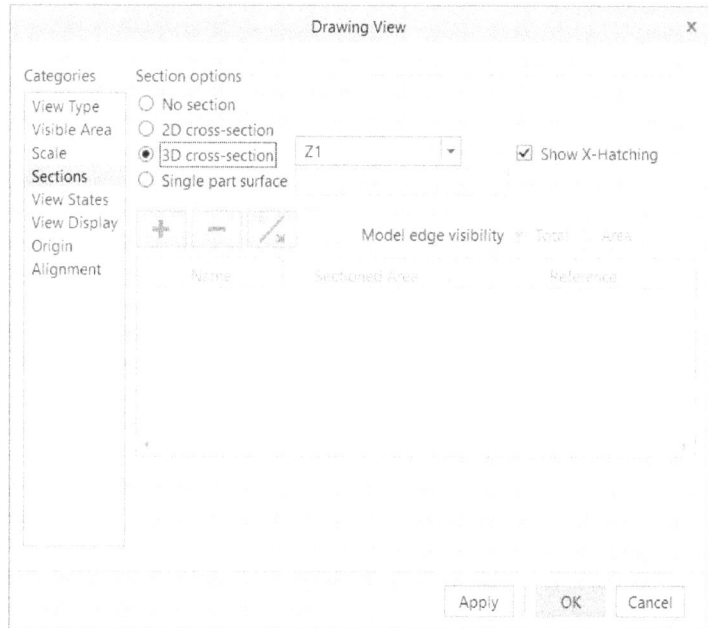

Figure 8–45

7. Click **OK** to complete the view. The view is shown in Figure 8–46.

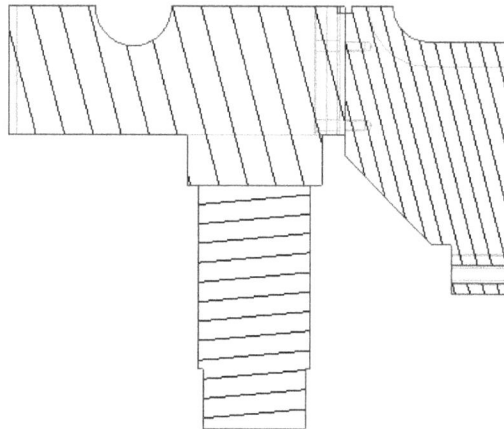

Figure 8–46

8. Change the drawing scale to **0.1**.

9. Create projection views, as shown in Figure 8–47. Set the Display style for each view to ⬚ (Hidden).

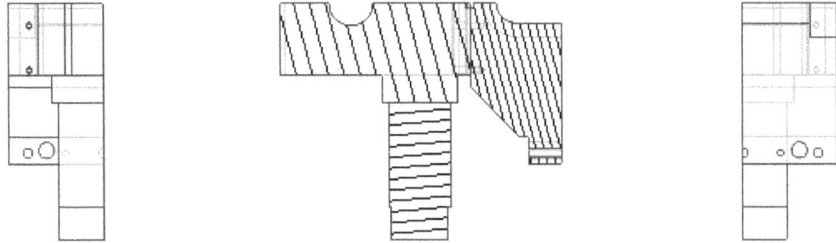

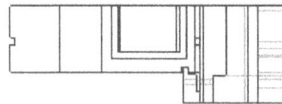

Figure 8–47

10. Save the drawing.

Task 3 - Create a simplified representation in the model and use it in the drawing view.

---

1. Open **08_holder.asm**.

2. In the In-graphics toolbar, click 🔳 (View Manager).

3. Select the *Simp Rep* tab to create a simplified representation. Select **New**, name the representation **S1**, and press <Enter>. The Edit dialog box opens. The default rule is to exclude all of the objects.

The use of a Simplified Representation in a new drawing differs from its use in already created drawings.

4. Include all of the components except **08_motor** and **08_adapter** by placing a checkmark next to them in the Edit dialog box, as shown in Figure 8–48.

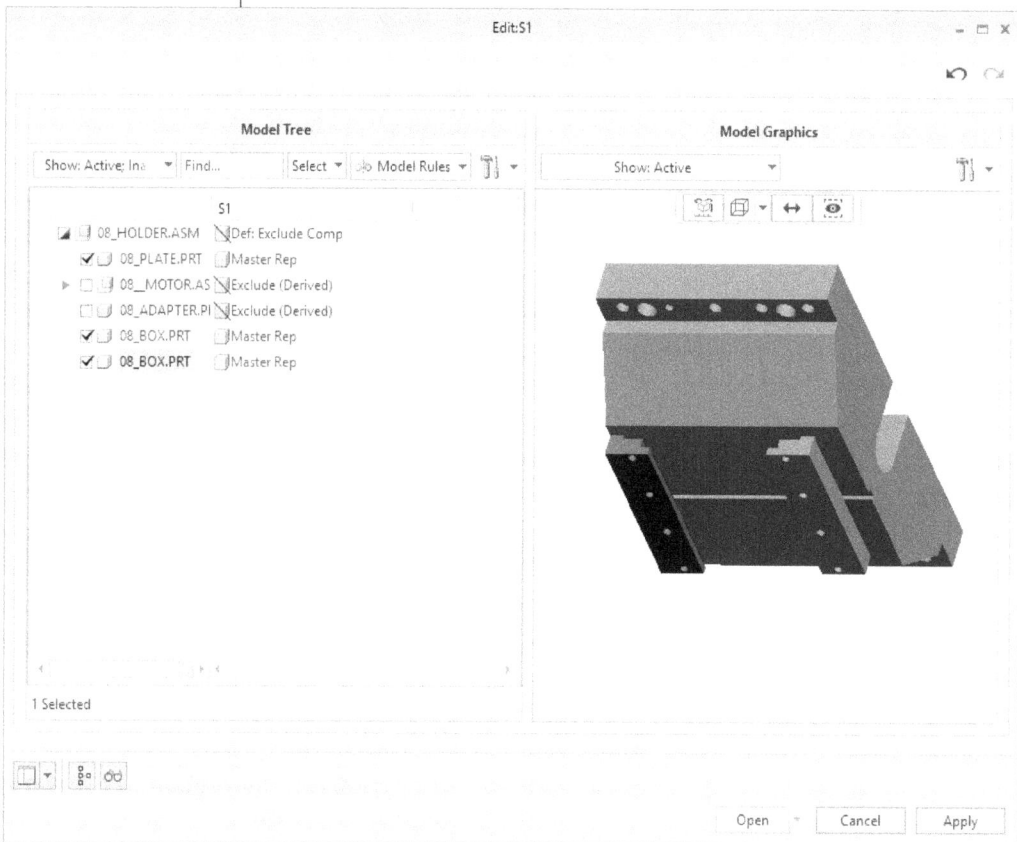

Figure 8–48

*The button may be labeled **OK** on your system.*

5. Click **Open** to complete the Simplified Representation. Double-click on Master Rep to activate it.

6. Save the model and close the window. **08_holder.drw** should now be active.

7. Click (Drawing Models)>**Set/Add Rep.** Select **S1** for the Simplified Rep.

8. Select **Done/Return**.

9. Create a new General view using the default orientation. If required, select **No Combined State**. Place the view as shown in Figure 8–49.

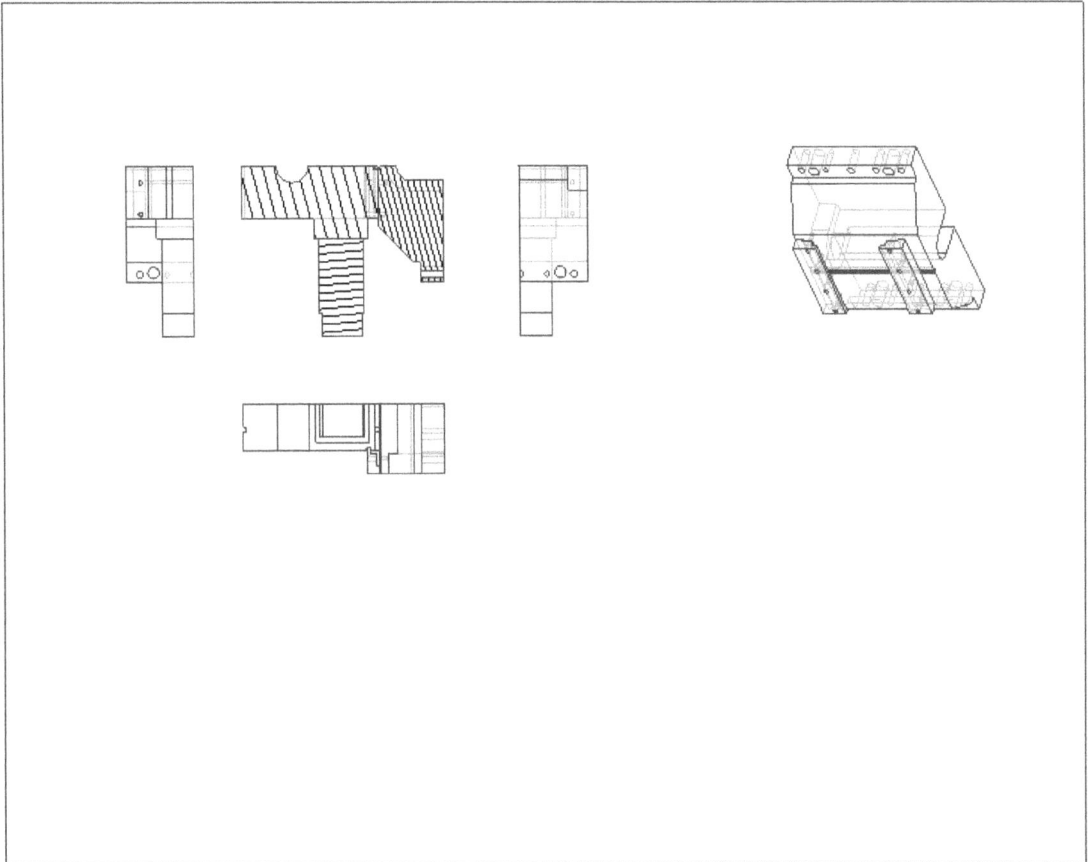

Figure 8–49

10. Save the drawing.

Task 4 - Create an ALL combined representation of the model and use it in the General view.

1. Open the Master Rep of **08_holder.asm**.

2. In the In-graphics toolbar, click 🖼 (View Manager). In the View Manager, select the *All* tab to create an ALL Combination State named **VS1**, as shown in Figure 8–50.

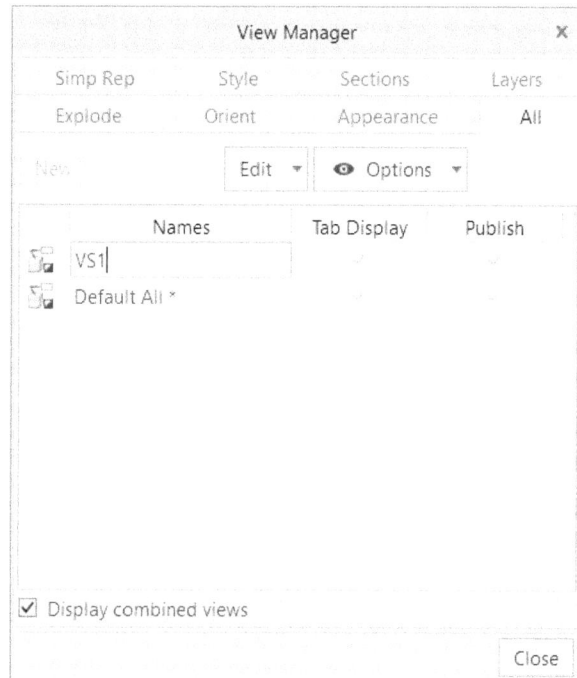

Figure 8–50

3. After entering the name, press <Enter>. Click **Reference Originals**

4. Click **Edit>Edit Definition** in the View Manager dialog box.

5. Set the following parameters, as shown in Figure 8–51:

- *Orientation:* **Default Orientation**
- *Simplified representation:* **S1**
- *Cross section:* **Z1**

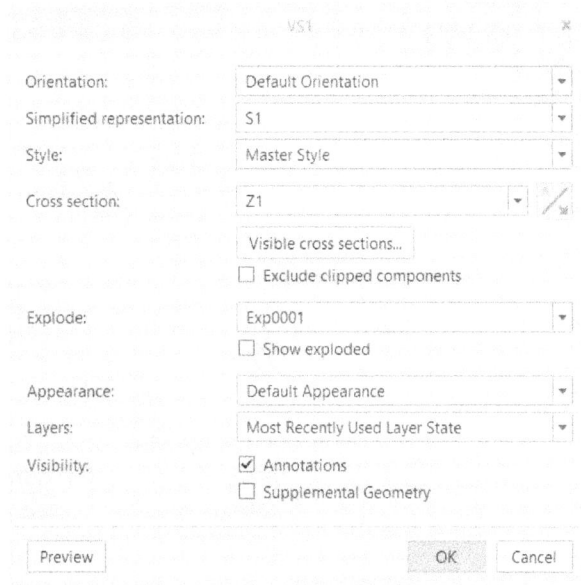

Figure 8–51

6. Click **OK** to complete the state. Close the View Manager. The model displays as shown in Figure 8–52.

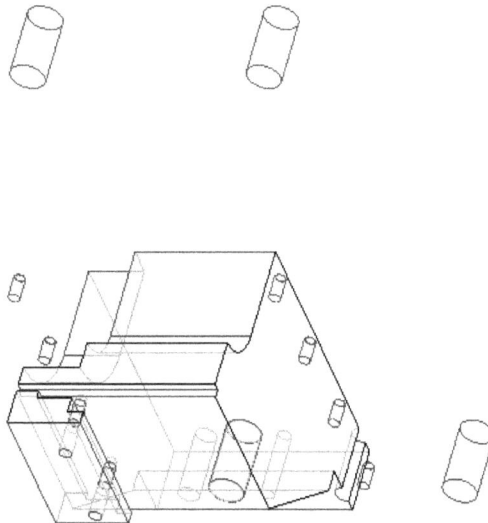

Figure 8–52

7. Save the model and close the window.

8. Return to the **08_holder.drw**. Create a new General view.

9. In the Select Combined State dialog box, select **VS1**, as shown in Figure 8–53.

Figure 8–53

10. Place the view under the previously created representation view, as shown in Figure 8–54. Complete the view using default options. Create two new general views as shown in the lower left corner of Figure 8–54.

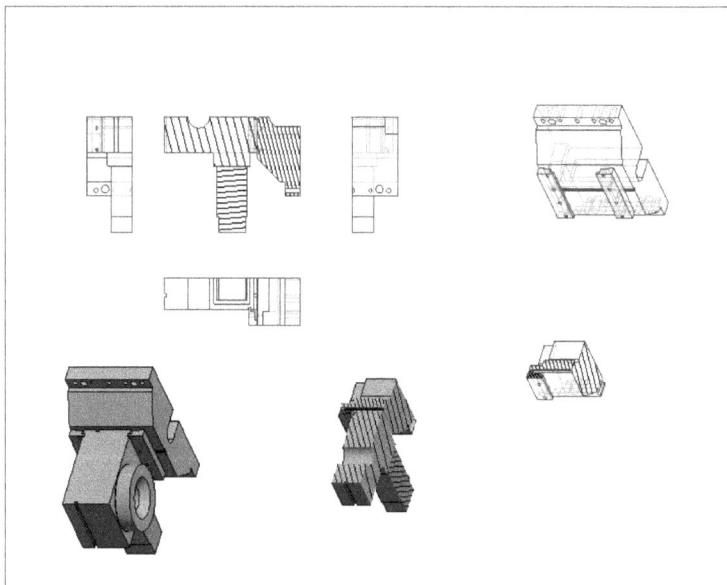

Figure 8–54

11. Save the drawing and close the window.

Chapter Review Questions

1. The first model added to the drawing is considered the current active model.

   a. True

   b. False

2. Which of the following is not a true statement?

   a. Adding models to a drawing increases a drawing's retrieval time.

   b. All of the associated models are retrieved into RAM with the drawing.

   c. It is important to delete any models that are not required in the drawing.

   d. If all of the drawing views for a model are removed the system automatically removes the model from the drawing.

3. Which of the following techniques do you use to set an alternate model as the active model? (Select all that apply.)

   a. Expand ⌐ ▼ (Set Active Model) in the Model Tree and select a model from the contextual menu.

   b. Double-click on the model name in the bottom border of the drawing in the Graphics window and select a model from the contextual menu.

   c. Select **Set Model** in the **DWG MODELS** menu and select a mode.

   d. Select the view of the model that you want to activate.

4. If an exploded state is modified in the drawing, it becomes independent of the exploded state in the assembly (i.e., if the exploded state changes in the assembly, that change is no longer reflected in the drawing)

   a. True

   b. False

5. Once the required component's hatching has been highlighted, which of the following items can you independently modify using the options in the **MOD XHATCH** menu? (Select all that apply.)

   a. **Spacing**

   b. **Angle**

   c. **Offset**

   d. Its hatching line style.

6. How can you remove a component from the cross-sectional display?

   a. Select **Exclude** in the **MOD XHACH** menu.

   b. Right-click on the components and select **Delete**.

   c. Select **Remove** in the Drawing View dialog box.

   d. You cannot remove a component from the cross-sectional display.

7. To display a 3D cross-section in a view you first need to define which of the following items?

   a. X Direction cross-section

   b. Offset cross-section

   c. Planar cross-section

   d. Zone

8. Which of the following categories enables you to specify a simplified representation for an assembly view?

   a. View Type

   b. View Display

   c. Visible Area

   d. View State

Answers: 1b, 2d, 3abc, 4a, 5abcd, 7d, 8d

Drawing Tables

Creo Parametric drawing tables are a powerful tool used to capture a drawing model's information in a table format.

Learning Objectives in This Chapter

- Learn to create a table by selecting the grids, using the Import Table dialog box, importing a table from a file, or using the **Quick Table** option.
- Define the origin and characteristics of a table in the drawing using the appropriate tools.
- Learn to add parametric information or text to the table cells, modify the table using various options in the *Table* tab, and save the table.
- Learn to create a Simple or Two-D repeat region and to enter text using the Report Symbol dialog box.
- Learn to update a repeat region table to display the parameters and model information.
- Manipulate the repeat region tables by filtering information, controlling the information displayed, displaying balloons associated with the BOM repeat region, and paginating the region.
- Learn to create tables automatically for created holes, datum points, and datum axes using the *Table* tab.

9.1 Create a Table

Drawing tables enable you to capture and organize a model's information in a table format. Examples of drawing tables include the following:

- Hole, datum points, and axes tables
- Bill of Material (BOM)
- Family tables

To create the table, you need to define its characteristics: how the table expands during creation (e.g., ascending and rightward), its cell sizes, and its origin. Once the table has been created, you can add parametric information or text to the table cells.

How To: Create a Table

1. The *Table* tab must be selected to create and modify tables, as shown in Figure 9–1.

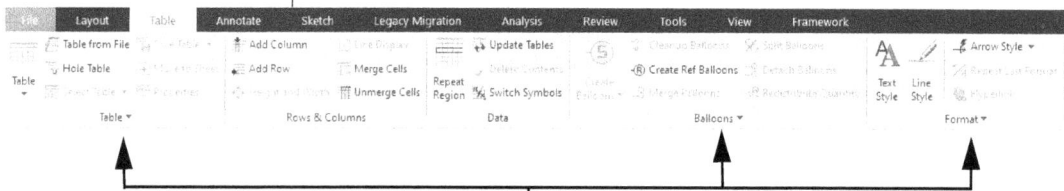

Additional options are located in the flyout

Figure 9–1

*You can also right-click and select **Create Table**. This opens the Insert Table dialog box.*

2. A table can be created by expanding ▦ (Table) in the Table group. This opens the flyout shown in Figure 9–2. The options in the flyout enable you to select the size of the table, open the Insert Table dialog box, import a table, or select from the **Quick Tables** options.

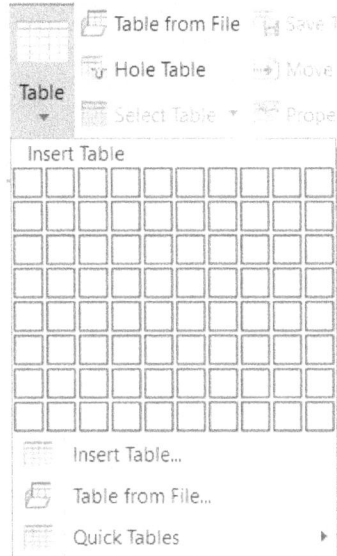

Figure 9–2

The Table flyout enables you to select the size of table by selecting the blocks on the grid. For example, you can create a 3x2 table (three columns and two rows) by selecting the blocks on the grid as shown in Figure 9–3.

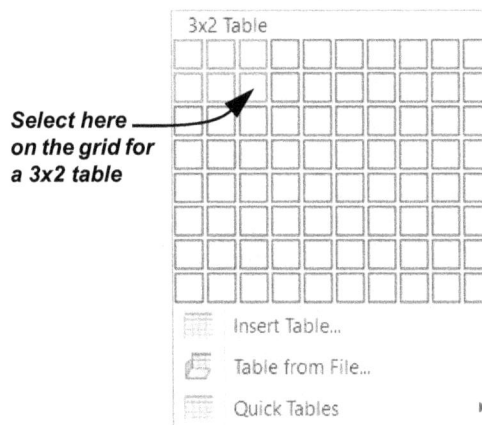

Figure 9–3

Insert Table

Creating a table using the **Insert Table** option enables you to specify additional options. You can specify the direction in which the table updates, the number of columns and rows, and the sizes of the rows and columns. The options are shown in Figure 9–4.

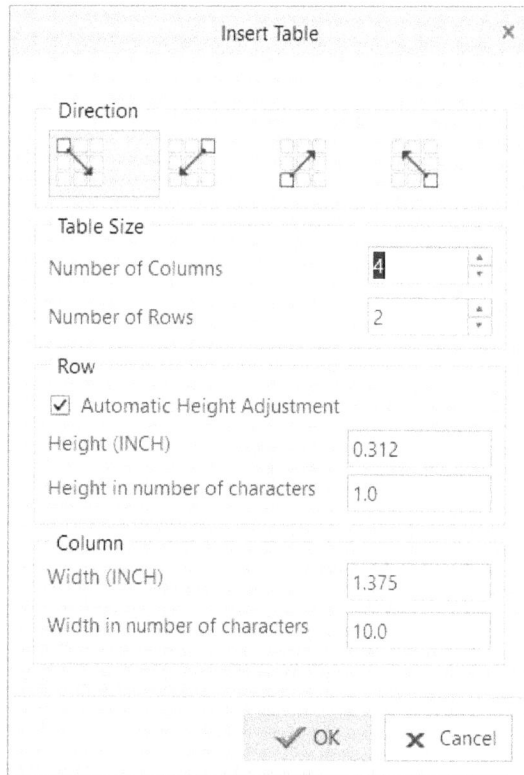

Figure 9–4

Table from File

Click (Table)>**Table from File** to retrieve a previously defined table. A table is saved with a .TBL extension.

Quick Table

Click ▦ (Table)>**Quick Table** to access a gallery of tables that are available for selection. These are commonly used tables for part and assembly drawings. **User Tables** and **System Tables** are the two categories of tables that are available. The User Tables contain tables that are stored in the **pro_table_dir** configuration option. If the configuration option **pro_table_dir** is not set, the system points to the working directory. The System Tables are predefined and located in the *<creo_loadpoint>/ text/tables* directory. If there are no .TBL files, the **Quick Table** menu is empty. An example of the Quick Table gallery is shown in Figure 9–5.

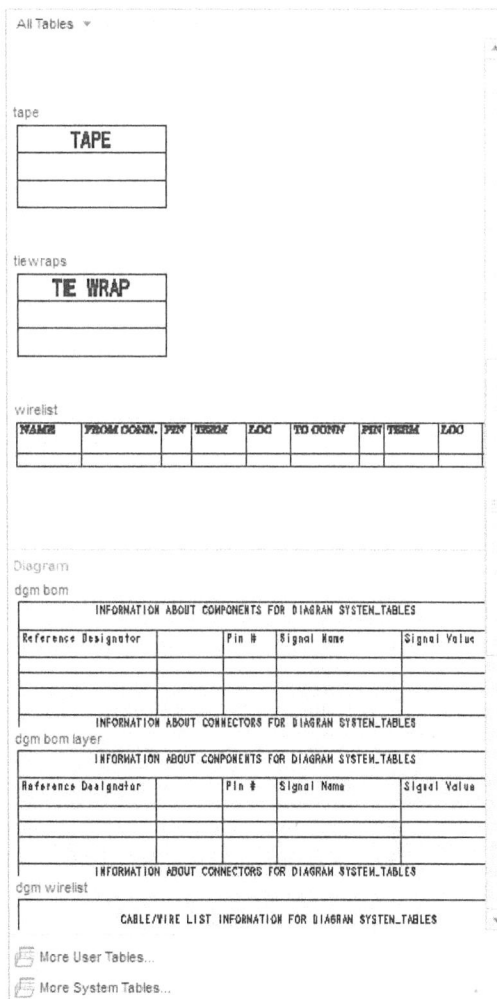

Figure 9–5

3. Each method requires you to locate the table location using the Select Point dialog box as shown in Figure 9–6.

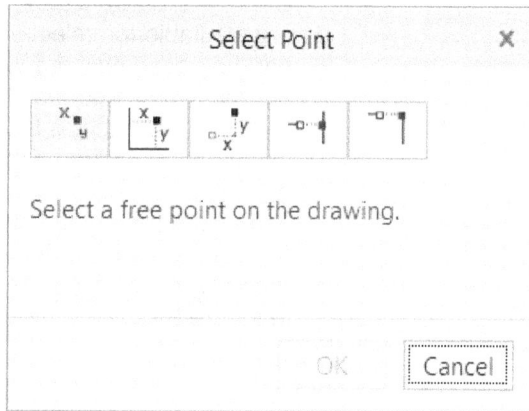

Figure 9–6

The options that you can use to place a drawing table are describe as follows.

Icon	Description
	Enables you to select any location in the drawing.
	Requires you to use an absolute coordinate system by entering an X- and Y-point location.
	Requires you to use a relative coordinate system by entering an X- and Y-point location.
	Requires you to select an edge or entity to locate the table.
	Requires you to select a vertex to locate the table.

4. The predefined table options are not always sufficient. You might need to define its characteristics: how the table expands during creation (e.g., ascending and rightward), its cell sizes, and its origin. This is done using the Table Properties dialog box. Select the table, right-click, and select **Properties**. The Table Properties dialog box opens as shown in Figure 9–7.

Specify the growth direction

Specify the row height

Specify the column width

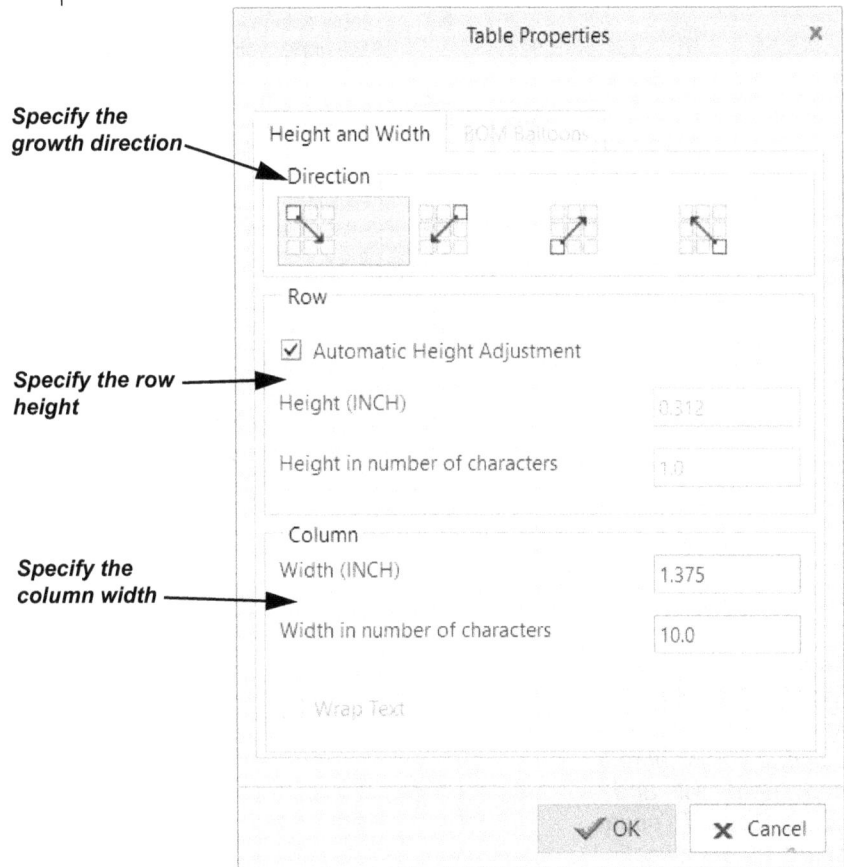

Figure 9–7

The direction options are described as follows.

Option	Description
	Expands the table rows below the table origin and expands the table columns to the right side of the table origin. (The origin is in the upper left corner of the table.)
	Expands the table rows below the table origin and expands the table columns to the left side of the table origin. (The origin is in the upper right corner of the table.)
	Expands the table rows above the table origin and expands the table columns to the right side of the table origin. (The origin is in the lower left corner of the table.)
	Expands the table rows above the table origin and expands the table columns to the left side of the table origin. (The origin is in the lower right corner of the table.)

5. Once the table has been created, you can add parametric information or text into the cells. To add text, double-click on the cell. The *Format* tab opens, enabling you to enter the required text. The text can contain dimension values, parameters, or special characters from the text symbol palette. The table shown in Figure 9–8 has been populated with text.

Hole Chart main_view : CS0			
Hole No.	X	Y	∅
A1	150.000	200.000	50.000
A2	150.000	400.000	50.000
A3	450.000	200.000	50.000
A4	450.000	400.000	50.000
B1	920.000	200.000	55.000
B2	920.000	400.000	55.000
C1	590.000	300.000	70.000
C2	690.000	300.000	70.000
D1	60.000	80.000	80.000
D2	60.000	520.000	80.000

Figure 9–8

*To copy cell content and formatting from one cell to another, select the cell that you want to copy, right-click, and select **Copy**. To paste, select an empty cell, right-click, and select **Paste**. You can also use the keyboard shortcuts <Ctrl>+<C> and <Ctrl>+ <V> to copy and paste.*

To edit the text, double-click on the cell and make any required changes. To modify the text attributes (e.g., style or height), use the options in the *Format* tab, as shown in Figure 9–9.

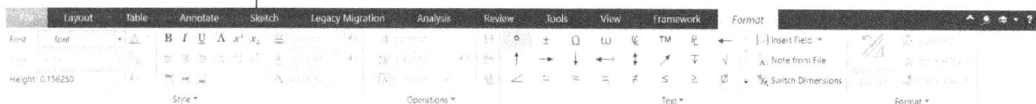

Figure 9–9

You can also right-click on the text to access a shortcut menu with various formatting options, or select **Text Style** to access the Text Style dialog box, as shown in Figure 9–10.

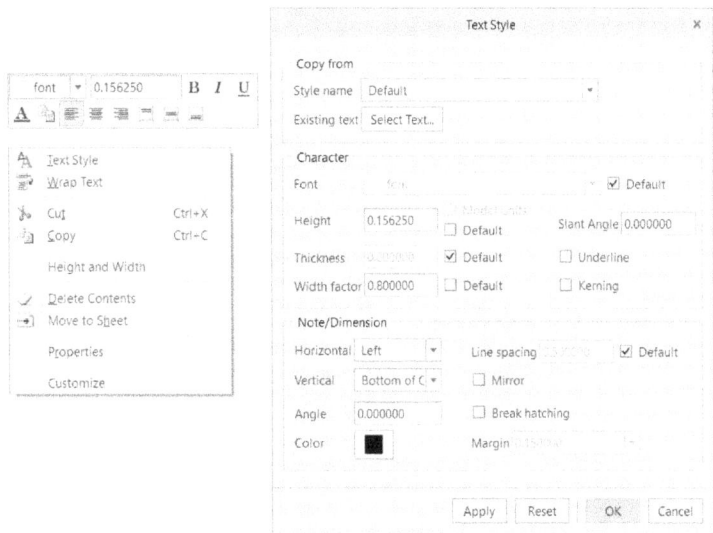

Figure 9–10

In general, similar types of tables are used in different drawings. By saving the table, you can quickly use it into other drawings rather than recreate it.

How To: Save and Reuse a Existing Table

1. Select the table by selecting a single cell in the table, expanding ▦ (Select Table), and clicking ▦ (Select Table) in the Table group. You can also select an entire table using the Table selection filter or by selecting the table from the Drawing Tree.

2. Once selected, click 🖫 (Save Table) in the Table group.

3. Enter a table name and click **Save**. The table is stored in the current working directory with a .TBL extension.

4. To open the saved table, click 📁 (Table from File) in the Table group and select the name of the .TBL file in the Open dialog box.

Alternatively, you can save the table as a text file by selecting the table, expanding 🖫 (Save Table), and clicking 🕮 (Save As Text) or 🕮 (Save As CSV) in the Table group. The table content is stored in the current working directory with a .TXT or .CSV extension, respectively.

Selection Methods

To select a cell, row, column, or the entire table, you can use one of the following methods:

- Set the selection filter to the required option (**Table**, **Table Cell**, **Table Column**, or **Table Row**) and select in the table.

- Set the selection filter to **Drawing item and View**. Place the cursor over the table, right-click and select one of the following options: **Next**, **Previous**, or **Pick From List**. Right-click to toggle through each item (i.e., **Next**) without having to display the shortcut menu.

- Set the selection filter to **Drawing item and View**. Select the cell, expand ▦ (Select Table) in the Table group and click ▦ (Select Table), ▥ (Select Column), or ▤ (Select Row) as shown in Figure 9–11.

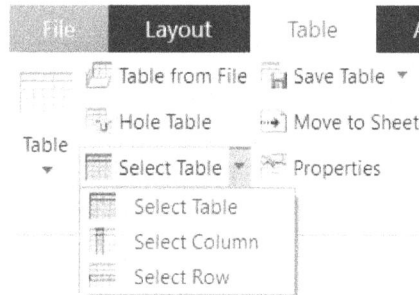

Figure 9–11

Copy Table

You can copy tables from one point to another. Select the table to copy, right-click, and select **Copy**. Clear the table selection, right-click, and select ▢ (Paste). The clipboard window opens, displaying the copied object. Select a point on the object in the clipboard to define the origin, and select a point in the drawing where you want to copy the table.

Rotate

To rotate a table in 90° increments (counter-clockwise) around its origin, select the table to rotate and select **Table>Rotate** as shown in Figure 9–12.

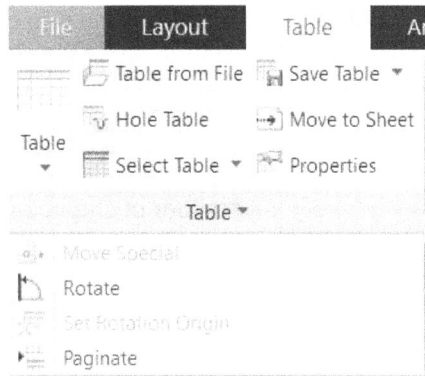

Figure 9–12

Justification

To justify the text, right-click in the cell, row, column, or whole table, and select **Properties** to access the *Format* tab. You can also click ⅍ (Text Style) in the Format group. In the Text Style dialog box, select the justification style in the *Note/Dimension* area as shown in Figure 9–13. Click **OK** to complete the justification.

To justify individual cells once the text has been entered, double-click on the cell, and define the justification in the Text Style tab.

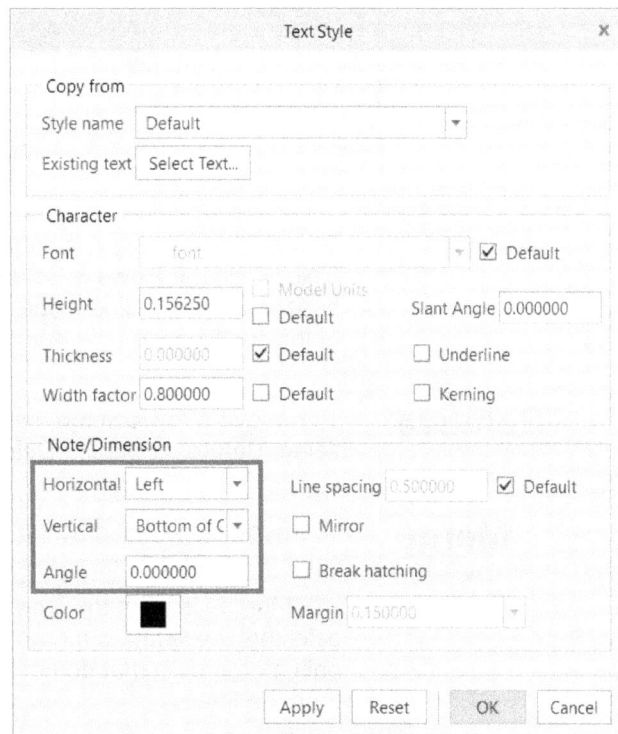

Figure 9–13

Size

To change the size of a row/column, select it and click ✛ (Height And Width) in the Rows & Columns group. You can also set the selection filter to **Table Column** or **Table Row** and double-click on the column or row. The Height and Width dialog box opens as shown in Figure 9–14. Use it to set the new size for the selected row/column. The size of the row/column can be defined by the number of characters or by length units.

You cannot change the size of individual drawing cells using this method.

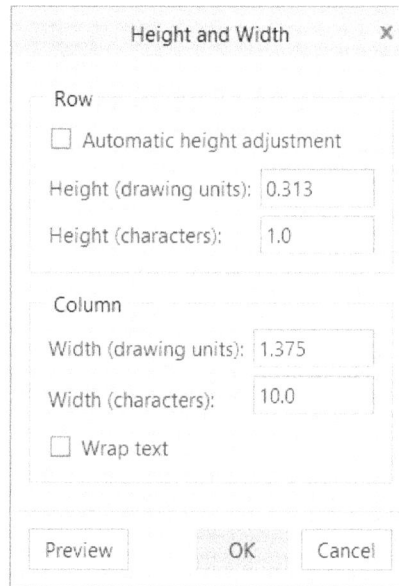

Figure 9–14

Insert

To insert a new row or column, click ✛≡ (Add Row) or 📏 (Add Column) in the Rows & Columns group. Select a horizontal/vertical line in the table. A new row/column is placed at this location.

Remove

To remove a row/column, select the row/column, right-click, and select **Delete**, or press <Delete>.

Merge

To merge individual drawing table cells across several rows or columns, select a cell in the table to identify the table, click 📄 (Merge Cells) in the Rows & Columns group, and select the cells that you want to merge, as shown in Figure 9–15. You can only merge cells that do not contain any text in any cell other than the first.

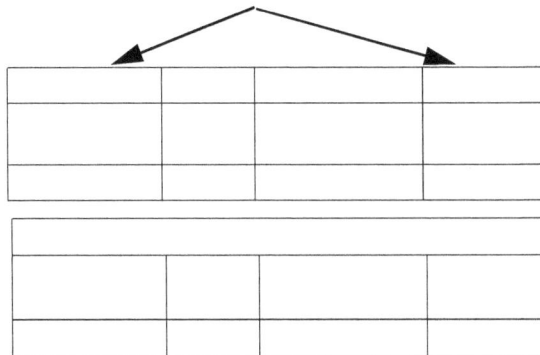

Cells selected to merge

Figure 9–15

Table Origin

The origin (i.e., fixed corner) of the table can be moved to a new location. Changing the origin of a table changes the direction in which the table expands when adding rows and columns (e.g., moving the origin to the upper-right corner of a table causes the table to build descending and leftward).

To modify the location of the origin, select the table, select **Table>Set Rotation Origin** in the Table group and select the new origin for the table. To set the new origin, select inside the table near its corner. The new origin is highlighted in magenta.

Blank Line Display

To blank cell borders in a table, select the table and click
⊞ (Line Display) in the Rows & Columns group. Only the internal cell borders can be blanked. You can also right-click on the table and select **Line Display**. The **TABLE LINE** menu displays as shown Figure 9–16.

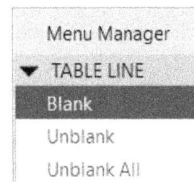

Menu Manager
▼ TABLE LINE
Blank
Unblank
Unblank All

Figure 9–16

- **Blank**: Blanks the selected line segments.

- **Unblank**: Re-displays the selected line segments.

- **Unblank All**: Re-displays all of the blanked line segments.

Figure 9–17 shows an example of blanked cell borders in a table.

Blank lines display as if the cells have been merged. However, text can still be entered and oriented in individual cells.

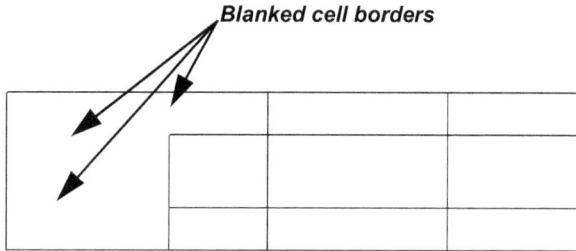

Figure 9–17

9.2 Create Repeat Regions

BOM or Family Table information that is pulled directly from the model is read-only.

You must create a repeat region to create a Bill of Material (BOM) or a table that is populated with family table data. A repeat region is a user-defined area of the table that resizes to accommodate the data with which it is populated. For example, if twelve rows are required to create a BOM for a twelve-component assembly, the system automatically creates the table to fit the assembly information. Additional cells are added or removed from the table if components are added or removed from the assembly.

How To: Create a Repeat Region Table in a Drawing:

1. The *Table* tab must be selected to create and modify repeat regions, as shown in Figure 9–18.

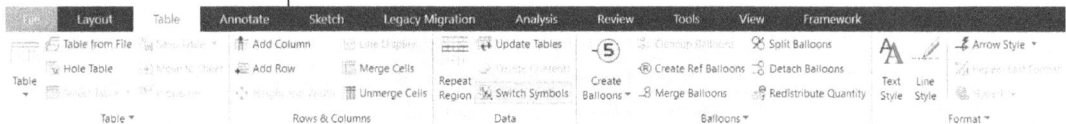

Figure 9–18

2. The table should contain a row that can be used to define the column's header and the number of columns that you want to repeat.

3. Click ▤ (Repeat Region) in the Data group. The **TBL REGIONS** menu displays. Select **Add** to define an area of the table to be repeated. Two types of repeat regions can be created: **Simple** and **Two-D**.

Simple

Simple repeat regions only expand the table in one direction, vertically or horizontally.

To create a simple repeat region, select **Simple** and select the cells to define the extent of the repeating region. This is done by selecting the cells that bound the area that you want to repeat. For example, if you want one row with four columns to repeat, select the first and fourth cell in the row, as shown in Figure 9–19.

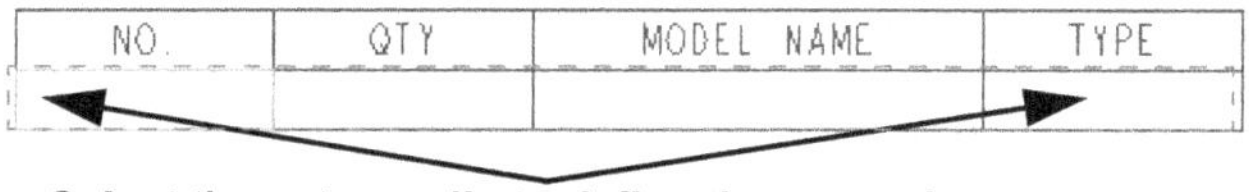

Select these two cells to define the second row to repeat.

Figure 9–19

Two-D

Two-D repeat regions are used for family tables. These repeat regions expand the table both vertically and horizontally.

To create a 2D repeat region, select **Two-D** and select the cells that you want to define the extent of the repeating region. To create a 2D repeat region, you must select the following three cells, as shown in Figure 9–20.

- Cell one represents the vertically expanding cells.
- Cell two represents the horizontally expanding cells.
- Cell three represents the cell that expands either horizontally or vertically.

This table was created to expand to the right and descending.

	Cell Two
Cell One	***Cell Three***

Figure 9–20

4. To enter text in a non-repeat region table cell, double-click on the cell and enter the text using the Note Properties dialog box. To enter text in a repeat region, you can also use the Note Properties dialog box. However, it is more efficient to double-click on the cell and use the Report Symbol dialog box to select the required parameters.

To select the parameters, select the first portion of the parameter name (e.g., asm). You are then prompted to select each additional portion until the parameter is fully defined. Figure 9–21 shows the menu selection used to define the asm.mbr.name parameter.

List items that are followed by ... indicate that the parameter definition continues to a further level in the Report Symbol dialog box.

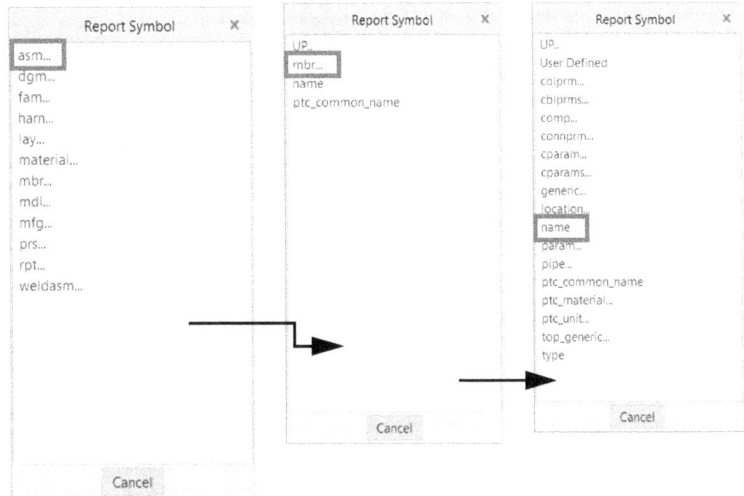

Figure 9–21

Figure 9–22 shows a table with text and parameters entered in its Simple repeat region, using the Report Symbol dialog box.

NO.	QTY	MODEL NAME	TYPE
rpt.index	rpt.qty	asm.mbr.name	asm.mbr.type

Figure 9–22

Figure 9–23 shows a table with parameters entered in its Two-D repeat region, using the Report Symbol dialog box.

	fam.inst.param.name
fam.inst.name	fam.inst.param.value

Figure 9–23

All system-defined parameters can be accessed using Creo Help Center.

Some of the parameters that you can use in a drawing table are described as follows:

Parameter	Description
asm.mbr.name	Component name in the assembly.
fam.inst.name	Family table instance.
fam.inst.param.name	Family table parameter.
fam.inst.param.value	Value of a family table parameter.
mbr.top_generic.name	Name of the generic (i.e., top-level generic in a nested family table).
mbr.top_generic.type	File format of the generic (e.g., part or assembly).
rpt.index	Numbers each item in the repeat region.
rpt.level	Recursive depth of the item.
rpt.qty	Number of occurrences of each item.

Using the Report Symbol dialog box is generally a easier and more accurate method of adding system-defined parameters to a table.

If you want to manually enter parameters in repeat region cells, right-click on the cell and select **Properties**. You can enter the report parameter in the Note Properties dialog box. To ensure that the report parameter is parametric, add an ampersand (&) symbol at the beginning of the parameter (e.g., &rpt.qty).

5. Once the table has been defined as a repeating region and all of required parameters have been added, you must update the table to display the model information. To update the table, use one of the following methods:

   • Click ☰ (Repeat Region) in the Data group and select **Update Tables**.
   • Right-click and select **Update Tables**.
   • Click ⟲ (Update Tables) in the Data group.

   To review the parameter symbols that were used in the repeat region, click ⛁ (Switch Symbols) in the Data group.

6. You can manipulate repeat region tables in the following ways:

   • Filtering information.
   • Controlling the amount of information displayed.
   • Displaying balloons associated with a BOM repeat region.
   • Paginating repeat region tables (same sheet or multi-sheet).

Filters

Once a repeat region has been established and parameters have been applied, some information might need to be excluded. This can be done by adding filters.

How To: Add Filters

1. Click ▦ (Repeat Region) in the Data group.
2. Select **Filters** and select the repeat region for which you want to add a filter. The **FILTER TYPE** and **FILTER REG** menus display as shown in Figure 9–24.

Figure 9–24

The **FILTER TYPE** menu options are described as follows:

Option	Description
By Rule	Excludes groups of items that match specific criteria.
By Item	Excludes selected items.

3. Select **Add** and enter the filter expression.

Filter information is entered using repeat region parameters and comparison operators: <, >, <=, >=, == (equals) or != (not equals). For example, the filter **&asm.mbr.type != assembly** would omit all of the assemblies listed in the repeat region.

Wildcards (*) are also permitted. Adding the filter **&asm.mbr.name != *bolt*** to a repeat region would omit all of the components with **bolt** in their names.

*Filters are available for both **Simple** and **Two-D** repeat regions.*

Figure 9–25 shows a filter added to a simple repeat region to exclude all of the parts from a Bill of Materials table.

The filter &asm.mbr.type != part would produce the same result.

Filter added to repeat region:
&asm.mbr.type == assembly

No.	Qty.	Model Name	Type
1	1	BASE_PLATE_FINAL_VISE	PART
2	1	BEARING_SUPPORT_FINAL_VISE	ASSEMBLY
3	1	GUIDE_FINAL_VISE	PART
4	1	SPINDLE_FINAL_VISE	ASSEMBLY
5	1	SUPPORT_END_FINAL_VISE	ASSEMBLY
6	1	SUPPORT_MIDDLE_FINAL_VISE	ASSEMBLY

No.	Qty.	Model Name	Type
1	1	BEARING_SUPPORT_FINAL_VISE	ASSEMBLY
2	1	SPINDLE_FINAL_VISE	ASSEMBLY
3	1	SUPPORT_END_FINAL_VISE	ASSEMBLY
4	1	SUPPORT_MIDDLE_FINAL_VISE	ASSEMBLY

Figure 9–25

4. Click **Done** to apply the filter. Existing repeat regions regenerate to accommodate the filter.

Attributes

The amount of information displayed in a simple repeat region can be controlled using the **Attributes** option.

How To: Set the Attributes for a Repeat region

1. Click ≣ (Repeat Region) in the Data group.
2. Select **Attributes** in the **TBL REGIONS** menu and select the region for which you want to edit the attributes. The **REGION ATTR** menu displays as shown in Figure 9–26.

*By default, the attributes displayed are **Flat** and **Duplicates**. These options report all of the top-level components in a simple repeat region.*

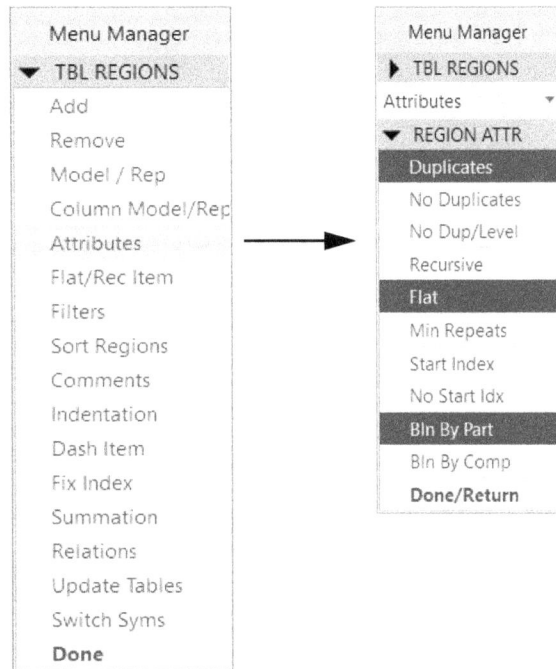

Menu Manager	Menu Manager
▼ TBL REGIONS	▶ TBL REGIONS
Add	Attributes ▾
Remove	▼ REGION ATTR
Model / Rep	Duplicates
Column Model/Rep	No Duplicates
Attributes	No Dup/Level
Flat/Rec Item	Recursive
Filters	Flat
Sort Regions	Min Repeats
Comments	Start Index
Indentation	No Start Idx
Dash Item	Bln By Part
Fix Index	Bln By Comp
Summation	**Done/Return**
Relations	
Update Tables	
Switch Syms	
Done	

Figure 9–26

The options in the **REGION ATTR** menu are described as follows:

Parameter	Description
Duplicates	Reports one row for every component (e.g., if **bolt.prt** displays ten times in an assembly, it is reported in ten separate rows of the table).
No Duplicates	Reports duplicate components on one row (e.g., if **bolt.prt** displays ten times in an assembly, then it is reported in one row of the table with a quantity of 10).
No Duplicates/ Level	Reports duplicate components at each level on one row (e.g., if **bolt.prt** displays four times in an assembly, twice in the top-level assembly and twice in a subassembly, it is reported on two separate rows each with a quantity of two).

Recursive	Reports components at every level (i.e., top-level and subassembly level), as shown below.

No.	Qty.	Model Name	Type
1	1	BASE_PLATE	PART
2	1	BEARING_SUPPORT	ASSEMBLY
3	1	BEARING_SUPPORT	PART
4	1	CRANK	PART
5	1	FLANGE	PART
6	1	FLYWHEEL	PART
7	1	GUIDE	PART
8	1	PIN	PART
9	1	SPINDLE	ASSEMBLY
10	1	SPINDLE	PART
11	1	SUPPORT	PART
12	1	SUPPORT_END	ASSEMBLY
13	1	SUPPORT_END	PART
14	1	SUPPORT_MIDDLE	ASSEMBLY
15	2	TENSION_PLATE	PART
16	1	VISE	ASSEMBLY

Flat	Reports only top-level components (i.e., components in sub-assemblies are not reported), as shown below.

No.	Qty.	Model Name	Type
1	1	BASE_PLATE	PART
2	1	BEARING_SUPPORT	ASSEMBLY
3	1	GUIDE	PART
4	1	SPINDLE	ASSEMBLY
5	1	SUPPORT_END	ASSEMBLY
6	1	SUPPORT_MIDDLE	ASSEMBLY

Min Repeats	Sets the minimum number of repetitions for a selected repeat region. The default minimum is 1 and a value of 0 avoids the blank lines caused by lack of data.
Start Index	Sets the index (value of **&rpt.index**) of one repeat region to begin where another repeat region index ends. This cannot be assigned for nested repeat regions.
No start Idx	Sets index numbering of a repeat region to 1.
Bln By Part	Enables you to have a BOM balloon reattach itself to another placement of the same part if the original component is suppressed or replaced.
Bln By Comp	Specifies that simple BOM balloons reattach themselves to whatever component replaced the one that originally owned the BOM balloon.

Pagination

Pagination can be used to break a long repeat region into separate tables. The table can be broken so that it can be displayed on a different sheet or elsewhere on the same sheet.

How To: Paginate a Repeat Region Table

1. Select the table.
2. Select **Table>Paginate**.
3. Accept the defaults in the **TBL PAGIN** menu.
4. Select the row at which the table is to be broken.
5. By default, the paginated portion of the table is moved onto the next sheet. If the sheet does not exist, one is created. If you do not want the table to continue to the next sheet, select **Add Segment**. Select an origin for the new table segment and locate the extent of the table on the same drawing sheet.
6. Select **Done** in the **TBL PAGIN** menu.

Creating BOM Balloons

BOM balloons can be displayed for any model with which a repeat region is associated.

How To: Display BOM Balloons in a Drawing

1. Expand ⑤ (Create Balloons) in the Balloons group, and select one of options shown in Figure 9–27 to define the placement of the balloons.

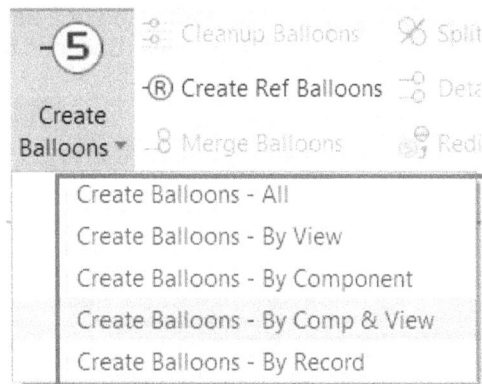

Figure 9–27

2. Select the repeat region.

When you select a balloon, the appropriate row in the table highlights.

3. Select a View or Component if required. If the **Create Balloons - All** option is selected, the balloons display automatically. Selecting **Create Balloons - By View** requires you to select a view to display the BOM balloons. The balloons display as shown in Figure 9–28.

Balloons update to reflect changes to the repeat region's model.

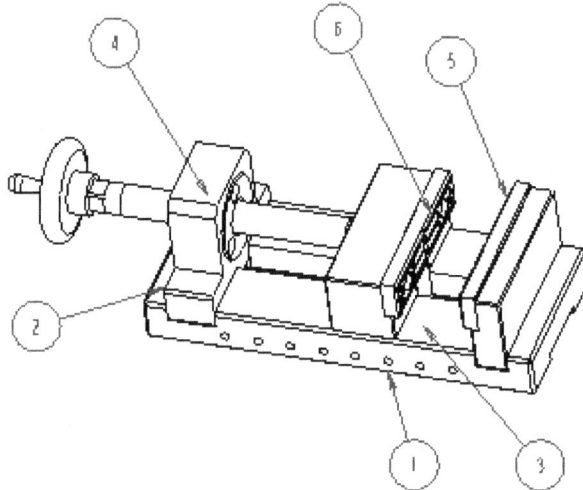

Figure 9–28

Modifying BOM Balloons

Click ✺ (Cleanup Balloons) in the Balloons group to clean up the positioning of a selected balloon. This option opens the Clean BOM Balloons dialog box, as shown in Figure 9–29.

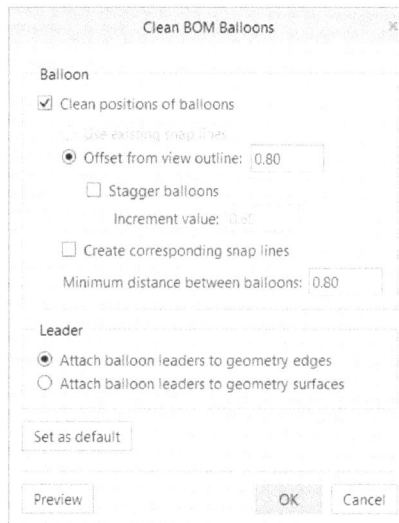

Figure 9–29

Additional balloons that maintain the same index number, can be displayed for multiple instances of the same component.

How To: Display Balloons for Multiple Instances

1. Set the drawing filter to **Component**.
2. Select the part to which to add the balloon.
3. Right-click and select **Add Reference Balloon** or click

   ® (Create Ref Balloons).
4. Select the view in which you want to display the reference balloon.

The formats to display reference balloons are shown in Figure 9–30. The **reference_bom_balloon_text** drawing setup option enables you to customize the text used to identify a reference balloon (i.e., REF), but the text cannot be removed.

- You can display balloons for every component by repeating the steps to display balloons. When all of the balloons are shown for the first time, the system assigns one balloon per row of the repeat region. If the step is repeated, the system prompts you to confirm adding a balloon to every component.

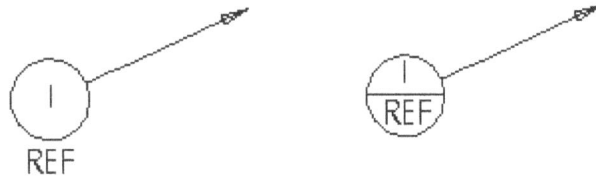

Figure 9–30

*To access the drawing setup file, select **File> Prepare>Drawing Properties** and select **change** next to Detail Options.*

9.3 Create Hole, Point, and Axes Tables

Tables can be automatically created for holes, datum points and datum axes. These tables are created so that they can be automatically updated with information from the drawing model. Figure 9–31 shows a table designed to display the drilled hole features in a specified view. The following information displays in a hole table:

- Location in X and Y coordinates

- Hole diameter

Datum point locations are tabulated in X, Y, and Z coordinates. The axis locations are tabulated in X and Y coordinates.

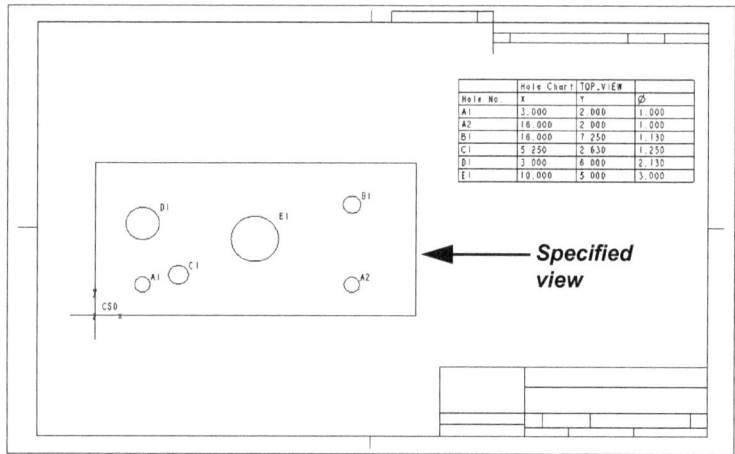

Hole Chart	TOP_VIEW		
Hole No.	X	Y	Ø
A1	3.000	2.000	1.000
A2	16.000	2.000	1.000
B1	16.000	7.250	1.130
C1	5.250	2.630	1.250
D1	3.000	6.000	2.130
E1	10.000	5.000	3.000

← *Specified view*

Figure 9–31

How To: Create a Hole Table in a Drawing

1. The *Table* tab must be selected to create and modify tables, as shown in Figure 9–32.

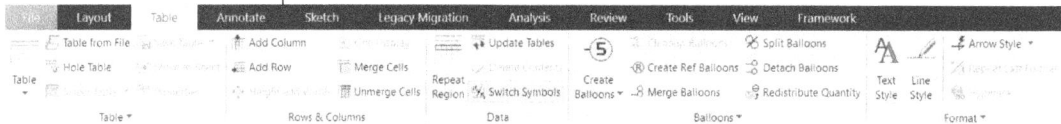

Figure 9–32

2. To create a hole table, click 🔲 (Hole Table) in the Table group. The Hole Table dialog box opens as shown in Figure 9–33. Select the table type. A table can be created for holes, datum points, or datum axes. Once the additional options have been selected, click **Create**.

Select Type

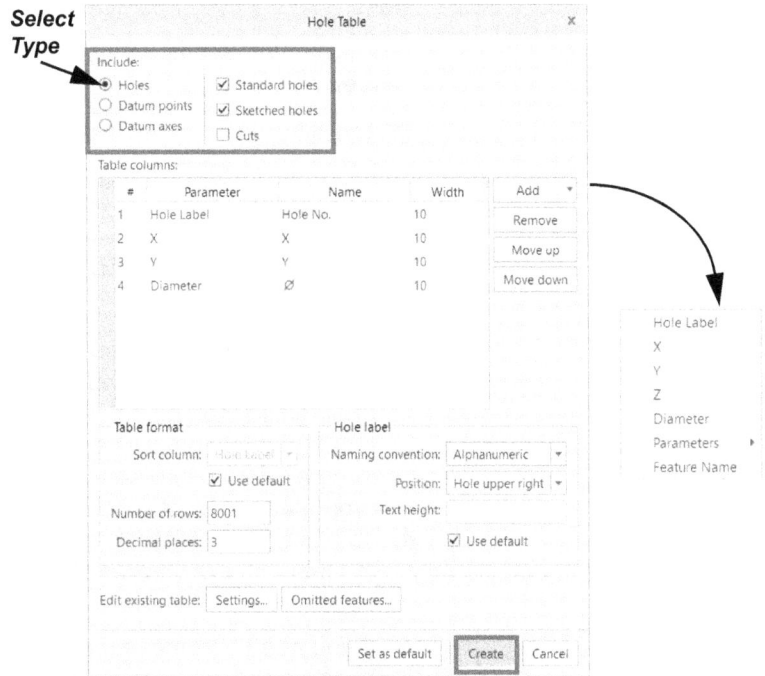

Figure 9–33

Additional options for hole tables are described as follows:

Option	Description
Add	Select a parameter to include as rows in the *Table columns* field as shown below. Hole Label X Y Z Diameter Parameters ▸ Feature Name
Remove	Removes rows from the *Table column* area.
Move up	Shifts a row up in the *Table column* area.

Move down	Shifts a row down in the *Table column* area.
Sort column	The Hole Label is the default option. Clear the default option to select a different method of sorting entities in the hole table.
Number of rows	Enables you to select **No limit** or **Maximum**. **Maximum** defines the maximum number of table rows.
Decimal Places	Sets the number of decimal places for the table values.
Text Height	Sets the text height for table labels.
Naming convention	Enables you to name entities (holes, axes, or datum points) using an alphanumeric or numeric format.
Position	Enables you to define the position of the text for the hole notes.

3. Select a coordinate system on the model to define the position values in the table. The coordinate system must be oriented so that the holes, points, or axes dimensions can be measured in the positive X- and Y-directions. If an inappropriate coordinate system is selected, you are prompted to select a new one.

4. To place the hole table, select the top left corner position of the table on the drawing sheet. Once selected, the hole table displays.

   If you need to remove the table from the drawing after it has been placed, you can delete the table by selecting it and pressing <Delete> after the HOLE TABLE dialog box has been closed.

5. To update the table based on changes that could have been made to the drawing model, right-click and select **Update Tables** or click ⟳ (Update Tables).

Practice 9a

Bill of Materials (BOM)

Practice Objectives

- Create a table in a drawing.
- Define repeat regions.
- Generate a Bill of Material (BOM) listing for an assembly.
- Show BOM balloons.
- Add a new sheet.
- Paginate a table.

In this practice, you will create the drawing shown in Figure 9–34.

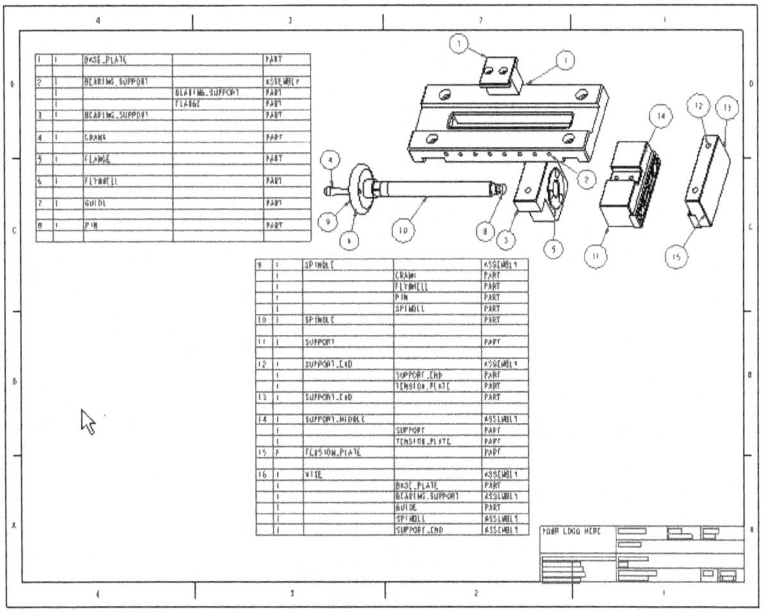

Figure 9–34

Task 1 - Open a drawing file and erase a view from it.

1. Set the working directory to the *Drawing_BOM* folder.

2. Open **vise_final_1.drw**.

3. Set the model display as follows:

    - $\overset{\times}{}$ (*Datum Display Filters*): All Off

    - (*Display Style*): (No Hidden)

Vise_final_1.drw references the model vise.asm.

4. Select the view shown in Figure 9–35, and then click
   ⬚ (Erase View) in the mini toolbar.

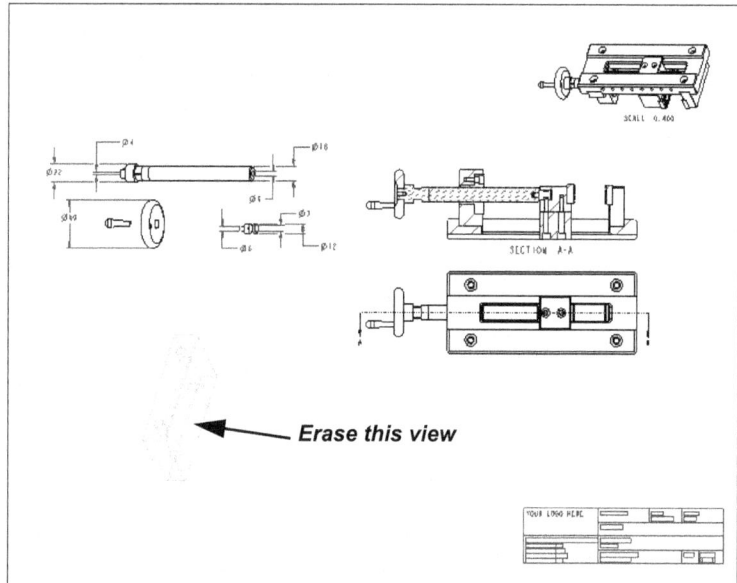

Figure 9–35

5. Press the middle mouse button, then click on the screen to
   finish the operation. The drawing displays as shown in
   Figure 9–36.

*Select **Resume View** in the Display Group in the Layout tab to display an erased view.*

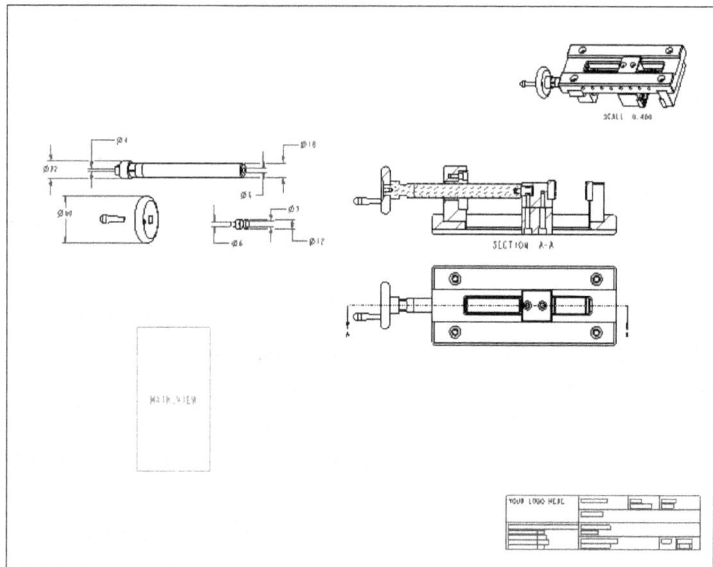

Figure 9–36

6. Select **File>Options>Configuration Editor** and click **Add**. Change the **highlight_erased_dwg_views** option to **no**. Apply and save the changes.

7. Relocate the view shown in Figure 9–37. The drawing displays as shown in Figure 9–37.

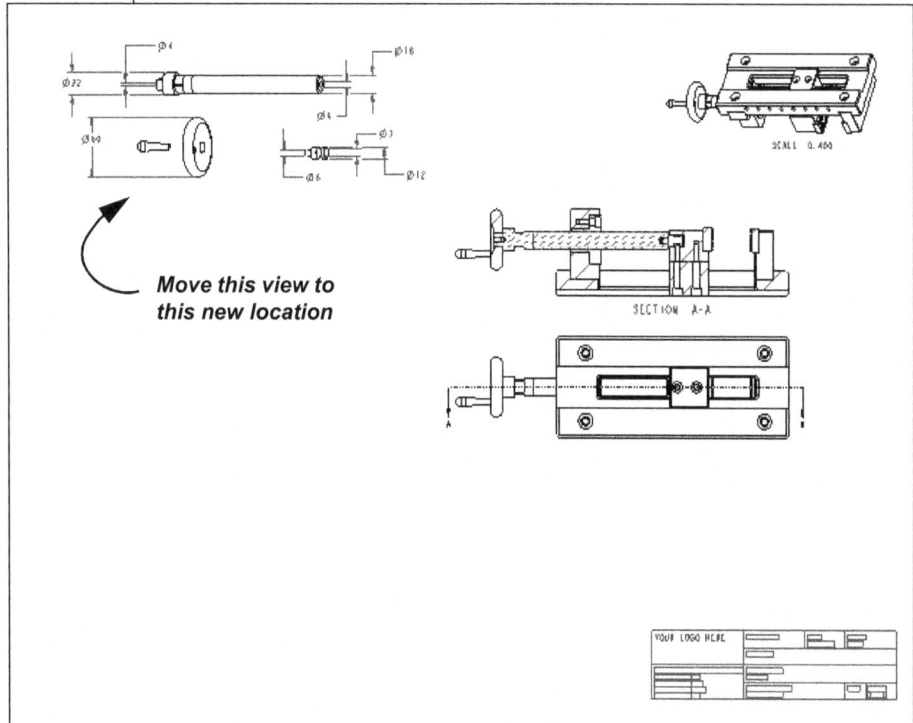

Figure 9–37

Task 2 - Set the current drawing model to spindle.asm.

You can also expand

▢ ▾ in the Model Tree and select SPINDLE.asm>master rep from the list.

1. If not already active, activate the spindle assembly by selecting the view in the upper left corner. Right-click and select Set/Add Drawing Model. This option will not be available if the model is already the active model.

Task 3 - Create a table with three columns and two rows.

You can also right-click and select Create Table.

1. Select the *Table* tab.

2. Click ▦ (Table) in the Table group.

You can also click

(Insert Table) and specify the number of rows and columns.

3. Create a table with three columns and two rows by selecting **3 X 2 Table** in the flyout as shown in Figure 9–38.

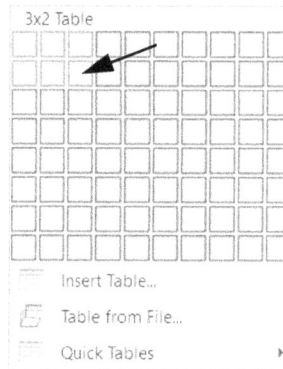

Figure 9–38

4. Locate the table, as shown in Figure 9–39.

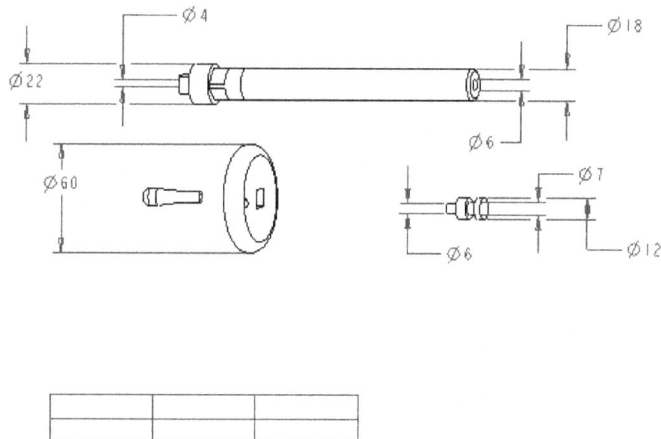

Figure 9–39

Task 4 - Change the sizes of the rows and columns.

1. Set the selection filter to **Table Column**.

You can also click

(Height and Width) to modify the size.

2. Double-click on the first column, as shown in Figure 9–40.

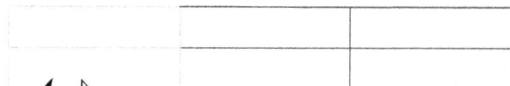

Double-click on this column

Figure 9–40

3. The Height and Width dialog box opens. Set the *Width in number of characters* to **3.0**, as shown in Figure 9–41.

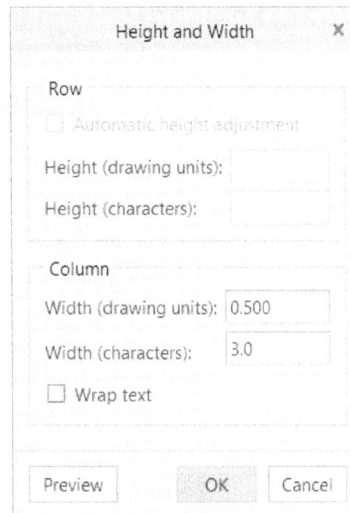

Figure 9–41

4. Click **OK**.

5. Continue modifying the number of characters for the width of the columns. The required character sizes are 6 and 18 from left to right. The table displays as shown in Figure 9–42.

Figure 9–42

6. Verify that the row heights are one character. (Hint: Set the selection filter to **Table Row** to select a row).

Task 5 - Enter text in the table cells.

1. Set the selection filter to **Table Cell**.

2. Double-click on each of the individual cells and enter the text, as shown in Figure 9–43.

Figure 9–43

Task 6 - Define a simple repeat region.

1. Click ≡ (Repeat Region) in the Data group. The **TBL REGIONS** menu displays.

2. Select **Add>Simple**.

3. Select the lower left cell and the lower right cell. Note that the lower right cell may not highlight.

4. Select **Attributes** in the **TBL REGIONS** menu and select any cell in the repeat region.

5. Select **No Duplicates>Flat>Bln By Part>Done/Return** in the **REGION ATTR** menu.

6. Select **Done** in the **TBL REGIONS** menu.

Task 7 - Enter report parameters in the repeat region.

Ignore any overlapping parameters and only consider the resulting text when defining the cell width.

1. Double-click on the left cell of the repeat region (under the *No.* column).

2. Select **rpt>index** in the **Report Symbol** menu. This adds the **rpt.index** parameter to the report table cell. Do not worry that the text extends into the next cell.

3. To review the parameter name, select the cell and click 🥄 (Properties). The dialog box opens as shown in Figure 9–44.

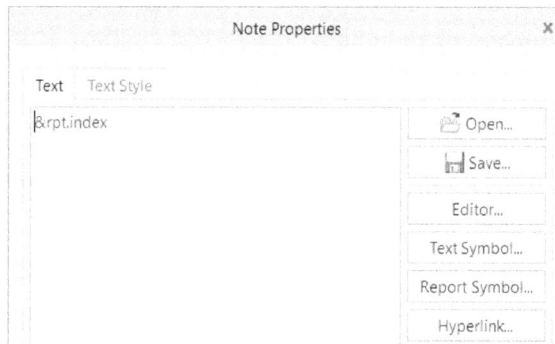

Figure 9–44

*Parameters entered by keyboard must be preceded by the **&** symbol.*

4. Repeat the process for the other cells in the bottom line. Select **rpt>qty** for the *Qty.* column and **asm>mbr>name** for the *Model Name* column.

You can also right-click and select **Update Tables**.

5. Click ⟳ (Update Tables) in the Data group. The table updates automatically with all of the model information from the assembly model, as shown in Figure 9–45.

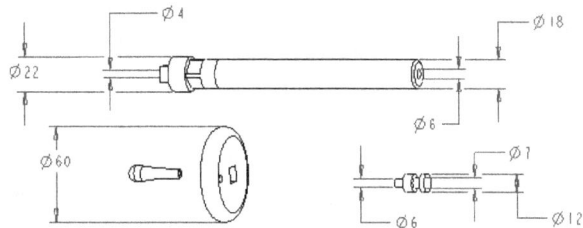

No.	Qty.	Model Name
1	1	CRANK
2	1	FLYWHEEL
3	1	PIN
4	1	SPINDLE

Figure 9–45

Task 8 - Display the balloons for the components of the spindle assembly.

1. Expand ⑤ (Create Balloons) and select **Create Balloons - By View** in the Balloons group. Select the General view for the **SPINDLE.ASM**. The view displays as shown in Figure 9–46.

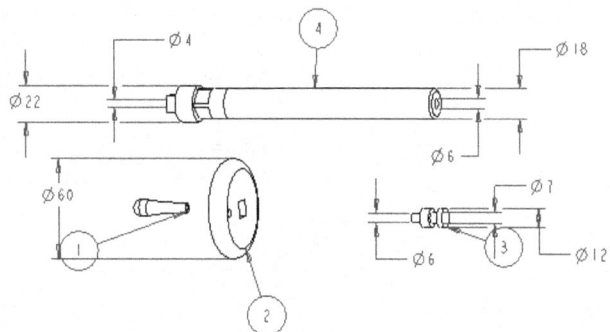

No.	Qty.	Model Name
1	1	CRANK
2	1	FLYWHEEL
3	1	PIN
4	1	SPINDLE

Figure 9–46

2. Set the selection filter to **BOM Balloon**.

3. Select and move the balloons as shown in Figure 9–47. To modify the attachment point, right-click on the balloon and select **Edit Attachment**.

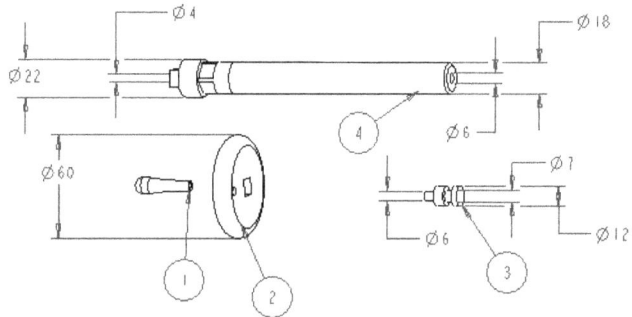

No.	Qty.	Model Name
1	1	CRANK
2	1	FLYWHEEL
3	1	PIN
4	1	SPINDLE

Figure 9–47

4. Change the selection filter back to **General**.

Task 9 - Set the current drawing model to vise.asm.

1. Select the view in the upper right corner, right-click, and select **Set/Add Drawing Model**.

Task 10 - Create a table with four columns and two rows.

1. Ensure that the *Table* tab is selected.

2. Click (Table) in the Table group and create a **4 X 2** table, as shown in Figure 9–48.

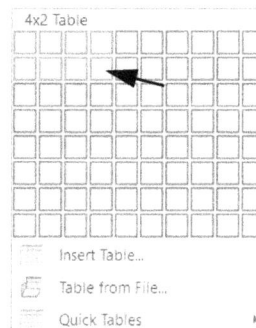

Figure 9–48

*You can also expand in the Model Tree and select **VISE.asm> master** from the list.*

3. Locate the table, as shown in Figure 9–49.

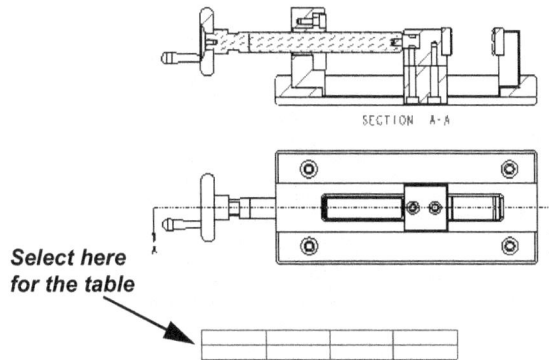

Figure 9–49

4. Change the column widths to the following measurements from left to right: 3, 6, 18, and 9. The table displays as shown in Figure 9–50.

Figure 9–50

Task 11 - Enter text in the table cells.

1. Set the selection filter to Table Columns and then double-click on each cell to enter the text shown in Figure 9–51.

No.	Qty.	Model Name	Type

Figure 9–51

Task 12 - Define a simple repeat region.

1. Click ▦ (Repeat Region) in the Data group. The **TBL REGIONS** menu displays.

2. Select **Add>Simple**.

3. Select the lower left cell and the lower right cell.

4. Select **Attributes** in the **TBL REGIONS** menu and select any cell in the repeat region.

5. Select **No Duplicates>Flat>Bln By Part>Done/Return** in the **REGION ATTR** menu.

6. Select **Done** in the **TBL REGIONS** menu.

Task 13 - Enter report parameters in the repeat region.

---

1. Double-click on the left cell of the repeat region (under the *No.* column).

2. Select **rpt>index** in the **Report Symbol** menu. This adds the **rpt.index** parameter to the report table cell.

3. Repeat the process for the other cells in the bottom line. Select **rpt>qty** for the *Qty.* column, **asm>mbr>name** for the *Model Name* column, and **asm>mbr>type** for the *Type* column. The columns overlap with information, as shown in Figure 9–52.

No.	Qty.	Model Name	Type
rpt.index	rpt.qty	asm.mbr.name	asm.mbr.type

Figure 9–52

4. Click (Update Tables) in the Data group. The table updates automatically with all of the model information from the assembly model, as shown in Figure 9–53.

No.	Qty.	Model Name	Type
1	1	BASE_PLATE	PART
2	1	BEARING_SUPPORT	ASSEMBLY
3	1	GUIDE	PART
4	1	SPINDLE	ASSEMBLY
5	1	SUPPORT_END	ASSEMBLY
6	1	SUPPORT_MIDDLE	ASSEMBLY

Figure 9–53

Task 14 - Redefine the table attribute to recursive.

1. Click ☰ (Repeat Region) in the Data group.

2. Select **Attributes** in the **TBL REGIONS** menu.

3. Select the repeat region that you created in Task 12.

4. Select **Recursive>Done/Return**. The table displays as shown in Figure 9–54.

No.	Qty.	Model Name	Type
1	1	BASE_PLATE	PART
2	1	BEARING_SUPPORT	ASSEMBLY
3	1	BEARING_SUPPORT	PART
4	1	CRANK	PART
5	1	FLANGE	PART
6	1	FLYWHEEL	PART
7	1	GUIDE	PART
8	1	PIN	PART
9	1	SPINDLE	ASSEMBLY
10	1	SPINDLE	PART
11	1	SUPPORT	PART
12	1	SUPPORT_END	ASSEMBLY
13	1	SUPPORT_END	PART
14	1	SUPPORT_MIDDLE	ASSEMBLY
15	2	TENSION_PLATE	PART
16	1	VISE	ASSEMBLY

Figure 9–54

5. Select **Done** in the **TBL REGIONS** menu.

6. Move the table if required.

Task 15 - Add an additional sheet to the drawing.

1. Select the *Layout* tab.

2. Click ⬜ (New Sheet) to add a new sheet to your drawing.

You can also right-click on the Sheet 1 tab and select New Sheet.

Task 16 - Add an exploded view to the sheet 2.

1. Insert a General view and select **No Combined States**.

2. Set the View State so that it uses the model's default explode state.

3. Set the *View Display* to **No Hidden**.

4. Complete the view. The exploded view displays as shown in Figure 9–55.

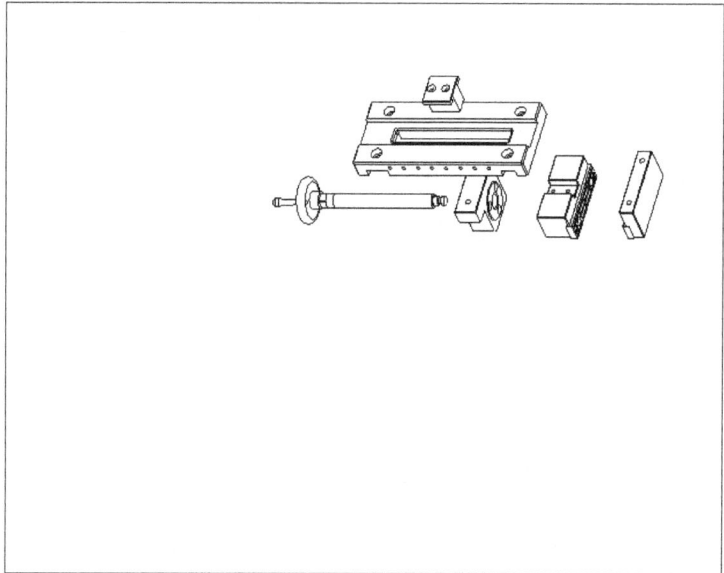

Figure 9–55

Task 17 - Create a table to display the components in the assembly.

1. Select the *Table* tab.

2. Create the table shown in Figure 9–56. The widths of the columns are 3, 6, 20, 20, and 10 from left to right, and the rows are both 1 character each.

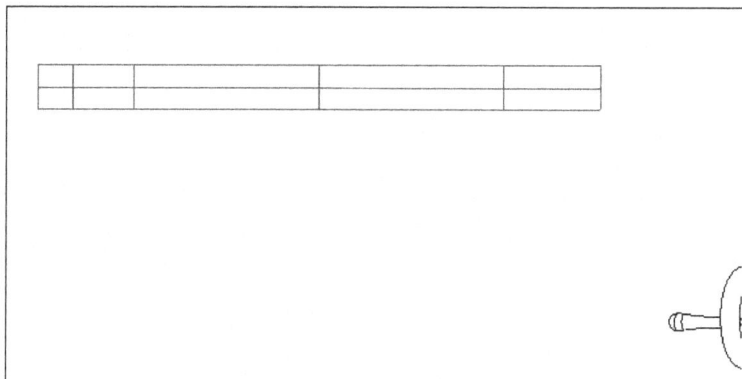

Figure 9–56

Task 18 - Create two simple repeat regions to display the components in the assembly.

---

1. Click ▤ (Repeat Region) in the Data group. The **TBL REGIONS** menu displays.

2. Select **Add>Simple** in the **TBL REGIONS** menu.

3. Select the two cells shown in Figure 9–57.

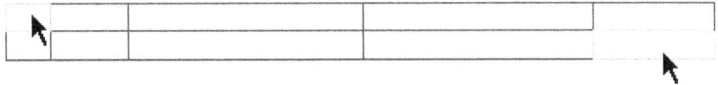

Figure 9–57

4. Select **Attributes** and select the repeat region that you just created.

5. Select **No Duplicates>Flat>Bln By Part>Done/Return**.

6. Repeat Steps 1 to 5 to create a repeat region between the cells shown in Figure 9–58.

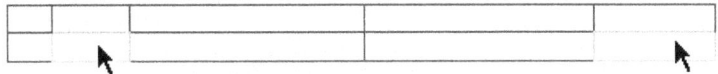

Figure 9–58

7. Select **Done** in the **TBL REGIONS** menu.

Task 19 - Add the report parameters to the table.

---

1. Set the selection filter to **Table Cell**.

2. Double-click on any one of the cells in the repeat region and enter the report symbols in the table, as shown in Figure 9–59.

rpt.index   *rpt.qty*

r p t	rptindexty	asm.mbr.name		asm.mbr.type
	rpt.qty		asm.mbr.name	asm.mbr.type

rpt.qty

Figure 9–59

---

3. Click ⇌ (Update Tables) in the Data group. The table should update with all of the assembly information, as shown in Figure 9–60.

I	I	BASE_PLATE		PART
2	I	BEARING_SUPPORT		ASSEMBLY
	I		BEARING_SUPPORT	PART
	I		FLANGE	PART
3	I	GUIDE		PART
4	I	SPINDLE		ASSEMBLY
	I		CRANK	PART
	I		FLYWHEEL	PART
	I		PIN	PART
	I		SPINDLE	PART
5	I	SUPPORT_END		ASSEMBLY
	I		SUPPORT_END	PART
	I		TENSION_PLATE	PART
6	I	SUPPORT_MIDDLE		ASSEMBLY
	I		SUPPORT	PART
	I		TENSION_PLATE	PART

Figure 9–60

4. Click ≡ (Repeat Region) in the Data group. Select **Attributes**.

5. Select the first row in the repeat region to select the larger repeat region.

6. Select **Recursive>Done/Return**. The drawing displays as shown in Figure 9–61.

1	1	BASE.PLATE		PART
2	1	BEARING.SUPPORT		ASSEMBLY
	1		BEARING.SUPPORT	PART
	1		FLANGE	PART
3	1	BEARING.SUPPORT		PART
4	1	CRANK		PART
5	1	FLANGE		PART
6	1	FLYWHEEL		PART
7	1	GUIDE		PART
8	1	PIN		PART
9	1	SPINDLE		ASSEMBLY
	1		CRANK	PART
	1		FLYWHEEL	PART
	1		PIN	PART
	1		SPINDLE	PART
10	1	SPINDLE		PART
11	1	SUPPORT		PART
12	1	SUPPORT.END		ASSEMBLY
	1		SUPPORT_END	PART
	1		TENSION_PLATE	PART
13	1	SUPPORT.END		PART
14	1	SUPPORT.MIDDLE		ASSEMBLY
	1		SUPPORT	PART
	1		TENSION_PLATE	PART
15	2	TENSION.PLATE		PART
16	1	VISE		ASSEMBLY
	1		BASE.PLATE	PART
	1		BEARING.SUPPORT	ASSEMBLY
	1		GUIDE	PART
	1		SPINDLE	ASSEMBLY
	1		SUPPORT_END	ASSEMBLY
	1		SUPPORT_MIDDLE	ASSEMBLY

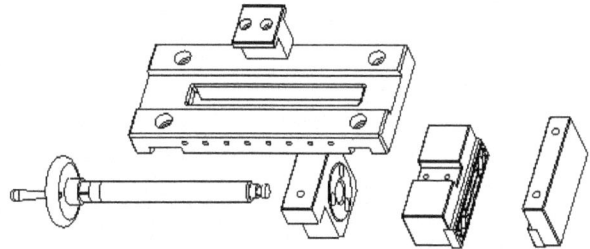

Figure 9–61

7. Select **Done**.

Task 20 - Split the table into segments.

1. Set the selection filter to **Table**.

2. Select the table and select **Table>Paginate** in the Table group. The **TBL PAGIN** menu displays as shown in Figure 9–62.

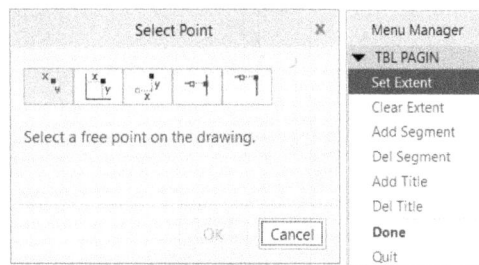

Figure 9–62

3. Accept the default settings (**Set Extent** in the **TBL PAGIN** menu and click $^{x}\!\!\!\blacksquare_{y}$ in the Select Point table) and select the empty row between index 8 and 9. The drawing displays as shown in Figure 9–63.

1	BASE_PLATE		PART	
1	BEARING_SUPPORT		ASSEMBLY	
1		BEARING_SUPPORT	PART	
1		FLANGE	PART	
1	BEARING_SUPPORT		PART	
1	CRANK		PART	
1	FLANGE		PART	
1	FLYWHEEL		PART	
1	GUIDE		PART	
1	PIN		PART	

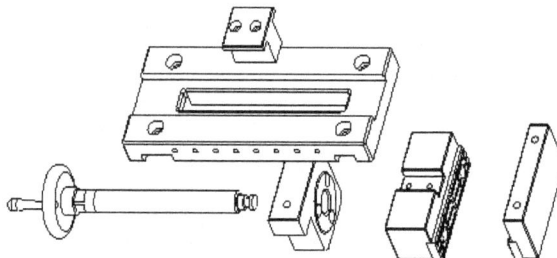

Figure 9–63

4. Select **Add Segment** in the **TBL PAGIN** menu, select an origin for the new segment, and select a point to define the extent of the new segment, as shown in Figure 9–64.

The diagonal distance between the origin and extent should be large enough to cover all of the remaining cells.

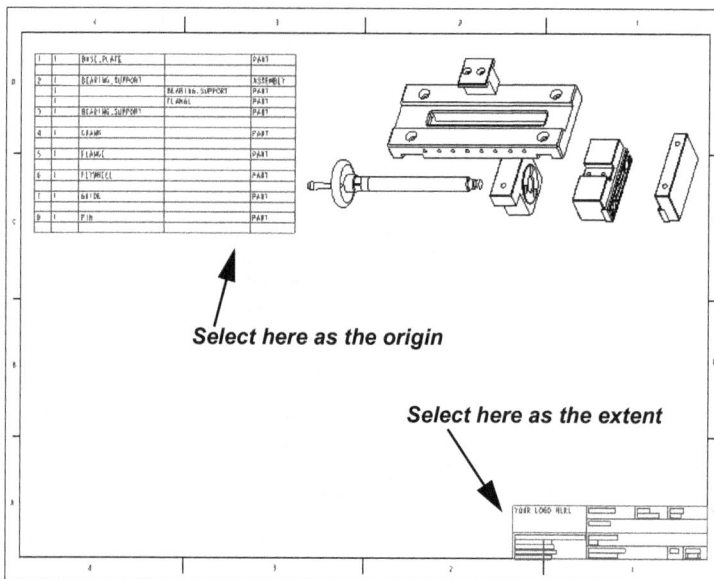

Select here as the origin

Select here as the extent

Figure 9–64

The drawing displays as shown in Figure 9–65.

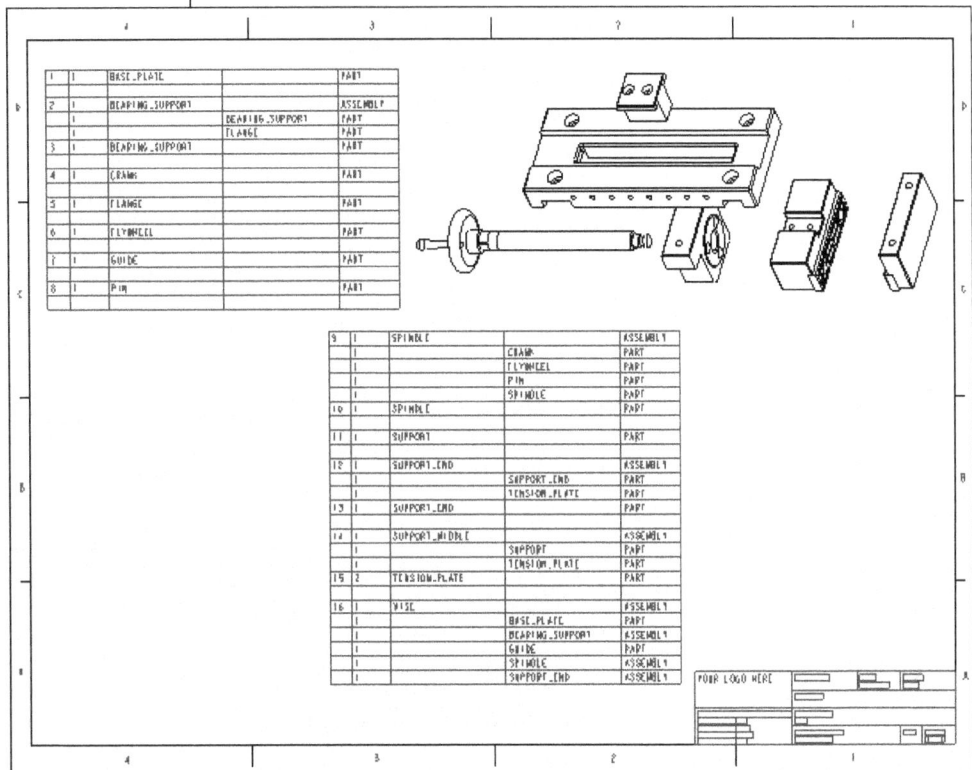

The table in the drawing (left side):

1	1	BASE_PLATE		PART
2	1	BEARING_SUPPORT		ASSEMBLY
	1		BEARING_SUPPORT	PART
	1		FLANGE	PART
3	1	BEARING_SUPPORT		PART
4	1	CRANK		PART
5	1	FLANGE		PART
6	1	FLYWHEEL		PART
7	1	GUIDE		PART
8	1	PIN		PART

The table in the drawing (center):

9	1	SPINDLE		ASSEMBLY
	1		CRANK	PART
	1		FLYWHEEL	PART
	1		PIN	PART
	1		SPINDLE	PART
10	1	SPINDLE		PART
11	1	SUPPORT		PART
12	1	SUPPORT_END		ASSEMBLY
	1		SUPPORT_END	PART
	1		TENSION_PLATE	PART
13	1	SUPPORT_END		PART
14	1	SUPPORT_MIDDLE		ASSEMBLY
	1		SUPPORT	PART
	1		TENSION_PLATE	PART
15	2	TENSION_PLATE		PART
16	1	VISE		ASSEMBLY
	1		BASE_PLATE	PART
	1		BEARING_SUPPORT	ASSEMBLY
	1		GUIDE	PART
	1		SPINDLE	ASSEMBLY
	1		SUPPORT_END	ASSEMBLY

Figure 9–65

5. Select **Done**.

Task 21 - Display the balloons for the components in the assembly.

---

1. Click ⑤ (Create Balloons)>**Create Balloons By View** in the Balloons group.

2. Select the first row.

3. Select the exploded view. The balloons indicating the components in the assembly are now displayed in the drawing.

Select **On Surface** as the attach type option to point the leader for the Balloon to the model's surface.

4. Move the balloons as shown in Figure 9–66.

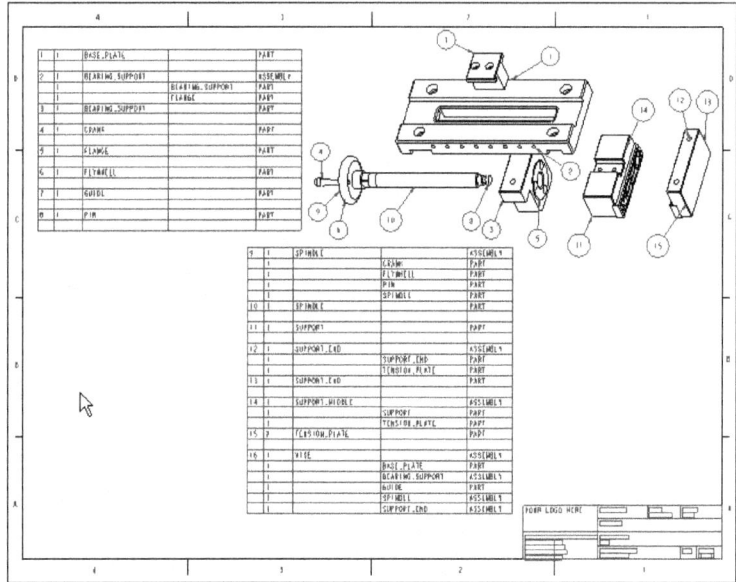

Figure 9–66

5. Save the drawing.

6. Erase all of the files from memory.

Practice 9b

Family Tables in Drawings

Practice Objectives

- Create a table listing all family table items.
- Save a table to the system disk.
- Retrieve a table from the system disk.

In this practice, you will create a family table and then open it in a drawing.

Task 1 - Create a table in the vise.drw drawing.

1. Set the working directory to the *Drawing_Fam_Tab* folder.

2. Create a new drawing named **temp** using an A-size empty sheet.

3. Set the model display as follows:

    - ⁕ *(Datum Display Filters)*: All Off

    - ◻ *(Display Style)*: ◻ (No Hidden)

4. Create a table anywhere on the sheet, two columns wide and two rows deep. The column spacing should be 15 characters and the row spacing should be 1 character.

5. Change the selection filter to **Table Column**.

6. Select the two columns that you just created by pressing and holding <Ctrl> as you select the columns.

7. Right-click and select **Text Style**. The Text Style dialog box opens.

Justification must be assigned before adding text.

You can also click
AA *(Text Style) in the Format group.*

8. Set the *Horizontal Justification* to **Center** and *Vertical* to **Middle** as shown in Figure 9–67.

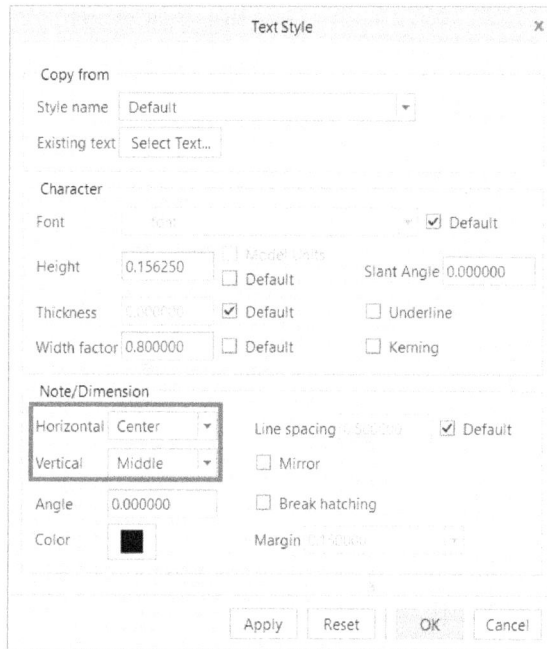

Figure 9–67

9. Click ☰ (Repeat Region) in the Data group. The **TBL REGIONS** menu displays.

10. Select **Add>Two-D** in the **TBL REGIONS** menu.

11. Select the following cells to define the 2D region: **C3**, **C2**, and **C4**, as shown in Figure 9–68 then select **Done**.

C1	C2
C3	C4

Figure 9–68

12. Change the selection filter to **Table Cell**.

13. Double-click on the cells in the repeat region and enter the text as shown in Figure 9–69 (**fam.inst.param.name**, **fam.inst.name**, and **fam.inst.param.value**).

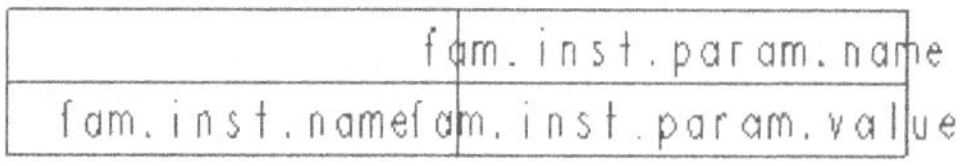

Parameters can overlap cells, depending on the length of the parameter value. Create the size of the cell so that it fits the parameter value.

Figure 9–69

14. Set the selection filter to **Table** and select the table.

15. Click ⊞ (Save Table) in the Table group.

16. Enter **family_table** as the name of the table, and click **Save**.

17. Right-click and select **Delete** to delete the table.

18. Close the window and erase the drawing from memory without saving.

Task 2 - Create a new drawing.

---

1. Create a new drawing. Enable the **Use drawing model file name** option and clear the **Use default template** option.

2. Select the generic model for **connector.prt** as the drawing model. Select **generic_b** from the Working Directory as the format.

3. Accept the generic model as the instance to retrieve and set the drawing to a **5.0** scale.

4. Create the two views and show the dimensions and axis, as shown in Figure 9–70.

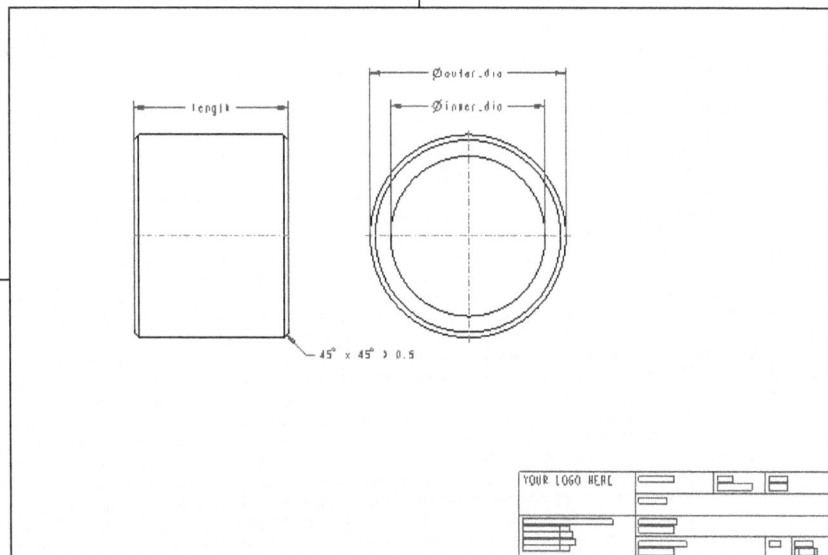

Figure 9–70

Task 3 - Retrieve the family_table table that you saved and place it in the drawing.

1. Select the *Table* tab.

2. Click ⛶ (Table from File) in the Table group. Select the **family_table.tbl** that you created earlier. Click **Open**.

The table automatically updates as it is added to the drawing. To update the table display if the model has changed, click ⟳ (Update Tables) in the Table tab.

3. Select the placement location for the table, as shown in Figure 9–71. All of the model instances are now displayed in the table.

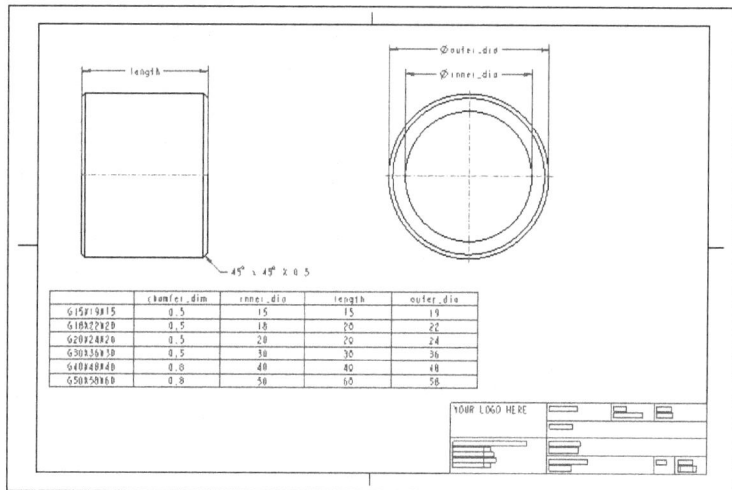

Figure 9–71

4. Save the drawing and close the window.

Practice 9c | Hole, Axis, and Datum Point Tables

Practice Objectives

- Place a Hole table in a drawing.
- Place an Datum Axis table and a Datum Point table in a drawing.

In this practice, you will create the drawing shown in Figure 9–72.

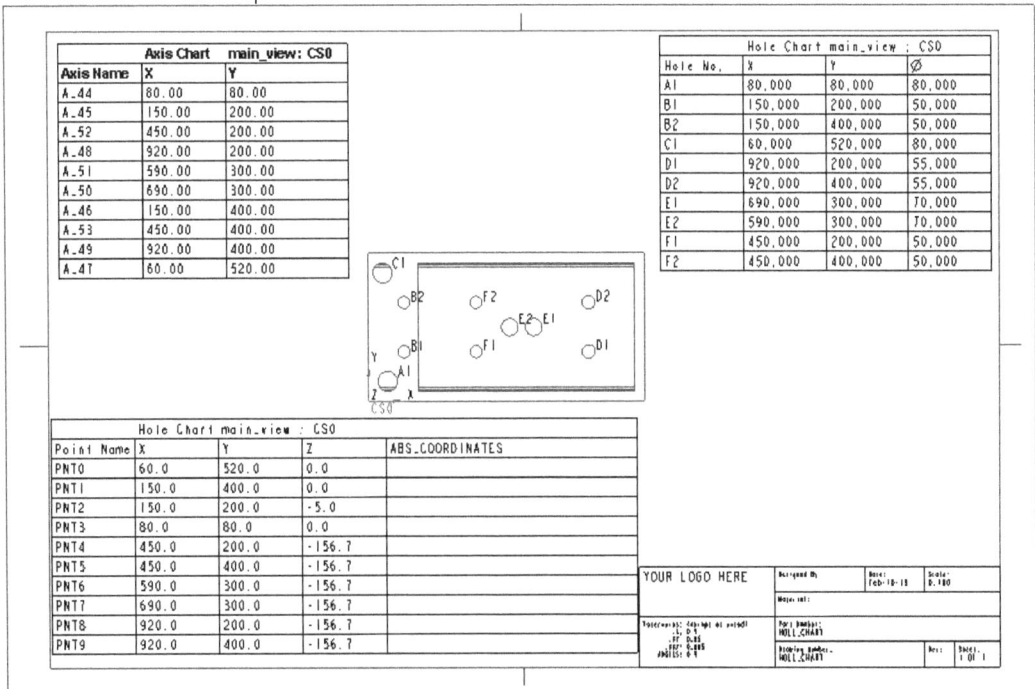

Figure 9–72

Task 1 - Create a new drawing.

1. Set the working directory to the *Drawing_Hole_Tables* folder.

2. Create a new drawing called **hole_chart** using the following options:
   - Clear the **Use default template** option.
   - Select **hole_chart.prt** as the default model.
   - Use the **generic_b format** found in the (Working Directory).

3. Set the model display as follows:

- *(Datum Display Filters)*: All Off

- *(Display Style)*: (No Hidden)

4. Modify the drawing scale to **.1**.

5. Display the coordinate systems and their tags.

6. Create the first General view as shown in Figure 9–73. Orient the view using the Saved View **TOP** and rename the view as **main_view**.

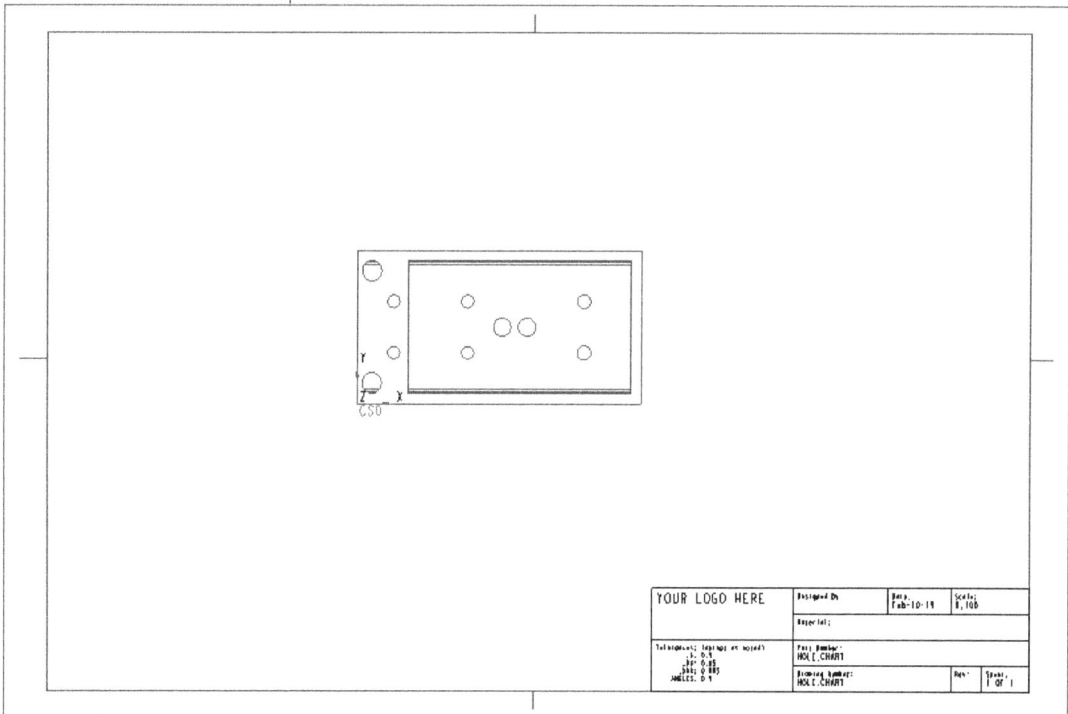

Figure 9–73

Task 2 - Create a hole table for the top view.

1. Select the *Table* tab.

2. Click (Hole Table) in the Table group. The Hole Table dialog box opens, as shown in Figure 9–74.

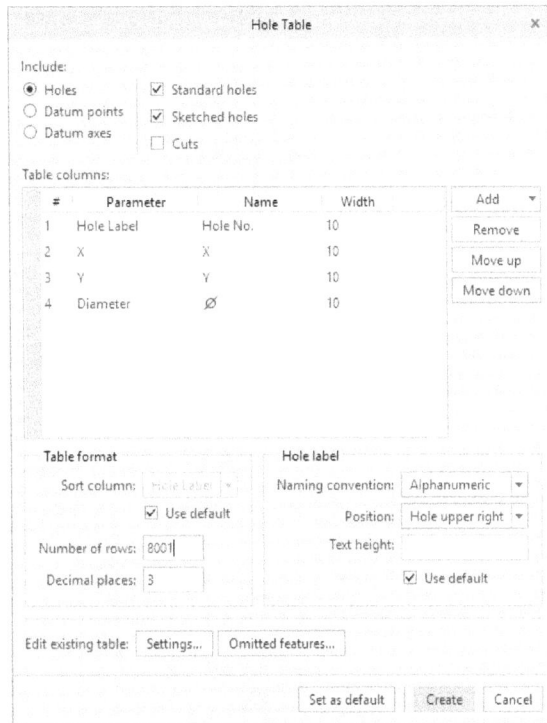

Figure 9–74

3. Accept the defaults and click **Create**.

4. Select the coordinate system **CS0** in the Model Tree or view.

To move the table, select it and drag it to a new location using the drag handles.

5. Click the position of the upper left corner of the hole table, as shown in Figure 9–75.

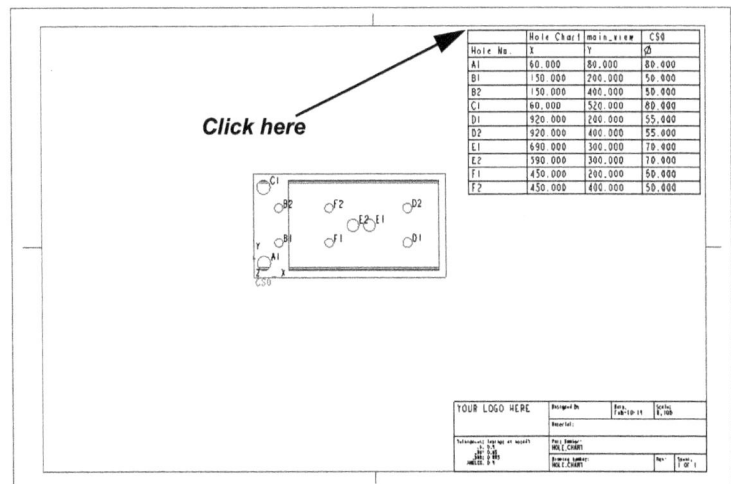

Figure 9–75

You can also click

⌗ *(Line Display) in the Rows & Columns group.*

6. Change the selection filter to **Table** and select the table.

7. Right-click and select **Line Display**. The **TABLE LINE** menu opens.

8. Accept the default **Blank**, and select the vertical lines in the top row to blank them, as shown in Figure 9–76.

Hole Chart main_view : CSO			
Hole No.	X	Y	∅
A1	60.000	80.000	80.000
B1	150.000	200.000	50.000
B2	150.000	400.000	50.000
C1	60.000	520.000	80.000
D1	920.000	200.000	55.000
D2	920.000	400.000	55.000
E1	690.000	300.000	70.000
E2	590.000	300.000	70.000
F1	450.000	200.000	50.000
F2	450.000	400.000	50.000

Figure 9–76

9. Press the middle mouse button twice to close the menu.

Task 3 - Modify a dimension in the model and update the hole table.

1. Open **hole_chart.prt**.

2. For the hole shown in Figure 9–77, change the dimension from **60** to **80**. Regenerate the part.

If required, select **File>Options> Configuration Editor** *to toggle off the* **tol_display** *option.*

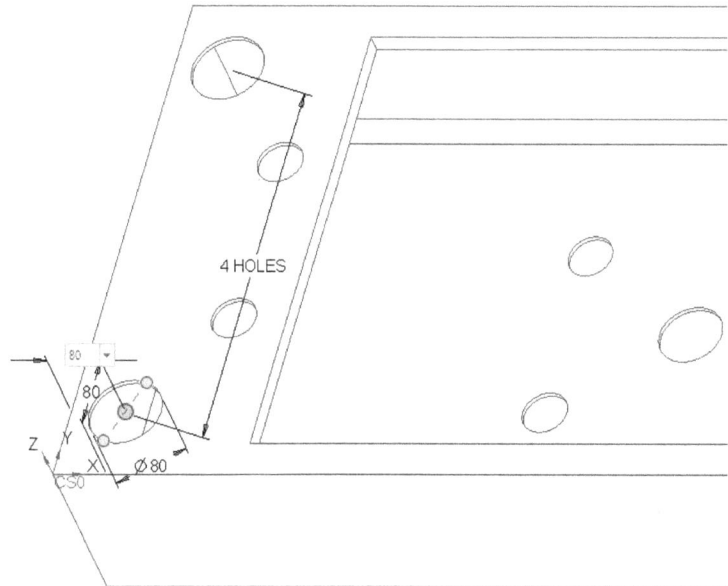

Figure 9–77

3. Save the part and close the window.

4. Switch to the drawing window.

5. Click ⟳ (Update Tables) in the Data group to update the value.

Task 4 - Create an axis table for the top view.

1. Click ⌙ (Hole Table) in the Table group.

2. In the Hole Table dialog box, select **Datum axes**.

3. Set the number of Decimal places to **2** and clear the **Use default** option for the **Sort column** option. Select **Y** in the drop-down list, as shown in Figure 9–78.

Figure 9–78

4. Click **Create**.

5. Select the coordinate system **CS0**.

6. Select the location of the upper left corner of the hole table, as shown in Figure 9–79.

Note that the axes table is arranged in increasing value of the Y-coordinate.

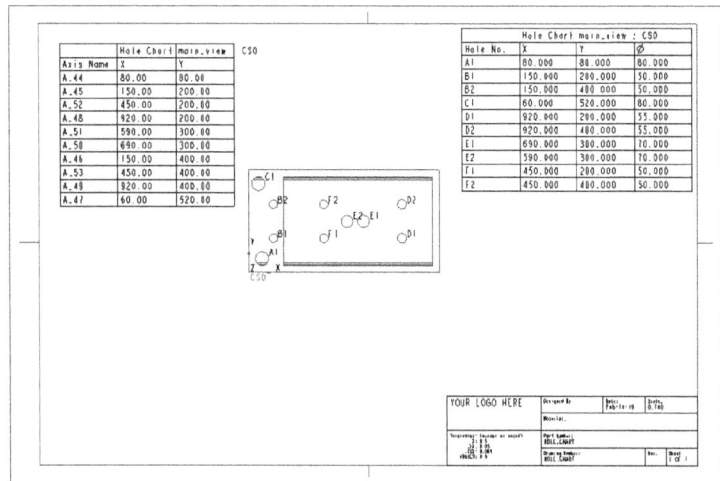

Figure 9–79

7. Change the selection filter to **Table Cell**.

8. Double-click on the cell containing the text *Hole Chart* and modify the text, as shown in Figure 9–80.

	Axis Chart	main_view
Axis Name	X	Y
A_44	80.00	80.00
A_45	150.00	200.00
A_52	450.00	200.00
A_48	920.00	200.00
A_51	590.00	300.00
A_50	690.00	300.00
A_46	150.00	400.00
A_53	450.00	400.00
A_49	920.00	400.00
A_47	60.00	520.00

Figure 9–80

9. Change the selection filter to **Table Row**.

10. Select the two top rows, right-click, and select **Text Style**. The Text Style dialog box opens.

*Any font type can be selected from the **Font** menu.*

11. Clear the **Default** option next to **Font** and select **Arial WGL Bold** in the **Font** drop-down list. Click **OK**. The table displays as shown in Figure 9–81.

12. Change the width of the right column to **15**.

13. Change the selection filter to **Table**.

14. Select the table shown in Figure 9–81, and blank the borders on the top row by right-clicking and selecting **Line Display**.

	Axis Chart	main_view : CS0
Axis Name	**X**	**Y**
A_44	80.00	80.00
A_45	150.00	200.00
A_52	450.00	200.00
A_48	920.00	200.00
A_51	590.00	300.00
A_50	690.00	300.00
A_46	150.00	400.00
A_53	450.00	400.00
A_49	920.00	400.00
A_47	60.00	520.00

Figure 9–81

Task 5 - Create a datum point table for the top view.

1. Click ⬚ (Hole Table) in the Table group.

2. Select **Datum points**.

3. Set the number of decimals to **1**.

4. Click **Add** and select **Parameters>Enter Name**.

Absolute coordinate of datum points can be entered manually in this column.

5. Set the parameter column name to **abs_coordinates**.

6. Click **Create**.

7. Select the coordinate system **CS0**.

8. Locate the upper left corner of the hole table, as shown in Figure 9–82.

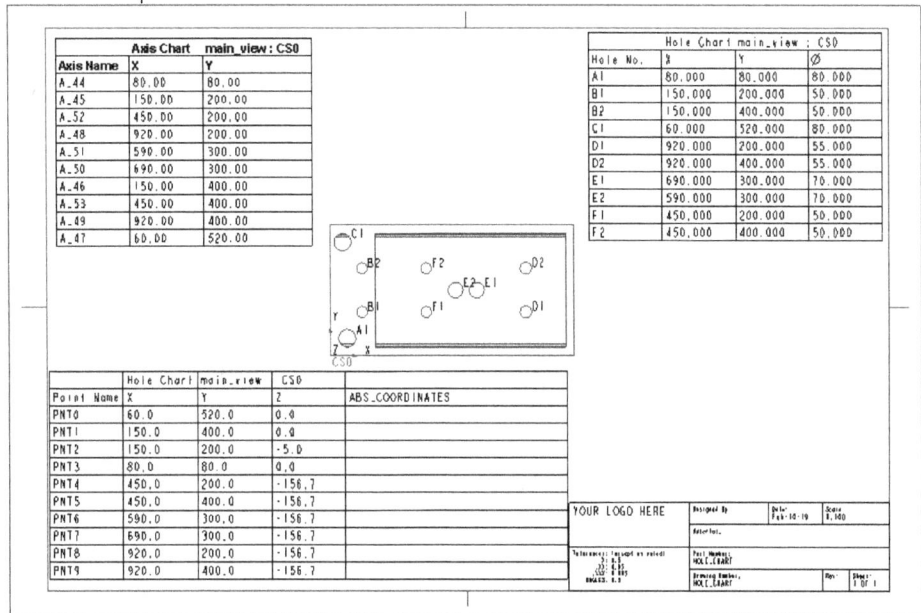

Axis Chart main_view : CS0

Axis Name	X	Y
A_44	80.00	80.00
A_45	150.00	200.00
A_52	450.00	200.00
A_48	920.00	520.00
A_51	590.00	300.00
A_50	690.00	300.00
A_46	150.00	400.00
A_53	450.00	400.00
A_49	920.00	400.00
A_47	60.00	520.00

Hole Chart main_view : CS0

Hole No.	X	Y	Ø
A1	80.000	80.000	80.000
B1	150.000	200.000	50.000
B2	150.000	400.000	50.000
C1	60.000	520.000	80.000
D1	920.000	200.000	55.000
D2	920.000	400.000	55.000
E1	690.000	300.000	70.000
E2	590.000	300.000	70.000
F1	450.000	200.000	50.000
F2	450.000	400.000	50.000

Hole Chart main_view CS0

Point Name	X	Y	Z	ABS_COORDINATES
PNT0	60.0	520.0	0.0	
PNT1	150.0	400.0	0.0	
PNT2	150.0	200.0	-5.0	
PNT3	80.0	80.0	0.0	
PNT4	450.0	200.0	-156.7	
PNT5	450.0	400.0	-156.7	
PNT6	590.0	300.0	-156.7	
PNT7	690.0	300.0	-156.7	
PNT8	920.0	200.0	-156.7	
PNT9	920.0	400.0	-156.7	

Figure 9–82

9. Blank the vertical lines in the top row.

10. Modify the text and text style in the top row, as shown in Figure 9–83.

Hole Chart main_view : CS0				
Point Name	X	Y	Z	ABS_COORDINATES
PNT0	60.0	520.0	0.0	
PNT1	150.0	400.0	0.0	
PNT2	150.0	200.0	-5.0	
PNT3	80.0	80.0	0.0	
PNT4	450.0	200.0	-156.7	
PNT5	450.0	400.0	-156.7	
PNT6	590.0	300.0	-156.7	
PNT7	690.0	300.0	-156.7	
PNT8	920.0	200.0	-156.7	
PNT9	920.0	400.0	-156.7	

Figure 9–83

11. Save the drawing and close the window.

Chapter Review Questions

1. Simple repeat regions only expand the table in one direction: vertically or horizontally.

   a. True

   b. False

2. You can manipulate repeat region tables in the following ways. (Select all that apply.)

   a. Filtering information.

   b. Controlling the amount of information displayed.

   c. Displaying balloons associated with a BOM repeat region.

   d. Paginating repeat region tables (same sheet or multi-sheet).

3. Tables can be automatically created for which of the following features? (Select all that apply.)

   a. Holes

   b. Datum Points

   c. Datum Axes

   d. Chamfers

4. Creating a table using the **Insert Table** option enables you to specify which additional options? (Select all that apply.)

   a. Cell text alignment,

   b. Number of columns

   c. Number of rows

   d. Sizes of rows and columns

5. Creating a table using the **Grid** option enables you to specify the sizes of the rows and columns.

   a. True

   b. False

6. The **Quick Table** command enables you to access a gallery of tables that are available for selections.

   a. True

   b. False

Answers: 1a, 2abcd, 3abc, 4bcd, 5b, 6a

2D Sketching

You can create drawings from 3D models, import drawing data from other CAD systems, and create 2D entities to supplement the existing information. This chapter discusses how you can add sketched 2D entities to your drawings.

Learning Objectives in This Chapter

- Learn the methods used to create and modify 2D entities using the *Sketch* tab.
- Learn additional tools in the *Sketch* tab to manipulate the 2D entities.
- Learn to move draft entities as one object in the drawing by creating groups or relating the entity to a view.
- Learn to ungroup, modify, and suppress draft objects in the drawing view.
- Convert drawing views into a collection of draft items that are no longer associated with their corresponding model.
- Use the Parametric Drafting tool to associate 2D entities with each other and create parent/child relationships.

10.1 Create 2D Entities

To start sketching in Drawing mode, select the *Sketch* tab, as shown in Figure 10–1.

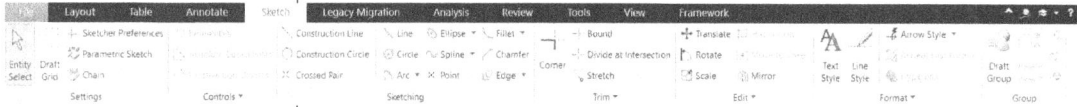

Figure 10–1

Sketching entities in Drawing mode is similar to sketching when creating a solid model. To sketch an entity, you select the start point (or center), move the cursor, and press the left mouse button to end the entity. As entities are added to the drawing, they display in the Snapping References dialog box and can be used as references to create other entities. You can continue to sketch entities by pressing the left mouse button or you can terminate entity creation by pressing the middle mouse button.

You can sketch the following entities in your drawing:

- Lines / Construction Lines

- Circles / Construction Circles

- Ellipses

- Arcs

- Fillets

- Chamfers

- Splines

- Points

- Use & Offset Edges

As you sketch each entity type, many of the same tools apply as in Sketcher mode.

Use the following common tips for sketching entities in your drawing:

- During the sketching process, use the options in the shortcut menu shown in Figure 10–2. These options enable you to select references and access other options that can help you accurately define the entity.

The options that are available on the shortcut menu vary depending on the type of entity that is being sketched.

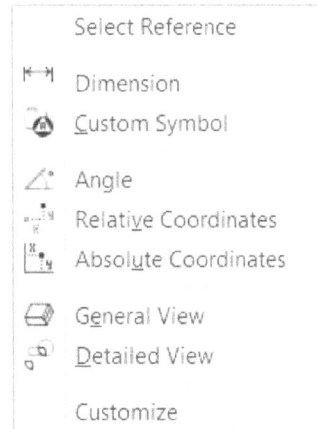

Figure 10–2

- The Snapping References dialog box opens once you have selected an entity type, as shown in Figure 10–3. This dialog box enables you to select references. To select a reference, click ⬚ (Select Reference) and select the reference entity (e.g., lines or circles).

*To remove references, select the entity in the Snapping Reference dialog box and click **Remove**.*

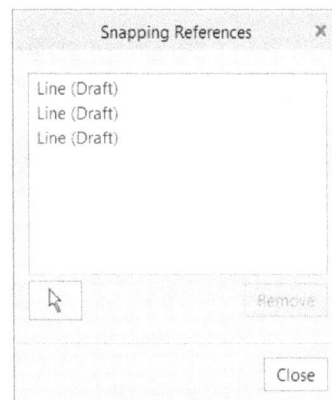

Figure 10–3

- The Sketch Preferences dialog box (as shown in Figure 10–4), enables you to set snapping rules for sketching. To open this dialog box, click ┼ (Sketcher Preferences).

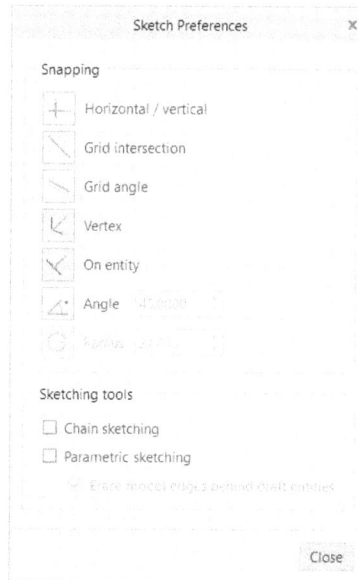

Figure 10–4

- The horizontal, vertical, midpoint, parallel, perpendicular, and tangent constraints can be applied automatically as you sketch.

- By default, all of the sketched entities are sketched individually and are not chained together. To chain entities at their end points, click ⟨ (Chain).

To sketch 2D entities, click the appropriate icon in the Sketching group, as shown in Figure 10–5.

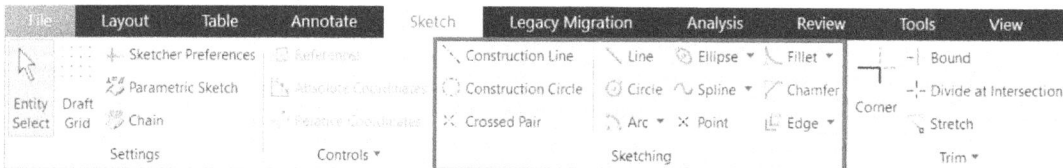

Figure 10–5

Line

To create 2D lines in your drawing, click ╲ (Line) or right-click and select **Line Chain**. Select the start and end points using the left mouse button. Right-click to access the menu options, as shown in Figure 10–6. Press the middle mouse button to complete the line.

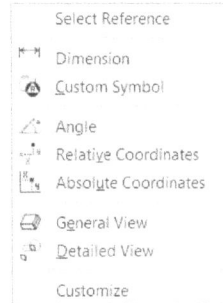

Select Reference

|⊢−⊣| Dimension
⚗ Custom Symbol

∠ Angle
Relative Coordinates
Absolute Coordinates

⊟ General View
Detailed View

Customize

Figure 10–6

The options used to define the line are described as follows:

Option	Description
Select Reference	Selects references.
Angle	Specifies the line angle counter-clockwise relative to the horizontal.
Relative Coordinates	Specifies the end point relative to the start point.
Absolute Coordinates	Specifies the end point using absolute coordinates.

Circle

To create 2D circles, click ◌ (Circle) or right-click and select **Circle**. Select the center of the circle and its radial extent. Right-click to access the menu options, as shown in Figure 10–7. Press the middle mouse button to complete the circle.

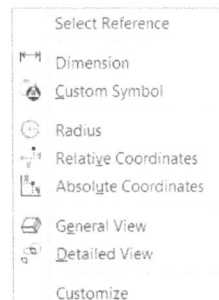

Select Reference

|⊢−⊣| Dimension
⚗ Custom Symbol

◌ Radius
Relative Coordinates
Absolute Coordinates

⊟ General View
Detailed View

Customize

Figure 10–7

Alternatively, you can specify the circle radius in the Sketch Preferences dialog box, and then sketch the circle with this radius.

The options used to define the circle are described as follows:

Option	Description
Select Reference	Selects references. This is useful to sketch a circle that is tangent to one or more entities.
Radius	Specifies the circle radius.
Relative Coordinates	Specifies the circle radius relative to the circle's center.
Absolute Coordinates	Specifies the circle radius using absolute coordinates.

Ellipse

To create 2D ellipses, expand ◔ (Ellipse) and select ◔ (Axis Ends Ellipse) or ◔ (Center and Axis Ellipse).

Select the center of the ellipse and the extent of the ellipse. Right-click to access the menu options, as shown in Figure 10–8. Press the middle mouse button to complete the ellipse.

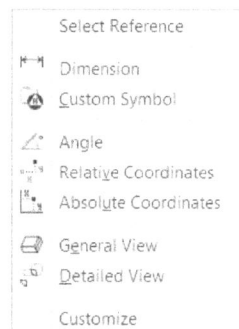

Figure 10–8

The options used to define the ellipse are described as follows:

Option	Description
Select Reference	Selects references.
Angle	Specifies the line angle counter-clockwise relative to the horizontal.
Relative Coordinates	Specifies the ellipse's major axis relative to the ellipse center.
Absolute Coordinates	Specifies the ellipse's major axis using absolute coordinates.

Arc

To create 2D arcs, expand ⟍ (Arc) and click ⟍ (Center and Ends) or ⟋ (3-Point / Tangent End). You can also right-click and select **Center and Ends Arc**. Select the center or end points of the arc. Right-click to access the menu options, as shown in Figure 10–9. Press the middle mouse button to complete the arc.

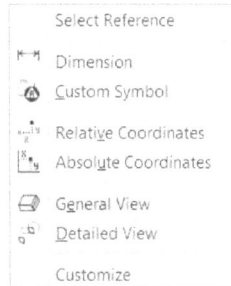

Select Reference
⊢⊣ Dimension
⊘ Custom Symbol
Relative Coordinates
Absolute Coordinates
General View
Detailed View
Customize

Figure 10–9

You can also specify the radius in the Sketch Preferences dialog box, and then sketch the arc.

The options used to define the arc are described as follows:

Option	Description
Select Reference	Selects references. This option is useful when you want to sketch an arc tangent to one or more entities.
Relative Coordinates	Specifies the arc radius relative to the arc center.
Absolute Coordinates	Specifies the arc radius using absolute coordinates.

Construction Line

To create construction lines, click ⟍ (Construction Line) or ⤬ (Crossed Pair). Select the start point and a second point to define the direction. The construction line does not have a defined length. It extends across the entire drawing. Right-click to access the menu options, as shown in Figure 10–10.

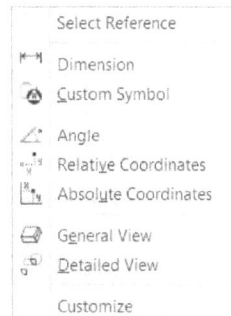

Select Reference
⊢⊣ Dimension
⊘ Custom Symbol
∠ Angle
Relative Coordinates
Absolute Coordinates
General View
Detailed View
Customize

Figure 10–10

The options used to define the construction line are described as follows:

Option	Description
Select Reference	Selects references. This option is useful when you want to sketch an offset construction line from an entity.
Angle	Specifies the line angle counter-clockwise relative to the horizontal.
Relative Coordinates	Specifies the second point relative to the first point.
Absolute Coordinates	Specifies the second point using absolute coordinates.

Construction Circle

To create construction circles, click ⊙ (Construction Circle). Select the center of the circle and its radial extent. Right-click to access the menu options, as shown in Figure 10–11. Press the middle mouse button to complete the construction circle.

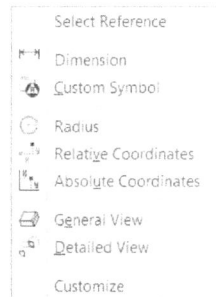

Figure 10–11

Alternatively, you can specify the construction circle radius in the Sketch Preferences dialog box, and then sketch the circle with this radius.

The options used to define the construction circle are described as follows:

Option	Description
Select Reference	Selects references. This option is useful when you want to sketch a construction circle that is tangent to one or more entities.
Radius	Specifies the circle radius.
Relative Coordinates	Specifies the circle radius relative to the start point.
Absolute Coordinates	Specifies the circle radius using absolute coordinates.

Fillet

To create a fillet, expand ⌐ (Fillet) and click ⌐ (2 Tangent Fillet) or ⌐ (3 Tangent Fillet). A 2 Tangent fillet requires a radius value. The radius for a 3 Tangent fillet is generated by the geometry. Using the **Trim Style** option, you can control the geometry that is removed when the fillet is applied. The Fillet options are shown in Figure 10–12.

Fillet Properties   X

Radius value:

0.271697   ▼

Trim style:

Full trim ▼

Full trim
Thin line trim
Solid line trim
Half trim
No trim   ncel

Figure 10–12

Chamfer

To create a chamfer, click ⌐ (Chamfer), or right-click and select **Chamfer**. Select the two references to chamfer. The Chamfer Properties dialog box opens as shown in Figure 10–13.

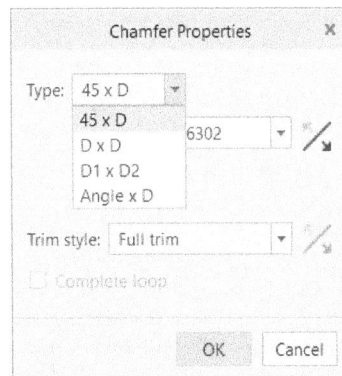

Chamfer Properties   X

Type: 45 x D   ▼

45 x D
D x D   6302   ▼
D1 x D2
Angle x D

Trim style: Full trim   ▼

☐ Complete loop

OK   Cancel

Figure 10–13

To define the chamfer, select the chamfer's dimensioning scheme (e.g., 45 x D or D1 x D2), specify the dimension values (use the ⌐ (Flip) option if required when defining Angle x D or D1 x D2), define the required Trim Style, and click **OK**.

Spline

To create a spline, click ᴎ (Spline), or right-click and select **Spline**. Select the start point for the spline and continue selecting points. Right-click to access the menu options, as shown in Figure 10–14. Press the middle mouse button to complete the spline.

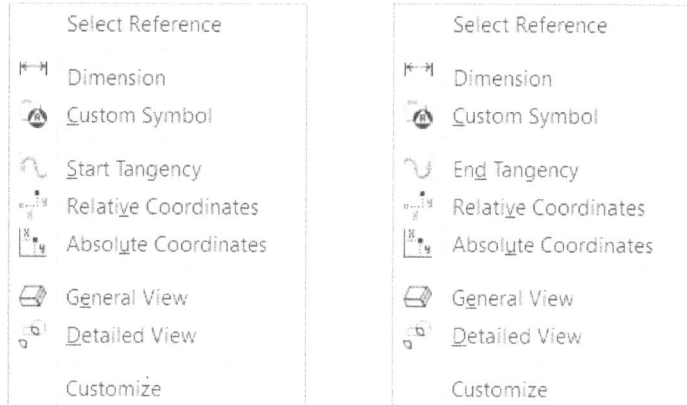

Select Reference	Select Reference
⊢⊣ Dimension	⊢⊣ Dimension
🔴 Custom Symbol	🔴 Custom Symbol
ᴎ Start Tangency	ᴎ End Tangency
Relative Coordinates	Relative Coordinates
Absolute Coordinates	Absolute Coordinates
🖪 General View	🖪 General View
Detailed View	Detailed View
Customize	Customize

Figure 10–14

The options used to define the spline are described as follows:

Option	Description
Select Reference	Selects references.
Start Tangency	Specifies the tangency at the spline's start point relative to the horizontal and counter-clockwise.
End Tangency	Specifies the tangency at the spline's end point relative to the horizontal and counter-clockwise.
Relative Coordinates	Specifies the spline point relative to the previous point.
Absolute Coordinates	Specifies the spline point using absolute coordinates.

You can sketch a horizontal spline curve by setting the start and end tangency angles to 180°.

Once all of the internal points of the spline have been created, right-click before selecting your final spline point and select **End Tangency**. This option specifies the tangency for the spline's end point.

Point

To create a point, click ✕ (Point). Place the point using the left mouse button. Right-click to access the menu options, as shown in Figure 10–15.

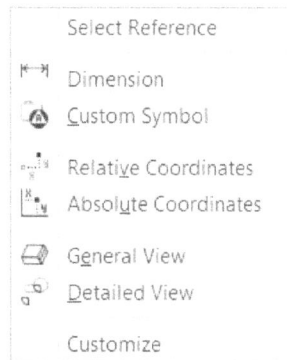

Select Reference

⊢──⫞ Dimension

◭ Custom Symbol

Relative Coordinates

Absolute Coordinates

General View

Detailed View

Customize

Figure 10–15

The options used to define the point are described as follows:

Option	Description
Select Reference	Selects references.
Relative Coordinates	Specifies point relative to previous point.
Absolute Coordinates	Specifies point using absolute coordinates.

Break

Select **Edit>Break** to break a draft entity. Select the entity you want to break and then select the first and second points to define the break. You can continue to break the same parent entity or press the middle mouse button to select another entity to break. Press the middle mouse button twice to finish breaking entities.

Offset and Use Edge

Expand ⌐ (Edge) and click ⌐ (Offset Edge) or ⌐ (Use Edge) to offset draft geometry from other draft entities and model geometry. This option opens the **OFFSET OPER** menu, as shown in Figure 10–16.

Menu Manager
▼ OFFSET OPER
  Single Ent
  Ent Chain

Figure 10–16

You can select an axis line or draft datum axis to create an offset draft entity.

The **OFFSET OPER** menu options are described as follows:

Option	Description
Single Ent	Offsets one entity.
Ent Chain	Offsets several entities.

⌐ (Use Edge) enables you to create a draft entity using a model edge. The new lines are automatically related to the view. When you erase the view, all of the attached detail items are erased as well.

10.2 Modify 2D Entities

Once you finish adding 2D entities to your drawing, you might want to modify them. Creo Parametric provides a number of ways in which you can manipulate 2D entities. Most options behave similar to the functions in the *Sketch* tab in part design.

Copy & Paste

To copy single or multiple draft entities onto the Drawing clipboard, select the entity, right-click, and select ▣ (Copy). Clear the entity. Once cleared, you can paste the entity by right-clicking and selecting ▣ (Paste). The entity displays in a sub-window for you to select the translator vector (a point on the entity). Once selected, you can place the entity on the drawing.

- You can also press <Ctrl>+<C> and <Ctrl>+<V> to copy and paste an entity.

Edit Group

Transforming draft entities enables you to move, copy, mirror, rescale, and stretch draft entities. To transform a draft entity, click the icon in the Edit group in the *Sketch* tab, as shown in Figure 10–17. Unlike copying and pasting, you do not have to preselect the entities for transformation.

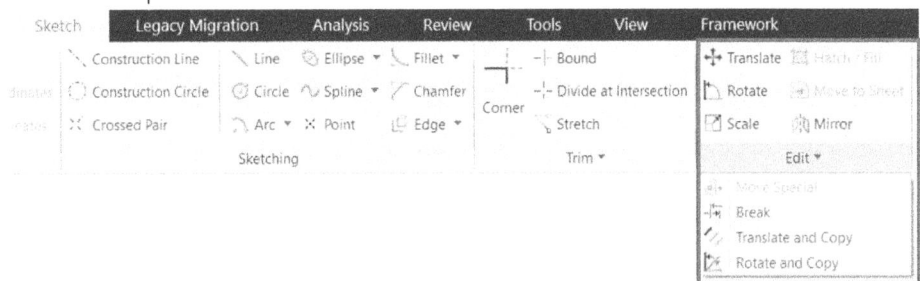

Figure 10–17

The options used to transform draft entities are described in the following table. When using any of these options, refer to the message window for information on what is required to transform the entity.

Option	Description
✛ (Translate)	Moves single or multiple draft entities.
▭ (Rotate)	Rotates single or multiple draft entities simultaneously.

☑ (Scale)	Increases or decreases the size of the entity.
✎ (Translate and Copy)	Creates and places multiple copies of draft entities.
➡ (Move To Sheet)	Moves a draft item to another sheet.
▷ (Rotate and Copy)	Creates a rotated copy of draft entities.
◫ (Mirror)	Creates copies of draft entities, unattached symbols, and unattached notes by mirroring them about a draft line.
➡ (Move Special)	Temporarily groups selected objects and stretches them in a specific direction. This option is useful if you have created a drawn object using several unassociated lines. Lines that join selected lines, but are not selected, also stretch to follow the moved lines.
▨ (Hatch/Fill)	You can manipulate the interior display of closed draft entities This option is only available if the closed draft entity is preselected before accessing the icon. The cross-hatching options are **Hatched** or **Fill**. The entities that are selected to be hatched or solid must form a closed loop. The display of draft entities as Hatched or Filled are as follows:

Original draft entities

Draft entities filled as Hatched

Draft entities filled as Solid

Trim Group

To lengthen or shorten draft geometry, select an option in the Trim group, as shown in Figure 10–18. You do not have to preselect the entities for transformation.

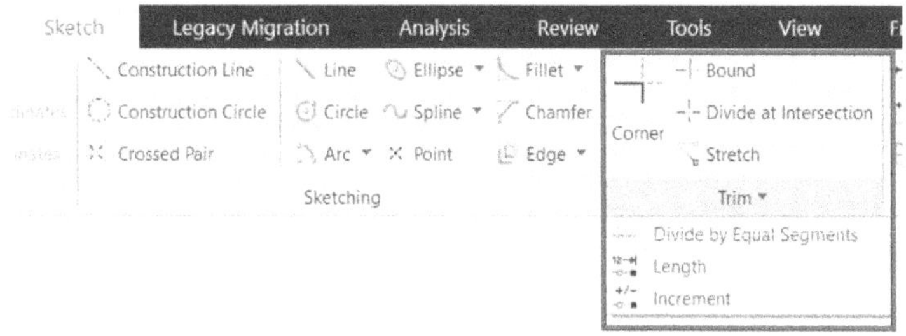

Figure 10–18

The options used to trim draft entities are described below. When using any of these options, refer to the message window for information on what is required to trim the entities.

Option	Description
(Divide At Intersection)	Creates two entities from one, divided at an intersection.
(Divide By Equal Segments)	Divides a selected line into a number of equal sections. You are prompted for the number.
(Corner)	Trims two entities to their intersection.
(Bound)	Trims to a specified entity or point. First select the boundary and then the items that trim to it.
(Length)	Trims to a specified length. Enter a length value and then select items to trim or expand to that length.
(Increment)	Trims or extends by a specified increment.

Format Group

To customize the display of draft items, use the icons found in the Format group, as shown in Figure 10–19.

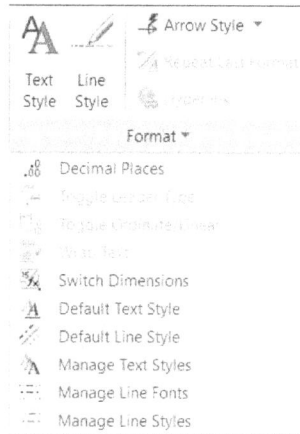

Figure 10–19

Line Style

You can set the line style of 2D entities using one of the following methods:

*   Select the 2D entities and then click ✎ (Line Style) in the mini toolbar.

*   Double-click on a 2D entity.

*   Click ✎ (Line Style) in the Format group.

The Modify Line Style dialog box opens as shown in Figure 10–20.

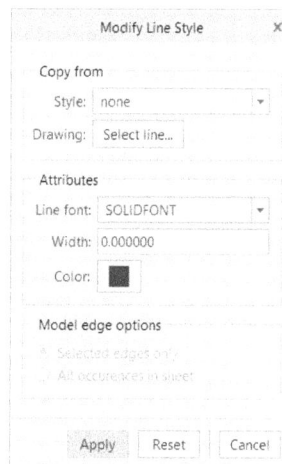

Figure 10–20

10.3 Group 2D Entities

The Group commands in the *Sketch* tab create groups of detail objects that move together as one object. The commands display as shown in Figure 10–21.

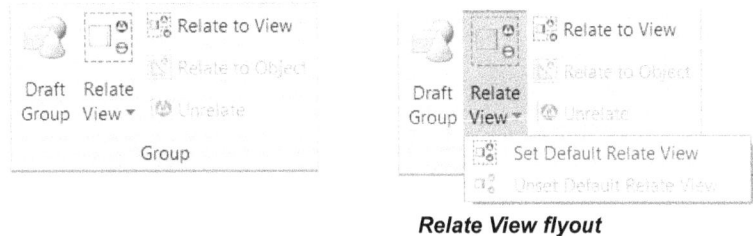

Relate View flyout

Figure 10–21

Drafting lines use a different grouping method from other detail objects, such as dimensions, notes, and GTOLs.

The options used to group draft entities are described as follows:

Option	Description
(Draft Group)	Groups drafting lines with other draft lines.
(Set Default Relate View)	Ensures that sketched draft entities are automatically related to the selected view.
(Unset Default Relate View)	Ensures that sketched draft entities are no longer automatically related to a view.
(Relate To View)	Groups objects with a view, including draft lines.
(Relate To Object)	Groups other detail objects with each other. For example, a note can be grouped with a GTOL.
(Unrelate)	Removes items from the group.

Once the items have been grouped, selecting one object selects the group and moves them all at the same time.

When using (Relate To Object) or (Relate To View), you select one parent to which the objects are related. When the parent moves, the related objects move;. You can also move the related objects separately. Use (Unrelate) to clear the relationship.

After associating items with a view, you can use the **Info** menu to identify the entities in any view or in a specific view.

Create a Draft Group

How To: Create a Draft Group

1. Click ⏚ (Draft Group) in the *Sketch* tab.
2. Select **Create**. You are prompted to select the draft items to add to the group.
3. Select the items and press the middle mouse button to complete the selection.
4. Enter a name for the group and press <Enter>. At this point, you can select draft objects for another group, or press the middle mouse button to complete the group.

Relate Draft Items to a View

How To: Relate Draft Items to a View

1. Select the draft items to relate to a view.
2. Click ⏚ (Relate To View) in the *Sketch* tab.
3. Select the view to which to relate.
4. To remove items in a related group, click ⏚ (Unrelate) in the *Sketch* tab.

Group Objects with Dimension Text

You can group a note, a draft geometric tolerance, or a symbol with dimension text so that it moves with the dimension when the dimension changes location.

How To: Group Objects with Dimension Text

When you erase, re-display, or delete a dimension, the system also erases, re-displays, or deletes all of the items that are related to it.

1. Select notes, symbols, or draft gtols to relate to the selected dimension.
2. Click ⏚ (Relate To Object) in the *Sketch* tab.
3. Select a dimension to which the selected items should relate.
4. To remove the grouping between the objects and the dimension text, click ⏚ (Unrelate) in the *Sketch* tab.

Ungroup a Draft Group

How To: Ungroup a Draft Group

1. Click ⏚ (Draft Group) in the *Sketch* tab.
2. Select **Explode**, select **Select** and then select a group. Alternatively, select **By Name** and select the group name. The selected group is ungrouped.

Ungroup Items from a View

How To: Ungroup Items from a View

1. Select the group.
2. Click ⚛ (Unrelate) in the *Sketch* tab. The selected items are unassociated from the view.

Set Drawing View as Current Draft View

When this option is active, all of the draft geometry is automatically related with activated view.

How To: Set a View as the Current Draft View

1. Select a view to be current.
2. Click ▨ (Relate View) and click ▨ (Set Default Relate View) in the *Sketch* tab. The system sets the selected view as the current draft view.
3. To deactivate the active view, click ▨ (Relate View) and click ▨ (Unset Default Relate View) in the *Sketch* tab.

Modify a Draft Group

How To: Modify a Draft Group

1. Click ▨ (Draft Group) in the *Sketch* tab.
2. Select **Edit** and then select **Select** to select a group. Alternatively, you can select **By Name** and then select its name.
3. Use the **Add** and **Remove** options to add or remove items from the selected group. Press the middle mouse button to finish.

Suppress a Draft Group

How To: Suppress a Group

1. Click ▨ (Draft Group) in the *Sketch* tab.
2. Select **Suppress** and then select **Select** and select a group. Alternatively, you can select **By Name** and then select the group name.

Resume a Suppressed Group

How To: Resume a Suppressed Group

1. Click ▨ (Draft Group) in the *Sketch* tab.
2. Select **Resume**.
3. Select the group to resume.

10.4 Convert to Draft Entities

Clicking ⊟ (Convert To Draft Group) in the Edit group in the *Layout* tab, enables you to convert drawing views into a collection of draft items that are no longer associated with their corresponding model. When you transform a view into a snapshot, the following changes occur:

*The **Convert to Draft Entities** option is available for part drawings and assembly drawings.*

- All visible geometry, axes, datums, and other entities in the view become draft entities.

- All draft entities that were previously associated with the view become free.

- All attached drawing items (such as notes, geometric tolerances, symbols, and draft dimensions) become unattached.

- All visible model dimensions are converted to draft dimensions.

- View dimensions become non-associative draft dimensions (i.e., if the model changes, the snapshot view does not reflect the change).

Notes and symbols attached to a snapshot view remain parametric unless you delete the model from the drawing.

In the case of a multi-model drawing, the model can be deleted from the drawing if all of the views and detail items of a model are snapshot. This technique is useful if an assembly view is required for a part drawing. Once the required assembly view has been placed, snapshot the view and delete the assembly model from the drawing. The assembly is no longer brought into session when the part drawing is opened.

10.5 Sketch Parametric Entities

Parametric drafting enables you to associate 2D entities with each other. The referenced entity becomes the parent, and changes made to that parent reflect in the child entity. The extent of the relationship depends on the type of references that are defined.

References can be made to other sketched entities in drawing views.

The sketched entities in Figure 10–22 are created using parametric sketching. The top horizontal line is the reference entity for the rectangular sketch. All of the other lines reference their start and end points when sketched. Therefore, the sketched entities can only be moved by selecting this referenced line. You cannot move any of the other lines in the sketch. In the example shown on the right in Figure 10–22, the lower parallel line references the upper line. The only constraint on these entities is that they remain parallel. Each line can be moved independently, but only the angle of the reference entity can be changed. Therefore, the lower line updates accordingly.

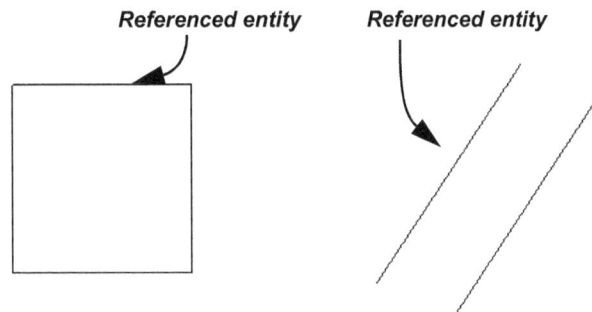

Figure 10–22

How To: Sketch Parametric Entities:

1. Click ⚞ (Parametric Sketch) in the Settings group.
2. Select an entity type (e.g., line, centerline, or arc).
3. Sketch the entity. The entity displays in the References dialog box and remains highlighted in the drawing.

*References can also be selected by right-clicking and selecting **Select Reference**.*

Practice 10a | Drawing Sketches

Practice Objectives

- Create sketched entities in a drawing.
- Use the Trim tools for sketched entities.

In this practice, you will create a sketch for installation instructions. The final drawing displays as shown in Figure 10–23.

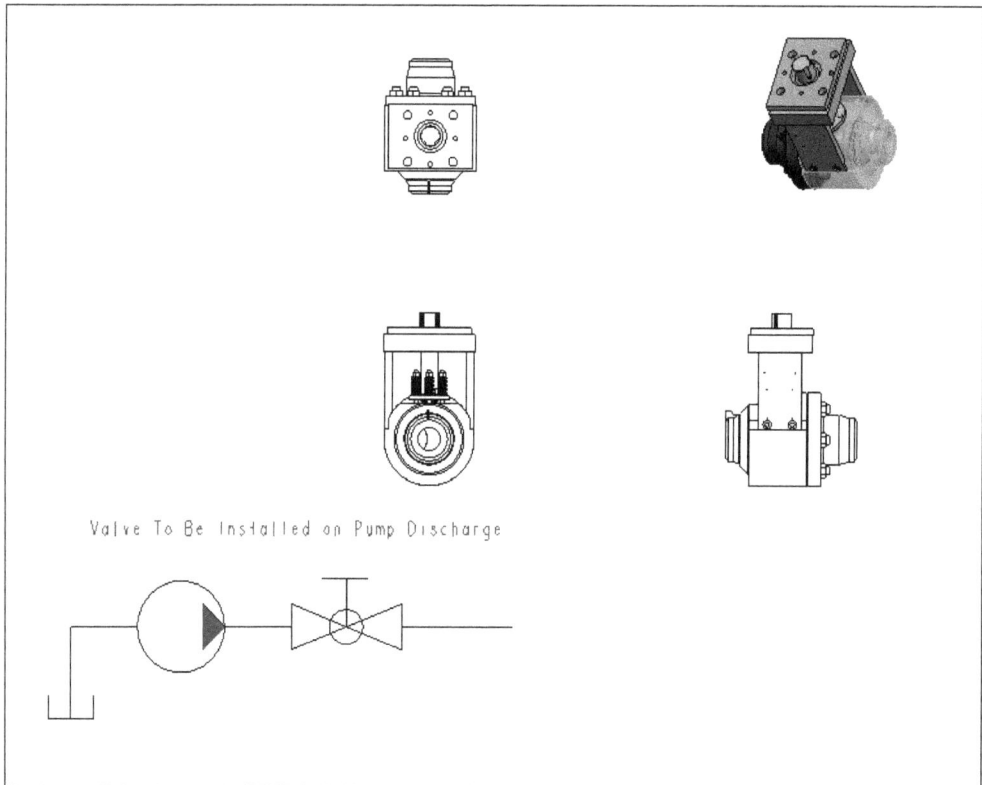

Figure 10–23

Task 1 - Open a drawing and add a note.

1. Set the working directory to the *Drawing_Sketches* folder.

2. Open **valve.drw**.

3. Set the model display as follows:

- ✳ *(Datum Display Filters)*: All Off

- 🗋 *(Display Style)*: 🗋 (No Hidden)

4. Select the *Annotate* tab.

5. Click ᴬ≡ (Note) and select a location for the note as shown in Figure 10–24.

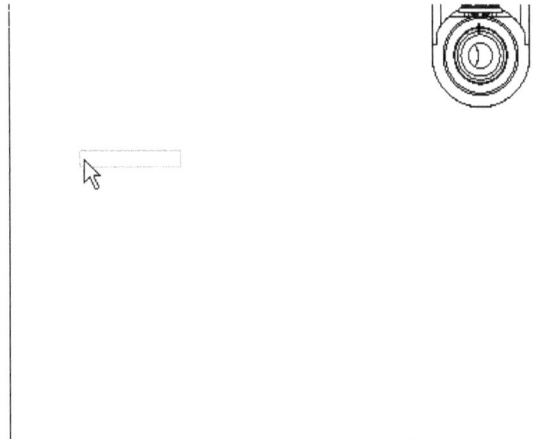

Figure 10–24

6. Type **Valve To Be Installed On Pump Discharge**.

7. In the *Format* tab, edit the text height to **0.3** as shown in Figure 10–25.

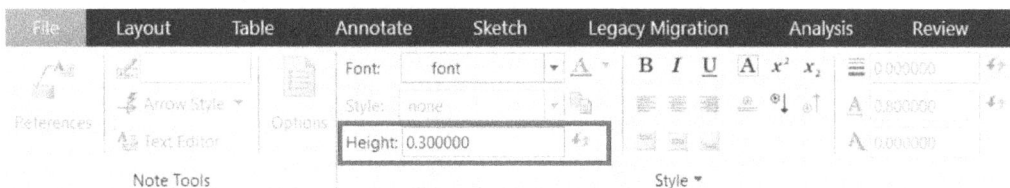

Figure 10–25

8. Select on the screen to complete the note.

Task 2 - Sketch a circle.

---

1. Select the *Sketch* tab.

2. In the Settings group, click ⠿ (Draft Grid).

3. In the Menu Manager click **Show Grid**.

4. Click **Grid Params>X&Y Spacing** and enter **.5** when prompted.

5. Click **Done>Return** and middle-click to complete the grid changes.

   The drawing updates as shown in Figure 10–26.

   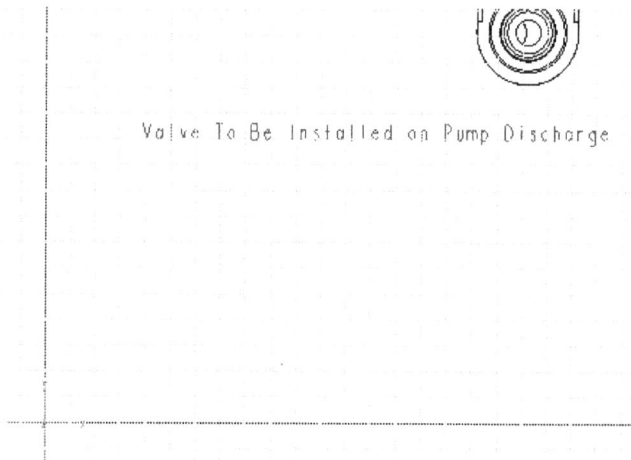

   Valve To Be Installed on Pump Discharge

Figure 10–26

6. In the Settings group, click ╀ (Sketcher Preferences).

7. Enable **Grid intersection** in the Sketch Preferences dialog box, as shown in Figure 10–27.

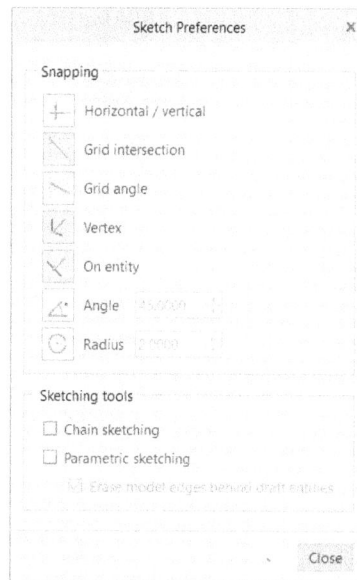

Figure 10–27

8. Click **Close**.

9. In the Sketching group, click ⊘ (Circle).

10. Click the center and radius locations to define the circle, as shown in Figure 10–28.

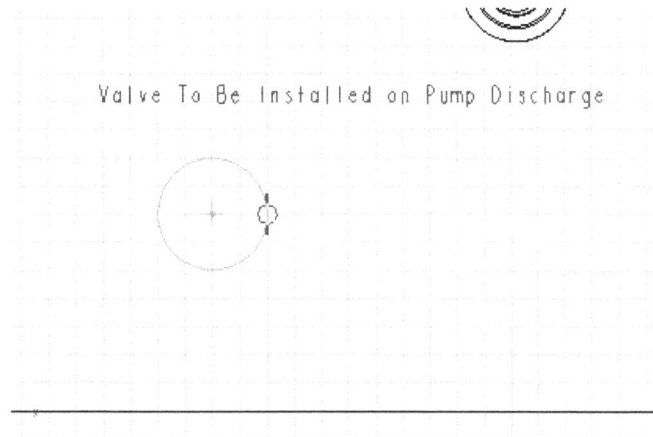

Figure 10–28

Task 3 - Sketch several lines.

1. Click ＼ (Line).

2. Select the two endpoints shown in Figure 10–29 to create the line.

Note that the cursor snaps to the grid vertices.

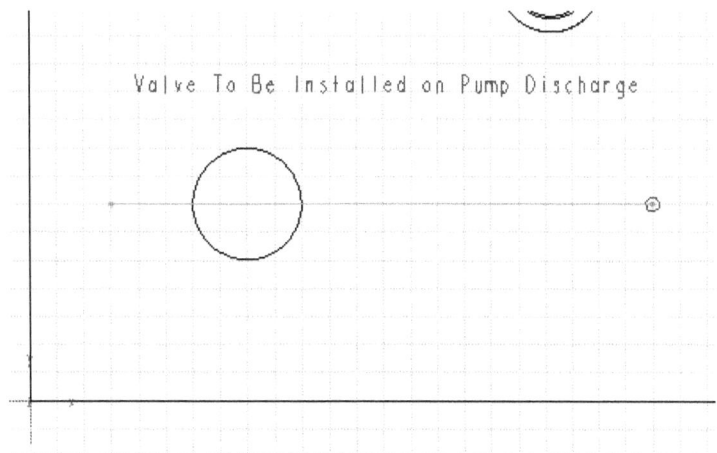

Figure 10–29

3. Select the two endpoints to create the vertical line shown in Figure 10–30.

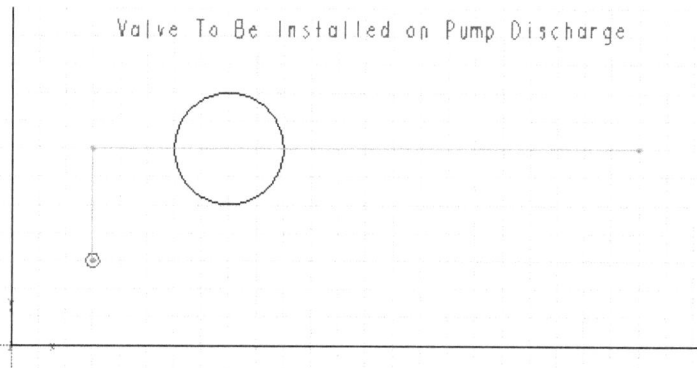

Valve To Be Installed on Pump Discharge

Figure 10–30

4. Sketch the three lines shown in Figure 10–31.

Note that you are sketching a single entity at a time.

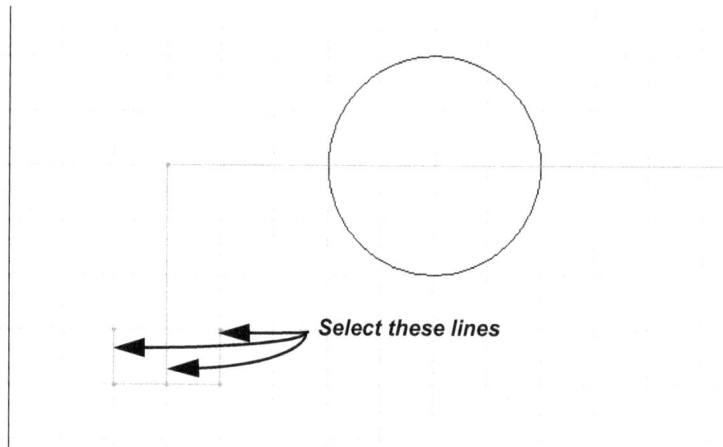

Select these lines

Figure 10–31

5. Press the middle mouse button to finish sketching.

Task 4 - Sketch a chain of edges.

1. In the Settings group, click 🖐 (Chain).

2. Click ╲ (Line), if not already selected.

3. Click the five points shown in Figure 10–32 to create the entities.

With the chain option, each entities continues from the previous.

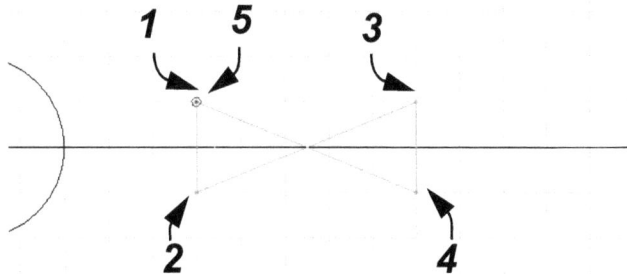

Figure 10–32

4. Press the middle mouse button to complete the chain. Close the Snapping References dialog box.

5. Click ╲ (Line).

6. In the snapping references dialog box, click ▷ (Select Reference).

7. Select the circle and horizontal line, as shown in Figure 10–33.

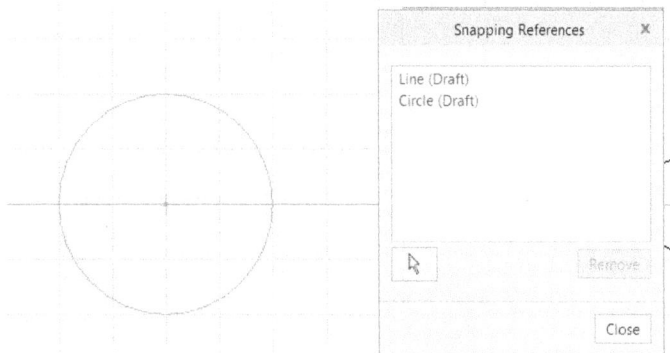

Figure 10–33

8. Press the middle mouse button to stop selecting references.

9. Click the intersection of the line and circle to start a new line chain, then create the three lines of the triangle shown in Figure 10–34.

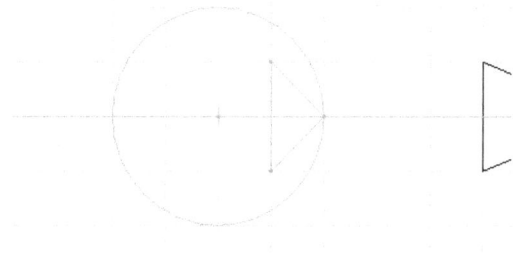

Figure 10–34

10. Press the middle mouse button to complete the chain.

11. With the triangle still selected, click ⬜ (Hatch/Fill).

12. Accept the default name for the section.

13. In the Menu Manager, click **Fill>Done**.

Task 5 - Finish sketching entities.

1. In the Settings group, click ✎ (Chain) to disable it.

2. Click ✛ (Sketcher Preferences) and disable **Grid intersection**.

3. Close the Sketch Preferences dialog box.

4. Click ╲ (Line).

5. In the Snapping References dialog box, click ⬦ (Select Reference).

6. Select the two lines shown in Figure 10–35.

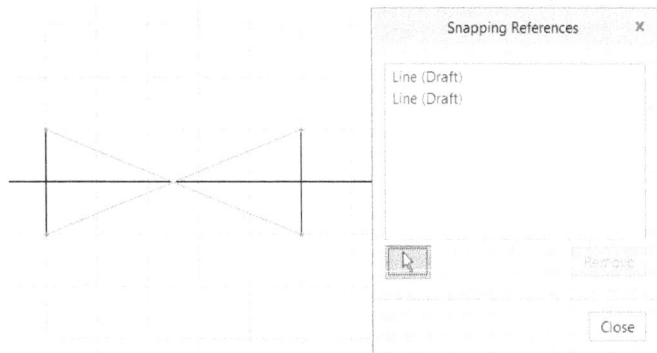

Figure 10–35

7. Press the middle mouse button to stop selecting references, then sketch the vertical and horizontal lines shown in Figure 10–36.

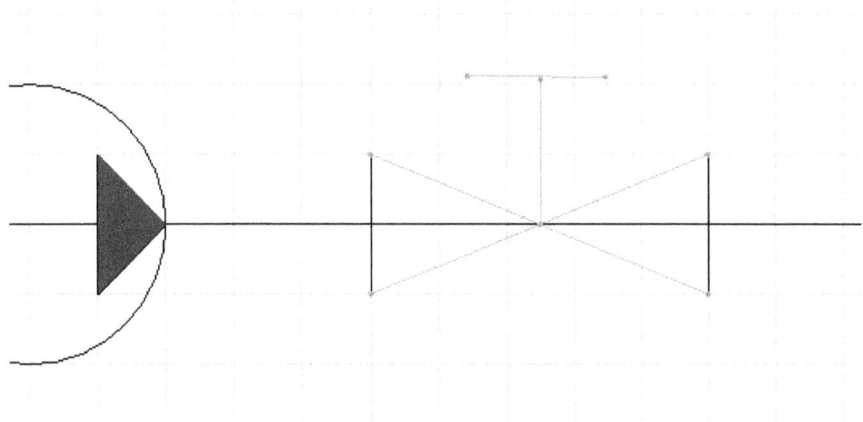

Figure 10–36

8. Press the middle mouse button to complete the lines.

9. Click ⊙ (Circle) and select the center and radius points to sketch the circle shown in Figure 10–37.

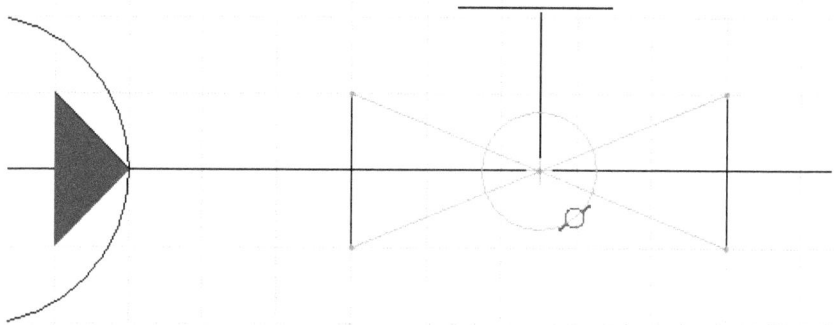

Figure 10–37

10. Press the middle mouse button to complete the circle.

Task 6 - Clean up the sketch.

1. Zoom in on the handle as shown in Figure 10–38.

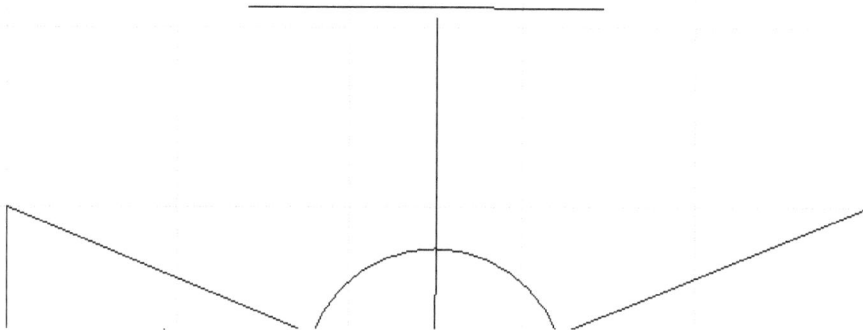

Figure 10–38

2. In the Trim group, click ⊣ (Bound).

3. Select the horizontal line as the boundary.

4. Select the vertical line to trim. The geometry updates as shown in Figure 10–39.

Ensure you select the vertical line below the horizontal line, if the lines cross on your sketch.

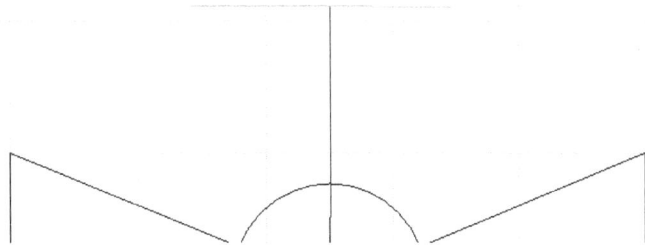

Figure 10–39

5. In the Trim group, click ⊣⊢ (Divide At Intersection).

6. Select the line and the large circle as shown in Figure 10–40.

The system breaks the line where it intersects the circle. If the entities disappear from display, simply repaint the screen. Intersect does not remove geometry.

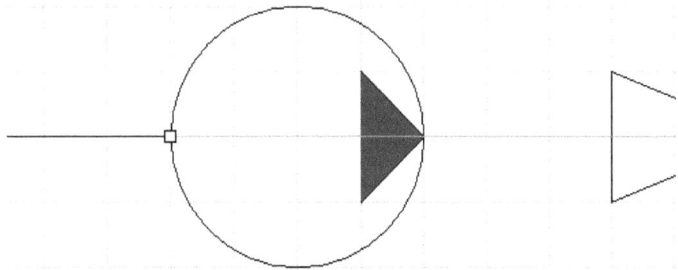

Figure 10–40

7. Repeat the previous step to create breaks in the line at the intersection with the other circle and the two vertical lines on the valve symbol, as shown in Figure 10–41.

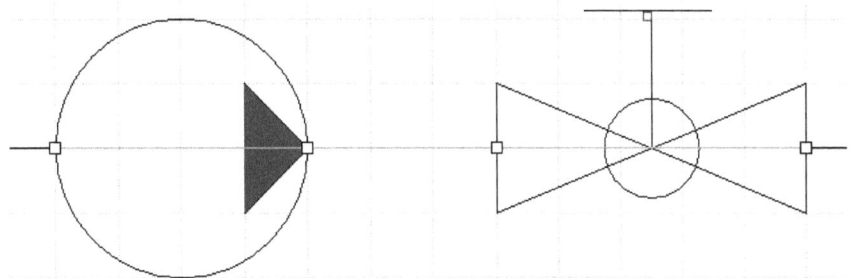

Figure 10–41

8. Select the line inside the circle and press <Delete> to remove it, as shown in Figure 10–42.

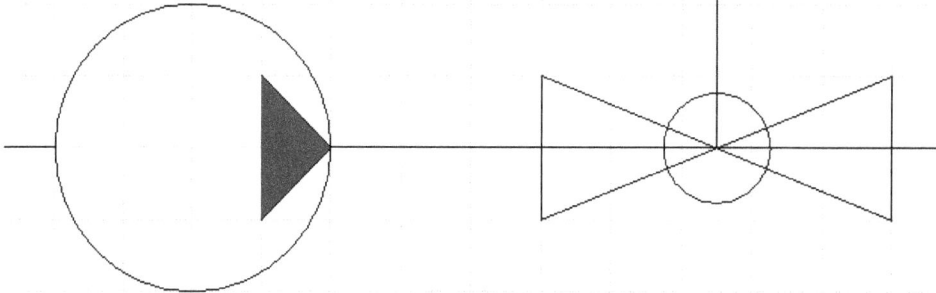

Figure 10–42

9. Delete the line segment running through the valve symbol, as shown in Figure 10–43.

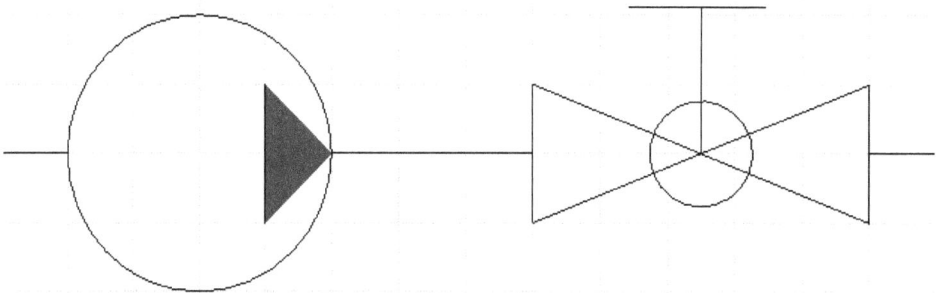

Figure 10–43

10. Click ▦ (Draft Grid)>**Hide Grid**.

11. Middle-click to complete the grid display change.

12. In the In-graphics toolbar, click 🔍 (Refit). The completed drawing displays as shown in Figure 10–44.

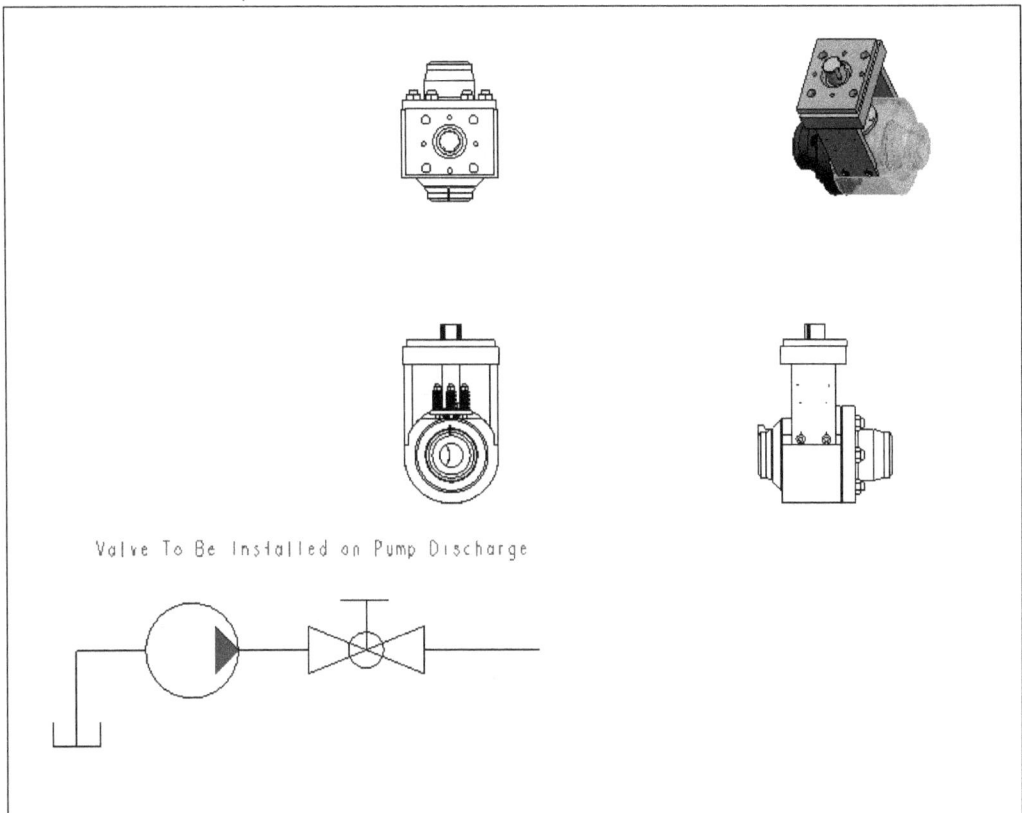

Figure 10–44

13. Save the assembly and erase all files from memory.

Chapter Review Questions

1. To create a chain of entities, which icon should be selected before sketching?

   a.

   b.

   c.

   d.

2. Which of the following entities can be sketched on a drawing (Select all that apply).

   a. Lines

   b. Circles

   c. Ellipses

   d. Arcs

3. Sketched entities can be grouped together into Draft Groups.

   a. True

   b. False

4. When using the **Divide at Intersection** option, Creo Parametric automatically removes a portion of the selected sketched entity.

   a. True

   b. False

Symbols

Symbols are used in drawings to communicate additional information for manufacturing. Symbols are groups of draft entities (e.g., 2D geometry or text) that are placed as a single entity (instance) in a drawing. Company-specific and commonly used information can be grouped as a symbol for efficient retrieval and placement in drawings.

Learning Objectives in This Chapter

- Create a new symbol using the Edit Symbol window to sketch the geometry and create text.
- Define the attributes in the SYMBOL EDIT menu to define the requirement for placing the symbol, text height, and general attributes.
- Create multiple groups from one generic symbol to create different variations of the symbol.
- Learn to define the symbol's placement, placement properties, groups, and variable text in the Custom Drawing Symbol dialog box.
- Learn to create a symbol palette to display frequently used symbols.
- Retrieve, create, and display surface finish symbols on the drawing.

11.1 Create Symbol Geometry

Specific feature-based symbols (e.g., weld symbols or surface finish symbols) can be displayed in drawings. Figure 11–1 shows some examples of symbols that can be created and used in a drawing. A custom drawing symbol consists of symbol geometry, text (if required), and its properties (e.g., placement type, instance height, and attributes).

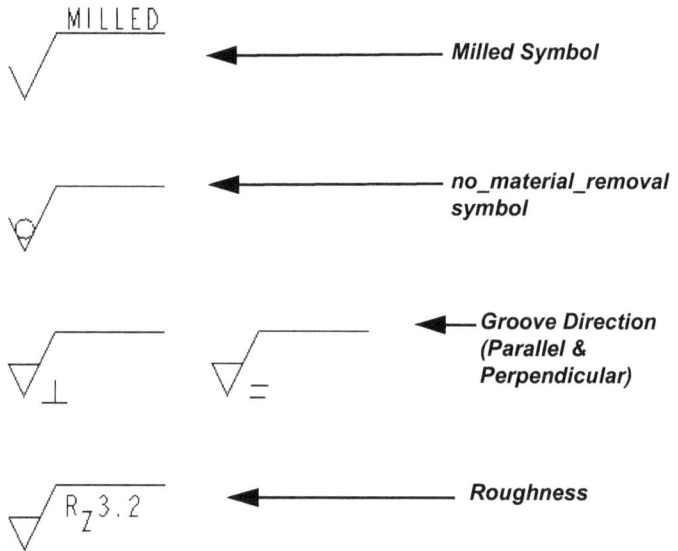

MILLED ←————————— *Milled Symbol*

←————————— *no_material_removal symbol*

←—— *Groove Direction (Parallel & Perpendicular)*

$R_z 3.2$ ←————————— *Roughness*

Figure 11–1

How To: Create a New Symbol

1. Select the *Annotate* tab to activate the annotation options.

2. To create a new symbol, expand ⊚ (Symbol) and click
   ⊚ (Symbol Gallery) in the Annotations group in the *Annotate* tab, as shown in Figure 11–2.

| Annotate | Sketch | Legacy Migration | Analysis | Revi |

Ordinate Dimension ▾   Symbol ▾

A Note ▾   ⊚ Custom Symbol

Dimension Geometric Tolerance   Surface Finish   ⊚ Symbol From Palette

⊚ Symbol Gallery

Annotations ▾

Figure 11–2

A different symbol icon might display on top of the Symbol drop-down list. The last used icon is on top.

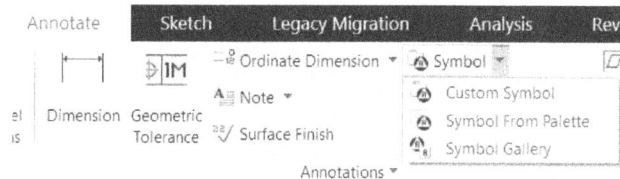

3. Select **Define** and enter a name for the symbol. The Symbol Edit window and menu opens as shown in Figure 11–3.

Menus

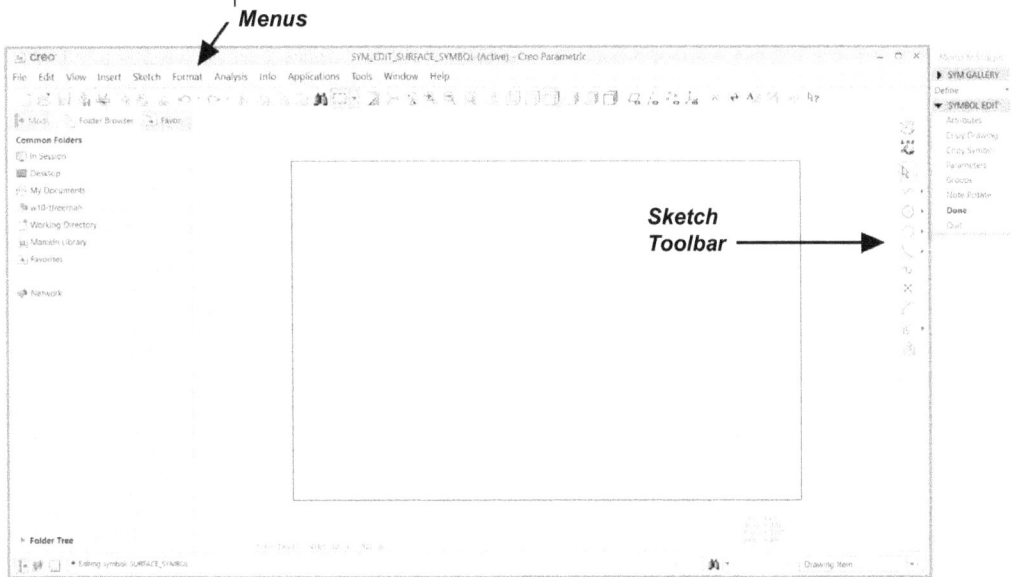

Sketch Toolbar ⟶

Figure 11–3

4. The symbol geometry consists of all of the 2D entities that are used in the symbol. For example, all of the entities in Figure 11–4 are used to create a surface symbol.

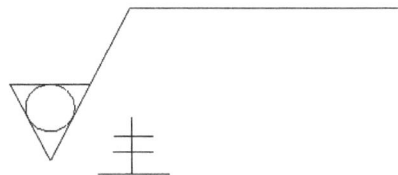

Figure 11–4

Use one of the following methods to create the 2D draft geometry that represents the symbol:

- Select **Copy Drawing** in the **SYMBOL EDIT** menu to copy existing entities from the current drawing. The selected entities are copied into the SYM_EDIT window.

- Select **Copy Symbol** in the **SYMBOL EDIT** menu to copy existing symbols from the current symbol directory. The selected symbol is copied into the SYM_EDIT window.

- Select **Insert>Shared Data>From File** and select the file in the Open dialog box. The following file formats can be used: DXF, DWG, SET, CGM, IGES, STEP, etc.

- Click the icons in the Sketcher toolbar or use the options in the **Sketch** menu to sketch 2D geometry in the SYM_EDIT window.

5. You can create both fixed text and variable text in a symbol. Fixed text remains the same every time the symbol is used. Variable text enables you to either select from predefined text that was assigned when the symbol was created, or you can enter a new value when the symbol is placed. The symbol shown in Figure 11–5 has both fixed and variable text.

Figure 11–5

To use system and user-defined parameters in notes, you must enter the ampersand (&) symbol in front of the parameter.

To create text, select **Insert>Note** or click (Note) in the toolbar. The note attributes for symbols are the same as those for creating drawing notes (e.g., leaders, text orientation, and justification). To add the note, select **Make Note** and enter the text in the message window.

To make text variable, you must use the following syntax when entering the note:

- \variable text\

To complete note creation, select **Done/Return** in the **NOTE TYPES** menu.

Attributes must be defined to successfully create a symbol.

6. The **Attributes** option in the **SYMBOL EDIT** menu enables you to define the requirements for placing the symbol. The *General* tab in the Symbol Definition Attributes dialog box is used to define the following attributes:

- Placement type and references
- Symbol instance height
- General attributes

The *General* tab in the Symbol Definition Attributes dialog box is shown in Figure 11–6.

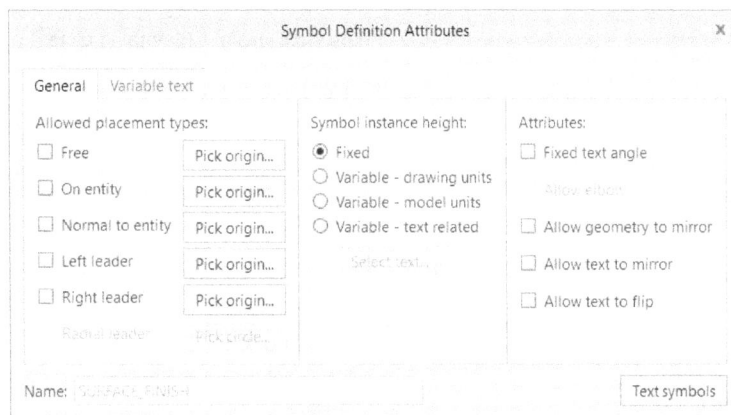

Figure 11–6

The **Allowed Placement Types** options are described as follows:

Option	Description
Free	Enables the symbol to be placed without a leader.
On entity	Enables the symbol to be placed on an entity.
Normal to entity	Enables the symbol to be placed normal to an entity.
Left leader	Enables the symbol to be placed with a leader to the left side of the symbol.
Right leader	Enables the symbol to be placed with a leader to the right side of the symbol.
Radial leader	Enables the symbol to be placed with a radial leader.

The **Symbol Instance Height** options are described as follows:

Option	Description
Fixed	Maintains the original symbol size.
Variable - drawing units	Modifies the symbol size based on the drawing units.
Variable - model units	Modifies the symbol size based on the model units.
Variable - text related	Modifies the symbol size based on the variable text used in the symbol.

The **Attributes** options are described as follows:

Option	Description
Fixed text angle	Maintains all text at the same angle.
Allow elbow	Creates an elbow that is attached with a leader. If this attribute is not enabled during symbol creation you cannot move the text.
Allow geometry to mirror	Mirrors all geometry entities when you mirror the symbol instance.
Allow text to mirror	Mirrors all text entities when you mirror the symbol instance.
Allow text to flip	Flips all text entities when you rotate the symbol instance.

The *Variable Text* tab is used to define the preset text values for each variable text entry. Each variable text entry has a different set of preset values. The *Variable Text* tab in the Symbol Definition Attributes dialog box displays as shown in Figure 11–7.

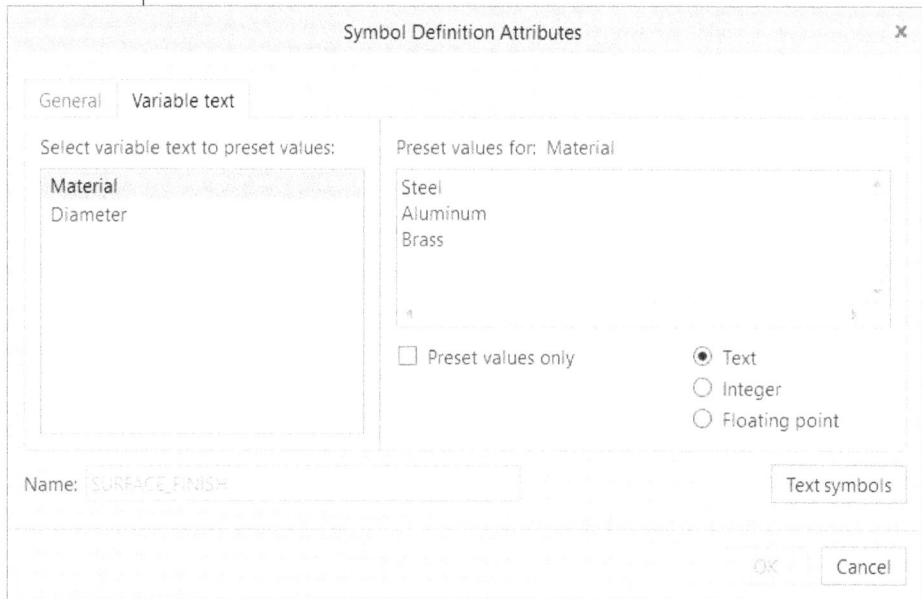

Figure 11–7

7. You can group the entities that make up a symbol (e.g., 2D geometry and text) so that instances (or variations) of one generic symbol can be created. Groups can be created as **Independent** (default) or **Exclusive**. Independent groups can be displayed together in the same symbol, while exclusive groups cannot be displayed in the same symbol. The symbol and all of the geometry and text that are required are shown in the example on the left in Figure 11–8. Selected entities and text are selected to create groups as shown in the example on the right in Figure 11–8.

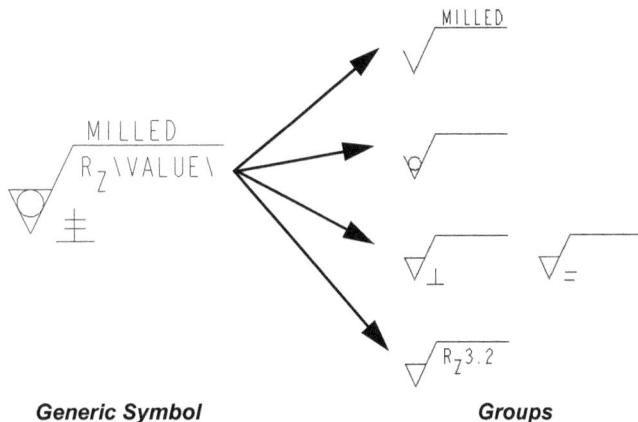

Generic Symbol   *Groups*

Figure 11–8

To create a group, select **Groups>Create**. The **SYM GROUPS** options are described as follows:

Option	Description
Create	Enables you to create a new group. Enter a name for the group and select the symbol entities to group.
Edit	Enables you to add or to remove entities from a selected group. For example, the menus shown add or remove entities from group 2.
Delete	Enables you to delete a selected group.

Clear All	Enables you to delete all groups in the symbol.
Group Attr	Enables you to set **Independent** or **Exclusive** as the group attribute.
Change Level	Enables you to divide a group into subgroups. For example, 2A is a subgroup of group 2, as shown below.

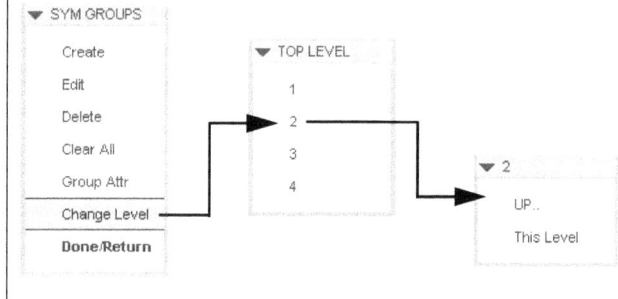

8. Select **Done** in the **SYMBOL EDIT** menu to complete the creation of the symbol. If you have not defined the attributes with regard to placing the symbol, you are prompted for this before you can complete it.
9. You can modify a symbol after it has been created using the options in the **SYM GALLERY** menu, as shown in Figure 11–9.

Figure 11–9

The options are described as follows:

Option	Description
Define	Enables you to define a user-defined symbol.
Redefine	Enables you to modify a user-defined symbol. The **GET SYMBOL** menu is shown below. 

Name	Redefines a symbol that has been retrieved.
Pick Inst	Redefines a visible symbol in the drawing.
Retrieve	Retrieves a symbol for redefinition.
Delete	Enables you to delete all instances of a symbol.
Write	Enables you to save a symbol to disk.
Symbol Dir	Enables you to define the symbol directory.
Show Name	Enables you to display the name and path for a symbol in a drawing.

11.2 Place a Custom Symbol

How To: Place a New Symbol

1. Select the *Annotate* tab to activate the annotation options.

2. To place a symbol in a drawing, expand ⚙ (Symbol) and click ⚙ (Custom Symbol) or right-click and select **Custom Symbol**. The Custom Drawing Symbol dialog box opens as shown in Figure 11–10.

Custom Drawing Symbol	✕

General Grouping Variable Text

Definition

Symbol name SURF_FINSH_SYM ▾ Browse...

New...

Placement

Type On Entity ▾

Properties

Height .3

Proportion

Angle 0.000000 +90

Color ▨

Preview

OK Cancel

Figure 11–10

Select the symbol in the **Symbol Name** menu or browse to select a symbol that is stored on the system. Only symbols that currently exist in the drawing are listed in the menu.

3. To define symbol placement, select an option in the **Type** menu in the *Placement* area in the *General* tab. The options vary depending on the placement type that was defined when the symbol was created. All of the available placement options are shown in Figure 11–11.

Free ▾
Free
On Entity
On Intersect
At Vertex
Normal to Entity
Offset
Absolute Coordinate
Relative Coordinate:

Figure 11–11

Once a placement option has been defined, drag the cursor onto the drawing and place the symbol using the left mouse button. The remaining two areas in the *General* tab enable you to define additional properties for the symbol. If available, you can customize the height, angle of display, and origin. The availability of these options is dependent on how the symbol was originally created.

4. The *Grouping* tab in the Custom Drawing Symbol dialog box is used to define the group that is placed in the drawing. Figure 11–12 shows a *Grouping* tab for a symbol for which groups have been created. To define the symbol, you must select the groups that you want to include.

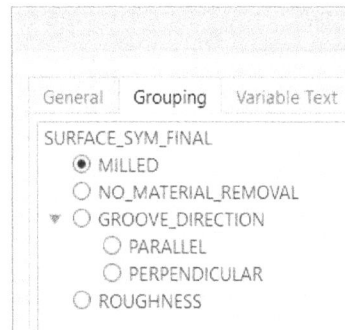

| General | Grouping | Variable Text |

SURFACE_SYM_FINAL
- ◉ MILLED
- ○ NO_MATERIAL_REMOVAL
- ▾ ○ GROOVE_DIRECTION
  - ○ PARALLEL
  - ○ PERPENDICULAR
- ○ ROUGHNESS

Figure 11–12

5. The *Variable Text* tab in the Custom Drawing Symbol dialog box is used to set the variable text values, as shown in Figure 11–13. If options are available for selection, they display in the **Value** menu.

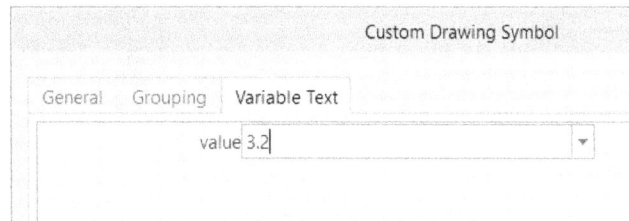

Custom Drawing Symbol

| General | Grouping | Variable Text |

value 3.2|

Figure 11–13

6. To complete symbol placement, click **OK** in the Drawing Symbol dialog box. This button is not available for selection until enough options have been defined to fully locate the symbol in the drawing.

11.3 Symbol Palette

The symbol palette enables you to display frequently used symbols in one location so that they can be easily added to a drawing. The symbol palette can be opened directly by expanding ⚠ (Symbol) and clicking ⚠ (Symbol From Palette) in the Annotations group in the *Annotate* tab. Symbols can be selected in the palette and placed in the current drawing. This increases your efficiency in creating and placing symbols.

*The **symbol_instance_palette_file** config.pro option can be defined with the path to the default symbol palette drawing file.*

Figure 11–14 shows the default Symbol Instance Palette, which displays generic symbols. The generic symbols can be placed using the free or on entity attachment types. The generic palette file is stored in the install location for Creo Parametic and is called **draw_symbol_palette.drw**. You can create custom palette files by creating drawing files and adding symbols to them. To switch between palettes, click **Open...** in the Symbol Instance Palette dialog box and select the file in the Open dialog box.

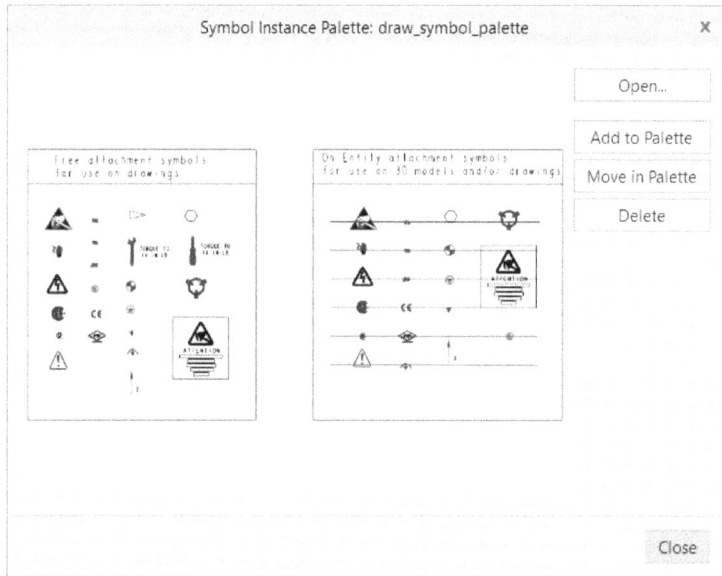

Figure 11–14

Symbols added to parts and assemblies can be displayed in a drawing using ⚠ (Show Model Symbols) in the Show Model Annotations dialog box.

11.4 Surface Finish Symbols

You can create and display the surface quality of a model using a surface finish symbol. Use one of the following three methods to add a surface finish symbol to a drawing:

- Display the surface finish symbol in Part or Assembly mode using the Show Model Annotations dialog box. The **Surface Finish Symbol** option in the Show Model Annotations dialog box is shown in Figure 11–15.

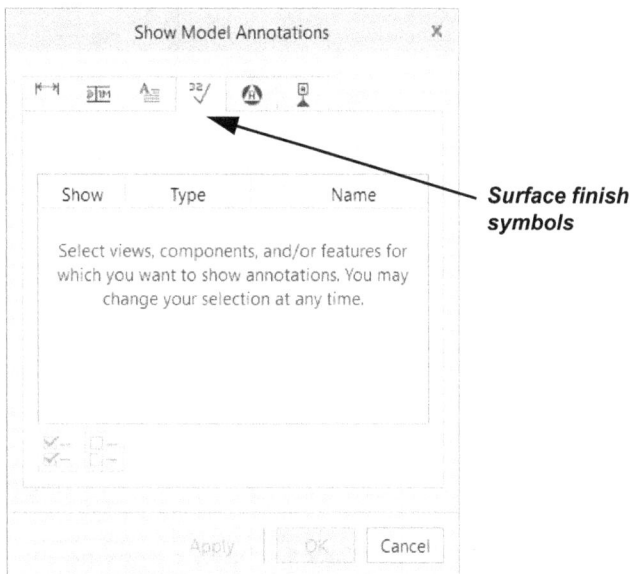

Surface finish symbols

Figure 11–15

- Retrieve an existing surface finish symbol (system-defined or user-defined) from your system by clicking ³²√ (Surface Finish) in the *Annotate* tab or by right-clicking and selecting **Surface Finish**. Select **Browse** in the Surface Finish dialog box.

- Create and place a surface finish as a custom symbol.

Practice 11a | Surface Symbols

Practice Objectives

- Create symbols, groups of symbols, and sub-groups of symbols.
- Place symbols and a system-defined surface finish symbol.

In this practice, you will create a symbol that contains groups and sub-groups so that you can place combinations of the symbols similar to those shown in Figure 11–16.

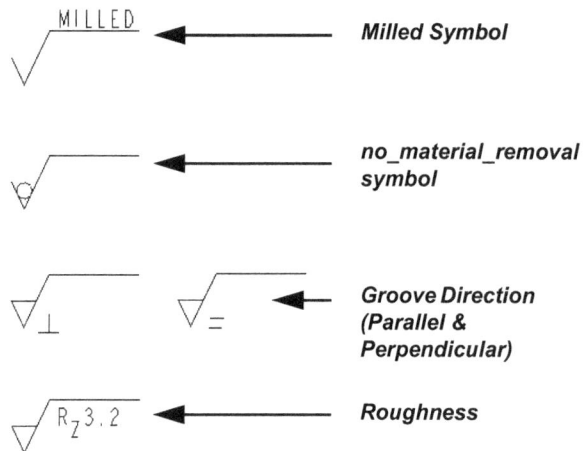

Figure 11–16

Task 1 - Open a drawing file.

Bracket_final_1.drw references the model bracket_final_1.prt.

1. Set the working directory to the *Surface_Symbols* folder.

2. Open **bracket_final_1.drw**.

3. Set the model display as follows:

   - *(Datum Display Filters)*: All Off
   - *(Display Style)*: (Wireframe)

---

4. The drawing displays as shown in Figure 11–17.

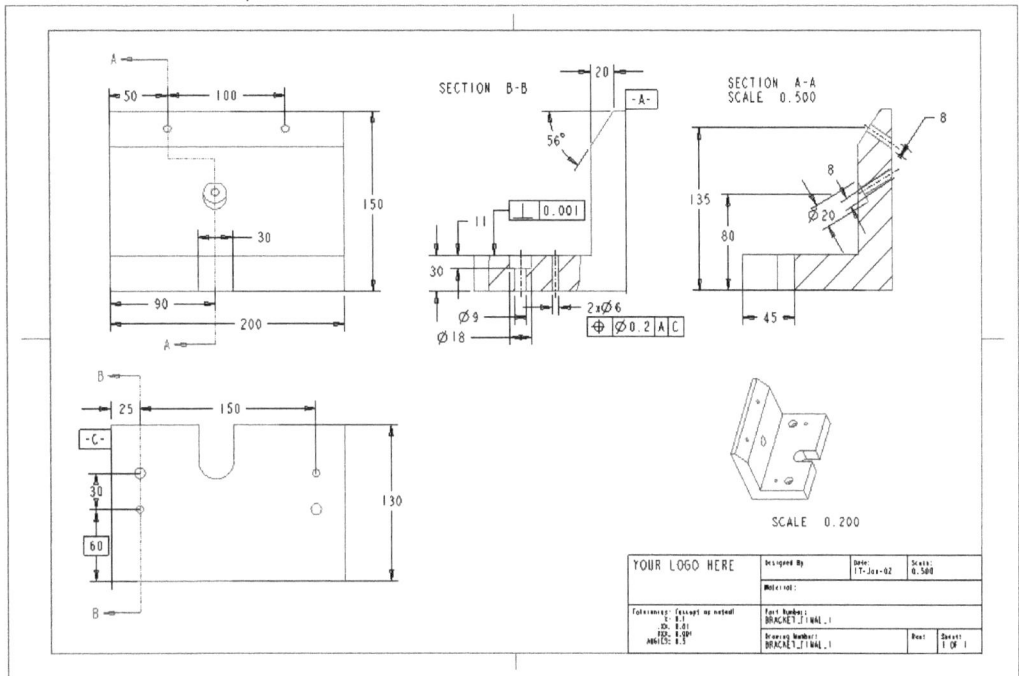

Figure 11–17

Task 2 - Create a symbol.

1. Select the *Annotate* tab.

A different symbol command might display on top. The last used icon is on top.

2. Expand ⚐ (Symbol) and select ⚐ (Symbol Gallery), as shown in Figure 11–18.

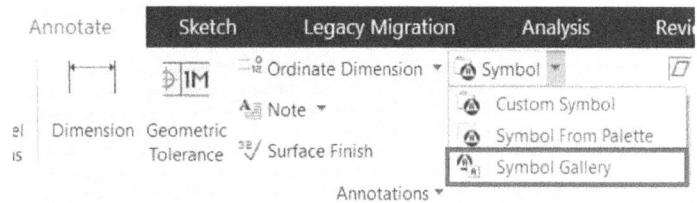

Figure 11–18

3. Select **Define** in the **SYM GALLERY** menu.

*The **Copy Drawing** option copies existing entities from the current drawing. The **Copy Symbol** option copies symbols from a directory.*

4. Enter **surface_symbol** as the name of the symbol. The SYM_EDIT_SURFACE_SYMBOL window displays in which you can sketch the symbol as shown in Figure 11–19. The **SYMBOL EDIT** menu also displays as shown in Figure 11–19.

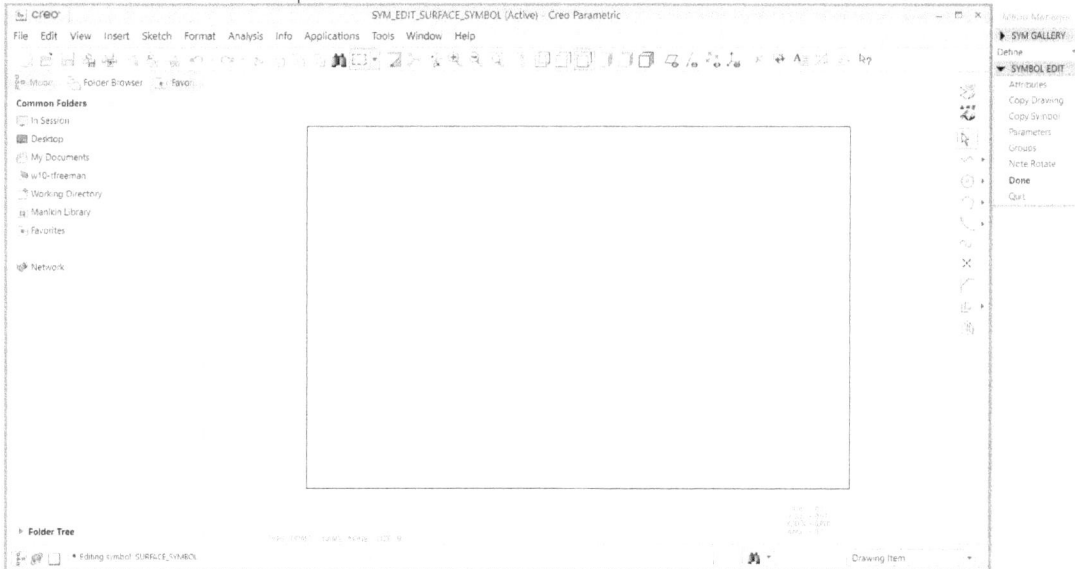

Figure 11–19

5. Select **View>Draft Grid** at the top of the main window. The **GRID MODIFY** menu displays.

6. Select **Show Grid**.

7. Select **Grid Params>X&Y Spacing** to change the spacing of the grid lines to **0.125**.

8. Select **Done/Return** in the **CART PARAMS** menu. The SYMBOL EDIT menu remains open. Do not close it.

9. Zoom in to display approximately sixteen vertical gridlines, as shown in Figure 11–20.

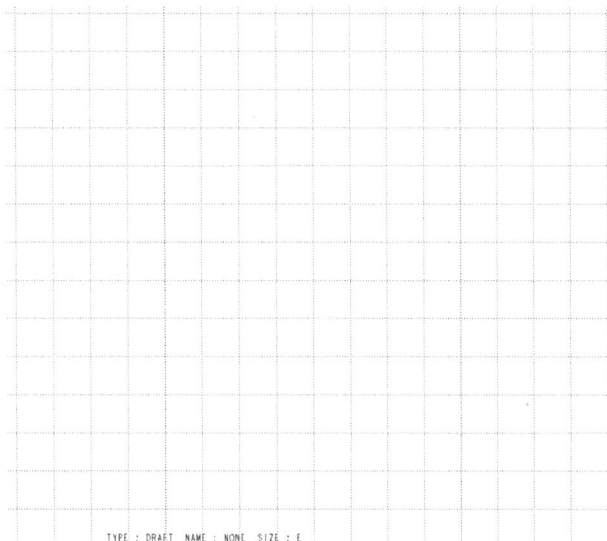

Figure 11–20

10. Select **Tools>Environment** and toggle on **Snap to Grid**. Set the other options to match those shown in Figure 11–21.

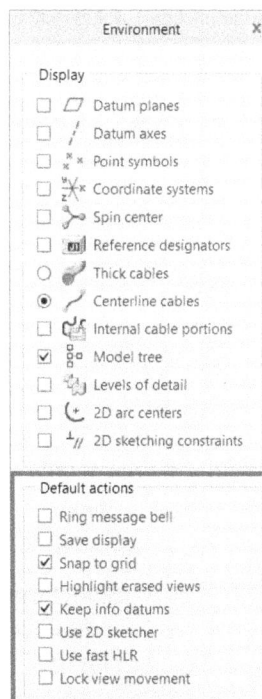

Figure 11–21

11. Click **OK** to close the Environment dialog box.

Task 3 - Sketch the symbol.

1. Click ⌄ (Line Chain). Sketch the four lines shown in Figure 11–22 and middle-click, when finished sketching.

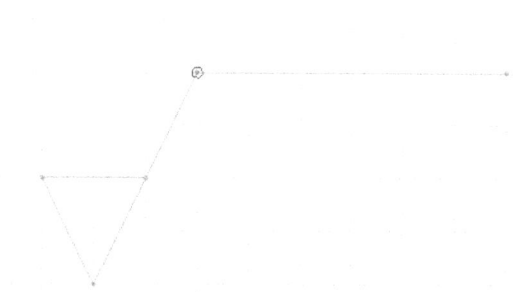

Figure 11–22

2. Select **Tools>Environment** and toggle off the **Snap to Grid** option.

3. Click ⊙ (Circle). Note that the References dialog box opens as shown in Figure 11–23.

Figure 11–23

4. Click ⬚ (Select References) in the Snapping References dialog box.

5. Select the three lines shown on the left in Figure 11–24. The lines display in the dialog box as shown on the right in Figure 11–24.

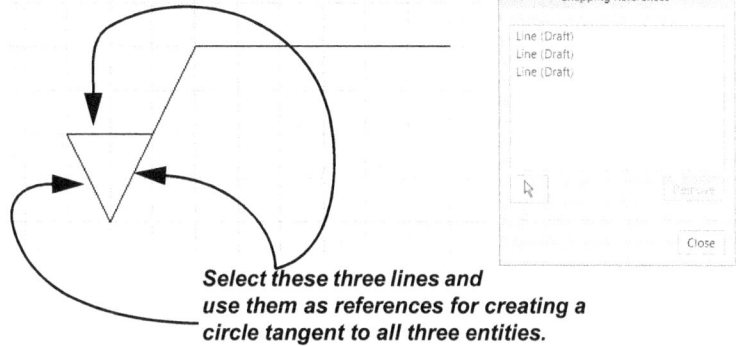

*Select these three lines and
use them as references for creating a
circle tangent to all three entities.*

Figure 11–24

6. Click ⟳ (Circle) again to sketch the circle.

7. Sketch the circle tangent to the three reference lines, as shown in Figure 11–25. Ensure the tangency symbol displays for all three lines.

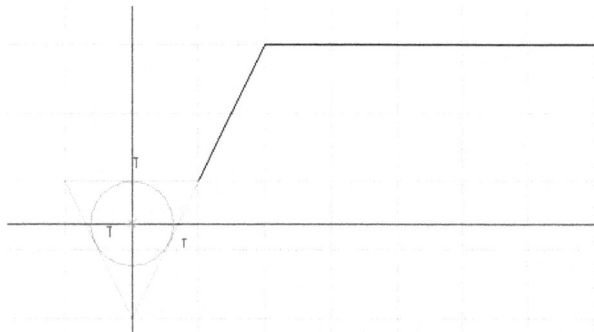

Figure 11–25

8. Press the left mouse button to complete the placement, then press the middle mouse button. The sketch displays as shown in Figure 11–26.

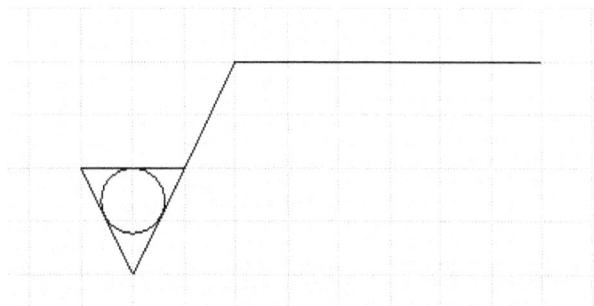

Figure 11–26

9. Click ⌒ (Line Chain) and sketch the horizontal lines shown in Figure 11–27.

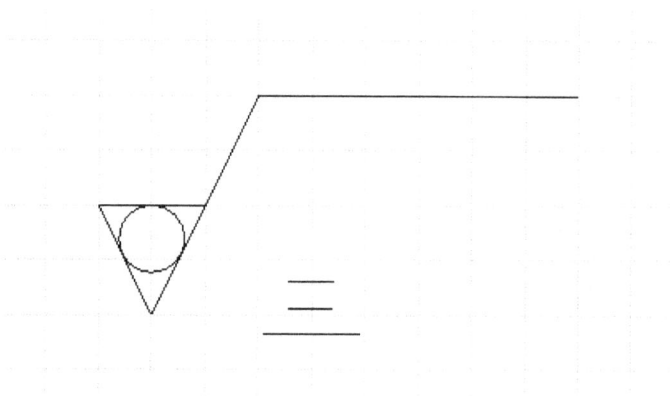

Figure 11–27

10. Sketch the vertical line shown in Figure 11–28.

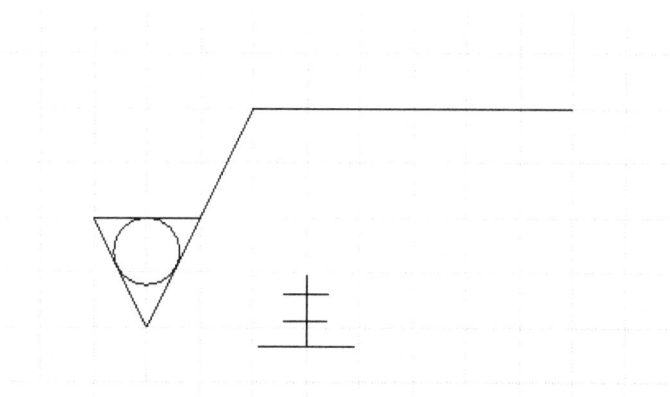

Figure 11–28

11. Click ᴬ≡ (Note).

12. Accept the defaults and select **Make Note** in the **NOTE TYPES** menu.

13. Select the location for the note, as shown in Figure 11–29.

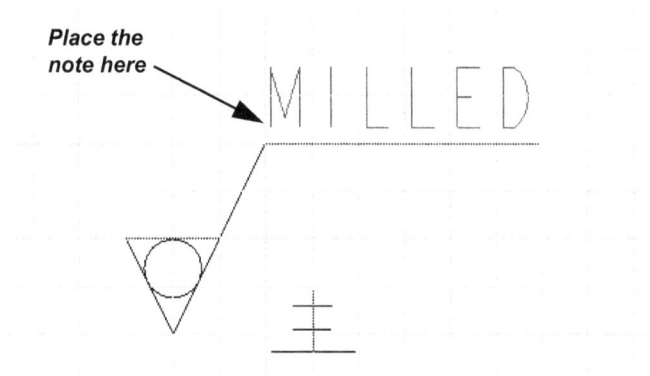

Place the note here

MILLED

Figure 11–29

14. Enter **MILLED** in the message window, press <Enter> twice, and select **Done/Return**.

15. If required, modify the text height. Right-click on the text and select **Properties**. Select the *Text Style* tab and change the text height using the *Height* field.

*The text height for the drawing can also be changed by modifying the **drawing_text_ height** drawing setup option.*

16. Create a second note, as shown in Figure 11–30. Enter **R@-Z@#\VALUE** in the message window and press <Enter> twice.

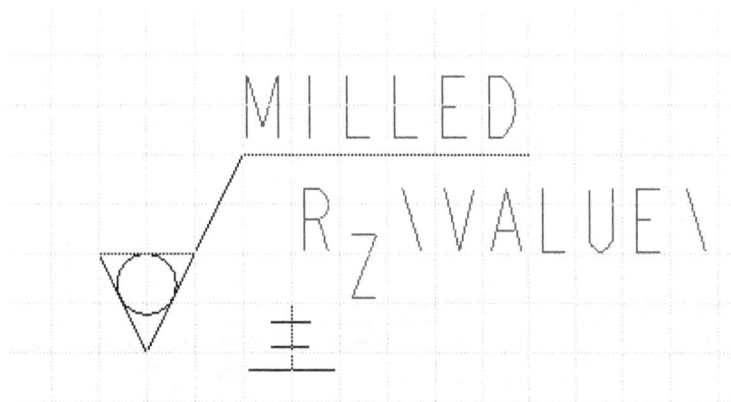

MILLED
R_Z\VALUE\

Figure 11–30

17. Select **Done/Return** in the **NOTE TYPES** menu. Modify the text height if required.

Task 4 - Define groups in the symbol.

1. Select **Groups** in the **SYMBOL EDIT** menu.

2. Select **Create** and set the group name to **MILLED**.

3. Press and hold <Ctrl> while selecting the entities shown in Figure 11–31 for the milled group.

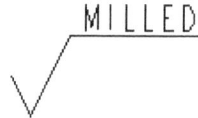

Figure 11–31

4. Click **OK** in the SELECT dialog box.

5. Repeat the Steps 1 to 4 to create the following groups:

   - NO_MATERIAL_REMOVAL

   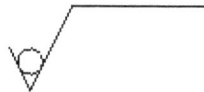

   - ROUGHNESS

   - GROOVE_DIRECTION

   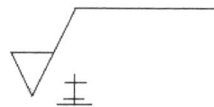

Task 5 - Create sub-groups of the GROOVE_DIRECTION group.

1. Select **Change Level** in the **SYM GROUP** menu.

2. Select the GROOVE_DIRECTION group.

3. Select **This Level**.

4. Select **Create** and enter **PERPENDICULAR** as the sub-group name.

5. Press and hold <Ctrl> while selecting the entities shown in Figure 11–32 that create the perpendicular symbol.

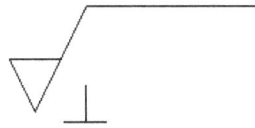

Figure 11–32

6. Click **OK** in the SELECT dialog box.

7. Create another sub-group called **PARALLEL** under the GROOVE_DIRECTION group.

8. Press and hold <Ctrl> while selecting the entities shown in Figure 11–33 that create the parallel symbol.

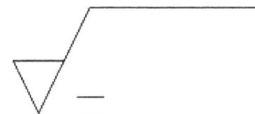

Figure 11–33

9. Click **OK** in the SELECT dialog box.

Task 6 - Determine the group attributes.

---

*Setting each level as **Exclusive** ensures that multiple groups cannot be displayed in the same symbol.*

1. Select **Group Attr** in the **SYM GROUPS** menu and **Exclusive** in the **GROUP ATTR** menu.

2. Select **Change Level>Up>This Level**.

3. Select **Group Attr>Exclusive**.

4. Select **Done\Return**.

Task 7 - Determine the symbol attributes.

---

1. Select **Attributes** in the **SYMBOL EDIT** menu. The Symbol Definition Attributes dialog box opens.

2. Use **Free** as the permitted placement type and select the lower tip of the triangle as the origin of the symbol. You will use this origin when placing the symbol in the drawing.

3. Repeat the same procedure for the following options: **On entity**, **Normal to entity**, and **Left leader**.

---

4. Select **Variable - drawing units** in the *Symbol Instance Height* area.

5. Select **Allow elbow** in the *Attributes* area. The Symbol Definition Attributes dialog box opens as shown in Figure 11–34.

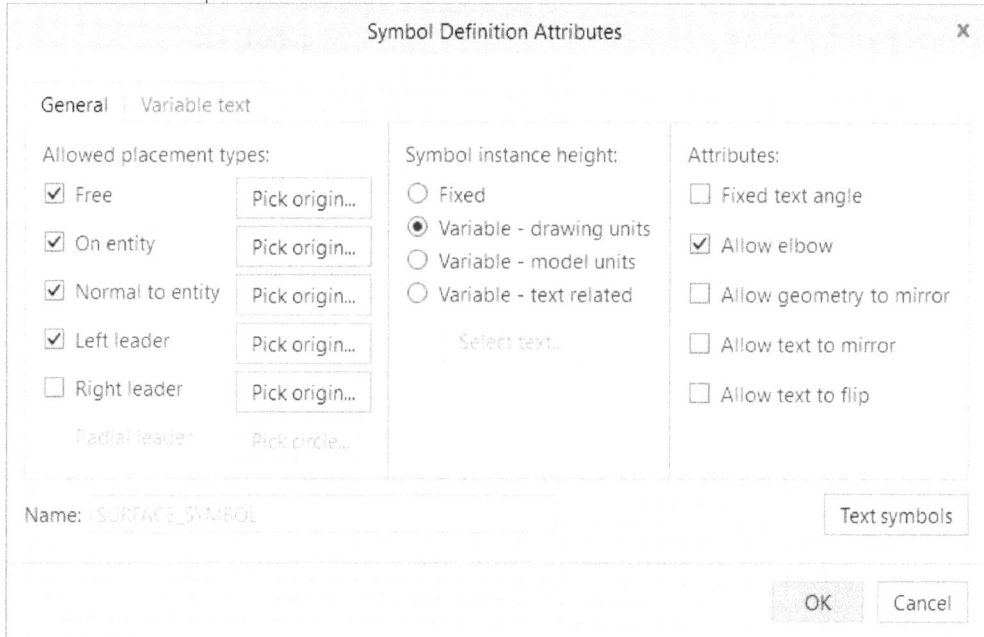

Figure 11–34

Task 8 - Set the variable text value.

1. Select the *Variable Text* tab.

2. Enter **3.2** in the *Preset Values for* area, as shown in Figure 11–35. This enables you to use the **3.2** value in the symbol. Any other values can also be entered here.

Symbol Definition Attributes ✕

General | Variable text

Select variable text to preset values:

VALUE

Preset values for: VALUE

3.2

☐ Preset values only

◉ Text
○ Integer
○ Floating point

Name: SURFACE_SYMBOL

Text symbols

OK | Cancel

**The word VALUE
should be displayed
in the Select Variable
Text to Preset Values
area. This is because
VALUE was enclosed
between backslashes
in the second note.**

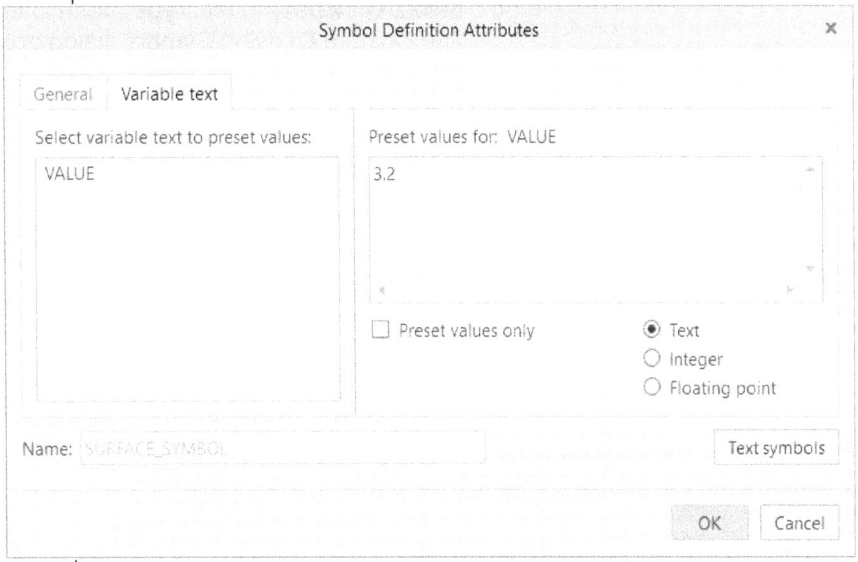

Figure 11–35

*Symbols are normally
stored in a symbol
library directory to
ensure that everyone
has access to all of the
symbols. Typically, they
are not retrieved from
local working
directories.*

3. Click **OK**. Select **Done** in the **SYMBOL EDIT** menu to complete the symbol creation. The symbol is now available for the current drawing. To use the symbol in another drawing, you must write the symbol to the disk.

4. Select **Write** in the **SYM GALLERY** menu and press <Enter> to save the symbol in the current directory.

5. Select **Done** in the **SYM GALLERY** menu.

Task 9 - Place the symbol in the drawing.

*You might have a
different icon on top
depending on which one
was used last.*

1. To place a symbol in a drawing, expand ⊕ (Symbol) and select ⊕ (Custom Symbol). The Custom Drawing Symbol dialog box opens.

2. Ensure that the **SURFACE_SYMBOL** name displays in the *Symbol name* field. If not, select the symbol in the Symbol name drop-down list or click **Browse** to select the symbol from the disk.

3. Select the *Grouping* tab and select the **ROUGHNESS** group.

*The default variable text
value is 3.2.*

4. Select the *Variable Text* tab. Enter **3.2** in the *VALUE* field. Select the *General* tab. Set the height for the symbol to **1**.

5. Select **On Entity** in the **Type** menu in the *Placement* area. The Custom Drawing Symbol dialog box opens as shown in Figure 11–36.

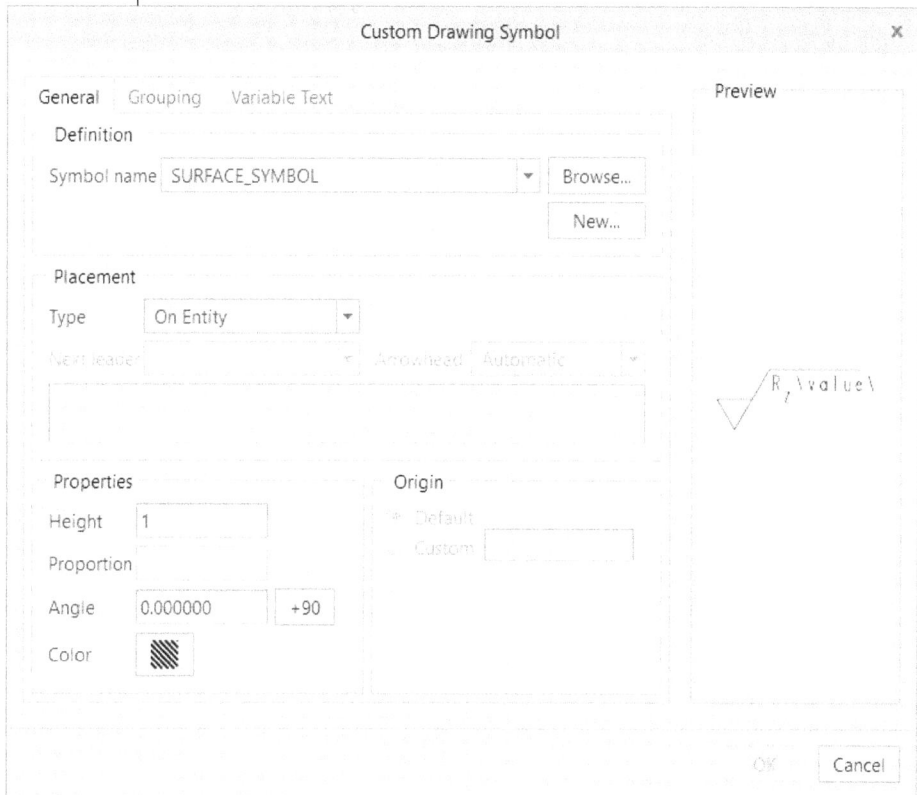

Figure 11–36

6. Place the symbol as shown in Figure 11–37.

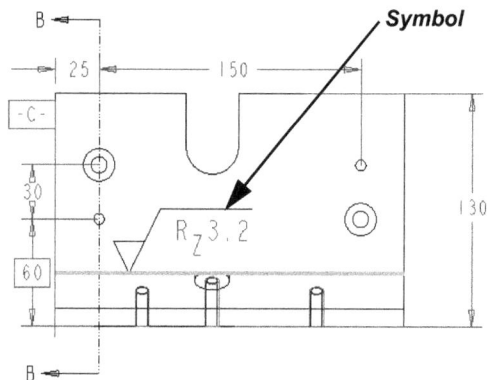

Figure 11–37

7. Press the middle mouse button to complete the symbol placement.

8. Click **OK** to close the Custom Drawing Symbol dialog box.

Task 10 - Place a system-defined surface finish symbol on the drawing.

You can also right-click and select Surface Finish.

System-defined symbols are stored in the Creo Parametric installation directory in the symbols directory.

1. Click $\sqrt[32]{}$ (Surface Finish) in the Annotations group in the *Annotate* tab.

2. Double-click on the machined directory.

3. Select **standard1.sym** and click **Open**.

4. Select **Normal to Entity** in the Type drop-down list and select the edge shown in Figure 11–38.

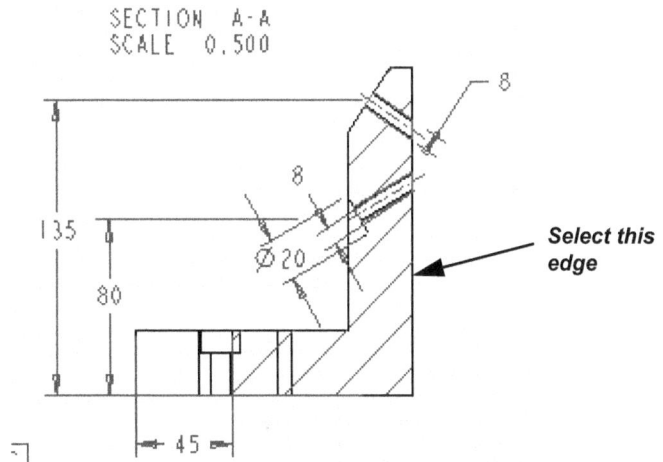

Figure 11–38

5. Set the roughness value to **16**. The symbol displays as shown in Figure 11–39.

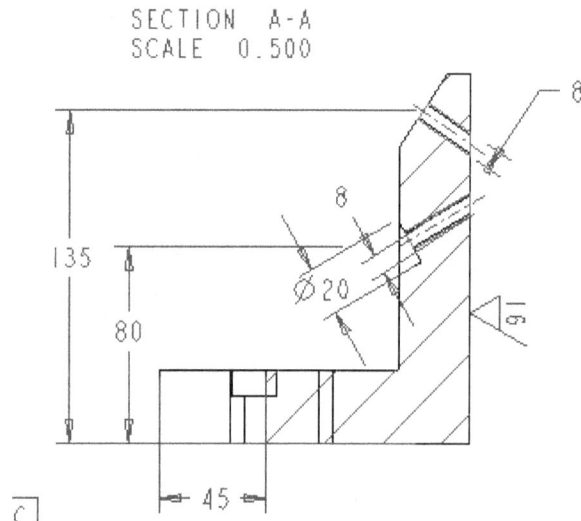

SECTION A-A
SCALE 0.500

Figure 11–39

Task 11 - Create and place a surface finish symbol.

Each entity in the symbol is now independent and can be manipulated (e.g., rotated).

1. Create the symbol shown in Figure 11–40 (create the text as variable text **\ROUGHNESS**). Place the symbol as shown in Figure 11–40. Select the symbol, right-click, and select **Convert to Draft Entities** to explode it.

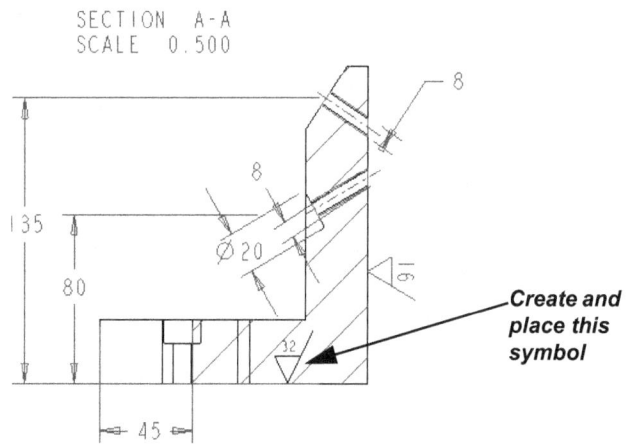

SECTION A-A
SCALE 0.500

Create and place this symbol

Figure 11–40

The symbol must be converted to draft entities to rotate it. System defined surface finish symbols cannot be converted or rotated.

You might need to translate the symbol as well.

2. Select the *Sketch* tab.

3. Click ⟆ (Rotate), in the Edit group in the *Sketch* tab to rotate the 2D entities and text. Select the geometry using a window box and click **OK** in the SELECT dialog box. Select a center point for rotation and enter the rotation angle. The geometry displays as shown in Figure 11–41.

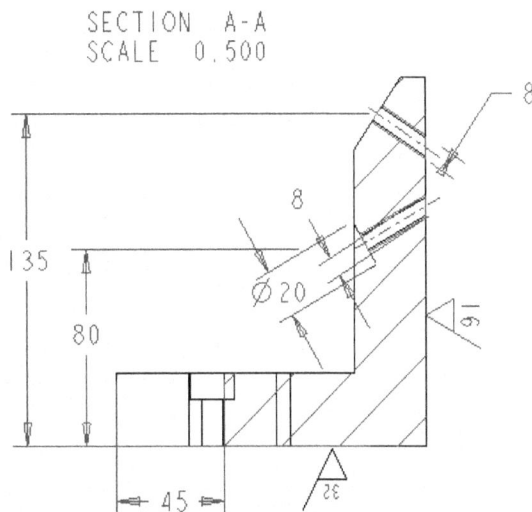

SECTION A-A
SCALE 0.500

Figure 11–41

4. Regenerate the drawing.

5. Save the drawing and close the window.

Practice 11b | Custom Symbol Definition Palette

Practice Objectives

- Create a drawing.
- Insert standard symbols.
- Insert custom symbols.
- Create a custom symbol palette.

In this practice, you will create a new drawing and insert both standard and custom symbols.

Task 1 - Create a new drawing.

1. Set your working directory to the *Custom_Symbol_Palette* folder.

2. Create a drawing called **CUST_DRW_SYM_PALETTE**. Clear the **Use Default Template** option. Use an empty template, landscape orientation, A-size sheet, with no model attached.

Task 2 - Insert custom symbols using Free Note placement.

1. Select the *Annotate* tab and expand ⊕ (Symbol) and click ⊕ (Custom Symbol). The Open dialog box opens. Click ⊡ (Working Directory).

2. Open **arrow.sym**. The Custom Drawing Symbol dialog box opens.

3. Using the **Free** note placement, place the symbol in the upper left corner of the drawing.

4. Click **Browse** and click ⊡ (Working Directory). Retrieve and place the **id_plate.sym** symbol below the arrow symbol.

5. Repeat this process for the remaining symbol files below. The drawing should display similar to that shown in Figure 11–42.
   - **rand_ww.sym**
   - **scale.sym**
   - **surf_finish_sym.sym**
   - **surface_sym_final.sym**

NOTE →

Year	1999
BRACKET_FINAL_I	

```
    10  20  30  40
  5 | 15 | 25 | 35 | 45
|,,|,,,,|,,,,|,,,,|,,,,|,,,,|,,,|,,
```

32 /
▽

milled
√

Figure 11–42

6. Click **OK** in the Custom Drawing Symbol dialog box.

Task 3 - Insert custom symbols using Normal to Entity placement.

---

1. Sketch four horizontal lines, as shown in Figure 11–43.

NOTE →

_____

Year	1999
BRACKET_FINAL_I	

_____

RAND

```
    10  20  30  40
  5 | 15 | 25 | 35 | 45
|,,|,,,,|,,,,|,,,,|,,,,|,,,,|,,|,,,
```

32 /
▽

_____

milled
√

_____

Figure 11–43

You can also use
<Ctrl>+<C> and <Ctrl>+
<V> to copy and paste
the symbols.

2. Add the following symbols to the custom palette drawing
   using the **Normal to Entity** placement type, and selecting the
   horizontal lines as the placement references as shown in
   Figure 11–44.
   - **arrow.sym**
   - **id_plate.sym**
   - **surf_finish_sym.sym**
   - **surface_sym_final.sym**

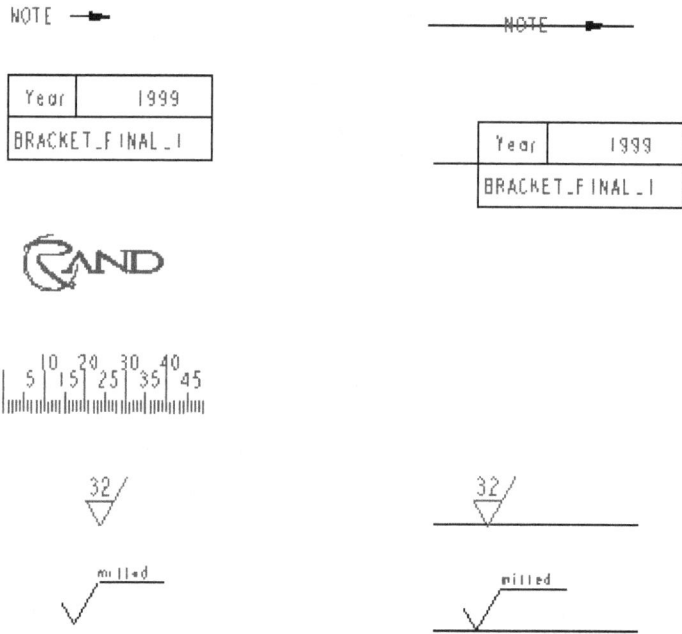

Figure 11–44

3. Save the drawing and close the window.

**Task 4 - Specify the symbol instance palette file in the
config.pro file.**

---

1. Select **File>Options>Configuration Editor**. The Creo
   Parametric Options dialog box opens, enabling you to set the
   config.pro file options.

2. Click **Add** and enter **symbol_instance_palette_file** in the
   Option field at the bottom of the dialog box. The option name
   should display automatically after typing the first three letters.

3. Click **Browse**. The Select File dialog box opens.

4. Click ⬚ (Working Directory) and open the
   CUST_DRW_SYM_PALETTE.DRW file.

5. Click **OK**, **OK**, and **Yes** to save the settings.

**Task 5 - Use the custom symbol definition palette to place
symbols on a drawing.**

---

1. Open **bracket_final_1.drw**. You will insert a logo symbol in
   the title box and attach a surface finish symbol to one of the
   views.

*You can also select
**Insert>Drawing
Symbol>From Palette**
in the menu bar.*

2. Select the *Annotate* tab, expand ⬚ (Symbol), and click
   ⬚ (Symbol From Palette) in the Insert group. The Symbol
   Instance Palette dialog box opens, displaying the symbols
   that you placed in the **CUST_DRW_SYM_PALETTE.DRW**
   drawing.

3. Click once on the RAND logo symbol in the Symbol Instance
   Palette window, as shown in Figure 11–45. Remember that
   the RAND logo symbol was placed in the symbol palette
   using the **Free** note placement type.

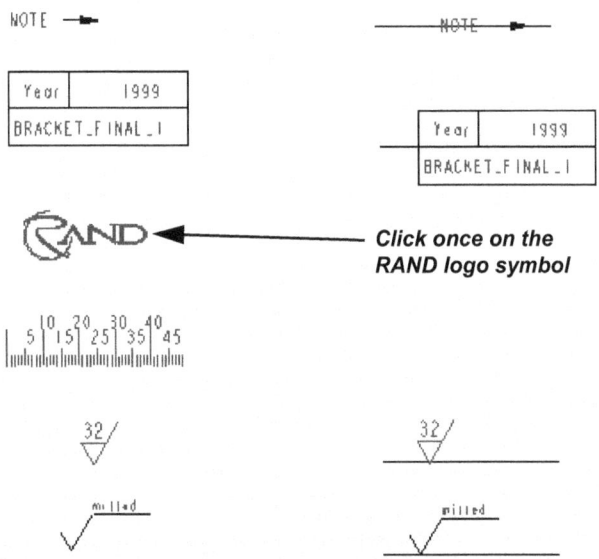

Figure 11–45

4. Drag the symbol to the location shown in Figure 11–46 and place it using the left mouse button.

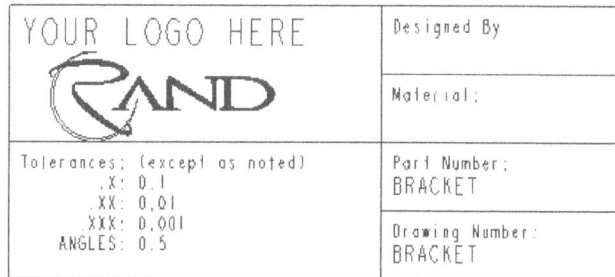

Figure 11–46

5. Right-click to complete the placement of the RAND logo symbol.

6. Close the Symbol Instance Palette window and remove the text that currently exists in this cell.

7. Expand ⚬ (Symbol), and click ⚬ (Symbol From Palette).

8. In the Symbol Instance Palette window, click once on the symbol for indicating material removal by machining, as shown in Figure 11–47. Remember that this symbol was placed in the symbol palette using the **Normal to Entity** placement type.

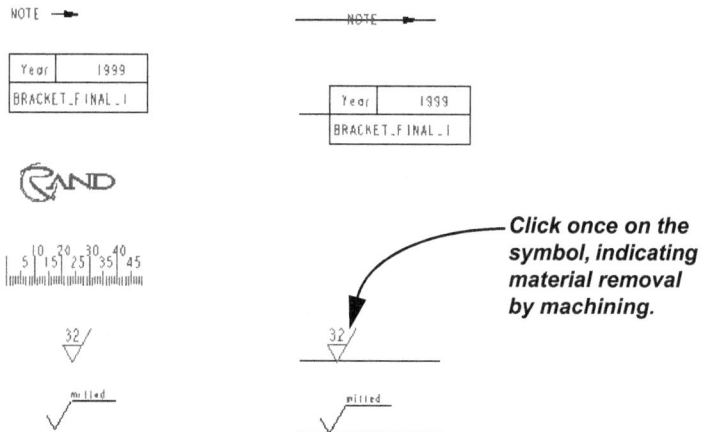

Click once on the symbol, indicating material removal by machining.

Figure 11–47

9. Select the right vertical edge in the Section A-A view, as shown in Figure 11–48.

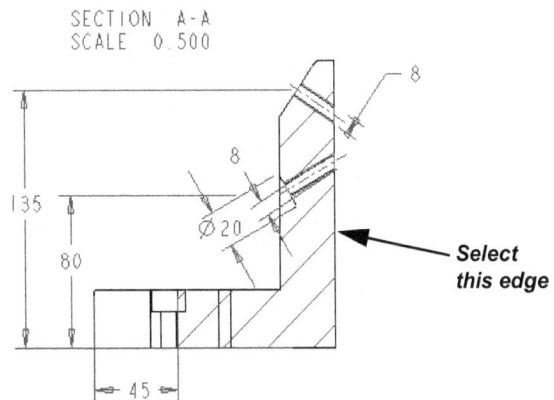

Figure 11–48

10. Set the roughness value to **32**. The symbol displays as shown in Figure 11–49.

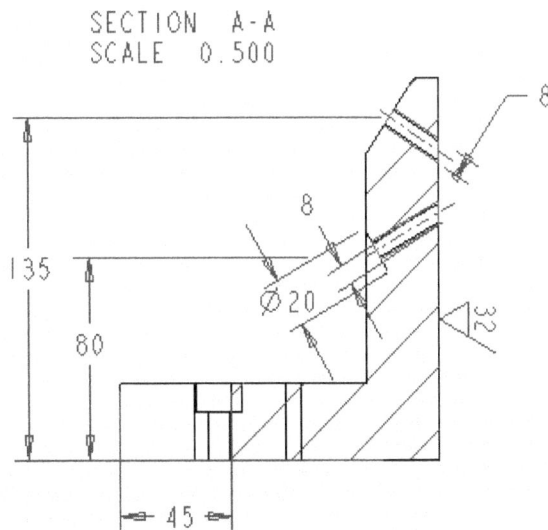

Figure 11–49

11. Click **OK** to close the SELECT dialog box.

Task 6 - Open the default palette.

Open... *enables you to open and switch between different custom palettes.*

1. Click **Open** in the Symbol Instance Palette dialog box.

2. Open **draw_symbol_palette.drw**.

3. Click **Close** to close the Symbol Instance Palette dialog box.

4. Regenerate the drawing.

5. Save the drawing and erase it from memory.

Chapter Review Questions

1. Which one of the following methods enables you to create the 2D draft geometry that represents the symbol? (Select all that apply.)

    a. Select **Copy Drawing** in the **SYMBOL EDIT** menu to copy existing entities from the current drawing.

    b. Select **Copy Symbol** in the **SYMBOL EDIT** menu to copy existing symbols from the current symbol directory.

    c. Select **Insert>Shared Data>From File** and select the file in the Open dialog box.

    d. Click the icons in the Sketcher toolbar to sketch 2D geometry in the SYM_EDIT window.

2. The fixed text remains the same every time the symbol is used.

    a. True

    b. False

3. Variable text enables you to select from predefined text that was assigned when the symbol was created. You cannot enter a new value when the symbol is placed.

    a. True

    b. False

4. Independent groups can be displayed together in the same symbol, while exclusive groups cannot be displayed in the same symbol.

    a. True

    b. False

5. What is the advantage of using a symbol palette?

    a. Enables you to place multiple symbols at the same time.

    b. Enables you to change the symbols.

    c. Enables you to set the variable text.

    d. Group frequently used symbols together.

6. Which command can be used to convert each symbol entity to be independent and can be manipulated?

   a. **Convert to Draft Entities**

   b. **Explode**

   c. **Group**

   d. **Independent**

Feature Management

Part and assembly drawings can be complex. Creo Parametric offers a variety of tools that enable you manage the display of features, components, drawing items, and views on the drawing. In this chapter you learn different techniques that can be used to simplify and clarify the drawings.

Learning Objectives in This Chapter

- Learn the differences between using the Hide tool in a part drawing and an assembly drawing.
- Learn the general steps used to hide features or components in a drawing.
- Temporarily remove features and components from the drawing by suppressing them in the model or assembly.
- Use layers to organize and perform operations on drawing items collectively.
- Learn how to hide, unhide, and isolate drawing items using layers.
- Learn to use the Activate tool to activate a layer to which new entities are automatically added.
- Learn the difference between part and assembly layer status and drawing layer status.
- Control the display status of drawing views independent of each other and vary the display of features, components, and drawing items.
- Use simplified representations to reduce the retrieval, regeneration, and display times of views in large complex drawings.
- Create part simplified representations and add the representation as a model in the drawing to simplify the drawing views.
- Use various tools in the *Review* tab to update, compare, and retrieve information about the drawing models.

12.1 Hide Items

Use the **Hide** option as a quick method of simplifying the drawing. Features or components that are hidden remain in the Model Tree and in the regeneration sequence. You can hide features or components in Part, Assembly, or Drawing mode. Due to the associativity between modes, the features and components are automatically hidden in all three modes. When manipulating the part, you can only hide non-solid features (e.g., cosmetic features). When hiding components in an assembly, the selected component is entirely removed from the display.

How To: Hide a Feature or Component

1. Select the feature or component to be hidden from the Model Tree or directly in the model. Parent/child relationships do not affect children of hidden parents because they remain in the regeneration sequence.
2. To hide a feature or component, right-click on the feature in the Model Tree and select **Hide In Model**. Hidden features are identified in the Model Tree by a gray box that surrounds the feature or component. Figure 12–1 shows an assembly drawing view and its associated Model Tree. The **spindle.asm** component has been hidden in the drawing.

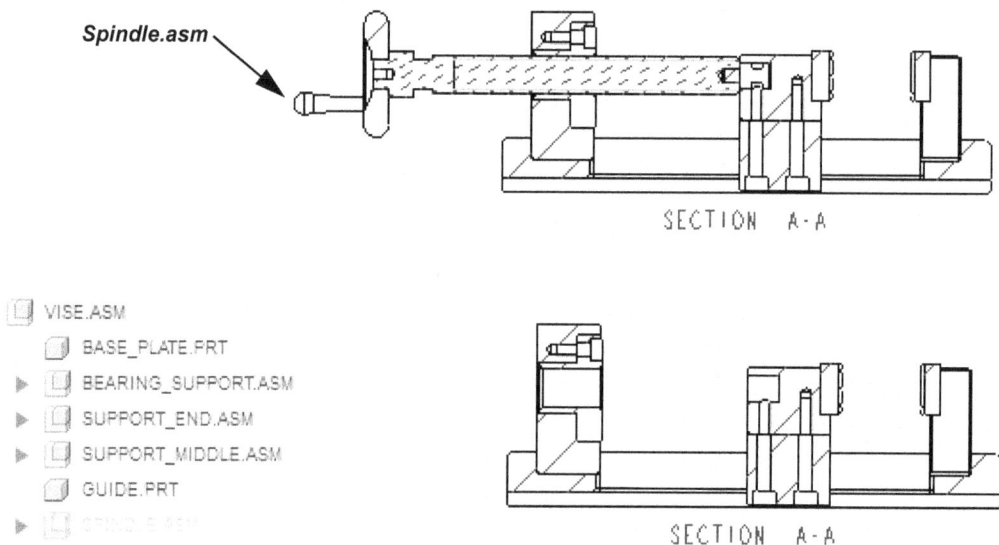

Figure 12–1

3. To unhide a feature or component, right-click on the feature or component and select **Unhide In Model**.

12.2 Suppress Items

Suppressed features and components are temporarily removed from the display and the regeneration sequence. This simplifies the appearance of the model and decreases the amount of time it takes to regenerate. For example, if you suppress a component and save the assembly, that component is not retrieved into session the next time you open the assembly or its drawing, as shown in Figure 12–2.

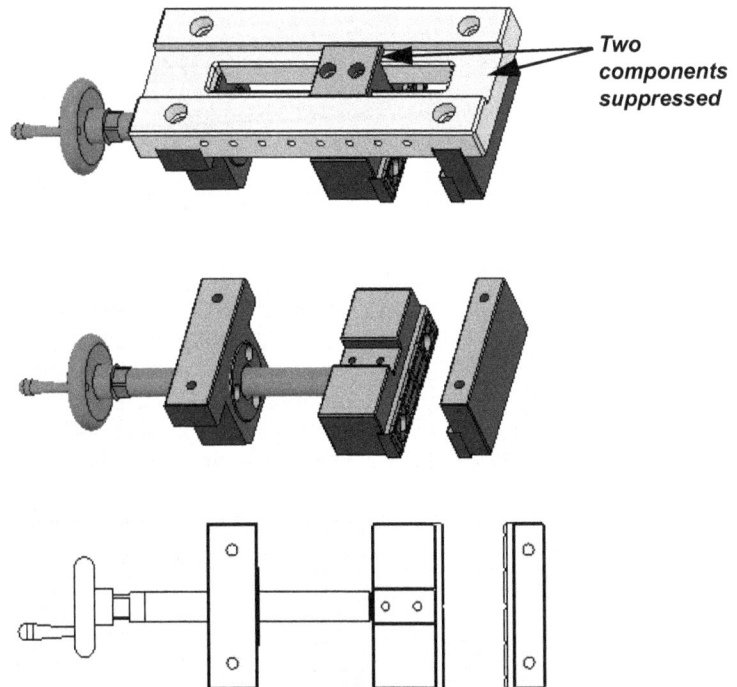

Two components suppressed

Figure 12–2

You cannot suppress or resume features or components in the Drawing mode. You have to suppress in Assembly or Part mode. Note that suppressed items are not displayed in the associative drawing.

To display suppressed features/components in the Model Tree, click 🔲 ▾ (Settings) in the Model Tree, select **Tree Filters**, and select **Suppressed Objects** in the *Display* area in the Model Tree Items dialog box. Suppressed items are marked by a black dot in the Model Tree, as shown in Figure 12–3.

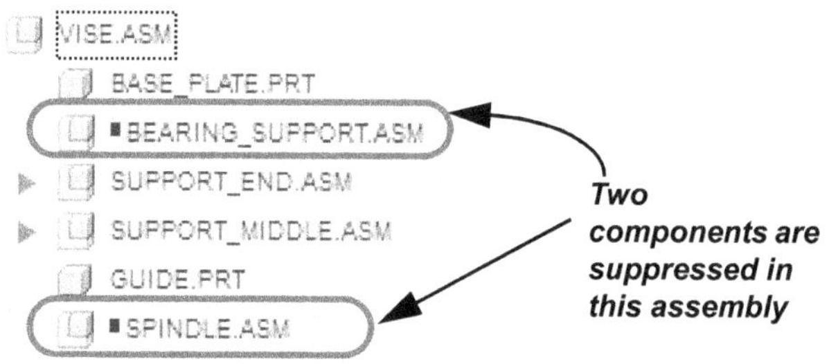

Figure 12–3

How To: Suppress Features or Components

1. Select the feature or component to suppress in the Model Tree or directly on the model. Carefully consider parent/child relationships. All of the children are suppressed with their parents by default.

All of the suppressed settings are saved when the model is saved to disk.

2. To suppress the selected item, right-click on it and select **Suppress** or select **Operations>Suppress>Suppress** in the *Model* tab. Note that any children are also selected when suppressing a feature/component with children. The Suppress dialog box opens as shown in Figure 12–4.

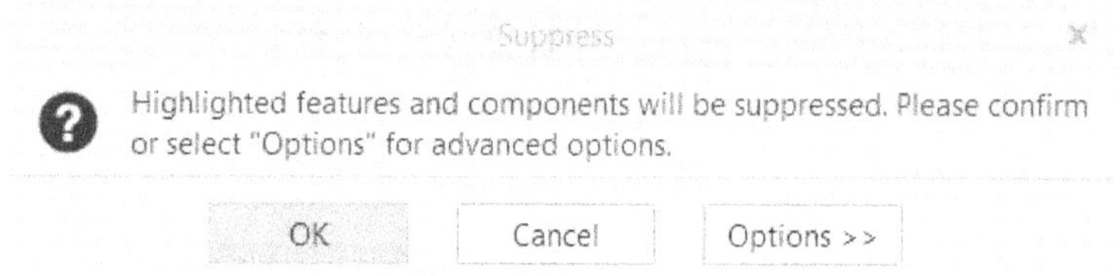

Figure 12–4

3. Click **OK** to confirm suppression of the feature/component and all of its children, or click **Cancel** to cancel the operation. Click **Options>>** for advanced options on controlling children. The Children Handling dialog box opens as shown in Figure 12–5.

Figure 12–5

You can set the status of any of the children to **Suppress**, **Suspend**, or **Fix**:

- The **Suppress** status suppresses the child with the parent. The status is set to **Suppress** by default.

- The **Suspend** status attempts to regenerate the child or children of the suppressed parent. It enables you to redefine or edit the references of the child feature. Suspending does not suppress the child. However, the child cannot be regenerated with its parent missing. If you attempt to regenerate the model, it fails and an Information Window displays, indicating that the parent of the feature/component is missing.

- You can assign a **Fix** status when suppressing a parent component or feature. Fixing enables you to lock the item in its current location.

4. Suppressed items can be restored to the display by selecting **Edit>Resume**.
   If the suppressed feature/component displays in the Model Tree, you can resume it by right-clicking on it and selecting **Resume**, or select **Operations>Resume>Resume** in the *Model* tab. By default, all of the suppressed items are removed from the Model Tree display when they are suppressed.

*The **Resume** option is only available if a suppressed feature is selected in the Model Tree first.*

12.3 Add Layers

The **Layer** option enables you to organize model items (e.g., features, components, or drawing items) in a drawing so that you can perform operations on those items collectively, such as displaying or hiding them. You can hide or show the layers, which enables you to control the display of multiple drawing items before plotting the drawing. Similar to the **Hide** functionality, you can hide components of an assembly that are placed on a layer, but you cannot remove the solid features of a part from the display.

A layer can contain any number of features, components, dimensions, notes, geometric tolerances, or tables. In addition, any one item can exist on more than one layer.

How To: Create a Layer

1. All of the Layer information can be found in the Layer Tree. To access the Layer Tree, click ≝ (Layers) in the *View* tab or click ▤ ▾ (Show)>**Layer Tree** in the Model Tree. The Layer Tree replaces the Model Tree, as shown in Figure 12–6.

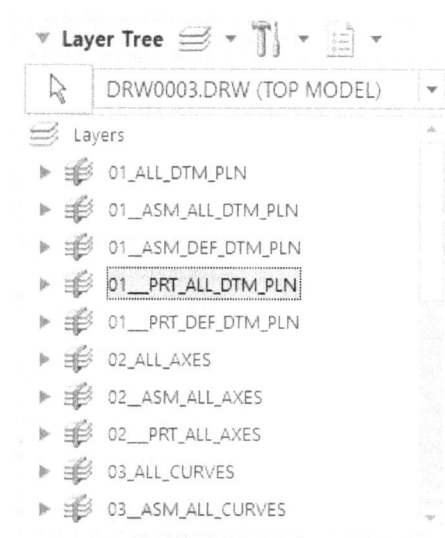

Figure 12–6

2. Click ⊜ ▼ (Layer)>**New Layer** to create a new layer. The Layer Properties dialog box opens as shown in Figure 12–7.

The default name of a new layer is **LAY00#**, where # represents the number of layers that are created in the model. For example, the first layer that is created in the model is called **LAY0001** by default. It is recommended that you replace this name with one that describes the contents of the layer.

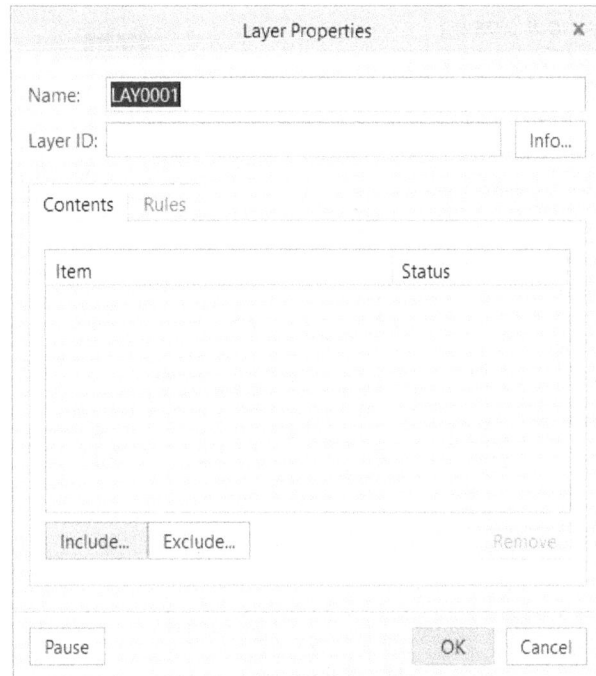

Figure 12–7

You can use the selection filter at the bottom of the main window to help select the correct items in the drawing.

***Pause** enables you to pause the selection of items without closing the Layer Properties dialog box. This is useful if you want to review items before adding them to the layer.*

3. Select drawing items, features, or components to populate the layer. The Layer Properties dialog box opens as shown in Figure 12–8, with all of the items listed in the *Contents* tab. Click **Include** to add items to the layer. Once added, the status updates to ➕. Click **Exclude** to exclude an item from the layer without actually removing it. Excluded items display ➖.

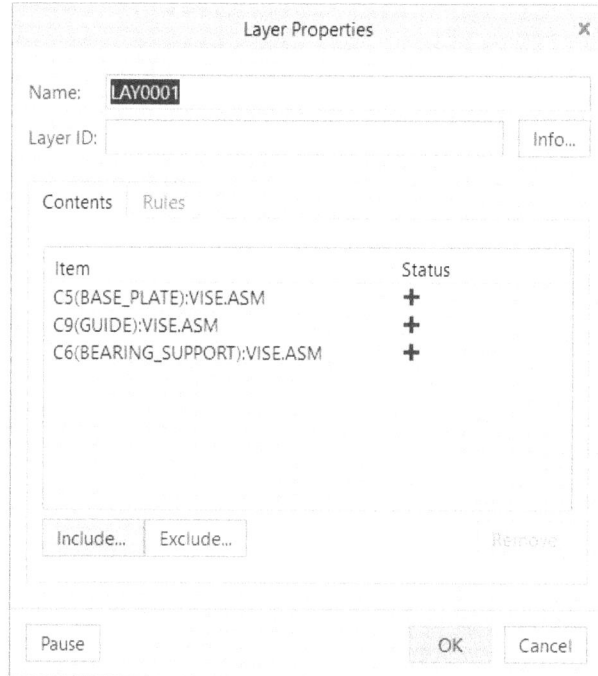

Layer Properties		✕

Name: LAY0001

Layer ID: _____ Info...

Contents | Rules

Item	Status
C5(BASE_PLATE):VISE.ASM	➕
C9(GUIDE):VISE.ASM	➕
C6(BEARING_SUPPORT):VISE.ASM	➕

Include... | Exclude... | Remove

Pause | OK | Cancel

Figure 12–8

4. Select it in the *Contents* tab in the dialog box and click **Remove** to remove an item from the layer. Click **OK** to complete adding items to a layer.
5. The display status of a layer can be set to **Hide**, **Unhide**, or **Isolate**.

Hide

The **Hide** status removes items in the layer from the display. To set a layer to **Hide** status, right-click on the layer in the Layer Tree and select **Hide** or click ≋ ▾ (Layer)>**Hide**.

Unhide

The **Unhide** status sets all of the items on the layer to be visible. This is the default display status for all new layers. To unhide a hidden layer, right-click on the layer and select **Unhide**.

Isolate

The **Isolate** status enables you to display layers that have their display status set to **Isolate** and all non-isolated layers as hidden. To set the display status of a layer to **Isolate**, click ⬓ ▾ (Layer)>**Isolate**.

To view the current display status of a layer, right-click on it and select **Layer Info**. The Information Window for the selected layer displays as shown in Figure 12–9.

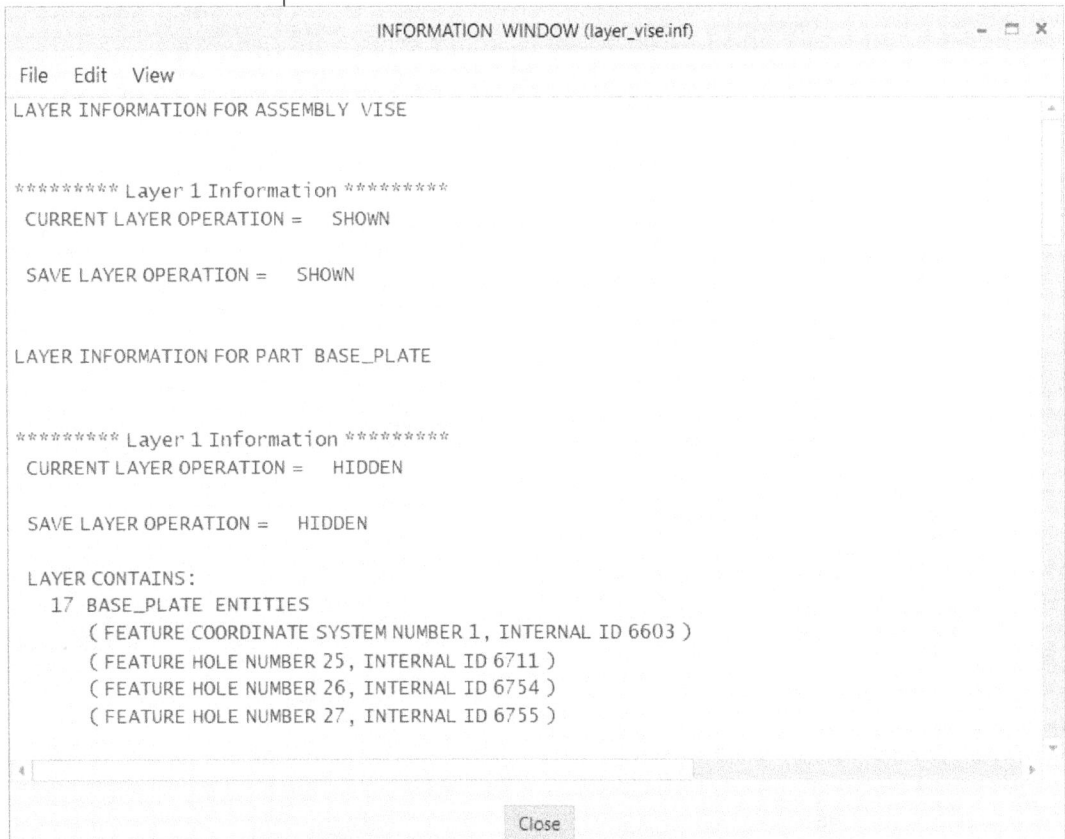

INFORMATION WINDOW (layer_vise.inf)   – ☐ ✕

File   Edit   View

```
LAYER INFORMATION FOR ASSEMBLY VISE


********* Layer 1 Information *********
 CURRENT LAYER OPERATION =    SHOWN

 SAVE LAYER OPERATION =    SHOWN



LAYER INFORMATION FOR PART BASE_PLATE


********* Layer 1 Information *********
 CURRENT LAYER OPERATION =    HIDDEN

 SAVE LAYER OPERATION =    HIDDEN

 LAYER CONTAINS:
   17 BASE_PLATE ENTITIES
      ( FEATURE COORDINATE SYSTEM NUMBER 1, INTERNAL ID 6603 )
      ( FEATURE HOLE NUMBER 25, INTERNAL ID 6711 )
      ( FEATURE HOLE NUMBER 26, INTERNAL ID 6754 )
      ( FEATURE HOLE NUMBER 27, INTERNAL ID 6755 )
```

Close

Figure 12–9

6. The following two lines in the Information Window identify the layer's display status:
   - Current Layer Operation
   - Save Layer Operation

The Current Layer Operation line identifies the display status of the layer in the current session of Creo Parametric. The Save Layer Operation line identifies the saved status of the layer. The model always opens using the saved display status for each layer. To save the display status for all of the layers in the model, right-click and select **Save Status**. To reset the layer display status to that which was previously saved, right-click and select **Reset Status**.

7. You can perform the following actions on a layer using the Layer Tree:

- Add items to a layer.

- Remove items from a layer.

- Delete the layer.

- Copy and paste items between layers.

Click 🖺 (Layers) in the View tab to display the Layer Tree.

The Layer Tree must be displayed to perform actions on a layer. You can add and remove items by right-clicking and selecting **Layer Properties**. Add or remove items using **Include...** and **Remove** in the Layer Properties dialog box.

To delete all of the items from the layer without using the Layer Properties dialog box, select the layer, click 🖺 ▾ (Layer) and select **Remove All Items**. All of the items on the layer are removed, but the layer remains in the model. To delete an entire layer, right-click on the layer and select **Delete Layer**.

Press and hold <Ctrl> while selecting items to select multiple items in the Layer Tree. To select all of the items between two selected items, press and hold <Shift> while selecting the first and last items on the tree.

Items from one layer can be copied and pasted to another layer by expanding 🖺 ▾ (Layer) and selecting an option or by right-clicking and selecting an option. Select it in the Layer Tree and select **Copy Item** to copy an item, and select the new layer and select **Paste Item** to paste an item.

Active Layer

The **Activate** tool enables you to activate a layer to which new entities are automatically added. For each new session in which a model/drawing is retrieved, you must reset the Active Layer. However, you do not need to reset it when switching between open windows.

*If you set the **floating_layer_tree** configuration option to **yes**, the Layer Tree displays in a separate window and it is not required to switch between Model Tree and Layer Tree.*

How To: Activate a Layer

1. Create a new or select an existing layer.
2. Right-click and select **Activate**, as shown in Figure 12–10.

Figure 12–10

Additionally, if you add draft content to an active drawing layer, it automatically adds it to a model layer of the same name if it exists.

3. A green star displays next to the activated layer, as shown in Figure 12–11. New entities are added to the Active Layer. If a layer in a top-level model is active, any layers with the same name in any sub-components are automatically active as well.

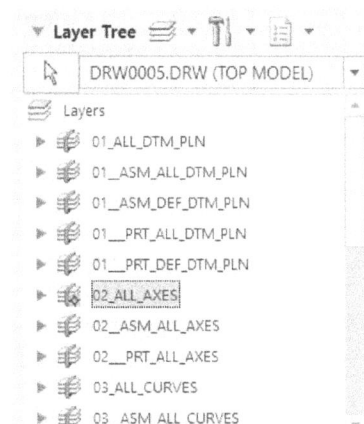

Figure 12–11

4. To deactivate the layer, right-click on it and select **Deactivate**.

Default Layers

All models created using the default template contain default layers. These are set up to include datum features (e.g., planes, axes, curves, points, and coordinate systems) and surfaces that are added to the model. You can define additional default layers by setting the **def_layer** configuration option and selecting the type of layer in the menu. As soon as the item is created or shown in the drawing, it is automatically placed on the defined default layer.

For example, if you add the **layer_dwg_table_<layer name>** configuration option, a table is placed on that layer as soon as it is created. A complete list of the default layers can be found in the Creo Help Center.

Display Status of Model Layers vs. Drawing Layers

You can control the display status of drawing layers in a drawing without changing the part or assembly in which the item is created. You can include items from parts and assemblies directly in a drawing layer without including them on a layer in a model.

To set a drawing so that it ignores the layer status of a model, you can do one of the following:

- Click 🖊 ▾ (Settings) in the Layer Tree and select the **Drawing Layer Status** option. Select either of the following options in the *Ignore display status of layers in the model* area in the Layer Status Control dialog box, as shown in Figure 12–12.
  - **Yes- Display status of common layers is controlled separately in drawing**
  - **All - Display status of all layers is controlled separately in drawing**

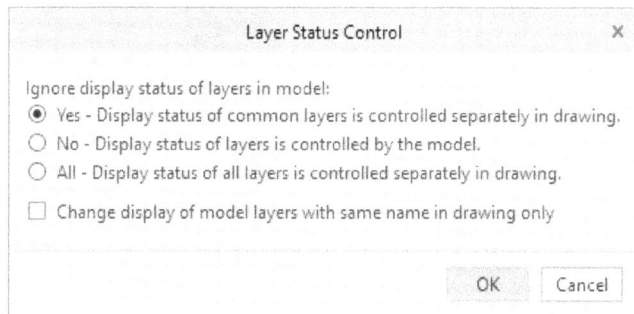

Figure 12–12

- Set the **ignore_model_layer_status** drawing setup file option to **yes** (default option) or **all**.

The advantage of setting the drawing to ignore the model layer status is that any changes made to the drawing layers are not reflected in the model layers. You cannot add or remove items from the model layers and you do not need to save the parts and assemblies after you have manipulated the drawing layers.

Layers with the Same Name

If you have created layers in Part, Assembly, and Drawing modes with the same name, you can set the model layers to have the same display status as the corresponding drawing layers. For example, if you hide the **datum_axis** drawing layer, the layer with the same name in Part and Assembly modes is hidden as well.

You can do one of the following to set the display of layers with the same name:

- Click 🗍 ▾ (Settings)>**Drawing Layer Status** in the Layer Tree. Select the **Change display of model layers with same name in drawing only** option in the Layer Status Control dialog box. This option is only available if either the **Yes** or **All** options are selected, as shown in Figure 12–13.

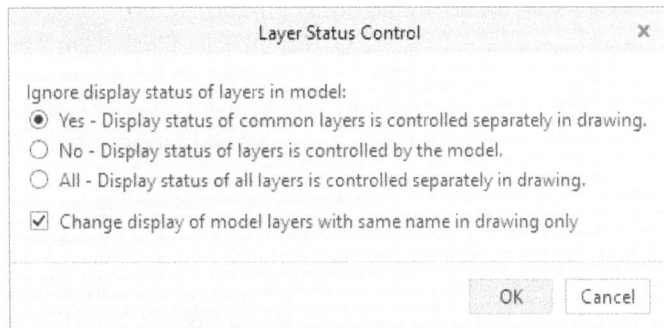

Layer Status Control   ✕

Ignore display status of layers in model:
  ⦿ Yes - Display status of common layers is controlled separately in drawing.
  ○ No - Display status of layers is controlled by the model.
  ○ All - Display status of all layers is controlled separately in drawing.
  ☑ Change display of model layers with same name in drawing only

                                                              OK   Cancel

Figure 12–13

- Set the **draw_layer_overrides_model** drawing setup file option to **yes**.

Controlling Individual View Display

Although drawing views do not have individual layers, you can control the display status of the drawing views independent of each other. Therefore, you can vary the display of features, components, and drawing items in different drawing views.

How To: Set a Drawing Display for a Selected View

1. Activate the Layer Tree by clicking ⬚ ▾ (Show)>**Layer tree**.
2. To set the layer display to the view level, select the *Active Layer Object Selection* field in the Layer Tree and select the view to manipulate in the menu, as shown in Figure 12–14. This menu enables you to set the layer display for the drawing, model, and view levels.

   If you do not know the name of the view to manipulate, you can also click ⬚ (Select) in the *Active Layer Object Selection* field and then select the required view.

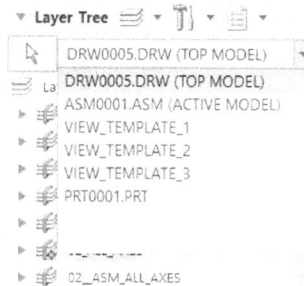

Figure 12–14

3. Right-click in the Layer Tree and select **Hide**. The items contained on this layer are not visible in the selected view.
4. Select the ***.DRW (TOP MODEL)** in the **Active Layer Object Selection** menu to return to the drawing layer level.

The following rules apply to the layer display status when you create views on a drawing:

- When you create an independent view, the layer display status is the same as the main drawing display. You can then modify the display using the steps described above.

- When you create a detailed view, the layer display status is the same as the parent view.

Active Layer

Active Layer is a new layer functionality that enables you to activate a layer to which new entities are then added. To activate a layer, use the **Active** command after you automatically insert new entities. To deactivate a layer, use the **Deactivate** command.

If you set the **floating_layer_tree** configuration option to **yes**, the Layer Tree displays in a separate window. Therefore, it is not required to switch between the Model Tree and Layer Tree.

12.4 Create Assembly Simplified Representations

Simplified representations enable you to reduce the retrieval, regeneration, and display times of large complex models and to focus on simplifying specific regions of models. They are used to control which components (parts or subassemblies) of an assembly are retrieved and how they are displayed. When the assembly simplified rep is retrieved, only those components in the rep are retrieved and other components are not brought into session.

If you are creating a drawing of a large and complex assembly, a view of a simplified representation can help clarify manufacturing specifications and emphasize important design aspects between components. A drawing is not limited to one drawing model, but can contain views and information from multiple models. Simplified representations are considered drawing models and have to be added to the drawing to create the views.

Three views were added to a drawing in the example shown in Figure 12–15. One of the views displays the original assembly, while the other two are created based on the two different simplified representations of the same model.

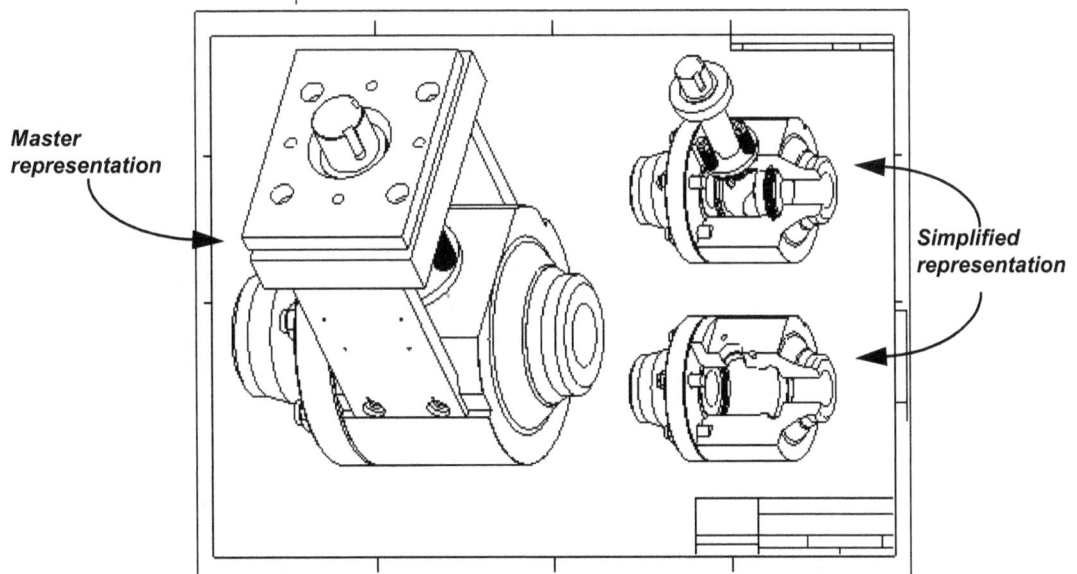

Master representation

Simplified representation

Figure 12–15

How To: Create a Drawing of a Simplified Representation

1. Click ☐ (New) in the Quick Access Toolbar to create a new drawing. Select the **Drawing** option in the New dialog box, and enter a name for the drawing. Click **OK**.

   The New Drawing dialog box opens. The *Default Model* field defines the drawing model to be represented in the drawing.

2. Enter the model name or click **Browse** to assign the model. Only one model can be selected, but you can add more models once the drawing has been created. If you select an assembly with a simplified representation, the Open Rep dialog box opens displaying all of the simplified representations, as shown in Figure 12–16.

You can select the original assembly (Master Rep) or one of the representations. This model becomes the current model for the drawing.

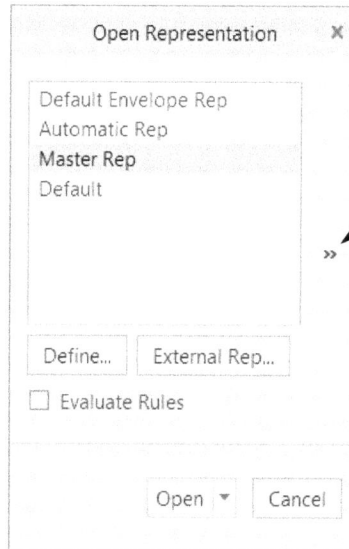

Select to preview the simplified representation

Figure 12–16

3. Define the template for the drawing and click **OK** in the New Drawing dialog box. Click a **View** icon in the Model Views group to add views of the current model. Add the views to the drawing as you would if the model did not contain any representations. The General view must be the first view added.

You can also click

(Drawing Models) in the Layout tab.

4. To add additional representations of the model to the drawing, ensure the *Layout* tab is selected and then right-click and select **Drawing Models**. The **DWG MODELS** menu displays. Select **Set/Add Rep** in the **DWG MODELS** menu, as shown in Figure 12–17.

Menu Manager
▼ DWG MODELS
Add Model
Del Model
Set Model
Remove Rep
Set/Add Rep
Replace
Model Disp
Done/Return

Figure 12–17

5. Select the simplified representation in the **SELECT REP** menu.

   This simplified representation is now the current drawing model, and the name of the selected representation displays at the bottom border of the drawing in the Graphics window. Any new views added to the drawing correspond to the newly selected representation. Again, the General view must be the first view added to the drawing.

6. The last simplified representation added to the drawing is considered the current active model. Select the *Layout* tab and use one of the following techniques to set an alternative representation as the active model:

- Double-click on the model name at the bottom border of the drawing in the Graphics window and select a model in the **SELECT REP** menu.

- Right-click and select **Drawing Models>Set/Add Rep** in the **DWG MODELS** menu, and select a representation.

- Click ⬛ ▾ (Layer) in the Model Tree and select the assembly and the simplified representation.

7. Deleting all of the views of a representation does not remove its association to the drawing. To break associativity between the representation and the drawing, delete all of the model's views, select **Remove Rep** in the **DWG MODELS** menu, and select the simplified representation to remove from the drawing, as shown in Figure 12–18.

Menu Manager
▼ DWG MODELS
Add Model
Del Model
Set Model
Remove Rep
Set/Add Rep
Replace
Model Disp
Done/Return
▼ RMV REP
Default Rep
Master Rep

Figure 12–18

Restrictions

Note the following restrictions of simplified representations in Drawing mode:

• Projected, auxiliary, and detailed views can only be created from the general view of the same simplified representation.

• Dimensions cannot be shown in Drawing mode for substitute parts.

• Changes to assembly-level simplified representations might result in a loss of information in a drawing.

12.5 Part Simplified Representations

Creo Parametric supports Part Simplified Representations in drawing views.

Creating Part Simplified Representations

To create a Part Simplified Representation, click ▣ (Manage Views) in the *View* tab or click ▣ (View Manager) in the In-graphics toolbar and click **New**. The View Manager dialog box opens as shown in Figure 12–19.

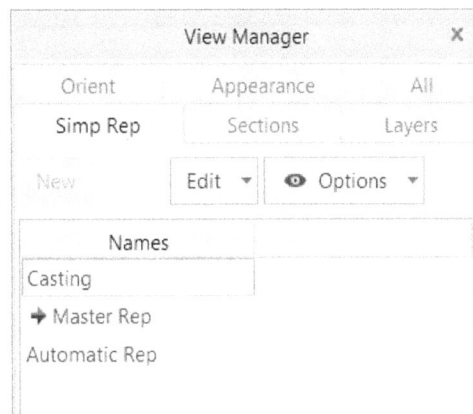

Figure 12–19

Select the appropriate operation (e.g., **Features**), as shown in Figure 12–20. Using the **FEAT INC/EXC** menu, select features in the model or Model Tree that you do not want to use in the Part Simplified Representation.

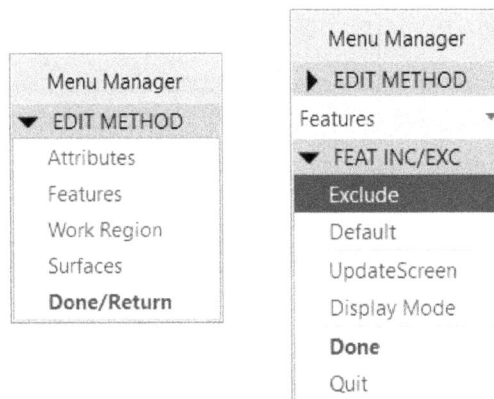

Figure 12–20

Creating a Drawing including Part Simplified Representations

If the model includes a Part Simplified Representation, you can select it from a list and use it as the default for the whole drawing. Usually **Master Rep** is selected, as shown in Figure 12–21.

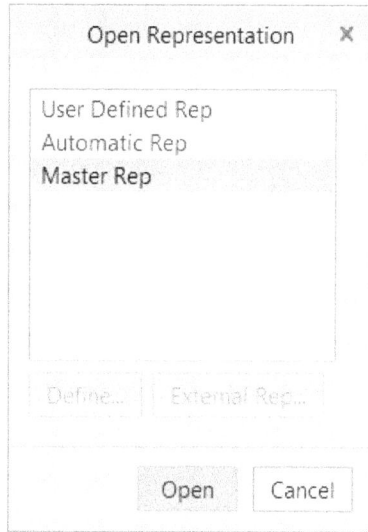

User Defined Rep
Automatic Rep
Master Rep

Open Representation ✕

Define... External Rep...

Open   Cancel

Figure 12–21

A Part Simplified Representation in a drawing is shown in Figure 12–22.

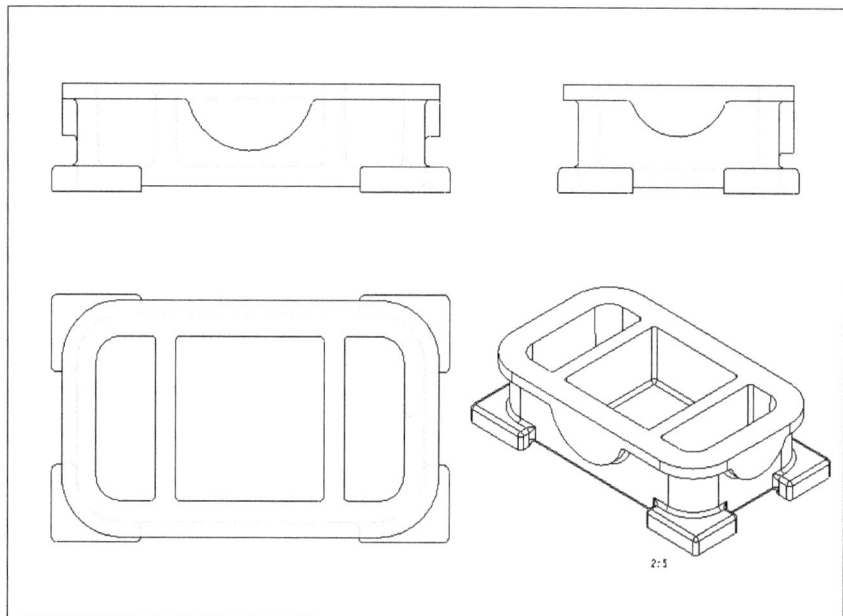

2 : 5

Figure 12–22

If you want to use Part Simplified Representations for another drawing view, ensure that the *Layout* tab is selected and click

(Drawing Models)>**Set/Add Rep**, as shown in Figure 12–23, and then create the new view. The Part Simplified Representation is then used for all of the new views until you change it again.

Figure 12–23

If you want to remove Part Simplified Representations from the drawing, you have to delete all of the views that include them

and then click (Drawing Models) and select **Remove Rep**. Figure 12–24 shows the drawing before the Part Simplified Representations are removed.

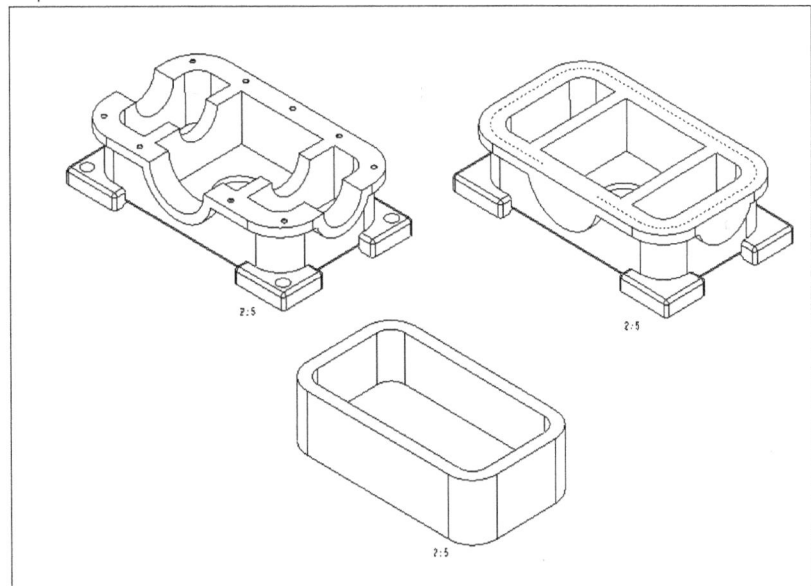

Figure 12–24

12.6 Review and Tools Tab

The *Review* tab includes information tools and icons that enable you to update your drawing. Using these tools, you can obtain information about the drawing, parts, and assemblies. To access these tools, select the *Review tools* tab, as shown in Figure 12–25.

| File | Layout | Table | Annotate | Sketch | Legacy Migration | Analysis | Review |

Figure 12–25

Update

The available icons in the *Review* tab enable you to update different aspects of a drawing. They are described as follows:

Option	Description
(Check Display Status)	Opens an information window. The window lists the sheet number, view ID, view name, missing information, and recommended action. This option only displays information if the part or assembly has been modified.
(Update Sheets)	Updates views and annotations on selected sheets in the drawing.
(Update Draft)	Updates any associative draft entities.
(Update Tables)	Updates all tables in the drawing.
(Regenerate Active Model)	Regenerates the drawing model.
(Update Drawing View)	Updates a selected view.
(Template Errors)	Displays drawing template errors.

Clicking ⚒ (Update Draft) in the *Review* tab enables you to update all of the numerical values in the model without physically updating the 3D model or geometry in the drawing. This method is useful when working with large drawings. You can update the drawing dimensions without needing to update the physical geometry. This is also a way to determine what has changed. The dimensions that have changed but are not regenerated display in a different color.

In an assembly drawing, clicking ⚒ (Regenerate Active Model) in the *Review* tab enables you to select what to regenerate using the Menu Manager options, as shown in Figure 12–26.

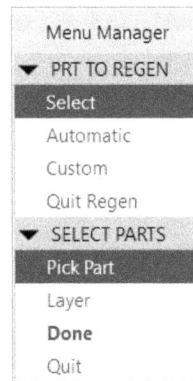

Figure 12–26

Selecting **Custom** opens the Regeneration Manager dialog box, as shown in Figure 12–27. This dialog box enables you to determine which parts and features are regenerated in the drawing.

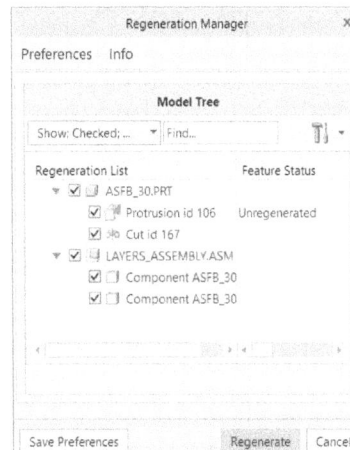

Figure 12–27

Compare

You can compare differences between drawings.

How To: Compare Two Versions of a Drawing

1. Select **File>Save As>Save a Copy** and select **.pic** as the file extension, as shown in Figure 12–28.

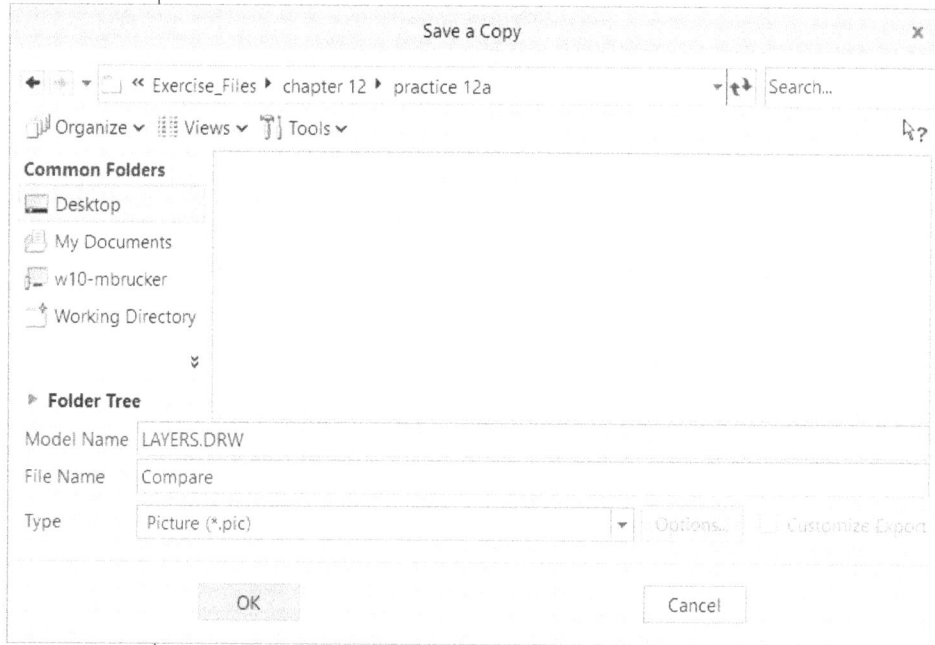

Figure 12–28

2. Open the version of the file that you want to compare.

3. Click ⊞ (Compare Sheet To Picture) in the Compare group in the *Review* tab.

4. Select the saved .PIC file.

5. Click ![icon] (Difference Report) in the Compare group to generate a report that lists the differences between drawings, as shown in Figure 12–29.

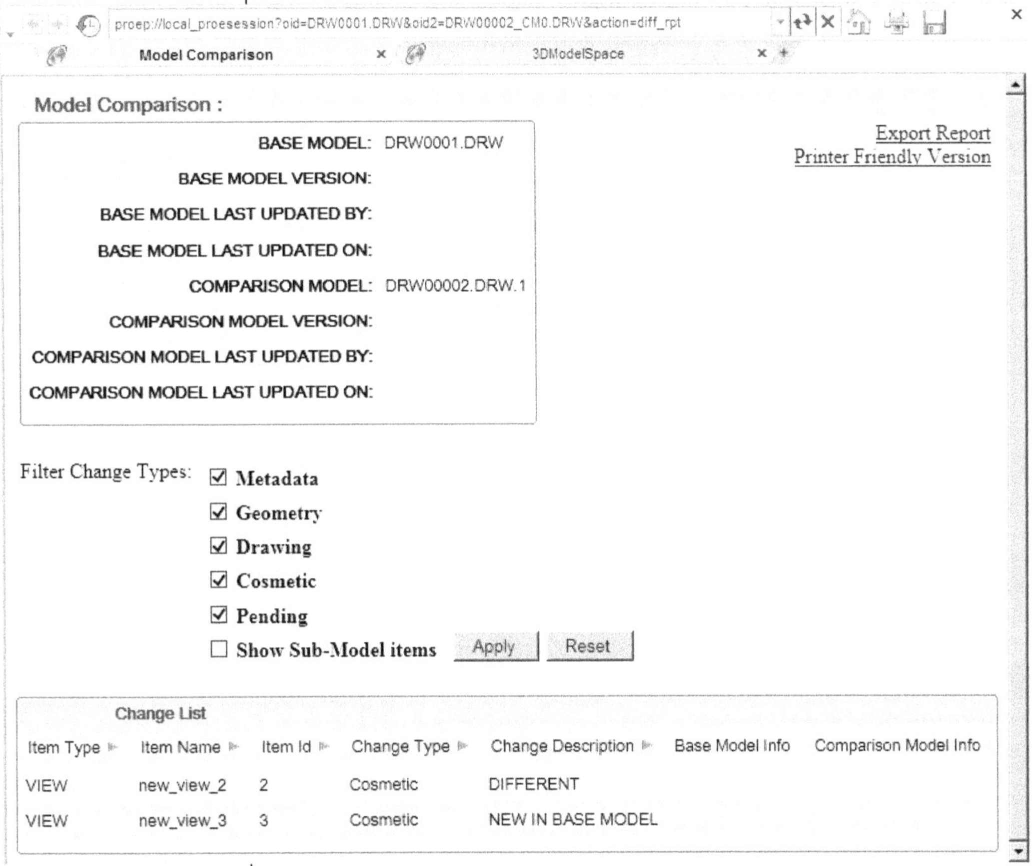

Figure 12–29

Information Tools

The Query group contains information tools.

Click ⬚ (Highlight By Attributes) in the Query group to open the Highlight by Attributes dialog box, as shown in Figure 12–30. This option enables you to specify the items that you want to highlight in the drawing.

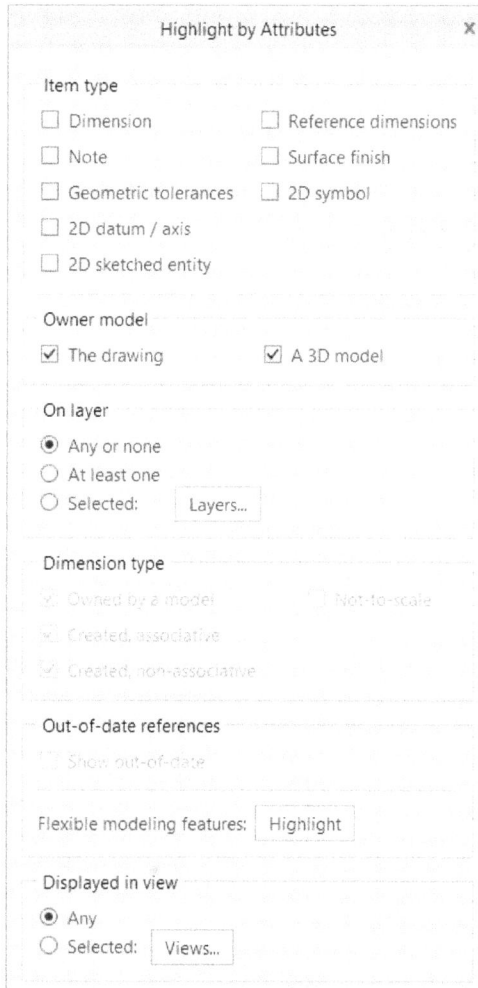

Highlight by Attributes	✕

Item type
- [ ] Dimension
- [ ] Note
- [ ] Geometric tolerances
- [ ] 2D datum / axis
- [ ] 2D sketched entity
- [ ] Reference dimensions
- [ ] Surface finish
- [ ] 2D symbol

Owner model
- [✓] The drawing
- [✓] A 3D model

On layer
- (●) Any or none
- ( ) At least one
- ( ) Selected: Layers...

Dimension type
- [✓] Owned by a model
- [ ] Not-to-scale
- [✓] Created, associative
- [✓] Created, non-associative

Out-of-date references
- [ ] Show out-of-date

Flexible modeling features: Highlight

Displayed in view
- (●) Any
- ( ) Selected: Views...

Figure 12–30

The *Owner Model* area in the dialog box has the following options:

- **Drawing:** Highlights items that were created in the drawing but are not associative to the component.

- **3D model:** Highlights items that were created in the model and displayed in the drawing.

Other options in the Query group are described as follows:

Option	Description
(Drawing View)	Displays a window with information about the selected view.
(Draft Entity)	Displays a window with information about draft entities in the drawing.
(Owner)	Displays the component that is the owner of the selected object in the message window.

Information tools are available in the *Tools* tab in the Model Info group and as follows. Many of the information tools are also available in other tabs and menus.

Option	Description
(Model Information)	Opens the browser window and displays model information.
(Feature Information)	Opens the browser window and displays information about the selected feature.
(Bill of Materials)	Opens the browser window and displays the BOM report.
(Reference Viewer)	Opens the Reference Viewer dialog box.
(Component Information)	Opens the Component Constraints dialog box and enables you to select parts in an assembly. Once the parts have been selected, the constraint information displays, as shown below. Click **Apply** to open a browser displaying more information. 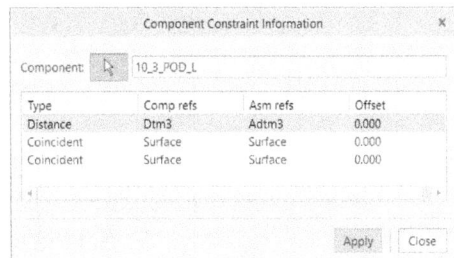
(Feature List)	Opens the browser and displays the feature list. Select **Investigate>Feature List** in the *Tools* tab.

Practice 12a | Drawing Layers

Practice Objectives

- Create layers in Drawing mode.
- Manipulate layers in Drawing mode.

In this practice, you will manage the display of features and components using layers. The final drawing displays as shown in Figure 12–31.

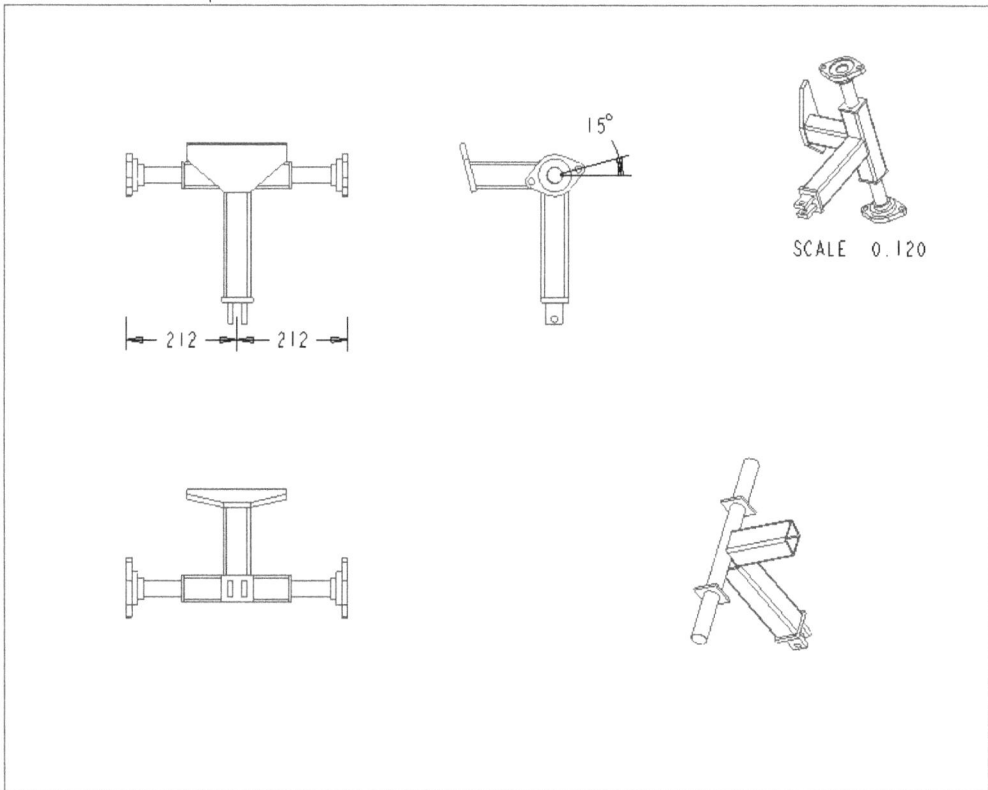

Figure 12–31

Task 1 - Open an assembly file.

1. Set the working directory to the *Drawing_Layers* folder.

2. Open **layers_assembly.asm**.

3. Set the model display as follows:

    - ⁺⁄✳ *(Datum Display Filters)*: All On

    - ⟩ (Spin Center): Off

    - ▯ *(Display Style)*: ▱ (Shading With Edges)

The model displays as shown in Figure 12–32.

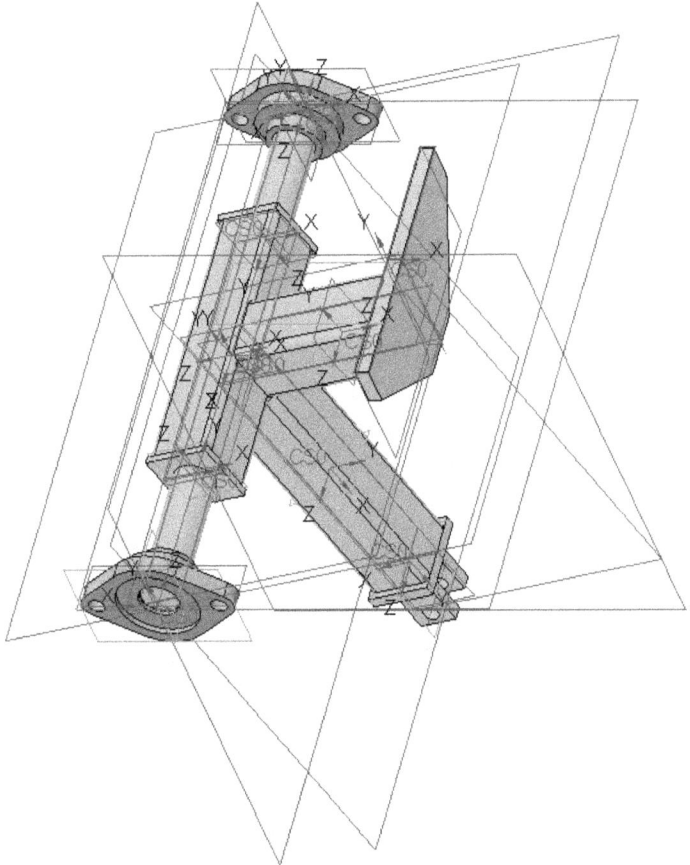

Figure 12–32

Task 2 - Open a drawing file and hide a layer.

1. Open **layers.drw**. Do not close the assembly window. This drawing is of the **layers_assembly** model. The drawing displays as shown in Figure 12–33.

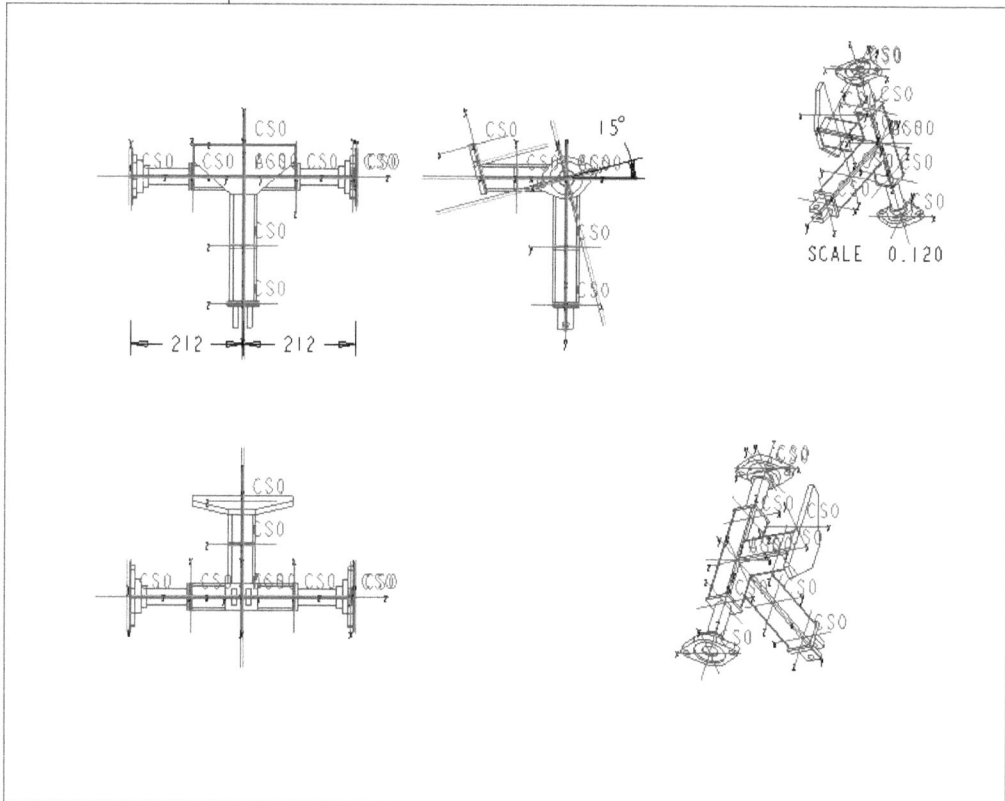

Figure 12–33

2. Display the Layer Tree by clicking 🗒 ▾ (Show)>**Layer Tree** in the Model Tree. The Layer Tree displays as shown in Figure 12–34.

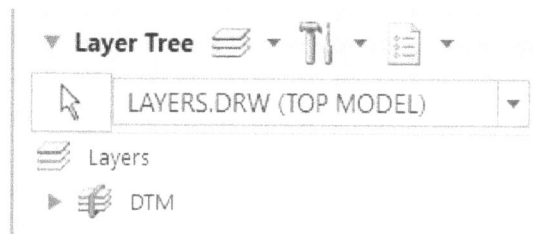

Figure 12–34

*The model has one layer, **DTM**. It contains part and assembly datum planes, coordinate systems, and axes.*

3. Click 🔨 ▾ (Settings) in the Layer Tree and select **Drawing Layer Status**.

4. Verify that the **Yes - Display status of common layers is controlled separately in drawing** option is selected in the Layer Status Control dialog box, as shown in Figure 12–35.

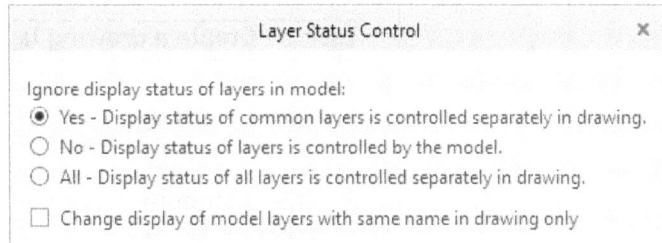

Figure 12–35

5. Click **OK** to close the dialog box.

6. Select the DTM layer in the Layer Tree, then right-click and select **Hide**. The drawing displays as shown in Figure 12–36.

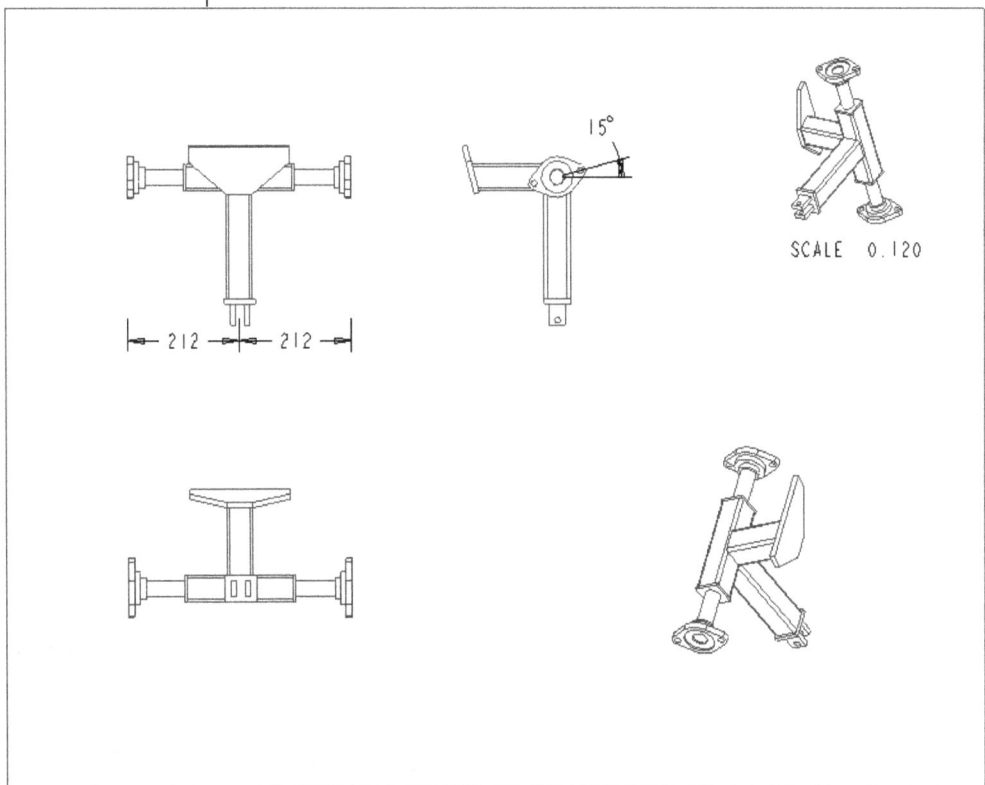

Figure 12–36

7. Save the drawing.

If you have closed the assembly window, open the **layers_ assembly.asm** *file.*

8. Switch to the **layers_assembly.asm** window to confirm that the layer was not hidden in the Assembly mode and that datum features are still displayed.

9. Switch back to the drawing window.

Task 3 - Create a drawing layer.

1. Click ≣ ▾ (Layer) and select **New Layer**. The Layer Properties dialog box opens.

2. Enter **components** as the name for the new layer, as shown in Figure 12–37.

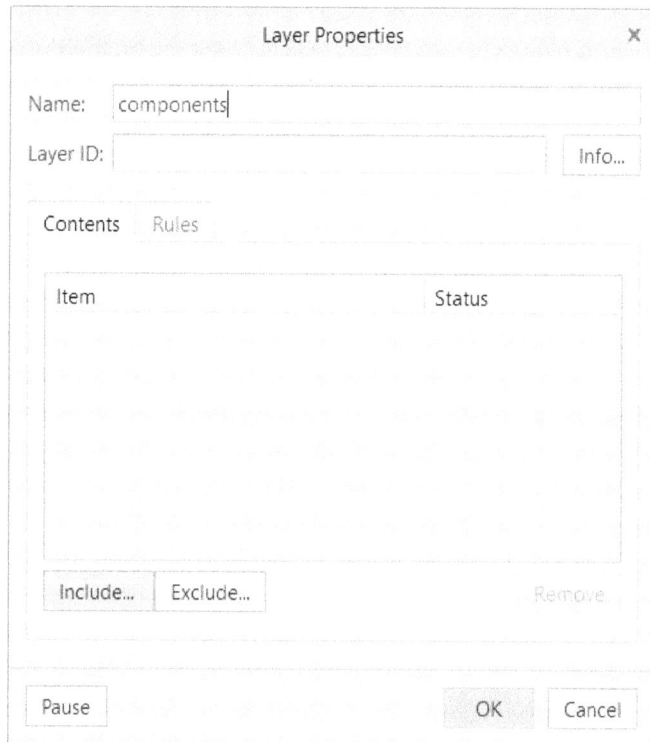

Figure 12–37

3. Click ≣ ▾ (Show)>**Model Tree** and add the following items to the layer:
   - Both **ASFB_30** parts.
   - Expand **5D1_SVAD_10.ASM** and select **10_2_STRED.PRT** and **10_4_BLOCK.PRT**.

The Layer Properties dialog box opens as shown in Figure 12–38.

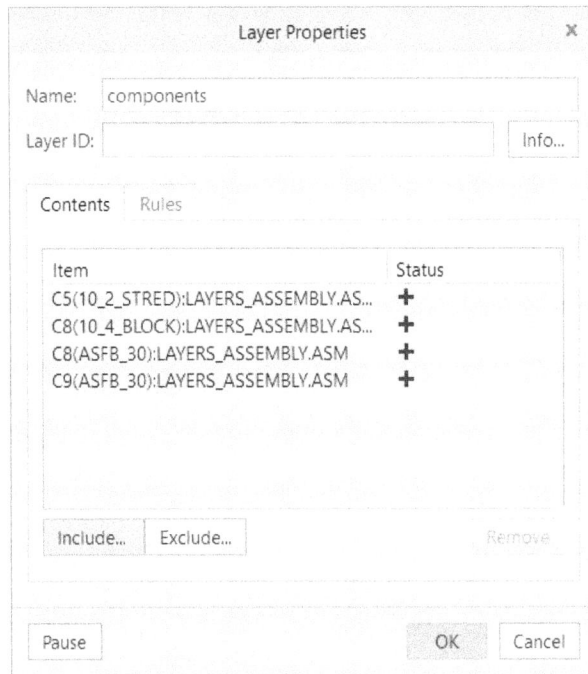

Figure 12–38

4. Click **OK** to close the Layer Properties dialog box.

5. Click 📄 ▾ (Show)>**Layer Tree** in the Model Tree to display the Layer Tree.

*Ensure that **Layer Items** is selected in*
📌 ▾ .

6. The new layer displays in the tree. Click ▸ to expand the layer and display the layer items. The Layer Tree displays as shown in Figure 12–39.

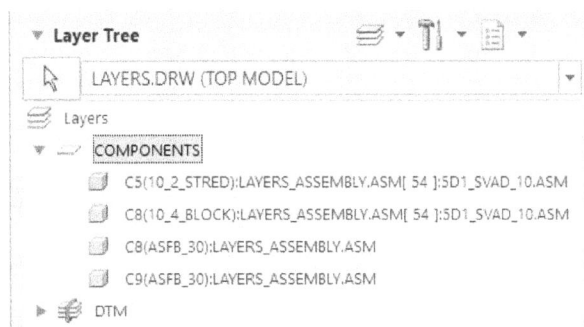

Figure 12–39

7. Switch to the **layers_assembly.asm** window.

8. Display the Layer Tree. The drawing level **COMPONENTS** layer was not created at the assembly level.

9. Switch to the drawing window again.

10. Hide the **COMPONENTS** layer. The components placed on the layer are not displayed in any of the drawing views, as shown in Figure 12–40.

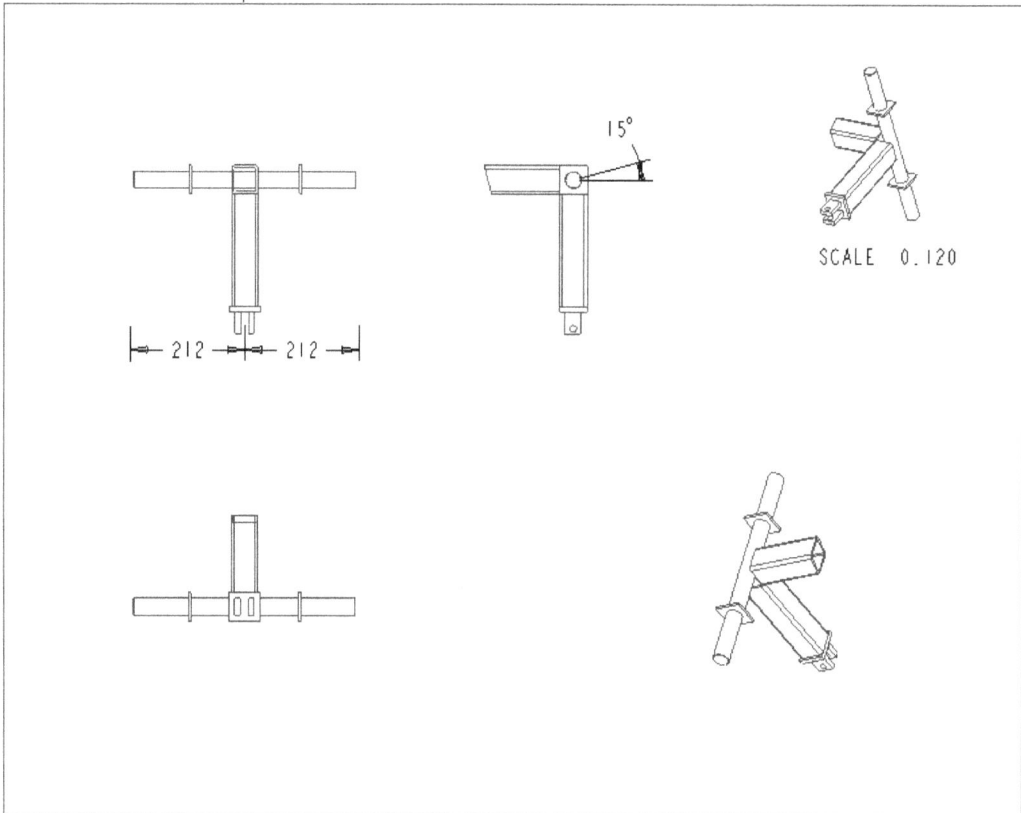

Figure 12–40

Task 4 - Set the display of a view independent from other views.

1. Show the **COMPONENTS** layer.

You can also click ⌖ in the Active Layer Object Selection field, and then select the view.

2. To control the display status of the bottom right view independently, select the *Active Layer Object Selection* field in the Layer Tree and select **NEW_VIEW_5**, as shown in Figure 12–41.

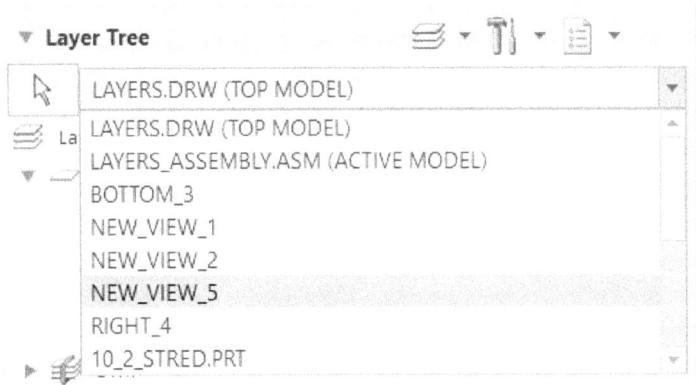

Figure 12–41

3. The layer display is now set to the view level. All of the layers at this view level are now handled independent from the layer status at the drawing level, including the **DTM** layer. Hide both the **DTM** and **COMPONENTS** layers. The four components are only hidden in the bottom right view, as shown in Figure 12–42.

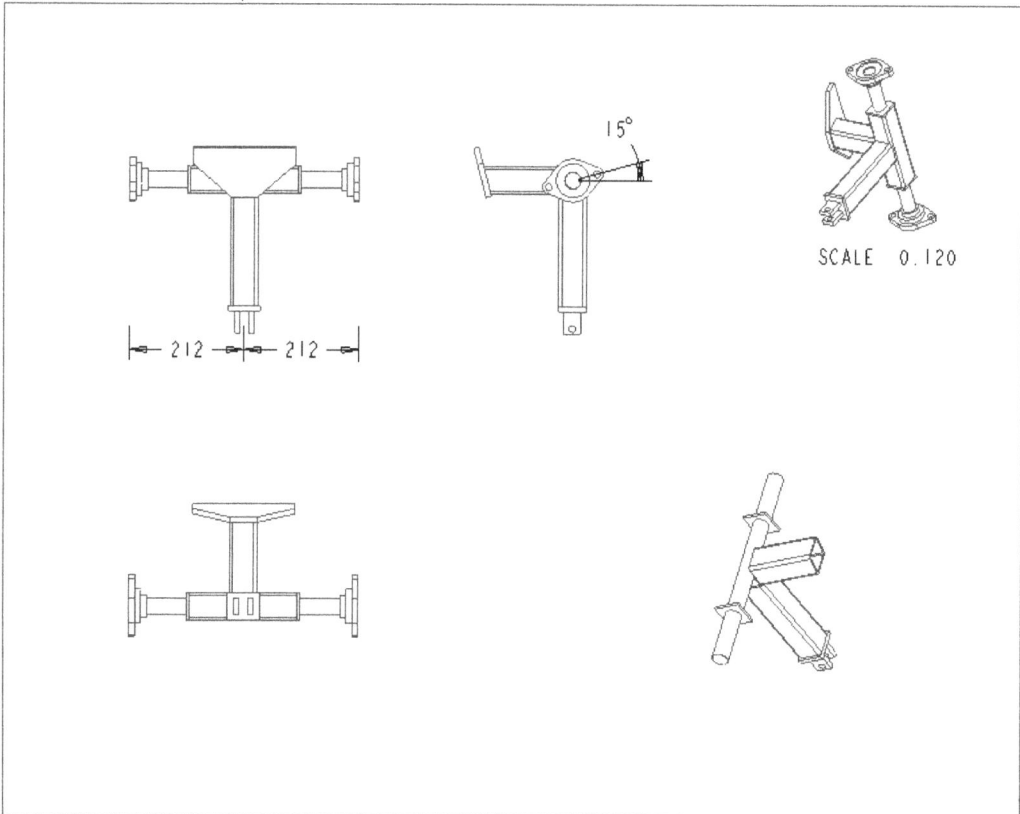

Figure 12–42

4. To set the layer display back to the drawing level, select the *Active Layer Object Selection* field in the Layer Tree and select **LAYERS.DRW (TOP MODEL)**. The **COMPONENT** layer displays at this level.

5. Save the drawing layer status. Right-click in the Layer Tree and select **Save Status**.

6. Save the drawing and close the window.

Practice 12b

Drawing of an Assembly Simplified Representation

Practice Objectives

- Create an assembly drawing of a simplified rep.
- Add a representation to the drawing.
- Set the current active representation.

In this practice, you will create a drawing of an assembly simplified representation and use the **Set/Add Rep** option to add additional representations to the drawing. The final drawing displays as shown in Figure 12–43.

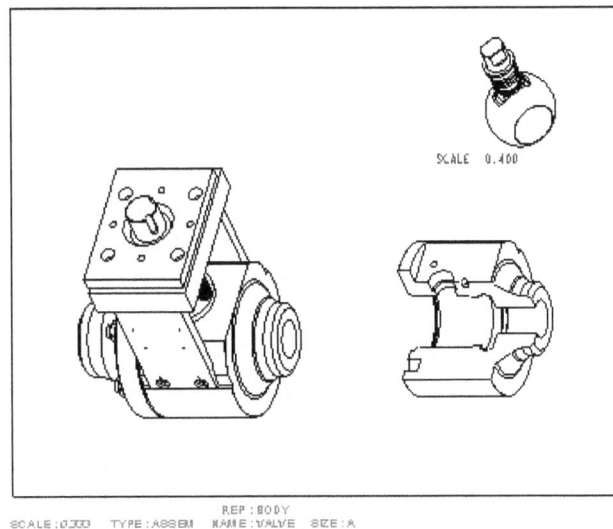

SCALE 0.400

REP : BODY
SCALE : 0.JJJ   TYPE : ASSEM   NAME : VALVE   SIZE : A

Figure 12–43

Task 1 - Create a new drawing.

1. Set the working directory to the *Drawing_Simp_Rep* folder.

2. Create a new drawing called **valve.drw** and clear the **Use default template** option.

3. Click **OK**. The New Drawing dialog box opens.

4. Select **valve.asm** as the default model for the drawing.

5. Select **Empty** in the *Specify Template* area.

6. Create the drawing using a standard **A** size.

7. Click **OK**. The Open Rep dialog box opens because simplified representations exist in the assembly.

8. Select **BALL** and click **OK**. This simplified representation is now the current model for the drawing.

9. Set the model display as follows:

   - ⁺⁄✳ *(Datum Display Filters)*: All Off

   - ◖ *(Display Style)*: ▢ (No Hidden)

Task 2 - Add a view to the drawing.

Verify that the Layout tab is selected.

1. Click ▱ (General View). Select the **Do not prompt for Combined State** option and select the **No Combined State** option.

2. Select the top right corner of the drawing sheet to define the center point for the drawing view. The Drawing View dialog box opens.

3. Select **Default Orientation** in the *Model view names* area and click **Apply**.

4. Select **Scale** in the *Categories* area in the Drawing View dialog box.

5. Select the **Custom Scale** option and enter **0.40**.

6. Click **OK** in the Drawing View dialog box. The drawing displays as shown in Figure 12–44. This view represents the Ball simplified representation of the valve assembly as it was created in Assembly mode.

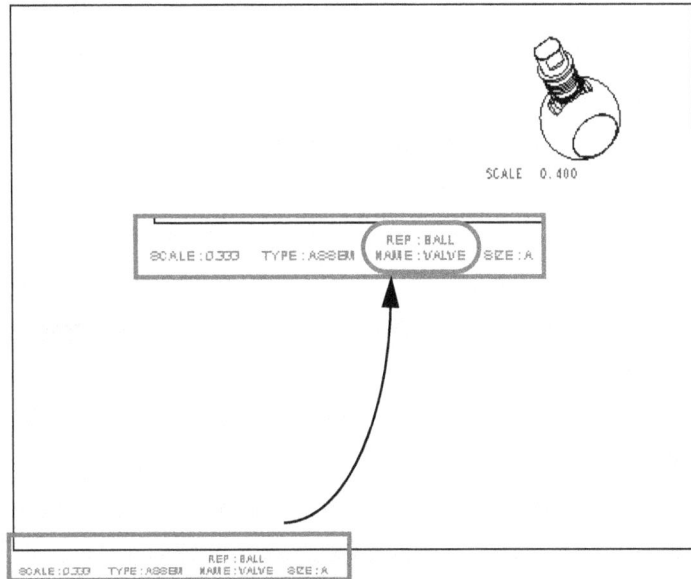

Figure 12–44

7. Select **File>Manage Session>Object List**. Review the list of the assembly part files that are currently in the session. Only the simplified representation Ball was added to the drawing. Therefore, not all of the valve assembly components are required in the drawing and in the session.

8. Close the INFORMATION WINDOW dialog box.

Task 3 - Add the Master Rep to the drawing.

You can also click
(Drawing Models) in
the Layout tab.

1. Ensure that the *Layout* tab is active. Right-click and select **Drawing Models**. The **DWG MODELS** menu displays. Select **Set/Add Rep** in the **DWG MODELS** menu.

2. Select **Master Rep** in the **SELECT REP** menu, as shown in Figure 12–45. The Master Rep is now the current model. The message window displays the prompt: *Current simplified representation for VALVE is now Master rep.* Select **Done/Return** in the **DWG MODELS** menu.

Menu Manager
▼ DWG MODELS
  Add Model
  Del Model
  Set Model
  Remove Rep
  Set/Add Rep
  Replace
  Model Disp
  Done/Return
▼ SELECT REP
  BALL
  BODY
  Automatic Rep
  Master Rep
  Default Rep

Figure 12–45

3. Click ▱ (General View) in the Model Views group in the *Layout* tab. Select the center point for the view, and click **OK**. The drawing displays as shown in Figure 12–46.

Ensure that the sheet scale for the drawing is 0.333. If required, double-click on the scale at the bottom border of the drawing in the Graphics window.

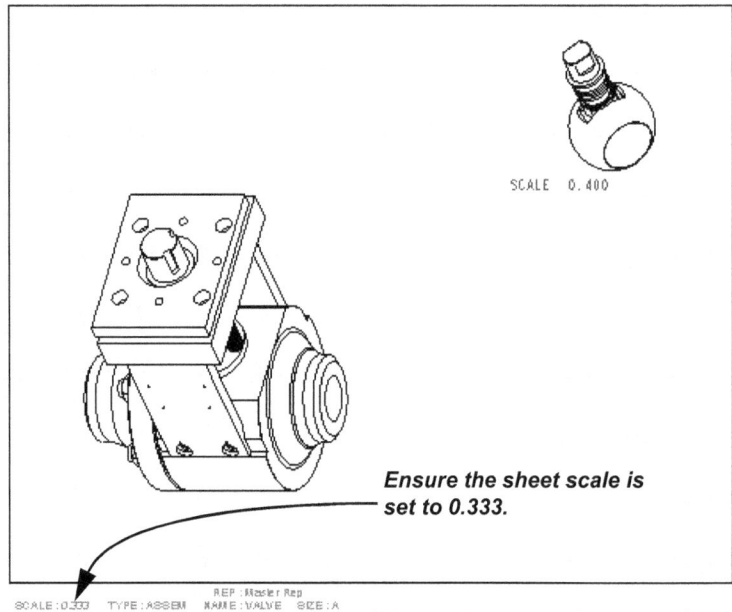

SCALE 0.400

Ensure the sheet scale is set to 0.333.

SCALE : 0.333   TYPE : ASSEM   REP : Master Rep   NAME : VALVE   SIZE : A

Figure 12–46

4. Select **File>Manage Session>Object List** to review the list of assembly part files that are currently in the session. More files are in the session now because you added the Master Rep of the assembly as an additional representation on the drawing. The Master Rep includes all of the components of the assembly.

5. Close the INFORMATION WINDOW.

Task 4 - Set an alternative representation as the active model.

1. Double-click on **REP: Master Rep** at the bottom of the drawing window. The **SELECT REP** menu displays as shown in Figure 12–47.

Menu Manager

▼ SELECT REP

BALL

BODY

Automatic Rep

Master Rep

Default Rep

Figure 12–47

2. Select **BODY** to set it as the active model representation.

3. Add a General view of the current representation, as shown in Figure 12–48.

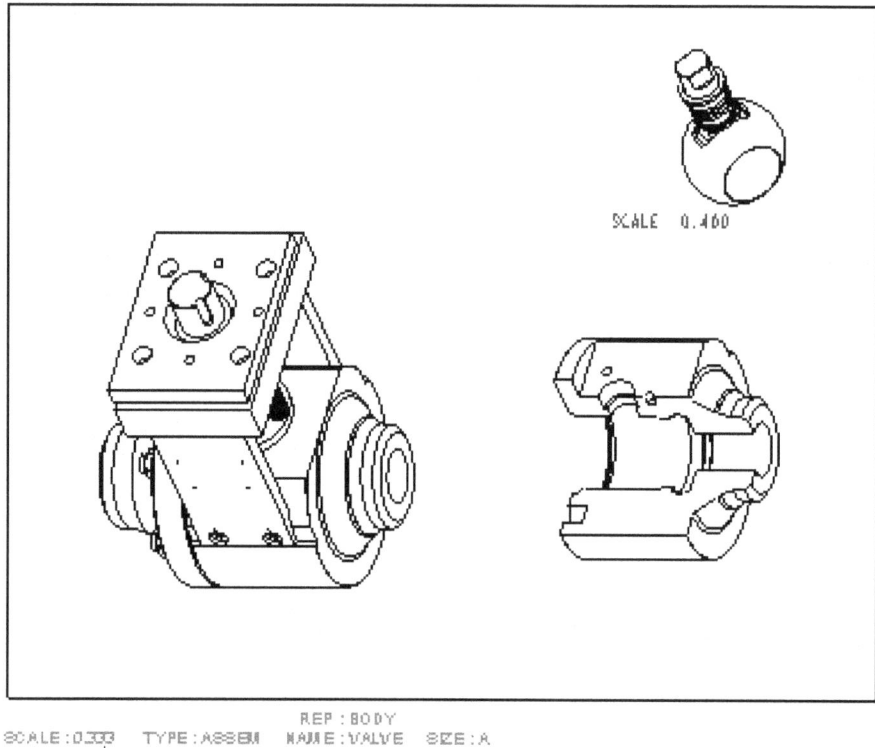

SCALE 0.400

SCALE:0.333   TYPE:ASSEM   REP:BODY   NAME:VALVE   SIZE:A

Figure 12–48

4. Save the drawing and close the window.

Chapter Review Questions

1. Which command enables you to update all of the numerical values in the model without physically updating the 3D model or geometry in the drawing?

    a. Click ⬚ (Regeneration Manager).

    b. Click ⬚ (Reference Manager).

    c. Click ⬚ (Update Draft).

    d. Click ⬚ (Regenerate).

2. If you want to remove Part Simplified Representations from the drawing, which of the following options must you perform? (Select all that apply.)

    a. You have to remove the simplified representation using **Remove Rep**.

    b. You have to delete all of the views that include them.

    c. You have to delete the drawing model.

    d. You have to remove the simplified representation from the assembly or part model.

3. What are some of the advantages of using a simplified representation? (Select all that apply.)

    a. Enable you to reduce retrieval time

    b. Enables you to focus on specific regions of the models.

    c. Controls how components display

    d. Reduces regeneration times.

4. A component is temporarily removed from the display and the regeneration sequence. Which of the following commands was used?

    a. **Hide**

    b. **Suppress**

    c. **Isolate**

    d. **Simplified Representation**

5. The **Activate** tool enables you to activate a layer to which new entities are automatically added.

    a. True

    b. False

6. You cannot control the display status of drawing layers in a drawing without changing the part or assembly in which the item is created.

   a. True

   b. False

7. When the status of a layer is set in an assembly drawing, the same status always applies to the that layer in the assembly.

   a. True

   b. False

Drawing Formats and Templates

A drawing format is a file that is imported into your drawing and provides a customized layout for your drawings. The format usually contains standard information, such as borders, title blocks, tables, and company information. A drawing template differs from a format in that templates can be used to automatically create more than title blocks, sketched entities, and tables. It is used to place views, placed notes, defined tables, and shown dimensions.

Learning Objectives in This Appendix

- Learn to create a drawing format using Empty or Empty with section and retrieve a 2D sketched section.
- Learn to create a format using imported data or different file formats.
- Learn to add tables to the format for title blocks and other tabulated information.
- Review methods of adding text to the format using parameters, notes, or text in a table.
- Learn the different methods of adding a drawing format to a drawing.
- Learn how to create drawing templates that can automate the creation of views, dimensions, simplified reps, etc., for a drawing.

A.1 Create a Drawing Format

The **Empty with section** option enables you to create a format that retrieves a 2D sketched section

In general, any text or tables that are common to all company drawings should be included in a drawing format to help reduce the amount of time required to complete a drawing. Once the format has been completed, it can be saved to the system disk for future use. Figure A–1 shows a typical **B** size format.

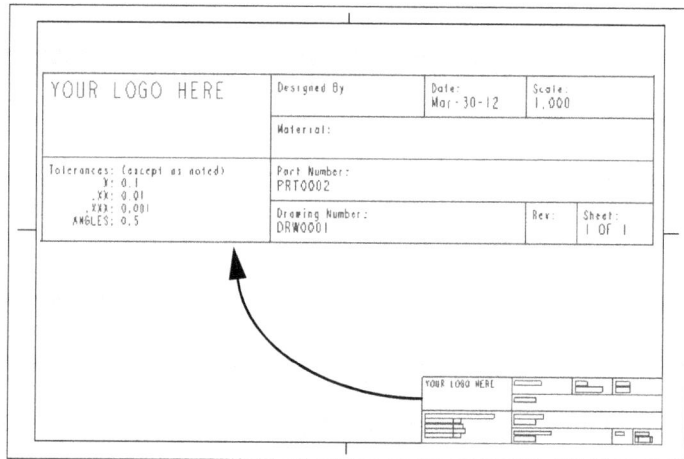

Figure A–1

*You can also select **File>New** to create a new file.*

Click ⬜ (New) to create a new drawing format. The New dialog box opens as shown in Figure A–2. Select the **Format** option and enter a name. Click **OK** to create the format.

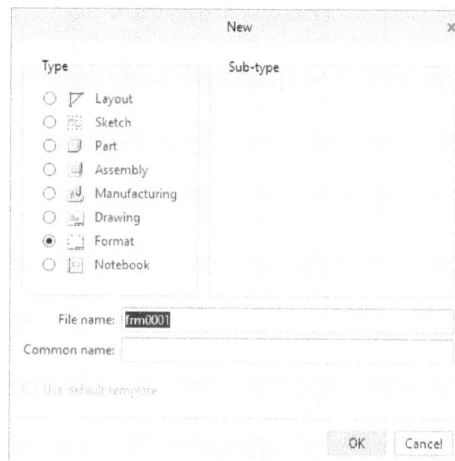

Figure A–2

The New Format dialog box opens. The *Specify Template* area in the New Format dialog box enables you to define the specifics of how the format is created. The options include:

- Empty with section

- Empty

Depending on which option is selected in the *Specify Template* area, the dialog box displays as shown in Figure A–3.

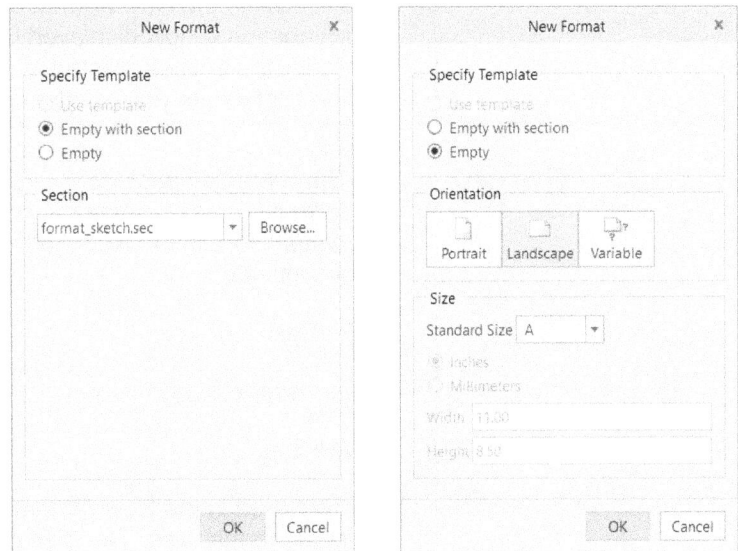

Figure A–3

Empty with Section

The **Empty with section** option enables you to create a format that retrieves a 2D sketched section (.SEC) that represents the boundary of the format. The sketched section is created using the sketching tools, which enable you to define a more precise boundary size.

How To: Create and then Import a Sketch into the Format

1. Enter the *Sketch* tab and create the sketch of the format.
2. Save the file (.SEC).
3. Click ☐ (New). The New dialog box opens.
4. Select **Format**, enter a name for the format, and click **OK**.
5. Select **Empty with section** in the New Format dialog box and click **Browse**.
6. Select the saved sketched section.
7. Click **OK** in the New Format dialog box. The sketched information is now displayed in the format.
8. Modify the entities created in the *Sketch* tab using **Format**. The entities are now 2D draft entities.

Empty

The **Empty** option enables you to define the orientation and size of a format. You can define the orientation of the format in the *Orientation* area in the New Format dialog box. The available options include:

- Portrait

- Landscape

- Variable

The *Size* area in the New Format dialog box enables you to define the format size. The **Size** options vary depending on the **Orientation** option that is selected. describes the standard sheet sizes available for the **Portrait** or **Landscape** orientation.

ISO	ANSI
A0 841 X 1189 mm	A 8.5 X 11 in
A1 594 X 841 mm	B 11 X 17 in
A2 420 X 594 mm	C 17 X 22 in
A3 297 X 420 mm	D 22 X 34 in
A4 210 X 297 mm	E 34 X 44 in
	F 28 X 40 in

The **Variable** option enables you to create custom sizes. For variable orientations, you can select the unit of measure and enter values for the width and height of the format, as shown in Figure A–4.

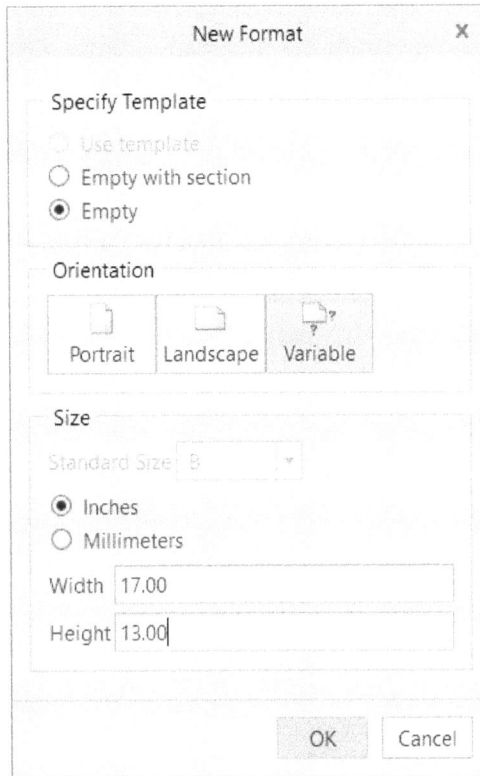

Figure A–4

The familiar 2D sketching tools and table creation tools are used for both options (**Empty with section** and **Empty**) to create the title block and any required tables.

A.2 Import Formats

Formats can also be created by importing existing data with different file formats, such as DXF, DWG, SET, TIFF, CGM, or IGES.

How To: Create a Format Using Imported Data

1. Create a new format. Ensure that the orientation is the same as the format being imported.

2. Select the *Layout* tab and click ⬚ (Import Drawing/Data) in the Insert group. Select the file that you want to import. The dialog box for the type of file you are importing opens, which enables you to change various settings, as shown in Figure A–5.

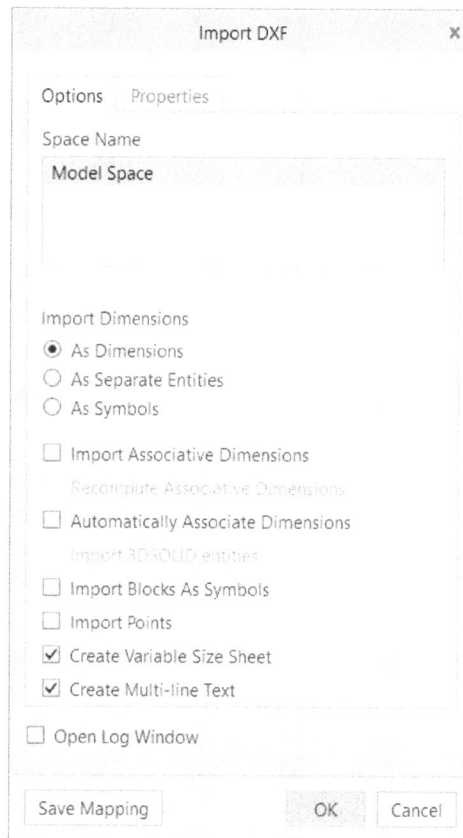

Figure A–5

3. Once imported, you can modify the entities created in the *Sketch* tab using the **Formatting** options. The entities are now 2D draft entities.

A.3 Add Tables to a Format

You can add tables to a drawing format to represent a title block or to tabulate model information. Once you have added a format to a drawing, all of the tables become independent and can be moved, modified, or deleted. When you remove or replace an existing format in a drawing, Creo Parametric highlights any tables that existed in the format and provides the option to remove or keep them.

You can also use
(Table)>Quick
Table.

The icons in the tabs are
the same as those used
when creating a
drawing.

Select the *Table* tab and click (Table from File) in the Table group to create a table in a format.

A typical title block in a table is shown in Figure A–6. The table contains text, system, and user-defined parameters.

Figure A–6

A.4 Parametric Text

Parametric text can be added to a format as a note, or as text in a table. The parameters used to create the text can be system- or user-defined. To populate the text, the parameter values are read from the model and then displayed in the drawing. For example, if you add the text **&dwg_name** to a note or table, the drawing name is automatically displayed once the format has been added to a drawing.

Some commonly used system-defined parameters are described as follows:

All system-defined parameters can be accessed using the Creo Help Center.

Option	Description
&current_sheet	Displays the current sheet number.
&dwg_name	Displays the drawing name.
&format	Displays the format size.
&model_name	Displays the model name.
&scale	Displays the drawing scale.
&type	Displays the model type (e.g. part, assembly).
&todays_date	Displays the date.
&total_sheets	Displays the number of sheets in a drawing.
&d#	Displays a dimension in a note (# is dimension ID). A dimension can only be shown once. If added to a note or table you cannot display it on a model.

User-defined parameters (e.g., **&designer_name**) are optional in a model. If the parameter value is defined in the model, the value displays automatically once the format has been added to a drawing. If the parameter value is not defined in the model, you can set the **make_parameters_from_fmt_tables** configuration option to **no** so that you are prompted for the value when the format is added. If the value is set to **yes**, the note or table text remains empty in the drawing. A value can be applied once the drawing has been created.

A.5 Add a Drawing Format

A format can be added to a drawing using one of the following methods:

- To add a format to a new drawing, select the **Empty with section** option in the New Drawing dialog box and click **Browse** to browse to the required format.

- To add a format once the drawing has been created, click ☐ (Sheet Setup) in the Document group in the *Layout* tab.

- To add a format once the drawing has been created, right-click on the *Sheet* tab at the bottom of the window, and select **Setup**.

The Sheet Setup dialog box opens as shown in Figure A–7. Use the cell in the *Format* column to set the format of the sheet.

Figure A–7

The drawing becomes dependent on the format once the format has been retrieved into the drawing. If you add 2D geometry, notes, or symbols to the source format, the change is automatically applied to the drawing. However, changes in the drawing do not reflect in the format. If you change the table in the format, the change is not automatically entered into the drawing. This is because tables are copied into the drawing when you retrieve a format.

How To: Update the Format Tables in the Drawing

1. Open the Sheet Setup dialog box and select a cell in the *Format* column.
2. Select the currently used format name in the menu.
3. Click **OK**. Keep or remove the format tables when prompted to finish the format update.

A.6 Create Drawing Templates

A drawing template differs from a format in that templates can be used to automatically add more information than a format.

Drawing Templates are useful for the automated creation of drawings. They automatically place views that include shown and cleaned-up model dimensions, cross-sections, combined states, simplified reps, explodes, notes, defined tables, and symbols. They are useful for detailing similar types of parts that have similar requirements. Using a drawing template improves efficiency and productivity because it automatically creates portions of the drawings. Figure A–8 shows an example of a drawing template, which has predefined views, a title block, and a table.

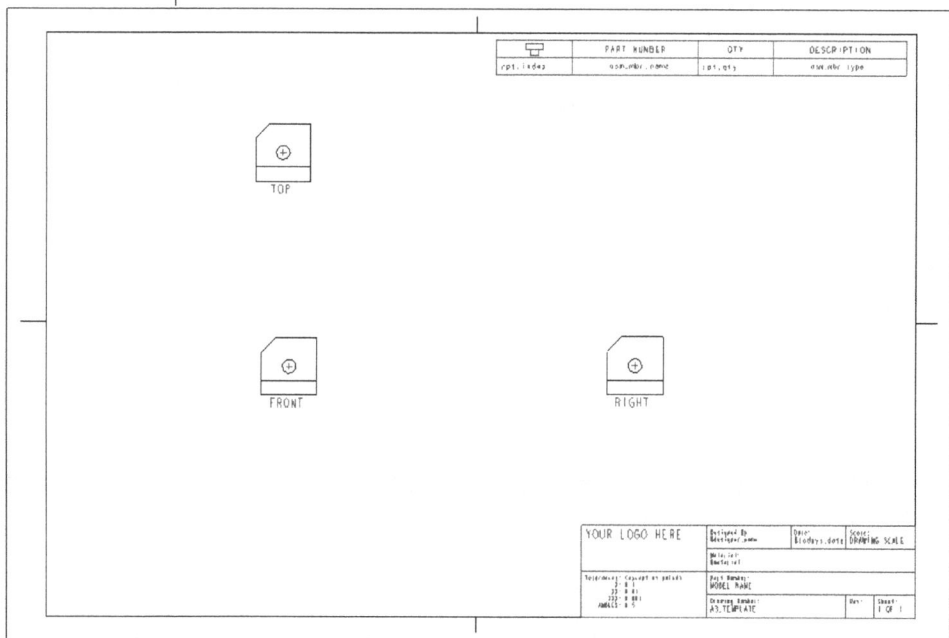

Figure A–8

Drawing templates are initially created in the same way as a standard drawing.

How To: Create a Drawing Template

1. Create a new drawing in the required size and company format.

2. Select the *Tools* tab and click 🔲 (Template) in the Applications group to enter Drawing Template mode.

3. Select the *Layout* tab and click ⬚ (Template View) in the Model Views group. You can also right-click and select **Insert Template View**. The Template View dialog box opens as shown in Figure A–9. Specify the **View** options and view values in the *View Options* and *View Values* areas. All of the values in the fields in the *View Values* area must also exist in the model that is used in the drawing.

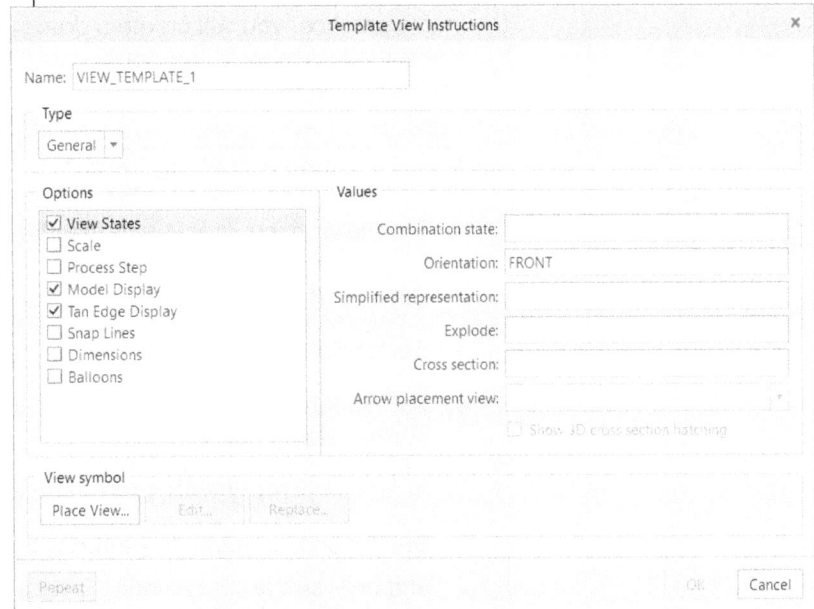

Template View Instructions

Name: VIEW_TEMPLATE_1

Type
General ▾

Options
☑ View States
☐ Scale
☐ Process Step
☑ Model Display
☑ Tan Edge Display
☐ Snap Lines
☐ Dimensions
☐ Balloons

Values
Combination state:
Orientation: FRONT
Simplified representation:
Explode:
Cross section:
Arrow placement view:
☐ Show 3D cross section hatching

View symbol
Place View...   Edit...   Replace...

Repeat   OK   Cancel

Figure A–9

4. Place the General View symbol as follows:

    •   Click **Place View** and place the view on the drawing sheet, as shown in Figure A–10.

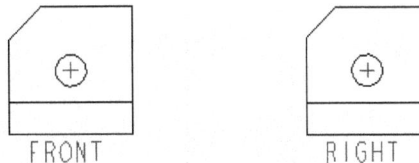

FRONT   RIGHT

Figure A–10

For the view to automatically display as shown in the template, the model must have a **Saved View** name that is defined in the Template View Instructions dialog box.

You must be precise when you place view symbols. Improper symbol placement can cause a failure when Creo Parametric places real model views.

Practice A1

Drawing Formats

Practice Objectives

- Create a new format using a sketched section.
- Create a table as a title block.
- Add the format to a new drawing.

In this practice, you will create a drawing format from a sketch. You will add a table to the drawing and then apply the format to another drawing.

Task 1 - Create a drawing format.

1. Set the working directory to the *Drawing_Formats* folder.

2. Click ☐ (New).The New dialog box opens.

3. Select **Format**.

4. Set the format *Name* to **format_1** and click **OK**. The New Format dialog box opens.

5. Select the **Empty with section** option.

6. Set the section name to **generic_b_1.sec** or click **Browse** and browse the ☐ (Working Directory) to select the file.

7. Click **OK** to create the format. The format displays as shown in Figure A–11.

*You can also create a new file by selecting **File>New**.*

Figure A–11

8. Create the table shown in Figure A–12 as a title block. Place the table in the lower right corner of the drawing. The table contains the following information:

- System-defined parameters (e.g., **&scale** or **&today_date**)
- User-defined parameters (e.g., **&material** or **&part_name**)
- Text

YOUR LOGO HERE	Designed By &designer_name		Date: &todays_date	Scale: &scale		
	Material: &material			Approved By &approved_name		
Tolerances: (except as noted) .X: &linear_tol_0_0 .XX: &linear_tol_0_00 .XXX: &linear_tol_0_000 ANGLES: &angular_tol_0_0	Part Number: &part_number			Part Number: &model_name		
	Drawing Number: &dwg_name			Rev: &rev	Sheet: &current_sheet OF &total_sheets	

Figure A–12

9. Save the format and close the window. This format can now be used in any drawing.

10. Select **File>Options>Configuration Editor** and ensure that the **make_parameters_from_fmt_tables** configuration file option is set to **no**.

Task 2 - Add the format to a new drawing.

1. Create a new drawing. Select the **Empty with Format** option in the New Drawing dialog box and browse to the **format_1.frm** format that you just created. Select any model in the current working directory as the default model.

Alternatively, you can create a drawing using the **Empty** option, and then add the format. To add a format in this way, right-click and select **Sheet Setup** or select the *Layout* tab and click ⬜ (Sheet Setup).

The Page Setup dialog box opens as shown in Figure A–13. Use the menu in the *Format* column to browse and set the format of the sheet to **format_1.frm**.

Figure A–13

2. Click **OK** to create the drawing. Note that the system-defined parameters automatically populate the table.

3. When prompted, enter text to assign values for any user-defined parameters that cannot be found in the drawing. The drawing displays as shown in Figure A–14.

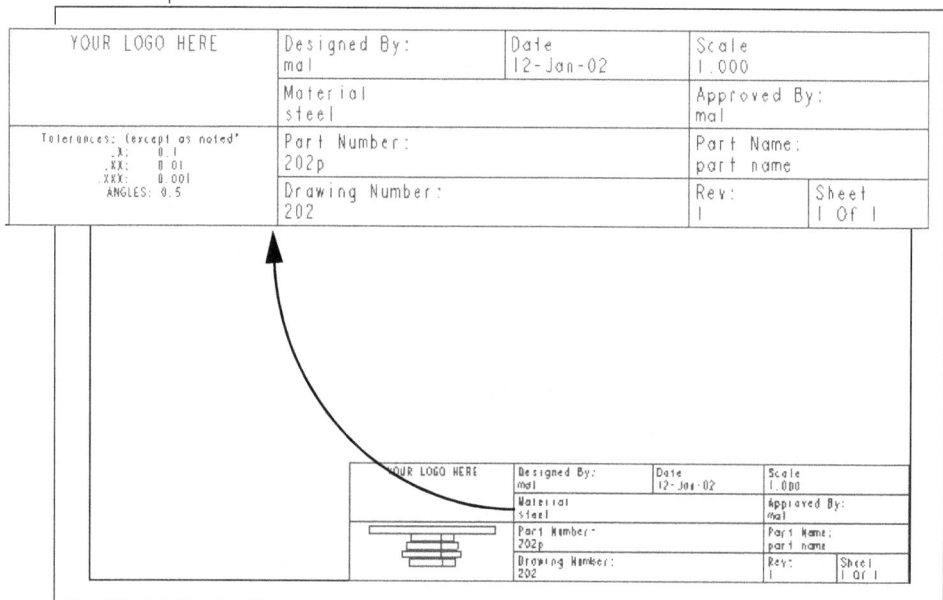

Figure A–14

4. Save the drawing and close the window.

Practice A2

Formats with Imported Data

Practice Objectives

- Create a Format using imported DXF data
- Create a Format using an imported sketched section

In this practice, you will create a format using imported DXF files. You will then apply the format to a sketch.

Task 1 - Create a new format with B size and landscape orientations.

1. Set the working directory to the *Formats_Imported* folder.

2. Create a new format named **rand_b**. Set the following properties in the New Format dialog box:

   - *Specify Template:* **Empty**
   - *Orientation:* **Landscape**
   - *Size:* **B**

3. Click **OK** to create the empty format.

Task 2 - Import format data from a DXF file.

1. Click ⬜ (Import Drawing/Data) in the Insert group in the *Layout* tab.

2. Select the file **format_import_data.dxf** and click **Open**.

3. The Import DXF dialog box opens. Click **OK** to confirm all of the default options. The imported DXF data displays in the drawing format.

4. Save the format to the system disk and close the window. This format can now be used in any drawing.

Task 3 - Import a sketch into a format.

1. Open **format_sketch.sec**. Note how the format layout is created with precise dimensions. Close the sketch.

2. Create a new format named **format_2**. The New Format dialog box opens.

3. Select **Empty with section**.

4. Click **Browse**, select **format_sketch.sec** and click **Open**.

5. Click **OK** to create the format. The imported sketch now displays in the drawing format.

6. Save the format to the system disk and close the window.

Practice A3

Drawing Templates

Practice Objectives

- Create a drawing template.
- Use a template to create a drawing.

In this practice, you will create a drawing template with three views. To complete the practice, you will use the template to create a drawing. The final template displays as shown in Figure A–15.

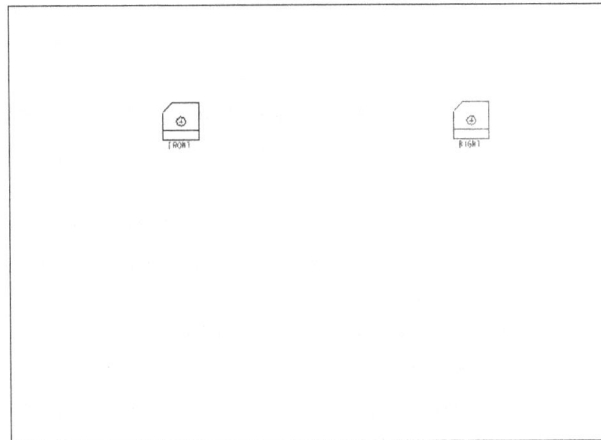

Figure A–15

Task 1 - Create a drawing template with a format A3_template.

1. Set the working directory to the *Drawing_Templates* folder.

2. Create an empty drawing and set the *Name* to **A3_template**. Clear the **Use default template** option if required. This field must be empty. Click **OK**

3. Set the following properties in the New Drawing dialog box:

   - *Default Model:* **None**
   - *Specify Template:* **Empty**
   - *Orientation:* **Landscape**
   - *Size:* **A3**

4. Click **OK**.

Task 2 - Create a template.

1. Select the *Tools* tab and click ⬜ (Template) in the Applications group.

Task 3 - Place the first General view in the template.

You can also click

⬜ *(Template View) in the Model Views group.*

1. Select the *Layout* tab, right-click, and select **Template View**. The Template View Instructions dialog box opens. It enables you to define the attributes of each view in the template.

2. Set the name of the view to **FRONT**.

3. Accept the default **General** as the *View Type*.

4. Enter **FRONT** in the *Orientation* field in the *View Values* area.

5. Enter **S1** in *Simplified Rep.* field in *View Values* area.

6. Enter **Z1** in *Cross Section* field in the *View Values* area as shown in Figure A–16.

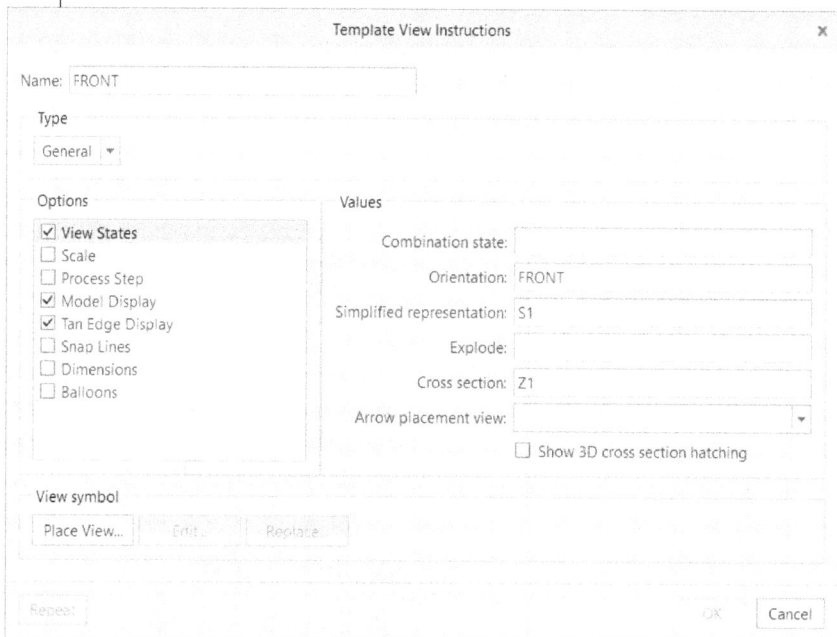

Figure A–16

*Click **Move Symbols** if you have placed the view template and want to move the view to a new location.*

7. Click **Place View** and place the view template on the left side of the drawing as shown in Figure A–17.

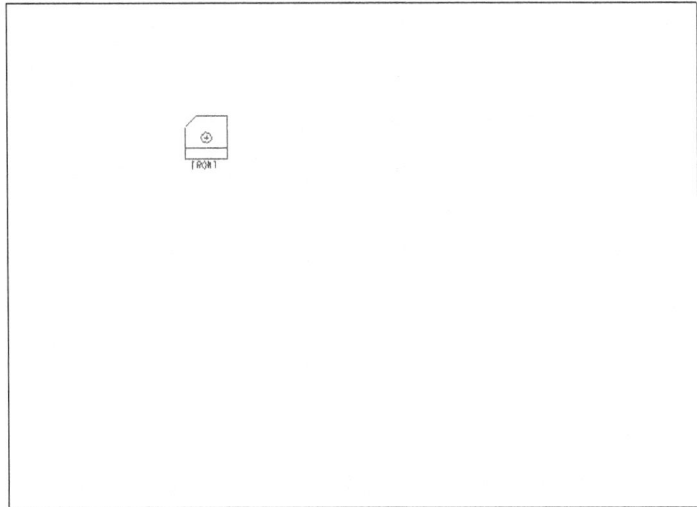

Figure A–17

Task 4 - Place projected views in the template.

1. Click **Repeat** to start a new template view.

2. Set the name of the view to **Right**.

3. Accept the default **General** as the *View Orientation*.

4. Enter **Vs1** in the *Combination State* field in the *View Values* area.

5. When you use *Combination State*, all other fields (such as *Orientation*, *Simplified Rep.*, and *Cross Section*) are defined by the *Combination State*, as shown in Figure A–18.

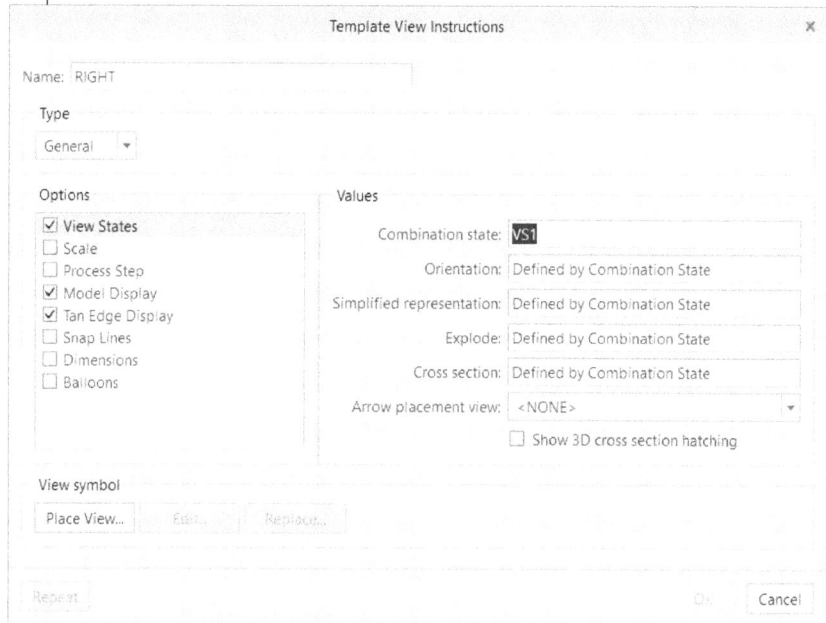

Figure A–18

6. Click **Place View** and place the view template on the right side of the drawing, as shown in Figure A–19.

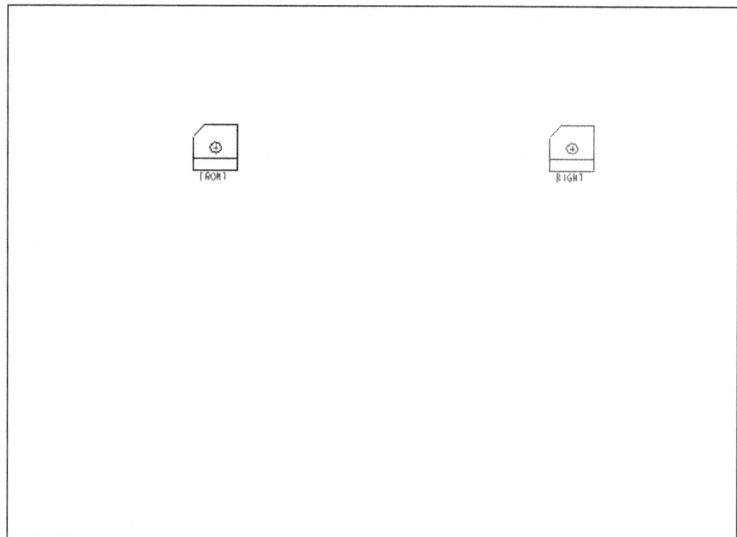

Figure A–19

7. Click **OK** in the Template View Instructions dialog box.

8. Save the template and close the window.

Task 5 - Create a drawing using the newly created template.

For the view to automatically display as shown in the template, the model must have FRONT as a saved view.

1. Create a new drawing using the new template. Enable the **Use drawing model file name** option.

2. Use the **bottom_plate_a** model as the Default Model.

3. The template is stored in the current working directory **a3-template,** as shown in Figure A–20.

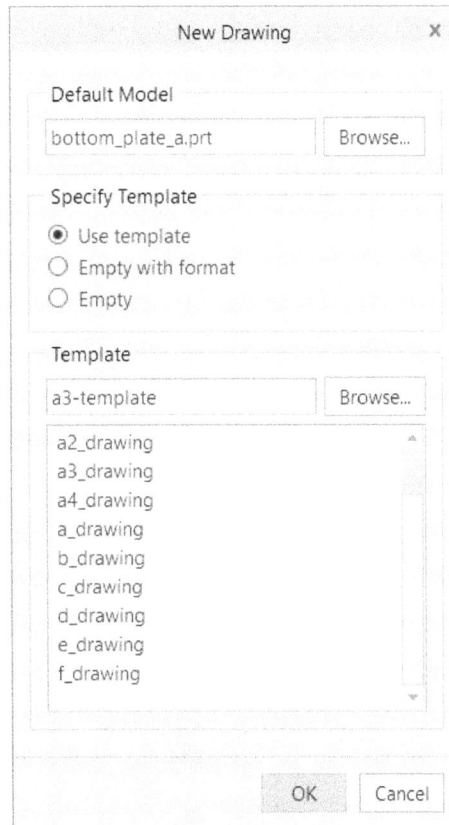

New Drawing

Default Model

bottom_plate_a.prt   Browse...

Specify Template
- ● Use template
- ○ Empty with format
- ○ Empty

Template

a3-template   Browse...

a2_drawing
a3_drawing
a4_drawing
a_drawing
b_drawing
c_drawing
d_drawing
e_drawing
f_drawing

OK   Cancel

Figure A–20

The view display might be different depending on the settings in your environment.

4. Click **OK**. The views in the drawing are created as shown in Figure A–21.

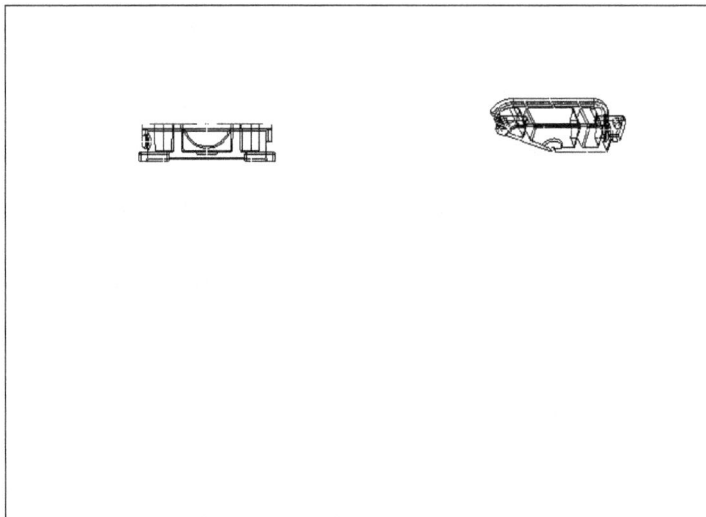

Figure A–21

5. Save the drawing and close the window.

Chapter Review Questions

1. Which of the following methods can be used to add a format to a drawing?

   a. To add a format to a new drawing, select **Empty with section** in the New Drawing dialog box and click **Browse** to browse to the required format.

   b. To add a format once the drawing has been created, click

       (Sheet Setup) in the Document group in the *Layout* tab.

   c. To add a format once the drawing has been created, right-click on the *Sheet* tab at the bottom of the window, and select **Setup**.

   d. All of the above.

2. The drawing becomes dependent on the format once the format has been retrieved into the drawing.

   a. True

   b. False

3. Which of the following enables you to automatically add more information?

   a. Format

   b. Template

4. A template enables you to automatically do which of the following? (Select all that apply.)

   a. Place views.

   b. Clean-up model dimensions.

   c. Create cross-sections.

   d. Create notes.

5. For the view to automatically display in the template, the model must have a **Saved View** name that is defined in the Template View Instructions dialog box.

   a. True

   b. False

Answers: 1d, 2a, 3b, 4abcd, 5a

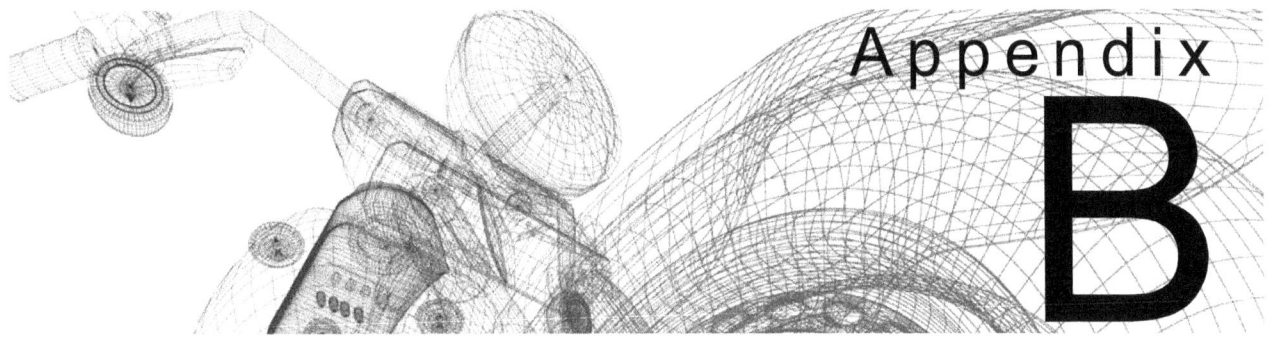

Object Linking and Embedding

In this appendix, you learn how to successfully create and insert MS Excel files in a drawing.

Learning Objective in This Appendix

- Learn how to use Object Linking and Embedding in a drawing file.

B.1 Object Linking and Embedding

Creo Parametric enables you to use Object Linking and Embedding (OLE) to insert objects into 2D Creo Parametric files. The OLE functionality can be used in the following Creo Parametric file formats:

- Drawings

- Reports

- Formats

- Layouts

- Diagrams

The insertion and editing of OLE objects is only supported on Windows platforms.

To insert an object, click ![icon] (Object) in the Insert group in the *Layout* tab. The Insert Object dialog box opens as shown in Figure B–1.

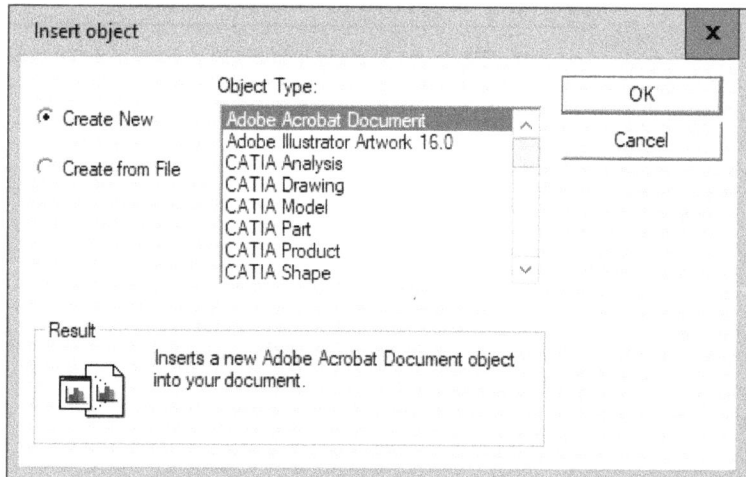

Figure B–1

Select the **Create New** option to create a new file. The *Object Type* area displays all of the file formats that can be used with the OLE functionality.

Select the **Create from File** option to insert an existing file. The Insert Object dialog box updates as shown in Figure B–2.

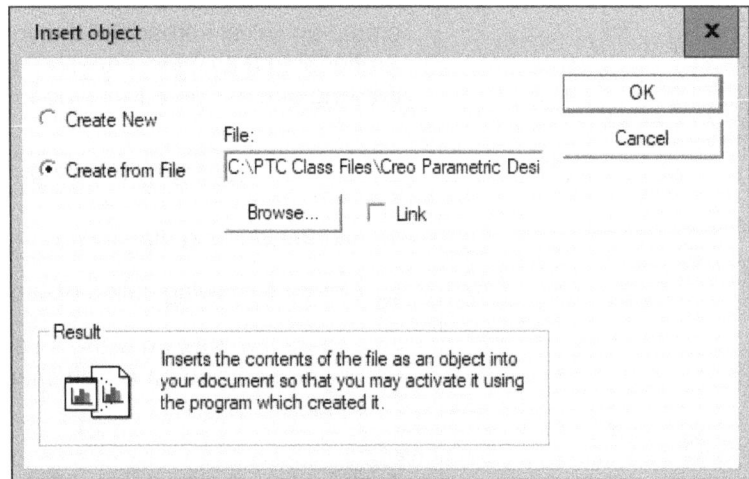

Figure B–2

When inserting an object from an existing file, it can be linked or embedded. Linked objects rely on the source file, while embedded files are standalone. In either situation, the object can be edited directly in Creo Parametric. If an object is linked, any change made to the source file updates the Creo Parametric object.

| Practice B1 | Object Linking & Embedding |

Practice Objectives

- Create and insert MS Excel files in a drawing

In this practice, you will create a new drawing and insert and create an Excel spreadsheet using the Object Linking and Embedding (OLE) functionality. You will also add a note to the drawing and assign a true type font.

Task 1 - Create a new drawing.

1. Set the working directory to the *Drawing_OLE* folder.

2. Create a drawing called **object_linking**.

3. Create the drawing using an empty sheet, landscape orientation, and an A-size sheet. Do not select a drawing model.

Task 2 - Insert a new Excel Spreadsheet into the drawing.

1. Click ⬚ (Object) in the Insert group in the *Layout* tab. The Insert Object dialog box opens.

2. Select **Create New** to create a new spreadsheet directly in the drawing.

3. Select **Microsoft Excel Worksheet** from the list as shown in Figure B–3.

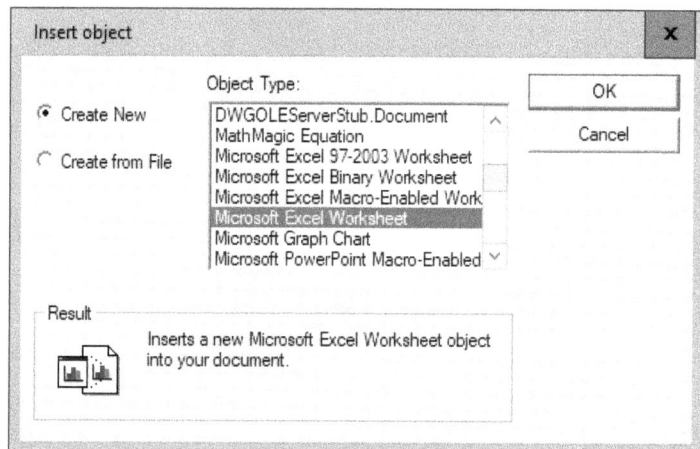

Figure B–3

4. Click **OK**. An empty Excel spreadsheet opens.

By default, the font is black and might need to be changed to enable the information in the drawing to be displayed.

5. Enter the information as shown in Figure B–4. The spreadsheet contains the same options as it would in the Microsoft Excel application.

	A	B	C	D	E	F	G
1	Top Level Bill of Material - VALVE.ASM						
2	Component Name	Product #	Quantity				
3	BODY.ASM	ra-t15433					
4	HOUSING.PRT	ra-t12003					
5							
6							
7							
8							
9							

Sheet1

Figure B–4

6. After entering the information, select the drawing to close the editor. To edit the spreadsheet, double-click on the text in the spreadsheet.

Task 3 - Move the spreadsheet to a new location (if required).

1. Select the spreadsheet. Drag handles display.

2. Place the cursor inside the spreadsheet.

3. Drag the spreadsheet to the new location.

4. To change the spreadsheet size, use the drag handles.

Pressing <Esc> while moving/resizing a spreadsheet resets the original location/size.

Task 4 - Insert an existing Excel Spreadsheet into the drawing.

1. Click (Object) in the Insert group in the *Layout* tab. The Insert Object dialog box opens.

2. Select **Create from File** to insert an existing spreadsheet directly into the drawing.

3. Click **Browse** and browse to **sample.xls**. Click **Open**.

4. Click **OK** to place the object. The spreadsheet displays in the drawing as shown in Figure B–5.

Notes for using OLE in a drawing:

(1) To modify the format of the spreadsheet, press the right mouse button and click Format Cells.

(2) The default font color is black, in order to see the font on a black background drawing you will need to change the font color.

(3) When inserting an object from an existing file it can be linked or embedded. Linked objects rely on the source file while embedded files are standalone. In either situation the object can be edited directly within Pro/ENGINEER. If an object is linked, any change made to the source file updates the Pro/ENGINEER object.

Figure B–5

5. Double-click on the drawing to edit and move the spreadsheet directly in the drawing.

Task 5 - Add a note to the drawing using one of the available true type fonts.

1. Select the *Annotate* tab and click ᴬ≣ (Note).

2. Select a location for the note on the drawing.

3. Enter **true type fonts are available**.

4. **Click** on the screen to complete the note.

5. Select the note and click ᴬ (Text Style).

6. Clear the **Default** option and select any of the ᵀᴛ fonts in the **Font** menu.

7. Click **OK** to apply the new font.

8. Save the drawing and close the window.

Appendix C

Print and Export Options

In this appendix, you will learn the various options available for exporting and plotting drawings.

Learning Objective in This Appendix

- Learn to export and plot drawings using the File options.

C.1 Print and Export Options

Creo Parametric enables you to export and plot drawings using the options in the *File* tab, as shown in Figure C–1.

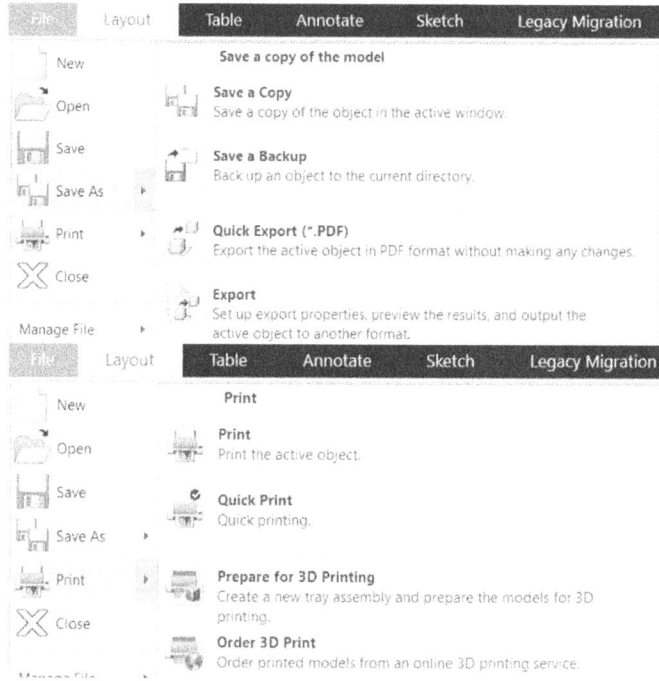

Figure C–1

Print

Selecting **File>Print** displays the *Print Preview* tab, as shown in Figure C–2.

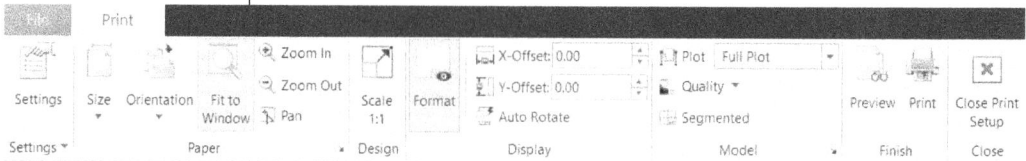

Figure C–2

Some of the main options are described as follows:

Option	Description
(Settings)	Sets printer configuration options, as shown below. 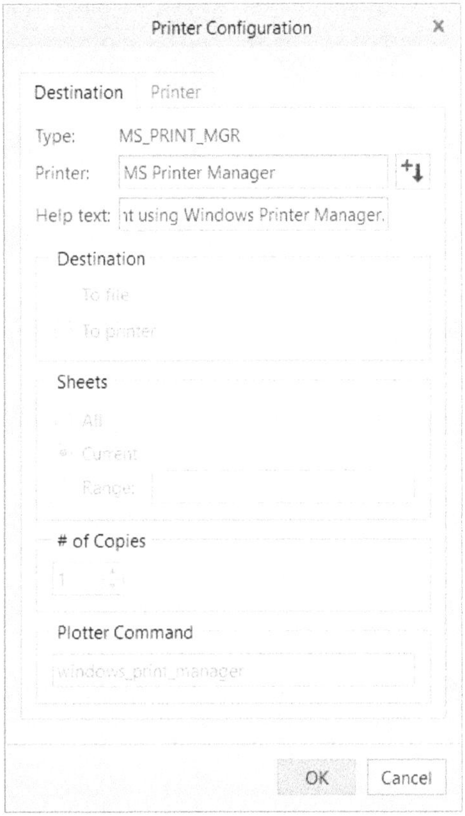
(Preview)	Previews the drawing before plotting.
(Print)	Selects the printer and prints the drawing.

For the Settings option:

Printer Configuration ✕

Destination Printer

Type: MS_PRINT_MGR

Printer: MS Printer Manager

Help text: nt using Windows Printer Manager.

Destination
  To file
  To printer

Sheets
  All
  Current
  Range

# of Copies
  1

Plotter Command
  windows_print_manager

OK   Cancel

Export to DXF

Creo Parametric enables you to select export options in the *Export Setup* tab.

How To: Export a Drawing as a DXF File

You can also select the ***Quick Export*** *option in the File tab to export a DXF using the default options.*

1. Select **File>Save As>Export**. The *Export Setup* tab activates in a new window, as shown in Figure C–3.

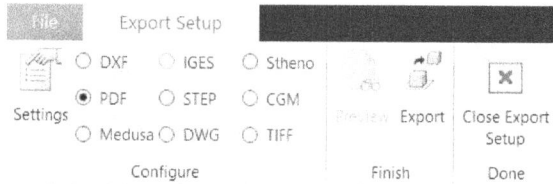

Figure C–3

2. Select the **DXF** option in the Configure group.

The Settings dialog box changes depending on which option is selected in the Publish group.

3. Click (Settings). The Export Environment for DXF dialog box opens as shown in Figure C–4.

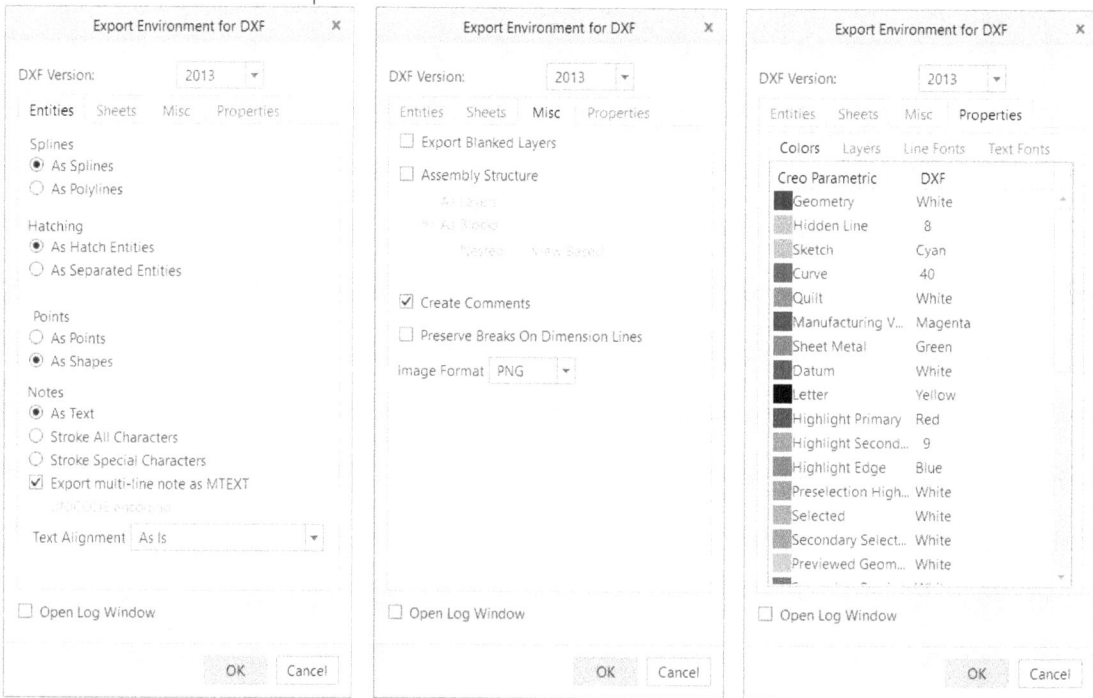

Figure C–4

4. Click (Preview).

5. Click ⬇ (Export). The File dialog box opens as shown in Figure C–5. Enter the name of the file and click **OK**.

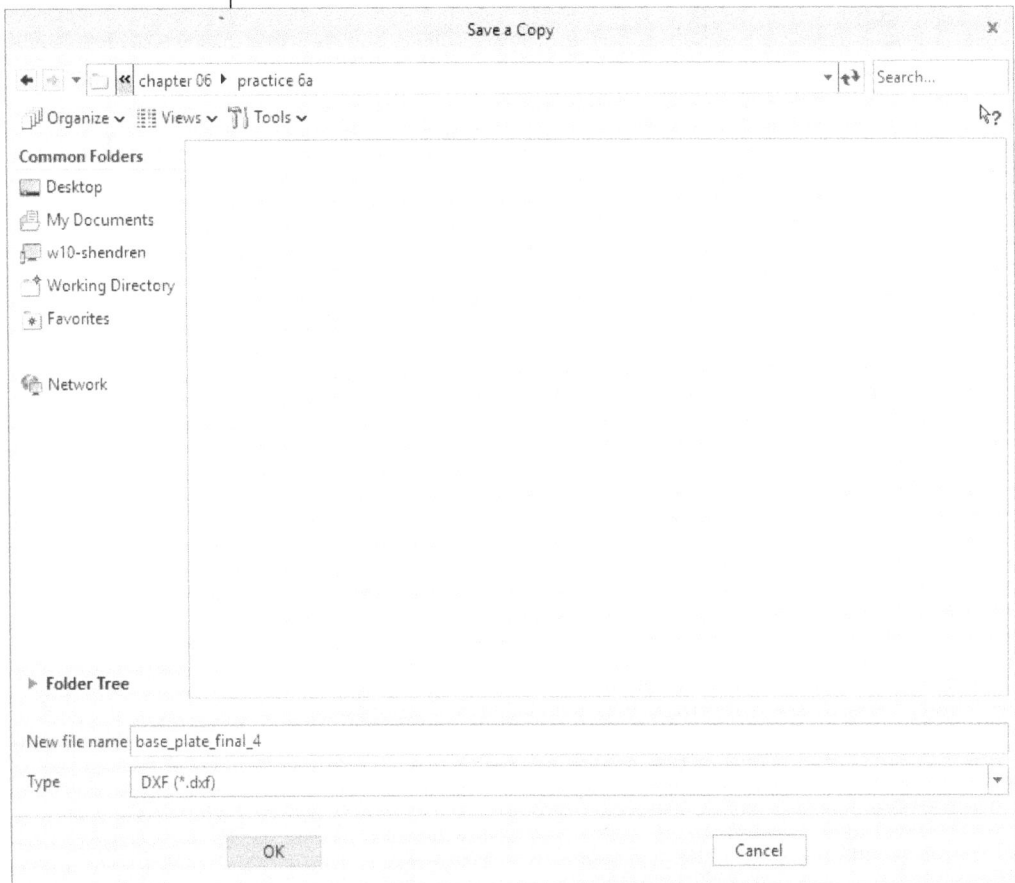

Figure C–5

6. Click ⊠ (Close Export Setup) to return to the drawing and close the Export mode.

www.ingramcontent.com/pod-product-compliance
Lightning Source LLC
Chambersburg PA
CBHW060945210326
41598CB00031B/4722

* 9 7 8 1 9 5 2 8 6 6 4 5 6 *